a funnel in the rock and soaks the lighthouse
placed on the meridian next the sea. From the platform where the lighthouse
stands, there is a magnificent sea panorama to the south from Fouls
round to Hillswick. The keeper & his wife (Mr & Mrs Wyclus) live alone here, their nearest
neighbours being the croft at the beach, and an occasional fishing man,
a crofter, who in case of need come over to help, on receiving a signal
from the lighthouse.

North of Eshaness, there is fine cliff scenery, the mainland
yielding to Yell, and then Yell to North West. Gradually the Muckle
Flugga Lighthouse came in sight. It gave me a thrill to see the
most northerly point (bar Canada) in the British Commonwealth. It
stands on a precipitous rock just to the north of North West. & although
we did not proceed beyond Yell this evening, we saw the lighthouse
clearly, its slopes neutralised by a great white patch of bird-lime.

Instead of anchoring for the night at Hillswick, we proceeded
eastwards through the sound between Yell and North West, and eventually
dropped anchor in Basta Voe. a favourite anchorage (the Captain told me)
of the First World War, chosen to-night because of the threatened gale
warning. But it remained peaceful during the evening, a change in the
weather being heralded by a heavy dew which so damped the deck as to
make our deck billiards difficult. There was another beautiful sunset,
and in other directions a soft mist tinged with a faint pink. In
the afternoon, after tea, whilst I slept on deck, Lithi did what he called a
caricature of me. It was good from the neck downwards. The head was
like Mr. Pecksniff, and when I remarked on its unlikeness to me, Lithi
explained that this was because it was a caricature! I always
thought the essence of caricature was to catch some likeness or painting!

21 July 1948   I am writing this in my cabin after tea. The cabin has every comfort, except a
place to write at. It is roughly 8 or 10 feet cubed, with two portholes. Opposite
the portholes is my bed and a wardrobe. On the other side, beneath the portholes, is
a long couch, between bed and couch is the basin, with some of his dad's
equipment.

Before I came down, Tom Simpson said "You will find it necessary to

THE JOURNAL OF SIR RANDALL PHILIP

Sir Randall Philip O.B.E., Q.C.

The Journal of
Sir Randall Philip, O.B.E., Q.C.

PUBLIC AND PRIVATE LIFE IN SCOTLAND, 1947–57

EDITED BY

FIONA CRADDOCK

The publication of this Journal
has been assisted by the Faculty of Advocates

The Pentland Press
Edinburgh – Cambridge – Durham – USA

First published in 1998 by
The Pentland Press Ltd
1 Hutton Close
South Church
Bishop Auckland
Durham

Typeset in 11/13 Sabon
by Carnegie Publishing, Chatsworth Road, Lancaster
Printed and bound by Bookcraft Ltd, Bath

Illustrations

Preface

by the Rt Hon. the Lord Rodger of Earlsferry

About ten years ago Fiona Craddock and I were engaged in a trial at the High Court at Stirling. For several weeks we travelled together and it was during those journeys that I first became aware that she was transcribing and editing the diary of her grandfather, Sir Randall Philip. Fiona was good enough to feed me with titbits which whetted my appetite. Some time later she married, became Mrs Jones and started a family. I heard no more about the project and supposed that it had been shelved. Earlier this year, however, I was delighted to receive a letter telling me that the diary was to be published and asking me to write a Preface.

I never knew Sir Randall Philip, but his name has come down to later generations of advocates as an impossibly diligent Procurator of the Church of Scotland and as one who might have expected to be appointed a Court of Session Judge, but who died before this could come to pass. The diary covers the decade from 1947 until his death. He made no secret of the fact that he was keeping it and he may well have intended that it should be read by others. This does not mean that it is bland, however. On the contrary he obviously enjoys describing his impression of those whom he meets. One dinner is enough for him to pin down Sir Compton Mackenzie's delight in discussing himself. The first Lord President Clyde is subjected to scathing retrospective criticism, while any future study of Lord Cooper will have to take account of the many entries where he appears, usually, but by no means always, in a sympathetic light.

The author held a variety of posts which took him into a wider world of public affairs. The diary went with him and so it records many events which were important in their day, even though they may now be largely forgotten. Much time and many trips to London were devoted to his work on the Central Land Board and the War Damage Committee. We hear of the arrangements for General Elections in the days before television dominated the scene and when a

Returning Officer could still travel by bus and Clyde steamer to perform his duties. Negotiations between the Church of Scotland and the Church of England, which were ultimately to bear little fruit, occupy much of Sir Randall's attention and give him a chance to observe various ecclesiastical stars in action. The insights he gains serve him in good stead when he enters with relish into a series of Byzantine negotiations with the Archbishop of Canterbury about the role of the Moderator at the Coronation Service in 1953.

It would be wrong to imagine that the diary is simply a record of the author's activities. On the contrary there is much which is intensely personal. The death of his son Gordon occurred four years before the diary opens, but the pain which he continued to feel surfaces in entry after entry. So also does his love for his children and for his wife, Ella. As the years go by he speculates on his chances of being made a Judge (not good, since he was a Liberal) and of being given a knighthood (better, since he was Procurator). When he ultimately receives the accolade in 1953, very properly he does not attempt to conceal his delight under any pretence of indifference. So we learn much about the man and his family. For many readers, however, the principal interest of the book will lie in the picture which emerges of the attitudes, preoccupations and way of life in a prosperous professional home in Edinburgh in the forties and fifties. They were certainly very different from those which are to be found in the chronicles of life in Fitzrovia during the same period and they are hard to recapture except from a contemporary account like this. It is a world in which the wireless reigns and in which television has made scarcely any mark. The prospect of seeing an amateur ciné film can still draw a crowd of Oxford students. Capital punishment is not questioned. So his description of his involvement in a case which resulted in the execution of his client is very matter of fact and, when he happens to be in the Old Bailey as the Derek Bentley case reaches its climax, he has no doubt about the inevitability of the verdict. The professional world is dominated by men – as one of the entries remarks, women have obtained equal rights but the opportunities are not yet open to them. Exclusively male dining clubs are still in vogue, with members composing ingenious poems and singing songs to provide the evening's entertainment. When holidays are taken the family set off on a proper expedition, whether by car or boat, and stay away for some weeks. Clearly Sir Randall relished these trips – though one suspects that at times some of his family may not have shared his enthusiasm for visiting quite so many obscure churches.

Fiona Jones has made a splendid job of editing the diary and selecting the passages which are likely to be of general and abiding interest. There are few diaries of prominent Scotsmen of this century. This is a notable addition. I wish the book all success.

Alan Rodger

Acknowledgements

I would like to express my thanks to the following people, without whom the publication of the Journal would not have been possible: the Hon. Lord MacLean for facilitating transcription from the manuscript; the Right Hon. the Lord Rodger of Earlsferry for his early encouragement and his enthusiasm in writing the Preface; Sheriff Principal G.S. Gimson Q.C. for his careful reading of the proofs and for his comprehensive and informative Introduction; Sheriff R.G. McEwan Q.C., the Hon. Lord Johnston, David Walker, and countless others for their enthusiasm for the project and their assistance in deciphering the manuscript; the Faculty of Advocates for their generous support of the publication; Meg Ross, for her patient and meticulous help in the publication; the Trustees of the National Library of Scotland for their assistance in enabling a copy of the Journal to be created and for their permission to reproduce many of the illustrations; Dr. Iain G. Brown, Assistant Keeper of the Manuscripts of the National Library for his help and advice; Lambeth Palace, T.H. Drysdale, the Hon. Lord Milligan and members of the family of the late Lord Normand for their assistance in relation to the reproduction of certain letters and poems; my aunt, Rosemary Philip, particularly for her expertise in tracking down obscure documents; Ian and Alison Craddock, for their unstinting support throughout; my brother Richard Craddock, for designing the cover; and my husband Michael Jones and my children Richard and Christopher for putting up with the disruption caused by this project. Finally, thanks are due to the lowly Amstrad PCW9512 word processor (and, of course, its technological successors), without which the transcription of the Journal would never have been started.

Fiona Craddock

Randall Philip – Biographical Notes

1900   Born to Rev. Adam and Mrs. Mary Philip, Longforgan, Perthshire.
        Younger brother of Harold
        Educated at Dundee High School
                Edinburgh University (M.A. in History)
                Glasgow University (LL.B.)
        Apprenticeship served at
            Maclay, Murray & Spens, Glasgow
            Morton, Smart, Macdonald & Prosser W.S., Edinburgh

1924   Admitted to Scots Bar

1926   Married Ella Wallace Gray
        Lived at 41 Great King Street, Edinburgh, and from 1935 at
        53 Great King Street

1927   Son, Gordon Francis Adam Philip born

1931   Daughter, Alison Mary Philip born
        Became Elder of St. George's West Church, Edinburgh

1939   Appointed Trustee of the National Library of Scotland

1943   Gordon died as a result of an accident playing rugby at school

1944   Daughter, Rosemary Kathleen Philip born

1945   Took silk

1946   O.B.E. for services rendered at Regional Controller's Office in
        War

1948   Appointed Commissioner, Northern Lighthouse Board
                Commissioner, Glenrothes New Town Enquiry
                Sheriff of Renfrew and Argyll

1949   Became Member of Central Land Board & War Damage
        Commission
        Procurator of the General Assembly of the Church of Scotland

1950–1 Church of Scotland Representative at Anglo-Scottish Church
        Conversations

1952   Church of Scotland Representative at World Faith & Order
        Conference, Lund, Sweden
        Convener of National Occasions Committee appointed by
        General Assembly of Church of Scotland which dealt with
        arrangements for Queen's Coronation & National Service in
        St. Giles' Cathedral

1953   Knighted at Holyrood House

1955   Sheriff of Perth & Angus
        Hon D.D. (Aberdeen)
        Appointed Commissioner, Cumbernauld New Town Enquiry

1956   Marriage of daughter Alison to Ian Dayrell Craddock
        Death of brother Harold

1957   Died 2nd May

Introduction

by Sheriff Principal G. S. Gimson, Q.C., LL.D.

Randall Philip died on 2nd May 1957, at the age of fifty-seven. (He was born in 1900.) For the last ten years of his life, he kept this Journal, recording the events and encounters of his astonishingly busy life. As he explained in the Journal, the occasion for its beginning was the appointment, as Lord President of the Court of Session, of Lord Cooper – a near contemporary (seven years older than Randall) and close friend whom he admired greatly, though not uncritically. In the Journal, he recorded the major events and concerns of his life, but also incidents of little importance and even trivial detail – for example what the Attlees had for breakfast on 26 August 1950! – all reflecting his delight in the variety of personality and experience that came his way. Embedded in his account are notably shrewd pen-portraits of Judges, Churchmen and others with whom he came into contact.

It seems scarcely possible that he could have been an effective member of the many committees and other organisations to which he was appointed, in addition to his Court practice, his core duties as a Sheriff (nowadays 'Sheriff Principal') and as Procurator of the Church of Scotland, and his long-term commitment to St George's West Church in Edinburgh. Yet the indications are that he *was* effective and very highly valued for the wisdom of his advice and his tirelessness. In the period of the Journal, there were a surprising number of special events which called for extra time and attention from him – the funeral of King George VI, the Queen's Coronation, her subsequent visit to Scotland including the National Service in St Giles' Cathedral and a flurry of other royal occasions. There were no fewer than three general elections, in which he was Returning Officer for all constituencies in his Sheriffdoms; Committees of the National Library of Scotland, and the supervision of the last stages of the fitting out of its new building (1954); and a Committee to advise on the choice of site for a new National Museum of Antiquities (that Committee reported in 1953 in favour of the site on which the building is only now being constructed!)

In the field of church affairs, he was instrumental in securing proper representation of the Kirk at the Coronation, and he was on a committee on representation on other national occasions. He was one of the Kirk's delegates at a series of discussions with the Church of England, exploring the prospects for Inter-Church relations. (From the Journal and from tributes by the English delegates, it is clear that he was an energetic and influential participant.) There were also a World Faith and Order Conference in Sweden and meetings of the British Council of Churches. To echo a phrase in a famous judgement of Lord Cooper's: 'His must indeed have been a busy life'!

In light of all these responsibilities, it is easy to lose sight of the fact that his profession was that of Advocate. His practice at the Bar must at times have seemed to him gratefully familiar and like the calm at the heart of a whirlpool. Fortunately his practice lay to a considerable extent in the field of trust, succession and estate law, involving the writing of opinions or pleading in Court on subjects which he had at his fingertips. At the same time, he had his share of other work, both civil and criminal. One this I notice – that the Journal seems remarkably free of complaints of the burden of legal research, which many advocates nowadays regard as a major burden: but then the law *was* simpler in those days.

There are two subjects which crop up regularly in the Journal on which a word of explanation may be helpful to those unfamiliar with them – the 'Round Table' and the appointment of Sheriffs as Lighthouse Commissioners.

The Round Table was just that – a more-or-less circular table which occupied a window recess in the advocates' lunch-room in Parliament House (the Court building in Edinburgh). It had come to be recognised as the preserve of a group of advocates who regularly occupied it, and who maintained its membership by invitation when vacancies occurred (usually through promotion to the Bench). This continued until at least 1975. There was no more to it than that, except that with eight or nine members covering the whole span of age and seniority and a variety of wartime experience, conversation was lively and varied. The senior members, including Sir John Cameron when Dean of Faculty, and Randall, were outstanding conversationalists.

The Northern Lighthouse Board was established in 1786, and there was obviously a need to set up a governing body. It seems likely that the requirements were for 'men of affairs' who also had some familiarity with the coastal and island regions of Scotland, and who had contacts there, and yet who could attend board meetings at the Board's headquarters in Edinburgh. The Sheriffs of the counties which included coastal or island areas filled that bill. Collectively, they covered the whole coastline and islands; being based in Edinburgh, but travelling occasionally to their Sheriffdoms and having contact with Sheriff-clerks, Sheriff Deputes and Honorary Sheriffs, they had the necessary qualifications. The Scottish Law Officers and representatives of local authorities completed the Board. In 1975 a reorganisation of the Sheriff Courts reduced the number of Sheriffs Principal to six, and a further six commissioners were added who had appropriate maritime or scientific skills or interests, including representatives of the 'users' such as shipowners and Master Mariners. In addition the Board has always had its own experts as well as its Marine Superintendent and the Masters of its tenders.

After that digression, what of Randall himself? His portly, even Pickwickian figure was matched by a puckish sense of humour. He was well inured to banter about his figure and was delighted with his nickname 'The Puffin', as he was also by the tales that when he was knighted, the Queen had called on him to rise as either 'Sir Roundel' or 'Sir Cumference'. He generally stood with his head slightly tilted back. His voice was light, very clear and with just a hint of dogged precision which marked him out as a Scot and made him one of the easiest pleaders or conversationalists to listen to. He was always eminently approachable and ready with advice or help. In court, he was a skilful and effective pleader. In the Inverness Free Presbyterian Church case (mentioned in the Journal) his duel with his friend Sir John Cameron was – on both sides – an outstanding display of forensic skill.

Among the many tributes which were published at the time of his death was one by Professor W. S. Tindal which was so true to him that, ignoring Samuel Johnson's caution, I must quote from it:

> . . . he entered with zest into familiar and unfamiliar situations. Things happened in his company. There was a point of historical interest to be verified, a scene to be photographed, a ploy to be invented, or a new acquaintance to make.

He was an establishment man, but one who never doubted that the establishment could be improved upon. He records a number of occasions when he declined offers of appointments or nominations, apparently being reluctant to abandon those to which he had already committed himself. Another facet of his personality was his indulgence of the oddities of corporate life – accepting such extravagances as the

Sheriffs referring to each other by the names of their Sheriffdoms –
'Fife' or 'Perth' – or, similarly, the bishops by the names of their sees
– 'Durham (gave a) . . . welcome, Derby opened the talk' – and similar
practices of the 'Monks of St Giles'. One matter on which he did not
feel that charity was called for was the chronic failure of the English
legal and ecclesiastical establishments to recognise the different traditions and institutions of Scotland.

When his menu at a Round Table dinner bore the description

> A man so large to some he seemed to be
> Not one but all mankind in effigy

it could have been a sober reflection on his multifarious activities and
his apparently unlimited appetite for work.

What readers of the Journal will soon learn is that behind this busy,
cheerful front there was one great and abiding sadness. Randall's only
son, Gordon, had died in 1943 at the age of fifteen as the result of
an accidental injury during rugby practice. In an intensely emotional
family the only mitigation of that blow lay in their unshakeable faith
in ultimate reunion. But the sense of loss persisted, as it was bound
to do, and there are several entries in the Journal recording conversations with other bereaved parents. How far that sad experience
influenced his seeking to fill every waking moment with activity is
impossible to say. What is good to learn from the Journal is that,
with his beloved wife and daughters, he lived an active family life,
taking every opportunity of having them with him, including journeys
on duty which he combined with detours to places of interest in a
manner reminiscent of Lord Cockburn's *Circuit Journeys*.

The last entry in the Journal ends with a typical incident – the
recovery of a book which he remembered from his youth – remembered because it contained a poem in Scots which he wished to recall.
The poem itself provides a fitting *envoi* to the Journal. You will find
it on page 587.

Stanley Gimson

CHAPTER I

1947

12th February 1947

If this Journal has any starting point, it may be taken to be the sudden change in Parliament House occasioned by the appointment of Lord President Normand to succeed Lord Macmillan as a Lord of Appeal, and the appointment of Lord Justice-Clerk Cooper to the office of Lord President. Most impending changes on the bench become common knowledge before their announcement. This one, announced during the Christmas Recess of 1946, was a well kept secret. The two men in Parliament House with their ears nearest to the ground, Peter Hook, doyen of Advocates' Clerks, and John Mitchell, Principal Clerk of Session, were for once surprised at their ignorance. The week before, I had sat on the Justice-Clerk's right at the dinner given by his advocates to Peter Hook, but on recalling my conversation can think of only one remark which might have suggested to me the impending change. Discussing the granting of 'silk' to a certain Counsel, the Justice-Clerk said to me, 'It is a matter for the Lord President alone. If I were Lord President I would not approve the grant.'

This change was one of special interest. The only recent precedents for a Justice-Clerk becoming President were Charles Hope (Justice-Clerk 1804–11; President 1811–41); Boyle (Justice-Clerk 1811–41; President 1841–52); and Inglis (Justice-Clerk 1858–67; President 1867–91). The only precedents for a President becoming a Lord of Appeal were Robertson (President 1891–9) and Dunedin (President 1905–13). Lord Dunedin had, however, the distinction of being both a Sheriff and a Secretary for Scotland, which offices had been held by neither J. P. B. Robertson nor Normand. The vacancy in the office of Lord Justice-Clerk led to interesting speculations. The Bar unanimously favoured the selection of Lord Patrick (I write while this office is still vacant). If he is appointed then this will follow a more remote precedent, for a Lord Ordinary has not been appointed to the Chair of one of the Divisions since Lord Colonsay (Lord Ordinary 1851) became, in 1852, Lord President. Someone remarked that it was the tradition for a chairman of the division not to use his judicial title (if he had one). Inglis was never called Lord Glencorse; Macdonald never Lord Kingsburgh. But I pointed out that Munro was always Alness. Even before he received a peerage, his vanity led him on occasion to sign as Alness – though he was always Munro *in praesentia dominorum.*

The appointment of Tommy Cooper (as he was always called) is of special interest to me, for I think I may claim both his respect and his friendship. At every stage of his career, he has been marked out for the highest promotion. Dux of George Watson's, Rector's Prizeman at Edinburgh University, he stepped at once into the largest and best junior practice. At first this may have been due partly to the fact that his uncle, Tom Mackay, after whom he is named, was Senior Partner of Macpherson & Mackay W.S., whose Parliament House practice was unrivalled and who sent him all their work. In this respect, he resembled Lord Dunedin, who was said to have made 700 guineas *per annum* from entail petitions alone, sent by his father's firm, Tods Murray & Jamieson. In other ways, however, the cases are not parallel. Cooper was essentially a product of the middle class backbone of Scotland, the product of professional man's home, Grammar School and the traditions of Thomas Chalmers and the Free Kirk. This has tended to give him socially a rather 'strict' outlook and one may almost trace the effect of it in his perhaps slightly censorious outlook towards those who have appeared before him in the dock of the High Court. It is also accentuated by his being naturally shy, and a bachelor who has always lived with his mother and brother James. I recall his telling me one time about an incident which occurred to him on a Mediterranean cruise. In the market at Algeciras, he bought, after much chaffering, a donkey, and then resold it at a profit. I replied, 'I thought you would have been spending your time with the bright young things on board ship.' He stopped and looked at me. 'Philip, do you not realise that I am shy?' I said I had never noticed it in Parliament House. He replied, 'Ah – professionally no; but – socially – yes.' This occurred while he was still a senior, and not yet a Law Officer. Since then, I have come to realise the truth of his self-analysis.

In describing him as 'strict', I am not so much criticising him as trying accurately to depict his personality. One of the things I have in common with him is that I have myself been brought up in a very similar atmosphere. It is no wonder that we both gravitated to St. George's West Church, the last stronghold of the Disruption tradition. We were ordained elders there the same day in October 1931, he being my immediate 'junior' and sitting next to me at the ordination service. This link has provided a common meeting place for us away from the immediate associations of Parliament House. In the old days when, while still in practice, he lived in Abercromby Place, I used regularly to walk home with him in the evenings and much of our early conversation took place then. When, in 1945, I became Joint Session Clerk, this brought us still more in contact with Church affairs. He constantly came forward with new ideas, often tending to be rather critical of Church organisation. I found that the most effective way to meet his criticism which was sometimes of the armchair variety was to set up a committee to deal with the matter, and invite him to join it. He would decline, saying, 'That was a good *Tu quoque*,' and there the matter would end.

Another link between us was our common interest in the historical side of the Law. Very quickly he discovered that I had taken a first class Honours Degree in History. His was a Classical Degree and his classical scholarship, so far as I could judge, was astonishingly accurate. But I think his academic hankerings were for legal history and this certainly appeared when he published his *Select Scottish Cases of the Thirteenth Century*. Over a period of years, there were quite a number of minor history inquiries which we pursued to some extent together. Intrigued by the reference to Nicholas de Vipont and the Manor of Aldenstone, among the documents which should have been returned to Scotland after the Treaty of Northampton and which we saw returned by the Public Records (Scotland) Act 1937 (cf. First Schedule), he induced me to track down information on Nicholas and this led me to write a short article about him in the *Juridical Review*. Earlier I was with him as third Counsel in The Duke of Richmond and Gordon casualty case (1927 S.C. 833), one of the last, I fear, of its kind. Later, when Lord Advocate, he took me as his junior in Mackay v. Lord Advocate (1937 S.C. 860), when the whole nature of judicial tenure in Scotland was explored. About the same time, he appointed me a member and secretary of his newly created Committee on Legal Reforms and he sometimes in fun referred to the Committee's first product as the Law Reform (J.R. Philip) Act 1940. At the time of the Abdication Act, he told me that Sir John Simon had submitted the Bill to the then Duke and Duchess of York (after George VI and Elizabeth). This was done as a matter of courtesy, but the Duchess took the matter seriously. Having studied the Bill, she pointed out that, in its then form, it would not carry the private estates of the Sovereign. The point had been overlooked by Sir John, and steps were

CONFIDENTIAL.   12th July 1936.

My dear Philip,

       I am much indebted to you for
the information you have supplied.

       For your private information I
may say that a project has been mooted from
the Palace for a coronation of the King as King
of Scotland, and this I am disposed to regard a
a breach of the Treaty of Union.

       Yours sincerely,

       T. M. Cooper,

then taken to make it clear that all private estates would also pass to the new Sovereign. Before the Abdication crisis, there seems to have been a proposal mooted that Edward VIII should have a separate Scottish Coronation, but Cooper's view was that this would be a breach of the Treaty of Union.

In appearance, he was small of stature and somewhat restless in manner, quick in movement and lacking in dignity. A slight deformity of one leg or foot made him intoed and almost, but not quite, lame. Physically, his one remarkable feature was the shape of his head, which plainly contained an unusual box of brains. When Lord Macmillan left his practice in Edinburgh and went to London, the common remark was that Tommy Cooper and Tommy Robertson (both small men physically) would each fill one of his shoes.

But intellectually, Cooper has been the first of his judicial and forensic brethren. 'The clearest brain since J.P.B. Robertson' was Condie Sandeman's remark to me about him on one occasion. A master of exposition, even more than debating, whose handwriting was as clear as his thinking, a coiner of telling phrases, with a never faltering gift of expression, a scholar and a businessman. As familiar with the House of Commons procedure, hydro-electrical undertakings, the port facilities of the Clyde, Thirteenth Century Law, as he was with the more immediate concerns of his profession; no-one who heard him plead or heard him deliver judgment could ever doubt his intellectual stature. But, with it all, he was entirely modest and unassuming, and it has been characteristic of him that, alone of the judges, he is constantly at the Parliament House fireplace, hob-nobbing with his friends still at the Bar.

I might mention other curious characteristics. An almost childish curiosity and inquisitiveness, he would push his head like a boy into the bonnet of my car. 'If I hadn't been a lawyer, I'd have been an electrical engineer,' he once said to me. Somewhat of (to use his own expression) an iconoclast, attacking traditions, reconstructing the Judges' quarters, framing new Acts of Adjournal and Sederunt, criticising the administrators of the National Library. In his radicalism, he was scarcely a typical Conservative politician and a generation earlier he would certainly have been an Asquithian Liberal. That may account for his popularity with other parties, for he was obviously on the best of terms with various politicians, like Tom Johnston and George Buchanan. On the Bench and in his professional work, bright, happy and humorous. Off the Bench and in his attitude to the World in general, somewhat of a pessimist. Like the rich young ruler, he had great, or at any rate considerable, possessions and took a peculiarly black view of modern economic conditions. His brother James and he were so lugubrious in the early stages of the War, that it was a standing joke that they should be prosecuted for spreading despair and despondency. When a judicial colleague took ill, it was 'the beginning of the end'. They were consigned to a lingering death, only to return a week or two later, hale and hearty, and falsify these gloomy prognostications. A younger man than James Forsyte, he nevertheless had certain of his qualities. Another characteristic was a fondness for Mozart. He was never tired of hearing the Larghetto in A from the Coronation Concerto. Yet another characteristic was a delight in pursuing some limited inquiry intensively. If an old case was not intelligible to him from the Reports, he always followed it up by obtaining the Decree itself from Register House. In this way, he succeeded in showing that the case of Bruce v. Lord Hamilton was really a multiplepoinding, and had no significance in the Law of the Crown as litigant.

The death of my Gordon opened a new chapter in my friendship with him. I sent a copy of my little book about Gordon to him and next morning in my box at Court, I found a delightful letter from him saying that his brother James and he had read it all from cover to cover the previous evening. This revealed a delightful trait in him, his love of children. Later he let me use his name as a reference when Alison went to St. Leonard's. But above all I shall not forget one snowy day, 8th February 1947, when I took Rosemary (aged 2¾) out in the motor for a run while her mother had a rest. We happened to pass Cooper on our way home, just outside his house. I stopped to speak to him about National Library matters, I having just been appointed as Convener of the Standing Committee of the Library Trustees in succession to Normand. Cooper said: 'Do come in. My mother would like to see Rosemary.' He lifted her in her Wellington boots out of the car and carried her over the snowy avenue to the house. She was as friendly as possible with him at once. While we sat at tea, she stood at the table between us, talking away and she was eventually so much at home that she dropped her woolly gloves into the cat's bowl of milk and took off her wellies and walked about the room in stocking soles. Such a scene would have been unthinkable in the presence of the last Lord President, but nothing could have been kinder than the way in which the President made friends with my little girl. As we went out, he showed me with pride a walking stick with the initials 'J. I.' on the handle, the walking stick of none other than John Inglis himself, presented to Cooper by Stair Gillon, on becoming President.

20th February 1947

My previous prognostications as to the new Lord Justice-Clerk seem to be wrong. This afternoon I learned from John Mitchell that it is to be Lord Moncrieff, that Blades is to become a Judge and that John Wheatley is to be Solicitor-General. I am delighted. I have always felt a touch of respect and affection for Moncrieff who once, at an earlier stage in my forensic work, gave me much encouragement and who, within the last year, presented me with his volume of poems. He is a powerful if somewhat erratic intellect. No-one is freer from prejudice or more ready to reconsider his view if wrong. But he is so quick that sometimes his logic errs. How he will work with Lord Mackay remains to be seen. The one dominating, quick, somewhat irascible, but always kindly. The other patient, prolix and pachydermatous. Blades and Wheatley took lunch with me at 'The Round Table', as we call it. Blades' father, minister of Allanton, died last month at the age of ninety-two; how sad he did not live to see his son's promotion. John Wheatley everyone likes and rightly. He is still a junior; but politics will inevitably secure his promotion.

21st February 1947

The appointment of Moncrieff is announced but not, as yet, of the other two. The talk about the appointment all hinged on how long he could work with Mackay. Moncrieff is seventy-six and rumours go that he is simply keeping the place warm for Patrick, who is expected to be home from the Japanese International Military Tribunal in Tokyo in the summer. He must be the oldest appointment ever, as he has celebrated his forensic jubilee.

There was much interest in the President's announcement to the Bar of the policy he means to follow in recommending for Silk. The alternative qualifications will be: (i) Eminence at the Bar; (ii) 25 years in attendance at Parliament House; (iii) Appointment to a Sheriff Principalship or (iii) (if a Professor of Law) the publication of some work of scholarship. It is much better that the principles should be so laid down. When I took silk, two others were refused it, one a Conservative and one a Socialist. After the Labour Government came in, the Socialist next year was given silk and then the Conservative.

There seemed little logic in refusing it one year and granting it the next. George Morton (Sheriff of Aberdeen, who has been fifty years at the Bar and is Chairman of 'The Round Table'), at lunch today recalled that, when K.C.s were first introduced into general practice in Scotland (in 1897 I think), those who were refused silk were Christopher Johnston (afterwards Lord Sands), Vary Campbell and Lees (later both Sheriffs). Christopher Johnston however had almost no practice, and spent most of his time standing in front of the fireplace in the Corridor.

22nd February 1947

Four years ago today, Gordon was taken from us almost ere we knew it. The day, as all days, was full of thoughts of him. Many friends sent us flowers, all the spring flowers of that early 1943 Spring. How different this year, when all lies under snow after a spell of frost and snow, lasting for almost a month. But the daffodils, tulips and mimosa (which Ella always gives me because it carries me at once to the Riviera) were there from kind friends, just as usual and also the unfailing sprig of rosemary from Lionel Smith, Gordon's old Rector. But the loveliest message of all, an unexpected telegram from fifteen year old Alison at St. Leonard's: 'Kindest thoughts today, Alison.' We could only look at each other when we read it.

Today, there came from Lord Patrick at the Imperial Hotel, Tokyo, a letter, thanking me for a Christmas card. It is dated 8th February 1947 and its description of the International Military Tribunal for the Far East is worth setting down:–

> Thank you for the kindly thought of me and for the picture of the happy people on the sun-lit road. That reminded me of an endless number of days I have spent on the hills in Scotland and made me long for home more than anything else has since I came here. I often think of our Bar at Parliament House. Indeed they are thrust on me. I used sometimes to grumble that I might have had a fuller treatment of such and such a topic from the Bar, a scantier treatment of another which I thought didn't much matter. Now I remember nothing but the anxiety and competence with which our fellows do their work, thus making my work easy. Here we have had about 100 American attorneys and not more than three of them would make a living in Parliament House. The result is that my work becomes difficult. All sorts of important things have not been enquired into, all sorts of ends are left untied, or if tied, they are invariably tied up with slip knots. Comyns Carr of the

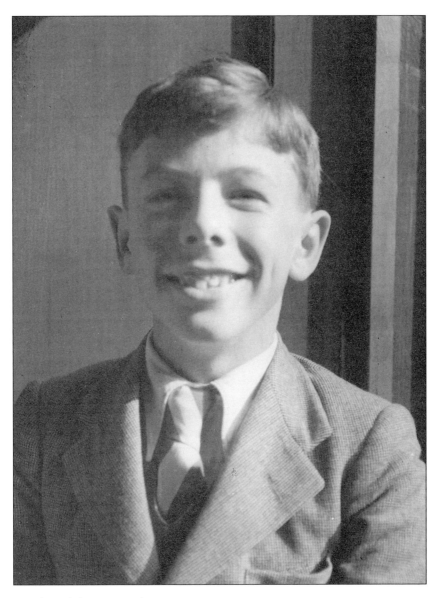

Gordon Philip, September 1940.

British section, we reckon at home a good competent K.C. – no more. Out here he shines like an arc lamp amidst a host of guttering candles. So I am now prepared any time you wish to maintain the competency of the Scots Bar against all-comers.

America must of course have hosts of competent people, but she has sent none of them here. I can only suppose that they are making too much money amongst the many minnows at home to make the long journey to Japan and to be away from their lucrative practice while America turns from War to Peace.

We have already 17,000 pages of evidence; Nuremberg had in all 16,000. I reckon that we shall have at least 25,000 pages of evidence before we have finished. I could do with one of our competent King's Counsel out here to help me pull the loose ends in all that evidence together, but I could not ask for that. It would take the fellow who came away for too long from the keen race in the P.H.

Yours ever,
W.D. Patrick

26th February 1947

Today Lord Moncrieff was installed as Lord Justice-Clerk and the news of Blades' appointment was published. He only learned of it himself on the 21st. The story is that the Lord Advocate simply said to him, 'Well you had better be ordering your new duds!' This terminates the colleagueship of two sons of the Manse as Lord Advocate and Solicitor-General respectively. By a curious chance, when my own father was nominated as Moderator of Assembly for 1921, his next rival, Dr. John A. Stutton, was proposed by G.R. Thomson's father, the late W.R. Thomson of Bellshill. I learned the news of my father's election from an evening paper in the University Union and G.R. Thomson, my fellow student who was sitting in the same room, was the first to offer his congratulations.

1st March 1947

Apart from my ordinary work, I have this week been occupied with a very urgent and important matter. At lunch with Dover Wilson in the University Club on Monday 24th, the President came up and told me that a Committee was being founded to consider the Scottish aspect of the proposed Crown Proceedings Bill and that its report had to be ready by the 28th. Then J.B.M. Young, the Clerk of Faculty, buttonholed me and asked me to be a member of this Committee, the President having apparently urged my name. Then on Tuesday, I was appointed Convener, the other members being Jock Cameron, Harry Guthrie, Douglas Johnston and Ian Fraser. We had two meetings on Wednesday and Thursday afternoons and I was able to lodge the completed report by Friday. I have to submit it (my first Faculty report) to the Faculty on Tuesday the 4th. The Bill makes some important changes, the chief being to abolish the rule that 'The King can do no wrong.' It also gives the Sheriff Court, for the first time, jurisdiction in actions against the Crown. But we have reported that certain of the usual grounds of jurisdiction of the Sheriff Court will not fit the Crown's case. We have also recommended that expenses should be awarded on the same scale to the Crown as to a subject and not on the High Court scale and that the time limit for proceedings which is six months should be extended for a year as in England. The most interesting features of the Bill from Scotland's point of view are that it proposes to make the Courts pronounce little more than findings, rendering the Judiciary powerless in face of the Executive, and that it seems to leave the English Courts free to entertain proceedings wherever the cause of actions arises in Scotland. I write before the Faculty has expressed its views. My Committee consisted of a most co-operative and efficient band of colleagues. Each one made his own contribution.

4th March 1947

Blades was installed today as Senator of the College of Justice, taking as his judicial title the name Lord Blades, not Lord Allanton. It was rather interesting to see my one St. George's West co-elder Cooper installing my other co-elder Blades. But for me it was a specially busy day, because, besides being all week in the new National Coal Board's first proof, I had at one o'clock to present the Crown Proceedings Bill Committee's Report to the Faculty. It was seconded by Jock Cameron and went through unanimously. Perhaps the need to find time for lunch as well as the speech made me more succinct than usual for three-quarters of an hour's lunch interval does not leave much time for a Faculty meeting and lunch. I am glad to think that the Faculty took a unanimous stand on preserving the independence of the Judiciary against the growing powers of the Executive and also on the safeguarding of the four centuries old privative jurisdiction of the Scottish Courts in proceedings against the Crown. This is one matter in which Scots Law has something to offer other countries for it succeeded in devising an ingenious and simple procedure in Crown suits, while England floundered among Petitions of Right, Latin informations, writs of *capias ad respondendum, sub poena ad respondendum*, appraisement and *scire facias*. No wonder the English lawyers hail this Bill as an advance, while Scottish lawyers, at any rate those who have studied it, realise that while it gives with one hand, it takes away more with the other. Quite a number of the Faculty came up to me afterwards and were kind to me about my speech. The Faculty realise fully the grave issues involved, and I was interested to learn from Jack Gibson, one of the Advocate's legal secretaries, that the point about the English Courts encroaching on Scottish jurisdiction had not been detected in official quarters.

9th March 1947

The National Coal Board case afforded a contrast which I have often seen before between Ronald Morison and Lawrence Hill Watson as pleaders. Since he took silk at the early age of thirty-six, after thirteen years at the Bar, Ronald Morison has been, so far as pleading is concerned, the leader of the Bar. He is almost exactly my own age and, even at the University, his debating both in the associated societies and in the Spec was distinguished by that charm and elegance which later have become the feature of his pleadings. I was admitted to the Spec on the same evening as he was and had many early opportunities of assessing his gifts. They are those of a really great Counsel – an unfailing clarity of expression, a strong and well-modulated voice, a quick brain and natural aptitude for selecting the right approach to any question, a plausibility of manner coupled with charm and tact; he is in many ways a good example of a product of an English School and a Scottish University. From his appearances in the Chair of the Spec, I used to question whether his judicial qualities were quite equal to his forensic. At the Bar he began with every advantage – the son of one judge married to the daughter of another and devilled to Tommy Cooper. He made a flying start and since then has steadily increased his lead. Although he was away for several years in the forties, in the Judge Advocate General's staff, no sooner had he returned than he immediately reassumed the leadership of the Bar and within four months of his return was elected Dean of Faculty when only forty-four. Yet in little more than six months he resigned from his position and one cannot help feeling that with all his success and charm, he yet lacks something. I think I have come to closer friendship with him in more recent days. He differs from Cooper in almost every way. He is not a scholar, his intellectual interests seem to be confined to this profession and he has little of the characteristically Scottish background. The two, if I mistake not, dislike each other just because they are opposites. But however Ronald may be judged he enjoys the warm regard of his contemporaries at the Bar and my own relations with him, especially as we have grown older, have been of the happiest. No-one who hears him in Court can but admire his art, the lucidity and power of his arguments, the searching ruthlessness of his cross-examinations and his tact and experience in the face of judicial interruptions.

Lawrence Hill Watson is quite a different type. Tall, handsome, prematurely white haired, a distinguished figure of very great intellectual ability and subtlety, he yet spoils some of his best efforts by annoying faults of manner. In a sense these only endear him to his fellows. He is always over-eager, possibly too optimistic and he has a way of sometimes ignoring his juniors or brushing others aside, as if he spoke to no-one below the rank of Lord Advocate. In the Tummel Garry Inquiry, in which I was his junior, he kept up a running commentary the whole time. His opponent, Ronald Morison was addressing the Commissioner, Jock Cameron. As Jock remarked afterwards, 'I at least had this advantage – that I was able to hear both arguments at one time.' With a somewhat untidy delivery in which sentences tumbled out without much form or comeliness, interspersed quite unnecessarily with high pitched 'D'ye see?'s, he is the despair of short-hand writers. But in spite of these undoubted defects of manner, he is a great Counsel. Give him a complicated question of statutory construction and he will elucidate it in a thorough and convincing way, for his informality of speech goes nevertheless with lucidity and incisiveness. His mastery of a case was never more surely proved than in the Excessive Profits Appeals, which arose under the Finance Act 1943, when, pitted against Sir Walter Monckton, he showed himself the greater exponent of this subject. I have always been on the best of terms with him ever since we occupied adjoining flats in 41 Great King Street in our earlier days at the Bar. He was always appreciative of my co-operation, and, out of deference to me, decorated his speech in the Tummel Garry Inquiry with a quotation I suggested to him from the opening chapter of *The Fair Maid of Perth*. In the present Coal Board case, he had Wheatley as his junior and we were entertained, on the fourth day of the case, to see John appear in his new silk gown, his appointment as K.C. having been announced only that morning.

I heard three good stories this week. One came from the case itself. The Clerk of the Forth Conservancy Board was describing a mineral refuse bing from which material was slipping down into the waters of the Forth. He said, 'I should describe the bing as a truncated cone' (then he thought for a little and added) 'except that it wasn't a cone and – it wasn't truncated!' The remaining stories concerned Lord Justice-Clerk Macdonald whose Second Division was a somewhat messy and divided Court without very much respect for their Chairman. One day, a lowlander Macdonald appeared as a party before the Division. Lord Moncrieff: 'I thought all the Macdonalds came from Skye.' Lord Justice-Clerk: 'Oh no, you find Macdonalds all over the world.' Lord Young: 'Aye and some of them in queer places too.' Lord Justice-Clerk Macdonald was a great volunteer. It was said of him, 'All the soldiers thought that he was a great lawyer and all the lawyers thought that he was a great soldier.'

I must mention a new interest which began for me in January and which, I hope, will grow with the years. I became a Trustee of the National Library in 1939 being appointed one of the Faculty Representatives in succession to J.S.C. Reid. I was, however, not a member of the Standing Committee, which really manages the Library. Since the transfer of the Library to the nation, Normand was Convener of the Standing Committee, except for two years when he was Lord Advocate, during which time James Keith replaced him. When in December 1946, Normand became a Lord of Appeal in Ordinary, the Convenership fell vacant. It never entered my head that I would be considered. One day, to my complete surprise, T.B. Simpson who was a member of the Standing Committee told me that the Committee would like to nominate me as Convener at the Annual Meeting of the Trustees in January. I could not but accept, though I first asked, would he not himself consider nomination. But he explained that he could not because of ill-health. He told me that Normand and the Committee had not been anxious to have Cooper though as President, he becomes *ex officio* a member of the Trustees. I think it may well be that I was selected as being more acceptable to all parties. The incident showed me, as I have often learned before, 1. that the best things come without any seeking and that the things we ardently desire we may not get and 2. that the tortoise may beat the hare. I was privately entertained later when Cooper informed that he could have had the position but did not want it and that no doubt I had been selected as a yes-man. It is good to be able to look facts in the face and laugh at them. About the same time, he complimented me on my Crown Proceedings Bill Report and said, 'You will be glad to know that I wrote a letter with my own views to the Lord Advocate and that your Committee's Report and my letter are 95 per cent in agreement.' The laugh was again with me, for I had had the advantage of seeing his letter before conferring with my Committee, but in truth our report did not follow the lines of his letter, for most of our major recommendations were entirely new.

Possibly a certain irritation at not being Convener led Cooper to be rather querulous in his criticisms at his first appearance among the Trustees. But while the form of his criticisms was not happy, the substance of them was sound and I determined that I would try to do my best to meet them as I have a sincere and deep regard for him even though I think he would be better married! I often compare my lot with his and with how much I have and he has not – dear wife, dear children, dear home.

His criticism was that too much was being spent on incunabula. He was particularly incensed over the past purchase of an early volume of sermons by an Italian which he said cost £800 and could only lie in a safe at Borthwick Castle. He kindly lent me a specimen report of the Library of the London School of Economics in order to demonstrate what he regarded as a properly balanced purchasing policy. I found this helpful and studied it carefully though manifestly it does not serve as a model to be uncritically applied, the National Library's purchasing being conditioned by the fact that it gets free of cost all Copyright Act publications and that its purchasing only begins where these end. However, I have tried to evolve a policy (he having protested that the Library had none and that Normand did not want to be disturbed) and I have put it in the form of a Memorandum which I intend to submit to the Standing Committee at its first meeting on 19th March. It is much more interesting to commit myself thus on paper before the meeting takes place than to record success or failure after the event. Roughly speaking the policy is fourfold:– 1. To produce a system whereby the foreign purchases will be more effectively reviewed and the agencies for obtaining information on current publications and for purchasing improved; 2. To obtain information of numbers and cost of incunabula purchased in the past in order that some guide may be obtained for the future; 3. To devise a better system for completing obvious gaps in the Library; and 4. To improve the particulars given in the Annual Reports. The Memorandum has, with minor adjustments suggested by Dobie, the Librarian, been approved by him and also by Cunningham, Librarian of Glasgow University, who is Convener of the Books and Manuscripts Committees.

I was amused that my first acts as Convener were an act of loyalty and an act of piety – the act of loyalty being to suggest an allocation of date for the summer meeting of the trustees so that they might be free to attend their Majesties' Garden Party at Holyrood House; the act of piety being to authorise a bid for the 1683 Edinburgh edition of the *Pilgrim's Progress* of which a copy turned up at Sothebys. An article advised that it may fetch £250. In the end the British Museum got it for £32 and we stood down to let them complete their set.

Before leaving the subject of the Library, I should like to record my tribute to Dr. Meikle. I think that he as Librarian and McIntyre as Dean were responsible for my becoming a Trustee. A kindlier man there could not be, always ready to give time and service by making the Library more and more accessible. Alison became a great borrower of books thanks to his interest. The Library is not the same without him.

The Scots Law Chair has fallen vacant through the resignation of Candlish Henderson. The President, the Vice-Dean and others have kindly said to me that I am the obvious successor if I care to stand and that my selection would be unanimous. But after much thought, I should prefer to remain at the Bar and they have told me that they are not surprised. The Professorship on its new conditions is much more lucrative but it is now to be a whole time job, the Professor being only entitled to deliver opinions, apart from the work of the Chair. But what opinions are worth anything unless the author of them has to defend them in Court? The new system of appointment is calculated to exclude the most ambitious and enterprising Counsel from competing.

Quite a number of advocates have asked me for copies of the recent lecture I gave on 'The Art and Ethics of Advocacy'. David Watson, who is almost filial towards me, asked me to autograph a copy for himself and a second copy for his father. I gave my three devils, John Wilson, Arthur Matheson and Ronald Kydd, extra copies. When David Watson's master, Archie Williamson, died I offered to come in his place and David is almost like a former devil now. Tommy Cooper also expressed great interest in it and on Saturday morning led me off to his retiring room to show me the page proof copy of his edition of *Regiam Majestatem*. He had deleted Lord Justice-General and Lord President from the title page but I urged him to restore it as it added interest for others to know that it was published when he held those offices. He is now planning an Atlas of Medieval Scottish History. He has plotted on a map of Scotland all the thirteenth century parish churches with a view to showing the different distribution of population. I mentioned to him that I was keeping this Journal and he said, 'Another Cockburn's *Memorials*?'

20th March 1947

Yesterday I attended my first meeting of the National Library's Standing Committee and I was, I confess, very diffident about taking the Chair at a meeting where everyone present, unless possibly R.S. Cant, the St. Andrews University Librarian, was my senior. The other Trustees present were Dr. Cunningham, Librarian of Glasgow University, Dr. Peddie, Secretary of the Carnegie Trust, Dr. J.S. Duncan (whom I had once addressed over ten years ago when he was a member of the Educational Endowments Commission), Professor Dickinson and T.B. Simpson. The remit, in terms of my Memorandum, went through unanimously, though I sense slight opposition from Cunningham, who remarked, 'I remain impenitent about incunabula.' I replied that I had no desire to take sides but wanted to keep an open mind until the facts had been duly ascertained. Cunningham also proposed Dover Wilson to fill a vacancy on the Books and Manuscripts Committee, which shows he has no desire that I should be on this Committee when it considers the remit. If that be his view, then I shall communicate my views to Dover Wilson, Dickinson and Peddie, all of whom are on the Committee. I am a newcomer and must walk warily, but I should be sorry if Cunningham took the view simply that, 'Whatever is, is right.' Peddie left the meeting with me afterwards and obviously thought that the remit would serve a useful purpose and I think that Cunningham is generally of this view too. The Standing Committee were obviously a most efficient body, with not a single passenger among them and a considerable volume of business was despatched in a short time, with no unnecessary talk. How different from most Committees!

Tom Simpson is Chairman of the Finance Committee. He was uncertain whether he would be able to attend, as he suffers from a weak heart. Therefore at the end of last week, he asked me to come and see him about a financial matter which he decided to raise. At our meeting we discussed other much more interesting topics. He has written recently two amusing works. The first is a day to day diary of the War from its start to its finish. This journal is already set up in print but the publishers are apprehensive about publishing it because it contains so many smart things about living persons. There is no doubt that when it is published it will be greatly enjoyed by all except possibly its victims. The second is an autobiography up to the age of thirteen. As it deals with the Academy, it has a special interest for me. He has lent me a copy to read. His recollections are all extraordinarily accurate and they faithfully depict the mind of a child but

Randall Philip in his mid-20s.

there is also present the characteristic art and cynicism of his later years. Of all members of the Bar, he has the greatest literary gift, being possessed both of a remarkable gift of expression and of an irresistible if somewhat acid wit. In the Spec when he rose to speak, he kept the Society either spellbound or rocking with laughter as no-one else could do. And as Treasurer of the Faculty of Advocates, he even succeeds in making the Faculty finances sound witty. But he has never succeeded in getting any real practice at the Bar. Some are surprised at this, but I am not. I had him in my mind when I expressed the view the professional humorist is almost certainly a forensic failure. He knows that a joke is expected of him and cannot resist giving it. In the Tummel Garry Inquiry, where he appeared for the National Trust, he marred an otherwise good afternoon by reading a lengthy extract from a work of humour in the course of his speech. Never did a joke fall flatter. Solicitors do not employ him in my view because they fear his witty tongue and never know whether he is collecting a joke about them to re-tell later to his friends. I urged him to publish some of his essays as I know that here his work could not but be admired. He has an amusing essay on the chronology of the *Pickwick Papers* and throughout the war he commented on Scottish Affairs in the *National Review*. Many of these comments came from the Journal already mentioned.

Two other events have happened this week. Today John Wheatley's appointment as Solicitor-General came out. And George Montgomery told me that he was to be a candidate for the Scots Law Chair. I have known him since 1921 when we began to sit at desks together as apprentices of Messrs. Maclay, Murray and Spens. He was known as Sunny Jim and that describes his nature. He is always pleasant, always smiling, always confident and untroubled. But these most attractive qualities have their obverse side. He is somewhat superficial in his work and pleading and never gets very deep into any subject. But he has an easy and lucid manner of speech. And his lectures (if he is appointed) should always be easy to follow. I certainly wish him well, although I do not think that he will add a textbook to the Law of Scotland. He told me of his intention to stand because before making it known, he wanted to know that I was not a competitor.

I have been reminded of two interesting survivals and record these here as both may soon cease to exist. Recently Mr. Hook, at the Dinner given in his honour, in recalling his fifty years of Parliament House, said that it used to be the practice to send fees to advocates not by cheque but in cash, the pound notes being carefully folded in a triangle round the shillings. But this practice still exists for this week I have received no fewer than four separate fees from Messrs. Morton, Smart, Macdonald and Prosser W.S. all in cash bundled up in this peculiar way. The other survival which I have met with though not recently is this: the old practice of folding the letter of instruction in such a way that it forms its own envelope. The letter when it is folded being thus sealed on the outside. Only one firm, Messrs. Henry and Scott W.S., have ever sent me letters in this form, but in doing so they followed the practices existing in the time of Sir Walter Scott.

As I want this to be a perfectly frank record of my experiences at the Bar, I set down the fees I have earned each year until now. I was called to the Bar on 14th March 1924 and from then till now, the position has been (in guineas):- 1. 71; 2. 29 (the year before my marriage, wasn't I an optimist? I remember I made only four guineas during that winter session); 3. 92; 4. 191; 5. 211; 6. 235; 7. 322; 8. 447; 9. 455; 10. 578; 11. 392; 12. 755; 13. 768; 14. 1,311; 15. 1,602; 16. 1,281; 17. 1,846; 18. 2,348; 19. 2,066; 20. 3,105; 21. 3,152; 22. 3,041; 23. 1,774. There are some interesting observations on this table. Year 1 was inflated by a shipping case in which I acted for Simpson, Spence and Young (the Simpson I understand being the one who gave his name to the Mrs. Simpson who later married Edward VIII after his abdication and became Duchess of Windsor!). The result with this qualification shows a very gradual progression until year 12 which was the point at which I gave up law reporting. Year 21 was my last full year as a junior and I think years 20 and 21 give a fair indication of what is about the normal maximum which a junior may earn at the Scots Bar. In one of these years I am sure Archie Williamson earned more but from exceptional circumstances and I wonder whether people do not sometimes imagine wrongly that a Scots junior makes much more. I doubt whether he does unless in exceptional circumstances. At this time I was certainly one of the busiest juniors. Year 22 is partly affected by my having taken silk midway through that year. Year 23 is the first full year as silk.

I have mentioned the shipping case of the first year – the Strathfillan. It is interesting to recall that in that case I was junior to the then Lord Advocate Watson (afterwards Lord Thankerton) and to Carmont K.C. (afterwards Lord Carmont) and that my opposing junior was Normand (afterwards Lord President and Lord of Appeal) his senior being Condie Sandeman K.C., then Dean of Faculty. It was the result of a golf match which brought me into this galaxy of talent. W.A. Allan of Fyfe, McLean was my opponent in a competition of the Glasgow Legal Golf Club in years before when I was an apprentice in Glasgow. He beat me in a match played at Wester Gailes and perhaps on this account and also because we were both sons of the Manse, he instructed me in this case. The Lord Advocate eventually returned his papers, Carmont absented himself one day and I had to cross-examine a skipper with Condie and Normand on the other side. I was so confused that to this day I recall having asked one question which was so complex that it contained 'isn't this the case?' or 'the case is' or 'in this case' four times!

31st March 1947

Last night the Round Table entertained Lord Blades to Dinner in the Committee Room of the Liberal Club. There were fifteen present, George Morton in the Chair, Blades, John Cameron, James Walker, Harry Guthrie, T.P. Macdonald, Norman Macdonald, F.C. Watt, John Wheatley, George Reid, Jeffrey Cunningham, James Crawford, John Wilson and Frank Duffy. John Wilson had composed the most delightful menu card I have seen. The epigraph ran: 'At a round table there's no dispute of place.' And on the back there was printed (I suppose to recall Blades' name and robust pleading) the line from *A Midsummer Night's Dream*:

> Whereat with blade, with bloody, blameful blade,
> He bravely broach'd his boiling bloody breast.

George Morton proposed the guest, 'Bless thee, Bottom, bless thee, thou art translated.' As Harry Guthrie remarked afterwards, George Morton is perhaps the most typical Scotsman alive. Twenty years senior to the rest of us, our respect and affection for him do not depend on his age but rather on his humane liberal outlook – always kindly, always receptive to new ideas, always on the side of moderation, what greater tribute to a man can there be than to win quite spontaneously the affection of those around him. Few of the Bench have won this in like measure, although I place D.P. Fleming alongside George Morton. As Jock Cameron said in proposing his health, George Morton has never lost the common touch nor his link with his native Carnwath. When in the days of Asquith and Lloyd George, dissension arose amongst the Scottish Liberals, it was George who wisely said, 'Nae tact speirin.' A sound and wise judge though not in the front rank of Counsel, he would assuredly have reached the Bench had not the political pendulum swung away from the Liberal Party. After Daniel had replied to the toasts, Frank Duffy sang a composition of his own to the Londonderry Air ('Danny Boy'). Then I proposed the health of the new Solicitor General, John Wheatley, and he replied. For this toast, John Wilson had selected as the appropriate motto: 'The pate of a politician one that would

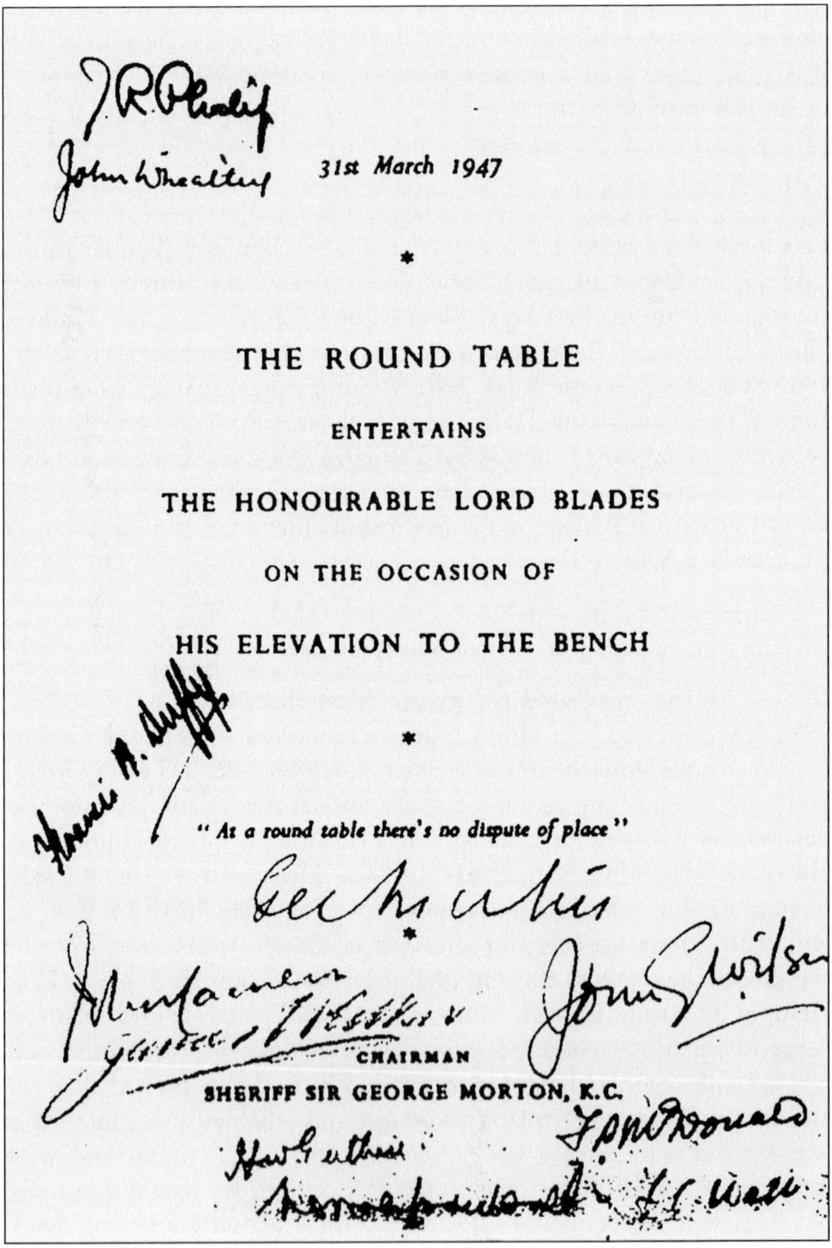

J. R. Philip

John Wheatley

31st March 1947

*

THE ROUND TABLE

ENTERTAINS

THE HONOURABLE LORD BLADES

ON THE OCCASION OF

HIS ELEVATION TO THE BENCH

*

" As a round table there's no dispute of place "

*

CHAIRMAN

SHERIFF SIR GEORGE MORTON, K.C.

circumvent God' (*Hamlet*). There followed songs which I accompanied to 'Vicar of Bray' and 'Passing By' sung by Jock Cameron, 'Clementine' in Professor Mair's French version by T.P. McDonald with all joining in the chorus. After that the Chairman nominated everyone in terms to propose or reply to a toast not on the list and this produced some ingenious *ex tempore* speaking, particularly from that subtle brain of James Walker who, not a politician at all, replied to the toast of the Labour Party proposed by F.C. Watt, (Conservative! – and until recently M.P. for Central Edinburgh). There were also two 'poems' read by Harry Guthrie and John Wilson, the latter fifteen verses cleverly taking off the fifteen present in terms. Finally John Cameron proposed that 'most potent grave and reverend signor' and at midnight or thereby the Dinner ended with 'God Save the King'.

One good story of the Crown Office was told by Harry Guthrie. A certain advocate depute who was troubled about a certain case and hesitated in his opinion, sent his papers to the Solicitor-General with the docquet 'this case requires consideration' hoping that the Solicitor-General would express his view. The latter simply wrote beneath the docquet the words 'I agree' and returned his papers to the depute. Harry Guthrie did not mention names but the Solicitor-General was King Murray.

The Round Table is, I think, in some ways a microcosm of the Bar. It well demonstrates the equality – which I have always regarded as a peculiar virtue of our profession – the singular good humour and freedom from jealousy of members of Faculty. In many ways there is ample scope for jealousy to take root, for many are called to the Bar, but few chosen for high preferment and the political situation often produces startling reversals of fortune. A good example is J.S.C. Reid, the present Dean of Faculty who as Lord Advocate appointed various judges but who is now himself in the wilderness. There have been jealousies of course but the absence of them is much more remarkable. Moreover, it is not a mere negative acquiescence in the success of others that is displayed by most members of Faculty. This was shown at the last Round Table to whose members it was a joy to do honour to their Chairman, to Blades and to John Wheatley. Another quality which I respect greatly in my own profession is their judgment. Ninety-nine per cent of them can be depended on first to try to ascertain the facts and then, and thoroughly, to express a considered opinion. This is the essence of sound judgment and in this respect the Bar is a great training ground of honest thinking. How often in other spheres this process is reversed thus, the opinion formed and facts then assembled to support it.

At this point I want to record my opinion and my general impression of the various members of the present Bench. I shall take the Lord Justice-Clerk first as I have already referred to the President.

Moncrieff took silk as long ago as 1912 and went on the Bench in January 1926. I was therefore less than two years at the Bar with him and indeed he had taken silk before the President and several of the other judges had been called to the Bar. He is therefore at the moment much the most senior member of Faculty on the Court of Session Bench. This brings a certain remoteness in age. But it would be quite wrong to suggest that he is remote in personality. He is a curious blend of the somewhat irascible and extremely affectionate. To some young counsel he may seem rather terrifying. But to me, both in Court and out of it, he has always been kindness itself, more than once telling me that he always listened to my arguments with interest. My first experience of this was in his second year as a Judge when, in the case of Sneddon v. Addie & Sons Collieries 1927 SN 164, he went out of his way to express appreciation of my arguments. This happens to many young counsel and the young counsel to whom it happens is never likely to forget the judge who said it. At last night's dinner, Blades expressed two views about Moncrieff. He said that in his view, Moncrieff was such a warm-hearted man that his irascibility was often due just to efforts to keep a good grip of his feelings. He also said that among the judges, Moncrieff was accepted as the greatest master of *ex tempore* delivery. He has a curiously subtle gift of expression which is intelligible to those familiar with it but puzzling to those who hear him for the first time. I recall his appearing in some sort of inquiry about 1925, at which Lord Constable was presiding. Constable was deaf in his left ear and the witness box in number 8 court (where he was sitting), which is usually to the judge's left, was specially moved to the right of the bench so that the steps leading down from it led backwards towards the bench instead of forwards towards the well of the Court. Moncrieff, who was cross-examining one of the witnesses, fired off one of his lengthy salvos which so surprised the witness that he stepped backwards in amazement and the next moment had disappeared from sight down the steps. Moncrieff was always absolutely fearless. On one occasion his junior, James Keith, was defending a judgment of Lord Blackburn's in the Inner House and was being constantly interrupted by the Division. Moncrieff came in at that moment, saw what was happening and leapt to his feet saying,

'I will not have my learned junior interrupted in the discharge of the somewhat august duty of supporting the judgment of the Lord Ordinary.' He then sat down and remained like a watchdog ready to spring while his junior completed his speech. With all his subtlety, he is the most logical of minds and if he errs it is not from prejudice but rather from a certain rashness for he is apt to be too quick. But if he is shown to be in the wrong, no-one is quicker to acknowledge his mistake. There is nothing petty about him. He has considerable literary and poetic gifts. At a Bar Dinner organised last summer by some young advocates who founded themselves into a society – 'The Friends of Jurgen' (Jurgen being the friend of the devil) – he made a speech on the traditions of the Bar which none who heard it will forget. He has also written a paper on the poetry of the law and a volume of poems, the latter of which he presented to me. It is called 'Fugitive Poems' and consists for the larger part of either short secular verse and classical translations or religious verse written partly before and partly after his reception into the Roman Church. Here is a short poem entitled 'Spindrift':–

> A throng of many voices,
> Hums to the wind-bewildered lea;
> And the summer breath that passes
> Bears the perfume of the grasses
> To the sea
> And the sharp salt spray rejoices
> In shrill ecstasy!

At the Round Table Dinner, Blades confided to me that Moncrieff was proud beyond measure at having succeeded to the office of Justice-Clerk. It is curious to think how accidental was his choice. Fleming went on the Bench along with Moncrieff as his immediate senior and had he not succumbed in an operation, he certainly would have been preferred. In the same way, had Patrick not been in Japan, he too would have been the more likely choice. Moncrieff is however a natural leader in any Division of judges. When Normand was President, it was Moncrieff, the quicker mind, who set the judicial pace. After Cooper had become President, while Moncrieff was still in the First Division, it looked as if that Division was going to work more uniformly, for Cooper was as quick as Moncrieff and the two ran in harness harmoniously. It is too soon yet to express a view on the new Second Division with Moncrieff in the Chair.

Since Moncrieff became Justice-Clerk, the First Division has consisted of Carmont, Russell and Keith. When I came to the Bar,

Carmont and Normand as juniors divided most of the shipping work. Carmont took silk a year before Normand but as seniors they again ran in parallel courses until politics intervened. Carmont had a rather more varied practice than Normand, although neither of them did as much work as either Graham Robertson or Cooper. As a young junior, Carmont edited a second edition of Armour on Valuation. Yet, I understood him to say that he was never instructed in a valuation case until he took silk. Such is the effect of literary efforts on practice. On the other hand, Candlish Henderson made his chamber practice out of the well-deserved reputation of his work on vesting. I once heard Cooper express the opinion that the three best legal works of our generation were Gloag on Contract, Graham Stewart on Diligence and Henderson on Vesting. Another curious fact about Normand is that apparently he never addressed a jury until he did so as Solicitor-General.

It was politics which first enabled Normand to draw ahead of Carmont and even then it was a pure chance. Carmont was Conservative candidate for East Edinburgh and Normand for West Edinburgh. In the General Election of 1931, one of these seats had to be relinquished to the Liberals and East Edinburgh was taken. As a result, Carmont never entered Parliament and instead, Normand became member for West Edinburgh and Solicitor-General, then Lord Advocate and then Lord President. Carmont practised three more years and then went on the Bench in 1934 after ten years as a silk.

As a counsel, Carmont was one of the great stylists of his day. He spoke slowly in a curiously high-pitched voice which had a tendency to break and yet was always pleasant to listen to. His words were always well chosen, he never faltered and he was always audible from any part of the Court. He once confessed to me that before he went in to speak in the Division, he was as nervous as a kitten and his thumbnails bitten to the core confirmed this. Yet to hear him speak would not have conveyed this impression unless one inferred it from a slight tendency to flush occasionally in anger and a certain mordancy of wit. As to his manner, I thought him a little inclined to fasten on debating points but his philosophical approach to a question and his capacity for independent thought, as well as his almost faultless manner, always secured him attention.

As a judge, he is the most silent of my time, sitting on the Bench with the sphinx like expression of a wise old owl. He has probably concurred more often than any other recent judge in the Division and he seldom gives the leading judgment. It was said of Lord Mure (I think by Condie Sandeman) that he was a sheep who always said 'Ba! Ba!' after the Lord President (Inglis) but if Carmont concurs, it is not from any sheeplike acquiescence. No man is more independent in his judgment when he likes. He may however be a little lazy. In one case where he had concurred with his brethren (who had proceeded on different grounds), his concurrence was the subject of comment in the House of Lords. Lord Russell of Killowen remarked, 'Whether all and each of these points of view commended themselves to Lord Carmont is uncertain, he simply concurred.' (Livingston's Trustees v. Livingston's Trustees 1939 SC(HL) 17 @ p35)

Carmont's independence of mind may however be illustrated by a story of, I believe, his uncle of the same name which well illustrates what must be the family character. Carmont belongs to an old Roman Catholic family (unlike Moncrieff who was a convert) and his uncle, the late Reverend John Carmont D.D., was at one time priest at Blairgowrie. Dr. Carmont was once involved in a very unusual litigation. A certain Captain Mitchell had died leaving a fund to the Roman Catholic Bishops in Scotland for the object of establishing and endowing an eventide asylum for aged and infirm clergymen. The Bishops having accepted the trust, decided to divide the fund into three portions, each portion to be administered by one Bishop without the concurrence of the others. This was plainly a breach of the trust and Dr. Carmont, who, as himself infirm had an interest in the due administration of the trust, drew the attention of the Bishops to their breach. When they persisted in it, he then, through his solicitors, intimated that he would take proceedings against them. The Archbishop of St. Andrews and Edinburgh then referred the matter to Rome and received instructions to censure Dr. Carmont. Dr. Carmont however persisted in his proceedings and the Scottish Bishops met and then formally directed the Bishop of Dunkeld, Dr. Carmont's Ordinancy, to intimate to him that he had incurred excommunication. Dr. Carmont however was not deterred by this and brought an application to have the Bishops removed from their office as Trustees and a Judicial Factor appointed. In the end, the Court, while not removing the Trustees from office, sequestrated the estate and appointed a Judicial Factor. I understand that the sentence of excommunication was afterwards recalled. But Dr. Carmont's action in face of so grave a threat carried into execution showed unusual courage. (Carmont v. Mitchell's Trustees 18R)

In private life, Carmont is a connoisseur in furniture, with a taste for good literature. To the Stevenson Club he read a memorable address on Robert Louis Stevenson and Edinburgh.

I'll gang nae mair whaur once I gaed
By Brunston, Fairmileheid or Braid
And far frae Kirk and Tron
And aye ayont the muckle sea
Still art thou dear, and dear to me
Auld Reekie, still and on!

Lord Russell, who comes next in the First Division, belongs to the group of judges of whom Lord Ormidale was one. While he had a considerable junior practice, he never had a large senior practice and as a judge he is not perhaps in the first rank. But he has many estimable qualities lacking in those more brilliant. Even at the Bar, he was very popular and attracted a disproportionate number of devils, all of whom have retained a warm affection for him. He was much in demand at Bar Dinners for he is a natural though untrained musician being able to extemporise with great facility. Unlike many musicians whose harmony is confined to their profession, Albert Russell carries about with him an air of constant good humour, pleasantness and charm. Sometimes on the Bench he flies into an unexpected tantrum, but it is momentary and the smile which is his usual expression quickly returns. He has a curiously mobile mouth, which expands from ear to ear when he smiles. One of his habits is to fix his eye on a point in the ceiling and, with a fixed smile on his face, slowly to propound some rather obvious proposition and you could almost imagine him knitting. It is this characteristic which has led him to being nick-named 'Aunt Mabel'. Another characteristic of his is a habit of building up extemporised judgments in the manner of 'The House that Jack Built'. Thus: 'The pursuer is a baker in Motherwell. On 16th May, the pursuer, who is a baker in Motherwell, was walking along the High Street. While the pursuer, who is a baker in Motherwell, was walking along the High Street, he saw a friend on the other side of the street. When the pursuer, who is a baker in Motherwell, saw his friend on the other side of the street from that side on which he was walking, he proceeded to cross and, in doing so, was run down by the defender's car . . . ' (and so on).

In two respects, Lord Russell excels. In the first place, he is extraordinarily successful in charging a criminal jury. In the second place, he displays never failing courtesy and attention.

Lord Keith, the fourth in the Division, was a counsel of large practice and equal ability. There was a time when every valuation case had

Cooper on the one side and Keith on the other. James Keith's special gift was, in my judgment, a fine legal imagination which enabled him to illustrate his argument and point to its practical bearing. As a pleader, he had a very slight nervousness of manner which produced a characteristic flickering of the eyelids and at times, almost a hesitation of speech. But these features only gave his pleading its characteristic charm and interest and the flicker of his eyelids was only the outward sign of a powerful intelligence at work. It is a tribute to the old Scottish Grammar School that Hamilton Academy has at this moment more former pupils in judicial office than any other school – Lord Keith, Lord Birnam and, in the Land Court, Lord Gibson. As a judge Keith has been criticised by those who plead before him for two tendencies. The one, a certain inscrutability and stubbornness, the other, a habit on every possible occasion of giving judgment *ex tempore* instead of taking his cases to avizandum. There is something in the criticism, but my own view is more appreciative of him than is the view of some others. He certainly does not give very much indication of the way his mind is working and the key to this may be a remark he once made to me. He said, 'In the great majority of cases, Counsel's argument has very little effect on the Court.' Certainly I have heard him address Lord President Clyde as if he knew that his argument was not likely to have much effect and when Clyde invited him to deal with a certain aspect, he indicated pretty plainly that he regarded it as having little bearing on his case. This quality which some label stubbornness (now that he is on the Bench) is in reality only extreme independence of mind. In the Division where he has just arrived he will not readily concur and he will have the energy when perhaps Carmont has not to express his own point of view. His fondness for *ex tempore* judgment is unusual in one who is not a very ready speaker. I attribute it partly to the incisiveness of his mind which quickly forms a view on a question and partly to the consequent desire not to have the burden of rethinking the problem later. Personally he is one of the most friendly of judges, youthful in appearance (so that one forgets his years) and a delightful companion in any outdoor pursuits for he is both a fine golfer and has, both on the bench and off, a keen sense of humour. I do not forget the fun I had in watching him wade almost waist deep in the Spey for a golf ball on a round at Newtonmore. Or another time when, as Chairman of the Youth Hostels Association, he accompanied me on a visit of inspection to the Youth Hostel at Kingussie. His boy, an Academy Dux, a year or two older than Gordon, is coming to the Bar and he asked me specially for a copy of my paper on Advocacy (of which he thought highly) to send to his boy. Keith became Dean of Faculty at a time when, but for his promotion to the Bench, a month or so before, Graham Robertson would have been the more likely appointment. As a businessman, Keith was particularly good. T.B. Simpson speaks highly of his short tenure of the Chairmanship of the National Library Standing Committee and he was responsible more than any other for the greatly improved financial position in which the Faculty of Advocates now stands.

14th April 1947

I must break off my impression of the present Court to record some recent happenings. Last week John Wheatley gave a dinner to some forty advocates and wives. This was the fourth Bar dinner of its kind in the last year, for there was the dinner of the 'Friends of Jurgen', the Dean's dinner and the dinner for Peter Hook. I sat between Mrs. Cameron and Mrs. Keith and we talked much about music and books. After dinner, quite a galaxy of talent was displayed. Cameron Miller sang two charming songs accompanied by Isobel Keith. Jock Cameron sang 'The Vicar of Bray' and 'Passing By', accompanied by John Wheatley, and Harry Guthrie sang two songs without any accompaniment. Mrs. G.S. Reid and Duffy also sang and a new performer, Mrs. Middleton, whose husband has just been called to the Bar gave two excellent Scottish recitations. John Wilson read his Round Table ode. Reference to this dinner leads me to say something relating to the earlier ones.

The Friends of Jurgen, who organised the first, are a group of young advocates who have revived the best traditions of the Bar with their *jeu d'esprit*. The first members were Arthur Matheson (Beau), David Watson (Vice-beau), Nigel Carrick-Allan (Macer) and Robert Taylor (Fool). Apart from Arthur, John Wilson and Ronald Kydd, my remaining devils were also associated with it and since Archie Williamson's death, his devil, David Watson, has gone some way to attach himself to me as a substitute 'master'. I am much taken by them. The first meeting which the Friends of Jurgen organised was a Stevenson commemoration on the jubilee of his death. I should explain that Jurgen was the 'friend of the Devil' and therefore the 'Friends of Jurgen' are 'devils'. John Oliver and Arthur Clark spoke on R.L.S.'s prose and poetry and I was invited to speak on 'Stevenson, the Man'. It was a very delightful evening held in Gladstone's Land and was instrumental in my being invited to become a Committee member of the R.L.S. Club of which I have recently become Chairman.

The second effort of the Friends of Jurgen was a dinner for Lord and Lady Birnam. This was the first Bar dinner to which ladies were invited and the Dean followed this custom when he gave his dinner after Christmas. The feature of the Jurgen dinner was the speech of Lord Moncrieff, which none who heard it will forget.

The dinner to Peter Hook was a remarkable affair. He has been fifty-five years about Parliament House, coming first when he was thirteen, and the dinner was given by the advocates on his 'list', though others, like myself, who were temporarily on his 'list' were also invited to be present. Lord Thankerton took the Chair and proposed Hook's health but it was the latter's reply which will be remembered. Peter Hook is so remarkable a man that I want to give my estimate of him. He began life without any advantages, starting as a choirboy in St. Mary's Cathedral and graduating from there as other boys have done to be an assistant in the Advocates' Library. Then he became Lord Advocate's Clerk. When Scott Dickson in 1906 lost his seat in Parliament, and in consequence the Lord Advocateship, he and the youthful Peter were 'out in the street'. They came back disconsolately to Parliament House. That day, an agent asked Peter Hook, who had never yet been an advocates' clerk, whether Scott Dickson would be available to act in a case. Hook saw his chance, said, 'Yes,' and arranged a consultation. From that moment he became the most trusted advocates' clerk in Parliament House. After forty more years, he is now the keystone of the whole Parliament House arch. 'Advocates' clerk' gives quite a wrong impression of him. It suggests perhaps some irresponsible assistant tripping along at Counsel's heels. But Peter Hook is a general in command. Wise, knowledgeable, courteous, tactful, yet courageous, full of the spirit of public service, an elder of the Kirk, the singer of a good song, Chairman of the Conservative Club, confidential adviser to hosts of country solicitors, fond of games and dancing, full of the zest of life, broad and sensible in outlook, a wholly admirable character who has learned the secret of life. Although I am not on his list, I have a shrewd suspicion that two of the advocates of recent years with whom he has been most friendly are Sorn and myself. Curiously my friendship was strengthened by bonds arising out of Gordon's death. His own son, Bill, had been missing at Dunkirk (though later he turned up) and, when Gordon died, he could not have done more to help me with my work in a difficult time. He was always good enough to say that when he entered our home, he at once became conscious of the spirit of harmony and love which truly prevailed there and it was out of this that our friendship grew. So is professional practice part of the bundle of life itself.

Last week the *Scottish Historical Review* resumed publication after a lapse of nineteen years. The *Review* came to an end in 1928 with its 100th number and now it has been revived this April with the 101st. The moving spirit is Dickinson, the new Scottish History Professor, whom I have met through Cooper. In this first number of the new series, Cooper occupied the place of honour with a lucid and ingenious article on 'The Numbers and the Distribution of the Population of Medieval Scotland'. Arguing backwards from population curves, he estimated the population of Scotland in the thirteenth century to be at 400,000 and thus, by means of taxation records, apportioned this figure among the medieval dioceses. My short paper on 'Sallust and the Declaration of Arbroath' also appeared. It was designed to show what I had discovered quite accidentally in reading through a *Times* War Anthology, that the famous passage of the Declaration: 'We fight not for glory nor riches nor honour but only for that liberty which no true man relinquishes but with his life' – was a free translation of Sallust's *Catiline*; and, also, that the variation in the translation, notably the substitution of the word '*vita*' for '*anima*', pointed to an ecclesiastic having been the author. We lawyers were in good company for the other contributors included a record scholar like Dr. Angus, and historians like Dr. Annie Dunlop and Henrietta Taylor. The most solid article however was probably that of Mr. McKerral, an ex-Indian civil servant on 'The Tack man and his Holding in the South-West Highlands'. I could not help contrasting Cooper's method with that of the historians. The latter wrote as if they were emptying their notebooks onto the printed page. His material was assimilated and presented with great lucidity and gift of exposition. Indeed I had a talk with him on the subject when he commented on the obscurity of the writing of such historians as Hannay and J.D. Mackie (in his introduction to Thomas Thompson's *Memorial on the Old Extract*). How much the various professions have to learn from each other. It would be well for an historian to have the experience of debating his thesis in the First Division. We both agreed that Dickinson was an instance of lucid historical writing and I think Rait was another. The same is true of the later portions of Hume Brown and R.L. Mackie's delightful *Short History of Scotland*.

I received today a letter from Lord Thankerton expressing appreciation of my paper on *The Art and Ethics of Advocacy*. He expressed the view that, in his experience, the most impressive pleader in appearance, manner and method was Alexander Asher. He thought J.B. Balfour (Kinross) was brilliant and placed Condie Sandeman between the two.

24th April 1947

On holiday at Grasmere we met, staying in our hotel, the Bishop of St. Edmundsbury and his wife. I had an interesting talk with him. When I remarked that William Temple had stayed in our hotel – Moss Grove, formerly Baldry's – he said that he had first come to this hotel himself in Temple's company. I observed that Temple had a much wider influence in Scotland than Lang. He argued that outwardly Temple had the greater influence but he said that, as a businessman, Lang was the greater. He also said that he united varying personalities. He was staying at Lambeth at the time of George V's death. Lang had many responsibilities suddenly thrust on him in connection with the funeral and other arrangements. He would attend Matins at 7.30 in the Lambeth Chapel. This would last for ¾ hour. Then, after attention to much troublesome correspondence he would, in the morning, meet the bishops and conduct business serenely. 'Something of a mouth' was the Bishop's further description of him. Temple on the other hand in business was for a man of his scholarship surprisingly uncritical. A suggestion would be made which he would seize on. Then the opposite view would be put by someone else and he would jump at that. The Bishop regarded Dr. Haigh of Winchester as the ablest of the present Bench. A 'devastating critic' – who would have been Archbishop but for ill-health. Dr. Fisher he regarded as the only man to be appointed to the Archbishopric a better businessman than Temple but 'no speaker'. He was much interested when I told him that I was named Randall after Davidson's great grandfather and grandfather, both parish ministers of Duckhill and the one the author of the 49th paraphrase. He did not know of Davidson's Scottish clerical ancestry, so I referred him to my father's book used by Dr. Bell at the beginning of his *Life of Randall Davidson*. I asked him about Hensley Henson who, I knew, lived in retirement in his Diocese. 'Yes,' he said, 'he is now gravely ill.' I remarked that I had read his Reminiscences and Bishopric papers which seemed to me much the most interesting modern books of their kind. 'Yes,' he observed, 'whenever Henson spoke, people crowded in to listen to him. But they never *voted* with him, for he somehow did not carry conviction.' I asked the Bishop if he took a turn of conducting prayers in the House of Lords and explained that Counsel appearing before the House had always to wait outside on tenterhooks until the officiating Bishop had concluded his devotions. He said: 'Yes, I take two weeks every year.' (I found out afterwards that he obtained his seat as a spiritual Lord only in 1946.) 'The senior Bishops select their weeks of duty first and always select periods in vacation! The junior Bishops take their duty during term.' I said that I had noticed that he had a suffragan, the Bishop of Dunwich, and expressed surprise at the name, Dunwich having been a rotten burgh, returning two members to the unreformed House of Parliament after the burgh was already under the sea. He explained that the present suffragan was only the second, that the name was the revival of an old name. The use of such a name with its unfortunate association even if picturesque seems doubtful policy. He was much interested to find that I knew Kersey and Nayland. When I expressed my delight in the Suffolk dialect, he took the contrary view, adding that he found the Suffolk people slow. I asked him about those mysterious twins, the two Deans of Bocking. He said: 'They are like Siamese twins, when one dies the other goes out of office.' The Bishop, Brook his name is, comes into dinner behind his wife as if they formed an ecclesiastical procession. He has a bald pate with dark hair surrounding it like a tonsure. His face is a Dickensian one. Mrs. Brook was 'sympathique', and I shall not forget her kindness to Ella. The friendship we made with them in the short time was a lasting one.

I cannot help at this stage contrasting Bishop Brook with another Bishop, Bishop Eivind Berggrav, the Norwegian primate and patriot who stayed with us one night in March 1946 on his way to the George Wishart Commemoration at St. Andrews. He had that humility and simplicity of the really great man as well as a warm humanity and humour. For over two years he was in solitary confinement in a forest camp twenty kilometres from Oslo. As he said, 'I had nothing but my Bible to read, my meals to cook and my pipe to smoke.' He added afterwards that he smuggled in a small wireless set with which he used to listen under the bedclothes to the BBC. His pipe was a magnificent one with a large square bowl and long pipe which enabled it to be held almost at the waist. He made friends with his German guards and was able to escape nightly to Oslo to address underground meetings there. At a meeting with Himmler, he stood up to him for

Bishop Eivind Berggrav.

an hour and a half. 'I suppose you would like to be made a martyr,'said Himmler. 'No,' said the Bishop, 'I have no such desire. But in any event, if you were to kill me, the whole of Norway is behind me.' Ninety-two per cent of the Norwegian pastors broke from the Nazi state and went out into the wilderness. 'We took as our example the Disruption in Scotland. What the Free Church in Scotland had done we also could try to do.' He was delighted that his captivity cost the Germans 250,000 kroner a year. As I had to go to a Glasgow murder case the same afternoon, I took him round Edinburgh in the morning. He signed the Lord Provost's visiting book beneath the names of Montgomery and Alexander. I introduced him to Normand, then Lord President, who took us both into the Judges' Retiring Room and was most courteous. Discussing the Nuremberg Trials, Normand expressed the view that Goering and the others should just have been shot. 'No,' said the Bishop. 'That would have been contrary to the Laws of War.' In Princes Street, with that delightful spark of humanity, he asked me with a twinkle in his eye, to stop my car near the Scott Monument while he rushed into a tobacconist's to buy a box of his beloved cigars. I took him to lunch with the Rev. Alex. King. 'This,' I said, 'is the first time that I have lunched alone with a King and a Bishop.' 'Yes,' he said, 'and you will be meeting a murderer in the afternoon.' I introduced him to the elderly waitress who has often attended to us and is kind to us because of Gordon. It was difficult to say which was more pleased to meet the other, this great but humble Norwegian patriot bishop or the kindly Scottish serving woman.

I must now resume my impressions of the present judges of the Court of Session, taking the other members of the Second Division than the Lord Justice-Clerk to whom I have already referred.

Lord Mackay is at the moment easily the chief character on the bench. Scarcely a day passes but there is a fresh story about him. Scarcely a day passes but he adds a new word to the English language. Originally he must have been a greatly gifted man. He was a dualist at Aberdeen, Cambridge and Glasgow. At Cambridge in the Moral Science Tripos, he took a First Class and Star. He was tennis champion of Scotland. He is a first class mountaineer. One of the buttresses of Sgoran Dubh above Loch Einich is named 'Mackay's buttress'. He is a beautiful sketcher. Every problem he seems to have thought of in advance. He has complete belief in himself, knows everything and can display much subtlety of mind.

But he has the faults of his kind. He is an unselfconscious megalomaniac. His subtlety has run to seed and he is prolix, turgid and confused in style. His fondness for new expressions has led him to devise a vocabulary of his own. He is pachydermatous and does not know when a joke is made at his expense. He is vulnerable to any amount of flattery. In spite of his pictorial artistry, he has no gift of selecting ideas and his judgments contain everything that comes into his head. Being an omniscient, he has rather a habit of crabbing others and is always correcting his colleagues, Sheriff-substitutes and members of the Bar. He is like Gladstone, inebriated with the exuberance of his own verbosity; as Cooper put it to me on 28th November 1946, his style is 'Thomas Carlyle intoxicated'! Physically, with his mouth forming a triangular opening to one side, he looks like a gigantic turbot lying on the fishmonger's slab. Certainly this is how he should be cremated. R.B. Miller, incensed at his verbosity, exclaimed, 'That man's got a face like a haggis.'

Yet he is one of the most lovable of men off the bench with a pawky Aberdonian friendliness that goes straight to the heart and he is much beloved by those colleagues of his own division who are most exasperated with his judicial behaviour.

Stories of him are legion. I shall give some which I have collected myself. First, verses of him by two of my devils (the third was asked to write a verse too but has not yet done so).

> As a patriotic lawyer, I dispense the law of Rome,
> When construing testamentary provisions,
> I much prefer a short dissenting judgment of my own,
> And my unreported Outer House decisions.
>
> (J. G. Wilson 1944)

> Oh my! Oh my!
>   Good Lord Mackay,
> Oh well of dicta never dry!
>   No interruption stays or stems,
> Your flow of wayward apothegms;
>   And slights that lesser men had curbed,
> Leave you completely unperturbed;
>   You vex the air, though no-one listens,
> With self-regarding reminiscence –
>   You adumbrate . . . you condescend . . .
> You amplify . . . you apprehend . . .
>   You 'state your view' . . . you 'put your point' –
> The whole debate slides out of joint.
>   Your brethren wince, and Counsel cry,
> 'Deliver us, ye hosts on high
>   From the unquenchable Mackay!'
> And so do I –
>   Oh my! Oh my!
>
> (A. A. Matheson 25/10/44)

Next, some examples of his use of language. He referred to a retired probation officer as a 'spent' probation officer. On another occasion

to some person having a 'sub-intention'; to the accumulation of income with residue as the 'balling-up of residue'; to a motor which
took a corner at 40 m.p.h. as coming 'peeping' round the corner; to
a female pursuer as 'unbonneted', that is, without a hat; to having
reached his 'almost conclusion' and getting mixed up with Alamein
and flamethrowers, to a certain litigant, a client of mine, Mrs. Allanly,
as a 'blamethrower'; to a trust fund as 'the corporeal quid to which
the trust attached'. As Lord Macmillan once explained to his colleagues in the House of Lords: 'You see, Lord Mackay has a
vocabulary all his own.'

Here are some longer examples of his Lordship:-

Lord Justice-Clerk Aitchison (deciding a case): 'This is a perfectly
simple case. But for certain authorities an ordinary man would have
no doubt as to the testator's meaning.'

Lord Mackay (dissenting): 'If I may for the moment place myself
in the position of an ordinary man . . .'

In Lord Advocate v. Hamilton's Trustees 1942 SC 426, at page 447:
'As the Crown are forced away, bit by bit, from one anchorage to
another, it is hard even to figure where it is that the flukes of their
anchor come at last to hold.'

In Allanly v. Allanly, Lord Mackay put a question to the Solicitor-
General (King Murray) (for the defender): King Murray: 'Yes, that
was a question which your Lordship has already put to Mr. Hill
Watson.' (my senior, for the pursuer). Lord Mackay: 'I did put that
question to Mr. Hill Watson but he just *puffed in my face.*'

Lord Mackay: 'I am prepared to follow Lord Dunedin who is a very
considerable authority especially when concurred in by myself.'

Lord Mackay: 'Counsel nowadays display an insane desire for brev-
ity.' Again, the same day: 'In this case I do not propose to deliver a
novum testamentium for the benefit of the drivers of motor om-
nibuses.'

Lord Mackay (to myself): 'Your argument has struck me almost
dumb.' (Lord Sorn to whom I told this the next day said, 'You should
have pressed your argument!')

In one case, it appeared that one of the parties had gone round various debtors and told them one after the other to write off their indebtedness. Lord Justice-Clerk Cooper to Lord Stevenson: 'This is like that parable of the unjust steward.' Lord Mackay: 'I am not sure that I agree with that parable!'

Lord Mackay: 'I shall have to act as midwife to this argument.' Counsel: 'I hope this will not involve a miscarriage of justice!'

I told Lord Mackay one day that I had been visiting the locus of an accident. 'Ah yes,' he said, 'What a pity that the Court does not do so too. We have to depend on plans and I notice that *my brethren* are not very good at reading them.' This recalls Lord Bowen's suggestion to his judicial colleagues for the opening gambit of a loyal address to Queen Victoria: 'Conscious as we are of each other's infirmities . . .'

Lord Mackay (in the Pringle Trust Case 1946 SC 353): 'I have never known the Court of Session to spin like a spider a scheme out of its own substance.'

On the functions of a judge: 'We don't like to add to Counsel's difficulties but after all that's what we're here for.'

Lord Mackay (in a Special Case): 'I shall not have begged out of me the answer to a question which was not argued.'

Lord Mackay: 'I shall be short if possible.' F.C. Watt (in whisper heard throughout the Court): 'Impossible!'

Harald Leslie: 'This appeal raises a short point.' Lord Mackay: 'No, Mr. Leslie, not "a short point", but perhaps "a point within narrow compass"?'

4th May 1947

At this point, I interject a curious incident which occurred to me at Grasmere and which records in a strange way the gratitude of a little bird. One day, the four of us went to Dove Cottage. We came in due course to a little room at the back, darkened by its low ceiling. The custodian opened the window to let in the sun and we looked out on the steep little garden with its grass slopes strewn with daffodils.

Perhaps it was a vision from the window that led Wordsworth to write:

> To me, the meanest flower that colour can give
> Thoughts that do often lie too deep for tears.

On a bush at the side of the window sat a robin, quite unperturbed by this opening of the window. The caretaker took some crumbs and laid them on the palm of her hand. In came the robin, settled on her palm and devoured the crumbs. Then the caretaker gave some crumbs to Alison and the robin, without any timidity, took the crumbs from her. In answer to our inquiry, the caretaker said that the robin had taken two years to train. He came every two hours for a meal and recently he had been somewhat perplexed by the introduction of double summer time. During the long frost, the robin seemed to be specially dependent on the supply of crumbs and seemed also to know that human beings might be short of food. For several times he arrived at the window with a worm dangling in his beak which he could well have devoured himself and solemnly laid it on the caretaker's hand for her to eat. Such is the gratitude of a bird.

This story leads me to refer to the cold spell of 1947, said to be the worst since 1841. Snow lay from 20th January to 20th March continuously and the bitterness of the cold was accentuated by the shortage of fuel. Windermere and Loch Lomond were frozen. In the Midlands every road was closed. The principal railway tunnel between Manchester and Sheffield was blocked. One million sheep were lost. We saw those left in the Lake District starved, skinny and diseased, though the Border sheep appeared as normal. The snow was followed at the thaw by unparalleled flooding particularly in the Thames Valley (where the river reached its highest recorded level), in the Fen country and at Gainsborough where Dutch engineers were brought to advise on the rebuilding of the embankments. As Gainsborough is George Eliot's 'St. Ogg's', I wonder if *The Mill on the Floss* dealt with the corresponding great flood of last century. George Eliot would be about twenty-two in 1841 and, if Maggie Tulliver was the author herself, the dates would seem approximately to correspond.

6th May 1947

At the resumption of the Summer Session, I had a meeting with the President about other matters, and he again tried to interest me in the Scots Law Chair, which has now been thrown open to people who would continue to practise. He did me the honour of saying that Hector McKechnie and myself were the only two at the Bar with the 'stature' to occupy the Chair. But as my mind was already made up, I told him so as tactfully as I could. In Montrose's words, which my own mother often quoted to me:

> He either fears his fate too much
> Or his deserts are small
> That puts it not unto the touch
> To win or lose it all.

I found afterwards that Hector McKechnie had taken the same decision. The candidates so far appear to be George Montgomery, William Garrett, J.L. Duncan, A.D. Gibb and a Dundee solicitor, Mr. Herd. The first three each approached me to propose them! But I was committed, first, to George.

16th May 1947

I proposed George Montgomery for the Chair of Scots Law and T.P. McDonald seconded. Hill Watson proposed Garrett, and Bill Grant seconded. George received 65 votes to Garrett's 10. One of the other two candidates, solicitors, received one vote and the other none. A.D. Gibb, Scottish Nationalist and Professor of Law at Glasgow, withdrew his candidature this morning. He would have been the most serious rival. The vote indicates the size of the active Faculty.

23rd May 1947

The General Assembly has been meeting. For the first time I am a Commissioner, my constituency being the Presbytery of Uist.

I made my third appearance, today, in the General Assembly. My first was about midnight in the old Church of Scotland pre-1929 Assembly in the Tolbooth Church where I appeared on behalf of an undeserving parish Maryton which a special Commission presided over by Dr. Joseph Mitchell of Mauchline (ex-Moderator) proposed should be suppressed. My only two arguments were that Maryton was the birth-place of Andrew Melville and also of Dr. Joseph Mitchell himself and therefore deserved a continued existence. We succeeded. The next appearance two years ago was for an undeserving Church in Dalry, Ayrshire which refused to enter into a reasonable union. We won again on technicalities. A Special Commission had been directed

Mrs. Mary Philip (Randall Philip's mother).

to visit Kirk Session and congregation and had not done the latter. I found this out and called on the Convener to admit his disobedience to the Assembly's direction. His doing so won us the case. But the Church was rightly forced into union the following year. Today's case was more deserving. St. David's and Old St. Paul's, Dundee, both High Churches, wished to unite but the Presbytery was against union

Dr. Adam Philip (Randall Philip's father).

on no very tangible grounds. We were able to put up a strong case on the merits which the opposition sought to criticise ineffectively without offering any stateable alternative case. We succeeded by a majority which did not require counting.

As I have now had as much experience of the Assembly as any present counsel, other than the Procurator, I can say this. It is, in law, a court but, in fact, a public meeting apt to be swayed by prejudice and full of much irrelevant talk. But there is something extraordinarily impressive about it which is unlike anything found anywhere else. That 1,608 Commissioners should attend day after day, morning, afternoon and evening with wives and camp followers, should display the keenest enthusiasm and interest in the work of the Churchmen in this secular age and should then return to their respective parishes up and down the land is one of the most amazing vindications of democracy. I am much more impressed with the triumphant democracy of the Assembly than with the Christian spirit of its business. Too often, the ecclesiastic is a man with little of real Christianity in his values. Even Dr. John White on a Committee on which I sat this last year shouted down his brethren on the Committee for 95 per cent of the time and when the Committee took, all of them, a different view from him, stomped out of the room in a rage. But let it not be thought that the Church does not number saints up and down the land. Ministers and their wives, living examples of great heroism and sacrifice, thinking not of themselves, regretting only that they cannot do better for their children, but the most happy natures in the world. I cannot but think of my own mother and father, the one an energetic, vivacious, tireless, practical Christian, the other a shy, self-conscious, almost mystical, Scottish George Herbert.

5th July 1947

The change in the position of a judge in the last fifty years is well illustrated by some circumstances which I set down here. Lord President Inglis always drove up to Court in his carriage and pair. In 1924, when I was called to the Bar, judges and counsel, almost without exception, ascended the Mound to Parliament House, at all events in Summer, in tall hats and morning coats as even Parliament House clerks had done a generation earlier. Now today I was talking to the President about the Library (it was Saturday morning). At the end of the conversation he said to me, 'I must go and collect my new ration book.' Four weeks ago he left me similarly saying, 'I'm off to buy fish for my lunch.' How are the mighty fallen. Another change of a different kind in my time is that, while in 1924 both Divisions sat regularly on Saturday mornings, now they never sit on Saturdays. I remember Lord Sands being very annoyed one Saturday when the President (Clyde) insisted on a case going on late in the morning. It was the day of the Anglo-Scottish rugby international at Murrayfield.

Lord Sands always attended these matches but Clyde never. He had no interest in games and did not mind how long the court sat on these occasions.

27th July 1947

During the later part of the summer session, I have had no time to touch this diary. I had a succession of long proofs which aborted my working time. One curious feature was that, for five weeks almost continuously, I was in proofs against Jock Cameron. I do not recall having been so continuously against one counsel for so long in different cases. We sat at lunch together each day, and remained throughout on the friendliest terms, though, in Court, battling against each other continuously. Jock Cameron is intellectually perhaps the most dexterous of the present Scottish counsel. He has a quick, powerful, subtle mind with a fluent and (what does not always accompany fluency) pungent gift of expression marked by an informality and tendency to slang which is very refreshing, if not always dignified. He is always in his kinder moments a very lovable fellow, though he does suffer from a certain egotism not immaterial in one of his pre-eminent ability. His legal judgment and his strategy and tactics are very good, if sometimes a little unscrupulous. The quality which he lacks and the presence of which would just complete his equipment is a certain dignity and moderation. One always sees in him something of the mischievous schoolboy or the *enfant terrible*. He served during the War in the Navy, and obtained the D.S.C. and was mentioned in despatches. The sea is in his blood, and his language has always a certain combination of nautical thickness and legal subtlety. Between us there is, I think, a mutual respect. One curious point is that, since his return from the War, although I have been against him in numerous cases, I have so far won every time. In the latest batch, however, is one which I shall lose. He once paid me a typical compliment at the conclusion of a War Office case which I won against him: 'This,' he said, 'is the first time I have seen the War Office represented by anyone with any intelligence!'

6th September 1947

Yesterday, apart from three drops of rain one afternoon in Glenfeshie, we saw the first rain since July. At Boat of Garten where we spent August, we had, except for half of one morning and two late afternoons, continuous sunshine and quite unclouded skies. I have seen nothing like it in this country, and it seems almost as if the long frost of the winter and this long period of sunshine had some connection.

While on holiday, David Watson, who was at Nethybridge, invited us on behalf of his mother and father to go and see them there. We met them at the Nethybridge Sheepdog Trials. We sat in a room overlooking the Nethy bridge, where people congregate as at the village pub, and exchanged stories of the law. Lady Thankerton looked frail but has the same charm as David. In her case:

> As a white candle
> In a holy place
> So is the beauty
> Of an aged face.

Lord Thankerton was anxious for any new stories of Parliament House, and I was able to give him a number about Lord Mackay. He spoke highly of the new Northern Irish Law Lord, Lord MacDermott. Lord Thankerton's hobby is knitting to which he was introduced on his honeymoon. David, for whom I have a sincere liking, went out of his way in every kind of courtesy to us, and told us that his father was anxious to meet me.

Mr. Wright, the minister of Boat of Garten, introduced me to Lord Erskine of Restormel, who opened his sale of work. Lord Erskine is a descendant of the famous Lord Chancellor, whose elder brother was Dean of the Faculty and Lord Advocate. His ancestor took his title from Cornwall, being a friend of George IV, who then held the Duchy and gave his consent to the use of the name. Lord Erskine was staying in a cottage which we very nearly took – The Shieling – in Boat of Garten. Alas! he has none of the eloquence of his sire, and in opening the sale made his two topics how his Cornish title came into being and how his ancestor secured the first Act for the prevention of cruelty to animals. He belongs to the Buchan Erskines, and is, I think, heir-presumptive to the earldom of Buchan but the head of his family is the Earl of Mar. Looking up *Who's Who* afterwards, I was interested to find that both the Earl of Mar and the Earl of Crawford state that they are the Premier Earl of Scotland.

Mr. Wright has the complete confidence of both the residents in and the visitors to Boat of Garten. It is easy to understand why. He is a good mixer, and his work in the pulpit is of a very high order. He never wastes a word and has a direct practical humour which appeals to all. I played the organ throughout the month as I have now done (omitting the War) for over ten years. It is a pleasure to do it especially when the church is so efficient and so much a focus of village life. Mr. Wright lost a child like myself, and, though others would not know, his prayers always contain some indirect reference to this, which is a further bond between us.

7th October 1947

Today is announced the resignation of Lord Moncrieff. Cruel fate seems to follow those Justice-Clerks who succeed Justice-Clerks promoted to be President. Witness Lord Justice-Clerk Patton who followed Inglis as Justice-Clerk. No Justice-Clerk can have acted for a shorter period than Moncrieff. Two long relapses due to heart trouble compelled him to be absent from the Bench for a considerable portion of his tenure of office.

Yesterday, I had lunch with Dover Wilson at the New Club and we met Dr. Lionel Smith who had with him Sir Donald Somervell, formerly Attorney-General and now a Lord Justice. He has the rosy countenance of a country squire with a humorous expression, and is well up on Walter Scott and Burns. I noticed too that he quoted, without difficulty, a passage from Masefield that I tried to recall. His father was a master at Harrow to whom Winston Churchill paid handsome tribute in his *Early Life*. His brother is a master at Tonbridge, D.C. Somervell, so school mastering is in the blood. I told him that I had once or twice appeared before Rowlatt J. when he presided over the Compensation Defence Tribunal and how delighted Rowlatt was when we were able to produce a real live litigant with the legendary name John Doe. The President told me after that Sir Donald Somervell had one week of heavy loss in which he lost his wife, his seat in Parliament and the Home Secretaryship.

Today we had a special meeting of the National Library Standing Committee to consider the Report of the Books and MSS Committee on the remit mentioned on 20th March 1947. I am glad to say everything went through satisfactorily. I had been put onto the Books and MSS Committee on Cunningham's suggestion half way through the discussion of the remit. I think that my previous judgment of Cunningham was quite wrong. During the last six months we have had the most happy co-operation. Going back to the policy outlined on 9th March 1947, I find that the remit has been wonderfully successful. We secured all the information we needed and found that the expenditure on incunabula, which had averaged £40 in 1939–42, rose to

£1,442 in 1943–7. It is now resolved (1) gradually to increase foreign purchases; (2) that purchases of incunabula in excess of £750 *per annum* should not meantime be made without the approval of the Standing Committee; (3) that a break-up statement of purchases should appear in the Annual Report each year, giving the purchases of the year set against those of the previous year, country by country. These were, perhaps, the chief proposals for revision of policy. The President, who was to have attended the meeting, (fixed specially for his convenience) had a chill and was absent. He rang me up later and I was glad to find that, although he had been the chief critic of the past purchases of incunabula, he approved generally of the proposed policy and was, I think, appreciative of the fact that it had gone so far to meet his views.

8th October 1947

Today's announcement is that the new Lord Justice-Clerk is to be G.R. Thomson; and John Wheatley, Solicitor-General, is to succeed him as Lord Advocate. At thirty-nine, I should think John Wheatley is the youngest Lord Advocate ever. His party has no older adherents at the Bar.

George Thomson goes on the Bench at fifty-four. Though he is my senior by seven years, in some respects he has been a contemporary, for the War delayed his studies. He went through some of his law classes with me, in particular civil law, and we were members of the Diagnostic Society together, he being Secretary while I was Assistant Secretary. He is a curious combination of opposites. A son of the manse but with not very much of the manse tradition. A conspicuously good student in law at the University, yet never acquiring the best type of legal practice which might be associated with scholarship. Rather a jury counsel, indeed, latterly our best jury counsel, before juries were suspended for the duration of the War (incidentally they resume on 14th October); but with a poor voice, and a curious sleepy manner. A Rhodes scholar, for although his father was later minister at Bellshill, for a time he went to South Africa I believe for George Thomson's health. I understand from both lobby correspondent and M.P. not a Parliamentary success, where he was regarded even by his own party very differently from J.S.C. Reid, who has become, possibly, the Conservative Party's best debater. George Thomson is impermeable like Lord Mackay, and, in the Second Division, there will now be a competition for which is the more pachydermatous. George Thomson's father, the late Rev. W.R. Thomson of Bellshill, was an able minister who died before he fully came into his own. He wrote a delightful volume of Dickens' sketches, called *In Dickens Street*. The son is joint author of a short textbook on Court of Session Practice, but does not take any special interest in legal scholarship. He had a good practice, though not commensurate with his present office, which has come through politics. But I think that although he was a good counsel, he may prove a better judge, for he has a gift of lucid informal exposition. I still remember a talk he gave on 'Guild Socialism' in the Diagnostic Society thirty years ago. When, during the war, I ran a team of volunteer staff officers at the Scottish Regional Commissioner's, he was a member of this team and he is now the third member of this team to go on the bench. The other two were Lords Mackintosh and Birnam.

10th October 1947

It was announced unofficially today that Douglas Johnston is to be the new Solicitor-General. I heard it from T.P. McDonald yesterday, as he had received the usual intimation from Douglas Johnston that he was to take 'silk' – a necessary preliminary. Douglas will be a year older than John Wheatley, and, politics apart, no one would have thought of him for the office, at any rate meantime. Indeed in August, when I saw him at Cromdale, he was thinking of Jock Cameron. Douglas is a very decent fellow, of considerable ability. Though the son of an Aberdeen solicitor, he is possessed of a rather overpowering 'Oxford' accent, a handicap which he shares with one other member of the bar. But this is only a veneer and, beneath it, he is a thoroughly good fellow. His wife is a sister of Margaret Kidd, our own lady advocate, herself a daughter of a Conservative M.P. I have never heard of him doing any political work, though he has always borne the description of a Socialist.

This afternoon, I lectured to the English Association on 'The Use of English in the Law Courts'. The President was to have taken the chair, but had a chill, and Keith replaced him. The meeting, though small, was very appreciative. In the discussion which followed, I was urged to make my paper an introduction to an anthology of legal judgments. But on what ground would the anthology be based? Not for the law contained in the judgments, for that can be had for those who want it in the law reports. Presumably for the literature, like Bowen, Macnaghten and Sumner (to whom I referred) in the *Oxford Book of English Prose*.

I have just completed a paper on 'R.L.S. – A Character Study from his Writings' to be delivered in December. The idea was to interpret his character not from any outside evidence, but simply from the writings themselves, particularly his intimate writings, like his letters.

15th October 1947

This afternoon, Lord Pethick-Lawrence, who is a Trustee of the National Library, appeared at our Standing Committee. It was interesting to have sitting beside me one of the three men who so recently had talked with Gandhi, Nehru and Jinnah, and taken a prominent part in the steps towards giving India Dominion status. A smaller man than I expected him to be, he sat throughout the meeting curled up with his eyes usually shut, and silent (not being a member of the Committee he had no vote). But, when after the meeting, he began to speak, he exhibited a surprising vivacity in conversation. 'Pathetic-Lawrence' is his nickname.

19th October 1947

Taking Rosemary (age three) to the Harvest Thanksgiving Service at St. George's West this morning, I met Dr. Warr on his way to St. Giles. He referred to the Court of Session service held last Tuesday in St. Giles before the start of the new law session. I remarked on the suitability of holding it in the chancel, where, this year, it was held for the first time. It was started about two years ago by Normand and until now held in the Moray Aisle. Dr. Warr had on this occasion chosen that the congregation should sing the 11th Paraphrase, and had heard the joke going round Parliament House as to whether this choice was not a fanciful compliment to George Thomson, the first Socialist to be appointed a judge by a Socialist Government:-

> In her *right* hand she holds to view
> a length of happy days
> Riches with splendid honours join'd
> are what her *left* displays!

I think I have already remarked that, if the President had not been a lawyer, he would probably have been an electrician or an engineer. Someone calling at Parliament House the other day asked for the President. He was told, 'You will find him mending the electric bells.' Sure enough, he was engaged in repairing one of the Division bells, which rings when a case is called. The President himself incidentally furnished me with another similar illustration. During the holidays, he was staying at Pitlochry and asked the engineer of the Tummel-Garry hydro-electric scheme to show him round the works. They came, during their peregrinations, to the Pitlochry dam. The President remarked: 'That dam is too low: if the water rises it will carry away that crane.' The engineer disagreed with him. But the President, with characteristic thoroughness, insisted on being lowered by crane to the top of the dam, where he examined the work at close quarters. Thereafter, he still adhered to his point. A few days later, a spate came and washed away the crane and part of the dam itself. In telling me about this, he chuckled with delight at his intelligent anticipation of this minor disaster.

25th October 1947

This afternoon Ella, Rosemary and I went out to the Dover Wilsons. They live at Three Beeches, Balerno, where Dover has just added a large study to his house, in which he does all his editing of Shakespeare. I always think of him as a man and a Christian, even more than as a Shakespearean scholar. This is not to minimise his great scholarship, but rather to emphasise that it is founded on his qualities as a man. He is one of the simplest, most generous-hearted and humblest men in the country. Today he tried skipping as we all did – to the delight of Rosemary. For many years, Ella was friendly with Mrs. Dover Wilson – an indefatigable, unconventional, positive, downright personality, overflowing with kindness, but not one to cross. For example, she does not like dogs, and, when we go to her garden, we always leave our dog behind! The friendship passed into a new phase the morning of 23rd February 1943 when we came out of the Infirmary after Gordon's death. There we met Dover and he was the first friend to hear. Gordon had been a great friend of his and he even kept and keeps his photograph always on his study mantelpiece. 'Now consider me Gordon's uncle and we will all talk of him like that. When A.W. Pollard lost his son, he adopted me as his nephew.' Next year, Dover had himself the same loss. His only son Godfrey died, while on service in Africa. His family, like mine, consisted of a boy, then some two years younger, a girl, and then over thirteen years later another little girl. Both Godfrey and the elder daughter were married and settled in Africa. The elder daughter, Audrey, went out as a Church of Scotland missionary to Blantyre, but has recently come home with her husband and one child and settled in Somerset. Today they were feeling lonely, because Carol, the younger daughter who was just a few years ahead of Alison at St. Leonard's, has gone south to London to volunteer for service as a landgirl. Dover Wilson took a great interest in my little book on Gordon, sent a copy of it to Sir Cyril Burt and the Dean of St. Paul's, and wanted it to be published. He it was, I think, who introduced me to the English Association and my subject was his suggestion.

Since his retirement from the Chair of English Literature here, Dover devotes his time to completing his edition of Shakespeare's plays. He works four hours in the morning, three in the early evening, golfs or gardens in the afternoon, and plays chess with Mrs. Dover Wilson at night. A year ago, when he had just completed editing *Macbeth*, he said to me, 'Shakespeare wrote three plays a year, I hope to edit them at that rate. But it was easier for Shakespeare to write three plays a year than for a nincompoop like me to edit three!' Again: '*Macbeth* is one of the shortest of the plays. The reason was that on James I's arrival in London, it was specially popular for Court performance. The present version is probably a shortened one designed for Court production with Banquo whitewashed because he was James' ancestor . . . Shakespeare must have read enormously with a prodigious verbal memory. Half of his vocabulary is his own invention – the words are not traceable beyond him. The other half, much larger than the vocabulary of other writers, could not have been acquired by mere conversation, only by reading. The passages about "germens" in *Macbeth* (Act IV, Scene i. 59) is found also in a similar sense in *Lear* (Act III, Scene ii. 8) and reflects the theology of Augustine probably derived through Neo-Platonism. It is next found in Boyle in 1691. But Shakespeare was not a scholar in the modern sense; such a scholar was then unknown. He knew his Latin but not Greek. He was not, however, an accurate Latinist. In *Anthony and Cleopatra*, he just spells his names in a manner which will enable the actors to pronounce them but not accurately . . . Shakespeare probably acted the prologue of *Henry V* and in other plays.'

To return to my impression of the Court of Session judges, I have still to refer to Lord Jamieson and Lord Stevenson, the remaining judges of the Second Division.

Lord Jamieson is, in some respects, the best judge in the Inner House at the present time. Certainly he is the most judicial. His is a career which has shown growth at each stage. As a counsel, Condie Sandeman always called him 'Dreary Dougal', and his style was certainly not lively. But the description is scarcely fair. He was peculiarly tenacious. He only put forward points which he had tested thoroughly and then no-one could shake him from his perch. He came late to the Bar having spent some years first as a solicitor. Rather unexpectedly, he became Lord Advocate. In the Outer House he was inclined to exhibit the worst side of his tenacity, tending rather to cling to little points and being difficult to move. But in the Division he has become a tower of strength, and the old tenacity is now united with a quite unprejudiced open-mindedness. Cooper, when Lord Justice-Clerk, leant on him, and seldom differed from him.

His personality is peculiarly deserving of respect. Lame through a physical deformity, he has latterly suffered greatly, and in the end required first to have a leg amputated and then to undergo an operation to his spine. During the war, before this happened, he went every week to a soldiers' hostel and helped to make the beds. His strong face, indicative of a strong personality, also shows the marks of suffering and of a sterling kindness which marks his whole nature.

Lord Stevenson is a handsome figure and an attractive personality. But he is a weak judge, and, indeed, just missed accepting the office of Sheriff-substitute at Dumfries. Craigie Aitchison's remark about him was 'Aye – he was always a master of discursive havering!' yet as an Outer House judge his conclusions, if not his reasoning, were frequently affirmed. He has one curious characteristic – a tendency to call everyone by the wrong name – which is, I believe, the real type of Spoonerism. Dr. Julian Huxley writing of Dr. Spooner: The Growth of a Legend (*On Living in a Revolution*: Chatto & Windus 1944) says of Spooner: 'A neurologist would doubtless tell us that he had something a little wrong with some of the association centres in his brain, which led him to saying the wrong word, or in some way making the wrong association.' For example, in referring to Bayswater Farm near Oxford, Dr. Spooner called it Piccadilly Farm. Land's End to John o'Groats he called Land's End to John o'Gaunt. He preached a sermon on Aristotle, and after concluding and descending absentmindedly from the pulpit, turned back and ascended the pulpit steps and leaning over the clerk said apologetically: 'Excuse me, dear brethren, I just want to say that in my sermon, wherever I said Aristotle, I should have said St. Paul!' It is this curious characteristic which Lord Stevenson also displays. In the Boswell MSS case – relating to the Boswell MSS found at Fettercairn House – a case which lasted before Lord Stevenson in the Outer House for a week, he persistently referred to James Boswell as James Ramsay, to Aberdeen University as Inverness

University, and to the Cumberland Infirmary (a claimant in the multiple poinding) as Cumberland University. The mistake was the stranger in that, through Lady Stevenson, he had some family connection with Sir Joshua Reynolds and the Johnsonian circle. Lady Stevenson's Christian name is Sophronia and their only son was named William Reynolds. 'Bill' as he was called was kept most of the war training troops in mountain warfare in Glenfeshie. He chafed to get to active service and, at last, persuaded General Wimberley of the 51st Division to have him posted abroad. After a fortnight in Holland he was killed in action. Lady Stevenson, one of the finest and noblest of women, has bravely borne this blow. They have shown great kindness to us.

12th November 1947

The Second Division was today described as the 'phoney' division. Someone asked 'Why?' The answer was: 'Well, one has a phoney voice, one has a phoney ear [Mackay has, this session, started to use an electric earphone, the first instance of its use in Parliament House], one has a phoney leg and one has a phoney brain!'

On the 8th, I took the Chair, as President of the Robert Louis Stevenson Club, at their annual Club lunch. The principal guest was Walter Elliot. He arrived late, and spoke on Stevenson in the Tradition of Scottish Letters, his theme being that the Scottish Tradition showed a preoccupation with the craftsmanship of letters, which sometimes distracted attention from the underlying thought the author had to convey. The address derived its motif from George Moore's description of Stevenson's prose as 'filigree English', which description Walter Elliot had obtained from Professor Renwick's reference to it in his R.L.S. address to the Club last year. As Renwick's address was published – in the *Edinburgh University Journal* – only about a fortnight ago, the preparation of Walter Elliot's address can only have begun about then. He eked out his material by reading extracts from Dunbar's *Twa Marrit Women and the Wedo*, Stevenson and Linklater. But, for a paper prepared in this offhand fashion, he got away with it wonderfully well. He is very anxious that some of the Buchan MSS (particularly the Montrose, Scott and one or two novels) and some Neil Munro MSS should reach the National Library. He was much interested to know that Stevenson's first act as President of the Spec was to admit a new member who was the future Lord Dunedin. In addition to Ella, I had as guests the Dover Wilsons, the Lionel Smiths,

John Dover Wilson.

Mr. Charles Matheson (father of Arthur, my late devil) and Mrs. Johnston-Gilbert, whose husband was one of the Club's guests – replying to the toast of the Corporation. I proposed Walter Elliot's health, pointing out that he must have been a 42nd cousin of R.L.S. (through Sir Gilbert Elliot, the latter's maternal ancestor) and also approximately rather more than an 18th cousin by affinity of Stevenson's greatest character, for Mrs. Weir of Hermiston was 18th cousin of Gilbert Elliot of Cauldstaneslap, who was a Border Elliot and a politician. 'Sit, ye eediot . . . what's this I hear of you? Poalitics, poalitics, poalitics, weaver's poalitics . . . gang your way back to Cauldstaneslap, and ca' your loom, and ca' your loom, man!' The Elliots were 'guid and bad like sang writers'. The bad had met their end suspended in mid air and from every ramification of their genealogical tree, there dangled a halter. But what of the good, the brave and the true? Sir Gilbert, the Lord of Session of Queen Anne; his son, Sir Gilbert, the Justice-Clerk; Jean Elliot, writer of that most exquisite of Scottish dirges, 'The Flowers of the Forest'; the first Earl of Minto, who was Governor-General of India; Hugh Elliot, who stood up to Frederick the Great, was not afraid to abstract a red dispatch box from beneath his nose and who when asked how he liked Berlin replied: 'Monstrously: the tallest grenadiers you ever saw, the most melodious drums, the sweetest trumpets, the most delicious artillery and the loveliest hussars', Norman Elliot, of whom it was was said that he and the devil alone understood the law of Teinds; the Minto Vice Roy of India who set it on the path to self-government; and Walter Elliot, statesman, politician, broadcaster, doctor, seven times doctor, University burgess, Lord Rector of Glasgow University, and foremost Borderer of the day. Might the courage and gaiety of Stevenson not come from his Elliot ancestors, and might they not have given the same courage and gaiety to Walter Elliot? Christine Orr proposed my health very gracefully.

14th November 1947

A political sensation has occurred, with which I have a faint personal link. Two days ago, Mr. Hugh Dalton, Chancellor of the Exchequer, presented his special autumn budget to meet the economic crisis. Yesterday evening at 10.40 p.m., the radio announced that, in Parliament, he had apologised for the 'grave indiscretion' of having communicated the outline of his proposals to a lobby-correspondent before the speech with the result that a London evening paper made advance publication of the proposals. The announcement went on to say that Mr. Dalton had tendered his resignation as Chancellor and that this had been accepted by the Prime Minister. To my amazement, I learned also that the offending lobby-correspondent was the correspondent of the *Star*. For this could only be Mr. John L. Carvel, well known to me. Today came confirmation that it was he and that, at his request, pending investigation by a Select Committee, he had withdrawn from duty as lobby-correspondent. Mr. Carvel, whom I first met two years ago at Kingussie, is one of the senior Parliamentary journalists, well known to all at Westminster and has been Chairman of the lobby-correspondents. He hails from Lesmahagow, and after a journalistic career in Glasgow, went to London, where he has been for many years. Last summer, when as Chairman of the Milk Services Committee, I had to pay a business visit to the Ministry of Agriculture and Fisheries, I spent the afternoon and evening till my train left King's Cross, with Mr. Carvel – first at the House, then at the Reform and Caledonian Club and afterwards at the King's Cross Hotel. It was the day when Mr. Attlee announced the creation of India and Pakistan and I met Mr. Carvel in the House just as the bell rang at the conclusion of the speech: so I just missed the historic announcement. Mr. Carvel is a liberal, or rather a radical, and, I should judge, on terms of confidence with members of the Government, for he wanted to introduce me (if I returned shortly) to Mr. Attlee and the Lord Chancellor, and he did that afternoon introduce me to the Under-Secretary of Foreign Affairs, Mr. Mayhew. But, on this occasion, he must have been somewhat indiscreet. It still remains to be seen what action the House of Commons will take in relation to both Mr. Dalton and himself.

I heard today also of a sad case – the arrest of a Sheriff Clerk for embezzlement. He was the most respected man in his native town and I believe when the news came out, the Marquis of Bute called on the Fiscal and himself offered to pay every penny of the loss, no matter what it might be. Only a few years ago, there was a similar case in the South of Scotland; in that case, as local observers remarked, the Sheriff Clerk in question was thought to be 'as sound as the Bank of England'. At the Round Table, where I heard the news, I also learned that a very presentable Parliament House clerk, who frequently sees me on business, and whom I know well by sight, though not hitherto by name, is none other than a former Stipendiary Magistrate of Glasgow, who resigned some years ago under a cloud.

23rd November 1947

This week I have been in Aberdeen conducting two Inquiries into compulsory purchase orders. As a result I had to return my first House of Lords case as a K.C. One of the Inquiries was at Dyce; the other in Aberdeen. No contrast could be greater. The Aberdeen Inquiry was held in the Council Chambers and I sat in the Lord Provost's chair, and was entertained by the Lord Provost. I was rather surprised to find him in Aberdeen that day as it was 20th November, the day of Princess Elizabeth's wedding, but he explained that the only Provost invited to Westminster Abbey was the Lord Provost of Edinburgh. The Dyce Inquiry began in the Carnegie Hall, Dyce. The temperature was below freezing point; the roads were ice-bound; I sat on a high platform between the two doors each admitting a draught; and melted snow dripped from the roof onto my papers. The case related to an acre and a half, used (insofar as it was used at all) as a strawberry patch and the District Council wanted to acquire it for a recreation ground. A section of the village opposed this course as 'depriving a man of his living' and the Inquiry was punctuated with applause or shuffling. Printed notices had been posted up throughout the village stating that Mr. J. Randall Philip K.C. would conduct a 'personal Enquiry' and that 'Objectors were cordially invited to be present!' After the hearing had lasted throughout daylight, I was asked to adjourn till the evening in order that persons in employment might give evidence then. We resumed, accordingly, at 7.45, but found the Carnegie Hall was then in use by a Masonic Meeting. Accordingly, we removed to a neighbouring church hall, tables being carried along the ice-bound village road by willing helpers. The resumed Inquiry reminded me of the hustings. At one point, I had to administer the oath to a mother with a babe in arms. I have now conducted a variety of these enquires – at Falkirk, Dumfries, Musselburgh, Kirkcaldy, and now at Dyce and Aberdeen. This widespread resort to compulsory powers is a new collectivist tendency of legislation, and it is curious to find that the chief opponents of its use in practice are the socialists in each community.

We also took the opportunity of calling on Lady Hamilton Fyfe at Chanonry Lodge. It is curious that this is the fourth Principal of Aberdeen University with whom I have a connection. Sir William Geddes was my grand uncle; Dr. Marshall Lang was distantly connected with Ella's mother; Sir George Adam Smith was a class mate both at school and at University with my father, and together they visited Germany and attended the Congress of Berlin, where they saw Disraeli bringing home the first 'Peace with Honour'; and Sir William Hamilton Fyfe, whose wife is my half-cousin, once removed!

At these Inquiries, I am always accompanied by a shorthand writer and an assessor or clerk from the Government Department concerned. This time, the shorthand writer, Mr. T.A. Kirkby, was a delightful personality, with whom I have now made many expeditions. He combines an energetic shorthand business, with over a dozen employees, with the work of a lay Baptist preacher. At Musselburgh, I was provided by St. Andrew's House with no fewer than three assessors, as well as a clerk – mineral, agricultural and planning. Such is bureaucracy, and this at a time when labour is short and people are being directed into essential work.

1st December 1947

A case which I had today before the First Division related to an accident which had occurred to a schoolmistress who, in order to ventilate a schoolroom, the windows of which had stuck with new paint, tried to open a window from the outside, and, in her efforts, received serious cuts on her wrists. The point was whether the education authority, having failed to have the windows loosened, were bound to anticipate that a teacher would herself try to loosen them in the manner indicated. I argued that the teacher was charged with the well-being of her pupils and her action was just what should have been anticipated. The Lord President: 'But here in Court, we manage to get on quite well without opening windows.' J.R.P.: 'Yes, my Lord, but the education authorities have to exercise a higher standard of care.' Lord President: 'It might be quite useful if, sometimes, Counsel were suffocated!'

6th December 1947

Sir John Fraser, Principal of the University, died suddenly on the 1st – the 'last great general surgeon' – a colleague described him. He was about to ascend the main staircase in the Old College to his room when an attendant offered to take him up in the lift. He said, No, he would walk. But, when he reached the first landing, he collapsed and fell down the flight of stairs. His remains were taken to the Infirmary, but refused admission, because death had already taken place. Truly, a prophet is not without honour, save in his own country and in his own house. The funeral, on the 4th, was the largest in Edinburgh since the death of Earl Haig. I first learned of the death at a St. George's West Session on the evening of the 1st and, Dr. Black being ill, arranged that our assistant, Mr. Scott Morton, should call that evening at the house. He, in the end, took the funeral service, Sir John having been a member of St. George's West, though always declining office. Curiously enough, I twice had the task of cross-examining Sir John, the second time in a case where the *amour-propre* of the Infirmary was involved. He was, perhaps, the most sincere of all witnesses I have met.

I was consulted by Dobie, the Librarian of the National Library, this week on a curious matter. Thomas Scott, the brother of Sir Walter, left descendants who ultimately became German nationals. One of the present descendants is a German baroness who lives in a Schloss near Dresden, in the territory at present in Russian occupation. She has family documents connected with Sir Walter which she desires to send to Scotland, but has no money to enable her to do this. Sir Walter Maxwell-Scott offered to provide part of the cost of transport, and I was consulted on whether the National Library would also assist in order that the papers should, if possible, come to the Library. It was agreed to make up a gift of £10 by Sir Walter to a sum of £50 to cover delivery to the British zone.

In a case in the High Court, counsel was asked why his client ran away at the approach of the police. Counsel: 'It is one of the few privileges still left to the subject!'

22nd December 1947

At the Standing Committee of the National Library on the 13th, there was a larger attendance and more interesting business than I have seen. The Lord Justice-General made his first appearance, and afterwards expressed himself very pleased with the review of book purchasing policy which I initiated. The Baroness von Oppel, Thomas Scott's descendant, is to get her books transported from Dresden to the Library if the Russians will allow it. On the very day of this meeting the Library was bidding at Christie's for the Campbell Papers. These are four volumes of documents – 543 in all – of Major-General John Campbell (afterwards Duke of Argyll), who commanded the Hanoverian troops in the West of Scotland in the years immediately following the '45'. They cover the period from July 1745 to September 1748 and have, it seems, not been finished. They were reported to the Historical MSS Commission though not by them. Dr. Maclehose and Sir Robert Rait were interested in them for the Scottish History Society. The Royal Library, Windsor, which has the Cumberland Papers, agreed to refrain from bidding against us. Perhaps, not being Jacobite papers, they have less interest to the mere curio hunter. But to the historical scholar, as coming from the Hanoverian side, their interest is all the greater. Quaritch advised us to bid £1,000, and Cunningham and Dobie proposed an even higher figure, which, on the information before me, I considered was justified, though I came to the meeting prepared to meet possible criticism and, accordingly, to have to defend it. To my delight and surprise, during the business there was thrust into my hand a note that the Campbell Papers had been acquired for only £350. I have had a glimpse of them since then. They contain one vivid account of the Battle of 'Prestonpans' (as it is called). This purchase has attracted much interest in the public press. This General Campbell is the one who figures at the end of *Redgauntlet*.

But the *pièce de résistance* at the meeting was the production of a number of Shakespearean quartos from Falkland Palace, which Major Crichton-Stuart has deposited with the Library. I took Alison to the Library today to see them. They contain, for example, two Elizabethan quartos of 1600 (i) a *Henry IV Part II* which bears on the title page that it was purchased on 31st December 1610 for 5d. (the same copy was sold in 1800 for £3 3s.); (ii) a *Merchant of Venice* printed for James Roberts for Thomas Heyes 'to be sold in Paul's Churchyard at the sign of the Greene Dragon'. Then there is a *Troilus and Cressida*, first edition (2nd issue with preface to reader) of 1609 'to be sold at the Spread Eagle in Paule's Churchyard, over against the great north door'; and a *Titus Andronicus* of 1611, bearing no author's name in front but with 'Shakespeare' written in, 'printed for Edward White and . . . to be sold at his shop, near the little North door of Pauls, at the sign of the Gun'. There are six other quartos, all before the first folio and all printed for Matthew Law and 'to be sold at his shop in Paule's Church-yard at the sign of the Fox'. A *Henry IV Part I* (4th quarto) says 'neare unto S. Augustin's gate. at the sign of the Fox'. There is another *Henry IV Part I* (3rd quarto) bearing the date 1599 in manuscript, but really 1604, containing a note that the only other known copies are in the Bodleian and Trinity College, Cambridge; and a *Henry IV Part I* (6th quarto) of 1622; a *Richard III* of 1612; and two *Richard II*s, one of 1615. The part played by the book in Paul's Churchyard is most curious. Beattie, who showed us these quartos, showed us also some Paires quartos of 1619, which however bear the dates of the 1st quartos, but the absence of the references to the shops where the earlier quartos were sold, is one clue showing that these Paires quartos are not of the dates they purport to bear. These quartos seem all to have come from the first Marquis of Bute, who acquired them just when Shakespeare, in the eighteenth century, was coming into his own. He purchased some of them for prices of from 2s. 6d. to 10s. Now, money would scarcely buy them at all.

Recently, I lectured to the eighty years old Heriot-Watt College Literary Society on 'R.L.S. – a Character Study from his Writings'. In the discussion which followed, one interesting fact was mentioned. Not merely is the lamp outside No 17 Heriot Row the lamp which Leerie used to light, but the little pond in the gardens opposite, with the island in the centre, is the original inspiration of *Treasure Island*. The pond was drained during the 1939–45 War, and a big water tank constructed in its place, but already this disfiguring landmark has been removed.

CHAPTER II

1948

3rd January 1948

This morning I had an interesting assignment. Dr. James Black of St. George's West is likely to retire shortly having sustained one serious heart attack two months ago and another this week; and a Committee, of which I am Convener, have been conferring amongst themselves and with him as to a colleague or successor. With his assent, and at the request of the Committee, I went this morning with Lord Cooper to interview Dr. J.S. Stewart to see whether he would be prepared to let his name go forward to nomination as successor. On personal grounds, I found this curiously interesting. J.S. Stewart was my senior at school by about four or five years at a time when for three years in succession duxes of the High School of Dundee took first place in the entrance competition at Edinburgh University, one of these ten years later taking first place in the (then supremely respected) Indian Civil Service examination. J.S. Stewart was second boy at school the year when this boy was dux. He is one of the most humble and Christian of men. He himself acknowledged that my own father had influenced him to enter the University, and, happening to preach in St. George's West on my father's diamond jubilee, he paid a very beautiful tribute to him then. He is quite the foremost Scottish preacher today, and, always scholarly and thoughtful, yet proclaims the gospel with apostolic fervour. Crowds flock to hear him and he has a deep influence over many Edinburgh citizens. In his first charge – Auchterarder – Lord Haldane came under his influence, and I noticed today, in Stewart's study, a photograph of Lord Haldane. As always I want to record my impressions at the time. Both Cooper and I thought Stewart, who had been a professor at New College for a year and a half, has come to realise that his true place is in the pulpit, and we today considered that he will let his name go forward to nomination. When he expressed some embarrassment at the thought of possibly leaving New College so soon after his appointment, I referred him to the precedent of Dr. R.S. Candlish who in August 1847 left

Free St. George's, as it then was, to succeed Dr. Thomas Chalmers at New College, but returned to St. George's within a year, when his successor who had been called – the Rev. Alexander Stewart of Cromarty – died before his induction to St. George's. When I said that this occasion brought to my mind the call of David: 'Arise, anoint him; for this is he,' (1 Sam. 16:12), Cooper remarked jokingly: 'Now don't you borrow Stewart's technique.' Stewart is, like my own father, the most unworldly of men, and was not concerned with the financial arrangements which I mentioned. But, as they may be interesting as an instance of one of the leading Edinburgh churches, and certainly the foremost preaching station, I mention that the proposal was that, during Dr. Black's survivance, the stipend to Stewart would be £1,100, with a manse, and motor car allowance of £100, fees for pulpit supply being also paid during the minister's absence on holiday for not less than two (and possibly three) months. How different from my own father, who when I was born, had a stipend of about £190 and manse; at the end of his active life, a stipend of £330 and manse. Yet I make bold to say that the little congregation over which he ministered was spiritually stronger than almost any other, and that there was an atmosphere of reverence there quite unknown in the St. George's West of my day. The 262 members in 1930, my father's last complete year as active minister, raised £778, with £419 for the schemes of the Church, figures which were, at that time, not exceeded by any other comparable country congregation.

17th January 1948

J.S. Stewart asked me to come and see him. His whole desire is to come to St. George's West, but, having decided eighteen months ago to accept the New College Professorship, he feels he has to abide by that decision. He was so manifestly obeying his call of duty that I did not attempt to overpersuade him. Lord Cooper did not accompany me on this occasion, but approved beforehand of my attitude.

24th January 1948

This week I gave in, as Convener of the National Library Standing Committee, my first Annual Report at the Annual Meeting of the Trustees. I dwelt on two points chiefly – shortage of staff and lack of accommodation. The Bodleian, with about 12,000,000 books, has an effective library staff (omitting patrols etc.) of 65; Cambridge, with about the same number of books, a staff of 53; the National Library of Ireland, with only 350,000 volumes, a staff of 33 (with a prospect of 18 more for MSS alone); the National Library of Wales, with 1,000,000 volumes, a staff of 31; and the National Library of Scotland, with about 2,000,000 volumes, a staff of 25 (if you count three night-patrols)! The new library building is, as yet, only up to three storeys, only one of which has a floor. This floor is now being installed with shelving which will, when completed (this Spring), take the inflow of books until 1950. Meantime, police cells and air-raid shelters in Parliament House are being pressed into use. These facts have made quite an impression in the press, and, even at the meeting, the M.P. for Central Edinburgh (Mr. Gilzean) rose and offered to raise the matter in Parliament; he has since drawn the attention of the Lord Advocate to the position. The feature of the meeting, for me, was a speech by Dover Wilson on the new Shakespearean accessions. He placed the National Library, with Edinburgh University, fourth amongst libraries possessing Shakespeare quartos – after the British, Bodleian and Cambridge.

Harry Guthrie was elected Keeper of the Advocates' Library this week at our Annual Meeting of the Faculty. Before his name went forward, I was asked to let myself be nominated, but, it seemed to me, a possible conflict of interest might arise between the Advocates' and the National Library, and so I did not stand. The clerkship of Faculty went to Jeffrey Cunningham with 38 votes against Ian Fraser's 35. I voted for the latter. Both were popular candidates, and it was generally felt that either would have been very acceptable.

This evening Ella and I had supper with Dr. Lionel and Mrs. Smith. Dr. Lionel Smith was Gordon's Rector at the Academy. He is an extraordinarily individual personality – classical scholar, hockey internationalist, famous sculler, son of a Master of Balliol, educational organiser of modern Iraq, etcher (he has only done four! – one of them, Jerusalem, is remarkable), twice pressed to be headmaster of Eton, Fellow of All Souls and Dean of Magdalen, tutor to Edward VIII, and Rector of the Academy – 'Reggie' to us, with a link which nothing can break between us, for Gordon was, I think, his best-loved pupil. He told me this story of Dr. Spooner. There was a function at New College to which some outsiders were invited. In a jovial mood, Dr. Spooner began: 'Some of us – ahem – have had the advantage of being educated at both Winchester and New College. Some of us – ahem – have had the advantage of being educated at the one but not the other. And – eh – ah – some of us – ahem – have had the advantage of being educated – at neither!' Another day, he passed an old lady in the street, and bowed deeply to her. A friend accompanying him enquired who it was. He replied: 'Ah yes' (in an absent-minded way), 'she is a widow now. Mr. and Mrs.—— were a devoted couple. They spent their lives among natives in the Congo. But he – alas – was eaten by – eh – ah – missionaries!'

29th January 1948

I had my first experience of broadcasting this evening, when I recorded a short talk on Sir Walter Scott and his Women Characters for broadcast on 3rd February. I enjoyed preparing the script much more than reading it. I think the meaning can best be brought out by somewhat slow reading, but evidently a more rapid pace is wanted for this type of literary talk. A technical hitch occurred in the recording, as a result of which, after I had concluded my reading, I had to read the last third again. It was Christine Orr who was responsible for the invitation, and she superintended the recording and gave me some useful practical hints. I had three practice readings before the actual recording, which was very considerate of her.

This week I have been engaged in a difficult and somewhat melancholy task. As Convener of a Committee of St. George's West, appointed in October, I have been conferring with Dr. Black, who has been laid up with a coronary thrombosis and threatened angina pectoris since the end of October. The Committee was unanimously of the view that it would be impossible for him to continue in the heavy charge, and latterly it became necessary for me to have certain correspondence with him about it. The Committee were extraordinarily loyal and most co-operative, and the President (who though invited to serve on the Committee declined) acted as a friendly adviser about the correspondence which was of a delicate nature. Last evening, Dr. Black reached a decision to resign, but I still await confirmation. The reasons which weighed with the Committee were five:- (1) that the experience of the Church, as witness a new Act of Assembly a year ago (1946), is against the practice of appointing a colleague; (2) that St. George's West needs, above all, a preacher and therefore above all an individualist, and that to have two individualists like Dr. Black would be like dog eating dog; (3) that, if we were limited to the selection of a colleague as distinct from a successor, the field of selection would be seriously narrowed; (4) that Dr. Black was certainly unfit to carry on alone, and almost certainly unfit to conduct the substantial portion of the work now required of a senior minister even with a colleague; and (5) that, as Dr. Black was sixty-nine in January and intended to retire at seventy, there was no point in having a colleague merely for a matter of months. It is curious that, at my final interview with Dr. Black, the only other person present was Rosemary (aged three).

13th February 1948

Dr. Black intimated his intention to resign as expected, and this was published on the 8th.

I was able to listen to my own broadcast on the 3rd. It is always supposed to be a shock to hear one's own voice. Perhaps because I was prepared for this, the shock was not as great as expected. My own voice was deeper and better modulated than I expected, with what seemed to me a faint suggestion of a West Country accent!

8th April 1948

For interest, I counted from my fee-book the number of opinions which I have written since 1st October 1947, and I find it is 122, which is not far short of one opinion every week day. This is pretty much what it has been for some years. I remember George Morton, who devilled to Craigie (of Conveyancing fame) telling us that Craigie wrote as many as three opinions a week. But I think this beats Craigie by quite an amount.

Last week I acted as Commissioner to hold, on behalf of the Secretary of State, the Public Inquiry at Kirkcaldy into the proposal to designate an area for a new town 'Glenrothes' to accommodate 30,000 inhabitants. The proposal is to provide accommodation chiefly for the additional numbers required to develop the Fife coalfield. The first 'new town' in Scotland was East Kilbride, and the Inquiry on that occasion went very badly, because the Objectors were allowed to make the inquiry an issue between the Government Departments and themselves. They cross-examined the Departmental representatives who were themselves not represented by counsel. The Commissioner was Tom Taylor. Since then, the House of Lords in the Stevenage case (Franklin [1948] A.C. 87) has decided that where a Minister conducts through a Commissioner an inquiry with respect to objections to his own draft order, the inquiry is limited to obtaining for the Minister information as to the objections. On this occasion, accordingly, I simply heard the evidence of the objectors – agriculturists and industrialists – and there was no cross-examination of them; neither did the Departments give evidence nor were they subject to cross-examination. The Inquiry went very smoothly. But, after the East Kilbride experience, the Departmental representatives were very apprehensive before the Inquiry, and great care was taken to follow strictly the lines of Franklin.

Today I have been appointed by the Minister of Health, in conjunction with the Secretary of State for Scotland, to serve on an independent legal committee to enquire into certain problems relating to medical partnerships raised by the recent National Health Services Acts of 1946 & 1947. The chairman is to be G.O. Slade K.C., Chairman of the English Bar Council. The other members may be Sir Cyril Radcliffe K.C., and J.H. Stamp, but of this I am not yet definitely informed.

9th April 1948

It was announced last night that the members of the Medical Partnership Committee are G.O. Slade K.C. (Chairman); Colin Pearson; Sir Cyril Radcliffe K.C.; J.H. Stamp; and, from the Scottish Bar, myself. G.O. Slade was the counsel who defended the notorious 'Lord Haw-Haw'; Pearson is Recorder of Hythe; Sir Cyril Radcliffe was Chairman of the Boundary Commission which settled the boundaries of India and Pakistan; J.H. Stamp is a well-known Revenue junior, coincidentally the senior in age. G.O. Slade is Recorder of Tenterden. It looks as if the common denominator was a recordership of the Cinque Ports, which is appropriate for a Committee of five.

5th May 1948

During April we spent ten days at Stratford-upon-Avon during the Shakespeare Festival. It was seventeen years since our last visit, though we have repeatedly been in the Cotswolds since. Alison and I had the unusual experience of being almost struck by lightning. We were passing through the churchyard when the spire of Holy Trinity was struck by lightning. All I knew at the time was that there seemed to be a ball of fire in front of and rather lower than my eyes. Some damage was done to stonework and brass inside the chancel on the south side, and also to stonework at the same point outside. The whole electric system was put out of action. Evensong was proceeding at the time.

Today, the President told me that he had been invited to become Principal of Edinburgh University. He wanted my views and immediate reactions. I advised: No, on two grounds (1) that it would not be *comme il faut* for the head of the Judiciary to accept such an appointment, and might unwarrantably suggest dissatisfaction with his present work; and (2) that a Senatus, two-thirds of which consisted of Englishmen out of touch with Scotland, would not be a congenial atmosphere for him to work in. Candlish Henderson, only the other day, unburdened himself to me about this aspect after twenty-five years or so as a Professor.

7th May 1948

I spent yesterday in London to attend the first meeting of the independent legal committee on Medical Partnerships. All the members were present. The meeting was held in a basement room of the Ministry of Health, just diagonally opposite 'Big Ben'. The two members of the Committee by whom I was most taken were G.O. Slade and J.H. Stamp. Slade is a more slender edition of Lord Carmont with, curiously enough, a faint resemblance to Oscar Slater, if you could imagine the latter converted into a good-looking genial personality. As the only Scotsman, I attended with some diffidence, but nothing could have been more considerate than Slade's treatment of me. At the outset he protested that he was a common lawyer, and knew far less about the matter than the others, who were Chancery lawyers. He very quickly showed his capacity, however, to absorb points put by others. J.H. Stamp was much the best informed, as he has been advising the British Medical Association all along. He has an extraordinarily acute mind, and would certainly be on the bench if in Scotland. He must be about seventy and white-haired, the kind of junior who simply does not exist in Scotland. He was also most courteous to me. The meeting resolved itself into Slade questioning Stamp for further information, and, when Stamp gave some peculiarly subtle theoretical explanation, Slade would say: 'Now, give me a simple example of what you mean, so that I may follow.' All the time he assumed the position of a common lawyer, always rather out of his depth with Chancery lawyers. I was interested, too, that each side had to explain branches of their law to the other, a situation impossible in Scotland, where there is no such sharp specialisation. Radcliffe did not open his mouth very much, but when he did it was much to the point. Pearson seemed more average. The conversation was so skilful and subtle that I felt almost a little out of my depth. My mind works more slowly, though, given time, I think its conclusions may be as sound. I took the opportunity also to look in at the law courts, where I saw the Chief Justice (Goddard) sitting with Tucker J., and another, and in another Court Birkett J. Later I went to the House of Lords, where Lords Porter, Simonds, Du Parcq, Normand and Oaksey (of Nuremberg fame) were hearing a workman's compensation case. The counsel, Paull K.C., was being hard-pressed, and seemed to me to be somewhat too precise and formal in manner, though with an experienced and finished style. I paid my first visit to the new statue of Roosevelt (massive, but not Roosevelt) in Grosvenor Square; and the Battle of Britain window in Westminster Abbey. I also saw Dean Matthews marching in procession at the Ascension Day Service in St. Paul's. The north transept is still closed because of bomb damage. I stayed for the first time (for nothing) in the Caledonian Club, whose new quarters are a delightful town house near Hyde Park Corner, once belonging to Hugh Morrison of Islay.

The President told me that Sir Walter Maxwell-Scott can no longer maintain Abbotsford and has offered it to the Faculty, with the Library which comes to them in any event. The difficulty is upkeep. It is to be held in trust for the nation, and would require an endowment of £50,000 to £75,000.

10th May 1948

In the Bar Foursomes today at Muirfield, my former 'devil' Ronald Kydd and I got through the first two rounds. In the first round, Lord Mackay was one of our opponents. He happened to refer, at one point, to Lord Simon's golf. I asked him how Lord Simon played against himself. Mackay's reply was: 'Oh, he has a pretty good opinion of his play, but he is not up to my standard. He's about Birnam's level!'

20th May 1948

Today, at a Faculty Meeting, it was decided to accept a proposal that Abbotsford should be handed over to the Faculty in trust for the nation. Lord Macmillan was present, and, as Chairman of the Pilgrim Trustees, explained that they were prepared to buy the house and nine surrounding acres, and also the objects of interest in the house which do not belong to the Library (the latter is already vested in the Faculty). He also mentioned that he had promises of £12,000 from various Scotsmen north or south of the Border towards an endowment, which should be of the order of £60,000. The Faculty appointed a Committee who were, in turn, empowered to invite prominent Scotsmen to become Trustees of the Endowment Fund and to make an appeal for the necessary contributions.

We have this week a young Frenchman staying with us, M. Alfred Westphal. He is studying divinity at Glasgow, and is a delegate to the General Assembly. He is much impressed with its international outlook. At its meetings, he has encountered a Swiss, a German, two Waldensians, a Hungarian, a Czech and a Finn. I am, again, Commissioner for the Presbytery of Uist, and last night I entertained to dinner the three minister-members at the University Club, along with my lay colleagues, Dr. Roderick Macleod and Mr. Hay Smith, and also my brother-in-law Donald and my former 'devil' Arthur Matheson. The ministers are extraordinarily up to date in their outlook, and it would be quite wrong to regard them as ultra-conservative. One told me, with misgiving, that he had once seen in a Lewis church the practice of the 'cutty-stool'. An illegitimate child was not baptised until its mother had appeared before the congregation. This must be a unique survival of a practice which I thought had died a century ago.

29th May 1948

I have just returned from London after making my first speech as a senior in the House of Lords. It was in a 'Chancery' case, whether a daughter, Lady Stainton, of the first Lord Forteviot had validly exercised a power of appointment by making an appointment *inter vivos* in favour of her son. The Court was a strong Chancery Court, Lord Porter in the Chair, Lords Uthwatt, Du Parcq, Normand and Morton. Uthwatt and Morton were the Chancery judges and Uthwatt, who is a vivacious forceful personality with a lightning mind in charge of the discussion. Morton is a good Scotsman who strayed onto the Chancery bench. He still speaks the language of Kelvinside and has quite a lucid way with him which does honour to Scotland. One of the humours of the discussions (as I learned after, though I noticed something wrong at the time) was that Uthwatt's collar stud had given way and his collar threatened to come off. My client, John Stainton, is the son of an official of the House of Lords, Sir John Stainton, and his whole family, the present Lord Forteviot and others were there. Lord Forteviot, as a peer, sat behind the judges. Sir John Stainton entertained us all to lunch in the Lords dining room – a party of about fourteen entertained royally, lunch ending with strawberries and cream. I spoke to several of the judges, Normand, Du Parcq and Uthwatt. During lunch, Sir John handed an envelope to Uthwatt. It contained a new collar stud, which had been ordered in the course of the morning. One new precedent was established by our case and the one in front. Since the House of Commons has been destroyed in the blitz, the House of Lords has vacated its chamber in favour of the Commons and itself occupied the King's Robing Room. That is where I appeared last in 1944. But now pneumatic drills working on the re-erection of the damaged portion of the buildings have made it impossible to conduct business there because of the noise, and the two Scots Appeals called after the Whitsunday recess were the first held in other premises – a Committee Room. To inaugurate the new practice, the Lord Chancellor (Jowitt) sat in the first case. He wears only court dress and bib, without wig, unlike Simon. From the angles at which he poses, he obviously likes to display his profile which is certainly distinguished. The hearings were described – that is the new precedent – as hearings before the Appeal Committee, and evidently the judges have to return and report their deliberations to the Lords. At one point, Lord Du Parcq invited me to put a certain verbal distinction which I was making into Latin. But I drew some laughter by declining in view of an unfortunate precedent which occurred recently when Hill Watson shocked the Court by calmly informing them that the word 'obtain' came from the word 'obtango'! I am glad to say that there is every reason to believe that we will win our appeal. We had a dissent by the Lord President in our favour. I spoke during the morning and, after James Walker had spoken for the Respondents, was not called on to reply. [*JRP did win the appeal, as he expected. 1949 SLT 39 – Ed.*]

13th June 1948

Yesterday it was announced that G.O. Slade, the Chairman of the Legal Committee on Medical Partnerships, had been appointed a Judge of the High Court, King's Bench Division. Today, returning from church, I met David Watson who told us he had just received word of the death of his father. It is interesting to recall that, in my first year at the Bar, in Carlile Steamship Co. v. Simpson, Spence &

Young, I was with him for the space of one consultation as his second junior. Carmont had taken silk, and I was brought in to cover him. William Watson left the case almost immediately after, on becoming Lord Advocate. I was then with Carmont as my senior, and it is good to recall that the opposing counsel were Condie Sandeman, the Dean, and Normand, then his junior, but now Lord of Appeal.

This evening I rang up the President to tell him about Lord Thankerton. He then said to me something which I should like to record, as, even if there were nothing in it, it is good to have had said to me by a Lord President. He said: 'If Reid goes to London, then some of those who are best able to judge think that you should be Dean.' I said: 'I think the Faculty's choice would be Fred Strachan; but in any event, I would never think of moving in the matter, because it is purely a matter for the Faculty, and my experience is that the best things come unsought.' He replied: 'No doubt, there are other pebbles on the shore. But there may be a vacancy on the bench this summer, and Fred Strachan should be appointed to that. No doubt, too, there are others senior to you. But you are respected for the moderation of your views, while there may be more forceful counsel.' I said that I believed myself to be in temperament a middle man, and that, at least, if ever it should be that the Faculty wanted me, with a real degree of support, I would place myself in their hands, and at least not draw back as Fred Strachan did when Reid was appointed, as at that time it seems likely that Fred would have received more votes. But that I would certainly make no move towards putting myself forward. I record this, as nothing may ever come of it, but, as our old maid Janet at home said when she received her first proposal of marriage at the age of sixty-nine from our seventy-five year old beadle: 'It's guid to have been askit.'

A very amusing incident happened this week at Parliament House. The President always parks his car in Parliament Square on one particular spot. John Mitchell, the Principal Clerk of Session, found another car parked on this spot one day this week. He went round trying to find out who had dared to appropriate the President's special preserve. No-one acknowledged ownership of the car, so he noted the registration number, and sent across to the City Chambers to ascertain the name of the owner. It turned out to be 'James M. Cooper'. The President was himself using his brother's car!

24th June 1948

I attended another meeting of the Medical Partnership Committee this week in London. Slade was in that twilight period between his appointment as judge and his knighthood, which he received the day after our meeting. At this meeting I had a pleasant experience. Hitherto, I had kept very quiet, in deference to my colleagues. But reading the transcript of last meeting's discussion, I came to the conclusion that it was very discursive and that nothing would help more than to try to focus our conclusions, or the conclusions at which we were groping, in writing. I spent part of the forenoon doing this, and then went out and visited Lincoln's Inn, Dr. Johnson's house in Gough Square and the Law Courts (to see Slade sitting on the Bench). At our committee meeting, Slade began by saying that, next time, we would have to hear some evidence, and could he formulate the views so far reached, namely three alternatives. I intervened to say that, tentatively, I had tried to formulate in writing the preferable of the three alternatives, and he invited me to read what I had written. When I had finished, he said: 'Now, read it again at dictation speed, and we shall have it taken down.' After I had done so, Stamp suggested the addition of the words 'less tax' after a reference to 'interest', and thereupon they all approved of my statement. Inwardly, I was greatly delighted, and I could not but notice the very cordial reception given to various other views I expressed later. I was glad that I had kept quiet until I had something to say. Before the meeting, I had an interesting discussion with Radcliffe on the components of goodwill in a doctor's practice. We came to the conclusion that, insofar as there was any goodwill, it depended principally on contract e. g. the introduction of the new doctor to the old doctor's patients, the implied recommendation in the transfer of the practice to the new doctor, the restrictive covenant not to compete with the new doctor, or the death of the old doctor (the practical equivalent), and also the use of the old doctor's surgery or house. I had dinner afterwards at my club with Masson, our Secretary.

Dr. Johnson's house just missed destruction, in the late war, from a flying bomb. The ground to the north of it is stripped bare. The house itself received minor damage from blast, the roof being damaged and doors blown in. It is in a quaint back alley, with a real Dickensian atmosphere. I was allowed to wander through the house unaccompanied. A copy of the dictionary (first edition) was lying on a table, and I looked up 'oatmeal' and 'Presbyterian' to remind myself of the definition of the first, and to discover what nasty things he had to say about the second. It will be remembered that the story goes that Boswell once asked Johnston what he would say if he were told that a hundred years later his *Dictionary* would be re-edited by a Scottish Presbyterian. 'Sir,' replied Johnson, 'to be facetious, it is not necessary to be indecent.'

On the train returning to Edinburgh, I found a plaque bearing that the sleeping carriage next to mine was called 'Bayonet' and during the late war served as Eisenhower's headquarters in the Normandy and Western Europe campaign.

The President tells me that he has been offered, and has declined, the Lordship of Appeal vacant through Lord Thankerton's death. He assured me that the naming by English newspapers of Tucker, L.J., as successor is not a mere flying of a kite. He is indignant that the Scots judges in the House of Lords should be reduced to one. In 1913, since when there have been two, the number of the English Lords was considerably less than it is now.

6th July 1948

The report now is that Lord Patrick is being offered the vacant Lordship of Appeal.

Yesterday, returning with Ella from Glasgow, where I had been conducting a local inquiry, we were hailed from the roadside by two youths in brown, whom we first assumed to be German prisoners of war. They asked for a lift in my car to Broxburn, where they intended to spend the night in a barn. We found out, however, to our surprise, that they were two Dutch boys, engaged on 'hitch-hiking' from Harwich to Aberdeen. Still further to our surprise, their surname turned out to be Ogilvie! Helmut Ogilvie was a medical student; his younger brother, Michael Ogilvie, a student of dramatic art. So charmed were we with them, that we invited them to come and spend the night in our house. They did this, and today have visited the Castle, St. Giles and John Knox's house. They talked German with the Swiss Mlle. whom we have at present (as Rosemary's Nannie) from Interlaken. Their father is a Dutch pastor. On their journey, they have been to London, Oxford, the Cotswolds, Shrewsbury, Liverpool and the Lakes. This afternoon, after helping Ella to top and tail gooseberries, they left for Queensferry on their journey further north.

8th July 1948

Yesterday, when at my London Committee, I took the opportunity to visit Dickens' house at 48 Doughty Street. It has not the charm of Johnson's house, and, even though it was the scene of *Pickwick* and *Oliver Twist*, there are no happy domestic associations. I went on to the law courts to hear a very effective cross-examination before Birkett J. by a K.C. named Havers! Strangely enough, in two days, I have heard a cross-examination by one English counsel called Havers, and read the opinion of another called Tonge!

5th September 1948

While at Boat of Garten during August, I had two visits to my London Committee. On the first, I managed to get a sleeper from Aviemore to Euston and back. But on the second, I could only get a sleeper back via Waverley. Between my two visits, the heaviest flooding known in Berwickshire occurred, when the Tweed rose to unprecedented heights, the Blackadder and Whiteadder rose in spate, and over thirty road and rail bridges were washed away, the worst interruption to traffic being the total disruption of the main east coast line between Berwick and Cockburnspath. As a result the line is closed for about two months, some six bridges on it being down. At first traffic on the east coast was, for a few days, diverted via Newcastle, Carlisle and Dalry to Waverley, but when I came north, we travelled via Tweedmouth, Kelso and St. Boswells.

The London Committee asked me to prepare the draft of our recommendations. At first I was somewhat indignant being on holiday, but, for the honour of Scotland, I vowed to myself I would do the whole thing! I have submitted the draft in three stages and the last was sent off yesterday. A propos Slade's delightful manner of assuming ignorance of everything until it is explained fully to him (only a genuinely modest man could adopt this attitude in such a committee), Colin Pearson was greatly delighted when I explained to him that this was what we call in Scotland – 'acting the daft laddie!' Masson, our Secretary, has been most appreciative of my drafting efforts (no doubt it relieved him!). I have had dinner with him at the Savile Club, and with Pearson and him at the Garrick Club. The former is mainly literary and social; the latter theatrical, literary and the bar (because of its nearness to the law courts). It is full of pictures of Garrick; and Zoffany and other eighteenth century painters. On my second visit, my club, the Caledonian, was closed for the holidays, but we had temporary privileges at the United Service Club – a most palatial place with portraits of all the admirals and generals who at one time or another got us into a mess. It reminded me of Siegfried Sassoon:–

> 'Good morning, good morning!' the General said.
> When we met him last week on our way to the line.
> Now the soldiers he smiled at are most of 'em dead.
> And we're cursing his staff for incompetent swine.
> 'He's a cheery old card,' grunted Harry to Jack
> As they slogged up to Arras with rifle and pack.
>
> But he did for them both by his plan of attack.

I remarked on this to a friend, Douglas Wimberley. 'Ah,' he said, 'but, you see, they were good club-men!'

9th September 1948

I have just returned from another two days at my London Committee. The parks in London were looking at their best. I amused myself by cinemato-photographing the cherry-trees, dahlias at the lake-side in St. James' Park, a huge bed of geraniums outside Buckingham Palace, and the families of tame birds – all in colour. I also went to the city to photograph in colour some of the bombed sites near St. Paul's and Bow Bells, and All Hallow's Barking and I visited Southwark Cathedral for the first time – where I was interested to find James I of Scotland had married Katherine Beaufort. Cardinal Beaufort's arms are still in the south transept, and there is a recumbent figure of Shakespeare, greatest parishioner of St. Mary Overie, whose brother is buried here.

I invited Slade to Lunch at the Caledonian Club. He asked me how long was it before I made my first £1,000-a-year at the Bar. I said, over ten years at least. Then I told him that I had never exceeded £3,500. He said: 'Latterly my income was £30,000. But this was because of brief fees in very special cases.' He has been Chancellor of Chelmsford and Southwark dioceses. The position, he considered, is much sought-after. It is worth £250 a year in fees for faculties, but it is also a public office of honour. We discussed various counsel, and agreed that two different types were attached to the bar, the advocate and the scholar, the common lawyer and the Chancery lawyer. The ideal was a combination of both. He thought Birkett best combined these qualities at present. Sir Patrick Hastings was a great advocate, but lacked the other side. He wants me, and Ella also, to go and stay with them. He is tall and athletic, a keen tennis-player in winter and summer; has four daughters and is now a grandfather. He said: 'Many people are almost afraid of Stamp. But I never feel too much deference to mere cleverness.' We discussed Lord Haw-Haw. ([1946] AC 347) He said he would never have been convicted, had not the Treason Act 1945 been passed shortly before, which made the evidence of one witness sufficient. One police officer happened to put on his wireless and heard Lord Haw-Haw broadcasting about Dover and Folkestone being bombed. He could remember nothing more, but this short passage which he identified as spoken by Joyce led to his conviction. I asked Slade if Joyce showed much animus, as in his broadcast. He said: 'No,' and added, 'He was a very brave man': no doubt referring to the way he took the sentence. He is going on circuit to Newcastle and Durham in October and means to visit Edinburgh.

This evening, at the Edinburgh Festival, we saw *The Thrie Estates*. It is the high-light of the Festival, and there is more history to be learned from it than from many text-books. It has much of Chaucer, and some of *St. Joan* about it.

16th September 1948

It was announced today that the Dean (J.S.C. Reid) is to be the new Scottish Lord of Appeal. For the third time the Labour Government has filled, or has been obliged to fill, a major judicial post with a Conservative (Normand, Cooper, Reid). Would that the Conservatives had done the same. Towards the end of their long tenure of office, they made some purely political appointments which could scarcely be justified on merit. Lord Pitman, who before his appointment was scarcely known to Parliament House, was precipitated onto the bench, in face of Graham Robertson, leader of the Bar, and Wark, two first-rate lawyers, but both Liberals. And more recently, there have been other political appointments, so that the bench is almost wholly conservative. The only non-political appointments of recent years have been Keith, Patrick and McIntyre (Deans of Faculty), Mackintosh, and Blades (who was non-political Solicitor-General).

My first experience with J.S.C. Reid was in a curious case of Capel v. Arbuthnot's Judicial Factor, where a certain Mr. Capel, after the death of Mr. Carnegy Arbuthnot of Balnamoon, sued the Judicial Factor on his estate and alleged a partnership in race-horses with Mr. Arbuthnot. We had great fun out of this case, as it involved a mastery of race-horses, and all types of race and race-meeting. When he was

Lord Advocate, too, I was quite often with him in Department of Health cases. He made a slow start at the Bar. Indeed, I remember when he was comparatively idle, and I saw him appearing in a Valuation of Teinds. But before he took silk, he came into a first-class Junior Practice. He is essentially a debater – showing great skill in fourth speeches, picking up information and points as the case proceeds. He has acquired quite a reputation in opposition in the House of Commons and would certainly have held high office if the Conservatives had returned to power. He has the reputation of being somewhat unapproachable. I have always found him very easy and friendly. He has, however, been absent from Parliament House far too much for a Dean of Faculty and has left the Vice-Dean (Strachan) to do the work. Fred Strachan will probably be the new Dean. McWhannell, my clerk, was 'tipping' me for Vice-Dean when he called today.

Mrs. Reid, who I think considers Ella as one of her best friends here, rang up this morning. I could see how pleased she was, though with a certain regret at abandoning the adventure of politics. She wants us to come and see them when they are settled in London.

In successive days, I have written opinions concerning two old school mates. My note-books have now the genealogical trees of a considerable number of Scottish families! In questions of succession and vesting, I always begin an opinion by making my own family tree. I was interested to find that the President, at the Bar and on the Bench, did the same. 'In every multiplepoinding,' he remarked, 'we should be furnished with a family tree.'

At this moment, my choice of minister for St. George's West would be Leonard Small of Cramond. I went out to hear him a fortnight ago, and, from start to finish, he could scarcely have been better.

Last week, I had a painful case of a schoolmaster who got into trouble, and, having pleaded guilty, received a sentence of one year. It is the second time that, within the last few years, I have thus appeared for a schoolmaster who was well-known to us. Each of them was a first-class teacher and devoted to his work, and, even after the tragedy came out, held in high respect by his colleagues. I felt the burden of this latter tragedy during the summer. It is good, however, to see the loyalty of friends.

18th September 1948

Yesterday I received word that the Lord Advocate wanted to see me at eleven o'clock today. At breakfast this morning, when the newspapers came in, I guessed the reason. Tom Taylor, Professor of Law at Aberdeen and Sheriff of Renfrew and Argyll, who was called to the Bar along with me, has been appointed by the Crown the new Principal of Aberdeen University. When I went up to the Crown Office, it was to be offered the Sheriffdom of Renfrew and Argyll. I accepted without hesitation. Of my last four predecessors in Argyll, Wark and Mackintosh reached the Bench, Fred Strachan is now Sheriff of Perth and Angus (the Sheriff of Perth 'never dies') and Tom Taylor is now to be Principal of Aberdeen. When Irvine returned from Renfrew and Bute, Bute was transferred to Ayr and Renfrew to Argyll. There are five Sheriff-substitutes, at Paisley, Greenock, Dunoon, Campbeltown and Oban. My jurisdiction extends from Kinlochleven in the North to the Mull of Kintyre in the South, and includes Dalriada and Iona, the two cradles of Scotland! I assume office on 1st October. Both John Wheatley (L.A.) and Douglas Johnston (S.G.) were most friendly in their good wishes, as also was Lionel Gordon, the Crown Agent. The salary is £1,100.

It was a day of mixed emotions. In the afternoon, clear and sunny, we went out to Black Barony for tea. It was here that we spent our two last holidays with Gordon, and this was our first visit these five years. The place was lovely as ever. We walked up the hill, his presence ever with us, and Rosemary, quite unconscious, plucked wild raspberries. Alison was unusually quiet: I think she felt as we did.

19th September 1948

I must complete my view of the present judges, as everything points to a change being imminent. Carmont, Jamieson and especially Stevenson and Patrick all seem unlikely to remain on the bench long. I finished with the Inner House judges on 25th October 1947. Let me now take the Outer House in their order of seniority.

Lord Patrick has now been away at the Tokyo War Crimes trial for over two years; and quite a number of the youngest members of the Bar would not know him. To the others, he is probably the best of our present judges. Cooper is his only competitor for this distinction. I once saw Patrick sitting in the Second Division with Cooper (as Justice-Clerk) and Stevenson. It seemed to me then that Patrick had the greater union of judicial qualities. In his own Court, there is something of the dignity and efficiency of the House of Lords. He does not begin to talk until he has read the case, as few judges do.

When he has read the case, he remembers the points as few judges do. He is singularly judicial in behaviour, cool and calm, always phrasing his points simply and lucidly, with a good memory for case law. He is also invariably pleasant to counsel who are trying their best. His career has been one of steady improvement, with one curious set-back. As a junior he was good with a slightly precious manner, but always much simpler and more lucid than most other counsel. As a senior, still a little sensitive about his position, he was almost condescending and a little chilly to solicitors. As Dean, where his position was assured, he was more approachable, though perhaps scarcely hospitable beyond what civility required. As judge, he has become positively genial, and friendly, indeed an ideal judge, both in talent and behaviour. The one set-back in his career was when, in the full flood of junior practice, he had to retire for almost two years to a sanatorium. No one then expected his return, but he came back seemingly restored in health, took 'silk' and stepped at once into large senior practice. To preserve his health, he made a practice of spending every weekend at the Crook Inn, Tweedsmuir. His long sojourn in Tokyo seems again to have affected his health, and for several months out of the last eight he has been in hospital there. It is hoped that he will return to Scotland this autumn, but unlikely that he will immediately be fit for work. Since Gordon died, he has been specially friendly towards me. He lost his own brother in a similar football accident.

Lord Mackintosh is a native of Nairn, and gravitates there still as often as he can during vacations. He was a dux of the Academy and is still Chairman of its directors, but he has a family of four daughters. He married a rich attorney's daughter (the daughter of Sir John Prosser), and the basis of his early practice was Morton, Smart, Macdonald and Prosser. His practice has lain, rather more than most, in Chancery work, and that is still his strong suit. He is a good example of *mens sana in corpore sano*, for he played Rugby at school and in the inter-city match, besides being a good scholar. But he is industrious rather than brilliant, somewhat lacking in humour, somewhat long-winded (though brief in comparison to Mackay), and for a father of daughters, curiously unpolished in his general behaviour. He has a curious habit of curling his forelock when in thought. On any legal question, he is distinctly good, and it is always a pleasure to address a legal argument to him.

Lord Sorn, like Lord Patrick an Ayrshire man, is a product of Glasgow's industrial aristocracy. His father, T.W. McIntyre of Sorn, was partner with Lord Mackay's in the shipping firm of Mackay and McIntyre, and left a large estate. Lord Sorn was head of the school at Winchester, and elected, when little more than forty, Dean of Faculty. He is gentle, suave and pleasant, with a keen and delicate humour – possibly the most popular judge on the Bench for his personal qualities. He enjoyed a very select practice of the best class, both as junior and senior. Cooper promoted Mackintosh to the Bench. Sorn was all along Normand's protégé. He is a good judge, but perhaps he is more remarkable for his unique charm of personality and lovableness than for his judicial qualities, great as they are. As counsel he enjoyed the highest reputation for fairness and reasonableness. His pleading was always artistic, though he had a curious hesitation of manner which, however, conveyed a certain charm.

Lord Birnam has, in many ways, an ideal temperament for a judge, quite imperturbable (if an atom bomb fell beside him, he would simply turn round and wipe the dust off his shoulder!) hard-headed and wise, with a pleasant and lucid expression. He is perhaps not a very hard worker, he manages to dispose of cases with the minimum of trouble (which is not quite the same thing). As a junior, when I had a choice of senior counsel, I always chose him; he was so intelligent and pleasant to work with and appreciative of the efforts of his junior. He has had the most unusual career at the Bar. After an excellent junior practice, he seemed to have put himself on the shelf by accepting appointment as Sheriff-substitute at Airdrie; he then left Airdrie to resume practice, and took silk; he was then appointed Chairman of the Land Court, with the title of Lord Murray; he returned to the Bar to become Solicitor-General, dropping his paper title and being knighted to become Sir David King Murray; finally, he went on the bench as Lord Birnam, taking this title to avoid confusion with the late Lord Murray (C.D. Murray), whose widow still survives. He very nearly called himself Lord Inverleith. The title 'Birnam' comes not from Dunkeld's twin, but from the name of his house – Birnam Lodge – in Airdrie. Thrice at the Bar and thrice on the Bench is surely a record. Finally, after reaching the Bench, he married, and Lady Birnam is as charming as himself. They both are fond of Kinloch Rannoch, and an old ghillie up there said once about him: 'I hear there's a man here they call Laburnum!'

Lord Blades is a son of the manse of Allanton. His father, about the oldest minister in the Church of Scotland, died just before his son went on the Bench. He was a leader of student life at Edinburgh University, and his success is attributable partly to a robust and forthright personality and partly to the friendship between himself and Craigie Aitchison, who gave him his first promotion. He is essentially a common lawyer, full of common sense; but he is less suitable to the finer distinctions of pure law. He has, on the whole, been a little lucky in his promotions, but he has always borne himself with modesty and simplicity, and he is much respected. His bearing in Court is also most judicial.

20th September 1948

Today, we motored to Tinto, Biggar, Kilmichael, Broughton, the head of the Manor Valley, and Peebles. We visited the Black Dwarf's Cottage and his grave in Manor churchyard. A small note-book contains visitor's names and I was interested to find all our three visits in this one book – the first in August 1942, with Gordon, the second in 1945 and the third today. It shows how few are the visitors when three visits in a period of six years all are recorded in the one book. There is, however, no sign on the road to mark the cottage, and Arthur Melville Clark, who was with us, did not know its location. Only this week curiously enough, in giving an opinion, I had to peruse a will which provided for the preservation of the Black Dwarf's cottage. How many literary associations arise in my chancery practice. I have at one time or another dealt with Burns' House at Dumfries, Boswell's Fettercairn MSS, Monkbarns, R.L.S.'s 'Peden the Prophet' at New Luce, the Pirates of Penzance, Lavengro, Burns' Falls of Bruar, the Fair Maid of Perth, Nicholas Nickleby, Barrie's Thrums and now the Black Dwarf! I was interested to be reminded that W.C.R. Chambers erected the stone to his memory at Manor. Only this year I purchased their book on the Black Dwarf; the first, I believe, they published; and, of added interest, because my copy bears the signature of the Great Unknown himself! Arthur Clark pointed out the position of Noblehouse, where Alan Fairford bade farewell to Darsie Latimer. Near Drumelzier, too, we saw, in a wooded circle, the supposed site of Merlin's grave. How curious are the names Kilbucho, Stobo, Posso and Fogo. 'O' seems to means a 'haugh', like Philiphaugh. We also saw the site which marks the site of Murray of Broughton's residence, near Broughton.

26th September 1948

Coming home from church today with T.P. McDonald, we noticed on the wall of No.45 Charlotte Square a stone inscription being carved. As this was my uncle Robert's former house, I went over to see what was written. The inscription was still incomplete, but was, as far as it had gone, to the effect that Sir Robert Philip, pioneer in tuberculosis, had lived in this house.

4th October 1948

This was an eventful day. In the morning, I took little Rosemary aged four to St. Monica's for her first day at school, photographing her in school hat and uniform before and after, greatly to her pride and delight. Then after conducting a planning appeal in the City Chambers, and visiting the locus concerned (Hanley Lodge, Gogar), I came home to find awaiting me His Majesty's Commission dated 29th September appointing me as from 1st October Sheriff of Renfrew and Argyll.

(Sgd) George R.

George the Sixth by the Grace of God
of Great Britain, Ireland and the British
Dominions beyond the Seas King, Defender of
the Faith, to all to whom these Presents
shall come
Greeting!

Whereas the office of Sheriff of the Sheriffdom of Renfrew and Argyll in Scotland will become vacant on the 1st October, 1948 by the resignation of Thomas Murray Taylor, Esquire, C.B.E., K.C.

Now Know Ye that we being well satisfied of the loyalty and ability of Our Trusty and Well-beloved James Randall Philip, Esquire, Officer of Our Most Excellent Order of the British Empire, One of Our Counsel learned in the law, have nominated, constituted and appointed and by the Presents nominate, constitute and appoint him the said James Randall Philip to be Sheriff *ad vitam aut culpam* of the Sheriffdom of Renfrew and Argyll as from the 1st October 1948.

Giving and Granting unto him the said Office of Sheriff with the salary and allowances assigned thereto by the Lords Commissioners of Our Treasury in lieu of all fees, allowances, expenses and emoluments what-soever, all which fees, allowances, expenses and emoluments in so far as drawn by him shall be paid into Our Exchequer.

And Also Giving and Granting unto him all powers, jurisdictions, authorities, privileges and immunities thereunto belonging or appertaining, he being bound while he continues in the said Office to accept such alterations in the nature of his duties thereof as may hereafter be prescribed by Parliament without claim to compensation or additional remuneration.

And Our Further Will and pleasure is that the said James Randall Philip do procure these Presents to be registered in the Chancery Department of Our General Register House, Edinburgh, within the space of three months from the date hereof.

Given at Our Court at Balmoral
the twenty-ninth day of September 1948
in the Twelfth Year of Our Reign
By His Majesty's Command
(Sgd) Arthur Woodburn

George VI no longer signs 'Imperator' as well as 'Rex', since the Empire of India became the two Dominions of India and Pakistan.

5th October 1948

The two most likely candidates for Dean of Faculty are Fred Strachan and Jock Cameron. So far as I can judge, the former is likely to have the support of the more responsible members of Faculty, and the latter that of the Third Estate. If service to the Faculty were the test, the chances of the former are the stronger, because for the last few years he has been in effect Dean already. If practice at the Bar be the test, the claims of the latter would prevail. There have been rumours that there might be a vacancy on the bench, which Fred Strachan would fill. As his sponsor at the last election, I felt I should find out the position before I approached him to see whether he would accept nomination. So last week I went straight to the President as the fountainhead and he told me that he knew of no immediate vacancy, though Fred Strachan would be quite likely to receive promotion within a year.

Today, I received this illuminating letter from the President:–

4.10.48

My Dear Philip,

Two points:- (1) Best congratulations on an impending announcement and (2) last week you asked me a question to which I gave you an answer which was true at the time it was given. I would not give the same answer today. *Verb. sap.*

Yours
T.M.C.

11th October 1948

Lord Stevenson's impending resignation is announced unofficially. But Ella has heard from Lady Stevenson that the news is correct. Fred Strachan will go on the bench. This will leave Jock Cameron's way to the Deanship clear. Hill Watson will stand, but, much as he is liked, will not get much support, as temperamentally he is unsuited to be Dean. I was sworn in today by the Lord President, and, in the afternoon, received the greetings of the National Library Standing Committee. My first two duties are to attend the funeral of Sheriff A.D. Donald, the father of my Sheriff-substitute at Dunoon, D.A. Donald; and to deal with a defaulting Sheriff Officer. Sheriff A.D. Donald was one of the strangest cases at the Bar. Prizeman in the Scots Law class, he came to the Bar expected to do brilliantly. For twenty-five years or more he walked the Parliament Hall doing almost nothing and when I knew him first, he was a quiet subdued old man, kindly when he spoke but rarely speaking to a soul. Then for the last ten years of his life, he became Sheriff-substitute at Dingwall, where he seems to have been well-liked. If the moves I have indicated are correct, the Sheriffdoms of Perth and Angus (Strachan) and Inverness, Elgin and Nairn (Cameron) will both fall vacant.

15th October 1948

Fred Strachan's appointment to the bench came out unofficially on the 12th and today he was installed. The appointment was approved in all quarters. His gifts are essentially judicial, and he has one of the best minds in Parliament House. He might well become another Kyllachy. I have been appointed arbiter by the parties in two arbitrations which he has given up. The Deanship is to be decided on the 29th. My selection is Jock Cameron and I am sure he will be appointed. For the Vice-Deanship, the three names mooted are T.B. Simpson, Bill Milligan and myself. I discussed the position last evening with Harry Guthrie, and we both reached the conclusion that it was not in my personal interest to stand, and that my attitude should be not to seek the position, and only let my name go forward if there was special pressure. We both agreed that Bill Milligan would be a suitable candidate, and had much more time to do the work.

Since the 12th, when it became definite that Fred Strachan was going on the Bench, many people have mentioned me, to my face, as the next Procurator of the Church. I am not going to count chickens before they are hatched, however.

On the 12th, Rosemary acted as trainbearer at Margaret Abbey's wedding in St. Giles. Though possessed of perpetual motion, she discharged her duties beyond all expectation, walking slowly the whole length of St. Giles, standing for half-an-hour during the service (yawning the while, making bright faces at her parents, and looking round to see where the sound of the organ came from), walking into the Thistle Chapel for the signing of the Register, walking out again, and then retreating down the nave quite unabashed. She made up for it by much wildness at the reception afterwards, when she lay on the floor while her toast was being proposed.

20th October 1948

I attended my first meeting of the Board of the Commissioners of Northern Lights. T.B. Simpson took the Chair. Apart from the Sheriffs, there were present the Provosts of Greenock and Campbeltown, with whom I shall meet again when I visit my Sheriffdom, and the Senior Bailie of Edinburgh. The slightly dim formal atmosphere reminded me of old days in the Spec. Wakelin, the Secretary, transacts the business with model efficiency. We accepted tenders for lighting buoys, supplying equipment for lighthouses, repairing roads, removing obsolete lights and also approved of raising lighthouse keepers' wages in response to an application initiated by their union. T.B. Simpson told me the President is still putting forward my name as Dean. But it would be premature for me, as yet, to stand. Still, even if nothing ever came of it, it is flattering to have been the President's choice.

Tomorrow, I go to be introduced at Paisley; and, on Friday, to Greenock. A.M. Hamilton, the Sheriff-substitute at Paisley, was at the Bar before I was born, and took silk before I was at the Bar. A terror to wrong-doers, and those who appear before him, he is, off the bench, one of the most hospitable of men, and, in accordance with his usual practice, has invited me to lunch.

An absurd rumpus has arisen between the Lord Lyon (Innes of Learney) and Sir Hector McNeill, Glasgow's Lord Provost. The Lord

Provosts of Edinburgh, Glasgow and Dundee wear ermine, whereas Aberdeen wears sable. Now Learney has ruled that ermine is reserved for peers and High Officers of State; and, by special privilege, the Lord Provost of Edinburgh; and that the others should follow Aberdeen's example and wear sable. To which Sir Hector replies: 'On 18th November 1619, the Privy Council ordained that the Provosts of Burghs should wear "black gowns, lined with some grave kind of furrings", but that the Provosts of Edinburgh, Perth, Dundee, St. Andrews, Glasgow, Stirling and Aberdeen should wear gowns of "red scarlet cloth, with furrings agreeable to the same".' ('We chose ermine,' says Glasgow's Lord Provost.) The Lyon, however, interprets 'furrings agreeable to the same' as 'agreeable to grave kind of furrings'. This is surely wrong. The antecedent of 'the same' is surely 'red scarlet cloth' – the nearest sensible antecedent.

23rd October 1948

I was introduced at Paisley on the 21st and Greenock on the 22nd. At Paisley, the procedure was:– I took the chair, and I presented my Commission and directed that it should be recorded. Then Sheriff Hamilton; the Dean of the Faculty of Procurators (Mr. Hunter), for the Bar; the Procurator-Fiscal (Mr. Hill), for the Court officials; and the Lord Lieutenant of the County (Mr. Hagart-Speirs) made speeches of welcome; and I replied. This completed the business. In Greenock, the procedure was the same, except that the Provost of Greenock was the fourth speaker. I remarked on his chain of office, and he said that it was presented by Sir Andrew Lusk, Lord Mayor of London (the granduncle of my friend, the Rev. D.C. Lusk).

At Paisley, I had my first initiation to administrative work as a Sheriff. (Actually my first interlocutor has been fixing a hearing at Campbeltown for an application to extend the boundaries of the Burgh.) I ordered a restriction of hours for a Registrar of Births, Deaths and Marriages at Neilston; and I appointed a Sheriff Officer. At Greenock, I had my first problem, a case where a Sheriff Officer had, through inability to get labour, been unable to carry out a physical ejection, and the holder of the decree had complained to his member of Parliament. I saw the Sheriff Officer, and reached the view that his explanation was genuine. No labourer will take on the work of eviction in Greenock, because of its unpopularity.

Harold and Kathleen came down to Greenock with me. The Chief Constable is kindly going to drive me from Queen Street Station in future. He gave me a police car to take me from Paisley to Harold's house, where I spent the night. Crossing Renfrew Ferry, I said to the police-driver: 'Let me pay for the fare; it will show them that I'm not in custody!'

After the Greenock ceremony, Harold drove me back to Glasgow where we had lunch in the Automobile Club. There we met Dr. John White, and he joined us after lunch for coffee. We discussed the vacancy at St. George's West. I asked him about a young Rev. John L. Gray of St. Stephen's and Buccleuch, whose name had been mentioned to us. It turned out that he had been an assistant at one time at the Barony. Dr. White, after consideration, said: 'He is the ablest young minister at present in Glasgow.' As we were leaving, Dr. White's conversation turned in a very general way on names which I knew were being canvassed for the Procuratorship. At the end of a rather general skirmish, he said: 'Your old father would like to see you wearing your wig in the Assembly.' Then with a smile, he added: 'Remember, I've not said anything about the Procuratorship.' I replied: 'Neither have I.'

In the evening, at our vacancy executive committee, Dr. Walton told me he understood I was to be the new Procurator. I said I was willing to stand, but wasn't saying more. He then told me that Dr. White Anderson had said to him: 'We must have Randall Philip.' This is interesting – especially as he is usually Convener of the Business Committee, and the other possible candidates, Matthew Fisher and Hill Watson, are both elders of his, and the first, his session clerk. The first has never had any practice, and was beaten in the contest with Strachan. The second himself told me on the 12th that he did not intend to stand. The matter has now been mentioned to me by quite a number, including the Rev. A.J.H. Gibson, Secretary to the Maintenance of the Ministry Committee, and Dr. Burnet of St. Cuthbert's. They always speak as if it were more or less certain.

Our vacancy committee is not making good progress. Three weeks ago, I proposed Leonard Small of Cramond, but the others, after hearing him again, though appreciative to a point, damned him with faint praise. I then suggested David Read, and, here, they were even less ready to approve. They are too good at depreciation. Other names at present canvassed are Rev. W. Yule (Crieff), Rev. John M. Kent (Cathcart South), the Rev. James Munn (St. Paul's, Dundee), the Rev. John R. Gray (St. Stephen's – Buccleuch, Glasgow) and the Rev. R.H.G. Budge (Troon). But I wish one member of the Committee would, as I at last have done, put forward a definite proposal. I would, as I told Dr. Walton, gladly welcome either Mr. Small or Mr. Read, and so would Dr. Walton. But, as yet, too many of the Committee are inclined to give their reasons for not liking a man, rather than their appreciation of him. One old lady spent exactly half-an-hour last night in dissecting one of Mr. Kent's services and sermons. It would have been quicker to hear the original.

The following is roughly what I said in reply to the speeches welcoming me at Paisley Sheriff Court:–

My Lords and Gentlemen, I thank you warmly for your presence here today, and for the welcome you have given. May I say, in turn, how deeply proud I am to preside over the Sheriffdom. There is surely no Sheriffdom which embraces a tract of country, industrial and rural, so varied as this and no Sheriffdom embraces friendlier people.

In the natural diffidence with which I take up my new duties, I shall rely on the ripe experience of my veteran colleague, Sheriff Hamilton. He has always united strict impartiality in the administration of justice, with a friendship and hospitality off the bench to the younger members of his own profession. I think I interpret today's welcome to me as, in one aspect, the mark of the esteem and, indeed, affection in which he is to be held in his own Sheriff Court.

To you, Dean of Faculty, I offer my thanks for the welcome from the Bar. Paisley has been a nursery of distinguished lawyers both for England and for Scotland [I was thinking specially of the McNairs and MacRobert]. It is my hope that we shall cooperate in maintaining and even enhancing the high traditions of this court. I shall always listen with appreciation and patience to the arguments addressed to me.

I thank you, Mr. Procurator-Fiscal, for the good wishes of the officials of Court. I know I shall depend on their support, and, in turn, they may depend on mine. I look forward to making their better acquaintance in the coming days.

My Lord Lieutenant, your presence today is a tribute to the place which the Sheriff Court occupies in the community. Recently, we have had some remarkable tributes to the merits of our Scottish jurisprudence. Only a year ago the simple and practical Scots rules of the Crown as Litigant were adopted for England, and extended in Scotland. Only today, we learn of unsolicited tributes to the merits of the Scots law of defamation [in the Report of the Porter Committee on the Law of Defamation]. I hope the day will not be far distant when the peculiar merits of that distinctive institution, the Scottish Sheriff Court, will be recognised even more widely than they are at present.

For myself, my aim will be to copy that judge whom I regard as the greatest Scottish judge in my time at the Bar, the late Lord Fleming, whose wisdom, common sense and humility won him the respect and affection of all with whom he came in contact.

29th October 1948

Today Jock Cameron was unanimously elected Dean of Faculty: No other name was even brought forward. The Lord Advocate presided at the meeting, there being no Vice-Dean since Fred Strachan's elevation to the Bench. Thus, Jock Cameron's former 'devil', John Wheatley, had the unusual distinction of being the one to announce to his old master the latter's election as Dean.

The *British Weekly* today couples my name with that of Hill Watson as the two names most frequently mentioned so far in connection with the vacant Procuratorship.

4th November 1948

I have just returned from visiting Argyll. I was introduced at Fort William, Oban, Campbeltown and Dunoon Sheriff Courts. I refused leave to appeal in a judicial separation relevancy point at Oban; extended Campbeltown Burgh boundary for the first time since 1832; and, at Dunoon, on the petition of the North of Scotland Hydro-Electric Board authorised the appointment of a special policeman at the Loch Sloy hydro-electric scheme!

At Fort William, I was entertained by Cameron Miller. He was in the R.N.V.R. and she was a Wren. He has a fine bass voice and played me some gramophone recordings of songs he had sung, including 'In Cellar Cool'. He has also made himself very popular through beating two professionals in throwing the discus at the Lochaber Games. He is expected to go to Portree every three weeks and instead of going via Mallaig now motors via Dornie to Kyle of Lochalsh. He made this change because on one voyage he found that he had to share the only cabin on the steamer with the accused whom he was going to try. He told me an amusing story of the 'Chimp' – otherwise 'Boris' – R.B. Miller, Sheriff-substitute at Stornoway, who is an 'original'. The two Millers were called the same day and after their admission to the Bar were walking away when Boris pushed his head unceremoniously into the First Division where Ronald Morison was pleading, and remarked (as he came out again): 'That fellow Morison is makin' a right hash o' yon!' Cameron Miller's remarks about me were very kind. The Fiscal at Fort William is an old fellow apprentice of mine, W.J. Cuthbert, and I called on him on arrival and had tea with him in his office.

As I came north of Tyndrum, my heart went up with a bound when I read the magic word 'Argyll' and saw before me my kingdom, Glenorchy bathed in sun, the mists over Blackmount, the bog which masks the massacre of Glencoe, James Stewart of the Glen's monument at Ballachulish and the glorious burnt sienna of the bracken and gold of the birches at the wood of Lettermore.

Chalmers, who is Sheriff-substitute at Oban, is a former solicitor, and a native of Perth. He lives in great state, in the finest house in Oban, Kilbowie, in the South Bay. The house stands at the edge of the Sound, the grass lawns descending straight into the water. From all the windows overlooking the Bay there are magnificent views. Chalmers is very popular and greatly respected, and has been invited to move elsewhere. Strachan wanted him to go to Perth, when he became Sheriff Principal there. The proceedings in Oban Sheriff Court were the most formal of my tour. My Commission was read in full, and there was a good representation of the County. A civic lunch was held afterwards, at which I sat on the right of the senior Bailie, Dr. Ivor Campbell (who was deputising for the Provost, who was unwell) and on my right was the Macdougall of Macdougall. One is here just at the watershed between Jacobite and Hanoverian. The Macdougalls were out at the '15 but not at the '45.

The same afternoon, I motored on to Campbeltown, in two hours forty-five minutes. Except for a short portion chiefly between Kilmartin and Tarbert, the road has most magnificent views of the islands to the west. The Council Convener, Mr. Matheson of Kilmartin, has promised to guide me to the stone of Dunadd which is on the estate of which he is factor.

At Campbeltown, I stayed with Sheriff and Mrs. Aikman Smith. The former, like myself, is a son of the manse, and this may explain the large attendance of ministers at my inauguration there. His wife was at St. Leonard's. Jim Aikman Smith is a mountaineer. I learned this from a lovely photo of Monte Rosa in his study. He had an interesting staff appointment at the Royal Palace, Caserta and met Sir Harry Wilson, Eisenhower, Bedell Smith and Marshal Tito. His introduction of me had the same friendly tone as that of Cameron Miller. Chalmers was also exceedingly friendly, though naturally he had less personal knowledge. Before leaving Campbeltown, the Aikman Smiths and I drove over to Machrihanish. Then on I went to Dunoon, leaving Campbeltown at 2.10 and reaching Hunter's Quay at 5.50 p.m. – a long run chiefly along the sides of Loch Fyne. Jura was magnificent from Kintyre and the autumn colourings around Inverary, like those in Appin. Argyll is more conservative than its neighbours to the east. Today, all the towns were observing the old Communion Fast-Day, and shops in places like Ardrishaig were shut as on a holiday. At Hunter's Quay, I stayed in the Royal Marine Hotel, as D.A. Donald does not live here but in Rothesay. Next morning, at Dunoon, I went through the same introduction for the sixth time and now my royal progress (as it was called) was ended. I returned home by Loch Eck, Rest and Be Thankful, Drymen and Stirling.

On reaching home, I learned that James Walker had been elected Vice-Dean. I was pressed last week to stand, but the President advised me not to do so, as it would prejudice my future chances of being Dean. Also, I am overworked as it is. But there was very strong backing. T.P. McDonald was the one who made the formal approach. When I declined, he went to James Walker. Up till this point, T.B. Simpson had considered his election sure. It soon became apparent that he had no prospects, and then, at a late stage, he withdrew and Bill Milligan was put forward in his place. But James Walker secured over 40 votes to about 31 for Bill. Had Bill stood originally, I think he would have been elected. This also reminds me of the other election result which came out when I was in Campbeltown – when the universally unexpected happened, and Truman was elected American President, instead of the favourite, Thomas Dewey.

10th November 1948

Two new sayings by Lord Mackay:–

In a joint opinion with Condie Sandeman, which I had to consider recently, he answered the final (Counsel will add anything) question:- 'We think it will appear that we have delivered a closely reasoned opinion.' Of a will partly printed, partly written: This 'irregular, piebald paper.' (Bridgeford's Exrs. v. Bridgeford 1948 SLT at p. 354)

Today, in a human moment, the President confessed to me that his heart was heavy because tomorrow a favourite cat of his which he had had for a dozen years was to be 'put away'. 'For a bachelor like me,' he said, 'animals are my closest friends. I cannot understand why the doctrines of the Christian Church deny immortality to animals. It's pure dogma.' He added that he had studied St. Francis of Assisi, hoping that he would say something on the subject, but that he had found nothing.

28th November 1948

This week I was appearing in the House of Lords. Our judges were Lords Simonds, Normand, Morton, Macdermott and Reid. The case was a Scots conveyancing case, from the legal point of view of absorbing interest, not least because there was a fundamental divergence of view on the question between the greatest of Scots judges – Inglis on the one side, Watson and Kinnear on the other. Inglis took the view of the feudal conveyancer, the others the view of beneficial interest. It seems to me a vindication of the feudal view. But I say this – deliberately – in advance of the decision (Mackintosh v. Westwood). On such a difficult subject as security created by *ex facie* absolute disposition, it was natural that the judges should be cautious. But it will be long ere I feel the same satisfaction as I felt on this occasion in all humility – receiving the uninterrupted attention of five of the best brains in the country, while, for over a day, I endeavoured to argue the questions of principle. Hector McKechnie who was for the Appellants made a very lucid speech, sometimes inclined to be flippant, but with a complete mastery of the subject. We had to be ready to explain almost anything. He gave a facile description of improper wadset: and I replied with an account of the *quaequidem* clause! *[see Bell's Principles, 10th Edition, paras. 901–8]*

Of the five judges, I think, possibly, Morton was the best. He has a quite remarkable gift of exact phraseology, which is never pedantic. It is an education to hear him state any point. He also seemed to be able to talk the language of Scots conveyancing, perhaps because although he is an English Chancery judge, he hails from Troon. Henryton from which he draws his title is a farm near Darvel or Galston. Simonds is that rare type, the robust scholar. He is a strongly built healthy man – at any rate in appearance – with almost the look of a farmer or one who has spent his days in the open air. When he opens his mouth, he has the same precise articulation as Radcliffe, and I hesitate to say whether he may not be better than Morton, though on this occasion, perhaps because he was less familiar with

Scotland, he was more diffident in expressing his opinion. Normand was the most familiar with the subject matter of the case. Reid's and his interventions were always helpful. I felt that Macdermott was not quite in the same class as the other four, though it is refreshing to hear the burr of Northern Ireland. My junior was my first 'devil' John Wilson. The case lasted three full days, and we sat as before in the Committee Room.

The first evening I had John Wilson to dinner at the Caledonian Club; next evening, Lady Reid invited me to dinner; and the third evening, John Wilson and I dined with Douglas Johnston (Solicitor-General) in the Halcourt Rooms at the House of Commons. The Reids live in a tiny but very comfortable flat high up in St. James' Court. We dined, the three of us, by candle-light, and I was shown Lord Reid's letters-patent, and received a description of his introduction as a peer.

Douglas Johnston gave me a card of introduction to admit me to the Inquiry which is being held into the allegations of bribery connected with Mr. Belcher, Parliamentary Secretary to the Board of Trade. The Inquiry is proceeding in Church House, Westminster. I obtained an excellent seat and heard the evidence of Sir John Woods, Permanent Under-Secretary to the Board of Trade; Harold Wilson, President of the Board of Trade; his private secretary; a tailor, Hersch Tieper, who had fitted Mr. Belcher for a suit supplied by Sidney Stanley; and a Margate hotel-proprietor, who had put up the Belchers on Stanley's instructions. Most of the examination was by Sir Hartley Shawcross (the Attorney-General). It was he who impressed me most. Harold Wilson, who is only thirty-two, though a very clever witness, did not impress me by his personality. The Court consists of Lynskey J.; Russell Vick K.C.; and Gerald Upjohn K.C. The first, like the Attorney, comes from the Liverpool bar. With a red face, he looks like an old ram, with tufts of white hair springing from his face. Russell Vick might be (in appearance) a genial shop walker in a second hand furniture shop. Upjohn is the Adonis of the three. I thought Lynskey's and Upjohn's questions were the best. Stanley and Belcher sat behind the solicitors, both anxious and fidgety. As I left (after spending the whole morning there) whom should I see sitting at the back of the Hall, but Bishop Brook of St. Edmundsbury, whom we met at Grasmere. He was at first surprised, and then greatly delighted to see me.

Since returning to Edinburgh, I have been approached by T.B. Smith, a young member of the Bar, who asks my support for a certain appointment. He gave me a list of his qualifications. Modestly, he has never mentioned these. But, just to show the quality of a younger member of the Bar, here they are:– Boulton Exhibitioner in Law at Christ Church; B.A. with 'First' in Jurisprudence; Eldon Scholar at Oxford University (£200 p.a.: open only to those with 'Firsts' or a Chancellor's Prize); First Class in English Bar examination; Lord Justice Holker (Holt) scholar, Gray's Inn (£200 p.a.); Lord Justice Holker Leaving Exhibition, Gray's Inn (£200 p.a.); a Lieutenant-Colonel and G.S.O. 1 of Political Intelligence Branch; Officer of British Resident Minister, Central Mediterranean Forces; member of Faculty of Advocates. He is as attractive as he is clever.

CHAPTER III

1949

12th January 1949

I have been too busy to keep this Journal. During the interval since my last entry, the Solicitors' Bill has received its second reading, before it had been considered by the Faculty at a Faculty meeting. This aroused much indignation and the Dean wrote a letter to all the leading papers. It may be, however, that there was a genuine misunderstanding as to the degree of consideration given, as the Lord Advocate had certainly met individual members of Faculty on the subject. But no misunderstanding would have arisen had there not been such haste. The Bill plans that all 'poor's work' now extended to include a much wider field will be paid on a 25 per cent basis. The Faculty have done their poor's work free for five hundred years. My objection to the Bill as framed is the overriding powers of regulation given to the Secretary of State which might interfere with internal Faculty discipline. But probably this will be modified when the Bill is in Committee.

Last night, we reached a decisive stage in the process of filling the vacancy in St. George's West Church. The Executive Committee (which numbered 25) then agreed to recommend the Rev. John R. Gray unanimously to the large Vacancy Committee (which numbered some 130).

It fell to me to submit the report and I was seconded by Miss Troup (sister of the Admiral) who had done yeoman service on the Committee, and Miss Hart. I dwelt on our objectives (1) evangelical preaching backed by sound scholarship; (2) a pastor young enough not merely to sustain the burden of a great congregation but also to rebuild it; (3) a man of wide sympathies with special influence with the young, and, for that reason, a man who had shared the hardship of war service. Then I reviewed his academic career, war service, pastoral experience, and the judgments of those best qualified to judge, giving also my own impressions. Finally, I expressed the hope that the large Committee would see their way to unanimity, because that

THE JOURNAL OF SIR RANDALL PHILIP

would be most likely to secure Gray's acceptance of the call. Lord
Blades said he had sometimes criticised the executive committee, but
now he was wholeheartedly behind them. He moved that Gray's name
be put forward and that was seconded by Miss Reid. The motion was
carried unanimously. It was, indeed, a satisfaction to see so large a
body undivided.

30th January 1949

The sequel to our Vacancy Committee meeting was as remarkable as
the meeting itself. Mr. Gray came to meet our Executive Committee.
We had time for dinner beforehand, and he made an excellent
impression. At the meeting I spoke first, and then Mr. Barrett, my
co-Session clerk. Then Dr. Walton said: 'Mrs. Esplin, as President of
the Women's Guild, perhaps you would tell Mr. Gray something
about its work.' Mrs. Esplin (to everyone's amazement): 'Well, Mr.
Gray, I think I should tell you that I am against your call, but still
you may rely on my cooperation and the cooperation of all the
women.' This from a woman who had twice acquiesced in a unanimous resolution to invite him – once in the Executive; and once in
the general Vacancy Committee! A dark pall descended on the meeting, and later speeches were somewhat stilted. Afterwards, as he was
slipping into Dr. Walton's car, Mr. Gray said to me: 'What did that
old warrior mean by her opposition? Does she object to me because
I am still unmarried?' I was, naturally, unable to give the clue. Needless to say, three days later Mr. Gray informed us that he was
unwilling to accept nomination. Since then, we have arranged as an
executive to place our resignations in the hands of the general Vacancy
Committee.

Last week, Harry Guthrie was appointed a judge, one of the two
new judges authorised by the recent Act to overtake the present large
volume of work. He will make, I think, a good judge, though possibly
prosaic, and I think he should be a good listener. He is painstaking
and considerate, and as an interesting side-light on his character, he
goes off each summer to attend a Summer School at Cambridge.
Anyone who remains a learner is bound to improve steadily as the
years go on. Incidentally, I think, last summer, his choice of subject
was Italian. I know he was much interested in my tracing of the
famous Declaration of Arbroath to Sallust, because he heard of it first
through a reference to it in a lecture on Italian.

I was at an interesting function a week ago. Two Communion cups, bearing the silver mark of 1685, which had belonged to the French Church in Edinburgh of that day, and which had fallen into the possession of Trinity College Church, were returned by their Kirk Session at a special Communion service of the French Church. Mr. Morrell of Trinity College Church preached in French.

13th February 1949

Dover told me a delightful incident last night. He and Mrs. Dover Wilson are to fly to South Africa, where he is to deliver a series of lectures on Shakespeare. He was visiting the blacksmith at Balerno, and told the latter's wife that he was leaving in a few weeks. 'When will you be back?' she asked. 'About May,' he replied, 'that is, if we don't crash.' She answered: 'Ah weel – if ye dae crash, ye're baith sure o' your wings!' A true remark; and in the true vein of rather grim Scottish humour. Dover repeated his offer to propose me for the Athenæum. I told him also of my recent visit to Greenock, where I had to propose the 'Immortal Memory' at the '43 Club Burns Dinner. I used two recent personal links I had with Burns (1) the story of how Murdoch read *Titus Andronicus* to the Burns family at Mount Oliphant, which Dover has now used in his edition of *Titus* and (2) the fact that I had discovered that the National Library had not, and never had had, a copy of the Kilmarnock edition. The rest of my speech was made up of an imaginary conversation with a young man in the train going to Greenock, the young man turning out to be Burns himself.

Yesterday, I proposed, and Harald Leslie seconded, T.P. McDonald as Keeper of the Advocates' Library. The motion was unanimous. He well deserves the honour. He is senior to Harry Guthrie, and would have been ahead of him, but for the fact that he was away for five years at the war. He is a sound, if not brilliant, lawyer. But, above all, he is a strong and attractive personality, with a natural gift of leadership which has been his since student days. He has been a very helpful member of our St. George's West Vacancy Committee.

Two very marked tendencies which I detect from my practice at the present time are (1) the devastating effect which taxation, and particularly death duties, are having on the hitherto very rich. Scarcely a week passes, but there is a Memorial on some *inter vivos* trust designed to avoid the worst effects of taxation; and (2) the growing public anxiety over new forms of public inquiry where a government department is exercising compulsory powers. This week, I attended such an inquiry at Ayr, where the Secretary of State is proposing to amalgamate the police areas of Kilmarnock and Ayr Burghs and the County of Ayr. The merger is opposed by Ayr. At that Inquiry, I represented Ayr. We tendered our evidence. But no one else came forward to submit evidence or be cross-examined, except that representatives of the Scottish Home Department were 'asked questions' by the Commissioner (Gordon Thomson) at the end of the Ayr case. We, however, were not allowed to cross-examine them. The procedure makes a mockery of the so-called public inquiry. This was in no sense the Commissioner's fault. In the first Police merger inquiry, at Chester, the Home Office did submit evidence in the ordinary way. I protested against the unfair procedure, and was on strong ground. The protest was well-reported in the press.

On my return from Ayr, I found awaiting me this typical letter from the President:—

Parliament House,
Edinburgh 1.
7th February 1949

My dear Philip

In your article on the DECLARATION OF ARBROATH (S.H.R. xxvi 75) you permitted yourself to insinuate that the letter never reached the addressee and was not intended to.

It was executed on 6th April, 1320. Allow about a couple of months for the journey overland by couriers from Arbroath to Avignon. John XXII should have got it in June and may have found time to study it in the course of July. When he read it he would find the threat that the Almighty would lay to his charge any prolongation of the war with the resulting 'corpora excidia, animarum exicia et cetera quae sequuntur incommoda'. If you will now look at *Theiner* p. 209 or *Rymer's Foedera* II Part I. 432, you will find that on 29th July John XXII addressed a strong appeal to Edward II not to prolong the war because of the 'corpora excidia, animarum exicia et cetera quae sequuntur incommoda'.

Is this a sheer coincidence or did John have the Barons' letter before him when the reply to Edward II was drafted?

Will you now say that you are sorry?????

Yours
T.M.C.

P. S. Don't ask me how the original got back.

T.M.C.

The L.A. on the 11th asked me to take Harry Guthrie's place on the Central Land Board. This involves a monthly visit to London, which quite frankly I will enjoy. To my surprise the post has a salary of £500, which will be added to my Sheriff's salary of £1100.

The Secretary of State has appointed the Lord President, with the help of two assessors, Professor Noble of Aberdeen University, and the acting Vice-Chancellor of Bristol University, to enquire into higher education in Dundee and St. Andrews University. I have already been retained on behalf of University College, Dundee. Broadly, St. Andrews University want complete incorporation; the majority of the Council of University College want 'dominion status' on the lines of Durham University; and the Town Council of Dundee want a new University. The situation has been blowing up for fifty years, but has become intensified with Sir James Irvine's concentration on St. Andrews, and his highly successful policy with that part of the University. Principal Wimberley of University College (formerly General Wimberley of the 51st Division) came to see me a week ago, and at the end of this week I visit him in Dundee to be shown over University College. I understand that I was retained on the recommendation of Lawrence Hill Watson and Kenneth Cullen who, as Sheriff and Sheriff-substitute respectively, are members of the Council. It is always flattering to be employed by professional brethren. Wimberley is a lanky enthusiastic restless personality, not the typical Principal. His methods which suggest Eighth Army shock strategy must have shaken the stagnating professoriate!

1st March 1949

I spent last weekend but one in Dundee with Principal Wimberley going over the case for University College. We inspected at high speed all the building development which has taken place since he took office (he is six-feet and long-legged and I trailed at his heels like a schoolboy). The rest of the time, we prepared the case. He is a great admirer of 'Monty'. After the North African campaign, Monty gave a group of generals, specially transferred from England (including American generals), a lecture on the campaign. Wimberley was much impressed with Bradley. Patton, on the other hand, did not impress the British generals at that stage. He sat in a corner and said, 'Oh yeah,' or, 'I may be old and stoopid, but somehow it doesn't make sense.' They soon realised, however, that they had misjudged him, and that he was one of the most enterprising of all the generals. His unconventional methods, however, would have impeded his promotion in the British Army. The Wimberleys have a most tastefully furnished house overlooking the Tay. They have two children. The career of their son well illustrates what the war has done, in one good way, for his generation. He is now only twenty-one. He was educated first in Scotland, and then in Tasmania, to which he was evacuated during the war. At 17½, he joined his father's old regiment, the Cameron Highlanders. He has been in Japan, in Malaya, round the Cape of Good Hope, through the Panama Canal, and now is about to go to the Middle East. His father asked him if he would like a trip to France. He replied: 'Very much: Europe is the only continent I've still to see!' The Lord Provost of Dundee is an ex-Sergeant of the Seaforths. Wimberley had to appear before a corporation committee, and received a formal letter stating that his speech should be limited to four minutes. When he appeared, however, the ex-Sergeant Provost whispered in the General's ear: 'As an old Seaforth to an old Cameron Highlander, I'll no gong ye till ye're done!'

14th March 1949

I have had repeated meetings over University College, Dundee, with Wimberley and Cumming, the College Secretary, here and in Dundee and have also discussed our evidence with the Committee formed to draft a precis. A weekend ago, I wrote continuously from lunch-time to bedtime (apart from meals) on both Saturday and Sunday, preparing the precis. When it was extended in type, it ran to 40 pages – over 10,000 words. Wimberley is like a big boy. Ella brought tea into our consultation this afternoon and was amused to find the Major-General sitting on the floor studying graphs.

I have received a Minute by the Secretary of State and Minister of Town and Country Planning appointing me a member of the Central Land Board (in succession to Harry Guthrie).

Today is my semi-jubilee at the Bar. The Oban Procurators were so discerning as to discover this at their dinner. This has been my best year yet as a Senior – 2633 guineas, which, with my Sheriff's salary, exceeds the remuneration of a Court of Session judge.

Last weekend, at St. Andrews, Ella and I saw Alison act the part of St. Francis in a Laurence Houseman play produced at a house party at St. Rule West. The acting of all was very good, and so was the production. But the girls disapproved of the play as they regard the house-mistress as too 'pi', and there was much deliberate applause at the wrong places!

In St. George's West our reconstituted executive committee has been busily engaged in searching for a new candidate. An informal approach through Blades was made to Prof. A.M. Hunter of Aberdeen, but he would not entertain the proposal. Now, we have arranged with the Rev. Murdo Ewen Macdonald of Partick Old that he should preach in Edinburgh next Sunday. He has made himself a reputation in Glasgow as a preacher, and during the war was first a Chaplain to the paratroops, then himself a paratrooper, and, finally, for two years, a prisoner of war. I took Dr. Walton a week ago to call on him in Glasgow. I was surprised to find in the house his brother, who also rejoices in the name Murdo Macdonald, though without the 'Ewen' and who is also a minister – at Milton, Glasgow.

22nd March 1949

Today my appointment as a member of the Central Land Board and the War Damage Commission was announced.

Last night our Executive and Vacancy Committee both unanimously decided to nominate Mr. Macdonald of Old Partick as minister of St. George's West. I heard him preaching twice on the 20th and he came to us for tea, and I had supper with him at Dr. Walton's. He is a native of Harris, educated at Kingussie and St. Andrews University. His previous charges were Portree and Old Partick. He was a chaplain with the Camerons; then a paratrooper; and on his third air jump was shot in both arms and taken prisoner. He just missed being shot by a German firing squad, and was for two years a prisoner-of-war. He has a very distinct preaching gift, but is still very Highland and some, though not I, complained a little of not hearing him. I have no doubt he will be a strong influence for good, for he is sincere and humble, a truly evangelical preacher and mingles the real Celtic fire and eloquence with a realistic modern outlook. This evening, a deputation consisting of Lord Blades, Mr. Carnon (former headmaster of George Heriot's), Miss Halden and myself went to meet him at Dr. Walton's. Only one member was unfavourable to his call, but he, the President, has decided to resign his membership and join a church nearer home.

I had a letter from Normand today stating that he had seconded my name, proposed by Dover, for membership of the Athenæum.

27th March 1949

We held a second dinner of the Round Table, to celebrate Harry Guthrie's elevation to the Bench. In the absence of George Morton, Jock Cameron, as Dean, took the chair. George, our beloved and universally respected 'permanent' Chairman, sent a message regretting his absence as inevitable, he having been called to the Bar some years before the new Judge was born. There were three official toasts after the King: 'Our Guest' proposed by John Wheatley, as Lord Advocate, and replied to by the Guest; 'The Round Table' proposed by Harald Leslie and replied to by myself; and 'The Chairman' proposed by Blades and replied to by Jock. Duffes sang two songs to my accompaniment. There were two unofficial toasts: 'The injustices of the Lords Commissioners of Justiciary', proposed by Frank Duffy and responded to by James Walker; and 'The memory of the late Viscount Simon' (who of course is still alive) proposed by Clifford Watt and responded to by Arthur Duffes. These impromptu efforts were sustained with great effect. It would be difficult to find a more complete sodality in Parliament House, or one which represents so many interests: two judges (Blades and Guthrie); the Lord Advocate (John Wheatley); the Dean (Jock); Vice-Dean (James Walker); and Keeper of the Library (T.P. McDonald); Arthur Duffes, head of the new Industrial Injuries Tribunal; F.C. Watt; Harald Leslie; George Reid, now Sheriff-substitute at Ayr; John Wilson (my old devil); James Crawford; Frank Duffy; and myself. How many of these others will yet be judges? I prophesy, in due course, at least five (if they survive). The toast-list was enhanced by apt quotations selected by John Wilson. Below my own name appeared:–

> A man so large to some he seemed to be
> Not one, but all mankind in effigy

> (Absolute and Abitofhell)

Another feature was that we were all guided to our places at table by cards depicting something associated with ourselves. The card for me consisted of a locked book with the title 'Diary–Top Secret' – together with a curved line indicating my rotundity. For Harry Guthrie, there was a grouse sitting on a daily paper – 'His daily grouse'. For John Wheatley, 'The Red Flag, with in front of it a bottle of orangeade' (he is a teetotaller). For F.C. Watt, who brought his K.C.'s gown from Ireland, 'a silk worm eating a shamrock'. For T.P. McDonald, who has recently conducted the Prestwick Ayr Inquiry, 'the letters K.L.M.' (of the Dutch Airlines, whose plane crashed). There was also a most magnificent printed menu, which had no relation, however, to what we were provided with.

Recently, at the National Library, we received a bundle of Jedburgh Charters, bound up in what looked like an old parchment. Some of the Standing Committee were for handing over the whole, as it stood, to the Register House. Others, more discriminating, thought that the cover should first be detached and examined by experts. This latter course prevailed. It now transpires that the cover consists of eight pages of a missal of the first quarter of the thirteenth century, which bears to have been used in an Augustinian house, and from its references to Kentigern probably in the Diocese of Glasgow. It seems almost certain that it is part of an early Jedburgh Abbey missal, in good condition and with the music.

30th March 1949

I have just returned from two nights spent in Gourock. For me, the two days were memorable for two incidents. First, Harold told me that Dr. John White had offered to propose me for the Procuratorship of the Church of Scotland. As he proposed the last three, this is, to say the least of it, propitious, but, whatever the outcome, I am proud to be thus honoured by one of the greatest Scotsmen, without any seeking on my part. Tom Taylor may second the nomination. Secondly, the Secretary of State has issued my Milk Services Committee's report, and the papers have so far given it an excellent reception, the *Glasgow Herald*, the chief organ of the milk-producing counties, giving it a leader.

5th April 1949

Last night, at a Congregational meeting in St. George's West, the Rev. Murdo Ewen Macdonald was unanimously elected our new minister. The attendance exceeded our highest hopes, the area of the Church being almost full. We had to organise four long queues for the signing of the Call. Some 399 appended their signatures last night, which is a splendid beginning. One mildly comic incident occurred. We had a strange organist, Eric Smith being on holiday. Dr. Walton, who as

Round Table Dinner 26th March 1949. Left to Right: Back Row: James Crawford, T.P. McDonald, John G. Wilson, Harald Leslie, Arthur Duffes, Frank Duffy, James Walker. Front Row: Clifford Watt, George Reid, John Wheatley, Jock Cameron, Harry Guthrie, Randall Philip, Daniel Blades.

Interim Moderator presided, gave out the 100th Psalm. The organist looked puzzled and said something which Dr. Walton could not hear. I therefore went down to the console to find what it was. The organist then asked me, 'What tune do you sing?' I said, 'The Old Hundredth, of course.' Whereupon he enquired, 'Where do I find it?' So I had the unusual experience of having to turn up the Old Hundredth for an organist.

21st April 1949

We have just returned from ten days in France. We crossed from Southampton to Le Havre on the night of the 9th (after I had spent the day at the War Damage Commission and Central Land Board) and we returned by Calais and Folkestone on the afternoon of the 18th. It was a period of continuous sunshine, with the hottest Easter in Paris for fifty years. On arrival at Le Havre, when the douanier looked over my passport (which had Rosemary's name though we had left her behind, as too young, in Scotland), he said: '*Et la petite Rose-marie? Elle n'est pas ici?*' Our first four days were spent in Rouen, and the remainder of the time in Paris. The havoc of the Normandy campaign is very marked. The harbour areas of Le Havre and Calais are both devastated. From Rouen Cathedral to the Seine, the town is flattened. Only the North Transept of the Cathedral was in use. Our chief impressions, however, were (1) of the remarkable recovery made by France; (2) of the vastly better fare available there (when contrasted with our austerity conditions); and (3) of the great vogue in France for the use of tartan, not Scottish products, but French (often inaccurate) tartans, no doubt prompted by the recent sight of Scottish troops. In Rouen, our hotel (de la Poste) had a restaurant which studied as a fine art the science of gastronomy. It was supervised by a Swiss manager, and besides French waiters, a young English waiter (learning French) and a Spaniard (who became very friendly, and whom we called – because of his home town – 'Bilbao'). We attended Palm Sunday services in St. Ouen, and were interested to see that everyone used boxwood in place of palms. We went twice, by the little tramway, to the viewpoint of Bon Secours. The railway from Rouen to Paris is most lovely. In Paris, besides ordinary sightseeing, we went to Versailles; we spent an afternoon in Chartres; we saw a Marivaux comedy and Molière's *Les Fourberies de Scapin* (with Jean-Louis Barrault, Madeleine Renault and Simone Valieu) at the Theatre Marigny; we attended Easter communion in the Scots Church, and saw a procession with the Cardinal-Archbishop in mitre at Notre Dame; and we had lunch with Mme Metzger and dinner with M. and Françoise Finet at 5 Rue Cernuschi. The most wonderful sight of all was Chartres, gleaming white in the brilliant sunshine with the unforgettable blues and reds of its incomparable stained glass – all undamaged by the War. At the Gare Montparnasse, we found a tablet commemorating the handing of Paris back to the French under General Leclerc. The Easter Communion in the Scots Church – with Dr. Caskie, a Scots hero of French resistance – was most memorable. The Church was packed – with schoolchildren who had come for their Easter holidays to Paris. Before being there more than a moment, I saw Willie Shepherd (of Dad's congregation in Invergowrie) now employed in Paris. So the influence of his fifty years' ministry in a Perthshire village lives on in the Scots Church in Paris. The sermon was preached by a young minister from Caithness, and we sang Rosemary's hymn 'There is a green hill' and Gordon's 'Rock of Ages'. It is not surprising that I was moved. In the afternoon of the day before, we saw an amazing display of three thousand different types of azalea in the Botanic Gardens at Auteuil.

Since returning from France, events have moved rapidly. I have spent the last two days in Dundee. Today the Council of University College gave its evidence in the St. Andrews Inquiry before Lord Cooper, with his two assessors, Professor Tyndall of Bristol and Professor Noble of Aberdeen. Our precis of evidence, which was expressed with care – Lord Cooper described it as cautiously expressed – contrasted with the very able but unjudicial production of the University Court, whose emotional tone was scarcely worthy of that august body. I stayed, for a second time, with the Wimberleys. The Principal told me that General Leclerc had, at one time in North Africa, been placed under his command. General Le Clerc's troops were West African and, to improve their morale, he determined that his own headquarters must be placed as near his front line as possible. Wimberley had to visit them there. General Le Clerc sat in his H.Q. with shells dropping all around, outwardly quite unconcerned, though Wimberley himself confessed that this required great courage.

29th April 1949

I have just returned from a two-day visit to my Sheriffdom (Dunoon and Greenock). I had Ella, Alison and Rosemary with me. At Dunoon Pier, we hailed a taxi and asked the man to take us to the Sheriff

Court. 'Oh, are you going there?' he said, 'I was there last week. I was fined five shillings.' When he dropped us at the door, he said: 'I hope you have better luck than I had.' I laughed and said nothing. After hearing my Appeal, I returned to the Pier for the Gourock Steamer. There was our taxi-driver. He came over to me, and said, 'Well, I hope things went all right with you.' Then I told him I was the Sheriff. Not in the least disconcerted, he then said: 'Oh, I've no complaint with the Sheriff. It's the Police I blame.' So I took up the cudgels for the Police, and argued that the law had to be observed.

2nd June 1949

On the 25th May, on the second morning of the General Assembly, Dr. John White, seconded by Mr. W.R. Milne W.S. (in place of Tom Taylor, who was ill) proposed me as Procurator of the Church of Scotland, and I was elected unanimously. I was introduced the next day, the 26th, and Principal Duncan, the Moderator, gave me a delightful welcome. I found myself in most congenial surroundings. Nothing could have been pleasanter than the friendship at once established with the 'circumtabular oligarchy' – Dr. Matthew Stewart (convener of the Business Committee); Dr. White Anderson (vice-convener) – two of the sturdiest and kindliest men in the Assembly; Dr. Caldwell (elected Principal Clerk the day before me), also a delightful colleague; and Mr. MacNicol, minister of my native parish in Longforgan (elected Deputy-Clerk to succeed Dr. Caldwell). Dr. White, too, was kindness itself; and I received a welcome on every hand from old colleagues of Dad's and friends of my own.

My first interjection in business was the following day. I had been out in the corridor, and, coming back, was suddenly asked would it make any difference if a proposal to make a certain children's allowance to ministers tax free? I took refuge in the view that they would require a considered opinion, because I had not heard the whole discussion and, in any event, an *ex tempore* opinion on income tax is not worth much. I spoke about six times in the Assembly, and made two quite substantial interventions, the one on the fiduciary duties of the General Trustees in relation to the Manse at Alves, and the other on the management of the Widows' and Orphans' Fund, when the Assembly (there at the time), on pure sentiment, made a wrong decision in face of legal and actuarial advice to the contrary.

The events of the Assembly were the two discussions on the Iona Community, in the first of which it was decided that George MacLeod was not eligible for nomination to Govan Old Church because as leader of the Iona Community he had 'undertaken employment not subject to the jurisdiction of the Church' and the second of which Dr. John White led the Assembly to appoint a special committee to endeavour to bring the Community within the Church. The first was a purely legal issue, argued for the successful view by T.P. McDonald (with Pirie) and for George MacLeod by Bill Milligan (with Harald Leslie). I was not called on for my view – fortunately for me. But my opinion would have been (1) that the Community work was not 'subject to the jurisdiction of the Church' but (2) that, having regard to the wider and narrower meanings possible for 'employment', *in dubio* that meaning should be preferred which did not result in disentitlement.

The Duke of Gloucester, as Commissioner, made an excellent and humorous speech at the close, which I learned from the Purse-Bearer was to a large extent his (the Duke's) own composition. The Moderator was on the whole good, if a little testy in some of his decisions. John White stood head and shoulders over everyone else, in every speech he delivered. George MacLeod was disappointing and almost incoherent, but was obviously under strain. In some ways, the men who most appealed to me were White Anderson, John McKenzie, Matthew Stewart and Caldwell, in that order – leaving John White as a case by himself.

We sat long hours, one day from 10.00 a.m. till 10.15 p.m. with only two short breaks. The speeches on Reports were mostly much too long, with some notable exceptions, but the shorter business (with which I was more concerned) was very interesting.

During my first week, we had staying with us Pastor Martin Niemöller, who was for eight years (less one week) a prisoner in a German concentration camp. Though he has preached all over the world, and, when he preached in St. Cuthbert's and North Morningside on Assembly Sunday, attracted quite phenomenal congregations, he is quite unspoilt – a very humble Christian, whose courage is not displayed openly. His sermon in St. Cuthbert's will be remembered by all who heard it as an experience of a lifetime. 'Thou alone art God.' His illustration drawn from personal experience showed how the attempt to set up another beside God failed. It was like listening to Paul after he came out of prison, and there was a simple solemnity of the occasion which was unforgettable. He was a delightful man in the house, and would hardly let me remove his shoes to be cleaned.

He told us much about his experiences in a concentration camp.

THE MANSE

INVERGOWRIE

29th.,May, 1949

Mr. J. R. Philip, K. C.,

E D I N B U R G H.

Dear Mr. Philip,

It was with very great pleasure that we, the Members of Session of the Church of Invergowrie, heard of your appointment as Procurator of the Church of Scotland. At our meeting today it was unanimously resolved to send to you our sincere felicitations, with the hope that this office which brings you great honour and places upon your shoulders great responsibility will also give you great joy and satisfaction in the execution.

With all good wishes,

and in the name of the Session,

Yours very sincerely,

Moderator

Session Clerk.

The German Court (after he had been detained without trial eight months) sentenced him to seven months, but, as he had already been detained that period, the Court was about to release him. Hitler then made him his personal prisoner, and he was detained for eight years, less one week. By a curious circumstance, although everything was taken from him in the concentration camp, he was allowed to receive back his Bible the day after. He was detained in solitary confinement.

Presbytery of Uist.

From:

The Rev. J. Campbell, M.A.,
Clerk.
Tel. : Lochboisdale 306.

The Manse,
Daliburgh,
S. Uist.

"

The news of the recent appointment by the
tne General Assembly of Mr.J.R.Philip,K.C.as
Procurator of the Church was received by the
Presbytery with much pride and satisfaction.
Mr.Philip has for a number of years represented
the Presbytery at the General Assembly and has
already won the deep respect and affection of
the members by his keen interest in their work
and by his generosity. The Presbytery rejoice
that this high honour has been conferred on hi
him and instruct the Clerk to send him a
message of congratulations and good wishes.

Extracted by

Clerk

16/6/49.

But each day when he had exercise in the compound, he memorised
a short passage of scriptures, and recited it at the window of each of
the other cells. Later, he was sent to the Pragser Wildsee in the
Dolomites. Near the end of his confinement he was allowed to meet
about half-a-dozen others, an Anglican, a Dutch Presbyterian, two

Norwegian Lutherans and a Danish Lutheran amongst them. Together they held communion, and they practised together hymns with lines which all knew, Dr. Niemöller making a translation for each language necessary. They sang these together in the prisoner corridor and the other prisoners heard them. It was like Peter in prison. He also gave Communion to a Nazi S.S. man who was condemned to death. He had only a prison mug with water and a crust of bread, but these served as the elements, and the two had communion together.

19th June 1949

On the 16th, Murdo Ewen Macdonald was inducted as minister of St. George's West. William McDonald of Palmerston Place gave the charge. The church area was full. Forty-six elders headed by Mr. Barrett and myself gave him the right hand of fellowship. This was the practice in St. George's West. Dr. Taylor of St. George's criticised it as not *part* of the Induction, which was by the *Presbytery*. I agree that it was not part of the Induction, but disagree profoundly as to its being inappropriate. It was a beautiful symbol of the Congregation's part, and where else could forty-six elders have assembled to do this! I recalled 'Suffer the little children'. It was, no doubt, not part of the arrangement that they should take part. Yet it is this part alone which is remembered.

The induction social gathering took place the following evening. Mrs. Barrett made the presentation to Mr. Macdonald, and two young people the presentation to his wife. I made presentations to Dr. and Mrs. Walton. To my complete surprise, Lord Blades got up at the end and presented me with a beautiful exposure meter for my share in the work, and made (for me) a most moving speech. In my speech to Dr. Walton, I wound up by quoting Isaak Walton: 'Let the blessing of St. Peter's Master be . . . upon (them) that are lovers of virtue; and dare trust in His providence.'

On the Sunday morning, Murdo Macdonald was introduced by Professor Donald Baillie of St. Andrews. In the evening, he preached his first sermon, and at twenty minutes before the service the queue for admission extended from the Stafford Street door of the Church almost to Melville Street.

28th June 1949

This last weekend, Ella and I have been in Aberdeen, where I was acting as external examiner in Law, Harry Shewan (who is about to take silk) being my co-examiner. Ella and I stayed at Chanonry Lodge with the Taylors. He and I were called to the Bar the same day; he preceded me as Sheriff of Renfrew and Argyll; and I have a close professional link with him, for I was his counsel in a seven judge case. It was a perfect weekend of continuous sunshine, and the garden of the Chanonry which has been a garden for a thousand years was a perfect sun-trap, full of birds, in which Tom Taylor took a special interest, studying a fly-catcher at work (by means of a 10x magnification field-glass). Mrs. Taylor is a doctor by profession, and a daughter of a former parish minister of Durrisdeer. They have two adopted children, Andrew and Margaret, which made a special link, as I had something to do with the adoption of the former (as a result of which a Birkbeck Hill edition of Boswell's *Johnson* now sits in my bookshelves as a memento). In the afternoon, Tom Smith (the new Professor of Law), Farquhar MacRitchie (the Professor of Conveyancing: a Lewisman of charm and modesty) and his wife; and Harry Shewan came for tea. We attended and took Communion at Old Machar Cathedral in the morning, where, in the roof, you can see the royal arms of the Empire, Spain, France, England and Scotland. In the evening, the Chaplain of the Episcopal Cathedral, a Mr. White, called, and turned out to be a remote connection of my own. Afterwards, Tom sang some songs, 'The Lake Isle of Innisfree', 'Home is the Hunter', 'O Waly, Waly' and 'The Bonnie Earl of Moray', and then he conducted family prayers – most memorably and beautifully.

14th July 1949

This last week I had a client who rejoiced in the unbelievable name of Aristophanes Plato. It equals the name of the pursuer appearing in the Rolls of the Court of Session on 24th February 1933 – Jessie Falconer Betsy Ajenith Catinka Mamelon Malacoff Christison or Martin (said to be the daughter of a Crimean veteran named after all of his battles).

Dobie (of the National Library) told me this week that W.K. Dickson, his predecessor ('Teakhead' was his nickname), who was born in 1860 and is dying just now, at the age of six in Paris met a lady who had seen Marie Antoinette's head roll from the guillotine. W.K. Dickson's father remembered the great Sir Walter hobbling about the fireplace in the Parliament House. 'But,' said Dobie (he is a grandson of Captain Marryat), 'my parents saw something even more remarkable – Sir George Mackenzie of Rosehaugh!' I enquired how. 'They happened to be in Greyfriars when his tomb was opened up, and they had a glimpse of the "Bloody Mackenzie" in a state of fine (mummified) preservation!'

Among other curious names I have met with in my own practice are Puig, Saqui, Phaup, Halfpap, Swinhoe, Virgo and Londragon – and, finally, Isaac Walton.

15th July 1949

Three events in the life of Parliament House have happened in the last twenty-four hours. The lead statue of Carolus II, the oldest in Edinburgh, which has developed a 'list to port', was removed from its pedestal in Parliament Square by crane last night at 6.30 after having stood there for 264 years. Today, Miss Kidd K.C., after being the only woman at the Bar for twenty-six years, was joined by two other advocates of her own sex. Today, Arthur Matheson, my second devil, spent his last day in Parliament House before taking up the new Chair of Law at St. Andrews University. He once signed himself to me as '*Paulisper decibolus: semper discipulus*'. Today, he gave me a lovely gold pencil as a keepsake. I had a share in securing his appointment.

18th July 1949

I am writing this in the *Pharos* off Montroseness at 6.40 p.m. We began my first cruise this morning as a Commissioner of Northern Lights. This year the cruise is to Shetland and Orkney. The party consists of Sir George Morton (Aberdeen), Maconochie (Stirling), Charles Milne (Dumfries), Lillie (Fife), Tom Simpson (Caithness and the Orkneys), myself (Renfrew and Argyll) and Gordon Thomson (Ayr and Bute), with Wakelin (Secretary to the Commissioners). We left Granton at 10.30 a.m. and no sooner had I unpacked than the Steward (Duncan Stewart) announced, euphemistically, the first ceremony – 'Waters on the Table'. After we had partaken of light refreshments, we went on deck and were weighed. Every Commissioner gains weight considerably on the voyage. I turned the machine at 17 stone 1 lb – the heaviest of the party. I beat the next by about 3 stone. Lillie was the lightest. I have since schooldays been heavy, but this is latterly due to constant sitting at my desk, writing opinions. We had lunch just off the Isle of May, which is a narrow island from

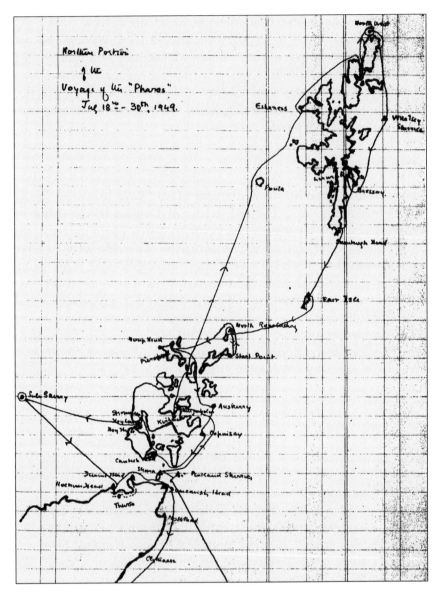

E. to W. but relatively long from N. to S. After lunch, we went ashore landing at a little rocky creek at the entrance of which the breakers roll in. The lighthouse dates from 1830, and has an atmosphere of Abbotsford Gothic. Just now there are three keepers: the head, who has just arrived, and two assistants, one with his wife from the Isle of Man, and the other from Orkney with a wife from Harris. The island is a bird sanctuary and there was a party of young people there. We were shown over the assistant keeper's house. The lighthouse is like one tower of a Scots castle. Off it are rooms with old oak furniture carved with the crest of the Commissioners. From there we returned to the ship and then began our passage to the Pentland Firth, passing the North Carr to the West and the Bell Rock, a gaunt lonely tower 150 feet high, with seas breaking over the rocks, on our starboard. South of the rock, we saw one basking shark. There were heavy clouds over the Isle of May, but, since then, it has cleared, and there is excellent visibility, the hills above the Howe of Mearns being clearly seen to our left.

Midnight. During the evening, we sailed up the coast of Kincardineshire and Aberdeenshire, and the last sight of the evening was the flashing light of Buchanness. Looking coastwards, we could pick out all the landmarks, Bervie, Stonehaven, Aberdeen and Cruden Bay. Aberdeen has presided today as Commodore. We sit round the table in order of seniority. Tomorrow Stirling becomes Commodore, and we go ashore at 8.30 at Pentland Skerries. Dinner was my most sumptuous since before the war – maize, kidney soup, turbot, chicken, peach flambé, strawberries, sardines, coffee, with excellent sherry, hock (Rüdesheimer 1933 especially good), madeira, port, coffee, snuff, cigars and cigarettes; later coffee again and kummel; and finally a night-cap when I took lemon squash! All evening we played deck billiards – first Fife and Argyll versus Stirling and Ayr; then the Secretary and Argyll against Captain MacLachlan and Ayr. Both times I was lucky to be on the winning side. Aberdeen and Dumfries were affected by a 'lazy swell' and disappeared most of the time, except at dinner. Ayr also felt sickly for a time. I never felt better.

19th July 1949

Just before six a.m. the assistant steward came in to close the port-hole because the deck was being washed down. I wakened early, and read Churchill's *Second World War*, vol. ii. I have brought it and Scott's *Pirate*, amongst other books, for the voyage. Today Stirling was Commodore. Before breakfast, we found ourselves lying off Pentland Skerries, a series of islands at the east end of the Pentland Firth. The sun was glistening; it was almost calm; and we could see far. On one side, to the south, rose Duncansby Head; on the other, to the north, the Pentland Skerries lighthouse – two lighthouses, one now the station for a fog-horn. We landed after breakfast. Instead of the barren grass of the Isle of May, there was lush green grass, with clover and buttercup, my first taste of Orkney. To the west lay Stroma, north-west Hoy, and north Scapa and the Orkney mainland, with Copinsay jutting into the sea on the north-east. The cliffs of Duncansby Head stood out clear in the sun. On the lighthouse buildings, I found an inscription commemorating the work of the Stevensons. The lighthouse is high, with a magnificent view in all directions. The principal keeper was married, and we met his sister-in-law, from California. The other assistant-keeper occupies a house by himself. The station is being converted into a rock station, the keeper's house being transferred to Stromness. The assistant-keeper whose house we saw is a self-taught violin player. I asked him what he played: 'Scottish songs' – he is an Orcadian. The island receives letters three times a month.

From there, we crossed to John o'Groats. The real reason was to send a message to Stromness for more food supplies, which, *pace* the crew, could not be transmitted over our own wireless. While lying off John o'Groats, I had a talk with Captain MacLachlan on the bridge. He hails from near Oban; the steward, Duncan (Duncan Stewart) from Campbeltown, and the bo'sun Andra' from Eyemouth. I last visited John o'Groats at the age of thirteen, in 1913. It seemed to me there were more houses. Dunnet Head, seen through the glass from John o'Groats, is a magnificent cliff, 300 feet high.

We then proceeded up the east coast of Stroma to near the lighthouse which lies at the north end. From the jetty, where we landed, we had a walk of about a mile to the lighthouse. There are cottages dotted all over the island, and a church and a school, but the population is migrating. One keeper told me that 17 persons (out of 100) had left in this year of low staff. The lighthouse is low (some 56 steps) but has a powerful beam. One of the assistant keepers had previously been on Skerryvore and Muckle Flugga. His name was Cameron. He had three nice boys aged fourteen, eleven and nine. The other assistant Ord had two charming little girls, Kathleen and Ruth, aged nine and seven. They all came down to the jetty to see us off. I left the greetings of the Procurator with Ord to convey to the minister. The school is a single-teacher school. The children stay there till twelve and then have to go to Wick, where they have to board out. The Ords had come from the Mull of Galloway. The station was the best kept we have yet seen, and the two families we saw, the Ords and Camerons, seemed very happy. The station was built in 1894. Eshaness is the most recent station built, and then Duncansby Head, both built between the two wars.

While we were at lunch, we proceeded on our way – 34 miles in three hours – to Kirkwall. When next I came on deck, Pentland Skerries were away to the South, Stroma out of sight and we were proceeding northways towards Copinsay in brilliant sunshine. I could see two of the causeways enclosing Scapa Flow, with the boom of sunk ships near where the submarines must have passed to sink the Royal Oak.

The entrance to Kirkwall is through a most lovely lagoon flanked on the right by Helliar Holm Lighthouse, and the mansion of the Balfours of Shapinsay. The steamer makes a wide curve sweeping round to the port, and the Cathedral of St. Magnus comes into view, dominating the whole town. It is of a curious mixture of stones, the oldest parts being apparently red sandstone, and restorations being done in grey or yellow stone. The blend of colours is not too effective, the dominating red being somewhat sickly. We followed an Orkney Steam Navigation Ship into the harbour, and berthed at the quay skilfully behind it. The Sheriff-substitute (Barrogill Keith, brother of Edward, who is about to take silk) was there to welcome us. I walked with Wakelin into the town which has stone paved tracks down its quaint streets, like a French town. At the Cathedral, I parted company with Wakelin and joined Maconochie. We two hoped to see St. Magnus' interior, but found it open today (Tuesday) only from 10 to 11. As we berthed only at 5 p.m. we were too late. The beadle was having his half-holiday and the minister lived a quarter of a mile away. So we did not succeed in getting inside. It seemed a pity to come two hundred miles to see a pre-Reformation Cathedral, and then to find it closed. We returned to the ship, where four guests were expected for dinner – the Lord Lieutenant (Mr. Sutherland-Graeme), the Sheriff-substitute, Colonel Henderson (a university friend of Tom Simpson's), and Mr. McLure, the local surgeon. I sat between the last and Gordon Thomson at dinner. The surgeon seemed to have some of the detective powers of Dr. Joseph Bell. First, he guessed my age – forty-nine – correctly. Then, he said (when I asked him for another deduction): 'I think you are a Christian in outlook.' I asked, why he said that. He replied: 'It's not what you say, but the way you behave generally.' T.B. Simpson told an amusing story. The same day as the Orkney paper reported his installation as Sheriff, they had a heading: 'T.B. scourge in Orkney.' On his next visit as Sheriff, there also appeared: 'Little bovine T.B. in Orkney!' After another sumptuous dinner, we emerged on deck where we saw a superb lingering sunset, the still waters of the lagoon being tinged with deep red. Little yachts sailed about in the hands of expert sailors. We played one game of deck billiards – the Lord Lieutenant and myself losing to the surgeon and Lillie. The sunset was still not over when we had finished. At

11.30 our guests left, headed by a slightly unsteady Lord Lieutenant. We sail at 4 a.m. tomorrow for Hillswick, so 'goodbye Kirkwall'.

20th July 1949

After a sound sleep, I was faintly conscious of the *Pharos* leaving Kirkwall quay. Later, I learned that it proceeded northwards by the Faray Sound, a route it had never taken before. When I first looked out, we were slipping past North Ronaldsay into the open sea. By breakfast time Fair Isle lay level to the East – over ten miles off, and ahead Foula. The sea was as calm as it is ever likely to be there. It was a day in a thousand, but the weather forecast at breakfast time predicted a shallow depression later – with gale warning for the Fair Isle area. After breakfast, the south headland of Shetland appeared – Fitful Point, and one by one the other humps appeared above the horizon, and two sets of wireless masts at Sumburgh. Lillie, who would argue the hind legs off a donkey, swore that the southmost point was an island. But it was simply that the land immediately to the north, where lies the Shetland aerodrome, was below the horizon. There were few birds about, but from now onwards we began to see skuas, chasing other birds, brown and often fat with their pilfered food. The sight of the morning, however, was Foula, with its precipice to the west, 1200 feet sheer down into the sea. Although we saw it well at 8.30, it seemed travelling ahead faster than ourselves, until (as Tom Simpson said) 'it stopped and we came up to it.' Captain Mac-Lachlan took the *Pharos* by the west side, to let us see the cliff, a never to be forgotten sight, the precipice with shades of different colours – one bright red; then, at the top, to the north-east, a green sward, with sheep grazing.

The Commodore of the day was Dumfries, who took his duties with painful seriousness, and was the butt of many shafts. To the north of Foula we stopped at a defective buoy marking a reef, and a boat went out to repair it. The Commodore was in his cabin at the time, but when he came up we told him he had missed the boat, which had had to leave without him. He was in quite a state as to whether he should have gone – although of course any other Commissioner would have known that a Commissioner could do nothing in connection with a buoy.

After lunch we landed at Eshaness to see the one-man lighthouse station there. There was a lovely little bay with dry-stane ruinous crofts round it, all except one which was inhabited. The bay was surrounded with low cliffs and caverns except at a small beach where we drew in. A cross on the hillside served not as a memorial but to guide mariners in to the bay. Above the cliffs great grassy slopes (the grass a bare scrub with sun-withered clover) rose to the small lighthouse quite a short distance away. Near the lighthouse, excavations were proceeding at the remains of a four thousand year old dwelling – pre-Pictish and said to be Mediterranean. The station is the newest in the service. It stands above the cliffs, but the spray from the Atlantic surges up through a funnel in the rock and soaks the lighthouse, so that shutters have to be placed on the windows next the sea. From the platform where the lighthouse stands, there is a magnificent sea panorama to the south from Foula round to Hillswick. The keeper and his wife (Mr. and Mrs. Wyllie) live alone here, their nearest neighbours being the croft at the beach, and an occasional relief man, a crofter, who in case of need comes over to help on receiving a signal from the lighthouse.

North of Eshaness, there is fine cliff scenery, the mainland yielding to Yell, and then Yell to North Unst. Gradually the Muckle Flugga lighthouse came in sight. It gave me a thrill to see the most northerly point (bar Canada) in the British Commonwealth. It stands on a precipitous rock just to the north of North Unst and although we did not proceed beyond Yell this evening, we saw the lighthouse clearly, its slopes marlized by a great white patch of bird-lime.

Instead of anchoring for the night at Hillswick, we proceeded eastwards through the sound between Yell and North Unst, and eventually dropped anchor in Basta Voe, a favourite anchorage (the Captain told me) of the First World War, chosen tonight because of the threatened gale warning. But it remained peaceful during the evening, a change in the weather being heralded by a heavy dew which so damped the deck as to make our deck billiards difficult. There was another beautiful sunset, and in other directions a soft mist tinged with a faint pink. In the afternoon, after tea, while I slept on deck, Lillie did what he called a caricature of me. It was good from the neck downwards. The head was like Mr. Pecksniff, and when I re-marked on its unlikeness to me, Lillie explained that this was because it was a caricature! I always thought the essence of caricature was to catch some likeness or peculiarity!

21st July 1949

I am writing this in my cabin after tea. The cabin has every comfort, except a place to write at. It is roughly 8 or 10 feet cubed, with two portholes. Opposite the portholes is my bed and a wardrobe. On the other side, beneath the portholes, is a long couch. Between bed and couch is the basin with most up-to-date equipment.

Before I came down, Tom Simpson said: 'You will find it interesting to look over the Register of the *Pharos*, and see all the Commissioners who have made the different trips. Their weights, too, at the start and finish of the voyage are given.' Just for interest, I looked back, I think, to 1901, and found I was the heaviest Sheriff by 3 lbs. Wark, my nearest rival, was 16 st. 10 lbs, but only at the *end* of one voyage. The *Pharos* has many interesting relics, and some five crystal decanters. Most interesting is a horn and silver snuff-mill presented by Sir Walter Scott, who (as the *Pirate* mentions) made the voyage in 1814.

Today, Fife was Commodore. We left Basta Voe at 8.30 a.m. and went first to the village of Uyeasound in the neighbouring sound of that name, where there has just been installed a minor light, kept by a crofter. The village itself was quite attractive – a stout little pier and harbour, some old cottages on the beach, scattered crofts round the bay, one shop (at least), two churches, and a big relatively modern house behind. The light consists of a concrete column about twelve feet high, with the small light on a metal framework above. It is meant to lead ships through the sound.

We had great fun last night, because we understood our anchorage was to be Uyeasound, and the Captain, instead, chose Basta Voe, which threw us out in our calculations, and we vainly tried to find our ship turning to port when instead she kept going to starboard. I also thought I saw two lighthouses, but was told there were none visible. One next day turned out to be a tower on, I believe, Fetlar, where Sir Basil Nevin Spence, the M.P. for Shetland, lives. Then Wakelin discovered that he had 'lost a lighthouse' – omitting to put Eshaness among his records – so, with two imaginary lighthouses gained, and our real one lost, the Commissioners' affairs were somewhat out of order.

From Uyeasound, back we went to the West Coast and then up the west side of North Unst to Muckle Flugga. It was again perfect weather. The caves are grander and grander, the further north you go and between Yell and North Unst the sound is flanked by a fair number of scattered dwellings. My chief impressions of Shetland are its vast size and sea spaces, the magnificent cliff scenery, the depopulated crofts, and the bare scrubby grass, sometimes with dandelions, but chiefly with wizened sea pink not unlike clover, and of course the birds.

Earlier in the morning, the principal lighthouse keeper at Muckle Flugga had been doubtful whether we could land, but it turned out all right, though only skilled and experienced seamen could bring in a boat there.

The cliff to the south is the last of North Unst mainland. The island to the north is the last outpost of Scotland. The lighthouse itself stands between two wireless masts on a high cliff. Behind are two striking rocks with points, one of them a sanctuary for gannets. The *Pharos* lay to the east, and from there we were taken in by our motor-boat to a creek between the lighthouse cliff and a projecting eastern spur. With difficulty the boat was piered. From here a cable draws loads up rails to the lighthouse. We ascended by steps partly built up, partly hewn out of the rock. The lighthouse itself is one of the best kept. But what interested me most was the puffins, colonies of attractive little birds which showed no timidity and sat on the rocks while I photographed them at my pleasure. There is something strange and majestic in the northern outpost of the United Kingdom.

Leaving Muckle Flugga, we proceeded up Burra Sound to visit the shore station, also a tidy well kept place, for the principal and three assistant keepers and a boatman. The boatman is the third generation to hold the office. His grandfather, uncle and he have brought the relief boat to Muckle Flugga for forty-seven years. This February for twenty-three extra days, keepers were marooned on the rock by bad weather, the longest recorded period (though at Skerryvore, it was once eleven weeks, Wakelin told me). The boatman proudly showed us his boat, the *Grace Darling*, and we met his mother, daughter and sister. I told him that Maconochie had a like ancestry in *his* profession. From Burra Sound, we returned to the open sea, and now after coasting southwards are anchored for the night in Balta Sound.

Being a Commissioner of Northern Lights is to have the thrill of a pirate's life without its disadvantages. As Lillie says: 'We're just like buccaneers.'

22nd July 1949

We left Balta Sound at 7 a.m. There was thick mist, but the sea was calm. Even as I write, the *Pharos* is sounding its fog-horn at regular intervals (11 a.m.). Our objective was Whalsay Skerries. When we reached their neighbourhood, an answering gun fired at regular intervals from the lighthouse warned us of our approach to the Sker-ries. We have no radar equipment. We have direction-finding, but, as the two nearest stations fitted with direction-finding equipment – Muckle Flugga and North Ronaldsay – are both separated from us partly by intervening land, the beam is affected, and the method cannot be used with accuracy in such circumstances.

Off the lighthouse skerry we halted, and a boat went ashore first to locate the lighthouse. From the ship, we could at first see nothing. Yet when our time came to enter the boat, we found that the *Pharos* was lying quite close to the islands. The lighthouse is a high one standing on a small low skerry. Between two sets of rocks is a small creek, from which a wire railway pulls loads up a gentle incline. This gave us an easy walk – up the track – to the light. You enter it from a short outside ladder. Then inside, there are five inside ladders, I think each with fifteen steps. Each takes you up to the next floor of the lighthouse. First, the stores, then, about two storeys up, a kitchen, then bunk beds, and finally the light itself. Most interesting here was the mechanism for the fog-gun. Acetylene gas operates a lever up, which then descends at regular intervals on a trigger which fires the gun. On the whole the gun was less noisy inside the lighthouse than out. In each lighthouse there is a visitors' book which we sign in order of seniority. George Morton, almost eighty, came up to the foot of the lighthouse, but could not go further, and the keeper kindly brought the book down afterwards to the jetty for him to sign. Everyone loves and respects George. The attention he receives from Mr. Hunter, the chief officer, who always takes charge of the landing parties is very affecting. With infinite care, he helps him onto the jetty, and back again on to the ladder up the ship's side. Between the jetty and the lighthouse, Mr. Hunter showed me an eider-duck's nest, of eider-down, with three pale grey-green eggs, about the size of a goose's eggs. Terns, which attack you if you go near their nest, were circling overhead, but none of them touched these eggs: a skua would, how-ever, do so. We saw there no sign of the parent duck, but later when we were back on the jetty, we saw her returning across the water to the nest. She is a small brown duck, and looks much like any other in the water.

From the lighthouse skerry, we coasted round the next island, Grunay, where there is a small pier. This used to serve the shore-station, but it was bombed by German aircraft in January 1942, and the lighthouse keepers are now billeted on a third island. Eventually they are to be housed in a shore-station at Lerwick. The boatkeeper,

Mr. Anderson, a native of the Skerries, met us at the pier, round which a few now empty houses and a boathouse are clustered. We climbed the hill, over fine grass supporting a few sheep, passed what used to be a garden protected by a wall, and reached the now abandoned shore-station. The German raider made a direct hit on the end house, killing the occupant, Mr. Anderson's mother. The ruins lie untouched as they were after the raid. The adjoining houses are intact. Nearby are a group of iron standards once used for the washing.

On the way back to the ship we used a klaxon-horn to indicate our position, to which we received an answering bell from the ship. The lighthouse gun, ship's bell and boat's horn made a queer blend of sound. The first time the klaxon sounded, Tom Simpson turned to me and asked: 'What did you say?!' Now we are back on the ship: 'waters' have been 'on the table', and we are crossing the open sea, so as to round the south of Bressay and enter Lerwick harbour. Tom Simpson, who is Commodore today, is taking an Appeal in Lerwick Sheriff Court this afternoon, and our arrival is timed for this afternoon, but the fog may delay us.

Last night, we had Captain MacLachlan at dinner. He is a typical West Highland master of the very best type. He says that, if he had to choose his career over again, he would be a doctor. While we were at dinner last night in Balta Sound, a boat left the ship. No enquiries were made, but it would not be surprising if sea-trout appeared at dinner.

On the Whalsay lighthouse skerry, although there was almost nothing but rock, there were sea-pinks, some green mossy seaweed, and green weed-like flowers.

George Morton is the acknowledged doyen, both because of his age and the respect in which he is held, of our party. He is tolerant, open-minded, and surprisingly young in outlook. I think he has felt the voyage pretty hard for his age, as some of the work is not easy, for one who is old and whose sight is so poor. Robbie Maconochie is a different type. He has none of George's simplicity, but seeks adulation and, while he can be very funny, is not quite so funny as he thinks. Charles Milne is the 'old-wife' of the party, always kind and courteous, but fussy and rather vulnerable to practical jokes, which, however, he has taken well. Lillie, with his yachting-cap on, looks like a Prussian officer – Charlie Peace we call him – who is at heart a thorough sound Scot of the old school in outlook, habits, prejudices and dress. Tom Simpson is much our brightest wit, with a well-informed mind and a never failing cleverness of touch; where he is, there is always entertainment; he and Maconochie both belong to families of distinction – the Maconochies associated with the law; the Simpsons with medicine. Gordon Thomson married the heiress of Skibo, and then overwhelming tragedy descended on him. His wife, still in her twenties, died two summers ago of polio leaving five small children. His old Napoleonic manner has been softened by this heavy blow. We are old fellow-apprentices from Glasgow days; yet till I saw him play deck-billiards I never knew that he was left-handed. Wakelin, the Secretary, is efficiency at every turn – a good host, a friend to the lighthouse-keepers, a born organiser and a connoisseur of good wine. Altogether, they are a group of men of very varied gifts and interests, yet united by real friendship.

(Later) As we entered the Sound of Bressay, we saw the *St. Clair*, the Aberdeen-Lerwick ship, lying there. It turned out that she had anchored instead of proceeding up towards Lerwick, because of the fog. Captain MacLachlan sent out one of the boats to see how far he was from the shore, and then we started off again, passed Bressay Lighthouse, and shortly found ourselves off Lerwick. The motor boat took us ashore, and later on the *Pharos* drew in to the quayside, much to the admiration of the citizens. The Commissioners, apart from Tom Simpson who went off to the Sheriff Court to hear an Appeal, set off to see the new houses which are being built to form the shore station for Whalsay. Then we all forgathered at the Sheriff Court, where Rob Wallace, the Sheriff-substitute, has gathered a fine collection of photographs of the previous Sheriffs and Sheriff-substitutes. In Lerwick itself, what was of most interest was the old paved streets (like Kirkwall, though more hilly) and the houses south of the quay dipping right into the water, and providing grand facilities for smugglers to slip in their ill-gotten wares. Lerwick is, I should judge, a larger and more go-ahead place than Kirkwall, but I prefer Kirkwall (though of course we saw it under more favourable conditions). In the early evening, Captain MacLachlan introduced me to Captain Macmillan of the *St. Clair*, an old friend of his from Tiree, and the latter, who was interested to meet a Sheriff of Argyll, took me over his ship, which, having followed us up the sound, was now lying at the other side of the quay.

In the evening, we had four guests at dinner – Rob Wallace, Mr. Norman Cameron (Laird of Bressay), Dr. Spence (a local doctor), and the Captain. I sat between Rob Wallace and Gordon Thomson. We had much talk of the 'Up-helly-a' and of Udal Law. It appears that, in the main, the land is held on feu-charters which usually reserve udal rights. What these are is not very clear. But, at least, Sir Basil Nevin Spence succeeded in a claim against the Crown to wreckage washed up during the war on his beaches, though, as a matter of grace, he gave the Crown a record of what he obtained. The Laird of Bressay was heralded by Robbie Maconochie (as an old Wykehamist) as a man of erudition who had either been a Clerk of the House of Lords or an official of the British Museum. We all plied him with conversation, but found him a dull dog.

Captain MacLachlan asked me if I knew the story of the Seven Hunters. These are seven rocks at the Flannans, to the West of Harris. In 1900, the three light keepers at the Flannans mysteriously disappeared, and to this day nothing is known of them except that they had all risen from a half-completed breakfast, the remains of which were afterwards found on the table. Tom Simpson also told me of the Trowy Glen, still haunted by the fairies, through which no Shetlander will go at night. If he left his horse and cart there, he would find the horse facing the shafts when he came back. Or, he added, the petrol in a private car's tank would be mysteriously transformed into red petrol.

23rd July 1949

I am the Commodore of the day. (7 p.m.) Here we are, anchored off the north-east side of Fair Isle, and white seagulls float above outside. I sit writing this in my dinner jacket. However customs may change, dinner on board the *Pharos* retains its old formality. Tonight we have the Captain's permission to splice the mainbrace.

It is now clear again, so clear that you can, from here, faintly detect Fitful Head, 21 miles NNE. When we left Lerwick today, however, there was thick mist. Down Bressay Sound, there was a succession of foghorns, and at length we heard the two-note horn of Bressay Lighthouse itself, the deeper note a rich diapason. Bressay Lighthouse is a natty little establishment. From the jetty, I went up to the light with a young assistant, Angus McCuish, from Harris, who, I found, knew Murdo Macdonald and his family at Plocrapool. The chief interest of Bressay was the working of its fog-horn, the two notes sounding through a cam on a wheel releasing gas into the appropriate pipe to produce the note from a rotating drum. We all felt the staff at Bressay (and later also at Sumburgh Head) were happy and contented. From Bressay we proceeded between Mousa and the mainland. Opposite the famous Mousa broch, the finest of its kind, Captain MacLachlan stopped his ship, and the more active of us went ashore to visit the Broch. It was a difficult landing – not for the elderly. The rocks were very slippery and the waves high. The broch is close to the water – 40–45 feet high, about 50 feet thick, shaped outwardly with the curves of a lighthouse, with an outer and an inner wall and rooms between, also a staircase leading to the top. It was probably also a tower of refuge.

From there we proceeded to Grutness Bay, beside Sumburgh aerodrome. There is an attractive sandy anchorage leading to a narrow isthmus of low lying land, from which a hill road ascends steeply the 300 feet to Sumburgh Head. A small bus was waiting for us, and in it we drove up to the lighthouse which commands a magnificent prospect in all directions. Fair Isle was clear to the south, and Foula faintly visible to the west; Nosshead a magnificent cliff away to the north-north-east. The principal keeper comes from Pentland Skerries. His wife, perhaps the most contented and finest type we have met, went straight from a house in Glasgow to be married to the then keeper at Muckle Flugga – what a change was there. About the stations, there were two children, a boy of eleven and girl of fourteen, and four dogs, an old spaniel (black) and a puppy spaniel (brown) and a Shetland collie and a rough-haired fox-terrier, quite a lively crew. The principal keeper works away at a violin and used to play with the assistant we met at Pentland Skerries. This one, who cannot read a note, nevertheless plays reels. Returning to the ship, we made a crossing here, and, as we passed Sumburgh, its flag dipped in salute and the inhabitants waved.

The principal keeper's wife at Sumburgh told me that the minister of Rothiemurchus (Rathbone) was coming to be parish minister of Sumburgh. Shetland is very depleted of ordained ministers. At present, there seem to be eleven on the group of islands, although there are some twenty-one principal charges. It is fair to add however that there are lay missionaries. At Fair Isle, there seems to be only a missionary. Fair Isle is very much cut off. Its only communication is by means of the *Good Shepherd*, a motor boat which sails the 21 miles from Grutness once a week in summer and once a fortnight in winter. The *Good Shepherd* is lying near by and I should not like to trust myself to her in all seas. In the Shetlands, too, there are only ten policemen – none in the north and four only in Lerwick. When a man is sentenced to a month's imprisonment, one of the policemen is deputed to take charge of him. Thus, the whole policing of Lerwick suffers. So they usually sentence to three months, when other arrangements can be made, and the prisoner is transferred to the Scottish mainland.

Mrs. Mathieson, the principal keeper's wife at Sumburgh, made the not unsensible remark to me: 'Do the Commissioners ever bring their wives with them?' I passed this on to Wakelin, who asked, 'What could they do that we don't?' I think they could get alongside the wives better and discuss domestic matters with them. Also they could pass on to them something about the latest fashions, which a woman wants even if she lives on Muckle Flugga. However, the idea though interesting is impracticable under existing conditions. But any one who knows something of the work of the Ladies' Highland Association knows its worth.

Opposite us in the anchorage stands a remarkable hill – the Sheep Craig – a high cliff to the west, lower cliffs on the other side, and a green sward on top. The shepherds climb up here, and then one by one their sheep are raised by sling from sea-level to the pasture on the heights. The practice has existed from the time of Sir Walter Scott's visit, and no doubt is very much older.

Fair Isle is now a bird sanctuary owned by Mr. Waterston of Edinburgh, and one nightingale has been seen on it.

24th July 1949

This is Sunday, and Ayr is Commodore. Lillie threatened to have a bathe this morning, but the water is too cold. (Later I heard he had taken it.) Last night Robbie Maconochie, Charles Milne, George Morton and myself had an animated argument on things ecclesiastical. Charles Milne, an elder of the Kirk, advocated Latin hymns to Gregorian chants about which he knows nothing, and decried the metrical Psalms. Robbie, an Episcopalian and Chancellor of the Diocese of Edinburgh, swore by the metrical Psalms, both music and, often, words. I advocated the best in both, and contested hotly Charles' suggestion that the metrical psalms were not many of them magnificent – even, to take an appropriate subject, in their references to the sea:–

> But yet the Lord, that is on high,
>   Is more of might by far
> Than noise of many waters is,
>   or great sea-billows are (Ps. 93)

I also swore by the prose Psalms, and the prayer-book version, but deprecated the use of no chants but Gregorian. It seems to me, and here all except Charles agreed, that the best of all systems should be used.

(7.20 p.m.) What stands out most in my thoughts of today is a conversation I had a few moments ago with the Captain. We were leaning over the side watching the gulls and some seals disporting themselves. I passed the remark: 'I suppose the sea has a great fascination for you – just as for me, a novice.' He replied: 'I'm afraid, sometimes, I'm very bitter about the sea.' I asked, why? He replied: 'It has taken from me my nearest and dearest.' Then he explained that his only child, a son aged twenty-four, who had distinguished himself in work and sport at George Watson's, and then in medicine at Edinburgh University, had in 1944 been medical officer on a ship sunk in the Adriatic, and that out of 120 on board, all except five were lost – including his son. He was to have been a medical missionary for five years, and then return to surgery in this country – to follow the example of Mr. J.M. Graham, F.R.C.S.E., also son of a master of the *Pharos*. I told him of my own loss, and a new bond of friendship was made between us.

Today was spent in visiting the South and North Lighthouses of Fair Isle. There is a Church of Scotland and a Methodist Church on Fair Isle. The schoolmaster normally conducts service at the former, but we learned that he was away and, in any event, the visit to the South Light took the morning. We landed at the nearby jetty. Thence a lorry transported us the two miles to the south of the Island. The driver declined any payment because it was the Sabbath. It is a hilly road. George Morton sat with the driver: the rest of us squatted on the back of the lorry. As we ascended the hill over the neck of land to the south of the island, we passed, first, a net set by the bird-watchers to catch birds. These they weigh, measure, and examine for vermin (to trace their origin). Next we saw by the roadside the remains of a German plane brought down in the war. On the other side of the hill, in a field, we saw two black and white oxen, which are used for draught and ploughing, the first I have seen in the United Kingdom. Then we passed a group of houses and the two churches, school, Fair Isle Post Office and general store. Finally, down we came to the South Lighthouse on a low promontory, with seas surging round it and high cliffs to the west. Here, a keeper's wife and daughter were killed in a German air attack in 1941; and the dwelling-houses demolished. They were in the process of being rebuilt. Inside the Lighthouse (both this and the North one were erected in 1891) we found that the light (as also that at the North) was constructed, partly, by a Frenchman, M. Bartier, of Paris. The North Light sheds the more powerful beam. While the new houses are being built, the keepers are living in temporary quarters, except that the principal keeper, Mr. Rae, at the North Light, superintends both the North and South, making his way from one to the other by motorbicycle. Returning the way we came, we took Mr. Fraser who is in charge of the building works to lunch on ship.

In the afternoon, we inspected the North Lighthouse, which is on a high promontory. This time the road was almost Alpine. We skirted cliffs and at one place a funnel through the rock down to the sea. The houses of the North Lighthouse are being installed with bath-accommodation, unlike most places. They have their own reserves of water on the hillside. A feature of this lighthouse is its foghorn which one reaches by a narrow fenced path leading between two cliffs. On the one side there is a cleft in the rock and you see the sea far beneath; on the other, the west side, great rocks and foaming eddies. In the lighthouse we met the young Fair Island wife of one of the assistant keepers. She displayed the quaint shyness of the islanders. She told us the curious fact that no girl had been born on the island for seventeen years: she must have been about the last: there have, however, been boys. The total population is some 65.

In the evening, the Captain, First Officer (Mr. Hunter) and Chief Engineer (Mr. Bremner) were our guests at dinner. There was a superb northern sunset, with a bright star and brighter planet, and away in the distance Fitful Head and to the right the (in comparison) lower headland of Sumburgh, with its lighthouse showing three close flashes every 30 seconds. Seals were disporting themselves in the bay during the afternoon and evening. The wonderful sunset over an expanse of more than twenty miles reminded me of George Morton's observations to me at Whalsay Skerries: why is nature so lavish with all kinds of matter? My answer was: If we knew the answer we should not be human: but may one reason not be to inspire reverence and awe for The Maker of all things?

25th July 1949

We slipped out of our anchorage at Fair Isle at 6 a.m. and made for North Ronaldsay. Through my porthole, I examined the cliffs on the east side of Fair Isle between the splashes of water from the washing of the deck, which from time to time made me suddenly slam it closed.

The Sheep Craig is an even finer precipice from the east side, where it rises right from sea level.

We had no sooner finished breakfast than the lighthouse of North Ronaldsay came in sight on our starboard, curiously marked with belts of brick interspersed with the usual white. As it stands on a low promontory, this enables it to be picked out easily against the sky. It is a high lighthouse and there are 178 steps on the main staircase. Fog came on while we were ashore, and then vanished. This allowed us to see the fog-horn start, continue, and stop: 'the birth, life and death of a hoot,' as Charles Milne would say. The most curious feature of North Ronaldsay is the walls which enclose the island, leaving only a small grass common and the shore outside. The walls are used to keep sheep out of the richer pasture, and thus scraggy sheep in great numbers graze on the poor grass outside the walls, and also on the foreshore, eating the seaweed. They some-times follow the tide as it ebbs, swimming out to eat the fresh seaweed. We did not see them swimming in the sea, though we did see them in a pond left from sea water. Never did seaweed smell so revolting as at North Ronaldsay. It is a flat beach, and the seaweed dries and rots in the sun. Mr. Hughson, the principal keeper, is a fine type, like Mr. Rae at Fair Isle. North Ronaldsay has 350,000 candle-power.

From North Ronaldsay, we went on, in less than an hour, to Start Point Lighthouse, on Sanday. It stands, like North Ronaldsay, on low land, but, here, the promontory is detached from the rest of Sanday by a ford which is open for traffic below half-tide. This was the most difficult landing we have yet had. The jetty and a hook which marks the safe channel were both submerged, and we might have landed on the hook, but for the care of the boatman in the bow. We had to 'walk the plank' onto slippery rocks, covered here and there with water and more slippery seaweed, and it took some short time to cover the rocks and reach dry land. The lighthouse has vertical stripes of brick and white, which enable it to be easily picked out from its background. Its light is wholly red, the relatively small lenses being surrounded by an outer cover of red glass, which reduces the light by 25 per cent. Near the lighthouse are the remains of an old lighthouse which must have been used in the days of Sir Walter Scott. A destroyer ran aground on the reef to the north, and its remains are still partly to be seen on the land nearby where they have been cast up. In the same way, we saw, just off the shore at North Ronaldsay, the wreck of a Norwegian fishing smack. As we proceeded outwards from the jetty, our motor boat grounded momentarily, which was awkward with the falling tide, but we managed to get off at once.

From there, we sailed (because of the fog) round North Ronaldsay (where we heard the fog-horn) and then set a course SW for Westray. It was mild, and, after a sleep on deck, I wakened to find Papa Westray to the north, and, in a few moments, we were anchored at Pierowall. Some of the Commissioners went by car to visit Noup Head Light. I took a walk round the bay of Pierowall and saw the quiet straggling Orkney village. There is an old ruined church, now an ancient monument, with fine seventeenth century heraldic memorial stones. In the evening we played deck billiards as usual.

Here, in Westray, there are no sheep to be seen, but cattle and hens in great numbers and the pasture is of quite a different quality, the richer pasture of Orkney.

26th July 1949

We left our anchorage at Pierowall at 9 a.m. in mist and rain and the deck was somewhat slippery. Our route lay, first, ESE, till we rounded Red Head, and entered the narrow channel made by Eday and the Calf of Eday. Here we passed a minor light (which we did not stop to visit), the house where Gow, the pirate, was captured, and a small lonely church with churchyard on the shore. This is a pregnant arrangement, as people and funerals seem to come by boat. Just after we had entered Eday Sound, the Captain pointed out to me the Covenanters' Memorial, near Mull Head at the east of the Orkney mainland. We were on the bridge at the time, and the weather had cleared and visibility from now onwards was excellent, the sun coming out later to make the day superb. I went to get my cap, and, as I was descending the ladder from the bridge, slipped and fell to the deck. I received a glancing blow from the bridge house on my head, and the next I knew was friends standing around me. Lillie, especially, was very kind, and propped me up. I was taken to the stern cabin, and soon found a lump on the right back of my head, and a bruised right elbow. I lay for a while, thinking that a blow like this was what Gordon received at football, and, strange to say, this brought all back to me, and tears to my eyes. The others went ashore, before lunch, to Auskerry Lighthouse, but I did not go. However, in the afternoon, we came to the anchorage at Copinsay, and then I visited along with the rest. It stands at the head of a cliff facing east, and on the west a shelf of green pastures descends to shallow water. The views south

On board the Pharos. *Glen Wakelin, Gordon Thomson and Duncan Stewart.*

(to Pentland Skerries) west (to the mainland) and north (to Auskerry and its light) were magnificent. Pentland Skerries, Copinsay, Auskerry, Start Point and North Ronaldsay stand, all practically in a straight line, and ships are handed on from one to the other. To the immediate north of Copinsay is a small island, not unlike the Bass Rock – the Horse of Copinsay. The head-keeper here plays the violin (like his colleagues further north) and the mandolin. One of the assistant-keepers had two beautiful little boys, healthy and handsome, aged five and four.

From Copinsay, we coasted down the side of Orkney, up which we had come a week ago. Near South Ronaldsay, we hailed a Granton trawler, curiously (for me) named the *Inchture*, and received from her a supply of fish, which is always – by custom – given free to the

Lighthouse ship, though we returned cigarettes etc. Then we turned WNW, past Pentland Skerries on the port and Swona and anchored off Cantick Head. The currents were very marked in the Firth and, in the clear sunshine, the rocks beyond Brough Ness stood out as clear as crystal in the sunshine. The lamp at Cantick Head is an old-fashioned one installed in 1858. It has a burner for each lens and so is less economical. We also had a demonstration of an old fashioned fog-gun, which the keeper operated specially for our benefit. The keeper had married his wife while at Ailsa Craig, and they had a dear little daughter, aged five, called Ailsa. I told her that I had a little daughter the same age.

Returning to the ship, we took dinner, while anchored off Cantick Head, in order to be on deck for the next part of the journey – which was of surpassing interest – through Switha Sound, by Lyness and between Cava and Hoy, and then across the western end of Scapa Flow to Stromness. In the distance with the glasses we could see the spire of St. Magnus and houses at Kirkwall; further to the east, the spot where the Royal Oak was blown up; the destroyer anchorage; and the place where in 1919, the German High Seas Fleet was scuttled. A beautiful sunset over calm waters greeted us as we approached Stromness Harbour. Here we anchored in the bay, and, after receiving our mail, spent the evening once more playing deck billiards.

27th July 1949

Today I went ashore with George Morton to post some letters. Stromness has the same narrow paved streets as Kirkwall and Lerwick, but they twist more, and the houses are more picturesque. One narrow alley leading up the hill from the main street is called 'Khyber Pass'! At one place, flags were hung across the street, for Stromness had just held its Gala Week, during which the *Pole Star* (the Northern Lights vessel which ordinarily services lighthouses in Northern waters) won first prize for a fancy dress display! The *Pole Star* is lying alongside us in the harbour. It is slightly smaller, but more modern, having been built in 1930, whereas the present *Pharos* (the fourth of its name) was built in 1909. Both have a certain likeness, the builders of both having been the same Beardmore's. The *Pole Star* supplies lighthouses along the Pentland Firth from Duncansby Head to Cape Wrath, and northwards to the Muckle Flugga; the *Pharos* the East Coast; and the *Hesperus*, the newest of the three, the West Coast.

We then crossed the Sound and inspected, first, Low Hoy and then

High Hoy. The latter is a fixed light with two red sections, indicating to shipping the islands in Stromness Bay, and the point of the island on which High Hoy stands, respectively. High Hoy is the first lighthouse where we found a cultivated garden.

In the afternoon, we visited the shore station for Sule Skerry and the shore stations now in progress of erection for Auskerry, Copinsay, and Pentland Skerries.

One problem which has recently arisen is whether all rock stations should have three keepers. At Start Point, for instance, there are only two, and, in winter, it is only light from 9.40 a.m. to 2.30 p.m. Accordingly, the two men have to cover the whole of the long dark period. Trinity House seems disposed to have three men in every such case. But in Shetland there were many cases, and, as yet, insufficient houses to provide for three keepers. Three men seem essential at least where there is not merely a light but a fog-horn.

28th July 1949

We were off at 6 a.m. this morning, bound for Sule Skerry, 38 miles due west of Orkney in a remote part of the Atlantic. It was very clear and also, for the greater part of the day, sunny, but there was a strong breeze, and the *Pharos* tossed and rolled, or, as the Captain put it, was 'a bit jumpy'. At least three of our party, George Morton, Charles Milne and Gordon Thomson were somewhat upset. I felt, as before, perfectly well, and, indeed, enjoyed the stern up one moment and the bow the next. About 9.30 a.m. we reached Sule Skerry, an island about a furlong in length, fairly flat, with the lighthouse at the highest point, in the centre. We had a little difficulty in getting into the motor-boat because of the swell, and Mr. Hunter forbade George Morton to come because of the risk to the safety of one so old and blind. It showed great spirit on George's part to try to go at the age of seventy-nine, when he is also so short-sighted that he can scarcely see the steps of the accommodation ladder.

We first visited the lighthouse, which has a powerful light of 450,000 candle power. We signed our names as usual in the album, and found few names in it, but those of Commissioners or officials. There were, however, the signatures of the survivors of at least two vessels sunk or mined in the vicinity. Sule Skerry has radio direction, and also supplies meteorological reports to Wick every four hours. They no doubt go to make up the B.B.C. weather forecasts for the area. The island's great feature, however, is its puffins. Hundreds and hundreds have made their home on the island. They fly about continuously and we found crowds of their young, still unable to fly, sheltering under the oil tanks from attacking sea-gulls. Mr. Hunter removed two of them from the engine-room. They lay their eggs, like rabbits, in holes in the ground, and, above the rocks, the island is virtually a bog full of these holes, of brown soft peaty soil, in which grow wild and rancid-smelling marigolds. Five miles to the south-west lies Stack, an island about half the size of Sule Skerry, inhabited only by birds. Mr. Hunter told me that the island of Rockall, 200 miles west of the Hebrides, which he has seen once, is about half the size of Stack.

From lonely Sule Skerry, we made a course south-east for Scrabster Docks. For long, we tossed and rolled without land in sight (the journey is 40 miles). Then, at lunchtime, the mainland appeared on our starboard, and Hoy to port. In the distance, we saw Ben Hope and later Morven, and in Scrabster, we saw the Old Man of Hoy. Landing among a bevy of outgoing Lowestoft trawlers (we had seen others near Sule Skerry), we proceeded by motor car, through Thurso, Dunnet and Brough to Dunnet Head. Here, the lighthouse stands 80 feet high, on a cliff itself 300 feet. Eight other lighthouses are in view – Holborn Head, Cantick Head, Stroma, Pentland Skerries, Duncansby Head, and three minor lights. The cliff is crumbling. One fog-horn has already fallen into the sea and the present one is likely also to fall unless precautions are taken. On exceptionally clear nights, the lights of Cape Wrath and Sule Skerry can sometimes be seen. We met the mother of the principal keeper's wife, Mrs. Campbell (aged eighty), whose father and husband were also lighthouse keepers and whose husband wrote a small book of Notes on the Bell Rock.

In the evening, we entertained the Captain, Mr. Hunter and Mr. Bremner to dinner. A great sight in the afternoon and evening was shoals of mackerel, threshing the water into spray as they chased the herring fry.

29th July 1949

I am writing this at midnight as we pass Rattray Head, and approach Peterhead and Buchan Ness. It is clear, and Kinnairds Head, the lights of Fraserburgh, Rattray Head, Peterhead, and Buchan Ness are all visible. There are one or two trawlers visible only by their lights crossing our track ahead and astern.

This morning, before leaving Scrabster Docks, we went ashore and visited Holborn Head light. Its feature is that the light itself is part of the keepers' houses, and is entered from the assistant keeper's house which is on the upper storey. The houses are substantial, built (I think) in 1861 by Messrs. Thomas and David Stevenson, and are almost unique among the houses we have visited in that they have both baths and running water. The light is 30,000 candle power, with red panels covering Scrabster Harbour and its entrance. The harbour was full of Lowestoft and Grimsby trawlers (some back from Ireland, where they had warm weather, feeling our weather in comparison cold). The fishermen are tough bearded young men. There are also fisher girls waiting to gut the fish. They tie strings round their fingers to prevent punctures from the bones and cuts.

At 10 a.m. we set out in the *Pharos*, past Dunnet Head, where the waves were raising foam around the cliffs. The fog-horn looks even more insecure, when seen from the sea. At the south end of Stroma, there was an amazing tide race of green water, and although our maximum speed is only 11½ knots, we were swept along by the tide at full 15. On the shore we saw Canisbay Church, a most picturesque building, and famed for its minister, Dr. Morison, the author of the greatest Scottish paraphrases. I like the thought that the imagery of the 30th paraphrase is drawn from the Pentland Firth, as seen from Canisbay manse. To the sea, we saw a large cargo vessel proceeding ahead of and faster than ourselves, and a big Blue Funnel liner fighting its way westwards against the tide. A smaller vessel behind it was making little progress. Had we been going in that direction, our speed might have been 3 knots. Duncansby Head is much less impressive than Dunnet Head. But there are two jagged rocks rising steeply out of the sea just beyond. When we had rounded Scotland's north-eastern corner, the sea became calmer as the west wind was now blowing off shore. After a heavy belt of rain, Morven came in sight and the Langwell Lodge and Berriedale in lovely colours. From this point southwards to Golspie, the coast was clear and sunny, and looked its loveliest – the Ord, Helmsdale, Loth, Brora, Dunrobin. Across the Firth we could see Ben Rinnes. We drew in close to Embo, the port of Dornoch, taking soundings on the way, and then Gordon Thomson and Tom Simpson left, the former taking the latter to stay with him at Skibo. An amusing incident occurred as they were leaving. On this trip, for the first time, the Commissioners have worn in their caps new badges produced at a cost of 35/- each. Tom Simpson, contrary to orders, wanted to retain his in his cap during his holidays, and he and Gordon Thomson stepped up to the accommodation ladder with the badges still in their caps. Waltolin insisted on them giving them up and they were solemnly unfrocked in front of the second officer and Captain.

From Embo, we set a course ESE by Tarbatness straight across to Kinnairds Head, the whole Morayshire coast now visible to us. Tom Simpson, who had been Commodore, having gone, I took his place for the rest of the day, and, in the evening, after dinner, George Morton and Robbie Maconochie played Lillie and Wakelin at deck-billiards, I scoring. Our game ended, and light began to fade as we reached Kinnairds Head. Sailing down the coast of Aberdeenshire was like driving at night along a wide boulevard. The lights of Fraserburgh, Kinnairds Head, Rattray Head, Peterhead and Buchan Ness glittered across the water, and trawlers with red and green lights passed and repassed.

I learn that there are various entrances or channels leading to the Bell Rock, 'Johnnie Gray's' on the north is the best. Then there is the 'Fairway' to the south, and 'McCarrick's' – coming from the south-west. I believe two others are 'Port Hamilton' and the 'Pool'. We hope for 'Johnnie Gray'.

30th July 1949

The ship was only just moving ahead when I wakened. This was because we must not be at the Bell Rock until the tide comes below the gratings at which we land, that is, below half-tide. The day was a perfect one, the sea calm, the distant views pellucid. The hills of Angus, the Sidlaws, the King's Seat and Dunsinane were all in sight, and you could pick out the houses and chimneys in Arbroath, and St. Regulus' Tower in St. Andrews. At 9.30 a.m., we proceeded to the Rock. The *Pharos* anchored about 200 yards off. We entered by 'Johnnie Gray', a winding entry between rocks, but quite easy in the perfect conditions of the day. It was what Mr. Hunter described as a day for 'a Commissioners' landing'! You first climb up about twenty steps on iron gratings fixed into the granite of the lighthouse base. I had heard about the unpleasantness of this from other Commissioners. But we were roped, and it was not too bad, though an experience. Inside, perhaps because of the thickness of the granite, each block of which is inter-locked, the space is pretty restricted, and there was much joking as to whether I would get up the top stair, because you have to pass through a very narrow hole. However, I managed it easier than the longer-legged Commissioners. Charles Milne and Lillie, with Wakelin were my companions. George Morton and Robbie

Maconochie remained on the ship. On one floor there is a neat kitchen, on the next six compactly packed box-beds; and on the next a 'library' or board-room, full of interesting relics: a marvellous scarlet and white flag, with the Bell Rock itself sewn on in coloured wool, and on one side a sailing ship and on the other the Abbot of Aberbrothock holding the cross of St. Andrews (this was worked by Jane Stevenson about a century ago); a marble bust of Robert Stevenson, the builder, and a marble base and this inscription:–

The Commissioners of the
Northern Lighthouses at a meeting
held in this apartment on the 20th
July 1824 when the Right Hon.
Sir William Rae, Bart. Lord Advocate
of Scotland presided
resolved
that a bust of
Robert Stevenson engineer
be placed in the Bell Rock Library,
in testimony of the sense,
entertained by the Commissioners,
of his distinguished talents,
and indefatigable zeal in the
erection of this lighthouse

There is also an old ink well; a pistol, I think, for igniting flints; and the ceiling of this room, domed shaped, has a fresco of a Greek temple (which is in need of retouching – Wakelin wondered whether an artist could be got to do it.)

On the next flat is the light itself, which gives a flash every 30 seconds, red and white alternately. Some of the lenses have been splintered by machine-gunning from German planes. This light was constructed by the Société des Etablissements Henri Lepaute, Paris, M. Dehesdin, Directeur. There is a beautiful old clock of 1811, telling the days of the week, and an anemometer, giving both speed and direction of wind. The prevailing wind is SW.

Here, again, I found a keeper with a violin. The three keepers, far from being morose hermits, were amongst the cheeriest and most laughing we have met. Their shore-station is at Arbroath.

From the Bell Rock, on we went to the North Carr Lightship, to which the *Pharos* was tethered, and we then were conveyed by motor boat from the one ship to the other. The North Carr is now the Commissioners' only lightship. There was one other, but it was handed over to Trinity House to replace a sunk lightship: all their lightships were attacked and sunk in the war. On the North Carr, there is a crew of about seven. It is a modern well-designed ship with light on top, fog-siren, and two ancient little brass guns used to send warnings of distress. The day had now become grey, and the Isle of May loomed out of a grey fog. The weather brightened as we entered the Forth, but the sun scarcely returned. We passed close by the masts of the *Silvestria*, sunk during the war, and passing Inchkeith by the north channel, entered Granton Harbour in rain. Just before we left, we received our second weighing, and I was horrified to find that, in spite of all the exercise on the voyage, I was now 17 stone 11 lbs, an increase of 10 lbs. We drove home in the rain, and so ended the east coast voyage of the *Pharos*. A wonderful experience, but even greater was my joy on coming home, to learn that Alison was being made Head Girl of St. Leonard's. This was the first news that greeted me, after Ella, Alison and Rosemary had met me on the doorstep.

8th October 1949

We spent August at Loch Awe, Oban and Dunoon. The most memorable days of the holiday, were a drive through Glencoe and Appin, two sails on perfect days to Iona, when we could see Skye in the North, Rhum, Eigg, Muck, Canna, Ardnamurchan, the Treshnish Isles, Coll, Tiree, Dhu Heartach, the Isles of the Sea, and Jura, Islay and Colonsay to the South; a visit to the Hill of Dunadd, which has been one of my objectives for twenty years, and another to Dunstaffnage and Ardchattan Priory, where we received much kindness from the Rev. Alex. Macdonald, minister of Ardchattan, followed by a journey over the high hill road from Loch Etive to Loch Creran and tea at Eriska.

I have had a very busy September, with two visits to the Central Land Board and War Damage Commission in London, and a complete circuit of my Sheriffdom. I conducted my first criminal case – a section 12 and section 15 of the Road Traffic Act case – at Oban on Alison's eighteenth birthday. Then last week, I heard one Appeal at Paisley on the Wednesday, one at Dunoon and one at Greenock on the Thursday, two at Greenock on the Friday, together with a conference with representatives of the political parties over Greenock Polling Places, the preparation of a stated case relating to my Oban trial, and a consultation in the evening as Procurator with Professor Riddell, Moderator of Glasgow Presbytery, over the question of George MacLeod's possible appointment to Govan; on Saturday I went to Campbeltown, and heard a further appeal there on the Monday.

30th October 1949

Since returning from holiday, I have paid three visits, at fortnightly intervals, to the Land Board and War Damage Commission. Hitherto, they have met once monthly, the meetings, except for two annually, being in Devonshire House, Piccadilly; the other two are in Edinburgh. The monthly visit I enjoy. Last summer, when from May to October I had to go almost every week – including twice from Boat of Garten in August – to the Slade Committee, I found it no joke. I wonder if the public, or for that matter Whitehall, realise the strain imposed on civil servants from St. Andrew's House, not a few of whom have to travel each week to London. This time, the extra visit paid to London was to attend a farewell meeting of the Board to Sir Malcolm Tristram Eve, and to welcome his successor. I may give my picture of the Board as it has existed during the first six months of my membership. There is, first, Sir Malcolm, a counsel of unrivalled experience in valuation and rating, but much more than that, a man of consummate ability, always able to unravel the most complicated legal problem in the simplest terms, and, at the same time, most conciliatory; over and over again, he has won over the Board and the public by his candour, fairness and open mindedness; his loss to the public service is very great. I rank him considerably above Slade in ability and rather of the quality of mind of Radcliffe. Next, Dame Myra Curtis, the author of the 'Curtis Report', formerly a civil servant, and now Principal of Newnham; she has what, in an olden day, would have been called a masculine intelligence, great subtlety, and also much valuable experience; her outlook I regard, however, as civil service rather than purely academic; she has a keen sense of humour as well. Sir Basil Gibson, formerly Town Clerk of Sheffield, a model to Town Clerks, shrewd, humorous, knowledgeable. Sir Luke Fawcett, a Trade Unionist, member of the T.U.C. General Council, but not I think what that would suggest in the public mind; a genial, incredibly stout, moderate-minded man, with a special intimate knowledge of the building trade. Mr. MacDonald, former General Manager of the Royal Exchange Assurance, a wise and mellow Scot, who has spent his life in London, and exhibits the best of both countries. Mr. J.R. Rutherford, former county convener of Dumbarton, our talkative member, who is rather inclined to keep bees in his bonnet, and has still, after a long time on the Board, to master the main provisions of the Act. Then there is our Secretary, Mr. Robert Fraser, formerly head of the Department of Health in Scotland, who now becomes Deputy-Chairman as well, quiet, popular, competent, just a shade lacking in personality. Usher, the Deputy-Secretary, a lone wolf, whose thinking cap is strong. Of the others who attend our meetings, I particularly single out Stout, a young civil servant, whose various memoranda on the complicated subject of minerals have been peculiarly competent, and who should go far. The new Chairman, Sir Thomas Phillipps, is a different type from his predecessor. Sir Malcolm is the best flower of an English public school. Sir Thomas is the Welsh 'lad o' pairts', who took a first in 'Greats' and in Mathematics and won the Fairford Prize. Sir David Milne said to me: 'He will master the Town Planning in six months.' As its difficulties compare with the old law of Teinds, it is obvious that he falls to be placed alongside the Devil and the Teind Clerk.

Dr. James Black died a fortnight ago, two days after a second major operation for cancer. I saw him ten days before, between the first and second operations, when he was serene and bright, and jumped out of bed and had tea beside me in his dressing gown. St. George's West was full, both at the funeral and at the Memorial service. At the beginning of his twenty-seven years' ministry there, he suffered an overwhelming personal bereavement, in the death of his wife; strange to say, for such an outgoing nature, he never mentioned her name; here, so much depends on how the loss is taken at the beginning. But the loss gave his ministry a new depth, and one would never realise from his radiant cheerfulness, the deep sorrow which was in his heart. As a preacher, he excelled in character study, for he had dramatic power amounting to genius, and could make any Biblical character live. In other forms of exposition, his preaching was not of the same quality; for his thoughts came in original flashes, rather than in sustained argument. He visited people who were sick, but partly because of the size of his congregation, and his outside commitments, there were gaps in his other visiting. In the business of Session and Deacon's Court, he was a poor chairman, for he was essentially a pleader rather than a judge, and always talked too much before others had expressed their view. He had a peculiar gift of perennial youth, which enabled him to win the hearts of small children. While I knew him very well, I never knew him intimately, and Mr. McCandlish, my predecessor as Session Clerk, had the same experience. One interesting fact he told me on my last visit to him. He was closely related to the McCaigs of Oban, and was at one time urged to bring an action for reduction of the famous will, but declined to do so. His was to have been one of the statues to be placed in McCaig's Folly! In the short time that I have known his successor, Murdo Macdonald, I have come to know him more intimately, however, than I ever knew James Black.

1st November 1949

George MacLeod of the Iona Community is at present at loggerheads with the powers that be in the Church of Scotland because they will not accept him for Govan Old Parish on his own conditions. Last General Assembly, he was, because of his occupation as Leader of the Iona Community, declared ineligible for nomination to Govan, and now he is willing to give up the leadership and be nominated, but on conditions. I have given three opinions this last week about him. With all his gifts, he has a most unreasonable disposition, and seems unable to think accurately. However, a rather amusing incident came to my notice today. Lord Gibson sent me a paper of his own on 'Christianity and the Law'. It recounted how Sir Alexander Gibson, Lord Durie, was kidnapped one day, while riding on Leith Sands, at the instigation of a Border laird who had a suit pending in the Court of Session, towards which Lord Durie was known to be unfavourable; Lord Durie was whisked off and detained in a Border peel till the suit was, in his absence, decided in favour of the laird. Lord Gibson had sent this paper to George MacLeod, and the latter's letter returning the paper has been sent me along with the paper. In his letter, George MacLeod says: 'I have it in me to wish that, shortly before the General Assembly another Gibson might have turned the tables and kidnapped certain ecclesiastical personalities had I been able to get them to Leith Sands, but it might have led to complications.'

7th November 1949

A week ago, in Dowell's Book Sales Catalogue for the 2nd, I noticed item 274 'MSS – Minute Books of the Diagnotic (sic) and Speculative Societies, 1816–87, 10 vols., and 2 others (12)'. Thinking this represented, in part, records of the Speculative Society, I asked Neil Macvicar, Senior President, to go and inspect them. He went, and later reported that 'Speculative' should be 'Speculating', and that some of the books were plainly those of the Diagnostic Society of the

University. I later was in touch with Mr. Braid, Senior President of the Diagnostic Society, and, with him, I went to Dowell's and inspected the volumes. Apart from an unrelated account book, they consisted of (1) Minute Books of the Diagnostic Society from its inception in 1816 – it was apparently first called the 'Speculating' Society; and (2) (more remarkable) the first Minute Book of the Edinburgh University Students' Representative Council, the first of its kind in the country. I arranged that Dowell's should withdraw the lot from sale, and also write the solicitor for the executry – William Saunders – which was selling them, pointing out that the executrix would no doubt want to return to the Society and S.R.C. the books that were theirs. Later, she agreed to do so. The effort cost nothing. One young advocate wanted to raise an interdict against Dowell's, but this way of peace was much simpler.

8th November 1949

Lord Gibson, Chairman of the Land Court, takes his judicial tenure very seriously, and, at agricultural inspections, is reputed to wander about the fields in his judicial robes. He has the same tenure as a Lord of Session. Once when the judges were attending St. Giles', he turned up, and claimed precedence over Lord Sorn; 'Ah,' said the latter shrewdly, 'we attend St. Giles' not as Lords of Council and Session, but as Lords Commissioners of Justiciary.'

5th December 1949

Just ten minutes ago, Alison telephoned from St. Leonard's to say that a wire had come from Lady Margaret Hall calling her for an entrance interview on the 8th. She goes down with a class mate, Margaret Harvey, on Wednesday the 7th. Two other girls, Jean and Pamela Morton, heard from St. Hilda's and St. Hugh's at the weekend, and Alison, and we her parents, have been on tenterhooks for three days. How proud Gordon would be of her. How well she has done, in work, play, and general character. This last term she has been head girl of St. Leonard's, and only to-day, she wrote saying that she had got into the best five at 'gym', for which there is a special distinction. She got her colours last year at lacrosse; has been a school monitor for a year; took five distinctions in her school certificate; and one distinction in the Senior school certificate; and with it all, is just a modest, natural, young-for-her-age 'wee lassie'. How proud I am of my children. Gordon was the same; and Rosemary bids fair to be like them.

10th December 1949

Alison and Margaret Harvey left for Oxford on Wednesday 7th. Last night, when in London, she telephoned me, and I was surprised to find she was in Tunbridge Wells. In Oxford, she had had a glorious time – three interviews, two very pleasant, one stiff, lunch with the Galbraiths, tea with Margaret MacGiven, a St. Leonard's senior, visits to Christ Church and Magdalen. But the College could not house them till news came from Cambridge, and so yesterday, after a day in London, they went on to Tunbridge Wells to stay with Margaret's aunt. Today at noon, we received a telegram from St. Leonard's that Alison has to go to Newnham for an interview on Monday. So that will be more excitement.

13th December 1949

Alison is still at Newnham. But this evening Miss Macfarlane telephoned from St. Leonard's to say that Alison has been offered a place at Lady Margaret Hall.

15th December 1949

Alison arrived home. After two days at Newnham, she went on to stay overnight with her class mate Julia Birley, the daughter of the Headmaster of Eton. Her account of life in the headmaster's house was most entertaining. Evidently there was a very keen family discussion as to whether the boys should wear white waistcoats at a coming dance. Alison has a strong preference for Oxford over Cambridge. At Cambridge, she went through six interviews, at Oxford three.

21st December 1949

Alison has accepted the vacancy at L.M.H.

CHAPTER IV

1950

4th January 1950

I leave in an hour on a new expedition – for me. I am one of a Church of Scotland delegation of seven appointed to confer with the Church of England. The conference arises mainly out of the Archbishop of Canterbury's Cambridge sermon on 3rd November 1946. Our delegation consists of Professor Manson, Professor John Baillie, Dr. Matthew Stewart, Professor Burleigh, Rev. Tom Torrance of Beechgrove, Aberdeen, and myself, with Professor Tindal as Secretary. I do not know the full English delegation, but I understand it includes the Bishops of Derby (Rawlinson), Durham (Williams *[later Bishop of Winchester]*), Manchester (Greer), two Durham Professors (Greenslade and Ramsey *[later Professor of Cambridge, then Bishop of Durham]*), Mr. Taylor (I think, a vicar in Birkenhead *[later Vicar of St. Andrews, Oxford and lecturer at Wycliffe Hall]*), and, as secretary, the Rev. R.R. Williams, Principal of St. John's College, Durham *[later Bishop of Leicester]*. The deputation is I understand mainly High Church – apart from Manchester *[Quite wrong. Manchester, Greenslade, Williams and Taylor were definitely not high. Derby is I should judge neither high nor low]*. The Scottish Episcopal church are sending 'watchers' in Bishop Graham of Brechin, and Hector Burn-Murdoch, my brother of the Bar; and the English Presbyterian, Professor R.D. Whitehorn of Cambridge. There was a risk that Prof. Baillie would not go, as he went into the Deaconess Hospital on Boxing Day, on account of a suspected ulcer; it would have been a calamity to go without him, and also without Dr. John White.

I am not very optimistic about the conference, not because we are not ready to do what the previous Joint Conference proposed, but because the Anglicans have withdrawn from the attitude agreed to by their previous delegation. As Derby was a member of both it will be interesting to see his attitude. The main facts, as I see them, before the conference begins, are worth setting down.

Resolution No. 43 of the Lambeth Conference of 1930 expressed the hope 'that an invitation may very soon be issued to the now fully united Church of Scotland to enter upon free and unrestricted conference with representatives of the Anglican Union on the basis of an appeal to all Christian people issued in 1920.' In pursuance of this Resolution, Archbishop Lang conveyed on 7th May 1932 an invitation to the Moderator of the Assembly, recalling the earlier Lambeth Conference of 1920 and the fact that the General Assemblies of the (then) two Scottish Churches had expressed their willingness to enter into the conference which the invitation proposed.

On 27th May 1932, Lang accompanied by Bishop Reid of Edinburgh addressed the General Assembly on the invitation, and, the same day, the Assembly adopted a motion, the main part of which was:- '(2) the General Assembly recognised that by the providence of God the re-united Church of Scotland is now at liberty to fulfil the solemn undertaking given in 1920 by the still separated branches of the Church in response to the appeal of the Bishops of the Anglican Communion and resolved that respectful intimation to that effect be communicated through the Moderator to His Grace.' This motion was carried by a majority; two amendments (1) opposing unrestricted conference; and (2) opposing conference *in hoc statu* were rejected.

Thereafter the Joint Conference opened. The following year an interim report was submitted to the 1933 General Assembly. On this occasion, the re-remit to the Church of Scotland delegates to continue the conference was hedged by an addendum, moved by Dr. Archibald Fleming of St. Columba's, Pont Street, and carried by 382 to 369 votes, to this effect:- 'The General Assembly, however, desire, with a view to prevent any misunderstanding, that the Committee should respectfully inform the representatives of the Church with which it confers that any agreement with regard to the Orders and Sacraments of the conferring Churches can only be based on the equal validity of the orders and sacraments of both Churches, and of the equal standing of the accepted communicants and ordained ministers in each.' I remember being present in the Assembly when this addendum was carried. All the most responsible leaders of the Church were against it, and it is a pity that Dr. John White was away from Edinburgh at the time. I also remember my Father's indignation at the manner, rather than the matter of Dr. Fleming's speech. However sound his position may have been, the timing of his addendum was unhelpful, and his speech irresponsible in tone.

Notwithstanding all this, it did not prevent the Joint Conference from unanimously reaching certain very valuable conclusions, chiefly six recommendations of 'Things that might be undertaken in common.' The first two were:- 1. Mutual admission to pulpits; and 2. 'That means be sought to recognise and place under a general rule the usage, already common in Scotland, and existing in many places in England, by which members of either Communion at home or abroad, where out of reach of their own accustomed ordinances, are welcomed in the other as members of the Catholic Church of Christ, to the Table of the Lord.'

In the 1934 General Assembly, these recommendations (all six) were expressly approved, and a Committee appointed for the purpose of considering how they might be carried into effect.

In January 1935, the Upper Houses of Canterbury and York both commended the Joint Report to the sympathetic and careful study of the Anglican Church. The Lower House of York passed a like resolution. The Lower House of Canterbury, before passing any resolution, expressed the desire to hear the corporate opinion of the Scottish Episcopal Church.

In May 1935, the Scottish Episcopal Church issued observations torpedoing Recommendations 1 and 2, in a document couched in most unfortunate terms. Thereafter, not unnaturally, the Lower House of Canterbury decided to adjourn the matter again; while the Lower House of York resolved that no further steps should be taken in regard to the report without full consultation with the Scottish Episcopal Church. In subsequent correspondence, Lang had simply to state, obviously regretfully, that he could give no definite response to further invitations for joint conference on Recommendations 1 and 2. The Lives of Temple, p. 462, and Lang, p. 370, both give glossed accounts of the incident which do not wholly agree with the recorded facts.

It is at this point that the Archbishop's (Fisher's) Cambridge Sermon comes, proposing, apparently (1) that the non-episcopal churches should 'take episcopacy into their systems'; and (2) that a system of mutual commissioning of individuals should be adopted. I say nothing about the proposal, until we hear it expounded by the Anglican delegation at the coming Conference.

5th January 1950

I am writing this at 5.30 a.m. as today is a full day – conferences at 10 a.m., 4.30 p.m. and in the evening – and a visit, guided by Canon Greenslade, to the Cathedral in the afternoon. Yesterday was an extraordinarily interesting day, marked by a certain initial impact of conflicting views; a remarkable demonstration of the calibre of Tom Torrance, who on theological questions at once made himself felt: and odd snatches of humour, not least when T.T., having torn his trousers at the knee in the train, tried to get some adhesive tape in a chemist, with which to make a temporary repair; or when Durham informed us that, in Castle Auckland, there is one part of the building called 'Scotland' where certain Scots of an earlier generation received a different kind of hospitality from that which we are now receiving.

On arrival, we were received by the Rev. R.R. Williams, Principal of St. John's, the Anglican Secretary, a young man who suggested to me rather the warden of a settlement than the Principal of a College. St. Chad's is the Tractarian College; St. John's the Evangelical. Torrance, Burn-Murdoch and I are in the 'new building', which is reached by ascending, descending and turning corners as one does in an old English Inn. Dinner was uncommonly good, but the beds are uncommonly hard; however, they let me hear the distant Cathedral bell chime out the hours more than I would otherwise have done. There is an unusual interval between the hour chimes and the bell which tolls the number of the hour itself.

After Durham had given a short and very attractive welcome, Derby opened the talk. The Conference, he said, arose out of the Cambridge sermon. That related primarily to Anglican relations with the Free Churches. The general proposal was that they should 'take episcopacy into their system – and try it out on their own ground first'. He then referred to the Church of Scotland Committee's report, and to 'one formidable sentence' that 'in Scotland, as in England, serious limits exist, at present, to what may be undertaken, even for high ecumenical ends, in the way of the alteration of ecclesiastical policy.' He also referred to Recommendations 1 and 2 in the 1934 Report, and stated that the Archbishop agreed that the Report of 1934 should be treated as equally relevant with the Cambridge sermon. Recommendation 2 raised inter-communion; and inter-communion would raise episcopacy; he hoped that episcopacy did not lie outside the scope of the discussions. Could the conversations be unrestricted? He suggested that we should not begin frontally, but by examination of the 1934 Report in the light of the Observations of the Scottish Episcopal Bishops.

Professor Manson, as Church of Scotland chairman, replied, and made, in some ways, a moving speech, beyond my expectations. He explained the Church's position on its report, and that our aim was fuller inter-communion, and the remit to us 'to take such action as may be deemed appropriate in the circumstances' (as stated in the report). We cordially acclaimed the Archbishop's view that inter-communion might precede constitutional union. With regard to the historical position, each church was national, and the nodal point of other communions: considerations which could not be left out of account. With regard to doctrine, this must be fully discussed, but how was episcopacy to be taken into the system of a church which claimed to retain episcopacy in a different form, though not prelacy; this would involve discussion of the Divine nature of the Church, succession and so on. The Church of Scotland, like its sister, claimed to have carried on the succession reformed. In reaffirming earnest desire for inter-communion, he stressed that, notwithstanding sub-sequent discouragements, there was the very marked measure of practical agreement in the Joint Statement of 1934. He hoped for ever wider communion; and each having access to, and a welcome at, communion in the other church.

After the conference, Derby, Torrance, Burn-Murdoch and I de-scended to the common room where we had a 'crack'. I fell through one chair and very nearly broke another: they seemed somewhat fragile for one weighing over 17 stone! (Next evening, Durham nearly fell through the same chair!)

Now, for my impressions of personalities. Of the three Bishops, Durham impresses me the most. He took no part in the discussion, but there is a kindly penetrating gleam in his eye, and a sincerity and charm, which I found most attractive. Derby is much more the prelate and man of the world, and, although the theologian of the three bishops, was, admittedly, carried quite out of his depth by Torrance. He confessed to me afterwards that he did not understand him. From my own experience, I felt that Torrance, speaking on difficult theo-logical matters, should have been very clear to any theologian and Ramsey and Baillie had no difficulty in apprehending the precise bearing of his argument, though I confess that, to a layman unfamiliar with the precise meaning of theological terminology, it was less easy. Manchester does not look like my idea of a bishop at all, but he is not the worse of that. He did not wear gaiters, and, at first, I took him for a young college representative, for he must still be in his young forties. He has not revealed the quality of his mind. Ramsey, the son of a Congregational minister, and now a High Anglican, is, Baillie considers, the strong man of their side, and has certainly appeared thus so far. So far, Torrance has made the deepest impression, with Manson, Baillie and Ramsey, I should say next, and

Derby adequate, but certainly not inspiring. Indeed, the strength of the Church of Scotland theologians is most impressive, when placed alongside their Anglican brothers. The observers have not yet spoken.

6th January 1950

All yesterday, except during the afternoon, the Conference proceeded. Generally, those who contributed most for the Church of Scotland were Manson and Baillie, with Torrance rather less prominent. Throughout the Conference, I got a new insight into Manson, who not merely revealed the depth of his wisdom and scholarship, but as greatly the depth of his Christianity. Baillie, too, more incisive and as charitable in outlook. On the other side, Durham not interjecting almost at all, but one whose sincerity and deep Christianity come out in all he says. For the Anglicans, the discussion was chiefly handled, in the general aspects, by Derby; in theology, by Ramsey, whom I find somewhat inscrutable as yet; and, historically, by Greenslade.

We broke off for lunch. Then, at 2 p.m., Greenslade conducted most of us, first, round the Cathedral, and, then, the Library – the shrine of Cuthbert (undergoing repairs); the list of Bishops – Wolsey was bishop for two years, but seems never to have come to Durham; the ancient clock; the statue of the last of the Prince-Bishops (whom Scott met), and the grave of Hensley Henson – of whom Dean Inge has written in his diary just published: 'Henson shows quite an affection for the Bloody Mary' (because of her statutes strengthening the position of Dean) 'who would have made short work of him.' (I am quoting from memory); the great bespangled and lighted Christmas tree in the north transept; the sanctuary handle on the door on the north side of the nave; the tomb of the Venerable Bede; with, close by, a manger-scene (Greenslade: 'Does the C. of S. regard that as rather high?') and the first of the three shepherds closely resembling a benevolent Dr. John White; the earliest Norman roof; the great solemn vista; the ship's bridge of an episcopal throne; Durham's one defect, the shoddy screen, still not too venerable to be removed (the wood, it is said, dates from 1650 after Dunbar when Scottish prisoners left in the Cathedral destroyed all the woodwork except the clock, saved, so the legend goes, because surmounted by a thistle); in the Library, the coffin fragments of Cuthbert (the coffin was only 5 feet 6½ inches long) and his relics, especially his cross (Brechin pointed out that he wore a replica of it); the echoing Chapter House, with its prison, again for Scottish prisoners; the College, as the close is called (leading to confusion with the University). Later, I observed to Tindal, who agreed with me, 'The Cathedral reminds one of the Anglicans' great defect, a great historical tradition which produces so noble a symbol of worship, but a symbol which is of meaning only if there are worshippers; otherwise it becomes simply a magnificent national monument.' (This morning walking through the cloister, I saw the Dean, Greenslade and another clergyman, robed, leaving after the eight a.m. service, and six worshippers, three of whom entered the Deanery itself.)

Before tea, I had a talk with Durham. He was for twenty years at Winchester, half of them as headmaster, and liked the Scottish contingent (among them David Watson); then Dean of Christ Church, and now here. He had a great regard for Lionel Smith, and wondered if I would know him; so I mentioned my close link. He must have been a fine headmaster. Mentioning the invitation to Lionel Smith to become headmaster of Eton, he said Mrs. A.L. Smith could never understand her son refusing it, but, in his view, Lionel Smith had no ambition for high office. He said A.L. Smith senior thought his own son and Sir Ernest Barker his two best students. I found that Greenslade had been at Oxford University as a don in St. John's when Heath and Seaman were there. Manchester came as a representative of the Trinity College, Dublin, Historical Society, to the Spec for an interdebate when I was a member. He is two years my junior, but looks more like ten; he was for four years a civil servant.

This morning, I walked through the Cathedral before breakfast, and finding Tindal stepping out to do the same when I came back, set out again with him. We left at 10.24. I had an intimate conversation with Manson, and later lunch with him and Baillie and Brechin. As we left the restaurant (I coming last), an attendant seeing so many black coats and a bishop popped out his head and asked me: 'Say, Sir – that man with the Cross – excuse me asking – is he a Cardinal?'

One other story about this visit. At one of our preliminary meetings, Dr. Taylor of St. George's said to me: 'But this will involve your being away two days from court.' I said: 'I'm delighted to go,' and then added, by way of reflection: 'The older you become, the more you like irrelevancies.' We walked on in silence after this, for a short time, and I realised I should have used 'one' and not 'you', to avoid ambiguity!

14th January 1950

Today I received from Alison's housemistress a letter with this sentence:- 'Miss Macfarlane' (headmistress) 'was telling me, at the end of term, that she never had a better or more trustworthy Head of School than Alison, that however difficult and unpleasant a duty might be, she would set about it immediately and carry it through.'

4th February 1950

Parliament was dissolved yesterday, and today I went to receive the writs for summoning the new Parliament. I received the writs for Paisley, West Renfrewshire and East Renfrewshire at Paisley; the writ for Greenock at Greenock; and the writ for Argyllshire at Dunoon. Together, they affect some 250,000 electors. The ceremony was very simple. At each place, the Head Postmaster attended the Sheriff Court, and delivered an envelope to me containing the writ. The writ is a short printed document, bearing the Great Seal. Even the name of the signatory 'Napier' was printed. The Sheriff Clerk at Dunoon, who has forty years experience, says that this is the first occasion on which the actual signature has not appeared. I strongly suspect that the writs were sent in advance of the dissolution to make sure of their arrival. On the back is a receipt which I signed, and, below, the return, which has yet to be made out. Another receipt is handed back to the Postmaster. Alison accompanied me. We went by car to Gourock. On the return steamer journey from Dunoon, we sailed back via Kirn, Blairmore and Kilcreggan, altogether a delightful and memorable day. With this today (Saturday); working my cinema-projector for a lecture by George MacLeod on the Iona Community to-morrow; an arbitration in Aberdeen on Monday; two special cases for Tuesday and Wednesday; receiving nominations in Paisley on Wednesday; a dinner that night in Glasgow; a committee on Thursday; to London on Thursday night for the Central Land Board and War Damage Commission and back here on Friday night; to Dunoon the following Monday – I can't complain of idleness.

13th February 1950

This last week, I have received four of the nominations for the five constituencies embraced in my Sheriffdom. On the 8th at Paisley, Major Guy Lloyd, Conservative candidate for East Renfrewshire; on the 9th at Paisley, Mr. J.P. Mackay, Liberal National candidate and

Mr. T. Scollan, Labour candidate, both for West Renfrewshire; and finally, one at Dunoon, for Argyllshire – of which more anon. The normal procedure is for the candidate with his wife, his proposer and seconder, and his election agent to attend. The nomination form, with signatures of proposer and seconder, and eight assenters – all of whom have to be checked as electors in the constituency – is handed in, with a signed consent by the candidate to nomination. These documents are checked. The candidate also hands over his deposit – of £150 – usually in bank notes, and a receipt is granted. That, and hand-shaking, completes the ceremony. In this election for the first time, candidates have had eight days in which to give in nominations; hitherto, they have had only one day.

Today, I went to Dunoon for the final day of the Argyll nominations. In the other places, as I could not be in three places at one time, the deputies appointed by me acted. In Renfrewshire, the deputy returning officers are A.M. Hamilton, Sheriff-substitute at Paisley; J.C. Bonnar, Sheriff-substitute at Greenock; and William Millar, Sheriff Clerk of Renfrewshire; in Argyll, Chalmers, Sheriff-substitute at Oban; and, for the period of nomination only, John D. Morrison, my stone-deaf Sheriff Clerk at Dunoon.

As I crossed to Dunoon via Strone and Hunter's Quay, the Cowal hills and Ben Lomond lay snow-white, bathed in clear sunshine. On board the *Marchioness of Lorne*, a talkative lady came up and spoke to me: 'Why don't English visitors come in February, when the Clyde hills are so lovely?' 'What a pity the *Queen Elizabeth* doesn't sail up the Clyde – there is no finer sea-approach to Britain.' 'Why don't farmers get a subsidy for their shepherds – why don't farmers get a subsidy for gathering sea-weed?' When I mentioned that Argyll had a coast-line of 2,000 miles, this led to her conjecturing as to the distance from Land's End to John o'Groats. I was relieved when we reached Dunoon.

At the Sheriff Court, Mr. Morrison told me that a dark-horse candidate was expected to submit a last-minute nomination – a lady from North Argyll, who had just failed to be in time for the last election. I said: 'Could it possibly be my garrulous friend on the *Marchioness of Lorne*?' Sure enough, at 2.55 p.m., five minutes before the list closed, in walked the lady, Mrs. Mary Stuart Macphail or Holt, describing herself by her maiden name, and as of 'Arisaig and Appin' – a 'small-holder, horticulturist, and house wife'. With some persuasion, I induced her to prune her description, and eventually she gave her surname as 'Macphail Holt' and deleted the 'horticulturist'.

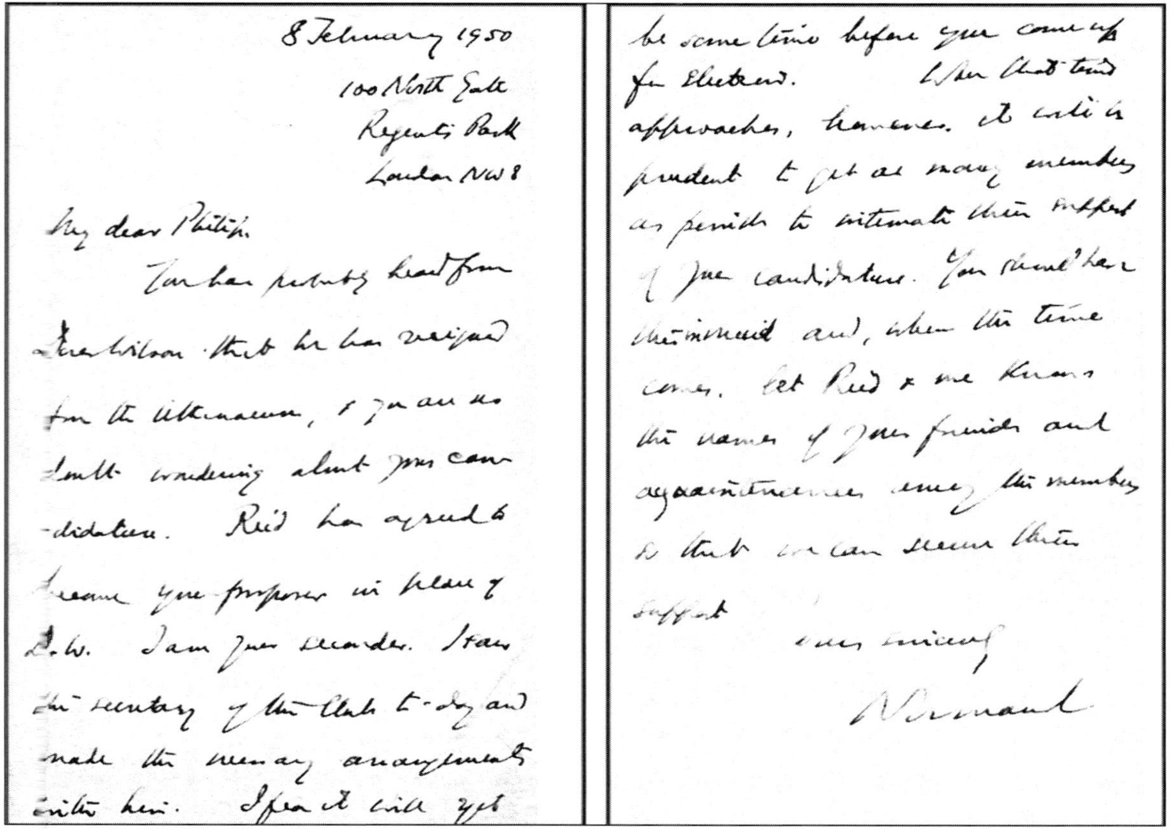
8 February 1950
100 North Gate
Regent's Park
London NW8

My dear Philip,
You have probably heard from Lord Wilson that he has resigned from the Athenaeum, & you are no doubt wondering about your candidature. Reid has agreed to become your proposer in place of L.W. I am your seconder. I saw the secretary of the Club to-day and made the necessary arrangements with him. I fear it will yet be some time before you come up for Election. When that time approaches, however, it will be prudent to get as many members as possible to intimate their support of your candidature. You should have this in mind and, when the time comes, let Reid & me know the names of your friends and acquaintances among the members so that we can secure their support.

Yours sincerely
Normand

Letter from Lord Normand.

She wanted advice about election agents, meetings, expenses. But beyond telling her that, as she had named no election-agent, she was deemed to be her own agent, I explained that the Returning Officer was not there to advise candidates, and that she must refer to a solicitor and to the provisions of the Act.

When in London on the 10th, at the French landscapes exhibition at the Royal Academy, I fell in with J.S.C. Reid (Lord Reid of Drem). It is amusing to recall that, when I came to the Bar, he was an idle junior, though highly thought of by his contemporaries. At my early stage, I had an amusing case with him about a partnership in race-horses. At the time, we mastered all the intricacies of horse-racing, but, alas, it has gone by the board. I remember seeing him in a proof relating to Valuation of Teinds, and thinking that was one of the few times I had seen him in Court. Another time, I gave an opinion; he as senior junior gave another one, to the contrary; and then Tommy Cooper as senior, agreed with my view. Now the one is a Lord of Appeal; and the other Lord President. J.S.C. Reid has a specially acute mathematical mind; and excels in a fourth speech, for he is at his best in picking other people's brains. He is coming to Edinburgh on the 17th to be admitted an Honorary Member of the Spec, and I am to have the privilege of introducing him. As Dover Wilson has just retired from membership of the Athenæum, J.S.C. Reid is now to be my proposer, with Normand as seconder.

15th February 1950

Today, my fiftieth birthday, we went as a family in the afternoon to Glencorse churchyard to gather snowdrops. The snow of the last few days had gone except on the hills and in dark hollows. The road to Biggar, and Flotterstone always reminds me of the days when Gordon was evacuated to Hartree and Alison to Belwood during the earlier years of the late war. And so, in this quiet outing, my little family of five was very much united across the years and beyond the boundaries of earth. We came back to a wonderful birthday cake with twenty-six candles, so that Rosemary would not be disillusioned as to my antiquity.

19th February 1950

On the 17th I attended the Speculative Society dinner and the sub-sequent debate: 'Is the day of the literary giant now over?' Lord Reid came down to my house before for a sherry; Sir Edward

Appleton was to have come too, but we joined him at the New Club. The dinner was held by candle-light in the Senate Hall, which I always think has the most superb collection of Raeburns to be seen anywhere: Principal Robertson, Adam Ferguson, and Professor Robinson, who, as a midshipman in the St. Lawrence, heard Wolfe as he crossed to Quebec repeating the lines from Gray's Elegy: 'The path of duty leads but to the grave.' Afterwards I introduced Lord Reid as an Honorary Member; and Matthew Fisher then introduced Sir Edward Appleton. Each of the honorary members afterwards made a short speech; and each of them, like two boys, took part in the debate. Sir Edward is one of the pleasantest and most easy natures one could wish to meet. Both of them entered thoroughly into the spirit of the occasion. I looked up the Spec members of 18th February 1925, and found that Mr. W.D.L. Greer of the Trinity College Dublin Historical Society (now Bishop of Manchester) spoke that evening on the negative in a debate on: 'Can Bachelors be Happy?' which was carried in the affirmative by 11–10. I had been present also.

25th February 1950

I am writing this at my hotel window (Saturday evening) at Dunoon. The General Election was on Thursday, and the Argyll count has still to be made – it is always later than the others except the Orkneys and Shetlands, Inverness-shire and the Western Isles: steamer transport causes delay in the return of the ballot-boxes. I see that, owing to storms, it is at present impossible to get the ballot-box off North Ronaldsay, and a steamer may have to be specially sent.

I left home in the morning of the 22nd, with 22 Opinions in arrear, all recent, for I did all I could to make up ground in the February week. On the way by road to Paisley, I called in at Balerno to be introduced by Dover (Wilson) to his daughter-in-law Monica Wilson (née Hunter), also a Professor of Anthropology at Grahamstown, South Africa. She has a Carnegie Fellowship and is proceeding to the U.S.A. Her older boy, Francis (age ten), whom I have never seen, calls me uncle, and when Dover went to South Africa last year I arranged to give Francis a carpenter's bench. Godfrey Wilson, father of Francis and Timothy, died a year after Gordon, and this visit on the 22nd was on Gordon's seventh anniversary – so between Dover and myself it was a special link – two fathers who had lost their only son. But it is not loss – for Gordon, Alison and Rosemary, and their dearest little mother are with me wherever I go.

At Paisley, in the afternoon, I swore in (1) presiding officers for polling stations (2) their clerks and (3) enumerators. (1) and (2) numbered over 300, and there would be 50–60 enumerators. These were for three constituencies – East Renfrewshire; West Renfrewshire; and Paisley. I also gave the first two categories an account of their chief duties. Later I saw the van-loads of ballot-boxes go out to the various stations – about a hundred in each constituency. In the evening Riddell of Glasgow University had dinner with me at the Paisley club, where I was staying. He came to discuss with me, as Procurator, the terms of an Assembly report on non-parochial work undertaken by ministers. It is intended to pass an Act of Assembly making all contracts for remunerative employment of this character (which is only to be undertaken in exceptional cases) subject to approval by the Presbyteries.

On the 23rd (Polling Day), I began at 9.30 a.m. and finished at 1 a.m. that night. In the morning, Mr. Robertson, Chief Constable of Renfrewshire, took me round polling stations, one in Paisley and the rest in West Renfrewshire – North School, Paisley, Inchinnan, Bishopton, Langbank, Port Glasgow, Gourock, Greenock, Kilmacolm, Bridge of Weir, Johnstone. Mr. Robertson is, like myself, a native of Perthshire – Strathtay – and looks like a sheep-farmer, a strong vivacious, humorous, rugged personality. He brought me back to the Sheriff Court at Paisley, at 2.30, and, while Mr. Millar (the Sheriff Clerk) made a similar tour of East Renfrewshire, I remained at the Sheriff Court, on call, filling in the time writing an opinion, which I completed before dinner. Mr. Goudie, Chief Constable of Paisley, joined me at dinner, and, afterwards, we visited Paisley Pollings till 9 p.m., the close of the Poll. The presiding officers and clerks had been on duty since 7 a.m., and appreciated the break caused by our visit. At 9 p.m. we went to the Clark Hall, where the count was to be the next day, and awaited the arrival of the returning ballot boxes. They came in mainly between 10 p.m. and 12 midnight, and when we finished at 1 a.m., some of the English burgh results, about thirty of them, were already out. They cannot have undertaken the full system of count.

On the 24th, we began at 8.45 a.m. The West and East Renfrew counts were completed by 3 p.m., and Paisley, shortly before 6. Mr. Millar took charge of East; I did West; and 'Hammy' (Sheriff A.M. Hamilton, K.C.) Paisley. East beat West by 30 seconds. I announced them; and left Hammy, whose last election it is, to announce Paisley. My two candidates were the Hon. John S. Maclay and T. Scollan. The vote was Maclay (Liberal-Conservative – whatever that means) 20,810; Scollan (Labour) 17,780; majority 3,030. For a time Scollan was leading; but, later, Maclay pulled ahead. The procedure is:- First, the absent (postal) votes are opened and the ballot papers placed in a box. Then all the ballot-papers are counted, and checked against the ballot-paper account, a return compiled from the returns made by the individual presiding officers. Then comes the second count, or separation of the votes cast for each candidate. The second stage is shorter, because, by then, the papers are in order. It began about noon. The Poll was a very heavy one, about 78%; Paisley was 84%, and Dundee, I see, 88%. Everything went very smoothly. I found both candidates and their agents most cooperative, and very courteous to each other. Indeed, from start to finish, the behaviour of everyone concerned was exemplary. My only criticism is of the superficial work of the polling agents. For a time, they watched the count, but, when refreshments became available, they left the count to look after itself. Apart from a cup of tea and three buns I had nothing to eat from 8.15 a.m. until 7 p.m. at night, when I went out to Gourock for the night. I signed the three Parliamentary returns before leaving. Mr. Millar, who had done yeoman service, had no voice left when I departed.

Today, at 9.30 I crossed to Dunoon by the *Loch Fyne*. The election is now settled. Labour has an absolute majority, but so small that it is virtually unworkable. Another General Election seems likely – not very far off.

At Dunoon, we spent the morning opening the postal ballot envelopes – some 888 of them. It was a picnic after Renfrew. I took the bus to Innellan, where I had tea, and then caught the *Loch Fyne* returning from Ardrishaig. On board were the Argyll ballot boxes returning from Colonsay, Jura and the Kyles of Bute. There were, it turned out, two messengers in charge, but they were pretty trusting. I saw no sign of them till near Dunoon Pier. I had only to drop one ballot-box overboard, and the Argyll Election would have been invalidated. It was a perfect day – sunny, clear, and bracing; two ships were engaged in trials off the Cloch and Wemyss Bay.

In Renfrew, the chief causes of rejected votes were:- failure to design witnesses in postal vote identity declarations; failure to stamp ballot-papers; insertion of voters' registration numbers on ballot-papers; and voting for both or neither candidate. Very occasionally, there was writing on the paper, as on one: 'a vote for Scottish nationalism' (and no vote marked at all).

27th February 1950

This morning we began the Argyll count at Dunoon Sheriff Court at 9 a.m., finished the first count shortly after noon, and reached the declaration of the poll about 2.30 p.m. The whole proceedings were similar to those at Paisley, only more 'Hielan' '. I announced the result in the Sheriff Courtroom – where the count took place – and then to the assembled multitude waiting outside – from the window of the Sheriff's retiring room. The Conservative won by 19,000 votes, to Labour's 9,000, with the horticulturist home-ruler third with 490 votes. Afterwards we sat in the lounge of McColl's Hotel, and listened to the three last Scottish results: Argyll, Inverness, and Orkney and Shetland. Jim Aikman Smith (from Campbeltown) accompanied me. After the count, too, I went on the bench and fined an Irish labourer £10 for breaking plate-glass windows at Kames by throwing stones in a drunken orgy. Labour now has an overall majority of only 7, the smallest (apart from the minority Labour Governments of 1924 and 1929) on record in the last century.

26th March 1950

Yesterday the Round Table gave a lunch in the Scotia Hotel to George Morton on attaining his eightieth birthday (which occurred on 1st February). Jock Cameron as Dean presided. George Morton sat on his right and myself on his left. At the other end of the table, James Walker, as Vice-Dean, was croupier, with Blades on his right, and John Wheatley, as Lord Advocate, on his left. There were also pres-ent:- T.P. McDonald (who, self-effacingly, had made the arrangements); John Wilson (whose forte is selecting suitable quota-tions to describe the speakers); James Crawford; F.C. Watt; G.S. Reid (now Sheriff-substitute at Ayr); Harald Leslie and J.J. Cunningham (the last two not strictly members of the Round Table, but close friends of it). Blades proposed George Morton's health; and George replied; John Wheatley, the Dean's health, to which the Dean replied. Apart from 'The King', these were all the toasts. The lunch began at 12.45 and ended at 5.15 p.m. The menu bore on the outside:-

> With his white hair unbonneted
> the stout old Sheriff comes (from Macaulay's *Armada*)

Blades had the caption: 'Well languag'd Daniel' and George: 'Sir, I perceive you are a vile Whig!' (Dr. Johnson).

George said it was now fifty-five years since he came to the Bar.

He came of bucolic stock, and (he said) he had, perhaps, a bucolic intellect. What turned his mind away from the agriculture of his yeomen ancestors was his reading, as a boy, a romantic tale in a local newspaper, about Fergus the Foundling who rose, like Dick Whittington, to become an advocate. In Lanarkshire, none of his acquaintances had ever heard of Parliament House, or John Inglis, who then presided there. But they all knew Lanark Small Debt Court, and one day, a great hero, the Sheriff-substitute, was pointed out to him. Little did he think that he would still be at Parliament House in his eightieth year, and receive a lunch from friends, few of whom were even born when he came to the Bar. In his fifty-five years, there had been little change in the traditions of the Bar, though its work had changed and expanded. The chief change he noticed was the greater courtesy of the judges. When he came to the Bar, he received nothing but courtesy in the First Division and Outer House, but, in the Second Division, Young and Trayner, especially the latter, made things very difficult for counsel. As he thanked us in his closing words, he broke down and was unable to finish. A more tolerant and noble character there is not to be found on the floor of Parliament Hall just now.

This week, we have entertained an Italian, Signor Teofilo Pons (from near Torre Pellice), a Frenchman, M. Monod (from Cannes), and a German, Dr. Bleibtreu (from Dusseldorf). The last is a legal adviser to the German Confessional Church. He has been a judge twice (deposed the first time by the Nazis) and defended Karl Barth, when he was prosecuted by the Nazis. I was asked, as Procurator, to show him hospitality, and after having him to dinner, took him next day to the Courts, and today to our Communion service in St. George's West, after which I introduced him to our Kirk Session. He was a most charming, vivacious and friendly man, and impressed all who met him. I was indeed proud to show him so much that signified Scotland at its very best. He said he was greatly moved by it all.

This week, and next, I conduct two Government Enquiries, the first, at Edinburgh, into a United Kingdom Wool Marketing Scheme; the second, at Lerwick, into a similar scheme for Shetland.

10th April 1950

On Monday 3rd April, with Ella, Rosemary and Mlle Monod (who is at present staying with us) set off for Lerwick. Alison is spending two months in France just now, and so was not with us. We went by train to Aberdeen, and there caught the SS *St. Clair* for Lerwick. It was a rough night, though towards morning the weather moderated. Not for long (if ever) have so many counsel gone to Shetland. The Dean (Jock Cameron) and Brand were for promotion of the Scheme; and T.P. McDonald and David Anderson for objectors thereto. I was, I think, the only one to survive unscathed by *mal de mer*. The light failed near Peterhead, and when I looked out at 5 a.m. we were abreast of the two lights of Fair Isle. Later I got my first real glimpse of Lerwick Harbour (last summer it was shrouded in mist). Noss Head is a magnificent cliff seen from the south, facing to the east as Foula faces to the west. We put up at the Queen's Hotel, where there were also staying Mr. Hunter and Mr. Davidson, my assessors from the Department of Agriculture and various witnesses at the Enquiry. Our host, Mr. Thomason, was most frank and hospitable, and two black-haired Shetland girls – like Minna and Brenda – waited on us. On the afternoon of Tuesday 4th, I was driven by Mr. Hunter, Mr. Davidson and a Mr. Smith, also of the Department, by Dales Voe, Tingwall, Whiteness, Weisdale, Aith and Voe and back by the main north road to Lerwick. We saw, in the distance, both Foula and Fair Isle and many of the scraggy Shetland sheep, whose precious wool has such a value to the island. Wednesday 5th and Thursday 6th were occupied with the inquiry. On Friday 7th, two young inspectors of the Department of Agriculture, Messrs. Esslemont and Paterson, motored Ella and myself to Brae and Sullom Voe, where, while they inspected a holding which was being improved by aid of a hill-farming subsidy, Ella and I walked along the side of Sullom Voe back to Brae, where Atlantic and North Sea are divided only by a narrow strip of land, across which a biting wind was blowing. In the evening, we went to the Wallaces for dinner. Rob Wallace did a wonderful work entertaining each week the navy, army and air force to dinner through the war. His guests included Lord Mountbatten, Prince Olav, and the Earl of Cork and Orrery, a fire-eater about whom he had many amusing stories. Rob claims to have suggested the use of Sullom Voe as a seaplane base, for, at an early stage, he pointed out that it was the only stretch of water in Shetland where seaplanes could land and take off in all weathers. Rob's house is situated at the south-west of Lerwick South Bay. The road to it is sometimes washed away, and even on our visit the sea was high. Bressay Lighthouse shone across the water. Rob keeps a diary of all his dinners – the menus and the list of guests – but he does not take the guests' autographs.

On Saturday 8th, we hired a car and drove over to Scalloway. It is one of the most attractive corners in the island – a harbour dotted with islands, the old seventeenth century castle of Patrick Stuart, with peculiarly fine turrets, a neat little yacht-builder's premises (where we saw a yacht on Shetland lines being built for Jock Cameron), the jetty where Prince Olav landed in the last war, in 1942, and the straggly village street, the fishing smacks in the bay. From Scalloway, we went up the Tingwall valley, stopping first to see the site of the old lawcourt or lawting.

My reading on this trip of Scott's Diary of his journey to the Lighthouses reminds me that he mentions 'Twaggers'. The name still survives in 'Twagoes Road', Lerwick. This means 'the two inlets', as 'wick' is a bay, and 'voe' a fjord. 'Point of Scotland' means 'Point of Scattland', and to this day common grazings in Shetland are referred to as 'scattald' – the grazings being allocated annually by a committee of crofters of the township who for this purpose elect their own chairman or grazings constable. On the outskirts of Lerwick, we could still see the tank obstacles and booby traps forming part of its perimeter defences. The Radar masts still stand, but most of the equipment has been pilfered, both there and at the air station at Sullom Voe.

16th April 1950

On the 14th, I paid my monthly visit to London, and, after a long sederunt lasting to 1.50 p.m., took Sir Basil Gibson and Mr. Rutherford to lunch at the Caledonian Club and then Mr. Sheldrake and I paid a visit to the Zoo to see 'Brumas' the baby polar bear. Its mother was almost human in her care for her baby. In the evening, four of us returned to King's Cross together in a taxi. Mr. Fraser, one of the party, senior partner of Fraser, Stodart and Ballingall, told me an amusing story about the Earl of Elgin. He says he always gets out the wrong side of the taxi, hoping that, by the time he reaches the pavement, some one else will have paid the fare! I met Lord Crawford on the platform. As he is the present Chairman of the Library Trustees, I work with him. He has very great charm, knowledge, and ability, and looks every inch an Earl. But it is a disadvantage to anyone not to have to work for his living. The sunrise over the Berwickshire coast, on a frosty morning, as we returned home, was unforgettable. The same evening Ella and I attended a farewell reception of the retiring French Consul, M. Philippe Monod, cousin of our Mademoiselle, and a member of the famous French Protestant family.

29th April 1950

This week I acted as Commissioner at Ayr on behalf of the Minister of Civil Aviation, Lord Pakenham, to hear objections by Scottish Aviation Limited (the owners of Prestwick aerodrome, or at least most of it) to a proposed compulsory purchase order issued by the Minister. This is the second of this type of hearing which I have heard – the first being the Glenrothes New Town Order. The procedure for such hearings has been laid down by the House of Lords in Franklin v. Minister of Town and Country Planning [1948] A.C. 87; and the Commissioner simply hears what the objectors have to say; and summarises and evaluates their evidence in his Report. There was a public outcry that the Minister did not order a public local inquiry, and certainly for a national issue of this kind he should, in my view, have done so, and has only done him harm and exposed himself to criticism by the alternative adopted.

The chief witness for the Objectors was Wing-Commander D.F. McIntyre. He is a remarkable man, with much physical courage and also intellectual drive and imagination. He and the Duke of Hamilton were the first airmen to fly over Mount Everest. They flew separately, in case one did not come back. He told me that the plane's speed was only about 120 m.p.h. and the wind was 140 m.p.h. He is a man of about forty-four, but his hair is prematurely white, no doubt with his air experiences. After the inquiry, we visited the Airport. I spent half-an-hour in the Control Tower and saw a Boeing stratocruiser from America arrive and land. I also inspected all the workshop buildings and saw two planes being fitted out for King Ibn Saud, and a wooden model of an atomic bomb, which was to be fitted for experimental purposes to another aeroplane.

In my view, in all these quasi-judicial tribunals, there should be evidence on both sides and cross-examination, and the report of the Commissioner should be published. Recently, I succeeded in getting procedure taken by Gordon Thomson, as Commissioner in the Ayr Police Amalgamation Inquiry, set aside, on the ground that though there was a public inquiry, government witnesses had been examined by the Commissioner without Ayr Burgh being allowed to cross-examine them. But the case which has recently aroused most controversy is the Public Inquiry into the disaster to the Dutch K.L.M. plane near Prestwick. T.P. McDonald, the Commissioner, found the Ministry officials partly to blame, and Lord Pakenham intimated, without giving any reasons upon the evidence, that he was not prepared to accept this finding. T.P. McDonald wrote a stiff letter in reply, and, it was only after a reprimand by the Prime Minister and an apology in Parliament, that Lord Pakenham was left in office.

2nd June 1950

The General Assembly has just ended, on 31st May. We had as our guest the Rev. Dr. Donald Caskie, of Paris. He comes from Islay, and is of a happy temperament, always cheery. His war record is most remarkable. He remained in France and was instrumental in enabling many British escaped prisoners to find their way to Spain. He was appointed Professor of English at Grenoble, and under this guise was able to carry on his resistance work for a time till he was imprisoned himself. One day, he had two British soldiers in hiding. They wanted to attend his service, but to do so openly would have risked their lives and his. He tried to dissuade them, but, when they persisted, he arranged to hide them in the gallery of the church, to which no-one else would have access. They were to lie on the floor, and simply listen to the service. By one of those curious chances, the Old Testament lesson was from Psalm 27, and, before he realised, Donald Caskie was reading: 'For in the time of trouble he shall hide me in his pavilion; in the secret of his tabernacle shall he hide me.' (v. 5) His eyes rose to the gallery, and there were the heads of the two Tommies peeping over, winking at him. With difficulty in keeping his face straight, he continued the lesson.

He was imprisoned first by the Germans, and then, in San Remo, by the Italians. When he saw my watercolour of the Madonna della Costa, he remarked: 'I could just catch a glimpse of it from my prison window.' Through four summer months, he was fed on bread and water, until he became so weak that he was almost unconscious of the transition from day to night. He had nothing to do, nothing to read, and while he still retained his strength, he used to close his eyes, imagine himself arriving in Edinburgh, walking along Princes Street, climbing to the Castle, descending to Holyrood, visiting his friends, and so passed many hours of solitary confinement. Outside, a French prisoner was made to march to and fro barefoot, without food, for four days, with a bayonet at his back. One night, Donald Caskie succeeded in passing a tiny portion of bread through the keyhole to this man. Later, when he repeated the operation, the Italians discovered him doing it, and nearly shot him.

Tonight Arthur Clark rang me up to say that he is amusing himself about the theory that Shakespeare may have visited Scotland. The particular point which had attracted him was that a Scots Act of 1587 created the offence of 'murder under trust' (which later figured prominently in the Massacre of Glencoe); and he wondered whether Shakespeare's reference to a 'double trust' in *Macbeth* might not indicate his knowledge of this crime.

20th June 1950

A fortnight ago, Ella and I set out on a wonderful itinerary. On Wednesday 7th, accompanied by Dr. Thomas Caldwell, Principal Clerk of the Assembly, we motored up to Oban. Next day, the 8th, we were joined by Tom Taylor, who as Principal of Aberdeen University, is also one of the Iona Cathedral Trustees. We all along with Chalmers (Sheriff at Oban) visited the new Roman Catholic Cathedral, the full length of which has been opened up since last summer. It is very impressive, except that the wall behind the main altar is rather heavy, and the roughness of the stone there is too obvious. At 1.30, we set off in the Lochinver for Craignure, accompanied also by Principal and Mrs. Duncan of St. Mary's, St. Andrews, Nevile Davidson of Glasgow Cathedral, and Mr. Anderson, the depute-Clerk to the Iona Cathedral Trustees. We were transhipped along with a young calf and cartons of Beattie's Bread on to the landing boat at Craignure, and so I set foot on Mull for the first time in forty-four years (my last time in Mull was when we spent two months in Salen when I was six). The rhododendrons along the Mull shore and near Duart gave the appearance of a garden. A specially-chartered bus took this gay party of ecclesiastics, lay men and camp followers through Glenmore (where scarce a house is to be seen) to Loch Scridain. Here we found a postal van waiting for the lifting of letters at a post-box, and the local postman filling in time by marching up and down with his bagpipes. Through Pennyghail, and Bunessan (where lived a hymn-writer of one of our new hymns) to Fionnphort we came, and then, after a short wait, we were carried by ferry to Iona. We stayed in the St. Columba Hotel, with the Taylors and Duncans and Nevile Davidson. It is kept by a brother of Professor Tindal. We expected an evening service in the Abbey, but there was none. Instead, George MacLeod took us up the tower from which we had a fine view. Earlier Ella and I climbed Dun-I. It takes less than an hour to ascend and descend. We saw our old friend the Dutchman's Cap. The island, and also Mull, is full of yellow irises.

On the 9th – St. Columba's Day – we had a full programme. First, we held a trust meeting. Then, at 11.00, the Trustees perambulated the buildings along with officials of the Ancient Monuments Commission from London and Edinburgh, Mr. O'Neil and Mr. Cruden. Lunch followed in the refectory – just completed. At 5.00, we resumed our trust meeting. At 8.00 there was a St. Columba Day service at which Nevile Davidson preached. At 9.00, we attended a sing-song for some Borstal Boys who were spending the night in the huts belonging to the Iona Community. The best item was one in which the whole audience began murmuring 'swish-swish-swish' (the waves lapping against the quay, as the troop-ship leaves for Hong-Kong). Then we all struck up the 'British Grenadiers' during the singing of which three Borstal Boys rapped out 'Eyes right – eyes front – eyes right! – eyes front! – eyes right! – eyes front!' At this point Tom Taylor (playing the role of general) called out by arrangement in the voice of Colonel Blimp 'Jolly fine show' – whereat the whole audience switched suddenly over to 'Auld Lang Syne' – to indicate the departure of the ship. One side then played the role of troops aboard; the other side, that of relatives waving good-bye; each acted their appropriate part; the singing gradually died down; and the proceedings ended with 'swish-swish-swish' of the waves at sea! After the sing-song, I talked alone with George MacLeod, far on into the night.

On the 10th, we walked out to the north end of the island, joining the Duncans there – where we saw the distant steamer approaching Staffa on its way to Iona. In the afternoon, the Duncans saw us off, and we and the Taylors with Mrs. Milne, a friend of theirs, returned through the Torran Rocks and by the south of Mull to Oban. Alison, Rosemary and Mlle. Monod, who had come from Edinburgh, were waiting for us at the pier, and we took the Taylors and Mrs. Milne with us for dinner, after which they left on the first stage of their return journey to Aberdeen.

22nd June 1950

Today T.P. McDonald showed me Sir Walter Scott's bar fee-book, which as Keeper of the Advocate's Library, T.P. had brought up from Abbotsford. It is a small leather note-book, very neatly kept. The annual aggregates show a small, though fairly steady, increase over the eleven years, to, I think 1803, when the book ends, but he never made more than about 250 guineas, which, I suppose, would be now at least three times that amount. There is no fee exceeding five guineas and most are single guineas. At the end of each year is a sum of fees received through his father.

To return to my account of our Argyllshire visit, on the 11th – Sunday – in the afternoon we crossed Connel Bridge to the north side of Loch Etive, then passed Ardchattan Priory, and climbed over the neck of land to Loch Creran. It was a broiling day, and the whins, and especially the rhododendrons, were quite unforgettable. We travelled past a mile of them on either side of the road at Barcaldine, and then finished with tea at Eriska. Later we called – Ella, Alison and I – at the Chalmers, at Kilbowie, where we sat out on the lawn enjoying the most superb view of Oban and the hills behind. Through a gap in the near hillocks beside Dunollie, there emerges a high distant peak, which would seem to be either Bidean-nam-Bian, or some mountain close to it.

On the 12th we met with a sudden emergency. Rosemary was diagnosed to have measles; the doctor came, and the best thing seemed to me to take her straight home; so Ella, Alison and I motored her home to Edinburgh. Then Alison and I returned to Oban. We left Oban at 10.45 a.m. and were back at 7.30 having spent from 3 to 3.30 p.m. in Edinburgh – quick time for 250 miles. It was a broiling day, but Rosemary was none the worse.

On the 13th, I set off alone for Campbeltown. The view south was superb in its variety – tumbling rocks and glens spring out on sudden seascapes. Kilmelford (where I stayed with Mother and Dad [when Moderator] in 1921), Arduaine (near where I stopped for lunch), more magnificent rhododendrons between Ardrishaig and Tarbert, and finally seals and cormorants disporting themselves south of Bellochantuy. I reached Campbeltown about 4.00, and found the town bedecked with bunting to celebrate its 250th anniversary. After tea with the Aikman Smiths, Jim took me to watch an exhibition golf-match (part of the ceremonies) at Machrihanish.

The 14th was a day of celebrations. I began by a five minutes' sitting in the Sheriff Court. Then we inspected two exhibitions – one containing a magnificent Mactaggart sea-scape just presented by his daughter to the Burgh, and also the Brooch presented by Bruce to the McNeils of Lossil, the other containing fine scale models of fishing smacks and a tug. At 1.25, Jim and I robed at the Sheriff Court, and, from there, proceeded in state (I wearing full-bottomed wig), preceded by a Police Inspector, to the Town Hall. Here, we were marshalled into the larger procession, I on the Provost's right, the Duke of Argyll on his left. The Provost of Campbeltown has only a chain of office, and no robes. But Provost Greenlees, who has a sense of humour (shown by his carrying on the profession of Stockbroker in the 'Wee Toon') had hired a fine ermine purple and black gown from a theatrical supplier in Glasgow. In a few minutes, the pipe band arrived; we formed up; and then off we marched to 'The Campbells are coming' – down to the cross. Here, some six of us ascended a red-carpeted platform. The Provost made a capital speech, on the history of the Burgh, prepared by Father Webb. The Town-Clerk read the Charter (translated) in three instalments, punctuated by specially composed fanfares. Jim Aikman Smith gave sasine with a twig, earth and stone (facetiously said to be 'Machrihanish coal'). The Provost accepted sasine. The Duke spoke. We sang the Old 100th. Prayer was offered and then we descended to the street to re-form as a procession. The only hitches were that the Provost almost dropped the three symbols of sasine; they were on a tray, and very nearly fell off; and the framer of the programme had forgotten to include the National Anthem. Back in the Town Hall, we had sherry, and the guests signed the visitors' book, I first, as Sheriff. Then Jim and I had our own little procession back to the Sheriff Court, where our obliging Inspector escort took our photographs. Then we returned to Duncarnoch, from where we saw the flag-bedecked *Duchess of Hamilton* leaving the harbour. On our way to the house, we called on Dr. Wylie Blue, who had achieved an all-time record in preaching for 56 minutes at the previous Sunday's civic service. To use his own expression, it was no doubt a 'variorum discourse', but there is something very lovable about him. In the evening, we turned to have dinner with the Provost and his wife and the Duke at the Argyll Arms, and from there went on to a civic reception at which I gave the toast of the Burgh, which two years ago I enlarged to twice its former size. I met all the celebrities of the county.

On the 15th I motored back to Edinburgh, and at once joined the Church of Scotland-Church of England Conference at the Roxburghe Hotel, which had started on the previous evening. The delegations were the same as at Durham, except that Dr. C.W.G. Taylor was present instead of Tom Torrance. I arrived in time for dinner which I had with Manson, Derby and Durham; we had a most lively conversation.

22nd July 1950 (Saturday)

I am writing this off the Mull of Galloway in the *Pharos*. The Court of Session term, prolonged under the new dispensation, does not end till the middle of next week; for the first time, the *Pharos* has left on the inspection cruise before the end of term. I just managed to finish my work yesterday afternoon. I had a two day case in Court, and another yesterday which however settled. I wrote two judgments in Greenock and Paisley appeals, a final finding in an arbitration, and I do not know how many opinions. I also attended a meeting of the Inter-Church Relations Committee, where Manson gave a report of the Anglican conversations. Supported by Torrance and myself, he received the support of the Committee to our further programme, after a certain amount of initial despair at the prospect of any immediate step being possible. The Church of Scotland is prepared for both inter-communion and interchange of pulpits, but the Anglicans are scarcely ready to widen their very limited measures for each at all. Not unnaturally the C. of S. ministers not engaged in the discussions wonder if anything will come of them. But even if the immediate way is barred, it would be a calamity if the discussions were to end. Maconochie, who is on the voyage with me and who has been Chancellor of the Diocese of Edinburgh, is entirely sympathetic with our side's difficulty, and considers that the fault is on the side of his own clergy. He considers Burn-Murdoch and the Bishop of Brechin both too high.

We had our termly celebration at the Round Table yesterday. We fine each other 1/- every time we both talk 'shop' and the proceeds, collected by John Wilson, go to provide one or two bottles of sloe gin and a bottle of orangeade at the end of the term. Another party of a different form took place later – the Birnams' sherry party, held in their beautiful house and garden at Colinton Road. He is the soul of common sense; she a vivacious outgoing nature; they always give the impression of being a very happy couple. I know he has a kind side to me; and she has too – when I arrived, she first kissed Ella and then – to my surprise – me!

This morning, I left from Waverley at 8.10 a.m. with Jack Lillie and Charles Milne. Harold met us in Glasgow and motored us to St. Enoch's, where we caught the 10.15 a.m. train for Ardrossan. Here the *Pharos* and the other Commissioners (who had come by car) were awaiting us. We are the same party as last year. Lady Morton had come to see George off (eighty years old now!). Two little Gordon Thomsons were there to give their father a send-off. We had to wait a few minutes till the *Lady Killarney* (of Liverpool), with a cargo of tourists for the Outer Isles, berthed – her hull is now painted green (it was yellow when we saw her at Oban last year) and is a rather cloying colour. We were hardly past the Harbour Bar, before the 'waters were on the table'. When we returned to deck, Arran lay on our starboard, and Ayr to our port. The Firth was calm, and the day much finer than we could have hoped. Just after lunch, we passed to the East of Ailsa Craig, behind which lay Kintyre, a clear blue. There was little traffic, a few fishing smacks, one cargo-ship, two submarines, one yacht, a tanker – but, quaintly, there sailed past us a little child's yacht, bound from Ireland to the Ayrshire coast!

23rd July 1950

At the end of June, I stayed in Aberdeen with the Taylors for the Law Orals. It would have caused no small delight to some people to see the last and present Sheriffs of Argyll playing duets on the Chanonry Lodge piano, chiefly slow movements from the symphonies – Mozart, Beethoven, and also Elgar's Enigma Variations. We decided that the only person who would have enjoyed the performance was the Sheriff Clerk of Argyll, himself, who is stone deaf!

Some days ago I paid a visit to our old friend Mr. J.W. Somerville, who was then dying of cancer. He was able to tell me that his nurse was a Miss Hately, and that she had told him that her grandfather was one of the last precentors of Free St. George's, and the author of the beautiful Psalm Tune 'Leuchars' used for Ps. 143. [*Thomas Leger-wood Hately 1815–67, now Hymn 70, tune (ii) - Ed.*]

In connection with proposals for a new War Memorial Chapel in St. Giles', which will involve removing John Knox's statue from its present position in the Albany Aisle and perhaps putting it outside, in Parliament Square, I had to look into the whole constitution of the authorities which control St. Giles'. They have been the Corporation; the Edinburgh Ecclesiastical Commissioners; the Managing Board; the General Trustees; the Kirk Session. The last three still divide the control, and there are different controls for different portions of the building, dating, historically, from the period before 1874, when the nave was occupied by West St. Giles' (or New North) congregation, and an earlier period when the South Transept was occupied by the Old Kirk. In dealing with the question, which involves a study of private acts since 1870 and some seven agreements affecting the Managing Board alone, I wrote my longest opinion ever. Controversy has arisen chiefly because 'structural alteration' is forbidden in the portion formerly occupied by West St. Giles' (under one of the Agreements) and a question has arisen as to whether certain of the changes proposed – the removal of John Knox, the alteration of pavement tiles, railings, wall tablets, and the like – involve 'structural alteration'. The type of 'structural alteration' previously contemplated is undoubtedly the partitioning of the nave once more into a separate church. I took the view that the particular alterations were not 'structural', since they did not materially affect the main fabric. Behind the dispute, there lies the fact that, whereas hitherto the Lord President has been Chairman of the Managing Board, after Normand's departure for London, Tommy Cooper was not selected, but instead Dr. Warr himself became Chairman, which Cooper does not like.

I give here one curious example of the President's methods. Recently, John Mitchell (the Principal Clerk of Session) told me that the President was sending me a letter about the National Library, and was sending a copy of it to Lord Crawford as Chairman of the Trustees. I said: 'Well, if it is coming to me, could you let me see a copy of it?' (I was up at Parliament House at the time). Mitchell showed me it. It contained certain criticisms, chiefly of Dobie, the Librarian, whom Cooper does not like. I thought no more about it, but the principal letter not having reached me, some days later I spoke to Mitchell, and remarked: 'That letter has never reached me.' 'No,' replied Mitchell, 'but the extraordinary thing is that the President has sent the copy of it to Lord Crawford. I pointed this out to the President, whereupon he said, "I shall be seeing Philip, to speak to."' This sending of a copy, but not the principal, seemed to me open to serious mis-interpretation; so, the National Library Trustees half-yearly meeting taking place shortly after, I took Crawford aside and had a word with him. He said: 'Yes, I have received the copy.' 'Well,' said I, 'I have never been sent the principal!' Crawford: 'The President put at the foot of the copy that he hadn't yet sent the principal, because you were at the time away from Edinburgh.' I replied: 'I was in Greenock for a day!' Lord Crawford was vastly entertained. *[I have not received the principal to this day! 9th June 1954]*

I heard an amusing story on the last day of Session about Cooper when he was Lord Advocate, and Millar Craig, then his Legal Secretary. One afternoon, Millar Craig returned to Dover House late from lunch. Lord Advocate: 'You're late coming back.' Millar Craig: 'I was having my hair cut.' L.A.: 'What – in office hours?' Millar Craig: 'Yes – it grows in office hours.' L.A.: 'Only part of it.' Millar Craig: 'Yes, Lord Advocate – but only part of it was cut off!!'

A good example of the President's lack of tact occurred recently at the Sheriff Court Rules Council. There were two alternative proposals for a change in the procedure relating to adjustment of pleadings – a major and a minor change. The President, who wanted to show that he was in favour of the major change, but could never induce the other judges to accept it: 'You know, my colleagues are such a lot of crusted old Tories that I could never get this proposal through!'

4th August 1950

I landed at Oban shortly after 8 a.m., and, having already arranged to leave my car in Oban, motored to Ord, Skye, to join Ella and the family. At the end of the voyage, I recorded 18 stone 5 lbs! As some wit remarked: 'The lighthouse inspection cruise would be quite perfect, if one could leave out the lighthouses!'

26th August 1950

Our fortnight at Ord House was a huge success. You approach it by five miles of the worst of roads, over a moor, past a tiny loch, down a gully, and finally along the Ord Burn. Here, once were houses accommodating sixty or seventy souls. The crofters lived an incredibly hard life, working for the farmer for a pittance during the day, and then carrying seaweed up to till their own cabbage-patches in the evening. There were no clearances on this side of Loch Eishort. The people just silently left. In the ruined cottages, a baby's cot, a spinning wheel and other furniture are still to be seen – it was cheaper not to remove them, when the houses were vacated. There were clearances across the loch. As Mr. Nicholson, the farmer, said to me: 'There might still be clearances even yet, but for the change in public opinion.'

Ord House is where Alexander Smith wrote: 'A Summer in Skye'. It is an old farmhouse with a fine garden (not kept in order) full of fuchsia, red-currants (as large as grapes) and a high palm tree. It commands the most glorious view of the whole range of the Coolins, as well as Blaven and the Red Coolin. One evening we crossed the bay – a fifty minutes' motor-boat sail – to the Spar Cave, once visited by Walter Scott – comparable with Cheddar Gorge – containing a steep wall of wet basalt, which we climbed, I with great difficulty. On the return journey, our boatman asked the company for a song, and we sang the whole way across. The sound on the darkening waters was very lovely. Another day, we visited Elgol (my last visit was in 1919); and another day, we went to Portree.

On the two Sundays, we crossed to the little church at Isle Oronsay. A Dr. Morrison, formerly of Kilmaurs, was preaching there. They had no organist, so I stood into the breach; the top notes of the organ scarcely sounded. Another afternoon, at Armadale, we visited Kilmore Church, and saw a memorial to J.A. Macdonald, the one advocate who was killed in the second World War. He was a Fascist before the War, and used to sell fascist newspapers in a black shirt at the foot of the Mound; he met his death in North Africa, strangely, fighting the fascist armies of Italy. He was a quiet pleasant fellow, the younger brother of the present Lord Macdonald; there was a tragic irony in his fate.

I learned that the Moderator, Principal Hugh Watt, was staying nearby. I called for him, but he was out. Next day, when the Ord Burn was in spate, we unexpectedly came across him as we were motoring up the Glen on our way to Elgol. He was preparing to fish the burn. Later, on our return, we met him again: he had taken eighty trout, but 'put them back into the burn because they were so small'. His chaplain (and son-in-law) G.T.H. Reid of Claremont, Glasgow, was fishing further down the Glen. They both, with Mrs. Reid and one Reid child, came for tea to Ord next day.

Now we are at Oban, and Ella and I have just returned from a night at Dunoon, where the Cowal Games were held yesterday. The occasion of our going was that the Prime Minister and Mrs. Attlee were visiting the games, and attending a dinner afterwards. We stayed at the Marine Hotel, where they also were staying, and had breakfast this morning at the next table to them. We were introduced to him at the Games, and then attended the dinner (sixty guests) given by the Provost. I was a little surprised at the 'ordinariness' of Mr. Attlee. In a group, you would scarcely notice him, and, in the stray conversation which took place, I saw little sign of outstanding quality. He is without any magnetism, or the personality which one associates with a leading politician. His speech after dinner, however, showed quite a clever turn of humour. I found conversation with him difficult. No one in the hotel dining-room seemed almost aware of his presence. But that he appreciated such courtesy as one could give was shown by the way he came back this morning into the dining-room, to say good-bye to me. I then went out to the doorstep to see him off. But not another person in the hotel went out. Whatever their politics, I think that this showed on the part of other guests a certain want of courtesy to a Prime Minister. It may seem a strange observation. But I felt just a little sorry for him. I found it difficult to accept him as

PROVOST E. F. WYATT

COMPLIMENTARY DINNER

to

The Rt. Hon. CLEMENT R. ATTLEE

P.C., C.H., F.R.S., M.P.

The Royal Marine Hotel
Hunters Quay
26th August, 1950   Argyll

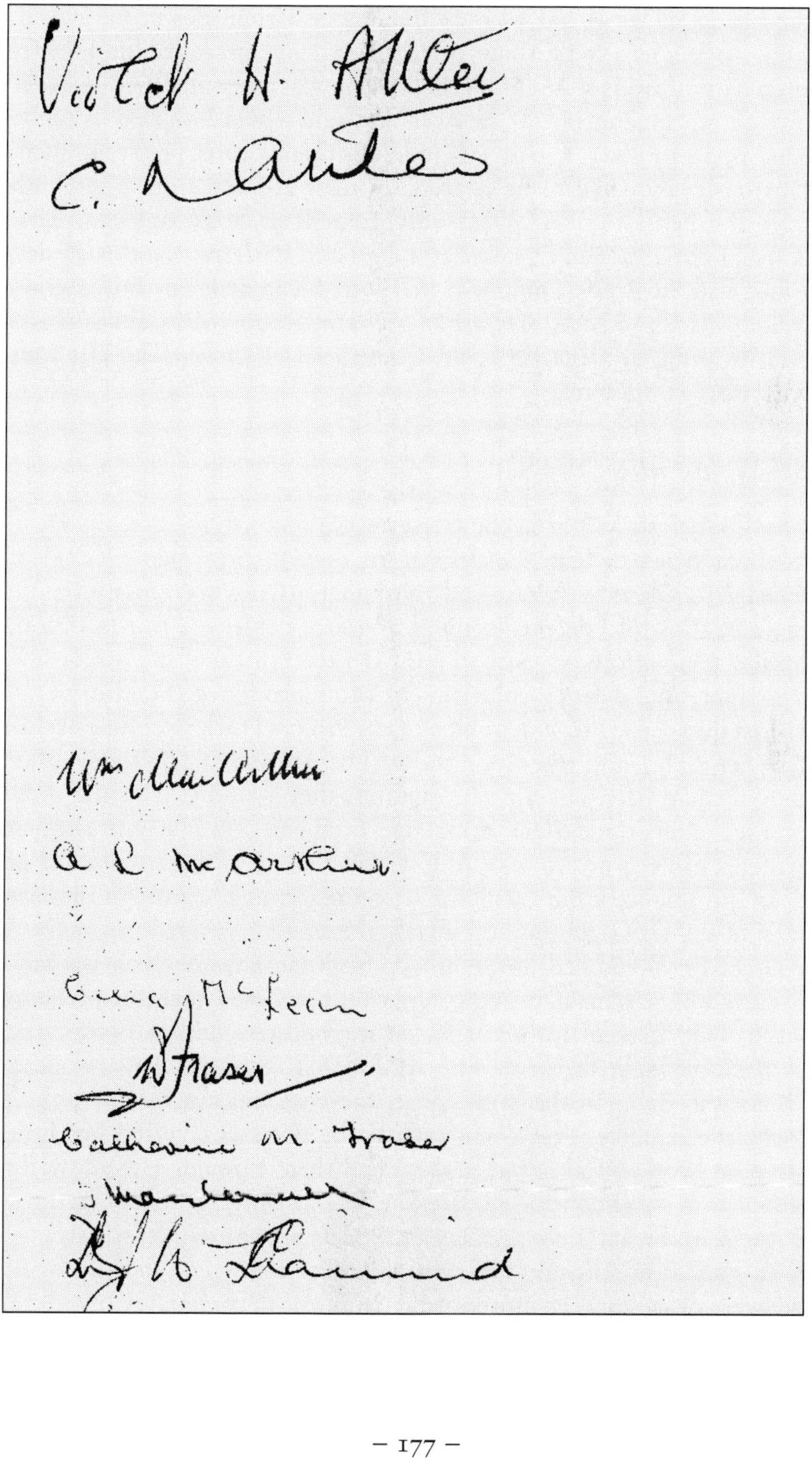

Violet H. Allan

C. D. Arthur

Wm MacArthur

A. L. McArthur

Ewa McLean

N Fraser

Catherine M. Fraser

J Mackenzie

A. H. Dermid

the fitting leader of one of the three greatest countries in the world. Mrs. Attlee was a pleasant person, with an attractive smile. Her simplicity of dress was most tasteful. She was presented with a silver brooch representing white heather and said a word or two in reply. The opportunities I had of judging them were pretty limited. Obviously, they had to be guarded in their conversation. They both took the lightest of breakfast, just grape-fruit, toast and tea. Mrs. Attlee, I noticed, read the *Sunday Times* and *Observer*. At the Games, I met also Sir Bruce Campbell, the Lord Lieutenant (already a good friend), Mr. and Mrs. Stewart of Acharn, Major MacCallum, M.P. and his wife, and the Earl and Countess of Balfour. The last four were also at the dinner.

8th September 1950

I have just returned from the Glasgow Circuit. On the 4th, the Dean nominated me to take the defence of one of three men accused of murder in Glasgow. I received the papers (Crown Precognitions in practice shown to defence counsel in murder cases – a fine tradition) on the same afternoon at 4.30 p.m. On the 5th I met my junior and the other four defence counsel. On the morning of the 6th, we all visited the locus, a tenement block near Princes Dock (Neptune Street, No. 151). The same afternoon the trial began, and at 1.30 today, after the jury had been out for 100 minutes, they found two of the three accused guilty (my client being one of them). As I was present at sentences in the previous case, I saw in four days three sentences of death pronounced. But the pathetic, yet redeeming, feature of the case was this:- The fight out of which the case developed began in a wretched two-roomed house at 151 Neptune Street, which we saw, occupied by parents and two young children. The father, the previous week, had 'beaten up' his wife, struck her arm with a bottle, and broken her right forearm. The wife's relatives decided to retaliate. Hence the fight. In the midst of it, the wife ran out for the police. Her little daughter, aged ten, one of the witnesses, seized her little sleeping brother and sister, and carried them through a window for safety to a neighbouring house. She was an intelligent, honest little witness, and what a courageous and lovely act she did. It was strange that, also, at my consultation with the other counsel on the 5th, while we were discussing the more sordid details of the crime, my own little Rosemary (now aged six) entered the study, and, in complete ignorance of the subject before us, came up and kissed me goodnight without a trace of self-consciousness in the presence of so many counsel. How much security had the one little child, and how little, the other.

While in Oban, I saw a fair amount of Mr. Lamb, the veteran Clerk of the Land Court, who was in the same hotel. He has 'sat under' five chairmen – Lord Kennedy, Lord St. Vigeans, Lord Macgregor Mitchell, Lord Murray (as he was then – now Lord Birnam) and Lord Gibson. I think that he would bracket Lord Birnam and Lord St. Vigeans first; then Lord Kennedy; then Macgregor Mitchell; and last Gibson. The first two were ideal; the third able, but not a good chairman; the fourth was a jury-pleader rather than a lawyer; and Gibson, well he's Gibson.

Mr. Lamb told me an amusing story about the Land Court's first visit to Wigtown – Gibson always likes a civic reception. He went out before breakfast on the morning of the hearing and seeing a postman enquired of him who was the Provost. 'Mrs. X,' the postman replied. Gibson then found where Mrs. X lived and sent Mr. Lamb to request her attendance. Mr. Lamb found her cleaning her brasses, but she agreed to come, when she had removed her curlers. The Court assembled, but the Provost was half-an-hour late in arriving. Mr. Lamb had primed her on the Land Court, its first chairman and its present one. In she came, and began by saying 'how glad she was to welcome the High Court of Justiciary on its first visit to Wigtown'. This mistake having been quickly corrected, she plunged on, and welcomed the Land Court and its chairman 'Mr. Kennedy'. 'Not Mr. Kennedy – Lord Gibson,' shouted Mr. Lamb. In a fluster, the Provost: 'Oh well, even if it's *Mr.* Gibson, still we welcome him just the same.' The title at last having been corrected, she subsided, and then Lord Gibson began a half-hour's oration in which he traced the connection of leading lawyers with the south-west of Scotland, beginning with Lord Stair and ending with himself!

At Oban, we visited some new places – Loch Sunart (which I knew at the top but not at the bottom); Lismore, where Mr. Carmichael, the parish minister, showed us over the remains of the Cathedral (three young Oxford undergraduates are engaged in excavations there); Beregonium or Selma, the seat of the Picts and Ossian, with an unrivalled view southwards through the Firth of Lorne; and the Isles of the Sea.

25th September 1950

Two evenings ago, we two made up a party of six at dinner in the N.B. Hotel, the others being Dover and Mrs. Wilson, and S.C. Roberts and Mrs. Roberts of Cambridge. It was Dover's invitation, and like all he does touched with unselfish kindliness. The Shakespearean and his wife, the Johnsonian and his wife, and Darby and Joan. It was Johnson's birthday, and we meant, but forgot, to drink his health. I first met S.C. Roberts two years ago when he delivered the Scott Lectures and then Dover had me to lunch with him. Each of us had lost our boy – perhaps that explains why one or two meetings made a friendship. S.C. Roberts afterwards sent me a memoir of his boy, and has inscribed it: 'To Randall Philip, who understands, from S.C. Roberts.' How I value books signed by a friend. Is it a sign of old age? Or of a heart grown more tender by loss? I've always had friends rather older than myself. I think the explanation is that, with being brought up in a home where there was always reverence, an old Scottish quality, I am at root serious minded. I fancy, all the same, that, if I left the Round Table, they would miss a good deal of fun. It is good to know oneself – if that is really possible. I know that what I lack in quickness of speech as compared with most of my fellows at the bar, I have made up with sounder judgment. Even as a student, other students used to consult me about their most intimate affairs. It is good to be trusted, however inadequate I know myself to be. Something of all this drew us three together. S.C. Roberts had just returned from the 500th anniversary commemoration of St. Salvator's College, St. Andrews, where he received an LL.D. The previous night, we had the Lionel Smiths at dinner. They too had returned from the same ceremony. Lionel Smith was representing All Souls; S.C. Roberts, Cambridge University and Pembroke College. He has had an unusual career. He became Secretary of the Syndics of the Cambridge Press, and Fellow of Pembroke College. A year or so ago (since my last meeting with him) he was elected Master of his College, and, then, by a strange coincidence, it was the turn of the Master of Pembroke to become Vice-Chancellor. So here is a Vice-Chancellor who has never done any academic teaching. He is none the worse of that. His boy was at one time Private Secretary to Attlee, and so we discussed the latter. His view is that he is very shy (Attlee told him so himself); and that he is better after a glass or two of wine. After dinner, we saw the Roberts off on the 10 p.m. train for London. The Vice-Chancellor was travelling in a 'third' sleeper! Then I drove the Dovers home. Their daughter, Carol, was jilted in her first engagement, and has broken off a second, having gone 'religious'. She is away just now trying to convert Motherwell. Through all the vicissitudes of this mortal life, Dover remains serene, a choice soul and a great Christian, and, though he would be the last to admit it, a holy and humble man of heart.

This month I have heard in St. George's West a series of sermons on the great temptations – Esau, Samson, David, Peter – from James Stewart. The church has been packed, and good it is, for he is not merely the first preacher of his day, but another humble Christian. I like to recall that I was a small boy at school three years or so behind him, and that Dad played a part in his entering the ministry. Today, I was at another full church, St. George's, and the funeral service of Dr. Taylor. He was not a lovable man; he had a nasty autocratic way and no humour; but he was a hard and efficient worker with a strong deep voice and an air of command which gave him considerable influence. On the Inter-Church Committee, however, he treated Manson, the chairman, like a schoolboy. Manson bore it like a Christian. Later this evening, meeting Tindal by chance, I went with him to the New Club, where we got into a spontaneous but deep discussion on Re-union. He is extraordinarily simple, unassuming and levelheaded.

26th September 1950

This afternoon, Rosemary (not yet 6½) came into my study with a bowl of flowers picked by herself from the garden, and laid it on my desk. It was her own idea, and she has done it before.

The other night, S.C. Roberts told us that a Norwegian Princess Astrid is starting at Lady Margaret Hall next week, at the same time as Alison.

10th October 1950

About ten days ago much interest was caused here, and later in Europe, by the unusual phenomenon of the sun and moon in turn appearing blue. Alison saw it, and came in quite excited; I did not. At the time, it was explained as caused by dust from forest fires in America. I was a little sceptical. Yesterday, Tommy Cooper told me that he had seen a spectrum produced by the Royal Society here, which showed quite clearly that it came from an atomic explosion in the United States. This was when I was lunching with him, Dover, A.H. Campbell and Dickinson before our National Library meeting.

Dover observed that 'once in a blue moon' is a saying which must have had some earlier factual basis – probably the result of an earthquake. He himself has pictures demonstrating the atmosphere effects produced by the earthquake in Krakatoa. They have stood over his study mantelpiece.

The Marquis of Bute's Kilmarnock Burns is for sale at the end of this month. It is not in the original covers but specially bound. Copies in the original covers are almost all in collections now. We decided to offer up to £1,000 for this copy for the National Library, which has not a copy.

Dover comes with me at the weekend to Oban, where on Monday I am installing Sir Bruce Campbell as a Honorary Sheriff-subsitute and doing certain other minor business.

Yesterday, I started employing a Secretary (Miss Johnston, to whom I was introduced by Sir John Falconer), as I have really too much to do, and have had so for about ten years now. Today, we heard that Alison had arrived safely at Lady Margaret Hall for her first term, and was in great form. She spent a night at Eton with the Birleys, and then next day they all motored to Oxford. When she arrived, she found lovely flowers waiting for her from Gordon's classmates, Jim Galbraith and David Symon. She already has decided to take up squash and punting.

14th October 1950

This has been a full week. In fact, just to give a picture of ten days:- on Sunday 1st October, I motored to Troon and addressed a meeting of the three Churches in the Concert Hall on the commemoration of the Reunion of the Churches twenty-one years ago on 2nd October 1929. That night I went on to Glasgow and next morning to Alloa. I spent three days in Alloa (going to and from it each day) at a planning inquiry at which I was commissioner. The question was whether the Coal Board was to get permission to work a mineral field from a new mine south of Alloa. £87,000,000 worth of coal (37,000,000 tons) are involved. The land is not very valuable agriculturally, but so flat that the mineral subsidence will cause permanent flooding from the Devon and affect roads and other services. Then on Wednesday afternoon, I went from Alloa to Lochearnhead, spending the night there. On the Thursday I attended a Probation Committee in Oban (my first experience of presiding over a local authority committee) and returned to Edinburgh. On Sunday, I repeated my Troon address – *mutatis mutandis* – at a similar meeting of three Edinburgh churches – St. Luke's, the Dean and St. Stephen's Comely Bank – held in the last church. This was the first time I had ever occupied a pulpit. On Monday, I had the National Library Standing Committee. Then on Tuesday I began the appeal in the Govan murder case before the Court of Criminal Appeal, consisting of Cooper, Carmont and Keith. There was some material for a real fight. The Crown could not prove which of the two Appellants struck the fatal blow, but had satisfied the jury that one or other did so, and that the two were acting in concert. I fought strenuously, without much encouragement from the bench, but in the end succeeded in compelling the Crown to reply. However, on Thursday the appeal was refused. After I had finished my argument and nothing was left but the Court's decision, on Wednesday night my solicitor here told me that it was my client who had actually struck the blow. Tommy Cooper seemed to think that, if a man was seen carrying beer bottles in his pocket on a Friday night in Govan, that was almost sufficient to justify the inference that he was a bottle-smasher. I countered by asking what would be the inference if the same occurred in Moray Place. Later, he referred to the Crown 'not bothering' to ask for a conviction against one appellant on an earlier charge. I demurred to the Crown's attitude not having been adopted with due responsibility. His comments during argument are often indiscreet, but, happily, he weighs his words differently in judgment. From the number of comments afterwards, I gathered that, at least, I had put up a good fight, and the Advocate (Wheatley) said to me: 'I couldn't help thinking that this case is a demonstration of one of the finest traditions of the Bar. Here you have given up infinite time and care to presenting these men's case for them.' I had, in fact, given up almost ten full days. I had a temperature on Monday evening before starting the case, through a heavy chill, but lived it down overnight thanks to Ella's ministrations.

Yesterday was the Edinburgh meeting of the Central Land Board. Tomorrow, off to Oban for a night and back next day. On the 18th, with Ella to Loch Sloy to see the Queen open the new Hydro-Electric Scheme. And all the time grinding out opinions, a lecture for Aberdeen, half-a-dozen dinner speeches, two new papers for Societies, not to mention many minor activities.

16th October 1950

Yesterday (Sunday) morning, Dover and I set off for Oban. We started in sunshine, but when we crossed the Highland Line, three wisps of cloud at times veiled the sun. This only added to the beauty, for shafts of sunshine broke through, making the russet browns of the bracken burn golden brown. We saw two rainbows, gloriously bright, and so close that we could almost touch the foot of them. We lunched at Crianlarich, and there met Dr. Miller now of Bunessan, formerly of Oban, returning from a London holiday to quiet Bunessan. He dined with us on the *Pharos* at Bunessan last July. At Oban, I ran Dover out to Ganavan, and there and at Connel pointed out all the land-marks – the Falls of Lora (I saw a steamer pass under Connel Bridge for the first time today), Beregonium, the seat of Ossian, Glen Salloch, Lismore, Kingairloch, Mull, Kerrera. Then I deposited him at the Station Hotel (the others are, mostly, closed for the off-season), and went out to Kilbowie. Mrs. Chalmers was in London (she returned this morning); Chalmers cooked supper, a most luxurious feast of lobster, cauliflower and sherry; steak; coffee; port etc.

This morning, we collected Dover and went to the Sheriff Court. We assembled in the retiring room. The first arrival was the Duke of Argyll in Campbell tartan kilt and M.C.C. tie – a colourful figure who gave an air of verisimilitude to the ceremony. Then came the MacDougall of MacDougall, Sir Bruce Campbell, Major Duncan McCallum M.P., the County Convener (Mr. Mathieson), the County Clerk (Mr. Jackson), Provost Calderwood, and Chief Constable Ross. We had a dignified little ceremony. The Commission was read; I swore in Sir Bruce; I then instructed the docquetted Commission to be recorded; I welcomed Sir Bruce; Mr. Milne spoke for the Procurators, and Mr. Macdonald, the Procurator-Fiscal for the Court officials and then Sir Bruce replied. Dover was introduced to all, and was greatly interested in the ceremony. The Duke asked us to lunch at Inverary, so on we went there next, after I had granted an increase in burial rates for various graveyards in Argyll.

On the way to Inverary, we started talking about the visit of Johnson and Boswell to Oban, and I remarked jocularly on the similarity of our relationship! Dover said: 'Nonsense.' So I offered to point out similarities, and we collected quite a number: Dover an Englishman, and I a Scot; Dover a literary man, and I a lawyer; Dover the older, and I the younger; Dover and Johnson, both Shakespeareans; I an admirer of Dover, and Dover able to suffer a fool gladly! Where, however, the comparison broke down was when we agreed that Dover was not an old bear like Johnson, nor was I a dissolute young scamp like Boswell! All this made natural talk, when only yesterday, the first extracts from Boswell's London diary were published in the *Sunday Times*.

At Inverary Castle, we were received by the Duke and had lunch with him, Sir Ralph Glynn (a cousin of his) and his private Secretary, a Russian. Venison pie and trifle, coffee and port, served on silver plates with the Campbell arms. The Duke was friendly and frank, and told me they had discovered an account of the Appin Murder by Mungo Campbell, which had never been published. Sir Ralph Glynn was a good conversationalist, with a robust forthright manner. Dover found the Secretary interested in his knowledge of Russia. (I remarked that our respective wives would probably not greatly like her; Dover agreed laughingly: 'They would probably object to her eye-brows!' [they were plucked]) The Duke speaks French well. He let us wander afterwards by ourselves through his various rooms. There were some Gainsboroughs, but the picture which interested me most was the Duke of the Appin Murder, robed as Lord Justice-General of Scotland. The house is mainly 1740–60. The Duke saw us off at the door: 'A Campbell always likes to see strangers off the premises,' he remarked laughingly. There is an interesting Library, with some quite modern books, like Coulson's Five Centuries of Religion and Mediaeval Village. They could not have been more cordial. Sir Ralph was full of stories of politicians. He seemed to have mainly Liberal affiliations, and talked of Asquith as 'Quith'.

From Inverary, we drove back to Balerno and Edinburgh in drenching rain. They had 27 inches at Inverary last month. We stopped for tea at Drymen. Dover was full of his Inverary visit and, on the way home, told me of schoolmasters who had influenced him, as well as innumerable scholars. He is a generous-hearted friend. It was strange to be in Inverary Castle again. I was there once before, in 1921, with Dad, when he visited Inverary as Moderator. I had just finished my History Honours examinations, and was then awaiting the results. Little did I imagine that my next visit would be as Sheriff to lunch with the Duke.

18th October 1950

We receive wonderful letters from Alison, now completely settled down at L.M.H. – wonderful coffee parties of ten each night in each other's rooms, walks through the parks, and boating on the river, the making of many new friends (I notice she already speaks of the Norwegian Princess who started with her simply as 'Astrid'). Jim

Galbraith and David Symon, Gordon's classmates, left flowers for her on her arrival, and David has already taken her up the river. She has also met Douglas Duncan, Principal Duncan's son, and toasted crumpets with him.

A series of letters have appeared in the *Scotsman* on inscriptions on Church Bells. So I sent in, anonymously, the lines Dad wrote and placed on the Bell at Invergowrie:—

> What time I toll
> > Bethink thee of thy Soul
> When so I ring
> > Praise God and sing
> What hour I call
> > Praise God for Christ, for all.

Like a mediaeval craftsman content to do his work, he placed his inscription on the bell, and there it hung in the tower, few knowing of the inscription. The Church is now closed, because of a union, and the congregation have given away the bell – I know not where.

Today, Ella and I went to see the Queen open the Loch Sloy Hydro-Electric Station at Inveruglas, Loch Lomond. The day was misty, the clouds hanging on the hills; last month, the Loch Sloy area had a rainfall of 26 inches, more than London's rainfall for the year. The whole ceremony was efficiently organised. A special train left Waverley at 10.50 a.m. and took us by the back of Glasgow to the North of Scotland Board's halt at Inveruglas by 1.20 p.m. We were served with a very special lunch on the way. On arrival we walked through the Power Station; a plaque on the wall records the name of workmen killed in the course of the works; it includes Polish, German and Irish names. Then we took up our position in a stand to the north of the tail-race, and facing the Power Station, beside which was the Royal stand. A third stand was situated on the far side of the tail-race. We found ourselves next the Norman Dukes, and others we saw were the Duke of Argyll, Sir Bruce and Lady Campbell, Chief Constable and Mrs. Ross, and Mr. and Mrs. J.G. Mathieson. I saw no other member of the Bar but Lord Gibson. The Sheriff of Dumbarton (Maconochie) was absent. After some music, and occasional deluges of rainwater from the canvas roof, the Queen arrived. Tom Johnston, Chairman, opened the proceedings after his four year old granddaughter had presented the Queen with a bouquet. The Queen, dressed in heliotrope, made a graceful reply. Then there was a speech by Lady MacColl, wife of the Deputy-Chairman, who made a gift to the Queen Tom Johnston made another gift, and then Sir Edward MacColl moved a vote of thanks. The scene was televised, but as the only television transmission is in England, this was not of much avail for those primarily concerned. After the ceremony, the Queen, leaving the car waiting for her, walked with umbrella up through the crowds of children, much to their delight. It was a strange spectacle to see 1,000 visitors and a total crowd of about 2,000 assembled there on the banks of Loch Lomond. When the Queen pulled the lever which started the flow of water, two indicators with red bulbs showed the acceleration of the turbines. I expected some foam at the tail-race, but there was little disturbance there, though the hum of the turbines was audible.

After the ceremony, buses drove us up the 2–3 miles to Loch Sloy – a wild and lonely spot between two steep hills. The last half-mile of the road is far in advance of Rest and Be Thankful, and can only be compared with an Alpine road. It ascends by steep gradients and acute curves, finally passing through a tunnel to emerge on a platform level with the top of the dam. We returned from Inveruglas at 5.22, reaching Waverley shortly before 8 p.m. We saw all the Fulton family: Angus, as water engineer, was presented to the Queen.

Dr. White Anderson of St. Cuthbert's, here, has been nominated as next year's Moderator. He is a really practical, loveable Christian, a good though not a great preacher, but, above all, a devoted parish minister, a servant of the Church at large, and one who brings charity into his judgments.

28th October 1950

Last night, the Justice-Clerk had a sherry-party for all those who attended the last Glasgow Circuit. Patrick, the other judge, was there. It is strange how political promotions reverse promotions resting on merit. Keith, Patrick, Sorn were all Deans of Faculty at a time when it would never have entered anyone's head to think of George Thomson. Yet now he takes precedence of them. Yet, he is, on his merits, a good judge, especially when he rouses himself out of his temperamental lethargy. His charge in the murder case in Glasgow was as good as any I have heard. But, while merit might have won him his present position, he has in fact attained it through the accident of being the only senior Socialist at the bar. He had, moreover, never been an active politician, before he stood as candidate with the Lord Advocate's office in his pocket. He was not a success in Parliament, because of his weary-Willie manner, but he looks fair to make an excellent judge. The present Socialist Government, just because they have not so many of their own supporters to choose from, have shown a wider range in their appointments. None they have so far made have been as bad as the Conservative appointment of James Stevenson as judge or Maurice King and Charles Milne as Sheriffs. All in all, the best judge of my time has been Fleming, and the worst Stevenson. Fleming united all the great judicial qualities: knowledge of the law, fair-mindedness, wisdom, and humility. Patrick is a great judge, too. To appear before him was like appearing before the House of Lords. He brought honour on us all, by being selected for the Japanese War-crimes tribunal – of which he would have been Chairman but for his ill-health. Just before this sherry-party, I received word that the Harris brothers, the two condemned accused in the recent Glasgow murder trial, were not to be reprieved. As I have since the Appeal heard that my client struck the fatal blow, I can scarcely complain. *[Later, my client, I believe, admitted striking the fatal blow, and his brother was reprieved on 31st October 1950.]* Another circuit opens next week, with two murder charges, one a particularly brutal case, where the Crown case against a police constable is that he struck a woman unconscious and then ran over her deliberately with a stolen car.

The President told me yesterday that he is to receive the honorary Doctorate of Paris University on the recommendation of its Faculty of Law. He will be the only British judge to hold this distinction at the present day, and the first Scots judge ever. He stays as a guest in the Hotel du Louvre, and has to give an address in French, for which he is to be carefully coached by Professor Orr of the Edinburgh Chair of French!

John Wheatley, at lunch yesterday, told us of an amusing incident the day before, when the opening of the new House of Commons took place. After the Dominion Speakers had moved in procession up Westminster Hall, an attendant came behind them with a carpet-sweeper. Then followed, in state, the Lord Chancellor, who, in voice and presence, is exactly the Lord Chancellor for *Iolanthe*. Behind the retinue came five attendants clothed in smart green overalls, also operating carpet sweepers in preparation for the subsequent arrival of their Majesties. As the green carpet-sweeper attendants proceeded up the Hall, the Band struck up 'Greensleeves'! I was glad to hear, in the wireless reproduction, that the band also played 'Over the Sea to Skye'.

31st October 1950

A curious development took place on the 28th in the Harris murder case. I first knew of it through a newspaper ringing me up and telling me that the Secretary of State had decided to defer the execution for a week in the case of Claude Harris, but not in the case of Paul (my client). The paper wanted to know if I could give any information. Needless to say, I refused; though I guessed that my client had confessed. The same evening and the following (Sunday) afternoon, other newspapers, including the *News of the World* (from London) rang me up, but again I refused to give any information. The Sunday papers and also yesterday's were full of the incident. Yesterday, Paul was duly executed but Claude's fate is still in the balance. In Greenock, where I was yesterday, I heard that the *Scottish Express* reporter had been seen on Sunday evening at the Bay Hotel, Gourock, with (if you please) the Harris family. Apparently, he had brought them down from Glasgow to keep them away from other newspapers. Certainly the *Express* produced the best copy. But strange behaviour engaging in social activities on the eve of an execution. No such incident as the differentiation between two persons convicted of acting in concert has happened before.

We are in mourning at Court for the King of Sweden, great-grand-father of Alison's Astrid. For the first time, today, I have been wearing 'weepers'.

4th November 1950

Yesterday, I went up to Aberdeen, to deliver a University Public Lecture on 'Public and Charitable Trusts in the Law of Scotland'. It was a great honour, of which I am sincerely proud. My predecessors were Daube (of Caius, Cambridge) who comes as Professor of Jurisprudence to Aberdeen in January, and Professor W.M. Geldart (of Oxford).

Tom and Ann Smith could not have been kinder. I think it was really an act of friendship because I had perhaps secured him the Chair of Law. I began my lecture by saying: 'I am not a graduate of this University, but, when I come here, I come home. My father's family hailed from the back of Bennachie. Seven of my family in the last two generations were graduates of the University, and your present Principal and I were called to the Bar the same day. He was my immediate junior!' I might have added that I had links with his four predecessors: Ella being related by marriage with Marshall Lang; Sir

William Geddes being my grand uncle; George Adam Smith my father's class mate at school and university and life-long friend; and Sir William Hamilton Fyfe having married my father's cousin. At least three of my family were honorary graduates of Aberdeen in the last two generations.

It is announced today that the young Oxford undergraduates, whom we saw working at Lismore, have, in their excavations, unearthed what is believed to be the Sacristy on the north side of the chancel of the thirteenth century Lismore Cathedral.

The Dean (Jock Cameron) made a good joke about my University lecture on Charities in the Law of Scotland. 'That,' he said, 'will be a subject appropriate for academic treatment in Aberdeen!'

12th November 1950

Yesterday after a day in London at the Central Land Board and War Damage Commission, I returned here and attended the Faculty's R.L.S. Commemoration Dinner in the Parliament Hall. The centenary of his birth falls on the 13th. This is the second time I have dined in the Parliament Hall – the other occasion being on the Scott Centenary in 1932. I just missed a third dinner – when Lord Birkenhead was the principal guest. This time I began with a sherry-party at my house, to which about thirty of the bar came. The oldest present was 'Hammy' (Sheriff Hamilton), and next Johnnie Jameson. Most of the others were quite young – among them men like Alex Thomson and Ian Shearer whom I should regard as coming leaders of the Bar. There was also a sprinkling of advocates from other places – Rob Wallace from Lerwick, Alastair Prain from Perth, and Allan Wallace from Glasgow, and two of our new women members, Miss Macintyre and Miss Smith. The former, if we in Parliament House mistake not, is about to become engaged to David Maxwell. We all watch the romance with a paternal interest.

Up in the Parliament House, we were received by the Dean in the corridor. About 130 came, rather more than at the Scott dinner. I had arranged for R.L.S. MSS to be displayed from the National Library, but I am afraid that, owing to the pressure of time and conversation, not many saw them. At the Scott dinner, the head table ran right down the west side of the hall, with the fireplaces behind, and with short cross tables running east and west. This time, the head table was placed across the hall, with the macers' 'pulpit' behind, and three long tables running down the hall from the head table to about the entrance. One curious effect of this arrangement was that many of the busts seemed to be looking down upon the Dean as he spoke, and, as his speech brought back legends of many of them, this was almost symbolical. Harry Erskine, for example, looked with approval on him as he spoke. Palm leaves divided the far end of the tables from the empty space beyond. At the head table – on the Dean's right – was the Lord Advocate (John Wheatley), then myself, Miss Kidd, and Jack Gibson; on his left, Lord Alness, Fenton (as Sheriff of Edinburgh), George Morton and Arthur Alison. The President sat at a side table, and so did the other judges. There was no judicial precedence, and, except at the head table, no places fixed. Only one member of the bar was unknown to me. He turned out to be J. Harper Orr, who has never attended before in my time.

The Dean proposed 'The Immortal Memory' and was quite excellent, though, I believe, not well heard at the far end of the Hall. His speech was prompted by Stevenson's pictures of Braxfield, Newton and Dundas of Arniston, and by reflections from 2 Rettie, the volume of the reports relating to the year of Stevenson's call. Tom Simpson, who proposed 'The Parliament House', was, as always, incredibly funny, his speech consisting mainly of reflections on Parliament from the as yet unpublished journals of Boswell. But it is dangerous to be expected always to be funny, and, with the difficulty some had in hearing him (though I heard well), his speech fell considerably short of the Dean's, which was dignified and eloquent, as well as full of imagination and allusive suggestion. Harald Leslie made a short reply to Tom Simpson's toast. No one is a more splendid specimen of human worth, and his deep natural voice carried well, but there was less of interest in his speech than in the other two. Without any question, the honours were with the Dean. After John Wheatley had called for a toast to the Chairman, Lord Alness got up and made a few remarks, as always in his perfect delivery (though now with an older voice); he told of the destruction of Skerryvore, Bournemouth, by a landmine during the war, and how, next year, the site would probably be converted into a commemorative garden, in Stevenson's memory. In John Wheatley and Margaret Kidd, I had two very congenial companions. The card at my place was prepared by Brown, our Faculty Officer, who is an adept at this kind of work. Tom Simpson told one good story. At dinner in Oxford Sir John Coleridge had to propose the toast of the University. He said: 'How can I do this adequately in faltering language such as mine? The Archbishop of Canterbury has proposed the toast of Balliol College with great excellence. But to me falls the duty of toasting the whole of Oxford. And what a hole it is!' I had an interesting talk with John Wheatley about the National Health Service Committee on which I served two years ago. The recommendations of the Report (which was mainly my draft) were adopted, and are now incorporated in the National Health Service (Amendment) Act, 1949. By a curious chance, it was John Wheatley who introduced this Act, although it was one affecting the United Kingdom, and not just Scotland.

17th November 1950

On the 13th (the actual Stevenson Centenary), we went, with the Duncan McGregors as our guests, to the R.L.S. Club Dinner. I sat between Betty McGregor and the Duchess of Atholl. I found the latter rather lacking in humour, though with a flood of well-informed conversation. J.B. Priestley proposed 'The Immortal Memory' in one of the best speeches I have heard made by a literary man. He is plain, and downright, sensible, humorous, and has a deep full Yorkshire voice that receives its resonance from his bulky person. He spoke without a note, in faultless, clear, simple prose, and, unlike lesser literary men who like to be outré, was content to be himself. He put the whole proceedings on a different plane. Arthur Matheson proposed the 'Guests'. With a narrower canvas than Priestley, he revealed that tender sensitive nature which makes his mind so distinctive.

On the 15th, I gave the Centenary Stevenson Essay at the Spec. Tom Smith came from Aberdeen to spend the night, and Ronald Kydd and Bill Hook joined us at dinner. The Society's Hall was full. There must have been about fifty, because the division in the debate recorded almost forty. Amongst other members there were:- Lord Mackay, Johnnie Jameson, Lord Mackintosh, Matthew Fisher, Hector Burn-Murdoch and some of my own contemporaries like Arthur Clark, Robin Notman and Hector McKechnie. My essay, I think, went down well, though I was nervous about it beforehand. I was asked to deposit a copy by the Society to be kept by it.

At the last Glasgow Circuit this month, there were six death sentences, and thirty-five years' worth of sentences for razor-slashing which had not produced fatal results – a record for these days; and it is to be hoped that the sentences will be a due warning to the perpetrators of this (for Glasgow) prevalent form of crime.

20th November 1950

After a long day in Greenock Sheriff Court, hearing an interminable pleader speak for three and a half hours on a point which could have been stated in five minutes, I returned home to find three interesting items awaiting me. A first-class Kilmarnock Burns (the Wilmerding) is to be sold in New York on the 27th. I appealed to Lord Macmillan for help to the Library to provide the necessary funds. This evening, I received a wire from him:- 'Pilgrim Trust will contribute up to £2,000 towards the purchase of Kilmarnock Burns; writing – Macmillan.' The Library can add at least £1,000. I am trying to tap one other source. Then Giles (A.F.) wrote me that he would be glad to receive my R.L.S. Centenary Essay for the *University of Edinburgh Journal*. Finally, the Warden and Chairman of Governors of Glenalmond come tomorrow evening to consult me about a master – some personal matter. Last night, I gave a talk on 'St. Luke and his Gospel' to a discussion group organised by Murdo Ewen's brother, Murdo Mac-donald, at Greenside. I pointed out the curious lack of interest in Luke – surely one of the finest of all the New Testament figures, whose writings are what we would treasure above all others' writings; and quoted Danti Gabriel Rossetti:-

> Give honour unto Luke Evangelist
> For he it was (the aged legends say)
> Who first taught Art to fold her hands and pray.

Only five of our churches are dedicated to Luke – one in each of Edinburgh, Glasgow, Broughty Ferry, Montrose and Milngavie. The same is true of the Roman Catholics – in Rome, the Accademia di S. Luca, but what else there? Here, in Scotland we often favour St. George, but I am afraid it is the Hanoverian, not the Cappadocian. Tomorrow evening, I give my R.L.S. essay once again, at the Association for the Speaking of English Verse.

28th November 1950

We learned today that we had secured the New York Kilmarnock Burns for $2,700 (approx. £965), though we were prepared to offer £3,000! The reactions of the different trustees to the proposed bid (even with £2,000 contributed by the Pilgrim Trust) was interesting. The President, Dickinson, the Dean, Hector McKechnie, Tom Simpson, Dover Wilson were all enthusiastic. W.R. Cunningham was so enthusiastic that he would have gone to £4,000. Dobie, Beattie,

Crawford and Muirhead were not keen, though the first two changed somewhat when they heard the excellent bargain we had made. Cunningham's remark was: 'What the First Folio is to the British Museum, the Kilmarnock Burns is to us.' (In view of this the Pilgrim Trust Contribution was not required, but we are grateful to them nonetheless for enabling us to go into the market.)

Lord Gibson told Tom Simpson the other day, when they were forced into conversation between Aviemore and Edinburgh, that the President always turned to him when he had some difficult point to consider. What nonsense and what vanity! I wish that the President heard him: he will be told. Lord Gibson is writing an appreciation of Lord Moncrieff for the Royal Society. The 'friendship' between the two would scarcely be owned by Moncrieff: what would he say if he were alive? It reminds me of George Morton's remark the other day about (the first) Lord Guthrie and R.L.S. He, charitable soul, was moved to observe: 'It was a rather one-sided friendship, and began on Stevenson's death.'

The other day Ella was shopping in a certain well-known butcher's. The shop-assistant said to her: 'It is always a pleasure to attend to you. You have the brightest face of all our customers.'

30th November 1950

I repeated George Morton's bon-mot about the Guthrie-R.L.S. friendship to Arthur Alison, the one member left in the Faculty who met Stevenson. He thought it was scarcely correct, and referred to what his own uncle Thomas Barclay says about the relations of the two men in 'I can remember Robert Louis Stevenson'. He thought, rather, that they were attracted to each other as opposites. Thomas Barclay lived with Alison's father, at the time when he (T.B.) and R.L.S. were together attending the Spec, when Stevenson was in his early twenties. Arthur Alison, as a small boy, used to come down from the nursery when about five or six for dessert with the grown-ups, and his uncle and R.L.S. would be having dinner there before going to the Spec. Alison remembers his sallow countenance compared with his uncle's rubicund complexion. The Alison parents never suspected R.L.S. to have any special gifts. On these occasions, too, Alison remembers R.L.S. wearing his velvet jacket.

5th December 1950

There is a good tale this week of David Anderson pleading in the First Division. He has many good qualities, but an over developed sense of humour is not one of them. The case involved the meaning of 'frivolous'. 'Well, how would you define it, Mr. Anderson?' enquired the President. Missing a heaven sent chance, David Anderson began: 'My lord, in Smith v. Smith (1932 S. L. T. 199), Lord Mackay –' Lord Carmont: 'You are not going to cite Lord Mackay on frivolity, surely, Mr. Anderson?' David Anderson, however, fetched out the 1932 volume of *Scots Law Times*, which happened to be a very thin one. 'You don't mean to tell us, Mr. Anderson,' went on Lord Carmont, 'that you are able to get the whole of one of Lord Mackay's judgments in that volume!'

I saw, today, a letter from Lord Gibson to the Dean of the Faculty of Procurators in Inverness, complaining that, at a recent visit of the Land Court to the capital of the Highlands, certain members of the Faculty had deigned to appear before him without gowns, and that no such indignity had been shown to Lord Sorn 'my immediate junior in Senatorial rank!' Obviously, Gibson's experiences at a recent St. Giles' service is rankling. He claimed to march in ahead of Sorn, but the latter ingeniously replied: 'We attend St. Giles' not as Lords of Session, but as Lords Commissioners of Justiciary, and you are not within that category at all.' Gibson is always claiming to have the rank of a Senator of the Court of Session.

14th December 1950

On the 11th, we reported the purchase of the Kilmarnock Burns to the Standing Committee of the National Library. Everyone was delighted, and I was congratulated. As usual I had lunch with Dover before the meeting (turn about, he takes me to the New Club, and I take him to the University). We were almost late for our meeting because Dr. Lionel Smith joined us, and knowing that I was proposing 'The Gentle Art' at the Dunrod Angling Club, Greenock, tonight, became deeply involved on the subject of Homer's allusions to fish! In the end Alick Buchanan Smith ran us up to the Library quickly in his 'milk-van', and this saved the situation. At tea, two of Alison's friends, Douglas Duncan and Dag Berggrav, were present, and I brought Dover and Dr. Smith. What a tea-party. Starting from Ella: – Dag Berggrav (son of Bishop Berggrav), Alison (Lady Margaret Hall), Douglas Duncan (son of Principal Duncan and a Scholar of Corpus), Lionel Smith (Scholar of Balliol; Fellow of All Souls; Dean of Magdalen), Mlle. Borel (from Neuchatel), Miss Johnston, my new Secretary (represents the Army, through her father), Dover (Hon. Fellow of Caius), myself, and Rosemary (age six). Dr. Smith and Douglas paired off as old Rugbeians; Dover and Rosemary, as the two with the childlike mind: what greater tribute could be paid to our greatest Shakespearean. Dag Berggrav is studying law. I have given him a Gloag and Henderson. He is at present resident at Mansfield College, Oxford: he strongly resembles his father. I took the two boys, with Alison, to see the Courts next morning; and in the evening, along with Mrs. Duncan, they came to tea again. The Macdonalds were there also.

There is a good story (which Dover gave me) about the Dean of Christ Church (The Very Rev. John Lowe – a Canadian Rhodes Scholar). He fulfils his engagements by helicopter. The story goes that one day he attended a meeting in Southampton. When he returned, he alighted in the Quadrangle. The choir were drawn up, and as he came down, they sang: 'Lowe! He comes with clouds descending!'

17th December 1950

I travelled to Greenock by car on the 14th, though the snow came on heavily, and there was as keen frost as I have seen for long. The reports give 33 degrees of frost in the Cairngorms, the coldest for thirty years. I would have gone by train, but at the last moment a young advocate consulted me on whether he should propose! This delayed me, so that I could only go by car. He had certain real difficulties which I tried to help him with, but, on the vital issue, I could only quote him Montrose's famous lines. At Gourock, where I spent the night, the frost was lying to the water's edge. I had a very good audience – about sixty – at the Angling Club Dinner, and did my best, though I was talking off my own subjects; it was a fair, but not my best, effort. A young Greenock minister spoke and sang well, with an untrained bass voice of concert proportions and unusual volume. Everyone must have been attracted to what he stood for by the way he took part in the evening's entertainment. The members of the Club have a 'bashed [pewter] mug', which is passed on each dinner from the holding member to another whom he chooses. The latter has to make an impromptu speech. No one knows who will be chosen, and every member is said to come with a speech prepared: this adds to the excitement. At Greenock dinners, there is a great deal of allusion to one's personal friends. All the members understand the allusions; but they may be lost on a guest from outside. It is a tribute to the closely-knit nature of the Greenock community. In any town with more of a floating population, this type of speaking would die out. Next morning, I heard an appeal in the Sheriff Court, and, finishing at 12 o'clock, motored up to Glasgow, and attended the Circuit as Sheriff. In the North Court there was a tumbler-smasher being tried. The principal witness was asked in cross-examination if he was not himself a dangerous character, given to assaulting other people. He said: 'Only my wife' (as if that were an extenuating circumstance). However, a series of previous convictions was then put to him, and among his previous efforts was one where, apparently, he had used a hatchet to a policeman. In the South Court, a fraud trial was at its fifth day. If it does not finish in two more days, the 110 days will be up, and the accused will go free. As the Crown case is still proceeding, the prospects of a finish are remote. The accused might himself go into the witness box and 'filibuster', but his counsel would not give any encouragement to such a course.

23rd December 1950

Two curious matters which came up this week were, first, that I have had to draft an Act to enable Kirk Sessions to function in Scottish Units of the services; and, secondly, that we had to consider whether cremated remains should be regarded as falling within an Act of Assembly of 1643 prohibiting burials within church. We considered that they did come within the principle of the Act, and, in any event, that any general practice to the contrary would now be repugnant to public policy. But, by a side-wind, this reflects an interesting social change. Almost all the churchyards have now been vested in county councils; people don't like the columbaria of the crematoria; and they have the old hankering for hallowed ground. It seems questionable if the local authorities should ever have taken over churchyards.

I am just now involved in a needless problem. Jim Aikman Smith, upon the death of Mr. Nimmo, Procurator-Fiscal at Dunoon, raised the question whether Lochgilphead District should not be attached to Campbeltown, instead of Dunoon. I have asked for reports from Jim Aikman Smith (Campbeltown) and Donald (Dunoon), and also from the Sheriff Clerk of Argyll. Today, the Dean of the Dunoon Faculty of Procurators writes me urging that no change should be made. *Prima facie*, I think the facts tend to support this view. I have to report to the Lord Advocate on the question.

I am toiling away with a paper I have been asked to give to the Leighton Club on 'What can a layman do towards Re-union?' It is a difficult task. If only those concerned with erecting difficulties would read their New Testament, the difficulties would vanish. The trouble, I think, is not merely that everyone has their own views, but many people think that others must accept their views also. He that thinks he has the Grace of God stands most in need of it. It seems to me that much 'Catholic' dogma of the later centuries has no real historical foundation, yet people are expected to swallow it or be dubbed schismatic. For me, the New Testament and the freedom for the individual conscience.

CHAPTER V

1951

1st January 1951

The opening of a new year. On the night of Christmas, the famous
Stone of Destiny was abstracted from the Coronation Chair and
removed from Westminster Abbey. Since then, the press not merely
in England and Scotland, but abroad in America and, for example,
Denmark has been writing up the incident. The first reports were that
a long-haired young man and woman, with a Scots accent, had been
seen in a Ford Anglia car beside the Abbey. Then it appeared that a
lorry had been abstracted from Glasgow, and left somewhere in Kensington. Then it was discovered that initials were scratched on the
Coronation Chair – 'J.F.S.' – incidentally, as lawyers have enjoyed,
Lord Strachan's initials! and a wristlet watch of Swiss make found
nearby. Then the police began dredging the Serpentine, only to find
a concrete block; and the River Crouch in Essex only to find nothing.
Then there was a telephone message from Newcastle from an unident-
ified person. Police have been patrolling all the main roads to
Scotland, but nothing is known of the stone. The Dean of Westminster, an Anglicised Scot, is 'distressed'.

The whole incident is significant like the Boston Tea Party. It is
incredibly silly, yet not so silly as the fuss that has been made about
it. Except for *The Times* which has reported even the shouts of joy
of the Scottish Nationalists objectively, the English Press only see it
as a demonstration without justification of wild Scots. Here, in
Scotland, although all reasonable Scots disapprove the act, there is
considerable satisfaction that, for once, England has realised the
existence of its neighbour, and considerable chuckling over the
Gilbertian efforts of the police. The only dignified thing that has come
out of it is a petition to the King which was left anonymously in the
office of the *Daily Record* in Glasgow. The petitioners for obvious
reasons do not sign, but to show their *bona fides* they identify the
watch found in the Abbey as known to them to have a soldered hand
and to have been recently repaired. Their petition, obviously framed

in the Scottish legal style, is a dignified and reasonable statement. The foreign press appreciated the Scottish reaction – after all the Stone was stolen by an English conqueror – but the English papers have no appreciation of Scots sentiment or the rapidly growing 'Irish' question, this time north of the Border.

3rd January 1951

The Scottish representatives travelled this afternoon to the third C. of E. – C. of S. Conference, this one like the first being held at Durham. Our C. of S. party consisted of Professor Manson, Principal Baillie, Professors Burleigh, Tindal and Torrance, Dr. Matthew Stewart and myself. With us were, from the Scottish Episcopal Church, the Bishop of Brechin and Mr. Burn-Murdoch. The Bishop's son, who is chaplain at St. Chad's College, was also travelling to Durham. Between Edinburgh and Berwick Manson and I poured over the draft report of the Conference, making various – as we thought – improvements. Afterwards, we all had tea, and then light-hearted conversation. At Durham, there was hard frost. I find myself in a bedroom at St. Chad's, between the Bishops of Manchester and Brechin. The matron, who recognised me from last year, gave me a kind welcome. Already, the clock of the Cathedral and its bells have announced its presence.

After dinner, we began the Conference. Derby, as first Chairman, made an opening statement, followed by Manson. The latter stressed the need of one being able to report back to the General Assembly that some immediate advance had been made, and that any long term policy would require to open upon two premises in particular: (1) that the policy did not start from a pronouncement with regard to the validity of Orders on either side, but rather from consideration of what should belong to the Fullness of the Church in that unity which, however far in the future, we were called to seek by our Lord's Command and in dependence on the guidance of the Holy Spirit; and (2) that the Conference recognised the principle of the sovereignty of the Divine Freedom in Grace within the history of the Church and of the World.

Before dinner, Greenslade gave me a full account of the staff and organisation of Durham Cathedral. As usual Hensley Henson's name came up with a crop of stories from his recently published letters. By a curious chance one of his letters comments on the appointment of the present Dean of Westminster. 'Could the Coronation Stone be safely entrusted to the keeping of a Scot as Dean?' Here, there seems fairly general agreement that a broadcast the other night by the Dean about the loss of the Stone was somewhat exaggerated, and showed lack of balance dwelling so much over the loss, when lives – more precious than stone – were being lost in Korea. The Bishop of Durham has not been well, and was unable to attend tonight's session.

6th January 1951

We returned from Durham by the 9.00 a.m. train. On the journey, my companions were Manson, Matthew Stewart, and Willie Tindal. We had an interesting talk about the Anglican service. I remarked on the absence of systematic scripture reading in many of our churches. Manson: 'There is no Church in which the Scriptures are so much, and so systematically, read as in the Church of England.' He then observed that prose psalms were, if anything, commoner in the Churches here formerly than now (which I doubt), instancing Claremont and St. Matthew's – both in Glasgow – where prose psalms had once been sung, but where he thought they were not sung now. Another: 'The Prayer-Book enables a man from any part of the country to go into any church as a stranger and yet find something familiar, and himself at home.' We all agreed, however, that this type of service produced one type of man, and that without other special prayers and good preaching, a liturgical service might lack inspiration. I remarked on the apparently larger proportion of men at our services. The others were inclined to agree, but this may be due either to the form of service or to the large place which laymen have in the services of the church. I remarked that, however, the Bishop of Manchester had told me that, in his diocese alone, with 378 parishes and 450 churches, there were no fewer than 250 lay readers, probably three times as many as in the whole Church of Scotland.

Two stories were told at the Conference. Prof. Burleigh mentioned how Sir Alexander Gray had come up to him about the Anglican-Free Churches Report and said: 'What kind of a report is this? I may be an atheist, but at least I'm a Presbyterian atheist.' Prof. Baillie told about a Rangers supporter who came away from a victory over Celtic, with the remark: 'There will be sair hairts in the Vatican the nicht!'

12th January 1951

I was conducting a Special Case in the First Division this week. The

President told me afterwards that one of the other judges had asked: 'Has Philip a black eye?' (evidently, for no reason, he thought I had). Cooper replied: 'Can you wonder? He's just returned from an ecclesiastical conference!'

There is much speculation as to who will succeed Fulton as Sheriff of the Lothians. My choice would be (from the Bar) James Walker; (from the Sheriff-substitutes) Norman Walker. A rumour was going round that it would be T.P. McDonald: he would be an excellent choice. The President told me, today, that Patrick was to have another operation. Why does ill-health dog our best judges, while the worst have painfully good health!

This morning, I had a two hours' inspection of the new Library Building with Dobie, Dr. Fairlie (the architect), and three officials of the Ministry of Works. The three lowest floors, G, H and J, will be ready for books about the middle of next month, but the next two floors, E and F, will also be required before all the books from the old building next George IV Bridge can be accommodated and a start made on the demolition of that building. There is a faint rumour that the new defence programme may again cause a suspension of work. I have been in touch with Lord Crawford about this (before he leaves for the U.S.A.). I suggested that, if necessary, we should ask the help of the National Commission on Museums and Galleries. He agrees, and says we should fight, and, if necessary, approach the Prime Minister.

24th January 1951

I had one of my most varied days. After breakfast, as usual drove Rosemary and her little friend Rosalind to school. At 10.30, appeared with Maconochie for the Northern Lighthouse Board before the Industrial Court in an hours of work dispute with the lighthouse keepers. The Chairman of the Court turned out to be G.G. Honeyman, now an English barrister, once my class-mate at Glasgow University, with whom I wrote a Joint Opinion only last month. I visited him in his Chambers then at the Middle Temple. He specialises in revenue and shipping law. This lasted till 1.20. Then, a quick lunch at Court. At 2.30, the Inter-Church Relations Committee, where our Anglo-Scottish Report (not yet in the hands of members, but only referred to from the Chair) appeared not to get a very good reception. This lasted till 4.50. At 5.00, a Church consultation at my house with Mr. Mercer Robertson, the Solicitor of the Church. That lasted till dinner. After dinner, I wrote an opinion after the consultation, and then began to prepare a case for the Second Division tomorrow, starting at 8.30. I've just finished. The case I first heard of by telephone at 5.00 p.m.!

This week I heard, with personal sorrow, of the death of my great mathematical master, Mr. Meiklejohn. Little over a month ago, he delivered a speech at the annual meeting of Dundee High School subscribers, and a week later I had a chance to pay my tribute to him at our School Dinner. I kept up correspondence with him till Christmas this year.

27th January 1951

Yesterday the Lord Advocate fetched me out of the Law Room up to the Crown Office, and offered me the Sheriffdom of Edinburgh! It is a difficult offer to refuse, and I asked time to consider. He was extraordinarily kind about it, pointing out that he may not have many more opportunities to make me an offer, and stating that he did not want to pass any by, without giving me the chance. Acceptance of this would mean my giving up Argyll, the Procuratorship, the Land Board, my practice – all of which have a strong hold over me. Until this offer was thrust on me, I scarcely realised how strong a place Argyll and the Procuratorship had secured in my life. Also, while practice is bound to go with advancing years, I have a very distinctive opinion practice of a kind which suits me down to the ground and which no one else has, and this offer would mean turning from this Chancery work which suits me to the modern ordinary legal problems of the Sheriff's civil court, and to criminal work, which the Sheriff handles in Edinburgh and which is not exactly my line. On the other hand, it would mean about half the work I do, security, a pension on retirement and a pension to my widow. The immediate financial loss would no doubt become later compensated by some gain. It would, of course, mean the end of prospects of the Bench, but, having no political claims, I must not put these too high. Ross McLean the other day told me that he was to stand as Conservative for Greenock, and added: 'Chaps like myself can only get by politics what you would get by your knowledge of law.' But, alas, when vacancies occur under a Conservative Government, and this is when they usually do occur, there are too many party mouths to fill. It is strange to hesitate about accepting a position which a few years ago I would have given any-thing to fill. I know some of my brother Sheriffs, Maconochie, in

particular, would give a lot to be offered the post. I have told only
Ella, Alison, Dover and Harold. Dover's initial reaction was a faint
'Yes' and Harold's definitely 'No'. But neither knows the whole circumstances, and, as in a legal opinion, unless you have the whole facts
before you, your opinion is not of great value. For example, health
counts as well as ambition; and also Ella's interests, and the children's.

30th January 1951

Yesterday we had the Annual Meeting of the National Library Trustees. The Report which I gave in was the most encouraging which I
have yet had the chance to present. The 'shell', the three lowest floors
(G, H and J) of the main building, next George IV Bridge, will be
ready to take books by the middle of next month, the two floors (E
and F) above the shell, are expected to be ready to take books by the
middle of July. Then we had to report the accessions of the Newbattle
Abbey Collection, with a number of John Donne's sermons, one
hitherto unpublished, the Kilmarnock Burns (in which the Press were
greatly interested), the superb facsimile of the Book of Kells, which I
saw in preparation last July at Trinity College, Dublin, and of which
we are to secure a presentation copy (in addition to one already
purchased) from the Provost and Fellows of the College. The speech
of the meeting was Janet Adam Smith's. She managed to infuse a good
deal of her own personality into it, and I felt amply justified in having
suggested her name as a Trustee. The President (as I discovered
afterwards) was piqued at Dr. Warr being asked to take the chair,
but he was one of the senior Trustees, and made an excellent Chairman even if he is not *au fait* with the Standing Committee's business.
Lord Crawford (me approving) invited him to do so: Lord Crawford
wanted me originally but, as I was presenting the Report, it seemed
better to do so from the floor, and Crawford preferred Warr to the
President. Alas, dog eats dog, and the President, I know, is sensitive
about not having been made, like his predecessors, Chairman of St.
Giles' Managing Board. Hence, although not pacifist, he has an anti-
Warr complex. He has others too – among them an anti-John Baillie
complex: he once called him a 'hot-house plant!' Here, his judgment
is on surer ground.

On Sunday, F.J. Taylor (of Birkenhead), my Durham colleague,
preached at the University service in St. Giles'. We had a large tea-party
for him beforehand. In the pulpit, his stout healthy figure recalls
Temple. He has, however, more warmth, without loss of light. It was

the best University service I have heard. He has a strong pleasant clear well-modulated voice, and is a man's man. His theme was that the University are concerned with means – how to make a bomb, how to produce literature or art – but that they must not sit on the fence and not declare themselves as to the end of life. All the professors, as well as the students, sat up. Dr. Matthew Stewart and I occupied the manse pew, behind the Senatus.

Tonight, I travel to London, in fulfilment of an offer I made at Durham, to attend the Church Assembly.

I have practically decided not to accept the Sheriffdom of Edinburgh. I may see the Lord Advocate in London tomorrow. I promised to let him know by then.

Mr. Peter Hook, doyen of advocates' clerks and most faithful of friends, a loyal and disinterested practical Christian, as well as a very shrewd business man, has just died suddenly. He was at Court on the 27th, and died next day. He began as a choirboy at St. Mary's, graduated (like others from the choir-school) to be a boy in the Advocates' Law Library, then became a clerk, then clerk to Lord Advocate Scott Dickson, and the trusted friend of a long succession of distinguished counsel from Scott Dickson to Thankerton, Cooper and Sorn. He acted – temporarily – as my clerk during the War, and we formed a close bond of friendship. He was Chairman of the Conservative Club, Chairman of West Edinburgh Conservative Association, an elder in St. Cuthbert's (where his wife sang in the choir), a good speaker and story-teller, a judicious critic of the opinions I wrote, and altogether a very versatile man. His son, Bill, the apple of his eye, is now at the bar, and a worthy son of his father. After fifty years at the Parliament House, Mr. Hook received a dinner, at which Lord Thankerton came here to preside, and he was then presented with an oil painting (there, too, he was a connoisseur).

1st February 1951

I spent yesterday in London at the Church Assembly, and have been in a proof today – after two nights spent in the train.

After lunch, Derby arranged to take me to see the House of Lords. I helped Derby into his robes. As I did so, he informed me that Bishop Weldon's waist measured 63 inches! He is a friendly wee man, when he gets to know you, and hung on to my arm. I mastered the mystery of the lawn sleeves, and wrist buttons, which he could not fasten himself. Then we processed to the Lords' Robing Room. He went in for prayers. I waited outside and saw the mace and Lord Chancellor arrive. As soon as prayers ended, I was admitted to the Strangers' Gallery. There I heard a discussion on safety of pedestrians, the best speech in which was by the (2nd) Marquis of Reading. After that the young Lord Mottistone made his maiden speech, on the new colonial office planned for erection beside Westminster Abbey. There was a question asked about the Coronation Stone (still missing) and I noticed the Dean of Westminster sprawling on the steps of the throne. The Lord Chancellor yawned with weariness, and I had a little nap. It was a pretty dull performance. The Bishops present were Gloucester, Newcastle, Derby, Southwell, who were afterwards joined by York and St. Edmundsbury. I came away before Lord Mottistone had concluded, and, after examining the bookshops in Charing Cross Road, returned to the Club.

As I went in to the House of Lords, I handed a note for the Lord Advocate to one of the attendants, and so gave up the Sheriffdom of Edinburgh.

10th February 1951

I was in London again yesterday at the War Damage Commission and Central Land Board. On the return journey, I saw Ronald Morison and Jim Shaw. They are giving evidence on Scots Law on different sides of the Fitzwilliam case. Jim Shaw has already been in the witness-box for four hours, having been cross-examined by Maxwell Fyfe. Ronald gives his evidence on the 12th. The latter was baiting the former with inventing a fourth type of Scots irregular marriage – by 'tacit consent'. Ronald says Pilcher, J. is a cross between Mackay and Sorn – a somewhat paradoxical description; but, in the end, he explained that he talked a great deal, and was not as good a judge as Sorn. The Central Land Board are full of appreciation of a judgment of Keith in a recent Land Board case (Sinclair v. Lockhart's Trustees 1951 S.C. 258).

In Bumpus's bookshop in Oxford Street, I met a delightful old Scot, Mr. Wilson. He began talking about books in general and Shakespeare in particular. From that we drifted to Bernard Shaw (whom he had known personally), Angela Thirkell, and Graham Greene. He said Bernard Shaw never could quite appreciate Jane Austen! Of Graham Greene, he said: 'Like so many others, he parades Roman Catholicism, which doesn't appeal to "Wee Frees" like myself or Christadelphians!' He has a soft Scots accent, faintly changed by years in London. He was greatly delighted when I said to him: 'You're Scottish,' and after our talk was over, thanked me for the 'crack' and hoped we would meet again.

17th February 1951

Dover, with whom I had lunch yesterday, told me that Mr. Wilson *is* Bumpus's, and the foremost bookseller in London and very much a personality. He did not know that he was Scottish. He and I went, after lunch, to the National Library to discuss the problem of control of export of books and MSS, which is the subject before a Government Committee to which we shall submit evidence. We have had only three cases, where proposed exports have had to be considered:- (1) a *Regiam Majestatem*, which Yale desired, but which we bought; (2) Caxton's *Dictae and Sayings*, an imperfect copy, which we let pass; and (3) a Boswell MSS on Scots Election Law, which had been stopped at the customs, and which we offered to buy from Lady Talbot of Malahide, but which apparently she is to keep in this country.

> Necessity and Cringletie
> Agree unto a little
> Necessity knows no law
> And Cringletie but little
> (Furnished to me by Robbie Maconochie)

James Gilchrist is, today, announced as the new Sheriff of Edinburgh. He is sixty-six years of age, and has been Sheriff-substitute for over ten years. He took silk in 1934, and was called to the Bar in 1910. An excellent choice: I had not thought of him.

19th February 1951

Dover has just asked me to go with him on the 22nd to a Bach piano recital by Sydney Newman in the University Music Classroom. How characteristically thoughtful of him: he is doing it because that is Gordon's eighth anniversary. And here, he would come in all the long way from Balerno just to do this sympathetic kindness to his friends.

23rd February 1951

Our house was full of flowers yesterday – it is eight years now since Gordon's accident, but most of his classmates, and many others remembered us once more. Geoffrey Shaw (now a Divinity Student) and Harold Nicolson (now a Law Student) came to tea; Dover was at dinner; then we went with him for a two-hours' Bach piano recital at the University; finally, I drove him home. He has asked me to go with him to see Laurence Olivier in *Anthony and Cleopatra* in London on 18th May.

I received a special retainer two days ago for Mr. 'Toby' Fitzwilliam, the plaintiff in the Fitzwilliam Peerage Case, as proceedings are now expected in Scotland. I was amused to find that the Dean, Vice-Dean and Chris Guest had also received retainers. Does he mean 'to call the whole Faculty out'? In the English proceedings, each day we read of extraordinary views being expressed on the law of irregular marriage in Scotland. There is still a complete ignorance among many people south of the border that Scotland has a law of its own. I remember Lord Romer, once in the House of Lords, obviously confusing Arran with the Aran Islands, and showing a faint belief that the inhabitants there still ran about in a half-savage condition.

Yesterday, I spent two hours in the morning chatting with Tom Taylor, who was speaking at the Inter-Church Relations Committee in the afternoon on the World Council of Churches. We discussed James Gow, now a law lecturer at Khartoum. He was Tom's best student. Gow began without any advantage as an office boy in an Aberdeen law office. In the War, he was taken prisoner at St. Valery and in prison camp fell into the company of an old classmate of mine at Glasgow University, J.A. Scanlan (now R.C. Bishop of Dunkeld). The latter instructed him in law and Italian and Spanish. Gow has a natural genius for legal principle. He was made a law tutor by Tom Taylor while still a student, and later became a law lecturer. I first met him conducting law orals at Aberdeen. He put his questions to the candidates with great fairness, but also with the consummate skill of an F.E. Smith. He was runner-up for the St. Andrew's Law Chair, and should eventually return either to a chair or to the bar, where he would (if he does not come too late) have an assured career. *[He received a Law Lectureship at Aberdeen. But he and Tom Smith did not see eye to eye, and Gow (now a member of the Scots Bar) has accepted a Lectureship in Tasmania: 22.6.54]* Tom made an excellent speech at the Committee in the afternoon. It is obvious that a good deal of justifiable pessimism exists at the small response of the Anglicans at our Conferences. As individuals they could not have been more co-operative, but as representatives they are loath to move too far. I like to think I have a letter from the Bishop of Manchester concluding: 'I believe that if we had a committee of two such reasonable beings we might rapidly reach general agreement.' Flatterous [*sic*], but true! General Eisenhower, Sir Dennis Lowson (the Carse of Gowrie Lord Mayor of London), and the Archbishop of York are expected to visit this year's General Assembly.

20th March 1951

Yesterday, Monday, I returned from a weekend in Aberdeen, staying with Tom Smith for the University Law Oral Examinations. On Sunday I went with him to the University service in the Chapel at King's, and processed in with the Senatus between Tom and Farquhar MacRitchie, and sat beside them and Tom Taylor in the stalls.

After we had attended the University Chapel service Tom Taylor went into the University Library and addressed the representatives of the Incorporated Trades of Aberdeen who had been present at the service.

Farquhar MacRitchie took me in to listen, and we took up our position beside some of the show cases containing the finest bindings possessed by the University. By pure chance I began examining these and was immediately attracted by one of the labels which bore that the bindings had been done by one John Philip, between the dates 1839–1847. It at once occurred to me this might be my great-grandfather and I arranged with Farquhar MacRitchie to pay a visit to the Library next day.

After finishing the Law Oral examinations and attending the usual lunch, Farquhar MacRitchie motored me out to Kings College, where we met the Sub-Librarian, Mr. William S. Mitchell, and told him of our quest. He immediately produced a paper of his own entitled 'Aberdeen Corner-Square Bindings' discussing these early Aberdeen Bindings with illustrations of two by John Philip, and gave me a copy. In the earliest Aberdeen Directory viz. for 1824 we checked that there was only one John Philip. He was described as a bookbinder (Philip and Moffat, 50 Queen Street, Aberdeen). His name continued to appear until the Directory of 1846/47 though his address changed to 46 Queen Street. 1847 was the date of death of my great-grandfather. In the Directory of 1847/48 the business had been taken over by John Edmond. I learned that it was still carried on in the name of Edmond and Spark, the business now being in the hands of a Mr. Douglas McD. Philip, however no relation. We then consulted the roll of Aberdeen alumni, where we found entries of for me extraordinary interest. My grandfather George Philip was recorded as a Master of

Arts under this note 'Georgius Philip f. Joannis, Librorum Glutina-toris, Aberdonensis.' His three brothers Alexander, John and Robert appeared under like entries. We then examined the bindings and they included (1) Aberdeen's earliest incunabule *The Epistles of St. Jerome* (1470) which bear the inscription 'Rebound, by J. Philip, Abdn, June 1834'; (2) A first edition of the Skene's *Regiam Majestatem* (1609); and (3) the first Minute Book of the Spalding Club. All these Bindings had a unique feature, namely that they are almost architectural in design having at each corner a square design. Mr. Mitchell says that no other corner-square bindings exist except, I think, one in Cambridge. One of the bindings was of peculiar interest because the four-square design by John Philip had been made to enclose a centre belonging to a much older binding. They have only recently been discovered and exhibited. Hence, no member of my family seems to have known about them.

Thereafter Farquhar MacRitchie took me to Messrs. Edmond and Spark and introduced me to my namesake, Mr. Douglas Philip. He was much interested. His firm is still in possession of some of the tools and designs used in producing these unique bindings. He pressed me to take on loan what he described as the first receipt given by my great-grandfather. It is dated December 1829 and bears also the signature of 'J. Edmond' who was presumably the employee who afterwards became the Edmond of the succeeding firm. I told both Mr. Mitchell and Mr. Philip that I had an old Day Book of my great-grandfather. On returning home I found that it contained an entry for 1st June 1807 'Commenced business in the bookbinding line in partnership with A. Hill, under the firm of Philip and Hill in the shop in the Lodge

Aberdeen Corner-square Book-Binding by John Philip: Minutes of the Spalding Club 1839–72, Vol.1

Receipt 1829, from John Philip, Book-Binder, Aberdeen.

Walk next to New Inn'. It is apparent therefore that the receipt, while an early one, is not by any means the first.

This was an exceedingly interesting discovery to make by the pure accident of looking over the show-case in the University Library.

Since returning to Edinburgh, I have learned further particulars from Beattie, Keeper of Printed Books at the National Library. Apparently, Mr. Edmond, who succeeded to John Philip's business, had a son, whom he named John Philip Edmond. The latter became Librarian to Lord Crawford, and afterwards Librarian of the W.S. Library. He was the author of the authority on Aberdeen printers. Beattie also told me that one of John Philip's bindings, which I saw at Aberdeen, turned up in England, and it was with information furnished by the National Library about it that Aberdeen managed to secure it for their Library. I returned from Aberdeen full of pride in this lovely work.

The other day Dr. Caldwell told me a story of an eighteenth century predecessor of his, Dr. Roy, in the parish of Aberlady. A villager of Aberlady owned a strip of land which ran into the lands of the Earl of Wemyss. It proved a veritable Naboth's vineyard, and the Earl coveted it. He and the parish minister laid their heads together as to how to acquire it. Eventually, the villager was inveigled up to Edinburgh on some fake pretext, and there conveniently press-ganged into the Navy. The Earl thought himself safe for a good time to come, and took over the plot. But the villager returned earlier than expected. When he learned what had happened, he thought twice about tackling the Earl, but went for his accomplice, the parish minister. He walked straight into the manse, took the minister by the scruff of the neck, conducted him into the garden, and then put him down the well! Shortly after, a rather bedraggled clergyman was brought out to return somewhat downcast and penitent to the manse.

Lord Crawford spoke to me after the last Standing Committee meeting of the National Library Trustees and said that he would like to suggest my name as Vice-Chairman of the Trustees in room of Dr. Baird Smith. However, it remains to be seen whether this will eventuate.

A fortnight ago, Lord Blades told me that Edward Keith (K.C.) is to be the new Sheriff-substitute at Edinburgh, in place of Gilchrist. But as yet there has been no announcement. His will be a very good appointment, as he is a first class lawyer. [He afterwards withdrew: Lindsay Duncan, from Kilmarnock receiving the appointment.]

Dover has invited me to go with him on May 18 to see the new production, in London, of Anthony and Cleopatra, by Laurence Olivier and Vivien Leigh, his wife. On the journey to Aberdeen, I read the introduction and First Act in Dover's newly published edition. Dover has also supplied me with particulars of the 'cuts' which Laurence Olivier proposes to make.

A week ago, when in London, I went to Olympia to see the Ideal Homes Exhibition, and was much interested to find a Books Exhibit including famous MSS, amongst them Sir Walter Scott's Abbot. It belongs to Col. Sir John Murray, the publisher and editor of the Quarterly. At the Library Standing Committee, three days later, I raised the question whether we might not approach Sir John to acquire this for the Library. Tom Simpson, who served under Sir John in the First World War, is to take an opportunity of approaching him.

10th April 1951

The Coronation Stone mystery still continues. Scotland Yard Detectives have scoured the West and West Highlands, and subjected a young woman domestic science teacher at Plockton to several hours' questioning. There is considerable indignation in responsible quarters at their activities. The Archbishop of Canterbury also made a most unfortunate reference to it in an Easter sermon, leaving the impression that those who took the stone were in some strange way linked with the violence of Good Friday. But 'do as you would be done by'. He should have referred to the violence with which the stone was first removed. My real regret about his utterances is the irrelevant harm it will do to the coming Inter-Church Relations report in the Assembly. Even one of the most staunch of Scottish Episcopalians has disavowed his views.

In a mild way, I have come in touch with the problem as Procurator. The Countess of Erroll, as hereditary High Constable, and others have publicly suggested that it should be deposited in a Scottish Church. Charles Warr discussed with me whether he should make a statement. On my advice, he stated to the Press that if it were deposited in St. Giles', he would have no alternative but at once to inform both the Secretary of State and the Police. Three nights ago, he called to see me. Feelers have been put out to him as to whether he could not receive it and at all events give it a dignified handing-over to Westminster Abbey, or suggest that it be held *in retentis* for a time until tempers had cooled, and some arrangement was made. We both agreed that this was an impossible course, and that he would personally be misrepresented in England. So, no doubt, it will either be handed over by whoever has it or remain concealed. What a Ruritanian romance for a novelist! How easily misunderstanding arises in England over things Scottish is shown by the fact that, when I was at the Church Assembly a day or two after the Covenant leaders suggested that the future of the Stone should be determined by the National Assembly, the Bishop of Derby thought this meant the General Assembly!

As an act of friendship, I gave the Bishop of Manchester my little book on Gordon, and he has replied with a little memoir he wrote of J.B. Gregg, a fellow undergraduate of his at Trinity College, Dublin, who died in early life as an Anglo-Catholic curate at Cullercoats, on the Tyne. I have a great affection and respect for William M., and we have now agreed to use each other's Christian names. He is a true Christian. I am glad Edinburgh is to give him a D.D.

The Secretary of State has just appointed me as Chairman of a Committee of Three to consider the functions and future administration of the National Museum of Antiquities. My colleagues are to be T.D. Kendrick, Director and Chief Librarian of the British Museum, and P.J. Rose, formerly Assistant-Under Secretary of State for Scotland. I shall find this most interesting.

Alison has just returned from three weeks in France. She went with Julia Birley (of Eton), Carol Robertson (whose father was with Harold at Merchiston) and an American girl. They travelled by bus from Paris to Lyon, Grenoble, Nice, Aix, Nimes, Avignon, and lived quite incredibly cheaply, at 4s. to 4s. 6d. each per night. It is good to hear of such independence. Alison had two nights also at Eton and attended Chapel twice during Holy week, hearing Alington preach. He is just resigning from the Deanery of Durham. Her account is that he spent his whole time either retailing stories or dashing (in so far as a man of his age can dash) into Boots for detective thrillers. De Valera was staying at Eton the week before Alison!

Two other invitations have come my way, of a novel kind for me, the one, to speak one Sunday morning at Merchiston (the result of my paper last month to the Leighton Club on The Layman and Reunion), and the other, from Melville Dinwiddie, to broadcast on 3rd June, in a Festival of Britain service, on 'Christianity and the Law' (the result of an after dinner speech recently at the Bohemian Club, Paisley, where he also was a speaker).

We leave on the 14th for a fortnight's holiday – Grasmere, Stratford-on-Avon, Oxford. We will return Alison there to L.M.H. and hope to meet some of her friends. The closest group are Julia; Carol; Eleanor Forshaw; and Astrid (in her own year); and Isobel Graham (a year ahead).

The Royal Commission for St. Andrews University is looming up now, and its appointment will soon be announced. I will be counsel for University College, Dundee, and Ronald Kydd my Junior. Tonight I have just written my last Opinion before going on holiday. One day last week, I produced four Opinions and two judgments, not all begun but all finished, the same day.

Rosemary got a perfectly lovely school report, just to match her big brother and sister. I went to the Botanic Gardens one day with her, and wandered among the rock-garden, and grass, and hot-houses, where I used to go with two other little children fifteen years ago. Her lovely little frank confiding nature was balm to me, as the gentians called up old memories.

11th April 1951

This afternoon, when I was walking with Rosemary, a newspaper reporter whispered into my ear that, three minutes before, word had reached the *Scotsman* that the Coronation Stone had been found laid on the High Altar of Arbroath Abbey! It is still not in the newspapers!

I had a visit this morning from Miss Connor, the Secretary of my new National Museum Committee. We have arranged for intimations and advertisements to go out for memoranda to be sent in by 30th June. In July, we will probably visit the British Museum, the London Museum, the Welsh National Museum (at Cardiff) and the Welsh Folk Museum at St. Fagan's Castle. We will probably hear the evidence in September.

12th April 1951

Last night, while Murdo Macdonald and David Smith (his assistant) were dining with us, Dr. Warr called. He was going to make a public statement about the Coronation Stone, and wanted me to revise it. I made several suggestions, which he adopted, and, as revised, it appears in today's *Scotsman*. He told me that the idea to deposit the Stone on the altar of Arbroath Abbey emanated from John Cameron. It was certainly a very much better solution than what Dr. Warr was contemplating, that it might be dumped at St. Giles'.

It seems quite obvious that the whole project at Arbroath was pre-arranged. No one took the number of the car which brought the Stone; no one could tell the type of car; no one seems to be able to identify the occupants. Two Arbroath Town Councillors 'happened' to arrive at the Abbey at the right moment.

Before I was dressed this morning, a trunk call came to me from a minister in Angus who wanted to take proceedings to interdict the police from returning the Stone to London. I guided him past this pitfall. Later in the day, I was rung up by the *Daily Mail*, and a very persistent newspaper man tried to find out whether I had been consulted about the letter left at Arbroath Abbey for the Church of Scotland. He revealed that the Moderator had today paid a visit to Glasgow, where the Stone now is, after having first been removed from Arbroath to Forfar. The hysterical Dean of Westminster is preaching at St. Andrews University this weekend. He will have a rather uncomfortable visit, I'm afraid, and scarcely get through without an incident. Even the Anglicans at Durham had little to say for his broadcast after the Stone was taken. The authorities seem to be thinking twice about taking the Stone to London.

1st May 1951

We returned on the 28th from a fortnight in England in which we motored to Grasmere, Bridgnorth, Stratford, Oxford, York, Otterburn, and home – these being our places of stay. Except for a wet Sunday at Grasmere, we had fine weather – ten days of unclouded sunshine. On the day we left, a letter of mine signed 'Rei Vindicatio' appeared in the *Scotsman*, and Professor Burleigh, with whom I held converse beforehand, adopted its suggestion in the Church and Nation Statement, which was printed prominently in *The Times* on 19th April, five days later.

We drove down to Grasmere in clear frosty sunshine. The fells were snow-capped, and we made a pleasant detour round Derwentwater. At Grasmere, we fell in with our old friends from Kingussie, Dr. and Mrs. Goldsbrough. He was Professor of Mathematics, at Newcastle, and from him I learned that the Durham Royal Commission took its evidence in private, without cross-examination. The same procedure may be followed in the case of St. Andrews. At Grasmere, Rosemary paid her second visit to Dove Cottage, and her first (my second) visit to Beatrix Potter's house at High Sawrey. From Grasmere we went straight south to Warrington, stopping at Wynwick for lunch. Then on by Tarporley, Whitchurch, Hodnet, Wellington to Bridgnorth, where we put up at Parlor's Hall, an old house now made into an hotel. Bridgnorth has a Caledonian Society of twenty-five members! Cheshire, especially Hodnet, charmed us on a clear sunny afternoon. Next day, after inspecting the old town of Bridgnorth and Worcester Cathedral, we lunched at Pershore and saw its Abbey, and stopped at Chipping Campden for tea. There we fell in with the vicar, an Irishman, who seeing us in his Church asked, was I in orders? An interesting conversation followed, and he promises, at some future date, to ring the 'Blue Bells of Scotland' on his chimes for our special benefit. At Stratford, we saw *Henry IV Part I*, with Michael Redgrave as Hotspur, and Anthony Quayle as Falstaff, we revisited all our old haunts, Campden (repeatedly), Bourton-on-the-Water (with its model village – building when last we were there), Bourton-on-the-Hill, Lower Slaughter (where we lunched by the stream), Stanway, Stanton, and two new sights, Great Tew and Dover's Hill. At Great Tew, a perfect Cotswold village, an inquisitive old villager plied us with questions while we lunched on the village green. We celebrated our Silver Wedding Day by attending the Shakespeare service at which a Father Tomkins (All Saints, Margaret Street) preached a 'sermon' half-essay, half-recitation, on Shakespeare (Anthony Quayle and

Michael Redgrave read the lesson, the latter Rom. 12 beautifully), and also by spending the afternoon at Dover's Hill, under superb conditions for the view. The cuckoo was singing in the woods. Another day to Compton Winyates; another to Coventry, Lichfield and the Mitchesons for tea; another day to Mary Arden's house. Then we took Alison to Oxford for her third term, and, at the conclusion of our Stratford visit, spent two days in Oxford to meet her friends. We saw her rooms and Miss Blochmann (her German tutor), had Isobel Graham with Alison to dinner one night, and the next evening, Julia Birley, Carol Robertson, Eleanor Forshaw and Princess Astrid of Norway and Alison. Astrid was just treated like everyone else, and called by her Christian name. It was rather sweet to see Queen Victoria's great great granddaughter curtsey twice to Ella when she left. We had coffee one morning overlooking the house of the Master of University College with some American friends of Alison's, the Bouwsmas, Dutch Americans from Nebraska and Michigan. On our way north from Oxford, we called at Akely to see the Hunters, a Stowe master and his wife, whom we met at Oban. Oxford was roasting, we lay in the Parks watching cricket practices. I saw the Balliol flag at half-mast, and learned later in the day that it was because of the death of Sumner. At York, we visited the Minster, at Durham, the Cathedral. There, we fell in with my friend, Greenslade, and afterwards had tea with the R.R. Williams at St. John's. At Otterburn, we stayed at the Towers with the Hendersons.

The Anglo-Scottish Church Report is out today. The *Scotsman* gives it a cool reception; the *Glasgow Herald* an appreciative one; the English papers say little about it, and only emphasise the difficulties.

20th May 1951

Gordon would have been twenty-four today.

I have just returned from two unforgettable days in London. I travelled there on the night of the 17th. On the morning of the 18th we had our Central Land Board meeting – a most exhilarating one. There was an incredibly difficult paper to be considered. It had been framed from the standpoint of administration, but it seemed to me to involve much that was outside the Act. I weighed in on this line, and found I was strongly supported by Dame Myra Curtis and Sir Basil Gibson. Against our view, the opposite view seemed to break down, and the paper is to be considered further. Sir Robert Fraser afterwards indicated to me that he was much encouraged by our line.

It was an interesting issue between law and administration, and was so difficult a question that I made it plain that I only expressed my view with diffidence, but this, I think, gave it in the result more weight.

After lunch with Mr. Rutherford and Mr. Sheldrake (Scottish head of the Board's Edinburgh Office), I went to the British Museum, where I had an interesting hour with Dr. Kendrick over the National Museum of Antiquities Committee. Afterwards, I met some of his principals at tea in their rather surprisingly third-rate canteen. Then I returned to the Caledonian Club in time to meet Dover. After an early dinner, we set off for *Caesar and Cleopatra* at the St. James's Theatre. We found that Sir Laurence Olivier had provided us with complimentary tickets, and Dover hatched the plan that we should invite him and Vivien Leigh for lunch, which I offered at the Club (ladies being admitted on Saturdays). He sent in word to Sir Laurence, during an interval, and the latter asked us to come round to see him after the play. *Caesar and Cleopatra* is a farce till the second last Act, when Shaw suddenly becomes absorbed in his theme, abandons his jokes and ends seriously. Sir Laurence, as Caesar, was quite superb. Art was concealed, and we saw only Caesar, a tolerant, large-hearted statesman afraid of being considered old. Cleopatra's part is disappointing for anyone to play, as Shaw suddenly drops her from the drama. The company included Norman Wooland as Lucius Septimus, Robert Helpmann as Appollodorus, and Esmond Knight as Belganos. Wooland (taller by a head than most others and a handsome figure) I found disappointing, reciting his lines rather than acting his part. Robert Helpmann has an unfortunate smirk which never leaves his face, and makes him never anyone but Robert Helpmann. Esmond Knight was inconspicuous. Of the lesser characters, Wilfred Hyde White, as Britannicus, was, I think, easily the best. His Victorian Englishman, in the guise of an ancient Briton, always brought the house down. Vivien Leigh, subject to the limitations of her part, was good. Olivier was really great – in Dover's judgment our foremost actor.

Afterwards we went round to his rooms, a suite of three, a parlour, office, and dressing room, with a bust of Caesar (on which his make up was modelled), but not really Caesar at all (as he confessed). He is smaller than I thought, no taller than myself, or only an inch or so more. Some dozen people joined us in the outer parlour. Each time he introduced us all to any newcomer, never faltering with our names. I remarked to him on this – I suppose it comes of quickly mastering his lines. I was introduced to Emlyn Williams amongst others, who

THE *NEW SHAKESPEARE*

ANTONY AND
CLEOPATRA

EDITED BY
JOHN DOVER WILSON

CAMBRIDGE UNIVERSITY PRESS

Randall
with an Editor's affection.
Christmas 1950

[Garrey]

[signature]

Intended of Sullivan as never truly Roman on 18th May 1951, after Shaw; Caesar and Cleopatra, and then Shakespeare's Antony and Cleopatra.

had called to see him. He was full of the lightness of Shaw and his slightness in comparison to the great tragedy of Shakespeare. 'And what a shame of the old man to give my wife such a poor part, and such poor lines to end on.' Then we – six of us – were taken in to his office, where he talked to us for twenty minutes, remarking on the failure of Alec Guinness in the present production of *Hamlet*, on Ivor Brown's criticism of his pronouncing 'Charmian' with a soft 'ch' (although Shakespeare's pun on it shows that was his way of pronouncing the name), and other like topics. He was still dressed in his Roman toga, and played with a necklace of 'gold' just removed. He was easy and friendly, without any 'side'. Before we left, he signed my copy from Dover of *Anthony and Cleopatra*, and then insisted: 'You must go and see my wife.' So we called next on Vivien Leigh. Dover went in first. I, not seeking to push my way in, remained outside, but Dover immediately brought me in, and introduced me as 'The Procurator of the Church of Scotland!' Notwithstanding this alarming introduction, she could not have been more kind and unpretentious, and talked to me in a most friendly and unsophisticated way. She is very small, has not a trace of colour in her cheeks, but is very beautiful. What, however, was most attractive was just her vivacious manner. We gave our invitation, but they both explained that the demands of their programme made it impossible. They give one performance of Anthony from 5 p.m. till 8 p.m., and start a second from 8.30 till 11.30. They are dead to the world at other times. Tomorrow was to be their first performance on this routine. Sir Laurence confessed that Shaw's lines were specially difficult to learn – 'Perhaps I'm getting old,' he said (he is only forty-three). I noticed, however, that, during the play, once or twice he fumbled slightly, once using Theodolus for Pothinius. But of course, this is only the first week of the production. Vivien Leigh also signed my *Anthony*.

On Saturday 19th, Dover and I visited the South Bank Exhibition of the Festival of Britain, visiting the main sights, drinking one pint of beer at the side of the Thames, and having a buffet lunch in the open air. The Exhibition has a unique site, and the exhibits show that a high level of intelligence is called for. Compared with other exhibitions before the War, it has, however, an ersatz quality. I was most interested in the exhibition of locomotives, and we also, like children, at noon watched coloured balloons released carrying free tickets of admission far and wide over London to those lucky ones who should find them. The wind carried them off in the direction of Lambeth. In the Lion and the Unicorn Exhibit, which included a symbol of 'British' justice, I was disappointed to find no hint anywhere that there was such a thing as the Law of Scotland – only Magna Carta, Habeas Corpus, and a collection of English Law Reports. I wrote afterwards to the director suggesting Stair and Erskine – with Stair's words, 'Surely they are most happy, whose laws are nearest to equity.'

In the afternoon, we visited the exhibition of books and early photographs in the Victoria and Albert Museum, where we received a special greeting from an effusive official who invited us to sign the Special Visitors Book, which we did beneath the names of Stephen Spender and Arthur Ransome. For me, the most memorable book exhibits were these: The Benedictional of St. Aethelwold (the finest surviving example of the Winchester school of illumination); Boswell's London Diary 1762–3 (lent by Yale University); the original MS of *David Copperfield*; and a lovely copy of Gilbert White's *Natural History of Selborne*, with a picture of Selborne (which I know) itself. The photographs included D. Octavius Hill's famous Disruption group, numerous pictures of Edinburgh midway through last century, an unusual but pleasing portrait of R.L.S., and a number of photographs by Dover's father's partner.

After tea at the Club, we walked across the Green Park past the tulips before Buckingham Palace, past Clarence House with its gay window boxes, through a Court of St. James's Palace to King Street where, once more, we entered the St. James's Theatre, and again took up the same seats, as we had last night, in the second row of the stalls. Sir Laurence said that he found the opening scenes of Anthony difficult, but from the meeting of Anthony and Octavius, the play moves on like an irresistible tide. Some one said it is at least one of Shakespeare's three greatest tragedies. The tragedy is certainly the most protracted, and the double tragedy is unique. Dover thinks *Othello* the most 'tragic' ending, with *Lear* next; though, I think, he would select as the three greatest, *Hamlet*, *Macbeth* and *Anthony*. The death of Anthony and the death of Cleopatra were superbly acted. It had all the solemn tragedy of the second movement in the Eroica Symphony. Both Anthony and Cleopatra played their parts with great feeling and depth. It was an unforgettable experience. After cheering ourselves with a late dinner at the Great Northern Hotel, we stepped on to the Night Scotsman for home. Dover breakfasted with us, and then left for Balerno.

2nd June 1951

The General Assembly has just ended. The Debate on the Stone of Destiny fizzled out, the Assembly, I think rightly (in the end), deciding not to deal with a matter so far removed from the concerns of a Christian Church. Our Anglo-Scottish Report went through with almost complete unanimity, two ministers being annoyed at the sentence providing for courtesy reference by Anglicans, invited to preach by us, to the Scottish Episcopal Bishop. On all else, there was unanimity. In submitting the Report, Manson spoke for forty-six minutes, and was almost stamped down. My speech was given a good reception: a pin could be heard dropping at the end, where I recalled Dad's 'Presbyter's blessing' conferred on Randall Davidson in 1921. Many people thanked me afterwards. Tom Taylor, following in the discussion, described it as 'moving', and Murdo Macdonald told me afterwards that it had been described to him by a Highland Minister as the best in the Assembly. I thought Field Marshal Sir William Slim's speech the best. Strangely, in the one week, I also heard two other generals, Sir Alan Cunningham (at the dedication of the Academy War Memorial), and Sir Gordon MacMillan (in the Assembly). Other distinguished visitors who spoke were the Archbishop of York (Garbett), Alderman Denys Lowson (of the Carse of Gowrie: Lord Mayor of London; married to a daughter of Lord Strathcarron), and the Ambassador of Jugoslavia. I seconded the General Administration Report, as well as the Inter-Church Relations Report, and my Kirk Session in the Forces Act was well-received both in the Assembly and in the Press. John Taylor (of Birkenhead) came for a night, and spent a whole day in the Assembly, hearing the M. of M. debate, and the Belford case. In the evening of his arrival, we drove him out to see Dalmeny Church, and the Priory Church at Queensferry. Dr. White Anderson made a first class Moderator. I give him full marks for everything, except the closing address in which he fell below the otherwise very high standard. His words of welcome, his prayers, and his control of business, could not have been better. Mr. Mathers made a good Commissioner, taking the place of Admiral Cunningham, just four days before the Assembly, owing to the latter's illness. The Assembly was the most interesting since I became Procurator: the Iona Community was integrated into the Church; the Inter-Church Report on the Anglican Conversations was approved; the Report of the Commission on Communion was an important document, as also the Report of the Commission on the Doctrine of the last War. The Assembly showed a healthy independence, and turned down the

Highlands Committee for a Deputy-Superintendent of Highland Missions and the Church and Nation Committee's report on the Stone. Burleigh was much upset at its view on the latter; but much harm was done to his most temperate report and speech by an inflammatory political diatribe by Sir George Waters, to which the sound sense of the Assembly reacted very badly. We had our usual dinner for the Representatives of the Presbytery of Uist; this time two ministers and two elders came – from Daliburgh, Benbecula and North Uist. I was greatly pleased when the Assembly appointed me to The Church Hymnary Trust, for over thirty years of organ playing I have got to know most of the leading Hymnaries backwards as well as forwards.

7th June 1951

Last Sunday, the 3rd, I broadcast on 'Christianity and Law' in the second of a series of broadcasts for the Festival of Britain on Christianity and the British tradition. I was given the choice of church or studio, and preferred the latter (especially for this kind of address). At my request, Murdo Macdonald conducted the service. I have had many grateful letters from up and down the country, and the address is to be printed in two places.

This week the Dean and I (on opposite sides) have been engaged in an incredible case, another – one hopes the last – of the 'Free Church' type of litigations. It relates to a split in the Free Presbyterian Church, and outwardly the dispute is as to which section of a congregation shall have the right to use a manse. The manse is held on a title under which the trustees are directed to hold it, in a disruption, for that section which adheres to the constitution and standards of the Free Church, as set forth in the Deed of Separation of 1893 of the Free Presbyterian Church. We have been raking through the Westminster Confession, the Order of Presbyterian Church-Government, Moncrieff's Practice and other like documents. The story is:- The Rev. Mr. Macqueen, now dead, once F.P. minister in Inverness, had a lady member of his congregation suspended for non-attendance at Communion. That was in 1924; and there were various irregularities about it, though the case was appealed up to the Synod, their Supreme Court. In 1937 the case was reopened with the result that, in 1938, the Synod restored the lady to membership. This was too much for Mr. Macqueen. He lodged a formal Protest over this latter decision. The Synod took the view that he thereby renounced their authority and separated himself from the Church – a rather startling view. However, he went out, followed by some of his flock (who were not put out) and started a separate congregation. He is now dead, but the congregation remains. It now has an 'honorary' pastor, and three 'elders' (two naively described as 'assessor elders'). Our short point – I acted for the Church – was that this 'congregation' was not a Presbyterian congregation but simply a self-constituted religious meeting, and, whether the Synod acted rightly or wrongly over Mr. Macqueen's protest, that did not concern the present members of this 'congregation', none of whom had been put out. The Dean, with his rather untethered eloquence, spoke of modern 'papal infallibility' and said that his 'whole argument related to the liberty of conscience' (for Mr. Macqueen). Guthrie could not help laughing, when I pointed out that, while that was his 'whole argument', his 'whole pleadings' related to other matters. The whole debate proceeded in an excellent atmosphere, and Harry Guthrie, who can be a little cross-grained but who, I know, likes me (and I him), gave me an excellent hearing. I was able to get in the comment on the Dean and his minority that their attitude was 'They're all out of step except oor Jock' ('Jock' being a veiled reference to the Dean). I was supported by almost the complete Synod, in old fashioned white ties and dickies. At the end, they expressed their warm appreciation of our argument. I could not help thinking what a fine set of men they might have been – with strong sharp features and keen intellectual faces – had their activities been directed to broad practical Christianity instead of the 'moribund orthodoxy' in which they vegetate, literal inspiration, prohibition of 'uninspired hymns' and 'instrumental music' which are included among their major tenets.

24th June 1951

The President told me a delightful story. Recently an Inverness Magistrate had ordered the destruction of a dog because it had bitten a child. When the case came on appeal before the judges of the First Division in the High Court, it transpired that children had been interfering with the dog, while it was having a meal, and the dog's behaviour was understandable. The Court therefore recalled the Magistrate's order. The other night, the President was walking up and down his lawn smoking his pipe, in the cool of the evening. Suddenly, the garden gate was pushed open, and a little girl entered, followed by a dog. She walked quietly over to the Lord

President, and shyly said: 'Excuse me, are you Lord Cooper?' He said: 'Yes, I am. What can I do for you?' The little girl replied: 'I just came here, because I wanted to thank you for saving the dog Laddie's life!'

Lord Crawford is going to propose my name tomorrow at the Library Standing Committee as Vice-Chairman of the Trustees in room of Dr. Baird Smith.

I have just returned from the Law Oral Examinations at Aberdeen University – always a delightful round of hospitality thanks to the Tom Smiths. I met David Daube, the new Professor of Jurisprudence, a most remarkable man, one of the three leading civilians in Europe. I expected a rather quick super-clever intellectual. But not at all – he is a quiet, gentle character, with a penetrating, almost hypnotic eye, a personality that conveys somehow supreme goodness and intellectual integrity. I took to him at once, and lost my trepidation immediately. With Tom Smith, David Daube, and now J.J. Gow (just appointed a Lecturer, and a natural legal genius) and Farquhar MacRitchie, a fine Scot of the Scots, Aberdeen has far and away the best Law Faculty in Scotland: it is indeed at the moment one of the first in Europe, though this has still to be discovered, as two of the appointments, Daube's and Gow's, have only just been made.

25th June 1951

The Standing Committee of the Library met, and I absented myself till they had discussed the Vice-Chairmanship. I gather from what I was told after that they think of approaching Dover first. Nothing could give me greater pleasure. They were all very nice to me, and, if it was in a sense a personal disappointment, there is nothing personal about their view, but only that Dover is very much senior and more worthy in every way, and I am already Convener of the Standing Committee. I shall show them that I respect their judgment and am not petty-minded. Ella, as always, was there to welcome me when I came home.

Alison, just back from Lady Margaret Hall, had an unusual distinction a week before the end of term – that of falling into the river from a canoe in company with Royalty. Astrid (just back the same day from Buckingham Palace, where she had been staying with her grandfather, King Haakon), Carol and Alison all went out in the evening in a canoe for supper. The canoe gradually turned turtle, and all went in, greatly to their own delight and that of the spectators on the banks. Alison goes to Heidelberg this August. Rosemary is to be the Sleeping Princess in a school-play.

10th July 1951

Yesterday was our half-yearly meeting of the National Library Trustees. Dover lunched me at the New Club. Lord Crawford joined us, and we had an hour's talk. Then our meeting at 3.15, at which I seconded the nomination of Dover as Vice-Chairman of Trustees. After the meeting, I brought Janet Adam Smith, Lord Crawford and Dover home for tea. They were all most pleasant. I had written Lord Crawford saying that, if Dover was proposed, nothing would please me more, and that I would be very glad to support his nomination. Lord Crawford replied thanking me for 'your kind and generous letter'. He made it very plain that he was most appreciative of my attitude, and I felt that I had cemented a friendship. Lord Crawford remained quite a time after the others had gone, discussing books.

12th July 1951

We were discussing politics at the Round Table today, where the law of defamation is suspended. I observed: 'The difference between the Dean and the Vice-Dean' (they were both present) 'is that the Dean is agin' everything and the Vice-Dean' (a genial agnostic) 'in favour of nothing!' There was general agreement that in this there was an element of truth.

The other night a Waldensian student who has been studying theology this Session at New College, called to say good-bye, before leaving that night for Italy. He said: 'There are seventy pastors in the Waldensian church, and I am the sixty-second to come to Edinburgh to New College!' He has been to Wales and Ireland, Iona, Oxford and Kent. He was full of appreciation for the spirit of friendship he had met in the Church of Scotland. J.S. Stewart and Tom Torrance were his favourite professors. Their theological outlook, he felt, was nearest to the Italian. He had never been able to read Karl Barth in Italy, because there was no Italian translation: 'but my visit here has let me read him in English.' He considers that the real life in the Waldensian Church just now is rather to be found in the South (where he comes from) than in its traditional home – the Valleys. His successor at New College will also come from South Italy. He goes now to a parish in Milan for a year, then to Paraguay or Uruguay.

14th July 1951

Saturday morning, Caledonian Club, London. I am sitting in my bedroom here at the window, overlooking a mass of red brick houses, some draped with creeper, chestnut trees dense with foliage coming right up to one of the windows, and to the south, over a sea of chimneys, Westminster Cathedral.

I came here on Thursday night. Yesterday morning, we had the Central Land Board and War Damage Commission meeting. Everything conspired to make the proceedings run into the afternoon, which could have been awkward as I had another engagement at 2.30. However, I had a meeting with C.J. Highton, the solicitor; then the Board meeting, with nine substantial problems on the agenda; then a conference with the Chairman (Sir Thos. Phillips), the Vice-Chairman (Sir Robert Fraser), the Deputy-Secretary (H.B. Usher) and Highton, about a case for counsel. Since Sir Malcolm Eve resigned from the Chairmanship, I have been the only lawyer on the Board. As a result of this conference, I will probably have to come for a consultation in September. I am always struck by the facility of expression of some, though not all, of my colleagues on the various Boards or Committees I have sat on here. If it were unusual, I could only put it down to the English classical training. But it is not unusual, though I think definitely more widespread than among the same classes in Scotland. On the other hand, it is not matched by an equal gift of written expression. The inferiority of which I am very conscious in oral expression, I do not feel in written. I think that the real explanation must be the much larger percentage of men trained in public schools in England: this at least inculcates an early confidence together with an early training in holding one's own. In another way, one gets the same training, in a fuller degree but at a later less receptive stage, at the Bar. I am often struck with the complete inability of very distinguished intellects in other walks of life to give ready answers to straight questions. One or two of my theological friends show up their weakness in this respect in presenting business in the General Assembly. They are excellent conversationalists, and yet when a question is put to them unawares, they are tongue-tied. I think that the reason is that answering questions in public is a test of one form of intellectual honesty; and, in a sense, every time a difficult question is answered, one performs a mild act of courage, and the more practice one has the more likely one is to give not merely a straight, but a satisfactory, answer.

I took Usher to lunch at the Caledonian Club. He was in the

Treasury and private secretary to Ramsay Macdonald. He knew Craigie Aitchison, Tommy Cooper and J.S.C. Reid, and placed the second highest in Parliamentary capacity. He was less impressed with Reid, but did not see him so much in his opposition days, when he excelled as a front bench critic. His mind is essentially destructive, whereas Cooper is essentially constructive (of the highest order), though somewhat petty-minded.

From this point onwards, I began my work as Chairman of the National Museum of Antiquities Committee. My programme was to visit (Friday afternoon) the British Museum; this morning the London Museum; tomorrow Caerleon Museum and St. Fagan's Folk Museum in Wales; and on Monday morning, the National Museum of Wales.

At 2.30 I went to the British Museum, and there met Kendrick, P.J. Rose, and Miss Connor, our Secretary. After a preliminary conference, we were taken to the Museum of Antiquities, and had a further conference with the Keeper, who then took us round the Department, introducing us to Brailsford his assistant. The Department is only recovering from bomb-damage, and not all the rooms were at their best. In particular, we were able to see relatively few of the British Antiquities, but we did see one room of items in course of preparation. I should like to have studied them longer. Actually what interested me most was in another room – as we were leaving – the MS of *Alice in Wonderland* and MSS of *Captain Scott of the Antarctic*.

Afterwards, we three (Rose, Miss Connor and myself) had tea together, and then I brought Rose here for dinner. He was at Dover House for many years first as a private secretary, and finally as deputy permanent secretary. The Scottish Office, which has been located at Fielden House since bombs damaged Dover House early in the war, is shortly to return to Dover House. Rose served under some fourteen Scottish Secretaries from Lord Balfour of Burleigh onwards, and some fifteen Lord Advocates. He had a special regard for Dunedin, Shaw and Ure. Both he and Miss Connor asked me about Uncle Robert, with whose work with tuberculosis they had come in contact.

(Saturday evening: Angel Hotel, Cardiff) This morning we visited the London Museum which is for the present housed in a portion of Kensington Palace. The taxi-driver brought me up the main drive to the Palace, a modest building surrounding a quadrangle, with pink geraniums at the windows and the doors. Mr. Grimes, the Keeper of the Museum, pointed out the only portion at present occupied by royalty the portion occupied by my Kilmory friend, Princess Alice and the Earl of Athlone. It looked very quiet and modest, an oasis in the heart of London. The policeman at the door stopped my taxi, but the driver explained that I was making for the Museum, which, it turned out, is properly entered from the Park. Coming the private way, I saw a delightful group of mews houses, now occupied by royal staff, almost (except for the dull brick) like a part of a Cotswold village, set in a London Park. A private gateway admitted me to the Park, and a hundred yards to the right was the entrance to the portion used as the London Museum. Here the museum has moved from bombed out Lancaster House. It may remain there for fifteen years; alternatively, its new home may be Holland House or a site near the South Bank Exhibition. It was a broiling summer's day, and the light came into the cool apartments making them very attractive. Mr. Grimes discussed the museum with us for over an hour, a lively voluble energetic man, full of ideas, who has made a wonderful thing of his temporary quarters – far more imaginative than anything I have seen in this sphere. The museum is on two floors. Great skill has been shown in choosing soft greens and pinks for decoration. The showcases themselves are delicately coloured. Each has concealed overhead lighting, and the museum itself especially the lower cellar-like floor is relatively subdued in its lighting, so that one unconsciously concentrates on the exhibits. It shows that good lighting in the museum itself is not important, if the exhibits are properly lighted. Mr. Grimes has also shown great skill in devising display cabinets out of the walls. There was even a small window showing children's furry toys through the years. But the whole museum was quite remarkable. There were London costumes from Tudor to Victorian times, the robes of a judge and a sergeant-at-law, Cromwell's death mask, Charles I's dress at execution, an early haberdasher's shop, Chelsea porcelain, and old glass, an eighteenth century interior, a wonderful sounding clock, with arts and crafts which functioned at 12 noon (we saw it striking then), quite unique models of London in different ages, the Globe Theatre, old London Bridge, with its arches which so stemmed the river as to create a lake which froze in winter, the Great Fire (actually taking place), Old St. Paul's, Roman London, old Cheapside, a showcase of suffragette items, Elizabethan jewellery, Coronation robes, royal cradles, children's toys and dolls' houses, a photographic survey of London, interesting prints of London throughout the ages, bone-shakers, the Holyhead coach (a model), and an old sampler with the quaint sentiment:-

> Sweet it is to see a child
>> Tender, merciful and mild
> Ever ready to perform
>> Acts of kindness to a worm!

After lunch, we caught the 3.45 express from Paddington for Cardiff (three hours: first stop Newport). It took me through familiar country, the line to Didcot, Swindon, near Malmesbury, near Castle Combe, and then to new country, the view south to Bristol, the Severn tunnel (5 minutes 10 seconds to go through) and so into South Wales without a sight yet of the Severn. What a change west of the river: poor houses, and untidy waste space in front of Cardiff station, few porters, fewer taxis, the austerity of a grim industrial area, grimmer than the worst of Lancashire. We put up at the Angel, where I overlook the park of Cardiff Castle. In the evening, Dr. John, Director of the National Museum, called, with his wife, to see us. What a contrast is this grim countryside to the soft quiet of Kensington Palace.

15th July 1951

Cardiff. The Angel. This morning, we motored to St. Fagan's Castle (not really a castle, but a Tudor house) to see the Welsh Folk Museum. St. Fagan's is the former seat of the Earl of Plymouth (Windsor-Clive), and the place where Royalty used to stay on their visits to Cardiff. It is four miles out, but beside the main line to Swansea, and stands in a beautiful garden, with part of the old Castle walls, with the little church beside from whose steeple the bells tolled the Sunday hymns, and the whole perched above a little valley with fish-ponds and beyond sloping wooded country. The grounds extend to 18 acres, and beyond the ponds, reached by a tunnel under the road, is another 80 acres to form an extension of the Museum grounds. The Castle itself will ultimately be only an exhibit, for the Museum proper is to be built in the 80 acres. The Castle is furnished in early seventeenth century style. As many as 80,000 visit it in the year. The garden contains a lovely statue of a boy by Sir W. Goscombe John. We also saw a tulip tree, with a flower with the fragrance of a melon. There are in the grounds a seventeenth century (reconstructed) woollen mill and barn, the first still in course of erection. Two other buildings – seventeenth century pavilions – are to be put up. All represent period buildings transported stone by stone from their original site. How splendid it would be if we in Scotland could have such grounds with specimens of a Hebridean 'black house', the broch of Mousa, and indoor models of such things as a section of the Roman Wall (Antonine), a medieval monastery, some of our first old bridges, and medieval Edinburgh, and folk-work such as the thatchwork done by Errol craftsmen and, at the other end, Betty Kirkwood's enamel and silver work. St. Fagan's was the scene of a Royalist defeat in the Civil War. We returned by Llandaff Cathedral. The main spire was partially destroyed, and the interior burnt out in the blitz. Beside is a statue of Dean Buckland, a celebrated Welsh geologist in clerical garb, a rather striking period piece. He it was who discovered the Red Lady remains of prehistoric origin (a man at that) which he placed as Roman, believing that the world was created in 4,004 BC. At St. Fagan's, they have craftsmen who do wood-turning and basket-making: and, by their work, make £600 a year. Dr. John of the National Museum, and Dr. Peate, Keeper of St. Fagan's, showed us round. It is curious how two of the chief figures in Cardiff have been Scotsmen – the Marquis of Bute (who inherited his Cardiff estate through a marriage with a Herbert), and the Mackintosh of Mackintosh.

After entertaining Dr. John and Dr. Nash-Williams (Keeper of Antiquities) to lunch – Dr. Peate had to leave us for other work – we set off by car in the afternoon to Caerleon Roman Museum and Camp, which lies upstream on the Usk from Newport. It occupies a rather unique situation. The Usk is a relatively broad and deep river – it could take 8,000-ton steamers but for its innumerable bends. At Caerleon, there is a great plain surrounded and sheltered by hills, and the site of the camp is surrounded by a great bend of the Usk. To reach the Camp and Caerleon itself, you cross the river close to the site of the old Roman bridge. The Camp itself, one of the three legion-centres in Britain – York and Chester being the others – covers a large area; and outside the Camp proper are the amphitheatre, baths and quarters for camp followers.

The Museum, to which we went first, occupies a rather absurd whitewashed little classical building, and consists of one hall with cellar beneath. Perhaps the most interesting of all the exhibits was a large inscription, found recently, recording Trajan's third consulate. The stone was Italian marble, and had been engraved in Italy during the second consulate, but the third had been reached by the time the stone reached Caerleon, and a less skilled hand had added another 'I' to the 'II' already engraved, making it look like this:- 'III'. There were large collections of coins of almost every emperor, fragments of Samian ware, tomb-stones, an amphora, and a statue of the god and goddess of fortune, a statue probably of a legionary commander, and sections of mosaic paving.

The amphitheatre lies close by. It was excavated by Dr. Nash-Williams himself. The arena is comparatively small, and the surrounding banking rose to 30 feet and is quite high yet. There is a fine system of conduits for drainage; the site of an old altar, probably to Nemesis, the goddess of the gladiator; and the entrance with traces of the gates which admitted the animals. They may have had dogs fighting larger animals, for this is depicted on a stone in the museum. The stone work was covered with plaster, on which imaginary stone work was depicted, the 'stones' being divided by red lines or cuts. One such section is depicted under glass; but the red is fading – and soon the paint will no longer be visible. The various sections of the work had the names of the officers in charge recorded, and the fact that these stones are hidden suggests that they were put there only for purposes of record: if any fault was afterwards found in the work, it would be traced to its author. The stone work nearest the arena was covered with a smooth concrete facing, probably to prevent animals from getting a foothold and jumping out.

16th July 1951

(10 p.m. in the train at King's Cross before departure.) This morning we made a lightning inspection of the National Museum of Wales. It is perhaps the finest of the three main buildings of Cardiff City Centre – the Museum, the Municipal Buildings, the Law Courts. The Municipal Buildings I certainly like the least. The Museum is particularly strong in its botanical and geological sections. In the Botanical, there are the most wonderful life-like replicas of Welsh flowers made by a lady who is both an artist and a botanist. The exhibits relating to the Welsh coalfield are the best in the Geological. In Art, there are magnificent works of Goscombe John, Augustus John, and Frank Brangwyn – all Welshmen. The Archaeological – with which we were specially concerned – is inadequately housed as regards exhibition space, but its storage and register system is particularly good, and the space ample. Folk-exhibits take up too much space – proportionately – the most interesting however being a spit for roasting an ox which is turned by a treadmill operated by a dog – we saw another yesterday at St. Fagan's. There is very little painting, apart from the artists mentioned. There is in Sculpture a fine Rodin. The Coronation robes worn in 1911 by the Duke of Windsor as Prince of Wales are

shown – what will the Queen, on her visit two days hence, think of them? There is fine Welsh china, Roman coins (the gold are replaced for exhibition by imitations, for security). There is a magnificent lecture-hall – the Reardon Smith – seating 480 in the fashion of a continental Chamber of Deputies. It has a stage for plays and concerts.

Dr. John, with Dr. Nash-Williams and Mr. Lee (the Secretary), entertained us at lunch, where we also met Captain Crawshey, a member of the Council, Lord-Lieutenant of Monmouth, and member of an iron founders' firm, who does much public service of all kinds and is greatly respected.

Mr. Rose and I caught the 3 p.m. London express and were back in Paddington by 6.10 p.m. The country was bathed in soft sunshine, and as we passed through the fringe of the Cotswolds, I thought with a pang of old days motoring through this very land with Gordon and Alison, then little children. After dinner at the Club, Mr. Rose and I came up here, and now this very moment the train has started for home.

21st July 1951

We left yesterday morning on the Northern Lights cruise. We joined the *Pharos* lying off Granton at 9.30 a.m., and visited Inchkeith, Fidra, the Bass Rock, and the Isle of May (the first lighthouse I have visited twice on these cruises). We lay off the Isle of May till 6 a.m. this morning, and now (6.30 a.m.) we are creeping up the coast of Fife towards the Bell Rock.

31st July 1951

Great indignation was caused by the announcement in Parliament of an increase in salary to all but the part-time Sheriffs. No one of course objected to the increase, but only to the discrimination. I read this decision as a first step towards the abolition of the office of Sheriff; if it were to go, it would mean the end of almost the last of the great historic offices; and it would certainly be more costly if the work now done by them is put into other hands – so many miscellaneous duties are at present paid for by the Sheriff's salary. Two very weak appointments, for which Lord Advocates Cooper and Reid were responsible, have not enhanced respect for the office. But, as an interested party, my views must be accepted *cum grano*.

When I went to bed, I found the usual last night apple-pie bed awaiting me. My pyjamas were sewn up; my shoe-trees placed beneath the sheets; and the sheets and blankets folded the wrong way. The Secretary – our 'paid-dog' as we affectionately call him – must be responsible, for whoever did it secured access to my cabin by means of a skeleton key. I retaliated by putting an ashet of salmon (what remained of it) under Gordon Thomson's pillow. In other ways, the evening was a gay one. There was the usual lightsome deck-billiards, George Morton's and Robbie Maconochie's 'buckies' being greased on the under-side with candle-wax, which made them travel unaccountably twice the usual distance.

16th August 1951

I returned home on 1st August, and next day motored with Ella and Rosemary (Alison being in Heidelberg) to start our holiday at Lunga House Hotel, Ardfern. We stayed there till the 7th, when we came on here (Great Western Hotel, Oban).

Lunga House is the home of the Macdougalls of Lunga, the senior branch of the clan after Macdougall of Macdougall (Dunollie). They have suffered the heaviest of losses. The then heir, in the Grenadier Guards, was killed in September 1914. His father, although sixty-one, went off in the Gordon Highlanders (in which he was a colonel), and was also killed in action in France in 1915. A grandson was left as heir. He grew up to serve in the Second World War: he also died in action. Now his widow is trying to maintain the house for the son, a boy of eleven years of age. The house is being conducted as an hotel by two ladies, the Misses Shankland, who have, I suppose, taken a lease of the house. It stands in a sheltered fold of the hills overlooking the sea, Shuna, Luing, Lunga and Scarba. We had superb sunsets over the Ross of Mull. A monument beside the sea commemorates the Macdougall's sacrifice.

We visited Crinan, Kilmartin (where we attended the really beautiful little perpendicular church, whose present minister, the Rev. Angus Macleod, is a native of Harris), Craignish, and the lovely Kilmelford-Dalavich road. Loch Craignish is a scene of depopulation. There was once a pier, which is now crumbling away, and the little hamlet, round the old parish church, is like the church itself in ruins. One day we overtook a party of boys walking from Kilmartin to Ardfern, and offered two of them a lift. They were charming little boys, one from North Shields, the other from Oxford, brought there by a boys' club run by New College, Oxford. The guiding spirit seems to be Keith

Hodgkin, son of Mrs. Lionel Smith (we knew that the Smiths had also stayed, with Freya Stark, at Lunga). The boys live on an old boat, made into a house, stranded above high water mark on an island opposite Ardfern.

Our fellow guests in the hotel included a charming Greenock business man, Mr. Nicol, who is fitting out the farm of Kilbride, near Kilmartin, as a sheep farm for himself and an ex-naval son; a Scots doctor from High Wycombe, with a very English wife and three boys (he was one of ten children of Mr. Craig, sometime parish minister at Ardentinny); and two French students, from Paris, who seemed to spend most of their time at Craignish Castle, which seems to be a centre for foreign students. The Chief Constable and Mrs. Ross came to dinner with us; and he told me that the police were keeping a watch on the activities at Craignish Castle. I must say, I found it difficult to suspect the two French boys: when I sat down one wet day in the large drawing-room and played the piano, they came in and said that they had just been remarking that the house needed music!

Here, at Oban, we have not sailed in one steamer yet this year, but we have met many friends and made new friends. We went with the Leslie Weatherheads, who are staying at Connel, to Lady Margaret's Tower, Lochnell, where there is an unrivalled view in all directions – we saw Colonsay, about forty miles off. We made friends with M. Rappoport, his wife, and daughter: he is an 'avocat' of the Court of Appeal in Paris, specialising in copyright law, very vivacious, a veritable M. Poirot. With them, we went, by invitation of Leslie Grahame-Thomson and his wife, the Maid of Lorne, to Barcaldine Castle for tea. It made it doubly entertaining to visit the sixteenth century keep in company with Parisian observers. At the castle, which is like a border keep, say Darnick Tower, you enter at the front door, and immediately climb the first flight, which takes you to a large lounge stretching the full width of the Tower. Off the lounge is a cache-cache, where undesirable guests would be put; at another corner, a narrow passage, too small for transporting bulky furniture, leads to a little smoking-room, where we drank to the health of our hostess and host and of our French friends or rather the 'auld alliance'. Leslie Thomson told some odd stories about the old Stewart-Campbell feud. Recently, he was summoned to give architectural advice at Glenure, at the head of Loch Creran – the old house of the 'Red Fox', to which he was brought after the Appin Murder. Before giving his advice, Leslie Thomson asked the purpose of all the rooms. Finally, they came to an empty room, and the hostess remarked that, here, the body of

Colin Campbell was laid after being brought from the wood of Lettermore. The hostess remarked: 'The blood-stains on the floor from his corpse used to be pointed out to visitors.' A workman standing by blurted out: 'It was never so. The old pig was bled white before he reached Glenure.' Again, a gentleman went in one day to a shop in Oban, and made a purchase, asking it to be sent to his hotel, and giving his name as Campbell. 'Have you ever heard of Glencoe?' asked the shop-girl. The Maid of Lorne also told us of the dismay she felt, as a girl of eighteen, when she was invited to be bridesmaid at a Campbell wedding. The laird of Barcaldine had his right of pit and gallows, and, to this day, the mound across the road from the Castle is called the Gallows Hill. When the Heritable Jurisdictions Act was passed, abolishing the two hundred or so heritable jurisdictions, that of the laird of Barcaldine (so Leslie Thomson said) was alone omitted – by misadventure. There was much laughter as to what would happen if the jurisdiction were now exercised, and the case came up afterwards for consideration by the Sheriff! Our French friends were delighted to be transported into this feudal atmosphere – so reminiscent of the Barony of Bradwardene. Another day we took them to Connel and Loch Awe. They were delighted to see the Captain of Dunstaffnage, having also met the Chief of the Macdougalls at Dunollie.

After our invitation to Barcaldine, we received an invitation to tea at Dunollie, and Ella, Rosemary and I went there. Rosemary played with Colonel Macdougall's grandchildren, whom she had also met at Barcaldine. Mrs. Macdougall was confined to bed with lumbago, but Ella went up to see her afterwards, while Colonel Macdougall, who, at the age of eighty, had entertained us and the three little girls at tea, took me through his policies and also up to the Castle. He is a charming, entirely simple, entirely natural old gentleman, and it is a delight to meet him – a tonic after all the 'go-getting' of the modern world. In his garden, he had a lovely desfontainea spinosa, which I have seen previously only in the manse garden at Lismore and at Lunga House. It has holly-like leaves, and a trumpet flower, the size of a cigarette, all waxy, scarlet, except at the outward tip, where it is bright orange yellow. It grows also in Torquay. He had some fine rhododendrons, though not to match Arduaine. The view from the old castle is one of the finest. There is an open view to Mull, and down the Sound of Kerrera – much finer than at Oban. The earliest portions of the Castle go back to the sixth century, though before Robert the Bruce defeated the Macdougalls in the Pass of Brander, Dunstaffnage was the Macdougalls' principal seat. Colonel Macdougall is, I understand, the 29th Chief. Because of his age, he was not going to the Clan Gathering in Edinburgh on 18th August, but sending the Maid of Lorne and his other two daughters instead.

17th August 1951

I heard my first jury trial, in Oban. A youth of twenty was charged with a serious assault on a girl of sixteen from Mull, who had just come to the mainland to take up her first job as tablemaid in a hotel in Oban. She gave her evidence simply and fairly, and David Brand, who was for the defence, told me afterwards that he felt he could not attack her in cross-examination as the accused would have liked, as it would only have antagonised the jury, who were bound to be impressed by her evidence, and the way she gave it. M. Rappoport attended the whole forenoon, and part of the afternoon, and gave me his criticisms afterwards. His chief criticism was that the cross-examination was too long. He said: 'What in America would take 200 minutes, and in your country 100 minutes, in France would take only 20 minutes!' He was delightfully fresh and humorous, and his criticisms were both lively and just.

21st August 1951

I adjourned the case after the jury, on the 17th, had found the accused, by a majority, guilty as libelled. I had, in view of the accused's age and the new Criminal Justice (Scotland) Act, 1949, to give consideration to whether there was any other practicable method of dealing with the accused than by imprisonment. My conclusion was 'No', and I sentenced him to three months imprisonment. The probation officer's report contained the opinion of the headmaster of an approved school, where the boy had once been, that this was the necessary treatment, and the accused's solicitor told me that the youth's father agreed with the headmaster's opinion. Whether the youth knew his father's opinion as stated in Court (for, as it concurred in that of the headmaster, it was necessary to know the latter's view), I do not know. I got the impression that the agent's desire was to convey the view to me, without hurting the boy's feelings, though the information was rightly before me.

On the evening of my sentence, the 20th, at the request of Miss MacPhee, of the Great Western Hotel, I showed my films of the recent Lighthouse voyage to the hotel guests. We raised over £12, by collection for a Church of Scotland Eventide Home for North Lorne. Dr. Ivor Campbell, of Oban, also gave a most instructive lantern lecture on 'Old Oban'. He had a quite unique series of slides of such antiquities as Macarthur's Cave, early folk-life and also of three shipwrecks, one of which I remembered, having seen it as a small boy of six, when, in 1906, I crossed from Oban to Salen, Aros, Mull, for our Summer holiday. The same evening, Mr. Cameron, of the *Oban Times*, introduced me to the Macneil of Barra, who had been attending the Clans Gathering in Edinburgh. He is an American from New York, and with his son, who had obtained special leave from the U.S. Army, had crossed the Atlantic for the occasion. He was to leave at 6 a.m. next morning, by the *Loch Earn*, to visit his ancestral home in Barra. He was greatly delighted that I knew Castlebay, Kisimul Castle, and the lighthouse at Barra Head. I suggested that he should persuade the Captain of the *Loch Earn* to wireless the Fishery Cruiser *Minna*, which was then conveying his clansman the Secretary of State for Scotland, round the Outer Isles and try to arrange a meeting with him.

We met many good friends in Oban, amongst them Mr. and Mrs. Hunter, from Akely, Bucks, whom we met at Oban last Summer, and at Akely in April. Mr. Hunter is a master at Stowe. Rosemary was very busy collecting wild flowers, and Mrs. Hunter helped her to identify them. Alison paid the Hunters a visit last Spring from Oxford.

Today, we left Oban and motored by Connel, Ballachulish, Kinlochleven, Fort William and Newtonmore to Boat of Garten, where we are staying at Moorfield, what a change of scene. Gone are the lovely colours of the West; gone is the land of hill and sea; but, instead, is the heather, at its finest, and the bracing air of the mountains. Still I have left my heart for the present in the West.

Today is announced the death of Dr. John White – certainly the greatest Scottish church statesman since Thomas Chalmers, and, I think, in his peculiar combination of first-class ability, personality, and judgment, the foremost Scotsman of his generation. He was a good friend of my own Father, as he made plain when he proposed my nomination as Procurator. He was always most kind and considerate to myself. His place will not be filled at once, for there is no churchman of the same stature.

His death follows that of Dr. R.J. Drummond – at the age of ninety-three the father of the Church of Scotland – Moderator in 1918, and practically a contemporary of Dad. Dr. Drummond was a descendant of the Relief and later United Presbyterian Church. He was the last distinctive representative of the old Voluntaries. He was the last wearer of the white bow tie in the Church of Scotland, still to be found among the smaller Presbyterian churches, and widely worn a generation ago. A man of extraordinary vigour, he played golf till ninety, and cycled and climbed till a few years earlier. I came to know him well when I became Chairman of the Destitute Sick Society, of which he was a Vice-President, and had been Secretary for many years. A volume of his reminiscences as a nonagenarian came out this summer, and I have just bought it. While it records some interesting facts of Church life over a century, which otherwise would be forgotten, it will not stand comparison with the recent autobiography of Dr. D.S. Cairns, which is unquestionably a minor classic.

Mention of these names reminds me that, one Sunday at Alvie Church, we heard Professor A.M. Hunter from Aberdeen University preach. We slipped away quietly from Boat of Garten, but found that the greater part of Boat of Garten had done the same. Professor Hunter is one of the authentic voices of the Church of Scotland, certainly of the Professors, the best preacher after J.S. Stewart. He was formerly Professor at Mansfield College, Oxford, and held parishes before each chair: going from Oxford to Kinnoull, and from Kinnoull to Aberdeen.

5th September 1951

We returned home to Edinburgh at the end of our holiday going one day by the Lecht, and Gairnside, to Crathie and Dinnet; and the next day from Dinnet to Braemar and the Devil's Elbow to Blairgowrie and Perth – two perfect days, during which we saw Ben A'an under perfect conditions, and Deeside at its best, with the Royal Standard flying from Balmoral, and the heather full out on Dinnet Moor.

8th September 1951

On our return to Edinburgh, we were greeted by Alison, back from Heidelberg and Holland, and her two friends, Carol Robertson and Eleanor Forshaw, and, immediately, pitchforked into the Edinburgh Festival. On the night of our return, I went to see Alison in *Murder in the Cathedral*, played by the Corpus Owlets (from Corpus, Oxford). The first part was played in the Lower Signet Library on a platform with the audience at both ends of the Hall; the second part, in the chancel of St. Giles'. Both, especially St. Giles', were most impressive. Douglas Duncan played Becket; and, from the children of the Scots Bar, there were Eileen Mackintosh, Alison and James Clyde. On other days, I heard Kathleen Ferrier sing Schubert, Mahler and Brahms lieder to Bruno Walter's accompaniment; the Amadeus String Quartet in the Freemasons' Hall; and the Théâtre de l'Atelier from Paris playing Anouilh's *Le Rendez-vous de Senlis*. The Corpus Owlets are producing *Murder in the Cathedral* in the ruins of Holyrood Abbey on Sunday afternoon the 9th, and next week in the University Chapel, St. Andrews; St. Andrews Castle; and Arbroath Abbey.

9th September 1951

Mr. Findlay, the beadle of St. George's West, telephoned me this afternoon to say that a stranger had called at the Church asking to see a minister. He was going into hospital, and wanted to confide in someone before he went. Mr. Findlay asked (since Murdo Macdonald was on holiday) what could he do? Would I speak to the stranger? I said, yes, and a Cockney voice came on the telephone at the other end, and asked could he see me? Although, since I was a Sheriff, would I not put him in prison? All this seemed very strange; however, I said I would see the man, and in twenty minutes, he came down to my house.

He was obviously in pain. He had a rupture, said he had been to the Infirmary; but they could not take him in. He said he had walked from London, and was on his way to Inverness where a cousin of his would put him up till he could secure a place in hospital. He had a certificate from an Essex hospital stating that he needed treatment, and that he should not walk or drive a vehicle. He asked me how to get to Inverness, and I suggested by the ferry and 'hitch-hiking'. He had been sentenced to six months at Lincoln for accession to house-breaking; but had been released after four months. He claimed to know Dr. Moffat of Crown Court Church, London. He never asked for money. I asked him what he thought I could do, and he said, give him a word of cheer and a word of prayer. I gave him a cup of tea and some eatables, and said, 'Now you feel better, don't you?' But he said, 'I'd like a prayer as well.' So I said the Lord's Prayer with one or two petitions for his needs. Then, he rose, thanked me, and went away. A strange case. I think, quite genuinely, he was in pain and despair, and wanted what he asked for, and not money.

13th September 1951

I am just back from a three-day 'circuit' in my Sheriffdom. On the 10th, at Greenock, I heard an appeal against an interdict preventing the showing of a ciné-film of the Robinson-Turpin World Championship Middle-weight Boxing Contest. One cinema obtained interim interdict against another showing the film. The first had, undoubtedly, exclusive rights under a contract with a renter to exhibit the film, but the second was not a party to the contract, not bound thereby. There seems no reason for Bonar to have given interim interdict, and I am going to recall his judgment.

On the 11th, having crossed the previous evening to Dunoon, I spent the forenoon examining the Sheriff Court Records of Argyll. Then I met Sir James Fergusson of Kilkerran at lunch, and took him to see the Records in the afternoon. We found some interesting records, particularly a Valuation of Teinds in Argyll in 1751, in perfect condition. As we were leaving, the Sheriff Clerk thrust a further bundle of papers into our hands. They are all to go to the Register House: I feel, by this step, I may have saved the last valuable records of Argyll. Sir James was a very pleasant companion at lunch, and we found much in common. He is going, next year, to make a special exhibition at the Register House, of documents relating to the Appin Murder.

On the 12th, I returned to Greenock, heard an applicant for admission as a Sheriff Officer, and then returned home.

Tonight – Ella's birthday – I go to London for tomorrow's Central Land Board and War Damage Commission meeting. In the evening, I am meeting a Mr. Gilmour, chief solicitor to British Transport Commission, for dinner at the Garrick Club. Sir Malcolm Tristram Eve asked me to meet him. Then, an invitation addressed from the Isle of Eigg (where Mr. Gilmour then was) came asking me to dinner at the Garrick Club! He wants my views about a new solicitor for the Commission in Scotland.

I was consulted today about two extraordinary Church matters. A claim of damages has been brought by an Israeli woman and her child against Tiberias Hospital, Palestine. It is alleged that, a few hours after the child's birth, a rat entered the ward and bit off the child's nose! St. Ninian's Old Church, Stirling, because of financial difficulties, has sought to introduce a scheme whereby each member shall be required to subscribe annually 26s. to Church purposes, or get a dispensation, for a lesser contribution, from the Kirk Session. To permit such a scheme would be to convert the Church into a closed society, membership of which was conditioned by a financial test. The scheme will be turned down by the good sense of the Church; but the wonder is that anyone would have seriously proposed it.

22nd September 1951

I have just finished a sitting, lasting five days, of the Committee on the National Museum of Antiquities, with Sir Thomas Kendrick and Mr. P.J. Rose. As a Committee we cooperated well. Sir Thomas knew everything about Museums, and Mr. Rose about the Departmental side of a Government Museum. They were most considerate to me, being junior, and expressed themselves in a most appreciative way about my Chairmanship. With a small Committee which had no passengers or politicians, it was easy to arrive at efficient and realistic conclusions on the merits; and, much to our surprise, the evidence tended to decide most questions for us. The one question on which there was some real difference of view on the evidence was, whether the new Museum should have a central-built-up, or a perimeter-park site. Before the enquiry, I favoured the latter, because I think that, with so many great prehistoric remains, so many of which are quite inaccessible to the public – witness the Broch at Mousa, for one example – there is room for open-air replicas of the smaller of these after the manner followed in a Folk Museum. Oddly enough, Professor Gordon Childe, whom Sir Thomas regarded as the most eminent of all our witnesses, himself advocated (without any prompting) this very idea, as also did Mr. Cant of St. Andrews University. But all the other witnesses who dealt with the matter favoured a central site. We had a wonderful variety of witnesses: for the Universities, Principal Duncan and Mr. Cant of St. Andrews; Professor Piggott of Edinburgh; Professor J.D. Mackie and Miss Robertson of Glasgow; Professor Lockhart of Aberdeen. For the Society of Antiquaries, Professor Piggott, Professor Robinson of Durham, Mr. Graham and Mr. Kerr. For the Royal Commission of Ancient Monuments, the Earl of Haddington and Mr. Graham. For himself and the Prehistoric Society, Professor Gordon Childe. For the Saltire Society, Dr. Oliver and Miss Ramsay. Miss I.F. Grant on behalf of her own Museum at Kingussie. Representatives of Edinburgh Education Authority and the Museums in Glasgow, Aberdeen and Dundee. Mr. Stevenson of the National Museum itself.

There was an excellent realism about the witnesses. They realised that we could not provide a new Museum with a wave of a wand, and turned their attention to a short term policy (for twenty years) to improve the existing Museum; and only thereafter a long term policy. Much to our surprise, too, they agreed almost to a man that a Folk Museum should be a separate project, some favouring Regional Folk Museums; others preferring a single National Folk Museum near the Highland Line, say, between Perth and Dunkeld.

We visited the National Museum, the Royal Scottish Museum, the United Services Museum, and the City Museum; also certain storage accommodation.

I had a violent bout of two-day influenza on the third and fourth days, and just managed to carry on; but it vanished as quickly as it came.

One, for me, amusing incident occurred during the week. I had to consider a Memorial in my practice, in which a father wanted advice about a draft *inter vivos* Trust Deed affecting his child, cutting her out of certain estate, and giving the residue, instead, to Glasgow University to found a Chair or Lectureship, 'for the purpose of teaching to Barbers, Hair Specialists, and the general public the proper treatment of Scalp and Hair, particularly in reference to falling hair and premature baldness'! I advised that the University would be most unlikely to accept a gift for so unacademic a subject, and, if they declined, the Truster's whole object would be defeated. That day, at our Committee, we had been hearing about the Archaeology Department of Glasgow University, which has no professor; and so, I went on to suggest, if it was of help to my client, that he might, instead, endow a Chair of Archaeology!

On the opening day of the Committee's work, I entertained my colleagues, along with Dover, to dinner at the University Club. Dover and Sir Thomas got on very well together, each enjoying meeting the other. I only hope Mr. Rose did not feel that the conversation fell into a groove. As host and spectator, one thing amused me with my English guests – how their conversation exemplified what I have always thought the difference between the Englishman and the Scotsman. The Scotsman, making a new acquaintance, thinks only of the man, and possibly of his principles: the Englishman, however, is not an individualist, but an institutionalist. Thus, the conversation had not gone far before the party was made aware, or discovered, that Dover was Lancing and Caius; Kendrick, Oriel; and Rose, a Johnian. From the opening gauntlet, the conversation developed into a discussion of institutional figures, supported by institutional points of view. To say all this is not to criticise Dover, who is the most understanding and open-minded friend imaginable of everything

Scottish, always praising the religious background and kindly humour of the Scot. It is rather to point out the essentially different cultural background in which the two nations grow up. I had forgotten another institution which figured largely in the talk – clubs, and the Athenæum in particular. The point might be put this way. Here, if you play Rugger, the question is whether you are good: there, it is as important, whether you are a Blue or play for an unknown club; in cricket, Sydney Barnes never quite lived down the fact that he played for Staffordshire, not a first-class club; in rowing, it matters whether you were at Eton and Trinity Hall, or at Wooloomooloo and Worcester (otherwise, why always publish the details when the Boat Race takes place); an episcopal theologian starts with a certain market advantage over a more acute theologian from the non-episco-pal ranks; Gladstone chose his bishops from Oxford and Cambridge alternately, and the idea that they might be recruited from anywhere else (Trinity College Dublin of course excepted) is one which has only occurred comparatively recently to the spiritual leaders of the Church. And so on; and so on; one could multiply the examples indefinitely. I once discussed it with Dover; he said: 'Yes, it is social snobbery, there is no doubt, but social snobbery is the glue that binds together the fabric of English society – whether in the village with squire and parson, or in education with the public schools and older universities and the idea of creating an essential ruling class, or in the Church, with the established Church and the non-conformists.' All this is strange to a Scotsman or a Frenchman: it seems to him to involve a certain wastage of intellectual merits in the less privileged sections of the community. But it is more important to see its merits than its defects; and it certainly gives a stability, or (as Dover put it) glue, to society.

3rd October 1951

The General Election – Polling Day is to be 25th October – will make me very busy. Three visits to Renfrew this week – Paisley tomorrow, Greenock the next day, and on the 6th, to Paisley, Greenock, and also, in Argyll, Dunoon, to receive the writs. As usual, after eighteen months inactivity in the political parties in Greenock, there is a last minute urge to challenge two polling-places, but the proposal comes too late. Incidentally, my receipts for acting as Returning Officer in five constituencies at last General Election came to £92 odds, or roughly half that after deduction of income tax – less than £10 net a constituency, for the work involved, about the poorest remuneration imaginable.

I had my meeting in Dundee last week, briefing our witnesses as to the line they should take on policy when they came to give evidence on the day following, before the Royal Commission on St. Andrews University. We discussed mainly – the federation versus the integration of St. Andrews University, the arguments for limited Arts teaching in Dundee, the arguments against a separate Medical College in Dundee, the proper assessment of the existing 'collegiate' system in St. Andrews. The following day, the Council gave their evidence before the Commission here in Edinburgh. Afterwards, they came down to my house to report results. They were, on the whole, well pleased. They expect (1) that Dundee will get adequate Arts facilities; (2) that the Commission will not countenance St. Andrews' proposal of a separate Medical College in Dundee; (3) that the St. Andrews Colleges will be retained; and (4) that the Commission will favour integration, but establish some kind of Dundee council with a Dundee head, more favourable to Dundee than even Lord Cooper's proposals. The Commission will probably propose that Commissioners be put in to supervise the adjustments for about ten years.

Today I attended an interesting function. The first volume of the Third Statistical Account for Scotland – on Ayrshire – has just been published, and at a ceremony in the Laigh Parliament Hall, it was presented by Sir Archibald Sinclair, great grandson of Sir John (who promoted the first Statistical Account) to the National Library and received on the Trustees' behalf by Lord Cooper. Sir Archibald acknowledged the great share ministers of the Church of Scotland had taken in compiling each account. A lunch was held beforehand at the Overseas Club. Mr. J.G. Kyd, formerly Registrar-General, who inspired the new venture, took the Chair. On his right were Sir Archibald and Lord Cooper. On his left, Sir John Erskine and myself. Next to me, on my other side, were Mr. G.P. Laidlaw and Dr. Hugh Watt (whose daughter has acted as Secretary to the new venture). Sir Archibald, at lunch, recalled how, to get some dilatory parish ministers to complete their work on the First Account, his great-grandfather had threatened to billet some fencibles at the manses. Mr. J.G. Kyd said that, for the Third Account, he would have an even more powerful lever, for, as Convener of the Aged and Infirm Ministers Fund, he could bring another form of pressure to bear! Sir Archibald asked me to be introduced to him, and I recalled having met him almost twenty years ago at the house of Mr. James Scott, then Liberal M.P. for

Kincardine. He has a considerable stutter, but uses it skilfully for emphasis.

17th October 1951

T.P. McDonald, today, gave me this rhyme about Sir John Cheyne, one of my predecessors as Procurator (1891–1906) and also as Sheriff of Renfrew. He was six feet six inches tall and known as 'Long Chain'. He received a knighthood in the Birthday Honours, and Queen Victoria conferred it on Midsummer's Day:-

> The Queen has done a marvellous thing
> A miracle of might
> For 'twas upon the Longest Day
> She made the Longest Night.

Yesterday, the General Administration Committee of the Church appointed a Committee *ad hoc* to consider and take the step if necessary to secure for the Church an appropriate place in national services, and at Coronations and the like. Dr. Matthew Stewart, to my complete surprise, went on: 'We have considered who should be Convener, and we recommend the Procurator.' Others proposed for the Committee were Dr. Warr, Principal Duncan, the Marquis of Aberdeen, Sir James Fergusson, Lord Cooper and Mr. C.C. Cunningham: the last will probably feel that he cannot act. I had to report on a large number of legal points. The Church is selling Boswell's Court, and a number of valuables have to be removed. There was much laughter when I reported that these included a portrait of my predecessor as Procurator who was hanged. My suggestion was approved that Ebenezer Erskine's pulpit and chair and a collection of communion tokens should be offered on loan to the Museum of Antiquities.

I have been through three times last week and once this week, in my Sheriffdom over the Election, and pay a further visit tomorrow. I was present one day at the founding of Paisley Abbey Trust, the deed which I revised as Procurator, and in which Trust I am, as Sheriff, a Trustee. Another day I attended a Conference about proposals for changes in certain Greenock Polling Places, but these cannot take effect at this election. To make this clear I also had to attend a meeting with two civil servants of Scottish Home Department, Mr. de Watteville and Mr. Hamford. I was able to satisfy them that, in one case, there was at present no satisfactory alternative to the present polling-station, and that, in another, a change projected could not be carried through at this election. Although the Greenock Conference was arranged as long ago as September, and representations had come from the Labour Election agent, neither the Labour nor the Conservative agents attended! Yesterday, at Dunoon, the Argyll Labour agent lodged a protest at the number of absent voters applications granted. If a Registration Officer refuses an application the applicant can appeal to the Returning Officer. But if the Registration Officer grants the application, the applicant is notified, and the Sheriff does not see the application. The agent has been asked for any specific case with regard to which he makes a complaint, and the Registration Officer has been asked to confirm that, in all applications, he duly applied, to the best of his information and judgment, the statutory provisions. I received yesterday a cheque from the Exchequer for £1,500 for the Argyll Polling Expenses, and today cheques for £1,300, £1,400, £1,000 and £1,500 for West Renfrew, Paisley, Greenock, and East Renfrew respectively. Have the electors any conception of what a General Election costs?

23rd October 1951

(London: Caledonian Club) Outside my bedroom window the London trees are turning to an autumn golden; and the sky is clear blue. I came here the night before last, and yesterday attended the British Council of Churches, which, this time (my first), met at the Congregational Union headquarters, Memorial Hall, Farringdon Street, E.C. It was, in every way, a most unsuitable place of meeting, the Hall too large to create an atmosphere of intimacy and induce discussion, no heating though we perished in a temperature near freezing point, inaudibility of all but the platform speakers, too much steam being let off by trains at Holburn Viaduct. On the other hand, the hall was interesting. In the Upper Hall, where we had tea, were the names of members like R.W. Dale and Joseph Parker and Silvester Home, as well as later Chairmen of the Congregational Union, like Sidney Berry (whom I met as long ago as 1921 when my father was Moderator) and the site was the site of the Fleet Prison! And the hall was the scene of Bernard Shaw's first speech. Those present from the Church of Scotland were John Baillie, J.K.S. Reid, J. Fraser McCluskey, J.D. Logan, myself and D.C. Bowser (his name reminds me of a dog: 'Down Sir!'). There were other well-known names, the Archbishop of Canterbury (in the chair), Bishops of London, Chichester, Lichfield and Sheffield, the Dean of Chichester (Duncan Jones), with a curious domed head like Walter Scott, M.E. Aubrey, Hugh Martin (whose manner I liked; though in appearance he is curiously unattractive), Mrs. Kathleen Bliss, and many others whom I have yet to know. Almost the first person I spoke to was the representative of the *Church Times*. He looked on me slightly askance, when I declared my Church: but was a little shaken when I told him that, as a boy, I had been a regular reader of the *Church Times* and the *Guardian*, both of which came into our manse, week by week. Would that non-Anglican papers entered every vicarage: there would be more understanding, and knowledge of other churches. There was a day when I could have named the complete composition of every Cathedral Chapter; without boasting, I am sure there are few Anglicans who have a like knowledge of other churches, and none who have of the Church of Scotland. The Anglican atmosphere, I thought, weighed rather heavily on the platform.

The conference itself was somewhat depressing. One report after another was presented in a speech dealing with generalities and there was little sense of urgency: the 'man in the street' would have formed a poor impression. There was practically no discussion, perhaps because the non-intimate character of the Hall stifled it. Yet this is a new, only some six years old, movement, and one must not be too hard; but the atmosphere could scarcely be labelled Pentecostal. I sat beside J.K.S. Reid and J. Fraser McCluskey, and had tea with members of the Irish Presbyterian Church.

The redeeming feature in the Conference was the Archbishop's chairmanship – so buoyant, humorous, and gay, resourceful and wise. It was a pleasure to watch him, not the heavy ecclesiastic, but rather a gay-hearted schoolboy, with all the wisdom of long experience and a most charming modesty. Whether he is a great spiritual leader is another matter.

The Archbishop has a curious mannerism. To read any document, he perches his glasses on his eyebrows, and reads without them. Then when he wants to look round the hall, he twitches his eye-brows, and his spectacles fall into their proper position.

After the Conference, I left with John Baillie, and we journeyed together along the Strand.

My destination was the Garrick Club, to dine again with Gilmour. This time he introduced me to quite a number of his friends. Last time I had met Casey, editor of *The Times* and Morrison, just retired from the *Times Literary*. This time we sat down at dinner, Gilmour on my right, myself on the right of Ian Hay (at the head of the large table), and on his left, Casey, and the Hon. Charles Russell, K.C., grandson of the 1st Lord Russell of Killowen, and son of the second (before whom I have appeared in the House of Lords). He is just forty-three, took silk at forty, and is manifestly built to succeed in the family tradition, handsome, a strong and attractive and debonair personality, with a keen sense of humour, who had appeared for the Earl in the Fitzwilliam case. Ian Hay, I had met several times. I acted for his wife's Trustees in a case which greatly pleased them, as it freed marriage contract funds which gave them a jaunt to South Africa. There was much talk of the Election. General expectations are a Conservative majority of at least fifty. Casey, whose ear must be near the ground, pointed out that, while Labour claims a victory, no one on the side of Labour has predicted what the majority would be, whereas many papers have estimated the probable extent of a Conservative majority. I noticed this morning (in the light of last night's talk) that *The Times* came out strongly for the Conservatives. Gilmour is coming to Dunoon next week. He wants to see Jim Aikman Smith and Cameron Miller (without their knowing his object) to see if either would suit as Legal Adviser in Scotland to the Transport Commission! I also met Sir Wilfred Bennett, who is, as from taking his seat tomorrow, Metropolitan Magistrate at Marylebone Police Court. His wife is a Maclaine of Lochbuie, and he said Sir Frank Lockwood had some connection with the Maclaines of Lochbuie – hence Frank Lockwood's island, off Mull; and (in passing) I met John Maude K.C., who was rushing off to a political meeting in the East End, and to suit the occasion, was wearing an old flannel suit, of which trousers and waistcoat did not meet.

This morning (the 23rd) I sallied forth to Marylebone Police Court, to which Sir Wilfred had invited me, saying that he would give me a seat on the bench. Not knowing where the Court was, I hailed a taxi, and asked for the Police *Station* by mistake. However, the driver thought I looked respectable and after driving quarter of a mile, asked me to confirm where I was going, and then learned it was to the Court. Lest he should still be in doubt, I explained that it was to sit on the bench! He deposited me at the Court, where no sooner had I alighted than I slipped and fell full length on the pavement. What he thought then is better left unsaid. I entered and found myself among a group of unwashed, but was quickly transported by obsequious clerks (nothing like those in Scotland) to Sir Wilfred's room. He was, I think, formerly magistrate at Woolwich. After receiving information about the day's cases, we entered the Court, and I sat with him on his left till 11.30, when he adjourned for ten minutes for a glass of milk. The work was handled most expeditiously, wives seeking maintenance from deserting husbands, three prostitutes sentenced for accosting, two loitering with intent to commit a felony, and a husband who admitted theft, and his wife who was charged, but acquitted, of receiving the goods. The saddest case was of an eighteen year old boy, whose mother was dead, whose father had disappeared in Birmingham, who was about to be called up in ten days, and when he was alone in London, had loitered with intent to steal cigarettes. He was put under probation for the ten days till he should join up. Obviously he had had no real chance in life. Two barristers appeared, and the one who prosecuted handled his case well. A Scottish-accented solicitor also appeared for one accused. A most interesting morning.

From there I went on to Farringdon Street, in time to hear the Bishop of Sheffield ending his speech on European Refugees. I found myself next a German, Von Halm. A Church of Scotland minister, Nisbet, made an excellent speech. Then J.K.S. Reid conducted devotions.

In the afternoon, there was a discussion on Laymen in the Church. I ventured to raise my voice for the first time, advocating a study of the different methods used in different denominations, It was decided, on the motion of Mrs. Kathleen Bliss, to appoint an *ad hoc* Committee to consider this problem. About eight spoke on this topic, the first real discussion which had taken place. Next on in the afternoon was a man wearing a Campbell scarf. I chanced my arm and said, 'Canon Macleod Campbell? I am the Sheriff of Argyll.' He was delighted: he is the grandson of the famous Macleod Campbell and superintends C. of E. missions and has just missed a bishopric. One who spoke was Mrs. Geoffrey Fisher, the Archbishop's wife. Not knowing her, I asked Canon Macleod Campbell who she was, and when he told me, I could only remark that then this was truly an *argumentum ad hominem*. But a more distinctive lady speaker is Mrs. Bliss, the first lady to obtain a First in Theology at Cambridge. There is a clarity and discrimination in her language which impresses you at once. John Baillie told me that she married an Anglican missionary teacher. She was a Congregationalist, but turned Anglican: her Anglican husband was meantime turning Congregationalist! Another extraordinary figure who spoke was Canon Vidler of Windsor, not extraordinary in what he said, but for his appearance – black beard, black shirt, white tie – for all the world he might have been Mussolini's last surviving Fascist.

After tea, I left with J.B. Logan, and being too late to see St. Paul's, we walked round by St. Mary-le-Bow and the ruins of Bread Street, to have a look at the tablet in memory of John Milton. And so back to the Club, from Mansion House Station.

In the evening John Baillie came to dinner, and, from his long experience of these conferences, gave me his impressions of the various speakers. He told me how when he, as not the senior Professor, had been made Principal of New College, he had arranged to have Manson made a Vice-President of the British Council of Churches, as some consolation. I could not tell him that Manson had consulted me at the time but, like the good Christian he is, had swallowed his disappointment in silence. According to him, Mrs. Fisher, Mrs. Bell, and Mrs. Hunter could each have occupied a place as distinguished as their husbands. He said Chichester would have been Archbishop but that he had angered the Government by his outspoken references to Peace. He said that Macleod Campbell was one of three Oxford undergraduates – the other two being Neville Talbot and Michael Furse – all of whom were marked out for bishoprics, but were rather too boisterous and high spirited to show the requisite episcopal control. Then Michael Furse was made a Bishop (St. Albans) but neither of the others secured a see at home. Neville Talbot's father, the Bishop of Winchester, was once asked why. He answered in a monosyllable: 'Mike.' Michael Furse had not been sufficiently discreet to encourage Laing to recommend the appointment of the other two. John Baillie has a high opinion of Oliver Tomkins, secretary of the World Council, who he expects will soon be a bishop. He recounted how Hugh Martin had built up the S.C.M. Press into the great undertaking it now is. He is a D.D. of Glasgow. When I remarked how I noted M.E. Aubrey had never received any honorary degree from a British University, he replied: 'No, but he is really not a heavy-weight. His name was brought forward in Edinburgh, but it was remarked that he had been somewhat lucky to receive a C.H.' John Baillie stated that, in the British Council, there was a strong demand for Scottish Secretaries; because they avoided the problem of Anglican versus Free Churches, and did not cause heart-burning among the various English Free Churches. He is convinced that, so far as England is at present concerned, the future lies with the Anglican Church and not the Free Churches. This arose out of my comment on the number of Anglican laymen who had taken part in the Council, and the comparative absence of Free Churches laymen. Also, in speaking at the Conference, I had stressed the use of laymen rather as office-bearers in the Church (as in the Church of

Scotland method) than as lay-preachers – it had been mentioned, for example, that 80 per cent of Methodist preachers were now lay. Without depreciating their services, I do not see how any Church built on such a basis could survive indefinitely. I ventured to point out that, in the Church of Scotland, while we had only some hundred lay preachers, we now had 38,000 elders (an increasing number), and, in the congregation of which I was a member, there were some 180 or so officebearers (only half elders). One other speaker, Professor Michael Foster, afterwards gave the membership of the Church of England men's society as approximately 20,000, but is this not rather an association of loyal laymen for conference purposes, rather than a band of office-bearers with definite duties assigned to them? This is the kind of matter which the new Committee will have to study.

26th October 1951

I have moved into a new world since my last entry. I travelled back to Edinburgh on the night of the 23rd, and, on the 24th, motored to Paisley where I am writing this entry in The Club, just after Polling Day (the 25th) in the General Election. On the afternoon of the 24th I swore in the Presiding Officers, Poll Clerks, and enumerators for the three Renfrewshire constituencies other than Greenock. On the morning of the 25th, the Chief Constable of Renfrewshire motored me round polling-stations in the West Renfrew constituency – Johnstone, Howwood, Lochwinnoch, Kilbarchan, Houston, Linwood. That afternoon, we opened the postal votes for the three constituencies, a tedious job lasting till 7 p.m. Then after dinner, I went to the Town-Hall for the count; for the first time, an evening count. We were allowed more enumerators this time by the Treasury: for West Renfrew (which I took charge of) I had forty, and, the count being at night, it was possible to get enumerators of experience, like bank and post office officials. Thus, we were able to complete the first count by 12 midnight, even though polling-boxes had to be brought in from as far as Inverkip, and, after twenty minutes break to allow the enumerators light refreshments, we resumed the separation of votes, and had this work completed by shortly after 2 a.m., a result with which everyone was highly pleased. Mr. Mackay was, again, returned, by almost the same majority as last year. Indeed, the Scottish results are so far almost the same as last year, no seat having yet changed. At present, the Conservatives have gained over the whole counting 11 seats, and the Liberals 1. The results are only available as yet for the towns and some of the counties, but it scarcely looks like the landslide predicted by the Conservatives. My impression is as it was last year – that the country is evenly divided at present, and that each major party should recognise that fact. Instead of this, many politicians have for the last year, and especially since the announcement of the Election, been behaving like children, and some of the most irresponsible. Two, who in my view have not adopted this attitude, and whose political broadcast was constructive and not vituperative, are Mr. Attlee on the one side and Lord Woolton on the other. I got into bed shortly after 3 a.m., after a very long day, but as fresh as a daisy. Today I go on to Dunoon for the Argyll count on the 29th, and certain preliminaries which take place tomorrow.

28th October 1951

(Sunday evening) I came to Dunoon on the 26th, and, on the morning of the 27th, we opened the postal vote envelopes. There were some 1,212 votes allowed, and some 28 defective, for some such reason as failure to vote, death, failure properly to complete the identification form.

In the afternoon, as last Election, I took the bus to Innellan, and returned with the *Loch Fyne* bringing in the boxes from Kintyre and the islands of Islay, Jura, Colonsay and Gigha. While at Innellan, I tried to gain entry to the Matheson Church, to see the window to Dr. George Matheson, whose famous hymn: 'O love that will not let me go' was written here – in its original form – 'I climb the rainbow through the rain', and not 'I trace the rainbow . . .'. The manse has a wonderful situation, and it is not surprising if the view from it may have, indirectly at least, inspired the words of the hymn. On the *Loch Fyne*, I found Jim Aikman Smith on his way from Campbeltown to join me at Dunoon.

M.H.A. Gilmour joined us in the evening. He had missed the connection from Glasgow, hired a taxi to Greenock, and then chartered a launch to take him across to Dunoon.

Today, we left at 10.15 a.m., and were driven by Inverary and Glenorchy to Bridge of Orchy, where we met and lunched with Cameron Miller, and then returned by Crianlarich and Tarbet and Glencroe to Dunoon. Our police driver pointed out many places of interest: Benmore estate, the Inverchapel estate at Loch Eck, Glenbranter (Harry Lauder's old estate), Ardkinglas, the Estate Office at Inverary, and a fine salmon pool in the Orchy, where some salmon poachers were recently trapped. The autumn tints especially towards Loch Awe and Cruachan were very fine. Constable MacVicar, a most frank and likeable young policeman, showed us his wireless in operation. At present it serves only for a radius of 10 miles from Dunoon. When Gilmour in a slightly condescending way referred to Hon. Sheriff-substitutes, the Constable rallied surprisingly, and said that he considered it the most honourable office a layman could hold, more honourable than the Provost of a Burgh. In turn we introduced into the conversation the name of Duncan Ban Macintyre, and said that, of course, Gilmour would know the works of so distinguished a poet. He was at first not quite sure whether we were 'pulling his leg'. The hotel at Bridge of Orchy is, surprisingly, run by an Italian, who (having received a warning telegram) entertained us in great style. I was, frankly, smitten in my conscience, when, after lunch, I looked through the hotel window, and saw a little congregation singing in an adjoining hall. I thought, too, of my own little family at our Communion in St. George's West. We came back by the Loch Sloy Power Station, which is now becoming part of the landscape. At the head of Loch Fyne, there is now being built a tunnel to carry the Glenshira water down the steep hill. It is, said P.C. MacVicar, the first of its kind. He also pointed out to us Neil Munro's monument on the heights between Inverary and Loch Awe: strangely enough, a Swiss (the only) car in front of us stopped to view the monument. The autumn colours on the trees were everywhere most lovely.

On our return to Dunoon, Gilmour indicated that, for the kind of work he had in view, he preferred Cameron Miller. It involves the amalgamation of the old L.M.S. and L.N.E.R. law offices in Scotland, and, for this kind of work, he thinks Cameron Miller's robust extrovert personality the more suitable. At Bridge of Orchy, Cameron Miller introduced me to the Town Clerk of Fort William, Mr. Dow, who was very delighted when I recalled having done work for him relating to a farm tenancy near Invergloy.

29th October 1951

We completed the Dunoon count today by about 1 p.m. – having started at 9 a.m. Major MacCallum was again returned. An amusing incident occurred during the count. I saw a stranger (to me) enter the Court room. I immediately went to him, and asked him, had he taken the declaration of secrecy? He said, 'No.' 'Well,' I said, 'you must go out at once,' and I put him out in five seconds. He was very apologetic, and informed me that he was the new Procurator-Fiscal and had just thought he would look in out of curiosity. He will not do it again.

The result of the Election is most inconclusive. The Conservatives have an overall majority of 17 seats, and Labour an overall majority of votes. Like the last Election, this shows that the extreme of neither party has the confidence of the country.

15th November 1951

Two nights ago, Dr. Warr asked to see me, and called in the evening. He referred to Dr. John White's death, and explained that various memorials to him were being considered – plaques in his Church Extension churches and the like. Then he added: 'And his biography will have to be written.' Then he looked at me and smiled. When I took his meaning, he explained that he had come to invite me to undertake the writing of the biography. He told me that this would be most acceptable to Dr. John White's family, who would gladly put all his private papers at my disposal. He also urged me to do it, as I was acceptable to both sides of the Church. I was very touched and said that I would like time to consider the invitation.

Alison writes us that, last Saturday, she was invited to dinner at the Mitre Hotel by Prince Olav, Astrid's father and the Norwegian Crown Prince. She greatly enjoyed the experience, but was not quite sure how to address her bread-and-butter letter!

I spent yesterday in strengthening our averments in the Free Presbyterian case for the hearing in the First Division two weeks hence. It will provide the Court with novel fare – a cornucopia of ecclesiastic favours.

25th November 1951

I accepted the invitation from Dr. Warr, and, at the Commission of Assembly on 21st November, it was announced that I had agreed to write the biography as part of a national Memorial to Dr. White. It turns out that Riddell was also behind the invitation – as Dr. White's successor in the Convenership of the Church Extension Committee. He wrote me:- 'In the close connection I had with John White in such affairs he several times spoke most appreciatively and affectionately of yourself.' In reporting to the Commission, he said that the biography was being entrusted to one who had Dr. White's fullest confidence. But the book has yet to be written!

Yesterday the Springboks beat Scotland at Murrayfield by 44 to 0, the biggest victory a visiting team has ever had. In the evening, I spoke at the English Association dinner on 'Public Speaking Today'. My theme was that public speaking took two forms nowadays:- (a) a cold factual statement making meaning clear; (b) prophylactic verbiage designed to obscure, or hide the absence of, meaning: that the beauty of noble words, the melody of a voice, the emotion behind all purposeful utterances was left out; that it was not Edward Everett's two-hour oration at Gettysburg that we remembered, but Lincoln's two-minute speech; that beauty and truth could be conveyed in even the humblest speech like a pebble cast in the water; that modern political speech was too synthetic and forgot good manners; that humility opened the door to all great thinking and should underlie all great speech; that just now there was too much pride, omniscience, and arrogance, and too much of the ignoramus who knew all the answers; that few had the courage to be really simple; and that what might not happen if a great man once more spoke the words of Lincoln at Gettysburg. I also read Humbert Wolfe's mountain flowers as an instance of poetry from the Civil Service – a favourite poem of mine, which Rosemary likes, too, as I have read it several times to her.

MOUNTAIN FLOWERS

Climb by the path, and you'll find mountain mallow,
narcissus, restless in the wind, as though
she heard a voice beseech her bloom to follow,
and softly drown in the reflective snow.

Or higher still, like little red macaws,
in green sequestered cages, brooding, see!
the Alpine rose, obedient to the laws
which rule that vertical mute aviary.

Then, last of all, only the edelweiss,
not soft like any other flower else,
but a small cuttle-fish against the ice,
clutching the rock with pale grey tentacles.

These and a thousand others, how small, how brittle,
how easily pulled, how folded in the hand,
and how long afterwards a single petal
is all we keep of vision's Oberland.

The President gave me an autographed copy of his latest book, *Supra Crepidam* – his four Presidential addresses to the Scottish History Society. The last address contains a reference to myself. The four addresses are all remarkable. Three of them (the last three) are so remarkable in their exploitation of new techniques as really to be a turning point in Scottish historical study.

17th December 1951

At the end of November and beginning of this month, we debated the Free Presbyterian Manse case for four days in the First Division. The Court was crowded all the time. Gordon Stott came up to me afterwards and surprisingly to my delight said that some juniors had remarked that it was the 'closest-knit argument' which had been heard in the Court for years. R.H. McDonald having had to return his papers, David Watson opened on our side coolly, skilfully and lucidly. Jack Hunter followed, at times becoming almost incandescent, with some of the heat engendered by his clients, but a good effort nonetheless. The President at one point hinted to him that a little less heat would be desirable! It runs in his family: his father almost spluttered at times with excitement over his case. Brought up in Raasay, he would have been a perfect Free Presbyterian: brought up at Rugby, he is what he is. I followed and enjoyed citing the First and Second Books of Discipline, the Westminster Confession, the Form of Presbyterial Church Government, Knox's history in Dickinson's edition, and even Milton's sonnet in which he refers to classical assemblies, an expression in the Westminster Confession which puzzled the President – who was deeply interested in the case. The Dean came last, paying delicate compliments to me, his real object being to suggest craftily that our case was skilful rather than sound. We rather expect the Court to hold that both sections of the Inverness P.R. Congregation have 'adhered to the constitution and standards', which is the legal question buried beneath a mountain of theology.

Last week, when in London, at the Central Land Board, I interviewed Hodder and Stoughton, who want to publish Dr. White's Life. It is amusing to be wooed by a publisher. The same evening, I entertained Alison and three of her friends, Janet Blyth (from Ludlow), Geoffrey Helliwell (from Halifax) and John Willmer (from London) at dinner in the Caledonian Club. A nicer company I could not imagine: it made me feel quite juvenile. Alison is one of a reading party of six staying for ten days with John Willmer's parents in

Hampstead; the father is Sir Gordon Willmer, of the Probate, Admiralty and Divorce Division. Their studies have not prevented a visit to Twickenham for the Oxford-Cambridge match, to the British Museum, the Mansion House, and the Law Courts. They left the Club, when I went to catch the night train back to Edinburgh. The following evening, I was Jock Cameron's guest at the Half-Century Club, a club formed to study famous crimes. I sat between Jock and Moray McLaren, whose book on the Scots has just come out as a Pelican. The old Cameronian referred to therein was the man who presented the picture of R.L.S. on the back of a donkey to the R.L.S. Club. I received the gift, as President, two years ago from Moray McLaren. John Wilson read a paper on the Aberdeen coffins case – H.M. Advocate v. Dewar and Forbes. The speech of the evening was a fascinating account by Superintendent Westland (now retired) who conducted the investigation, and had a dossier on Dewar, two years before he was arrested. It was an amazing story of patient investigation.

CHAPTER VI

1952

12th January 1952

We have now practically decided to publish the biography of
Dr. White through Hodder and Stoughton. I had suggested to the
Memorial Committee an approach to Nelson's, as, other things being
equal, I should have liked a Scottish publishers. But they showed
little real interest. Mr. Hardie, joint managing director, enquired,
'Was Dr. White really loved?' and wanted a subvention from the
launch, contemplating about 2,000 of a circulation. Mr. Cutts of
Hodder and Stoughton thought in terms of a circulation of 5,000
minus. Also the format of H. & S.'s books was more attractive than
those of Nelson's. But the real point which decided me was Mr.
Hardie's rather damping reception. On the subject of a literary agent,
Janet Adam Smith advises me against employing one, and Moray
McLaren was rather in favour of one. I think I will not employ one,
since it might be well to reserve power to reduce the royalty, if it were
desirable to sell at a lower price. Mr. Cutts' royalty proposal was 15
per cent against Mr. Hardie's 12½ per cent. I met the Dr. White
Committee yesterday, and they approved of these arrangements. I
hope to see Mr. Cutts the week after next, when I am in the House
of Lords.

I called to see Dr. Warr this afternoon about the business of the
next Church Committee on Representation of the Church of Scotland
on National Occasions, of which I am Convener. For an hour we
talked about everything under the sun except our business, a most
delightful conversation which we both enjoyed – Russia, Liberalism
(he and I are both Liberals, I discovered), *Ferdinand the Bull* (a child's
book), remarriage after divorce (on which I had to speak in the
Presbytery this week), the Sir Walter Scott Club, team-ministries in
parishes, and so on. We then turned to business. The chief 'national
occasions' we both considered were: Coronations, Royal marriages,
Royal funerals. At the Coronation, he thought there were four representatives of the Assembly (sitting to the south of the crossing), three

chaplains (Lang says four, so one may have been absent) to the north of the Sanctuary, in a gallery behind the seats for Royalty. The other two Royal occasions are more personal, and only about 2,000 are present at a wedding as against 6,000 at a Coronation. But, at these, the Moderator and Dean of the Thistle were present. At the Coronation, Dr. White and the other Assembly representatives sat; the bishops stood. Only the two Archbishops and the Bishop of London took part in the service. The Archbishop of York read the Gospel; and the Bishop the Epistle; Cantuar did the rest. Temple's father divided the Coronation with the then York; but that was because Temple senior was aged and needed help; this was the reason given by William Temple to Charles Warr. Dr. Warr thinks there is not much wrong with Scotland's representation at a Coronation. In what is a sacramental service, it may be difficult for others to take part in a Church of England service, though there would be no difficulty the other way round. Dr. Warr also told me that he was often called on in a personal way to help on Royal occasions. He wrote a Christmas broadcast for the King; a prisoner-of-war broadcast for the Queen; and the Lord High Commissioner's address for the Duke of Gloucester. The latter had said to him: 'They have plenty of humour in the Assembly. I would like some in my speech.' The speech was greatly appreciated! In the Queen's broadcast Dr. Warr had a sentence to the effect: 'I hope that you will all shortly be at home again.' A blue pencil was put through this, lest it be interpreted in Germany as a forecast of a Second Front.

I am going to the Faith and Order Conference of the World Council of Churches at Lund from 15th to 28th August as the sole lay representative of the Church of Scotland. We will go as a family and make it our holiday as well.

This week the First Division decided the Inverness Free Presbyterian Manse case. They held by a majority that neither side had shown the other to be in non-adherence. The result was that the action failed. Lord Russell dissented in our favour. The Lord President accepted our argument almost entirely, but, in the last two or three sentences of his judgment, after saying in effect that the defenders had done everything they could to secede, held that non-adherence by them was not made out. But for this, I thought his judgment a model of clear reasoning. The Dean was as puzzled by this last stage as I was. I wonder whether the L.P. had written the point the other way in the first instance, and then realised that the result was 2 to 2. The matters in the judgments were, however, very fair, except Lord Carmont who went off at a tangent, and made a lot of criticisms about points raised by neither party.

Since before Christmas, I have been overhauling opinions which came in shoals: the Election put me into serious arrears.

We went out one day to see the Candlish Hendersons. He has now retired from practice. He told me that, in the Church Union negotiations, his father got on much better with Lord Sands than Dr. John White. He also told me that Lord Strathclyde had told him that he (Strathclyde) was told by Horn, Dean of Faculty, a good judge of men, that Jeffrey was very popular, whereas Cockburn was not. This is odd because a few days later I received this information in a letter from Alick Buchanan Smith: 'My eldest brother George (killed in action in 1915) studied law at Edinburgh in 1913 and 1914 when he graduated LL.B intending to go on to the Bar. During that time my Grandfather, George Smith, born 1833, who lived in Edinburgh spoke to him of his life as a student about 1850. Here is an extract from a letter from my brother written about then: *"Grandfather was telling me of the days when he used to go about the Court of Session sixty-three or sixty-four years ago, about 1850, and of Lord Jeffrey and Lord Cockburn. He was most interesting. He said that Lord Jeffrey was always fidgeting and poking up the fire in Court and causing great annoyance to his brother judges and the advocates; but that Lord Cockburn was a much worthier judge than he . . ."* As to whether that impression was a fair one another question. I should think that his estimate of the comparative worth of Lord Cockburn would be a reflection of the opinion of another?' The opinions differ! The same is true of today. I always considered that, great intellect as he was and first of pleaders, L.P. Clyde lacked almost all the judicial qualities. L.P. Clyde himself held Wark and Normand in respect as counsel, but somehow did not seem to care for Fred Strachan. L.J.C. Alness, on the other hand, found Wark a red rag. Alness, who intellectually was scarcely fit to unloose the latchet of Clyde's shoe, had very considerable judicial gifts, and used his gifts to the best possible advantage. In the days when you could choose your division, everyone chose Alness's division in preference to Clyde's, which must have been mortifying to that infinitely greater intellect and yet he seemed unable to diagnose the reason. Clyde and Sands were each giants, but individualists; Sands was the really great judge of that First Division. But Alness, Ormidale, Hunter and Anderson (Hunter alone being of the stature of Clyde) made an excellent judicial team. Normand and Fleming (the wisest judge of all) made a far surer combination. It was of Alness that John Buchan once remarked rather acidly: 'Is he still polishing his one talent?'

Gilmour and Cameron Miller told me that the latter has been appointed legal adviser to British Transport Commission in Scotland. Bobbie Kerr telephoned me this evening to say that he has been offered Fort William.

8th February 1952

This week has been full of sudden unexpected happenings. On the morning of Wednesday the 6th, I was standing in Parliament House beside my box, talking to a solicitor-friend, Mr. Hay-Smith, when up came someone and whispered: 'We've just heard the King is dead.' The rumour came from Mr. Rhind, Parliament House clerk of J.&F. Anderson W.S. I caught hold of him. 'Yes, I've just confirmed it at the Post Office. The news came out at Sandringham at 10.15' – so we heard in less than an hour. No one can have expected it – otherwise Princess Elizabeth would never have started on her Australian tour. She was in Kenya still, when the news reached her. The news set wheels working at once in Parliament House. Thirteen judges assembled in the First Division (Blades being on circuit in Perth) and the President made a formal intimation that the Court would rise. I whispered along to the Dean: 'Do you realise this solemn thought – we will probably never be K.C.s again?' (We're Q.C.s now!)

The next excitement was to arrange for the reading of the Proclamations (if and when they arrived). I fixed Friday (today) with the Town Clerk of Paisley. I asked him the drill. He said: 'The Provost reads the Proclamation in Paisley; and you read it in Renfrew.' I heard later of trouble in Elgin where a question had arisen whether Sheriff or Provost should read it; so I telephoned Mr. Millar, the Sheriff Clerk, to see whether the 'Elgin compromise' would not suit – that I should intimate having received the Proclamation, and then request the Provost of Paisley to read it. All this time I had not seen the Proclamation. I first saw it today half-an-hour before it was to be read:

WHEREAS IT HAS PLEASED ALMIGHTY GOD TO CALL TO HIS MERCY OUR LATE SOVEREIGN LORD KING GEORGE SIXTH OF BLESSED AND GLORIOUS MEMORY, BY WHOSE DECEASE THE CROWN IS SOLELY AND RIGHTFULLY COME TO THE HIGH AND MIGHTY PRINCESS ELIZABETH ALEXANDRA MARY,

WE, THEREFORE, THE LORDS SPIRITUAL AND TEMPORAL OF THIS REALM,

BEING HERE ASSISTED WITH THESE OF HIS LATE MAJESTY'S PRIVY COUNCIL, WITH REPRESENTATIVES OF OTHER MEMBERS OF THE COMMONWEALTH, WITH OTHER PRINCIPAL GENTLEMEN OF QUALITY, WITH THE LORD MAYOR, ALDERMEN, AND CITIZENS OF LONDON, DO NOW HEREBY WITH ONE VOICE, AND CONSENT OF TONGUE AND HEART, PUBLISH AND PROCLAIM THAT THE HIGH AND MIGHTY PRINCESS ELIZABETH ALEXANDRA MARY IS NOW, BY THE DEATH OF OUR LATE SOVEREIGN OF HAPPY MEMORY, BECOME QUEEN ELIZABETH THE SECOND BY THE GRACE OF GOD, QUEEN OF THIS REALM AND OF ALL HER OTHER REALMS AND TERRITORIES, HEAD OF THE COMMON-WEALTH, DEFENDER OF THE FAITH, TO WHOM ALL HER LIEGES DO ACKNOWLEDGE ALL FAITH AND CONSTANT OBEDIENCE WITH HEARTY AND HUMBLE AFFECTION, BESEECHING GOD, BY WHOM KINGS AND QUEENS DO REIGN, TO BLESS THE ROYAL PRINCESS, ELIZABETH THE SECOND, WITH LONG AND HAPPY YEARS TO REIGN OVER US.

GOD SAVE THE QUEEN

Later, I got into touch with the Scottish Home Department, and they said that in 'Head Burghs' i.e. County towns, the Sheriff read it; in other burghs it was usually the Provost. So that the 'drill' originally proposed by the Town Clerk was in order – Renfrew being the 'Head Burgh', not Paisley. When I reached Paisley today, I at once told the Provost that I had been proceeding on a misunderstanding, and every-thing was solved to everyone's satisfaction.

At Paisley, we processed from the Municipal Buildings to the War Memorial, and then, facing south, the Provost read the proclamation. There was a slight echo, producing a boomerang effect, from the loud speakers. There were two guards of honour, naval and military. The spectacle took place in brilliant sunshine, which lasted all day. In the procession, there were first two halberdiers, dressed unusually in a purple-brown, then the mace bearer with draped mace; then the Provost, with myself on his right, then Interim Sheriff R.R. ('Bobbie') Kerr, who is deputising for 'Buggins' Young (who is off for a term with an ulcer), then the Town Council and so on. A feature was that, although there was a huge crowd, there was not a cheer – not I think because the people lacked enthusiasm (indeed tears have been shed over the King's brave fight against death; and the courageous fulfil-ment of duty by the young Queen), but rather because people are shy to begin the cheering. I suggested beforehand to the Provost that he should have a cheer-leader placed in the crowd, but he thought the cheers would come. Seeing what had happened, I told the Town Clerk of Renfrew for the afternoon ceremony, and at Renfrew the children present cheered lustily to the call of a schoolmaster chosen to lead on

Randall Philip reading the proclamation at Renfrew Town Hall (Courtesy of The Herald and Evening Times, Glasgow).

my suggestion. In reading the Proclamation, the Provost of Paisley omitted 'the Second' after 'Elizabeth': it occurred twice, and Scots people, for whom she is 'the First' don't like it. I thought – whatever a democratically elected Provost might do – as a Crown officer, I should read the Proclamation as it was expressed – and so I did.

Some half-dozen of us assembled in the Provost's Room, the Provost (Stewart Black), Mr. Morrison (Town Clerk), Bobbie Kerr and myself, Mr. Millar (Sheriff Clerk), Mr. Hill (Procurator-Fiscal), the naval Captain in charge of his guard (from Abbotsinch), an army officer, in charge of the military guard, Monsignor Pirie, the senior Roman Catholic priest, Rev. W.H. Logan of Paisley Abbey, and soon we were joined by the Lord Lieutenant, Sir Guy Shaw Stewart, in uniform. I wore full bottomed wig, court coat and waistcoat and trousers, not knee-breeches. (I think I should have had white gloves and three-cornered hat.) At lunch – a party of about forty – we toasted Her Majesty and also 'the Baron of Renfrew and Snowdon' (pronounced Snawdon) – Prince Charles (age 3½!). The name of Snowdon survives in Sneddon and Back-sneddon Shirts.

Then Sir Guy took the Sheriff Court party to a special meeting of the County Council. I sat on his right, and a message of sympathy to the Queen Mother and loyalty to the new Queen was passed

From there we were driven to Renfrew. At the boundary where Paisley meets Renfrew, we stopped, and there were welcomed by the Provost (Gibson) and Magistrates of Renfrew – a most picturesque and courtly ceremony, which I much enjoyed, the Provost of Renfrew being a model of courtesy. We then drove on and entered Renfrew Town Hall at the rear, to find ourselves in a large company of the county and the burghs. We passed through the front door out to a platform in the square – county representatives on the left and burghs on the right. Then out I came, with the Provost in the centre, and I read the Proclamation. The loud speaker worked excellently, and I read without a mistake (not even saying 'King' instead of 'God save the Queen'! – a very easy error to fall into) and also tried to keep my voice on its lower notes and read with real expression what were, after all, moving words reminiscent of the introduction to the Authorised Version. Afterwards we had sherry and tea in the Town Hall, and I met innumerable acquaintances. Then after saying goodbye to Sir Guy, my companion of the afternoon, who, beneath a guardsman's exterior, conceals a kind heart, I returned with Bobbie Kerr, Mr. Millar and Mr. Hill to the Sheriff Court – and from there drove home in my own car. On reaching Edinburgh I found a telegram reporting that all had gone well at Inverary. There Chalmers from Oban read the Proclamation in my place.

Yesterday, and the previous evening I had another interesting ploy. At George VI's Coronation, the Church of Scotland was represented by three persons within the sanctuary, by other representatives elsewhere (the Clerks and Procurator [Campbell Black] included), and by four chaplains to the King. At Princess Elizabeth's marriage, the Moderator in person was given a seat within the sanctuary with the King's special approval. The question was now to make sure that the claims of the Church to a like place at His Majesty's funeral service should be recognised or at all events made clear. Fred Strachan telephoned me and referred me to the correspondence in 1947 concerning the Royal Marriage. With this before me, I drafted letters to the Lord Chamberlain and the Dean of Windsor (to be signed by myself) and to the Archbishop of Canterbury (to be signed by the Moderator [White Anderson]) and took them out to the Moderator at 9.15 a.m. yesterday. I had a conversation with the Scottish Home Department on one point. I had thought to drop the Dean of Windsor, but they recommended me to write him as well as the Lord Chamberlain. They indicated that, in any event, the Moderator would receive an invitation as a guest, but I felt it my duty to make plain that we had in view a like place to that expressly accorded by George VI at Princess Elizabeth's wedding. They were also to pass on this indication. The three letters went off yesterday. We will await the result. It is amazing to a layman that there should exist at a national service a kind of ecclesiastical colour-bar operating against a church whose protection it is the first duty of a new Sovereign, on accession, to secure. A fortnight ago, when in London for the House of Lords, I heard a courageous sermon by the Archdeacon of Rochester (Harland) in St. Paul's urging, in a most ecumenical spirit, the re-thinking of Anglican episcopacy. Then followed Communion for which I waited, but the printed invitation was so couched as to make it plain that only Anglicans were welcome. Much as I should have liked to take Communion, especially in the spirit of the sermon, I felt I could not in face of such a closed door without saying I was a Presbyterian, and felt it better not to go forward. I felt very much the feelings of a black man, turned out of a fashionable restaurant because of the colour of his skin. And yet R.R. Williams of Durham was kind enough to call me an ambassador of good will between the Churches. Surely the harm done to one sincerely desiring Communion by such a repulse is more evil than the admission of one not confirmed according to Anglican use to Anglican Communion.

9th February 1952

There was great newspaper excitement this evening. The Provost of Alva proclaimed 'Queen Elizabeth' without 'the Second', and the Rev. Dr. Drummond of Alva prayed afterwards for Queen Elizabeth 'First and Second'. The Lord Lyon has declared the Proclamation null and void, and stated that the Minister will be prosecuted. The newspapers rang me up as Procurator, and asked, would the Church take action? I refused to say anything.

13th February 1952

Yesterday I received a letter from the Dean of Windsor saying: 'I will gladly arrange that the Moderator shall have a place in the Sanctuary of St. George's Chapel on Feb. 15,' and inviting him to join an early morning rehearsal with the Archbishops and others taking part. So I have succeeded in establishing a few precedents.

2nd March 1952

John Sparrow, whom I met at Dobie's and again with Gilmour at the Garrick Club last September, has (rather surprisingly) been elected Warden of All Souls. Gilmour told me, all the same, that it was expected. I saw A.H. Campbell today: he told me that, when it was mooted last summer on Sumner's death, John Sparrow's comment was: 'One Sparrow does not make a Sumner.'

This week has been a busy one. I drafted three loyal addresses from the Church to the Queen, the Queen Mother, and Queen Mary. In the first, especially, I tried, beneath the usual formularies, really to say something. One paragraph was added to my draft, but the addition also was my own. The Moderator proposed that we 'greet' the Duke of Edinburgh, rather than 'welcome' him – which was the better phrase. But every word of the remainder was, I think, my own.

19th March 1952

Alison came home a few days ago from Oxford, and announced that one of her suitcases had had the distinction of having visited Buckingham Palace. Astrid was short of a suitcase when she went to attend the Royal Funeral, and so Alison lent her one! Alison has been elected Treasurer of the Junior Common Room at L.M.H.

At the end of February I was one of the guests at the inauguration Dinner of the Aberdeen University Law Faculty Society. It was a big splash in the Elphinstone Hall. Tom Taylor presided. Tom Smith proposed 'The Guests' and Professor Kunkel of Heidelberg replied. Professor Ehrenzweig of the University of California proposed 'the Scottish Legal Tradition', and this was replied to by the Justice-Clerk (for the Bench); Jock Cameron (for the Bar); Dr. R.M. Williamson (for the solicitors); and myself (for Scottish Legal Scholarship): I in turn, Janus-like, proposed the new Society which was replied to by Malachi Mulligan, one of my examiners, who bears a delightful name. Prof. Kunkel stayed with us in Edinburgh earlier in the week, and we had a little dinner party for him and for Ehrenzweig, to which we invited the Fishers and David Watson. The President and A.H. Campbell, who were also invited, could not come. Travelling back from Aberdeen, I had as my companion Ross Parsons, a law professor from Perth, Western Australia, who was also at the dinner. At the dinner, I sat between the President of the Glasgow Students' Law Society, and Prof. Kunkel. The latter is a quiet, rather tired-looking man, who grew on acquaintance, and though his English comes slowly, made an admirable speech. Daube was his best student. Ehrenzweig is a vivacious Austrian, who, because he had one Jewish grandparent, had to flee from Austria in the late thirties, and is now at Berkeley, California. I learned from him that Berkeley is now the richest university in the States, better endowed because of state support than Harvard, and has 8 campuses and 46,000 students.

This week I received an invitation from F.H. Lawson, Professor of Comparative Law at Oxford, to write a paper on 'Administrative Law in Scotland' for the *Journal of Comparative Law*. I have taken the proposal to avizandum.

A week ago the House of Lords decided an appeal which I argued in January. We were appealing against a unanimous judgment of the First Division, and we won the appeal. The judges were Normand, Reid, Tucker and Cohen. The case was 'The Hay Memorial', Lerwick. It seems to have been the first case on a question of charitable trust which has gone to the House of Lords from either England or Scotland for over fifty years. We were given a very courteous and considerate hearing. So far, I have won each case in the House of Lords since I took silk. James Crawford, with Inglis, was against me. The Dean was in London for the next case, which was subsequently postponed. He wasted the best part of a week. Ian Fraser was on the journey from Edinburgh to King's Cross for the same case, when he was stopped at Newcastle. I have heard of Graham Robertson being similarly stopped at Carlisle twenty years ago. Latterly, House of Lords arrangements have been much more considerate of Scottish Counsel than they used to be. But it does seem absurd that the Dean should have to kick his heels for several days in London, and then be told he could go home. He had his wife with him, and I entertained them and the counsel in my appeal at a jovial little dinner in the Caledonian Club.

I have now signed the contract with Hodder and Stoughton for Dr. John White's Life. It is to be 'after the style' of Lockhart's Cosmo Gordon Lang. On the first Sunday evening in June, I am to broadcast on John White before an appeal for the national memorial fund to commemorate his work.

The statue of Charles II, reinforced so that it will sag no longer, has been restored to Parliament Square. The Faculty gave £100 towards its restoration, but like many another generous act, it has passed unnoticed.

29th April 1952

On the 19th we left Alison because of her impending return to Oxford, and Ella, Rosemary and I, with Fräulein Dankert, went for ten days to Belfast, where I was a Church of Scotland representative at the first meeting there of the British Council of Churches. It was my first visit to Northern Ireland, though mother had Workman cousins there, and in the Irish accent, I could almost hear my Uncle Keir speaking again. In fact, I have a touch of the brogue myself. We were struck by the brilliant greens, the rich agriculture, the friendliness of the people, the absence of tenements, the different religious situation. We had two lovely motor runs:- (1) to Antrim, Bally (which we liked especially), Cushenden (for lunch at the Bay Hotel), Cushendale, and back by the Antrim coast; and (2) to Newcastle and round by the sea and the Mourne Mountains past Kilkeil and Killowen to Rostrevor (lunch at the Great Northern Hotel), and home by Newry and Hillsborough. Another remarkable feature of Ulster is its incredible number of generals, and of U.S. Presidents (some two-thirds of the whole number). Our day at the mountains of Mourne was our best. There were miles and miles of whin and gorse, and, at Killowen, lovely rhododendrons and periwinkle.

For me, the most interesting experience of the meeting of the British Council of Churches was a half-hour's tête-à-tête with the Archbishop. Manson introduced me, and then, as I wanted to speak to the Archbishop about Coronation matters, he kindly and tactfully withdrew. I explained my purpose, and came straight to the subject, mentioning that the Church of Scotland desired the same official representation as at last Coronation, but that the special Committee of which I was Convener, supported by the General Administration Committee, were going to recommend to the Assembly that no claim be *asserted* to share in the service, as it was, under present circumstances, essentially an Anglican service. This did not mean that we would not welcome an *invitation* to take part. The Archbishop said: 'Well, I'm most grateful to you for telling me this, and since you have been so frank I can explain that I have been discussing with Don,' ('a good Scotsman', he called him), 'what place we could give the Church of Scotland, and we were thinking of proposing that the Moderator be asked to carry from the altar the Bible which is presented to the Queen. This would also mean that the Moderator would be placed within the sanctuary.' He added: 'It's my special desire that the Church of Scotland should, as the established Church, have a different place from the Free Churches.' At Windsor, he mentioned, the Dean had proposed that the two Moderators should process together, but he (the Archbishop) countermanded this, and placed the Church of Scotland Moderator behind the Moderator of the Free Church Federal Court. I enquired whether any invitation to the Moderator could be given before the Assembly, but he thought not. He stated that the Queen appointed a Committee to make the Coronation arrangements, and then that this Committee delegated the arrangements for the service to him. (Actually this Committee is announced today 29th April.) I enquired whether the Church of Scotland could have a representative on the Committee; he thought not as such, since it was made up of the holders of certain offices. He remarked at one point that he thought the decision of the Assembly last year over the Coronation Stone showed great wisdom.

3rd May 1952

I was asked by Cunningham of Scottish Home Department (Sir Charles Cunningham) to meet him to discuss the Church of Scotland's attitude towards Coronation arrangements (the date of the Coronation having been announced on 29th April). I met him with Anderson, one of his chief assistants. I explained that the Church authorities – the special sub-committee and the General Administration Committee – had approved a three fold proposal: (one) that the C. of S. representation at last Coronation – as guests – was fair and reasonable. I outlined what this was; (two) that the C. of S. would not *assert* a claim to take part in the service, as it involved an Anglican communion and as this seemed the proper attitude for a Christian Church, but that things would be different (1) if an invitation was given to participate and (2) if the dominion representatives insisted on a reconstitution of the service; (three) that the C. of S. would propose a national service in St. Giles' after the Coronation – not a re-coronation, but one in which the regalia of Scotland might be used. Cunningham seemed most favourably impressed with the line taken. He asked, would we want proposal three put to the Queen before the Assembly? I said: 'I thought not,' (as I thought the view expressed by the Assembly on the proposal might help her in her decision). I had also in view that the point might have been unofficially mentioned to her by Dr. Warr. Cunningham asked me if I had mentioned the Dominion proviso to the Archbishop (I having told him of my conversation in Belfast). I said I thought not, because at that stage the matter was not in issue, the Archbishop having made no suggestion that there might be such a reconstitution. I also explained that I had not referred to proposal three to the Archbishop since it was a purely Scottish matter; he agreed that was quite right. He said he would keep in view our attitude.

The same morning I had a meeting with Mr. P.J. Rose about the National Museum Report. I completed my draft in January, but there is one outstanding issue in that he would like the Board to be purely Crown appointed. I indicated that I was inclined to his view that the representative of the Society of Antiquaries and of the Universities should be appointed by themselves, but that I rather agreed with the idea of a smaller Board of 'effectives' without a standing Committee, rather than the big Board after the style of the National Library, with a standing Committee. He is to consider this further.

On 1st May, the President (who is on the Coronation Committee) asked me for the Church of Scotland views. I explained what I had told Cunningham. He seemed favourable, and said: 'I would like to see the Queen put the Scottish Crown on her head.' I said it would have to be momentarily, because Cunningham told me that it weighed 5 or 6 lbs! Oddly enough, the President's only other comment was, would the place of the national service not more fitly be Glasgow Cathedral? I am sure he took this line because of a certain jealousy towards Charles Warr who is Chairman of the St. Giles' Managing Board, a position which has hitherto always been occupied by the President for the time being! I headed him off this idea.

Last evening Fred Strachan called in a great state. He considers that the President is 'so irresponsible in his views' that it must be made very plain that he does not voice the official opinion of the Church of Scotland. He had expressed some certainly very rash views to Fred, and added that the C. of S. would get less than last Coronation, and that he was seeing the Archbishop on the 5th. I told Fred that I had already seen the Archbishop and Cunningham; he was greatly relieved about this. I also told him that what the President was doing on the 5th was to attend the Coronation Committee; that he had shown me the plan of seating of the Committee (round a large table); and that I thought it unlikely that, at so large a meeting, he would have much, or any, opportunity to speak privately to the Archbishop. Fred told me that the President is very hot about the Coronation Stone; and would virtually like it brought back to Scotland by force; and that the President had said that his views were the same as Dr. White's. In point of fact, I know that Dr. White's view was that expressly in the decision of last year's Assembly, and had that decision not been taken, Dr. White had another similar motion to put to the Assembly. There is no doubt that the President indulges in a lot of loose talk behind the scenes, and is always meddling with other people's business, but Fred Strachan seemed to be excessively sensitive to his views which, in public, are expressed more guardedly.

The St. Andrews Royal Commission has reported. Its solution is a unified University, with, however, substantial devolution to Dundee and St. Andrews, and the whole of the academic institutions in Dundee to be made into one College is nearest to the view we in the College Council have maintained. Indeed the *Times* Leader referred to it as a Durham-Newcastle solution, with some modification, which was substantially our case. The Commission's reflections on the outlook displayed by St. Andrews towards Dundee will not be liked by Sir James Irvine. I wrote Wimberley. He had also written me, and he expressed appreciation of my advice over the last two years. It is a good example of the reasonable view triumphing, and the extremist, but very vocal, views receiving a distinct repulse.

I should have mentioned that Cunningham referred to the proposal at the last Coronation that there should be a civil ceremony at Holyrood, but explained that, after being carried a good way, it had been dropped because it savoured too much of a re-coronation. I said that I was aware of this previous proposal, but thought our proposal number three better because it avoided all suggestion of a re-coronation, and because a religious service was more in accordance with the sentiments in general of the Scottish people. I also mentioned that we were not happy about the way in which the oath had been tinkered with, and that it had gradually been altered from a strictly Church of England oath to a general oath for the United Kingdom, which the Archbishop was scarcely entitled to administer, relating as it did, *inter alia*, to maintaining the Protestant religion in Scotland. But I said that we did not want to raise legal points of this nature, however much we disliked the trend of alteration made in the oath (without consultation with the Church of Scotland). Anyone who compares the first post-union oath with the last one taken will see at a glance the extraordinary alteration which has been made. Initially, the correct view was (a) that the accession oath covered the Church of Scotland and (b) that the Coronation oath covered the Church of England. There were obvious historical reasons for this differentiation, but now the Coronation oath has been greatly widened to overlap the statutory accession oath relating to Scotland, and this could not have happened had the one partner to the Union been consulted with the same fairness as the other.

18th May 1952

A week ago I received a letter from the Archbishop of Canterbury which began: 'My dear Procurator, I look back with the greatest satisfaction to the conversation which we had in Belfast. It established at once friendly and informal relations between us with regard to a matter which is full of potential difficulties.' He mentioned that he had had a further talk with the Dean of Westminster, and that the latter was prepared to relinquish the hitherto accepted privilege, of bringing the Bible from the altar, to the Moderator. I replied that I deeply appreciated the Dean's attitude.

At the beginning of this week, the Moderator, Willie Tindal and I went to Aberdeen to attend the meeting of the Representative Church Council of the Scottish Episcopal Church. On the way, I told the Moderator, as the Archbishop agreed I should do, about the Dean's offer. As we were to be in London later presenting the loyal address to the Queen, I suggested holding a small dinner party at the Caledonian Club, and inviting the Dean to it. To our surprise on reaching the Hotel in Aberdeen, we found the Dean having dinner there, and gave him our invitation. But he is unable to come. He is attending the R.C.C. meetings as an Honorary member, and then having a week's fishing on the Don. We talked about general matters. As we parted, he shook my hand warmly and said: 'I hope that things will work out to your satisfaction for the Coronation.' I thanked him, and added how much I appreciated his action.

We had a further talk, the Moderator, Tindal and myself, about how much should be said at the Assembly. We came to the conclusion that, if possible, I should confine my statement to general terms. To say much would provoke supplementary questions, and raise a press discussion. Above all, we incline to the view that, if the Queen thought well of a St. Giles' service, it would have far the best effect, were the first announcement of it to come from the Palace itself. We will mention this to the General Administration Committee on the 19th and get their approval. The Moderator will by the time of the Report be out of the Chair, and Convener of the Business Committee, and he can weigh in and advise the Assembly, as leader of the House, not to press for further detail at this stage.

On the 15th, I travelled to London with Dr. Caldwell and Mr.

Loyal Address from the Church of Scotland to the Queen at Buckingham Palace, 16th May 1952. L-R: Bailie F.H.M. Walker; Rev. Thomas Caldwell (Principal Clerk of Assembly); Right Rev. Dr. W. White Anderson (Moderator of General Assembly); Rev. William MacNicol (Deputy Clerk); J.R. Philip (Procurator); Rev. W. Roy Sanderson; Mr D.W. Bogle (Law Agent)

MacNicol to be ready for the presentation of the Church's loyal address to Her Majesty on the 16th. The journey was enlivened when a young mother with two small boys – two years and eight months old respectively – joined the train at Grantham. She was to fly with her husband to Canada that night to visit her parents in Prince Edward Island. What between children and luggage, she had more to manage than she could by herself undertake. So Dr. Caldwell and I and another lady in the compartment helped to entertain the bigger boy throwing a stuffed elephant from one to the other round the compartment, and also taking a turn to see that the baby did not fall out of his 'carry-cot'. She was most grateful to us. Mr. MacNicol read his book, and did not seem interested in children. Dr. Caldwell, on the other hand, revealed a new side of his character; he is a fine Christian. We also had a good laugh when, on our arrival at the Rembrandt Hotel (opposite Brompton Oratory) he was hailed by the Head Porter as 'Father' Caldwell! Our party at the Hotel was enlarged by the arrival, first, of Roy Sanderson of the Barony, and then of the Moderator and F.H.N. Walker (just become a Bailie of Edinburgh). David Bogle (who is staying in the Club) joined us next morning.

We set out from the Hotel on the 16th at 11.15 a.m. in full regalia – myself with full-bottomed wig, and black gloves in one pocket, white in the other. In the end it did not matter which – so I wore white. A battery of pressmen took photographs of us before we left; I also took some. As we drove down Constitution Hill, we were met (accidentally) by a troop of Life Guards. Then outside Buckingham Palace, we had a wait till the changing of the Guard was completed, and the crowds began to disperse. Numerous Americans came up to our car window, and photographed me in my wig. After we had rounded the fountain, on the south side of the entrance square, we were again stopped, and made to come out onto the pavement to be photographed. Then we drove in, through an arch under the facade to the main courtyard. We were met at the entrance by the Queen's piper, from Coupar Angus, to whom the Moderator spoke, and who was greatly delighted to see us and to hear that Mr. MacNicol came from 'just over the hill from Coupar Angus'. We then ascended a long stair to the first floor, where we were met by Sir Terence Nugent, Comptroller of the Household. We entered a large ante-room overlooking the garden to the west, where we could see a stretch of lawn leading to the Grosvenor Place Wall, with a pond half-way. To the south was the still unrepaired wing, which received bomb damage. The ante-room had a deep rose carpet, pictures of George IV (by Sir Thos. Lawrence), George III and

Queen Charlotte (by Allan Ramsay) and other monarchs on the one wall opposite the windows, and ormolu tables with huge vases between each window, a heavy mausoleum of a room. Sir Terence rehearsed what we were to do and then retired. Shortly after, the doors opened. The Moderator led us through with Dr. Caldwell, Mr. MacNicol and myself three paces behind him on the left and David Bogle, Roy Sanderson, and F.H.N. Walker three paces behind him on his right. Opposite us on a small portable dais stood the Queen, a mere slip of a girl, in black simple dress with side pleatings, with three rows of pearls round her neck, pearl earrings, two diamond clasps on her left shoulder (one, I think, a maple leaf from Canada) and open toe-less shoes. The Secretary of State for Scotland introduced us. Then we bowed; the Moderator stepped forward three paces, bowed again and read our address; this was then handed to the Queen; who, in turn, gave it to Mr. Michael Adeane. She then read her short reply, in a clear pleasant voice, and handed it to the Moderator, who then took his place at her side. Then, in turn, we moved up to be introduced:- Dr. Caldwell; Mr. MacNicol; myself; David Bogle; Roy Sanderson; F.H.N. Walker. Her hand was taut when I shook hands with her, as if she felt a certain strain. To David Bogle, she remarked: 'How pleasant to see you again,' – he had danced last summer with her in Deeside. We then filed out into a side-room and downstairs again. Everything went smoothly, except that the Secretary of State seemed at first to forget that he had to introduce us. The Comptroller was flashing messages to him.

Otherwise, the ceremony went perfectly. Below, we exchanged farewells with our piper, and then entered our cars and drove off. I could not help feeling a certain pity for a young Queen as burdened with official duties, when she might have been enjoying her children. Of those who stood round her, I recognised only the Lord Chamberlain (the Earl of Clarendon) with beard and stick. I believe Sir David Maxwell Fyfe was there. There was one lady-in-waiting; the rest were men.

Outside the Palace, just as we were about to proceed up Constitution Hill, we were again ambushed by photographers. While we waited for them, the guard passed, and one guardsman had his shoe-lace undone; I wonder what the sergeant of the guard had to say about it afterwards. Then we drove back to our hotel. It was a broiling hot day. My collar, at the end of the ceremony, was becoming quite soft. I was relieved to learn afterwards that others than ourselves had felt the heat: a guardsman slumped down in a faint. But a full-bottomed wig on a day like this was almost as oppressive as a bear-skin.

4th July 1952

Much has happened since my last entry. The Assembly was the most turbulent, and least satisfactory, so far as legal business is concerned, that I have yet encountered. The behaviour of some members in the Melrose case was quite disgraceful. They were so anxious to vote for their prejudged view, that they would not let me speak, until I said plainly that such conduct in a judicial proceeding was disgraceful. I spoke on the Report of the Committee of National Occasions, of which I am Convener; on the Report on Marriage and Divorce which I largely drafted; and on Communism. The first with highly controversial matter in the background went through quietly. In the second, our Report was adopted with only a trifling verbal exchange. I was roused by having heard the night before from Dr. Luecking, our guest, of the position of Communism in Eastern Germany. Dr. Luecking, the head of the Evangelical Church in Westphalia, stayed with us for ten days – a charming guest. He was touched by his welcome, and said he never believed that he would find in another country such 'brethren in Christ'. He was due to go on to the Sacred Mission at Kelham, and then to Cuddesdon for a few days. But he willingly left out the first to remain longer with us. He was one of the most gay and charmingly Christian characters I have met.

In the middle of June I had a visit first to Iona for the meeting there, in the alternate year, of the Cathedral Trustees, then to Oban where I presented to the Faculty of Procurators a photograph of Chalmers reading the accession proclamation at Inverary; then to Campbeltown where I installed three honoraries, Mr. MacKelvie, Dr. Mackenzie, and Colonel Taylor, and also welcomed Sir Bruce Campbell on the Bench, and gave a small lunch at the Argyll Arms. Tom Taylor was the only other Cathedral Trustee with me at Iona. I attended a communion service at the Community, which had some beautiful and instructive features, and we had lunch on Sunday in the Refectory with the Community. Dr. Kenneth MacLeod – of 'The Road to the Isles' – was there, and I photographed him next day with Rosemary. He has that Highland wistfulness in his smile, like the music of Chopin. The journey was remarkable for the birds I saw: cormorants, a fulmar, herons, oyster-catchers, and a cock and hen pheasant. It was cold weather, but the views were unbelievably clear.

On our way to Iona – we came and returned via the Sound of Mull – we could see Skye, Jura and Tiree all at the one time. On the Sunday afternoon, we walked over to the west shore via the machair, and were caught, on the way back, in drenching rain.

Next week, I was in Aberdeen in my last year as law examiner. The students presented me afterwards with a Faculty of Law tie – a new invention at Aberdeen.

I was asked to broadcast as second speaker, after the Moderator, Dr. Johnstone Jeffrey, in the series 'Why I believe'. I recorded my broadcast yesterday. It is a very difficult broadcast to do. Ronnie Falconer on receiving the script wrote: 'All I can say is to thank you from the bottom of my heart for your very brave and moving script. If it does for the listeners what it has done for me, then LAUS DEO!' I felt I had to speak about learning Christianity from the love, gentleness, charity, forgiveness and courage in my own home, and discovering the real love of God at the time of Gordon's death, and the real meaning of immortality. I quoted the second verse of 'I vow to thee, my Country' and ended by stating my belief that neither life nor death . . . should separate us from the love of God which is in Christ Jesus Our Lord.

The Queen paid her first official visit to Edinburgh as Queen. The Duke had jaundice, and dropped out at the last moment. The *New York Times* headline ran: 'Queen visits Scotland. Edinburgh has jaundice!' We went with Alison to the Holyrood Garden Party on the 27th. She had just returned that morning from Oxford, having in the last week played in *Ralph Roister Doister* at Eton, Harrow and Radley.

19th July 1952

We left yesterday morning at 9 a.m. from Granton for this year's Northern Lights cruise, and now I am writing this in my cabin at Kirkwall. I set out with a 'fan-mail' relating to my broadcast on the 15th – most kindly appreciation. I had a kind telephone message from Lady Fleming who rang up when we were in the midst of a sherry-party which we gave on the 15th for about seventy-six guests, mainly young advocates and their wives. On the *Pharos*, our company this year is quite different. Robbie Maconochie, Lillie and I remain from last year's company. The others are:- James Gilchrist (now Sheriff of the Lothians); Bailie Campbell (senior Bailie of Edinburgh, a railway union official); Provost Boyd of Greenock (a baker to trade); and Glen Wakelin. Ross MacLean is joining us later. This might seem a less well-assorted company than a band of professional brethren. Actually, I consider it a great improvement. The Sheriffs have tried to show special courtesy to the magistrates; and the magistrates have responded by entering into the spirit and tradition of the *Pharos*. So far, the weather has been less favourable than usual. Yesterday, we visited the Isle of May again, and I paid my second visit to the Bell Rock. The new company were game – all except Robbie climbed the Bell Rock, the base of which was still under water. We went in by Johnnie Gray's channel: Mr. Hunter, as usual, navigated us superbly through it, over still uncovered rocks. We had with us Mr. Parker of the Caledon Shipbuilding Yard, Dundee. He has prepared plans of the proposed new *Pharos*, which is expected to be built by about 1955, provided that the contract is placed soon. It will be a larger ship, 1,200 tons against the present 920 or thereby. There will be nine cabins for Commissioners and Secretary against the present eight. A whole deck will be set apart for the crew instead of their very limited present quarters, and there will be more room to play 'buckies'! Mr. Parker mentioned that, when in 1909 the present *Pharos* was built, life-saving apparatus for the crew was estimated at £5! What a change from now. I think the loss of the *Titanic* in 1912 led to a new outlook – that and other causes. Mr. Parker exhibited both plans and a sketch. The new ship would have a cut-away bow, and cruiser stern, as against the cut-away stern, and straight bow of the present *Pharos*. We put Mr. Parker off at Arbroath.

I weighed in at 17 stone 9 lbs, the same as at the start of last year's trip. Our last sight of the coast last night was of Girdleness and the lights of Aberdeen. Radar picked out the cliffs beautifully and the trawlers dotted about the vicinity. We had no Radar on our last trip here: it was installed in 1951.

30th July 1952 (Wednesday)

We lifted our anchor shortly before nine a.m. and sailed in to Oban in time to catch the 12.05 train for Edinburgh. This was a brilliant sunny warm day – so different from the chilly weather of this cruise. I weighed 18 stone 10 lbs. at the conclusion of the voyage. Gilchrist also put on a stone and a lb., and the Provost a lb. I paid a visit in Oban Bay to Mr. Hobb's yacht *Torlundy*, as I saw Sir Bruce Campbell on deck. They could not come over to join us, as the Regatta races were just beginning.

The following story was invented on this year's cruise. When the

World Faith and Order Conference, Lund. Back Row L-R: Rev. William Stewart; J.R. Philip; Rev. J.K.S. Reid; Dr. T.F. Torrance; Dr. W.D. Maxwell. Front Row L-R: Dr. A.C. Craig; Dr. Donald Baillie; Dr. Nevile Davidson.

Commissioners came to embark at Granton, Mr. Walker, the second officer, went up to James Gilchrist, and asked: 'Sheriff Gilchrist, I think?' 'Yes, that is so.' 'Then, may I mention that your cabin is on the port side of the ship. Sheriff Philip's cabin is on the starboard side. We want the ship properly trimmed!'

11th August 1952

Tomorrow, we leave for Newcastle, from which we sail to Copenhagen and thence to Lund for the World Conference on Faith and Order. Sir Charles Cunningham telephoned me today to say that, although the announcement would not be made till, at earliest, September, the Church of Scotland's proposals in connection with

Coronation arrangements will probably be acceded to. It has been announced that the Queen is to visit Scotland from 23rd to 29th June 1953, but, beyond this, nothing has yet been announced with regard to Scotland.

12th August 1952 (Tuesday)

We set out for the World Faith and Order Conference at Lund, travelling by the M.S. *Parkeston* from Newcastle to Copenhagen. Before we were out of Waverley I saw two other delegates, Donald Mackinnon and the Bishop of Brechin. After lunch in Newcastle we went down to the quay-side and in the Custom House were joined by W.D. Maxwell who had motor-cycled there from Whitekirk and who intends after leaving the Conference to return by motor-cycle via Oslo. On board the ship we also met Archie and Mrs. Craig and Bishop and Mrs. Graham. The *Parkeston*, in spite of its name, is a Danish ship, which used to be on the Harwich to Esbjerg run. The sail down the Tyne was fascinating. We backed the first mile and then swung round in a special canting basin. Just as we were sitting down to dinner the ship emerged from the river and began its crossing of the North Sea. The weather was excellent though it showed some sign of deterioration as we neared Denmark. We saw many trawlers particularly in the Dogger Bank area; a magnificent sunset over the sea; but almost no sea-birds (so different from the Lighthouse voyage).

At our table there sat a Danish father with daughter and son. They behaved most charmingly to each other and could not but attract our attention. On the last evening when we were on deck watching the first Danish lighthouses show up I noticed that the daughter was wearing Mackenzie tartan gloves, and I asked jokingly was that her clan. She replied that her cousin had been a Seaforth Highlander and was in the Royal Scots now. The father then said that his sister was the widow of Sheriff Martin Laing, late of Kilmarnock. The father gave me much useful advice about exchange and tipping.

We had a pleasant run past Elsinore with good views of both shores, the Swedish side distinguished by its windmills, the Danish side by its beautiful houses. We reached Copenhagen about 10.50.

Our travelling companions, particularly Maxwell and Mackinnon, were a source of great delight and entertainment. Maxwell is an inveterate snuff-taker and carried several varieties about his person. He and I snuffed our way across the North Sea and through the Conference. He introduced me to some varieties of Danish and Swedish liqueurs, on which he seemed to be already expert. Maxwell and I became great friends; he expressed the view that we would both have been extremely happy in the eighteenth century.

Mackinnon, however, was the really eccentric character both of the voyage and of the Conference. He arrived in the most disreputable suit with an untidy sports shirt held together by a bedraggled Wyke-hamist tie. At the Conference he abandoned the tie but clung tenaciously to the shirt. After wearing it for a considerable period, one day he appeared with a white shirt and collar, but confessed to me that he had forgotten to put a tie on. He had a big patch of elephantine design on the seat of his trousers which Rosemary labelled Professor Mackinnon's 'zoo'. As he looked exactly like a Displaced Person it is not surprising that one day a large parcel arrived at the hostel where he was staying. It was from a wealthy burgher of Malmö, who wrote that he had heard of Mackinnon's intellectual work and services to the ecumenical causes, and heard also of how difficult the rationing situation was in Scotland and would like him to accept one of the three suits enclosed. Mackinnon himself told this story, quite unaware of the effect which his curious appearance had caused at the Conference. Mackinnon also told me of another story about himself. Shortly after his arrival at Aberdeen University, he was walking along Union Street, Aberdeen, when he became conscious that the police were following him. They came up to him and asked for his Identity Card. It was too much to expect Mackinnon to carry an Identity Card. They took him up a side street to question him. After they had discovered who he was they confessed that they had suspected him of being a Pole who was being sought as a suspected murderer. Mackinnon is quite an unselfconscious eccentric. It is certainly not a pose. At Oxford when he visited friends all the wine glasses had to be removed from the table, otherwise he would either crunch them in his hands in the intensity of his conversation or sweep them in a wild gesture off the table. No one could be more friendly than Mack-innon. I had long and interesting talks with him and he showed the same friendship to Alison and to Rosemary that he showed to me.

14th August 1952 (Thursday)

We arrived at Copenhagen and went straight to the quay from which the ferry crosses to Malmö. The passenger ferries take approximately two hours. We crossed in one of the Swedish boats. At Malmö we found a very helpful porter. He carried our four suitcases on a bicycle with a big rack in front from the quay to the nearby station. We were interested to see two advertisements of Loch Awe and Kilchurn Castle in the station. The Swedish electric trains are most clean and comfortable usually of the non-compartmented type. In quarter of an hour we were in Lund. Our hotel is beside the station. The proprietrix, Fru Mortenson, speaks no French, German or English. Until we learned a little Swedish we had to communicate chiefly by signs. Our two rooms are spotlessly clean but there are no baths and no hot water. The hotel simply provides bed and continental breakfast, which is exactly what we wanted. It overlooks a very lovely square with grass plots, flower beds and a fountain. On another side of the square is the Grand Hotel where many of the chief delegates were staying. They paid dearly for staying there, as most of them found that on the travel allowance they were unable to take breakfast in the hotel without their allowance running out. We had dinner in a nearby restaurant along with Bill Stewart. Bill Stewart is a Church of Scotland missionary at Nagpur, but was a delegate from the Church of Northern India. He is one of the finest of the younger missionaries, with an extraordinarily good academic record. Tom Torrance is one of the *enfants terribles* of the Conference, thirty-nine years old, but quite amazingly learned and a theologian of the slightly pugnacious type, but a very charming and frank nature. In the evening, while Rosemary was being put to bed, I wandered out into the square and before I knew where I was I had fallen into the arms of Mrs. Rawlinson and the Bishop of Derby. They were as delighted as I was. We had a long talk together, about their boy Anthony, Jim Galbraith, and Gordon. Shortly Ella joined us and I introduced her. This friendship renewed became one of the most pleasant features amongst our friendships at the Conference. They took us in to the Grand Hotel that evening and there we had a long and very pleasant talk with the Archbishop of Quebec (Carrington), Dr. Ernest Payne (secretary of the Baptist Union), the Bishop of Derby and Jack Reid. Afterwards I was introduced to Archbishop Brilioth. I was able to establish some interesting links with the Archbishop of Quebec. I told him that I had a Canadian brother-in-law. He was greatly delighted when he discovered that I knew of Drummond's 'habitant' poems. 'They are a minor classic, scarcely known outside the province of Quebec,' he said. I also told him that Professor Robison whose Raeburn portrait hangs in Edinburgh University was, in early life, the midshipman who heard General Wolfe say 'Gray's Elegy' as he crossed the river to the siege of Quebec. He confirmed that the story was quite authentic historically. The

Rawlinsons had amusing tales about the absence of baths in Sweden. On an earlier visit the Bishop and Anthony ordered baths. Anthony arrived first and was somewhat astounded to find in the bathroom a powerful Amazon awaiting to scrub his back. When the Bishop heard of this he decided he would rather forgo a bath. The Bishop can be a very forceful personality indeed, but in his wife's presence he becomes quite subdued. Mrs. Rawlinson is quite irrepressible. She had a wonderful story about staying in a convent in Paris where there were English nuns. It was about the time of the birth of Princess Anne. The nuns were having their silent hour but it was arranged that Mrs. Rawlinson should indicate whether the new baby was a boy or a girl by lifting her skirt if it was a boy and a little more if it was a girl. When she raised her skirt the nuns were tremendously delighted. After the hour's quiet was at an end, the nuns explained that their joy was two-fold, not merely that they were delighted to know that it was a girl, but also that they had, for the first time, been privileged to see nylon underwear.

15th August 1952 (Friday)

We went up to the University this morning to let me register. There I found a queue waiting and joined it. I was resolved to speak to as many strangers as I could. Behind me there was a young American. The moment I mentioned my name a man alongside said, 'I have been waiting to see you.' He turned out to be Principal Allan of Knox College, Dunedin, who had travelled from Dunedin to Lund, via San Francisco, in five days. He told me that in 1923 he, with Henry Adamson, had occupied Dad's pulpit at Invergowrie while we were in Rome. Amongst the papers which we received was a Conference document No. 11 entitled 'Towards Church Union, 1937–1952', compiled by Bishop Stephen Neill. I at once turned up the account of the Anglo-Scottish Conferences and found it to be unfortunately a very inaccurate and one-sided one, containing no reference whatsoever to the action which the Church of Scotland had taken upon the joint reports of 1934 and 1951. The mistakes were so glaring that with the approval of all the Church of Scotland delegates I prepared a Memorandum which was later submitted by them, drawing attention to the inaccuracies. It is regrettable that such a document should have been put out, but I am afraid it is explained by the fact that the secretariat is at the moment too exclusively Anglican and the documents had apparently not been checked by any representative of the Church of Scotland.

The delegates obtain all their meals in the Akademiska Foreningens Restaurant or students union, a very well equipped building at the other end of the quadrangle from the University. Between the two buildings lie beautiful gardens with a large fountain playing in the centre. In one corner stands a small tree which is said to belong to the oldest species in the world – a ginkgo tree. The meals in the restaurant, like the meals on the *Parkeston* were quite a revelation to Britons accustomed to rationed food. Everyone was served in buffet fashion from a centre table, the delegates helping themselves. The drink consisted of milk or a drink which looked exactly like beer but which was really sweet mead with an alcoholic content less than ginger ale. The delegates sat informally anywhere and meals provided an excellent opportunity for extending friendships. We paid our first visit to the Cathedral which contains an astronomical clock like Strasbourg. At 12 o'clock two knights in armour at the top hammer each other with their swords twelve times, then a door opens and the three Kings followed by attendants pass in turn in front of the Virgin and Child and bow. At the same time the clock plays out very slowly and simply with varying crescendos and diminuendos the tune 'In Dulci Jubilo'.

We had tea on the square at Bantorget outside our hotel, and in the evening Ella and I attended the opening service of the Conference in the Cathedral. The really impressive thing was the magnificent singing of the German chorales. The hymn-book of the World Christian Movement with hymns in English, French and German was used throughout the Conference, each delegate using the language most convenient to himself.

16th August 1952 (Saturday)

Today the Conference opened with a General Session. Archbishop Brilioth presided and conducted the whole business in excellent English. He has a deep, almost guttural voice and a grave and wise manner. A short address was given by Archbishop Athenagoras. He is perhaps the most picturesque figure at the Conference with a white pointed beard and flowing purple coat over his black cassock. He is extraordinarily good-looking and knows it. When I asked permission to photograph him he carefully combed his hair before he allowed me to do so. At the dinner given later to the Conference by the city and parish of Lund, he unashamedly combed his hair in the middle of dinner. The whole Conference is being divided into five sections, three relating to the Church, the fourth to Ways of Worship, and the fifth to inter-communion. In the evening there was held a pre-Communion service in the Cathedral at which Donald Baillie preached, this time from the pulpit. Every word was heard of a most simple and impressive sermon. The singing of the German chorales was quite magnificent – 'Nun Danket', and the well-known Stralsund chorale. It was refreshing also to hear the great Swedish congregation sing the 23rd Psalm to 'Crimond', and Dr. George Matheson's 'Make me a captive, Lord', to one of Bach's own hymn-tunes.

17th August 1952 (Sunday)

Today there was held in the Cathedral morning service with Communion to which Archbishop Brilioth had invited all the delegates. The sermon was preached by Bishop Nygren. The Communion was administered by the Dean of Lund with three other clergy of whom I afterwards came to know two, Pastors Dahmen and Schlyter. Archbishop Brilioth explained the form of the Swedish rite to the whole Conference. The number of communicants appeared to be very large but I afterwards learnt that the figure was about 550–600. Communion was given to about twenty at a time; each group continued to kneel until all had been served and did not move away after the next had been served as in the Anglican practice. The words of the Swedish rites are beautiful. The wafer is placed in the communicant's mouth with the words 'The Body of Christ given for thee.' The wine is then given with the words 'The Blood of Christ shed for thee.' The repetition of these words for so many communicants left an indelible impression. The service was conducted with great dignity. At its conclusion the four priests in turn served each other in pairs. In addition to the delegate communicants there were many young people. The offering was taken up with ladles after the old Scottish style, except that the money was placed in leather bags instead of boxes and great skill was required in conveying the ladles among the crowded congregation. With boxes many heads would have been cracked. Amongst those who took the collection were women, both young and old.

In the afternoon I went with Alison and Rosemary to the Folk Museum. On the way we fell in with Professor Clavier of Strasbourg (whom I had met at the French Church in Edinburgh), and M. Hoyois of Belgium. I took the chance of speaking to them and they were most friendly both of them and for the remainder of the Conference. We were fascinated by the Folk Museum. There are some twenty period houses and some white goats graze in one of the small parks. Almost the most interesting of all the exhibits is the little Swedish church. There is also a series of rooms for different uses and one unusual feature is homemade tapestries after the sampler or paisley shawl idea, containing all manner of biblical scenes in which the characters wear nineteenth century Swedish costume. There was also an unusual exhibit, a *kyrkabåt*, a special boat built for rowing people to church, the Swedish equivalent of the old Scottish kirk boat.

Later I was introduced by the Rawlinsons to the Bishop of Washington, Dr. Angus Dun. He was a stalwart, well-built, pleasant man with much greater informality than his Church of England colleagues often have. He told me that he was the great-grandson of the Relief minister of Kilsyth.

He told me also that he was connected with Dun in Angus; hence his name. He, too, never afterwards passed without exchanging a word with myself or the family.

In the evening the Conference met to hear papers from Professor Schlink of Heidelberg and Oliver Tompkins. Dr. Schlink's address was one of the most remarkable and caused a certain fluttering amongst the dove-cotes of the German Lutherans. At the Second Advent Christians would be differently divided from their present divisions in the Church; the best Christians would be found in all branches of that Church. Unity was most likely to be achieved by looking to the future instead of to the past. Oliver Tompkins' paper described the progress since the last Conference in Edinburgh in 1937. He suggested that the limit might have been reached in making explanations; that the Conference had willed the death of our denominations; that there should be a new outlook on the Christian teaching of unity; that the Churches should unite to a greater extent in common prayer. One sentence from his paper was commonly referred to later: that the attitude of the Churches should be to remain together except in so far as they were compelled to be separate, not that they should remain separate except in so far as they required to be together.

18th August 1952 (Monday)

A further General Session took place this morning. Dr. Obendiek of Wupperthal spoke on 'Social and Cultural Factors in our Divisions.' One point he made which interested me was that the Reformation itself developed in the orbit of a German-Scandinavian Anglo-Saxon culture and society. He was followed by Professor Garrison of the

Disciples of Christ, U.S.A., who made a very provocative and also humorous and trenchant speech. I later came to work with Dr. Garrison in my section and found him a most honest and realistic and at the same time humorous colleague, with a gift of expression and great skill in drafting.

Dr. Garrison was followed by Professor Hromadka of Czechoslovakia. He spoke with great fire and was too diffuse. I cannot help thinking that his reputation arises partly from the fact that he had come from behind the Iron Curtain. He was followed by Bishop Peter of the Reformed Church of Hungary, the only Reformed Church which has bishops. He urged the need for the Conference to be available to both east and west; otherwise it might be interpreted as the Conference of an Atlantic bloc. He also was my colleague later in the section already mentioned. I found him one of the best of colleagues with a warm side to Scotland where he had studied. I was interested to find that quite independently of me the Davidsons had also formed a high opinion of him; indeed they thought him one of the best people in the whole Conference. I discussed with him the position of the Church behind the Iron Curtain. He said that their position was better at the present time than it had been previously, chiefly because the Roman Catholic church no longer held such dominance and the Reformed Church was free to develop itself. It has been possible for Lutherans and Reformed to have inter-communion and also, in some instances, inter-celebration. Bishop Peter was followed by Pierre Maury of France who looked exactly like a successful banker or consultant physician. He spoke in French which was at first translated by Dr. Visser't Hooft. I could not help being amused at the combination. It was exactly like a Punch and Judy Show. Pierre Maury swung his arm backwards and forwards in big circles exactly as if punching Judy on the head. After one big sweep which seemed finally to dispose of Judy, he cast off his interpreter and spoke in perfectly good English for the rest of his discourse.

19th August 1952 (Tuesday)

The forenoon and afternoon were devoted to section meetings when the reports of the various confessional groups were given in. In the evening I attended a special meeting of the Reformed Confession group. There were 120 present and every continent was represented. Professor Hromadka occupied the chair. His chairman's remarks were vivacious and humorous. The other speakers were, first, Dr. E.C.

Blake, the Clerk of Assembly of the Presbyterian Church of the U.S.A. He comes from California and was commendably brief. It is rather surprising to find that there are three different Presbyterian denominations in the United States: the Presbyterian Church of the U.S.A.; the Presbyterian Church of the United States; and the United Presbyterian Church. The difference between the first and the second is accounted for by the Civil War, the first being mainly North American and the second South. The third is mainly derived from voluntaries. Dr. Blake told me that a union is in prospect.

The next speaker after Dr. Blake was Tom Torrance whose speech was the *tour de force* of the evening. He stressed the influence of the Reformed Churches as occupying a bridge position in the ecumenical movement. The great Reformation truth was that the word of God was exalted over tradition. With regard to the essential nature of the Church the Lutherans paid little attention to form and order, the Anglicans very much. The Reformed Churches mid-way between the two. On the doctrine of the Episcopate he stressed that the priesthood of all beliefs was really a corporate priesthood; and that the true Reformed Doctrine was that the Church contained a corporate episcopate embodied in the Presbytery which ensured corporate continuity. He spoke with such confidence that at the end of his speech Professor Hromadka remarked, 'We cannot be blamed for being afflicted with an inferiority complex.' Principal Allan sitting beside me observed in more homely language, 'Well we've got a guid conceit of ourselves.' The third speaker was Dr. Ralla Ram of the Church of North India. He considers that the Presbyterians had taken the greatest part in the unions of the South Indian Church and the Church of North India. 'Of all those who are doing harm to the cause of organic unity, the Presbyterians are doing the least! No Bishop will reach Heaven because he was a Bishop here on earth; he will be there because he was a sinner saved by grace!' He urged, however, that the older Reformed Churches should not impress their traditions on the young churches of the East.

After him came a gallant little Pastor from Colombia, South America, Dr. Luis Quiroga. He described his Church as the youngest Reformed Church. It had been subjected to very grave persecution from the Roman Catholic Church which dominated the political parties. Eight of his churches' pastors had been assassinated; twenty-two to twenty-three of its churches had been blown up or burned. They had no political liberty just now, but their Church membership had doubled. He concluded: 'We are thankful to the Lord for the persecution', then added that it had disillusioned the Roman Catholic lay people.

20th August 1952 (Wednesday)

In the afternoon we went on a motor tour where we were the guests of the Church of Sweden. Alison and I travelled in a bus and Dr. Niemöller, who had a private car and was accompanied by Mrs. Niemöller and his son took also Ella and Rosemary. In our bus we found ourselves in the rear seat, with as a companion on my left side Dr. Leiper, U.S.A., and on my right side a German who could speak no English and only a little French. Immediately in front of us were the Bishop of Derby and Mrs. Rawlinson. We had a most jovial time. Dr. Leiper was quite irrepressible. He had told fifteen stories before the bus started, and talked in a loud voice making indiscreet remarks about the Anglican Church which the Rawlinsons greatly enjoyed. I cannot remember all the stories. One was that the minister of a rather thinly populated church had noticed a man for several Sundays sitting in front under the pulpit. After some days he spoke to the stranger and asked why he always sat at the front of the church, whereas most of the others sat at the back. 'Oh,' said the stranger, 'I must explain that I am a bus-driver and I wanted to find from you how it was that you made everyone sit at the back.' We visited two exquisite parish churches, both in the Danish style, for Skåne was originally a Danish province. They were beautifully white-washed and clean, the one simpler than the other. At the simpler one which we visited in the evening all the parishioners were drawn up awaiting the arrival of this gigantic party. The first church was at one time served by the late Archbishop Eidem. We visited various chateaux and had tea at Skaralid. Here there is a beautiful lake like Loch an Eilean. I asked Dr. Niemöller if he did not also think it seemed like the Pragser Wildsee in the Tyrol where he was at one time prisoner. The lake has, like Ordban by Loch an Eilean, a cliff from which one has an extensive view over the little lake to the rolling country beyond. At the cliff, I was introduced to a delegate from the Argentine and just at that moment an explosion occurred at a nearby quarry. I said: 'That must be president Peron,' which seemed greatly to delight my Argentine friend.

From Skaralid we went on to Knutsdorp where we were conducted over the chateau by the lady of the house. This is a magnificent chateau in red brick, its interior almost a museum of Swedish domestic furniture and art, with beyond a beautiful lawn and lily-pond. We went out to the lawn afterwards and found that the grass was full of tiny frogs from the lily-pond. Rosemary enjoyed greatly picking them up and seeing them jump from the back of her hand. The lady of the house, who belongs to the Wachmeister family, has divided the chateau into three sets of apartments. The first is occupied by herself and the other two by her sons and their families. The children were all playing about. One small boy took a great fancy to one of the Armenian delegates, Bishop Poladian, from the Lebanon and when we were about to go would not leave him. As we drove down the avenue the branches of the chestnut trees caught the roofs of the buses and numerous chestnuts dropped into the bus. The landscape of Skåne is incredibly wide, almost like the sea. There are no hedge-rows or fences. The cows are all tethered and eat a little circle of grass within their reach; horses run wild. The fields were being harvested by combined harvesters of an American pattern. There were numerous windmills. Dr. Leiper considered the landscape very like an American one. As we returned home there was an exquisite sunset and from a vantage point at the second church we visited it was possible to see, faintly, the spires of Copenhagen.

21st August 1952 (Thursday)

In the afternoon our section met in the chapter house of the Cathedral, a building which extends across the close some distance from the chancel. There is a most delightful brick courtyard with, in the centre, one of Lund's numerous fountains. Round the low fountain basin are carved figures representing faith, hope and charity, with texts in Swedish deeply carved. The rooms in the chapter-house were most exquisitely furnished. Indeed, the excellent condition of all fabrics is a feature of the Church of Sweden. Its close connection with the state gives it certain advantages as well as the obvious disadvantages of such a state church. The advantages which I noticed were that the fabrics were invariably in first-class condition; that Lund was not over-churched (there were only three parishes though the buildings seemed adequate); that there is practically no non-conformity; that the clergy are well-housed and paid. For example, the Bishop receives the salary of the Governor of a Province and the ordinary clergy seem to be able to run their own cars.

After our meeting I met the family for tea at the Conditori beside the University. We were joined by Bishop Angus Dun. I was struck by how different his outlook was from a Church of England bishop. When I called him the Bishop of Washington he said, 'We don't use territorial titles like the English.' He also explained to me that in America they look at the re-marriage of divorced persons quite differently from the Church of England. Each case is dealt with on its merits by the Bishop. This is, *mutatis mutandis*, the system which the Church of Scotland seeks to introduce and he was much interested in this.

22nd August 1952 (Friday)

I rose early and went to the Swedish Communion in the Cathedral. My object was primarily to attend Communion, following it with a Swedish text which Pastor Dahmen had given me. Also Pastor Dahmen had said that Pastor Schlyter would let me photograph him in his vestments. There was quite a considerable attendance but only three members of the Conference: myself, the Anglican Prioress of St. Hilda (the only nun present at the Conference) and Dr. Floyd Tompkins from America. I think that the Prioress (judging from the attitude of the *Church Times*) must have been horrified at having to take Communion with a Presbyterian. The service was so beautiful that I felt it would be quite wrong to take the suggested photograph after it, so I slipped away to the restaurant for breakfast. There I met a man helping himself to porridge. I thought this obviously indicated a link and sat down beside him. He turned out to be an ecclesiastical journalist from Finland who knew almost no English, but was able to explain that porridge was a favoured dish in Finland. After breakfast I went outside and there fell in with the Bishop of Derby. He told me that while I had been attending the Swedish Communion he had been attending a Communion of the Church of South India in the crypt below. He was deeply impressed with the beauty of the South Indian rite. When the Bread and Wine are given the words used are: 'Christ the Bread of Life' and 'Christ the true Vine'. I asked him whether the Church of England was likely to go further in recognising the Church of South India. He opened his heart to me about this. 'We have to consider the matter further in two years. I think that the majority will want to give full recognition and I hope that the majority will act even though they are only a majority. The Church of England must either act in this way or be prepared to become an isolated communion.'

One or two of my colleagues thought that Brandreth was one of the most unapproachable of the Anglo-Catholics. After lunch I happened to be walking across the quadrangle and fell in with him. I found he was doing nothing till 2.30 p.m. so asked him to spend the next half-hour with me. I found that his outwardly stand-offish manner was simply due to shyness. Before the half-hour was over we were good friends and I had introduced him to Maxwell and the Davidsons. Later in the afternoon official photographs were taken, first of the Reformed Confessions' representatives and secondly of the whole Conference. I was also able to get interesting pictures of Archbishop Brilioth to whom I was re-introduced by Dr. Garrison and Dr. Gresham. Dr. and Mrs. Niemöller are most friendly to us as is also their son, who spent some years in a Russian prison camp. I took to Archbishop Brilioth. He is what a chairman should be, friendly and considerate of everyone. After tea we had another meeting of the section. It is curious how the further east one goes the more eccentric become ecclesiastical costumes. To see Dr. Horton talking to Father Florovsky is like watching a modern business man speaking to an inhabitant of the Ark. Dr. Horton made an excellent chairman. Our section met in a most up-to-date lecture room with beautiful wood fittings, a feature of all Swedish premises. We sat there with the windows wide open but every day at noon Dr. Horton closed the windows nearest him for the deafening chimes of the Cathedral made conversation difficult to hear.

In the evening the Conference was invited to dinner in the restaurant by the town and Parish of Lund. I sat next the end of a table with Pierre Maury on my left and Ella on my right. Opposite me were M. Bagnier of Nice and M. Westphal of Paris. Westphal is an uncle of Alfred Westphal who once stayed with us. Opposite them were Professor and Mrs. Stachlin of Basel. Mrs. Stachlin is trying to organise the ladies of the Conference. They are to write her each November giving any news of interest in their churches and she will then issue a circular letter to all. Tom Torrance afterwards told me that Professor Stachlin belongs to a family of old pre-Reformation merchant princes of Basel, some of them millionaires. He himself lives quite simply in a large house and for the mere love of it takes in students to lodge. The three Frenchmen all knew Mme. Metzger and later Pierre Maury wrote a post card to her saying that he had met her 'Fille d'Écosse' and then all the Frenchmen and Ella signed it. At the dinner speeches were made by the Mayor, the Dean of Lund and Dr. Douglas Horton. Swedish students sang Swedish folk songs.

23rd August 1952 (Saturday)

This morning, the Conference wasted a whole Session discussing amendments to the constitution and other procedural matters. One hour was all I could stand. Thereafter Maxwell and I went out. He wanted to introduce me to Bishop Lakdasa de Mel and the three of us went down to the coffee room where we were joined by Donald Mackinnon. Bishop Lakdasa is quite one of the most charming personalities of the Conference with a bright, vivacious and friendly manner. We had a most interesting talk about T.S. Eliot and the new liturgy of Ceylon which is used by the Bishop and in the preparation of which material was drawn from some of Maxwell's books. In the morning Ella attended a talk for the ladies by Frau Niemöller who described the years during which Dr. Niemöller was in and out of prison. She has a small boy, called Martin after his father. Her hair is pure white after all her troubles. One day she said to young Martin, 'How do you like having such an old mother?' and he replied, 'I thought it strange at first, but I'm getting used to it now!'

In the afternoon we went as a family to Malmö. We stopped to have refreshments at a café on the quay-side and a Swede from New Jersey befriended us and interpreted our orders to the waitress. Then we visited the square where Rosemary played with the tame pigeons and where there is a statue of King Charles XII, the town house and St. Peter's Church.

Finally we went to the canal and from there took a motor-boat in which we sailed round the harbour, past the shipbuilding yards, with two archaic submarines and two 16,000 ton Norwegian ships building. Then round the town by canal, which traverses it like a canal in Amsterdam. We passed under eighteen bridges and saw a windmill and the beautiful royal park. Near one of the last bridges a small urchin leaned down and handed an envelope to the driver of the boat. It turned out to be photographs which had been taken at the start of the voyage and which had been developed and printed and while we were making our circuit the small boy had rushed across the town and handed them from the bridge. Many of the bridges are so so low that you have to duck to pass under them.

In the evening I went back to the Conference Hall and fell in with the irrepressible Dr. Leiper. He immediately furnished me with some American religious statistics which were most interesting: 70 million members of Christian churches in the United States of which 25 million are Roman Catholic; 11 million Baptist; 9 million Methodist; 6 million Lutheran; 5 million Presbyterian; 2 million Episcopalian; and 1½ million Congregationalist. He said that while the Christian membership was growing amongst those denominations which represented the earliest settlers, the Episcopalians, Presbyterians and Independents still numbered under 10 million.

24th August 1952 (Sunday)

In the afternoon I took Rosemary while Alison went out for a cycle run. We visited first the statue of Linnaeus and then saw a squirrel disporting itself in the trees near the University. At 4 p.m. Ella joined me and Alison took over Rosemary. Ella and I went to an At Home by Bishop Nygren for the delegates. There I had long talks with two Norwegians, Bischof Skard and Pastor Stoylen. The latter is Pastor at Bergen. They were very friendly from that moment onwards. I also met Dr. Niemöller and talking about inter-Communion with him I referred to the exchange of letters which had occurred between the Church of Sweden and the Church of Scotland and asked him what the attitude of the United Church in Germany would be. He told me: 'We would welcome inter-Communion with the Church of Scotland.' Mrs. Graham told Ella later that Dr. Niemöller had said that Ella was the nicest hostess that he had ever had.

After an early dinner the delegates marshalled in the Conference hall and walked in procession from the University to the Cathedral. I found myself sitting immediately behind Dr. Niemöller in a very good position about six pews from the front. After the delegates were all in position the King and Queen of Sweden walked in along the passage by my side quite simply and sat down before the front pews, surrounded by the delegates on one side and crowds of Lund citizens on the steps up to the altar on the other side in a most democratic manner. Nevile Davidson and I were together; the other delegates, Donald Baillie, Craig and Reid, were with us in the procession but became separated from us in the Cathedral. On the way back to the University I was accompanied by a Swedish pastor from Stockholm. The sermon at the Conference service was preached by Archbishop Brilioth and in his breadth of vision could scarcely have been better. He preached in English and was heard by all.

25th August 1952 (Monday)

Today we deserted the Conference for most of the day and went *en famille* to Falsterbo; a little steam train ran us there from the West

Station at Malmö by easy stages out to the promontory on which Falsterbo stands. The railway crosses a canal, which cuts off this isthmus from the remainder of Skåne. After crossing it you enter a land of heather and sand dunes. Falsterbo is itself practically built on sand dunes. There is an old church which has been buried on more than one occasion by the sand. The run to Falsterbo was fascinating because of the tiny stations and the many level crossings where we got glimpses of Swedish street scenes. We also traversed a country of lovely orchards and windmills. At Falsterbo we had a gorgeous Swedish lunch in a hotel near the station and then walked the mile to the sand dunes, through the picturesque little village. Alison and Rosemary danced a *pas de basque* in the sea, but it was too cold to remain in the water long. In the distance we saw the lighthouse which marks the south-west point of Sweden and far beyond the faint outline of the coast of Denmark.

26th August 1952 (Tuesday)

In the evening I attended an organ recital in the Cathedral, sitting in the front of the nave in order to be some distance from the organ. The organ playing was quite different from what we are accustomed to. Almost all legato and the music taken at a much slower tempo – I think the kind of playing which Dr. Schweitzer advocates. But then practically all the programme consisted of music of the chorale type. The recital ended with some music for voices and strings.

As I was leaving the Cathedral I fell in with Pastor Dahmen and he took me, along with Canon Cockburn whom we met, to his house for coffee. On entering his drawing-room I was surprised to see on one wall a portrait of Gladstone and when I commented on this Dahmen said: 'Yes, but he was a great European.' When in Glasgow, Dahmen had acted as interpreter in Aberdeen at the trial for murder of a Swedish seaman who was, however, acquitted. Lord Jamieson had been on the bench, Calver prosecuting and Blades defending. Dahmen was much impressed by the fairness of the trial. Both he and Mrs. Dahmen were most kind.

27th August 1952 (Wednesday)

The Conference continued intermittently from 10 a.m. to 3.45 p.m. At 4 p.m. I went with the family and Maxwell to tea at the Bjorlings. They have a beautiful house with a garden which is for the great part an orchard, but as it was wet we could not go outside. Apples are so plentiful that no one thinks of stealing them. 'Tea' consisted of both tea and coffee. It is the recognised thing to put all that you want on your plate at the first selection. There was a most wonderful cake like a gigantic pineapple, open in the middle and you put your hand in and helped yourself. It is called *spettkaka* into the making of which go no fewer than 30 eggs. It is made only in Skåne and is turned on a spit like a roast so that it is hard on the outside. Tea was followed by sherry. Then Mr. Bjorling took me to his study and showed me the Swedish Legal Code. The law of property is called *Jordabalk*, *Jorda* being pronounced very like our Scottish word 'udal' and being obviously of the same root. There are five Appeal Courts in Sweden. Mr. Bjorling is shortly to be transferred to Stockholm. He tells me that it is a recognised practice to sail across from Malmö to Copenhagen in order to buy cigarettes cheaply on the twenty mile crossing. On the other hand the Helsingborg ferry, being too short for the purpose, does not afford the same privileges. We also discussed the Scot in Sweden. Mary Queen of Scots' husband, Bothwell, once stayed at Malmöhus. The great agricultural reformer of Skåne was Rutgar Maclean.

28th August 1952 (Thursday)

In the evening the closing session of the Conference took place. There was an ovation for Archbishop Brilioth, whose work as chairman has been immensely appreciated. Then we parted. As we left Bishop Peter, who had stayed in Scotland, came up to me and said, 'Bless you, bless your home, bless your Church, bless your land. My heart's in the Highlands, my heart is not here, my heart's in the Highlands wherever I go.' Then we parted, he to return behind the Iron Curtain.

We attended the closing service in the Cathedral. Dr. Horton preached. Oliver Tompkins conducted the service most beautifully and was one of the most audible of all the speakers.

Canon Cockburn had introduced me to a young St. Andrews graduate who had married a Swedish girl and was lecturer in English at Lund – Elliott by name. Elliott wrote out some sentences in Swedish at my suggestion to express our very warm thanks to our hotel proprietrix for all that she had done and later in the evening we handed her the paper and she was obviously greatly delighted. She had a fox-terrier puppy which Alison was greatly interested in. The word for puppy in Swedish is *valpe* and I had a sentence prepared asking her to allow her daughter Margaretta to be photographed with Rosemary and the puppy but unfortunately it was too late in the evening to do this.

29th August 1952 (Friday)

We left at 9.15 a.m. At Malmö we had an hour's wait. Eventually we crossed in a Danish steamer at 10.45 a.m. The sea was quite choppy and we thought we were going to have a rough passage across the North Sea, but later the wind died down. We had lunch on board, and then went up to watch our entry to Copenhagen. This time both coasts were quite clear at the same time. Our companions on the ship included Bishop Poladian from Lebanon, and one of the most charming of the dark-skinned delegates, I think a representative of the Coptic Church, an old man with a white beard dressed in a long flowing black robe and carrying a handsome silver-mounted stick or wand. I took this picturesque group on board, with Copenhagen in the background. Bishop Poladian was anxious to get a copy of my coloured film of the Conference procession. It would certainly be amusing if it were to find a home in a monastery in Syria. When we landed we took our luggage to the *Parkeston* which was lying at a different quay from that where we landed. Then we drove to the square beside the Tivoli where Rosemary enjoyed feeding the pigeons and we looked round some shops; then we hailed a taxi and had a most wonderful drive through this most lovely city. We then had tea at the Tivoli and discovered the Amusement Park where we were fascinated first by the model railway and afterwards by a replica of mediaeval Copenhagen. It was a lovely afternoon and I am sure that we saw Copenhagen at its best. Before returning to the *Parkeston* we hailed another taxi and drove out to see the famous Organ of Grundvig church. When we returned to the ship we found the Davidsons and they became our companions along with Torrance and the Grahams on the ship. We left at 6 p.m., sailing much further down quay-sides than we did on our inward voyage; it was quite unbelievably beautiful. We were able to pick out lights on the coast and lighthouses on both the Swedish and Danish sides until quite a late hour in the evening.

30th August 1952 (Saturday)

When we went into breakfast we found ourselves at the quay-side in Aalborg which turned out to be in some ways the most interesting of all the places we had visited. First we went to the market-place where the market was in full swing with magnificent flowers and fruit and vegetables and geese pushing their heads out of baskets and chickens and hens and all sorts of country produce. The square was laid out in brilliant sunshine. We then visited the Budolfi Cathedral, the name being the same as St. Botolph e.g. at Boston. This was a glistening white church. Inside its colour scheme was the same white with numerous lofts and galleries, with most exquisite wood-work, coats-of-arms and wall-paintings. One loft, the royal gallery, bore an eighteenth century British coat-of-arms. In the porch there were ceiling-paintings of the kind which seems common in Danish churches, the scheme being a dull terracotta fresco painted over the white. The whole church was quite fascinating. From there we went to the house of Jens Bang, which is said to be the largest domestic building in Denmark, a beautifully preserved merchant's house. Then we visited the monastery of the Holy Ghost which dates from 1432 and is now used as a home for old people. It has an outer courtyard and both this and the cloister are covered with creeper growing up the walls. The refectory is a plain and beautiful arched building with a brick floor and the general scheme of colour being a soft pink. A Danish man and his wife were taken round with us and the former did much to increase our interest by translating as best he could the explanations of the guide. While we were here the Davidsons and Torrance, who had become separated from us after visiting the Cathedral, rejoined us and we then visited the small chapel of the almshouses. We then returned to the ship for lunch.

In the afternoon the Davidsons and the four of us hired a motor and drove to Blokhus. This journey was full of unforgettable surprises. At one point Nevile Davidson suggested diverting to look at a little church perched on an eminence. We were rewarded. Inside were the most superb roof-paintings which we had yet seen with all sorts of quaint pictures of biblical scenes done in simple mediaeval style, for example, the Crucifixion with the angels pulling the soul out of the repentant thief and the devils pulling the soul out of the other. Behind the altar was a little recess with a window open to the church and also a window behind open to the recess. This recess contained an old chalice and a light in the vestry could be used to illuminate it so that it was shown up through the window in the church. The church had no village round it but the place was apparently Jetsmarck. Another two miles by car brought us to Blokhus, where the sands were quite the finest that I have yet seen. Ten miles of the purest yellow sands stretching for miles in either direction, several hundred yards across and the breakers coming in from the west.

On our way back we took a more northerly route across a moor and came on another little church which, however, was closed. We returned at 5 p.m. after perhaps the most wonderful day of the whole fortnight. All day long 56 lb. barrels of butter had been rolling into the ship from the railway wagons on the quay-side and our cargo of butter must have been sufficient to supply quite a large part of the United Kingdom. In the evening we sailed down the Limfjorden. The sun was setting behind us as we reached the open sea. Then the moon rose and travelled across the sky until it too set. We first steamed in an east-south-east direction and then turned northwards, the clear sky enabling us to pick out the Pole Star. The sea was calm and the wash of the ship lit up with phosphorescence. Our last views were of the one or two lighthouses and buoys and the lights of Fredrickshavn on the Danish side.

Before dinner Nevile Davidson had discussed the possibility of having a ship's service next morning and we planned to raise the matter with the Brechins and Tom Torrance. To our surprise, at dinner Brechin got up and intimated that he was holding a Communion for Anglicans only at 8 a.m. next morning. However, we went on with our plan and invited him to take part. Afterwards he came up, I think slightly shamefacedly, and both he and his wife tried to be very friendly. It was a little unfortunate because, apart from British on the ship, most of the people were Scandinavians and at least they might have been invited to his Communion.

31st August 1952 (Sunday)

This was another quite superb day with a pleasant breeze and sunshine. In some fear and trembling we carried on our project of the service. We had only three hymn-books, viz. the 'Cantate Domino' in three languages, which had been used at the Conference. I found some Scottish ladies who were greatly delighted to hear of Nevile Davidson's project. I handed one hymn-book to them and they helped to lead the singing. We used again 'Nun Danket' and the Stralsund chorale; the hymns set to them could be sung in English, German, and French. To our delight the ship's company responded quite amazingly. There was a large attendance on the aft promenade deck. Even the Captain, First Officer and Purser turned up. The singing was very good. Nevile Davidson conducted the service and preached a quite

admirable four minute sermon. He asked me to read the lesson
(1 John, 4, vv. 7–16) and the Bishop took one of the prayers. We
raised a collection of over £4 for Danish seamen's charities. The
venture upon which we had embarked with some anxiety proved a
complete success and was much appreciated. Afterwards the Captain
came and thanked Nevile Davidson. It was Peggy Davidson's birthday
and the resources of the Steward's cupboard were able to provide her
with a suitable birthday present. In the afternoon Mrs. Graham introduced me to a lady – Lady Simonsen – who wanted information
about the best dictionary of Scottish words for a Danish friend who
was much interested in Scottish etymology. I recommended the *Scottish National Dictionary*, and also Jamieson's *Dictionary*. This lady
and I had a most interesting talk, and her husband Sir John Simonsen
joined us and later also Ella. It turned out that he was a Professor of
Chemistry with Danish ancestry. He had worked at the Imperial
College of Science and Technology in London with my cousin, Professor James Philip, and, even more surprising, Lady Simonsen turned
out to be a native of Nairn who had been a student of medicine under
Uncle Robert. We had a very interesting talk about Sir Edward Appleton and Sir Thomas Holland, the latter of whom they had known
intimately and for whom they had a very high regard. They gave me
a number of addresses in Denmark at which to stay and the name
also of the editor of the leading Aalborg newspaper who they said (if
I mentioned their names) would give me all the information I desired
about Aalborg.

Once again there was an exquisite sunset, the last glimpse of the
sun like a great platform just above the level of the horizon. Then
the moon rose, equally wonderful, lighting up the waters in the direction of the Dogger Bank.

1st September 1952 (Monday)

Shortly after breakfast we sighted the coast and soon were being
towed up the Tyne. Every passenger went ashore with some wine or
tobacco. As in every case I declared everything which was likely to
raise any question, and again not one of our suitcases was even opened
though I noticed that the Customs were pretty careful on this occasion
with some of the passengers. Our first reaction on returning was a
sense of the dirt of Newcastle Central Station after the brightness of
Malmö Central and a feeling that somehow the everyday people of
Britain were more shabbily dressed than their Swedish and Danish

counterparts. We reached home at 3.30 p.m., having travelled north with the Grahams. The Davidsons motored from Newcastle to Nethybridge, where Alison and I are to join them for a very short stay next week. Some of the delegates, such as Greenslade and Cockburn, were going to a further Conference in Finland. Maxwell had left by motorcycle for Oslo where I have just heard that he saw the famous Kon-Tiki raft on exhibition. The eastern delegates with whom we travelled were going home to the Middle East via Paris and Rome. Mackinnon was flying to Bossey, and Donald Baillie and Jack Reid were flying home. Thus we all scattered with memories of a wonderful fortnight and many friendships.

14th September 1952

Yesterday, Ella's birthday, we had a memorable day in East Lothian, lunching at Gullane, and having tea at Whitekirk, with the Maxwells, who showed us the church.

In the morning, I went up to Court before going to Gullane, to borrow Lindley on *Partnership* for an opinion. The President buttonholed me to discuss (a) the new National Librarian, and (b) Coronation arrangements. I had Rosemary (age eight) with me, and he took us to his private room. As we were leaving, I said to Rosemary: 'You are the first little girl of eight to have an interview with the Lord President in his private room.' The President then said: 'Rosemary, we will do better than that. You must come and sit in my chair on the bench.' He took her by the hand along to the First Division, and led her up to the President's Chair, and sat her down there. Then the two of us went to the Bar, and he made a little speech to her, she smiling all the time. He remarked: 'How tiny she looks sitting there.' I replied: 'It's like Lord Kincairney!'

17th September 1952 (Wednesday)

On 6th September I motored to Longforgan, where I spent the night at the Manse. Mr. MacNicol took me over the newly decorated Church which was to be re-opened next day. He introduced me to a Mrs. Loudon (formerly Miss Sellar), the first child to be baptised by Dad when he came to Invergowrie seventy-one years ago. The service on Sunday the 7th was crowded. Harold, who came from Glasgow for the day, read the lessons. I gave the address on the Goodly Heritage of the Parish. Mr. MacNicol conducted the service,

Practically every surviving friend from Invergowrie was there, and the Leslie Weatherheads and David Bells, both old school-mates. I enjoyed meeting all, including the Longforgan elders, and got a wonderful welcome. It was twenty-one years since I had attended a service in the District. On the last occasion, Dad celebrated his jubilee in Invergowrie, and baptised Alison, who will be twenty-one on Monday 22nd September.

Miss Johnston, late of Templehall, who remembered me as a child, was at lunch. Then in the afternoon, I motored her into town, and met Alison (who had come by train) at Ninewells. The two of us motored over Tullybaccart in gorgeous clear sunshine to Glenshee and over the Devil's Elbow to Braemar, where we put up for the night at the Fyfe Arms. At the Devil's Elbow, Scottish Nationalists had written on a boulder: 'Elbow the devils out.' Next day, we crossed to Donside and over the Lecht to Tomintoul, Grantown and Nethybridge, calling at Crathie (a dull little church), the Waltons at Gairnshiel (where we saw Mrs. Walton who showed us over their shooting-lodge), and the Wrights at Boat of Garten who were the next day celebrating the jubilee of their church. They asked me to come to it, but as I was staying with the Nevile Davidsons, I could not. We spent the next two nights at Forest House with the Davidsons, delightful hosts. Peggy had her mother (Mrs. Martin) and a Mrs. Mackay Forbes also staying. We had two lovely evening walks on the moors, the four of us the first evening, and Nevile and I the second. I took the whole party to lunch in Grantown, and afterwards, we visited Castle Grant, derelict since 1942. What a change in my lifetime. Once the chateau of Strathspey, and now a neglected castle beginning to disintegrate. We returned to Edinburgh next day via Drumochter and Queensferry. Since then I have been in Paisley as Sheriff and in London for the Central Land Board.

Yesterday, I attended a Committee meeting convened by George Dryburgh at Community House, Glasgow. A Miss Nyasa Livingstone was present, and she and Ralph Morton showed me the Bachuil [pastoral staff - Ed.] of St. Moluag, which, after a dispute with the Duke of Argyll, is now in her brother's possession. She was surprised when I told her that the Committee on the National Museum had considered whether there should be compulsory powers to acquire such precious antiquities in private hands: but I explained that we had recommended against such powers [see the Report, Cmd. 8604, p. 11, para. 21 - Ed.].

27th September 1952 (Sunday)

This has been a busy, varied week. Last Monday was Alison's twenty-first birthday, a very happy day for us all, spent in family. In the evening, I travelled to London for the tenth anniversary meeting of the British Council of Churches, held this time at the Baptist head-quarters, 4 Southampton Row. They have a beautiful little hall, with one strange feature in its acoustics. Anyone whispering at one side of the hall is heard easily by another, sitting at the other side: the round hall creates a kind of whispering gallery.

On Thursday I set off by car with Ella, and, after a Committee meeting in Glasgow and a call on the Nevile Davidsons, spent the night with Harold. On Friday, we were up betimes, and drove on via Tarbet to Inverary, for the lunch to Mr. Morrison, who retires on 3rd October after fifty years in the Sheriff Court service of Argyll. We had time on our arrival to visit the Justiciary Court, and also the Argyll Estates office, where Mr. Hamilton, the factor, showed us the room in which the Appin trial is supposed to have taken place. It is on the first floor, and now his office. Evidently, however, Sir James Fergusson thinks the site may have been nearer the Castle, where once the Mercat Cross was situated. Mr. Hamilton's room has a passage behind it, and, if the trial took place there, the passage must have been part of the Court. Even so, the room was very small.

The lunch to Mr. Morrison was given by the Sheriffs, and the solicitors of Dunoon, Oban and Campbeltown. He has served nine Sheriffs-Principal, and under six sovereigns. He began his duties in 1900, in Inverary, his native town. I spoke and made the presentation, and was followed by Chalmers and Donald; and also by the following Solicitors: Mactaggart of Campbeltown; Orr of Oban; and Dobie of Dunoon. Mr. Macdiarmid of Dunoon was in the Chair; and Mr. Stewart of Campbeltown expressed our thanks to him. Mr. Morrison made an interesting reply, recalling his experiences in the ice-cold winter election of 1910, when Loch Fyne itself was partially frozen. I gave him a copy beforehand of my speech, since, being stone-deaf, he would not hear a word of the proceedings. Then Ella and I motored back by Arrochar, Faslane, and Helensburgh to Edinburgh. I have never seen the Cobbler clearer, nor the autumn tints on Loch Fyneside more lovely.

3rd October 1952

I heard appeals in Greenock and Paisley on two days this week. In

Greenock, I had counsel on both sides, which helps greatly. I was able to send off the judgment there to Mr. Fletcher, the Sheriff Clerk Depute, in three days of the hearing. The Court of Session reopened yesterday. The President told me that Normand is about to resign his seat in the House of Lords. Will the President succeed him? He declined on the last occasion before Reid was appointed. Tonight is the President's beginning of term Reception. Yesterday, we had the usual St. Giles' service at the start of the Session. It was first introduced in Normand's day. Yesterday, all the bar, practically, attended.

I was able last week to piece together an interesting story. When dining with Sidney Smith at the Caledonian Club in London and discussing Tommy Cooper, I told him that, after Sir John Fraser's death, Cooper came up to me one day in the Parliament Hall, and said: 'I want your immediate reaction to the suggestion. It has been proposed that I should consider standing for the Principalship of Edinburgh University.' I replied: 'I think it would be a mistake. You are head of the legal profession and judiciary in Scotland. To accept the Principalship would reflect on your position as head of our profession.' Cooper then left me. Sidney Smith told me the other side of this episode. He said he had approached Cooper to become Principal. Cooper said he would think over the matter. Some days later, he came back and told Sidney Smith: 'I've thought it over, and must decline. It would seem to involve a certain reflection on the profession of which I am already the head!'

Lord Macmillan has left £7,000 to the National Library.

20th October 1952

A fortnight ago, Dr. Warr telephoned me one evening, and then came round to see me. Principal Baillie had approached him to be nominated as Moderator for 1953. He asked my views. I said he was the obvious man, and all regarded him as so. Because of the Coronation, no one in the Church of Scotland could quite occupy his place. He was minister of the metropolitan Church, and knew the Royal Family better than others; he was also familiar with organisation of ceremonial in St. Giles'. I urged him to accept nomination as a duty. Unexpectedly, he seemed hesitant and asked for details of the procedure in the nominating Committee, as to which I could say little, not having been a member of it till this year.

A week later, Dr. Warr wrote me that he could not see his way to be nominated: this has caused dismay in the Church. There is no obvious alternative. Other names mentioned are:- Pitt Watson; Jarvis; Urie Baird (as an Aberdeen nominee); and Stewart Thomson. It will probably be one of the first two.

7th November 1952

Pitt Watson was nominated; Jarvis, second; Stewart Thomson, third; and Urie Baird fourth. Pitt Watson will make an excellent Moderator. I had tea with him in the University Club the following day, and was with him at Committees before and after. He was quite excellent in the Chair, and has a distinct gift of informal oral expression. His modesty is most attractive. In prepared Assembly speeches, he can sway votes as few can: but in business and private conversation his feet are firmly planted on the ground.

I am having a strenuous time as Sheriff. The same week, I heard an appeal in Greenock, another in Paisley, a licensing application in Dunoon, and gave my address on 'The Art and Ethics of Advocacy' to the Dunoon Business Club. I have since heard another Appeal at Greenock, and go to Paisley on the 10th. I also go to Paisley quite a number of times before Christmas and to Oban and Campbeltown. Every Monday is taken up till the Christmas vacation, as well as some other weekdays. I have also been in Court every week, except one, and four opinions came in today.

I have now received the official information (although it is not to be made public till the 18th) that the Queen is to attend a National Service in St. Giles' on her Coronation visit to Scotland, that the Honours of Scotland are to be used, and that the arrangements are to be entrusted to my Committee. This afternoon, Dr. Warr and I met Sir Charles Cunningham, Mr. Anderson and Mr. Pottinger at St. Andrews House to make preliminary plans for a meeting of a 'Working Party' to start immediately after the announcement. The Lord Provost, the Q. and L.T.R., the G.O.C., Lyon, Dr. Warr, Pitt Watson and myself will be present amongst others. The meeting is to be on the 29th.

In addition, I received yesterday a letter from the Archbishop indicating that his proposals to invite the Moderator to take a part in the Coronation (the bringing of the Bible from the altar for presentation) were almost complete, and that, probably, the formal invitation will reach us in the next fortnight. The efforts of our Committee have been most rewarding.

Two days ago General Eisenhower scored a great victory to become

President of the U.S.A. The general expectation, on the whole, was that Adlai Stevenson would win; but it was a landslide in favour of Eisenhower. All the same, everyone feels that Stevenson conducted his side of the campaign on a very high level; and it cannot be often that two such excellent candidates stood against each other.

20th November 1952

This last week has been eventful. On Wednesday night the 12th, Ella and I travelled to London. We both had a morning's shopping: it was such a happiness to see her dropped from a bus at Piccadilly Circus, and make a bee-line for Swan and Edgar, from which time, 9.30 a.m., I didn't see her again till 11.45. Meantime, I did my own humbler masculine shopping – handkerchiefs in all types from fine lace to cheap but nice embroidery at Robinson and Cleaver, a toy for Rosemary at Hamley's and a walk round Bumpus, though I bought nothing there. Then we rejoined each other and, after buying a coloured guardsman postcard to send Rosemary, arrived at Church House, after walking through the Abbey and the quadrangle of Westminster School. At Church House, we had lunch with William Manchester as our host – this was the first time Ella had met him. What a fine friendly and upright nature. It was worth having been Procurator to meet him and Cantuar alone. They are a wonderful pair. After lunch, he took us up to the gallery of the Church Assembly, where we spent the afternoon listening to a quite fascinating debate on the method of appointing bishops, and heard a wonderful variety of Church leaders – the two Archbishops, the one in the chair, the other speaking twice, Chichester, whose speech on the method of appointment under Queen Victoria was the masterpiece, like a page of the best biography, Selwyn, Dean of Winchester, who was presenting the report, assisted by Joynson-Hicks M.P., a vague and wordy Archdeacon of Doncaster obviously out to bat for a bishopric, and others. As we were tired after our night-journey, the comfortable hall and pleasant atmosphere was a delightful place to snooze. Later, we heard a debate on the parochial church council, where, it seemed to me, some speakers had really not thought out the implications of membership. One speaker even went the length of suggesting that a Church of Scotland member might also, when in England, be a member of the Church of England. Another said the Queen was a member of both the Church of England and Church of Scotland: to which the Archbishop rejoined: 'No, protector of both; but member of one.' Did he recall that, after Queen

Victoria had been 'spoken to' by another Archbishop for taking Communions in both churches, she rejoined: 'Very well, I'll confine myself to Communion in the Church of Scotland,' and never afterwards took Communion in the Church of England. Surely, too, the taking of Communion by the Monarch in the Church of England is really a constitutional rather than personal act, or if regarded as a personal act, he would be being compelled against conviction to take a sacramental test. Queen Alexandra was, I believe, very unwilling to take C. of E. Communion; and the Duke of Edinburgh was embraced as an Anglican only by the skin of his teeth, and just in time. What a mercy we do not have the problem of requiring the Monarch to be head of the Church.

Jim Galbraith dropped in at 6 p.m. He and his sister Mary each got identical marks in the Civil Service exams. At the Foreign Office, she is in charge of Nepal and East Indonesia.

In the evening, we had a little dinner at the Caledonian Club with the Rawlinsons, and their son Anthony, and Lady Reid of Drem. We drove the Rawlinson parents home afterwards, and Mrs. R., a warm hearted soul like my own mother, now signs her letters to me 'affectionately'. Anthony is quiet in comparison with his parents: a great mountaineer, and on the reserve list for the next Himalayan expedition. I had a most interesting talk with him on reason and faith. It was good to be amongst such genuine friends all day. And, as we came out of the Church Assembly, we also fell into the arms of John Taylor, who was delighted to see us there. With the Bishop of Derby, I discussed the afternoon debate, and reminded him of the fact which he did not seem to know that, in Gladstone's day, the practice was followed of suggesting alternately an Oxonian and a Cantab for the vacant bishoprics. He said that, recently, there had been one bishop who had no degree!

22nd November 1952

On the morning of the 14th, I left Ella to have a quiet morning and thereafter lunch with Janie and Richard Coleman. I went to the Central Land Board. It was an interesting meeting for two reasons. First, we have now moved from Devonshire House, and met for the first time in the even more palatial 6 Carlton House Terrace. The Board Room, a heavy panelled over-ornamental room, overlooks the Mall, where workmen were starting to erect stands for the Coronation. I saw the Scots Guards Band marching up to assume the guard at Buckingham Palace. Across the Park lay the tower of Westminster Cathedral. The one really lovely feature of the house is its marble staircase, supported by Romanesque arches which might have been brought from Ravenna. Secondly, we got the news which was to be announced on the 18th that development charge was to be abolished. The Act as it stands is at least consistent, even if the housing scarcity made it difficult, except by compulsory purchase, to enforce land-sales at existing use values. But the new proposals, involving two bills, the first a vote-catcher, and the second, likely to be more complicated than the Act of 1947, have not the merit of following a principle. They appear to involve a tangle of expedients in an effort to turn the clock back. They may produce the rebound of a boomerang. I should not like to be the minister in charge of the second Bill.

I had lunch with Mr. Rutherford and Mr. Sheldrake at the Union Club, of which I am now a corresponding member, by virtue of my University Club (Edinburgh) membership. Then I hurried back to the Rembrandt, where I found Ella with the Colemans. After tea, they drove us to Paddington where we caught the 4.45 p.m. express for Oxford, Mr. Hugh Dalton travelling in the same coach.

Alison met us at Oxford Station, and we were hardly into our hotel – the Golden Cross – before we were entertaining six under-graduates – Alison, Julia Birley, Eleanor Forshaw, Jenny Nias, Douglas Duncan and Mark Sheldon. It was like being young again, and they were all so kind to us. They greatly enjoyed the evening, I think, and left about 11 p.m.

On the 15th, we went to have eleven o'clock coffee at Corpus with Mrs. Hardie (Isobel Macaulay), and met her two small boys. They have a Danish girl staying with them. I told her I knew only one Dane in Denmark just now – Professor Söe: whereat she said: 'He's my Godfather!' From there we went to the Bodleian, where I called on Myers, and he very kindly showed us the old fresco in process of being uncovered and retouched, and the endless railway for books, linking the two portions of the Library. We also visited Blackwell's – both adults' and children's shops – and, after lunch, sat recovering from lost sleep, and then after visiting Christ Church Hall, and the Cathedral, had tea in Mackay's tearoom, on the way there meeting Dr. Hugh Mackie, who shook me warmly by the hand. Then to New College chapel, to see Wykeham's crozier and Epstein's unmistakably great 'Lazarus rising from the Grave'. In New College nave, in the dark, who should we fall in with but Principal Allan (staying at the Mitre, not at Wycliffe Hall, as he intended). We invited him to dinner, to which Alison also brought her friend Janet Macgregor, grand-daughter of R.W. Barbour (on her mother's side). Janet is President of the L.M.H. J.C.R. this year; but she is also most charming, intelligent, smiling, and with every quality for popularity. After dinner, we all went on to St. Columba's Hall, where I showed my Lund cinema film to a crowded meeting of undergraduates, and then answered, as best I could, many very searching questions.

On the 16th, after lunch, Alison took us out to L.M.H. where we first had coffee in Jenny Nias' room, and then saw a series of other rooms, Julia's, Daphne Proctor, and finally, after watching the last engage in archery, and spending some time with Alison alone, walked on to the Galbraiths for tea. They were very insistent that we should have visited the Principal. Alison, who took the other view, had a lively argument in the best of humour with Mrs. Galbraith, while the Professor, also in the best of humour, tore reputations to shreds, praising however John Fulton (University of Sussex), and urging that he should be made Principal of St. Andrews, from his present Principalship at Swansea. Mrs. Galbraith who knows the Principal of L.M.H., Miss Sutherland, well, said that the latter had a high opinion of Alison's ability, and should be allowed to see her parents! We then returned to the hotel, where Alison left us, as we set off to catch the 7.58 train for Paddington, and later the 10.15 p.m. at King's Cross for home. A full, and rich weekend.

On the evening of the day of our return home, the B.B.C. came out with the news (1) of the abolition of development charge and (2) of the Queen's intention to attend a special national service in St. Giles', my own special triumph. She has requested that the arrangements should be carried through by my Committee in co-operation with Dr. Warr, as minister of St. Giles'. Next morning, the 18th, the latter news was greeted with the liveliest satisfaction in all the Scottish papers, and, since then, I have had incessant calls from journalists.

On the 19th I made a full statement of completed plans to the Commission of Assembly. This went very well: not a question was asked, and the speech was reported almost wholly verbatim in the Scottish papers.

One thing I could not mention, that the Archbishop of Canterbury has invited the Moderator to take a part in the Coronation service. That will not be announced until the Coronation service is made known. My Committee met on the afternoon of the Commission to consider an answer to the invitation. It was decided to accept it, but also that I should be sent to get the further views of the Archbishop

It was felt by some that the pew offered lacks real significance for the head of a Church. The Archbishop is to hand the Bible from the altar to the Moderator. The Moderator is then to carry it to the Queen. The Archbishop is then to present it, saying the appropriate words. The Bible is then to be handed back by the Archbishop to the Moderator who will convey it to the altar, where the Archbishop will receive it back from the Moderator and lay it on the altar. In the Committee, views were expressed that this was to treat the Moderator like an acolyte, and it was suggested that the Dean should hand the Bible to the Moderator; that, in the presentation, the Moderator should either speak or present the Bible; and that the Moderator might have the Bible in the procession. It is suggestions like these which I shall have to mention to the Archbishop. Personally, my own preference would be simply to accept the invitation. By the time of the next Coronation, the ecclesiastical doors may have opened wider. I wonder, however, how they would feel if we offered them such a part. If possible, I think, our St. Giles' service will be more practically ecumenical.

29th November 1952 (Saturday)

Last Sunday I motored to Oban, heard an appeal there on the Monday and then motored to Campbeltown; heard an appeal there on the Tuesday, and then returned to Edinburgh – about 400 miles. I had three days of brilliant sunshine, and frosty weather. The Perthshire and Argyll peaks were magnificent in sunlit snow, and snow came to the water's edge in Oban and at Kilbowie where I stayed on Sunday night. But the icy roads were quite phenomenal at places on the Monday. Between Ardrishaig and Tarbert, I was within an ace of losing my life. I came round a corner at Ernie's boathouse, to find one car (which had already skidded) with one wheel hanging over the beach on the loch-side of the unwalled road, and another car on the other side which had stopped in sympathy. With this unexpected predicament and the icy condition on the curve, I skidded first towards the beach (where I thought for a moment this was the finish) then in the opposite direction, my rear which began the skid sideways, turning first right to hit the off-wing of the 'sympathetic' car, and then left to strike with a glancing impact the already skidded car. The latter car saved me from going on to the beach. I ended up between the skidded car and the wall opposite, the two cars being incomprehensibly back to back. I got a bump on my right chest, which is still sore, but the engine was unaffected, and I was able to complete my journey.

The car is now receiving attention, and the repairs are not too serious. The journey was also memorable for the quite amazing view at 5 p.m. after the sun had been down for an hour, of a D.Y. Cameron aftermath of sunset with Jura and Islay silhouetted clear as crystal against a dark red sky, and the coast of Ireland with one flashing lighthouse standing out in the night clearness.

This morning, I attended a 'working-party' conference at St. Andrews House about the St. Giles' service on June 24th. It was attended by Scottish Home Department representatives, representatives of the Corporation, the Q. and L.T.R., Scottish Command, the Chief Constable, Lord Lyon, Dr. White Anderson and myself – Sir Charles Cunningham in the Chair. The chief question was, who should carry the Honours. Lyon was strong for the hereditary bearers, and indicated that they would be in the present instance, the Duke of Hamilton the Crown, the Earl of Crawford the sceptre, the Countess of Erroll, the sword. She might appoint the Marquis of Tweeddale or Earl of Home as her deputy. The Church's chief concern was that those who bore the Honours into St. Giles' should be worthy bearers.

13th December 1952

I was in London the last two days. I had to give evidence before the House of Commons Committee on Clergy Disabilities viz. as to whether the Act of 1801 should be altered as regards the Church of Scotland, and I had also to meet the Archbishop of Canterbury to convey the views of my Committee dealing with the Coronation arrangements. The Committee met at 4.30 p.m. on the 11th. And my meeting with the Archbishop was at Lambeth at 5.30 the same afternoon. This left me free in the morning. I went to the Old Bailey, hoping to be admitted to hear Lord Goddard's charge in the Craig murder case. I had no difficulty in getting into the Old Bailey, but the police, though sympathetic, were unable to let me into the Court. However, I called at the Public Office and there met a barrister who arranged to get me in. The Craig case was one where Craig, aged sixteen, and Bentley, aged nineteen, were engaged in house-breaking in Croydon. The police followed them to the roof of the house where Craig shot a policeman. In the possession of the two accused was a revolver, a very brutal cosh which could be fixed to one's hand and which had a sharp point so that a blow struck with the fist was equivalent to an attack with a dagger. They had also two daggers. The police put up a great fight and were complimented by Lord

Goddard at the end of the trial. I sat amongst the police, the Z Division; and a few yards from Craig's mother, father and sister. It was an incredible case of youthful murder. Craig's elder brother, aged twenty-six, was already serving twelve years for an armed hold-up and this seemed to have turned the younger brother against the police. Craig had one peculiarity, that he seemed unable to read, even up to the age of fifteen. The two accused were just in front of me in the dock – Craig rather a peculiar small-headed boy, Bentley with every appearance of normality. The Lord Chief Justice sat at the side of the bench with his clerk. In the centre of the bench sat the last but one Lord Mayor, Sir Denis Lowson and the two Sheriffs. This is to my way of thinking quite wrong. It reminded me of King Edward, when a witness in the Baccarat Case, sitting on the bench beside the Lord Chief Justice. How could a judge ever hold that a man who sat beside him on the bench is incredible? I heard the whole charge which was strongly for murder, and could not be otherwise. I did not wait for the sentences. But after the jury had retired the Court went on the deal with a plea of guilty in another case where another accused had been concerned with Craig in another act of house-breaking. I was rather surprised that when the Lord Chief Justice sentenced Craig he referred to Craig's participation in this other case, in which Craig was neither a party nor had pled guilty. It seemed to me that this reference was quite improper. Then I heard the opening speech in an incredible case of thuggery. A Lyons' van was carrying £2,000 of wages to an address in Wembley; suddenly a small car ran into it by a glancing blow and then stuck across its path. Masked men got out, attacked the occupants of the Lyons' van, took the money and escaped in a Jaguar car already conveniently placed at the side of the road. They were identified because a neighbour, interested in high-powered cars, had seen this same Jaguar going over a rehearsal of the attack a day or two before. Outside the Old Bailey whom should I fall in with but Mr. Cutts of Hodder and Stoughton.

In the afternoon I had more than three-quarters of an hour with the House of Commons Committee. Mr. Richard Law, son of Bonar Law, was in the chair. I was chiefly questioned by Mr. Arthur Woodburn, Mr. Griffiths and Mr. Bing, a young Labour Q.C. Mr. Woodburn was well-informed upon the Church of Scotland and his questions were very helpful. Some of the others obviously wanted to take me quite a long way beyond the scope of the Committee's work. But the experience was a very interesting one. From there I rushed by taxi to Lambeth. In the dark the taxi driver and I searched for a door-bell and eventually an old retainer opened a door in the entrance arch-way, and I was ushered into the quadrangle. I was surprised at how plain and relatively austere the place looked. There was a large quadrangle flanked on one side by the palace, on another by the chapel, on the third by a high wall and on the fourth by Lambeth Parish Church. It was so dark I could scarcely find a door. I crossed to the first obvious door and rang the bell, but peeping through the windows discovered that it appeared to be the laundry. I then edged my way along the wall to a big closed door and tried the bell there. A lady answered. She appeared to be a European refugee. She took me up a long flight of steps like those in the Deanery at Durham. There a young chaplain met me and I was ushered straight in to the Archbishop. Though the room was larger, it was extraordinarily like my own study. At the side of the fire with his back to me, the Archbishop was struggling with endless sheaves of what looked like drafts which he was preparing. Some of them on the left hand side lay on the floor. He was so absorbed that he did not at first notice me enter. Then our talk took place. As always, he could not have been more friendly. I said to him at one point that I felt I could speak to him as a friend, not as an Archbishop. After our meeting, he ushered me out to the top of the stairs and said: 'You will find your own way out, I hope.' I replied: 'It will be much easier to find my way out than it was to find my way in!' The house is plain to a degree. The room in which I was had un-stained wood panelling, and while comfortable was very simple. The impression I got was that the endowments are no longer sufficient to keep the Palace up in its old style. I was let out from the postern door by the same elderly retainer, and remarked that there was room for an excellent detective story, 'The Mystery of Lambeth Palace' – mysterious stranger disappearing in the dark.

I made a Memorandum of my interview with the Archbishop:

I had a most friendly conversation with the Archbishop for three-quarters of an hour. He is so straight and friendly that it is easy to discuss even difficult things with him. I went straight to the point. I began by explaining (i) that my Committee was deeply touched by the attitude of friendship he had shown, and (ii) that there was no part of the Coronation service in which the C. of S. would more gladly participate than in the presentation of the Bible to the Queen. I went on to add, however, that the Committee were very uneasy about one aspect of the invitation, viz. that the Moderator would be no more than a bearer of the Bible and have no significant part; that, while as individual Christians, we were most ready to accept the humblest part, it did seem wrong that the titular head of the national Church of Scotland should occupy a role which had no significance; that this might only produce the very criticism which all wanted to avoid: and that the criticism would be the more serious in that it would have justification. The Archbishop at once said, in the most friendly way, that he realised the force of this; that it had been in his mind; and that the change he had proposed that, instead of himself, the Dean should hand the Bible from the altar to the Moderator had been made with this in view. I said I appreciated this; and also that we fully realised that, if the Moderator were himself to take the Bible from the altar, that might introduce theological embarrassment for him, which we wanted to avoid. But all that was left was that the Moderator, 'under his own steam', would carry the Bible ten paces in the one direction, and then ten paces back again; and this would provoke the justifiable criticism that he was acting as a 'mere acolyte'. If any critic used that word of the part offered to him, the criticism would be difficult to answer, and the well-meant invitation might result in harm instead of good.

I then said that my object in coming to him was frankly to put this difficulty before him; and that my Committee wanted, without raising any theological embarrassment for him, to see whether some more significant part could be added to the Moderator's duties. I said I had three suggestions:- The first was that the Moderator should, if there was no historical claim to the contrary, carry the Bible in the procession into the Abbey. He said this would not be possible. The Bishop of London carried the patten; the Bishop of Norwich the Bible; and the Bishop of Winchester the Chalice. My second suggestion was that the Moderator should utter the words of the presentation of the Bible to the Queen while the Archbishop handed the Bible to her. I pointed out that this would let Scottish radio listeners hear the Moderator's voice. He objected to this because, throughout the service, everything said to the Queen was said by the Archbishop. My third suggestion – which I emphasised as the best – was that the Moderator should complete the bearing of the Bible by also presenting it to the Queen while the Archbishop uttered the words of presentation. He said that this was a new idea to him; and that there was some precedent for another than the Archbishop *presenting* something to the Queen, since the Dean of Westminster presented the royal robe to her. He also said that he realised that the words 'We present' would, in any event, take on a new meaning. Hitherto, they had been simply a royal or ecclesiastical 'we'. Now, in any event, they would mean the C. of E.

and the C. of S. He said this idea was 'not impossible', i.e. that personally he was 'not allergic to it'. Personally, he seemed very favourable to it; so I impressed on him that this step would remove all criticism which might otherwise have been justifiable. I said also that I realised that I could not expect an immediate answer; and he stated that there were some of his colleagues whom he would have to consult. He also mentioned that he would be seeing the Queen next day. He ran over the relevant rubric, indicating that only a small change would be needed. I said my Committee was meeting on Tuesday 16th and that it would be a great help if he could let me know the views before then. He replied that he thought he would be able to do so. I said: 'Quite frankly, I feel greatly embarrassed by making this suggestion in face of so kind an invitation.' He said, he appreciated the delicacy, but fully understood the reasonableness of our position. I said that, if this additional part were given, I thought I could say that the invitation would undoubtedly be accepted; but that, if the invitation were limited, as at present, my Committee would require to give further consideration to their attitude. I left with the impression that he personally means, if he possibly can, to give us this additional part, and I am distinctly hopeful.

He also discussed various other matters:- the resumption of the Anglo-Scottish Conversations; the recent unwise effusions of the Bishop of Monmouth (whom he described as scholarly but impractical and Welsh to boot); the attitude of the Episcopal Church in Scotland (Bishop Warner alone was helpful); the national service in St. Paul's; the national service in St. Giles'; and the Dalkeith wedding in St. Giles'. He was most appreciative of our attitude (which I explained) in the last two.

17th December 1952

On the 15th, I received the following letter from the Archbishop:–

Lambeth Palace S.E. 1
13th December 1952

My dear Procurator,

I have now consulted all those whom I thought it proper to consult, including Her Majesty the Queen, and I am happy to say that there is complete readiness on all sides to accept the proposal that the Moderator should actually put the Bible in the hands of The Queen and receive it back from her. I am proposing to alter the rubric to

1952

run as follows:-

'When the Queen is again seated the Archbishop shall go to her Chair; and the Moderator of the General Assembly of the Church of Scotland receiving the Holy Bible from the Dean of Westminster shall bring it to the Queen and present it to her, the Archbishop saying these words:

[then follow the words]

Then shall the Queen deliver back the Bible to the Moderator who shall bring it to the Dean of Westminster to be reverently placed again upon the Altar; this done, the Archbishop shall return to the Altar and begin the Communion Service.

I hope that this revision will give complete satisfaction to the Church of Scotland. Indeed you gave me to understand that this would be so.

Thank you very much for making our conversations on this subject so friendly and happy. It will be a cause of deep satisfaction to us both if we have been instrumental in achieving a right thing in the right manner.

Shall I leave it to you to tell the Moderator, or would you like me to write to him as well?

Yours sincerely,
(Sgd) Geoffrey Cantuar.

J. R. Philip Esq. Q.C.
53 Great King Street,
Edinburgh 3.

Our National Occasions Committee met on the 16th. Both it and the General Administration Committee have received news of this letter with the liveliest satisfaction, and the Moderator is now replying to accept the invitation in its adjusted form. The news is to come out to the public when at the beginning of the New Year, the Archbishop is to hold a Press Conference to explain this and other changes in the Coronation Service. Pitt Watson and others were very kind in their references to my efforts.

18th December 1952

I met Sir Charles Cunningham and Mr. Pottinger about two matters. First, the Church of Scotland (Dr. Mackintosh, Mr. W.R. Milne, Mr. Mercer Robertson and myself); the Roman Catholic Church (Father

- 317 -

Glancy); and the Episcopal Church (Mr. Fenthican), met them to discuss a more uniform rating exemption for Church Halls on the lines of sec. 43 of the Edinburgh Corporation Act, 1950. Then, after this Conference, I waited on to discuss with Sir Charles and Mr. Pottinger the forms of invitation to the St. Giles service on 24th June, and the preliminary allocation of seats in St. Giles. It is quite out of proportion that the Scottish Peers, many of whom are quite unknown in these modern days, should require all to be present.

One amusing incident occurred at the Committee meeting on the 16th. There was a lengthy discussion as to whether the Queen should, on the title page of the Form of Service for use in the Church at the time of the Coronation should be described as 'Elizabeth' or 'Elizabeth the Second'. Considering that the first post box labelled in the latter form in Scotland was smeared with paint, and a stick of gelignite put in the second, and also considering the need to avoid harmful controversy, I with the majority of the Committee preferred 'Elizabeth'. Dr. White Anderson, I think somewhat out of touch with public feeling, wanted 'Elizabeth II', though it would lead to a public row. During the discussion, I suggested: 'Why not just say "Her Majesty the Queen"?' All agreed on this! I was interested to find that Scottish Home Department proposed, in the St. Giles' invitations, to adopt the same expedient.

19th December 1952

In the preliminary list of allocations for the St. Giles' service, each Protestant Church apart from the Church of Scotland has been allocated two places. I proposed that the Roman Catholics should also have an allocation. I also suggested that the youth of Scotland should be represented by at least a school-boy and a school-girl, and that there should be other youth representatives, e.g. students, boy scouts, girl guides. The organised industries, town and rural, would be duly represented. I suggested that there should be representatives of remote unorganised rural workers e.g. a shepherd, a lighthouse keeper, and the like. The Bench, all fourteen, are, in my view, over-represented, and the Bar, so far only the Dean of Faculty, under-represented. I must see if I cannot secure a better distribution among the College of Justice as a whole: but this may be difficult.

Just now I am very busy clearing off arrears of opinions, and Sheriff Court judgments, of which I have had more than at any one time since becoming Sheriff. I had six at one time to write, and have disposed of three of them. I am still struggling with November Memorials. I was proposing the Paisley Faculty of Procurators at their annual dinner; addressing the Irvine and Kilmarnock office bearers' union; addressing the students at Trinity College, Glasgow; and hearing two Appeals, and introducing a Sheriff Officer candidate, all in two days this week.

CHAPTER VII

1953

28th January 1953

A fortnight ago our Round Table lunch party at Court lost one of its members. James Crawford, a Moray 'lad o' pairts', son of a schoolmaster at Hopeman, won a Foundation Scholarship at Fettes, and, after serving for some time in J. & F. Anderson W.S., came to the Bar later than most. He had recently taken silk and died in a moment from heart-failure at the age of forty-seven, in the presence of his wife and eleven year old boy. He leaves also a little girl aged seven. We all liked him. He had various endearing mannerisms, revolving his spectacles as he pleaded, tidying cigarette ash daily into a little heap. He was a persistent rather lengthy pleader, but knew his law well. I was against him in his last House of Lords case, where he was very fair. The President spoke very kindly yet humorously about it saying that he always was dangling his spectacles and that he adopted the manner 'I will be brief but tedious!' I wrote a little appreciation of him for the *Scotsman*, and Joan Crawford his widow called in the evening to thank me.

This last weekend I gave the address in Aberdeen University Chapel, my subject being Mark 9:24 – 'Faith in Christ'. It was a wonderful experience. I was very anxious to speak to the students, and say something that would really help them, and I was richly rewarded. They listened most attentively, and many kind things were said to me after, and Professor John Macleod wrote me, and Nellie Taylor Ella. I stayed with the Donald Mackinnons at Tillydrone House opposite the West front of St. Machar's. He is a loveable eccentric. His wife is most charming and ideally suited for him, quiet, even posed, thoughtful, and yet bright, such a contrast to his restless eccentricity. On Saturday, after Donald took me to the Chapel, they had, later on, a sherry party where I met many professors. Then I had dinner at the Athenæum with Donald, and David Cairns. On the Sunday, the Mackinnons and I had lunch at Chanonry Lodge with Nellie Taylor. Tom is not yet back from India, where he has been for a month. Later, I had tea with the Tom Smiths at their new house 50 College Bounds, where I met a Professor Price from Capetown, whose subject was Roman-Dutch law. After supper, Donald and I went for coffee to the Ian Pitt Watsons and saw their new baby. We were joined there by A.M. Hunter. A full weekend, but most distinctive was just the friendly courtesy of the Mackinnons whom it was good to meet. I travelled back to Edinburgh with Farquhar MacRitchie. There was a long delay because of vacuum brake trouble at Arbroath, so that we reached Edinburgh 70 minutes late, and not in time for the start of the National Library Trustees' Annual Party.

Tonight an exciting bit of news came in. I found, on coming in for tea, a letter marked 'Personal and Confidential. Very Urgent.' It was from the Archbishop of Canterbury – in these terms:–

27th January 1953

My dear Procurator,

As I am not quite sure what address would reach the Moderator quickly, and as I have to have a speedy answer, I am writing to you on one further point in connection with the Presentation of the Holy Bible. As you will remember I maintained that the words of presentation must be spoken by me since all the words accompanying the presentation of any object throughout the Service are spoken by the Archbishop and by me alone, and it seems to me that if the Archbishop said nothing at the presentation of the Bible it might look as though he were depreciating the Bible as compared to the other objects. I still think this argument was sound: on the other hand the result is not very happy in that it deprives the Moderator of saying anything and leaves him nothing to do but bring the Bible to and fro. Accordingly, I put a new suggestion to my committee at its final meeting last night by which this part of the service will run as follows:-

The Presentation of the Holy Bible.

When the Queen is again seated, the Archbishop shall go to her Chair; and the Moderator of the General Assembly of the Church of Scotland, receiving the Holy Bible from the Dean of Westminster, shall bring it to the Queen and present it to her, the Archbishop saying these words:

'Our gracious Queen; to keep your Majesty ever remindful of her Law and the Gospel of God as the Rule for the whole life and government of Christian Princes, we present you with this Book, the most valuable thing that the world affords.'

And the Moderator shall continue:

'Here is Wisdom: This is the royal Law: These are the lively Oracles of God.'

Then shall the Queen deliver back the Bible to the Moderator who shall bring it to the Dean of Westminster, to be reverently placed again upon the Altar. This done, the Archbishop shall return to the Altar.

Personally, I think this is a very happy solution; it makes the presentation in every way a joint action. I speak the words full of solemnity, and then the Moderator adds the grand conclusion.

We must give the Printer the all clear as soon as possible. May I ask you to let me know by telegram whether the Moderator approves this new order which I am, of course, also putting before the Queen.

Yours sincerely,
(Sgd) Geoffrey Cantuar

J. R. Philip Q.C.,
53 Great King Street,
Edinburgh 3.

I telephoned Pitt Watson, the Moderator-Designate, at Bearsden, and he warmly approved. Then after telephoning round Glasgow for the Moderator, Johnstone Jeffrey, I ultimately learned that he was at a sherry-party at the French Institute. I immediately searched him out there, and, having obtained his approval, wired the Archbishop:—

'Your letter of 27th January stop Moderator and Moderator-Designate both approve new suggestion. Sgd. J.R. Philip.'

6th February 1953

Today, Tommy Cooper wrote me that, when Normand returned to Edinburgh, Normand should be put on to the National Library Standing Committee; that then there would be two Lord Presidents on it; and that then he (Tommy Cooper) should retire. I protested, and pointed out that they were very different types and their contributions would be quite distinct. 'You,' I said, 'are the radical, to use your own terms, something of an iconoclast: while Normand is a dyed-in-the-wool-Tory!' He took it quite well. We talked for a considerable time about everything under the sun.

Two events occurred this week at the Bar. Jock Cameron is to fly to Singapore to act as arbiter in a dock labour dispute there. He will be away for three weeks. Lord Alness appeared on the bench of the

Second Division – from which he resigned twenty years ago. He is now eighty-three, and looked very much the same, with the same clear voice, only a little wizened, and very shaky on his legs.

This evening I went to the Northern Lighthouse Board Office. There is a Conference of the three Lighthouse Authorities next week. I will be presiding as Chairman. We confer on the *Pharos* in the morning, then have lunch, and, if it is fine, sail to the Isle of May and round the Bass. Our thoughts are full of the sea this week with the incredible loss of the *Princess Victoria* with about 120 passengers between Stranraer and Larne, and the devastating floods in Holland and South-East England. I also had a talk with Glen Wakelin about the Spithead Review. The *Pharos* will probably sail from Granton, and return by the West Coast. We are also having a Lighthouse Conference in London on March 26th, so that this summer, with Coronation and Coronation visit, there will be many diversions. I have tickets for the Coronation for Ella and Alison in the Royal Household Stand, thanks to Pitt Watson and White Anderson. I turned down other offers from the Northern Lighthouse Board and the Sheriffs, who were also offered tickets. The Church of Scotland were offered sixty seats in a stand. The tickets for the Sheriffs were addressed to George Morton as 'The Sheriff's Principal and Chairman of Land Court'. When will Whitehall learn something about Scotland? I am meeting the Earl of Home as Minister of State about the St. Giles' Coronation service, along with Dr. Warr, on the 9th.

I was also invited, this week, to act as one of three judges at a University debate, in the Union, between Edinburgh and Toronto. My fellow-judges were Ronald Selby Wright of the Canongate and J.G.S. Macgregor, a schoolmaster, himself a member of last year's Edinburgh debating team which visited Canada. The subject of debate was 'That the essence of greatness is to align oneself with the inevitable'. Edinburgh led in the affirmative – the speakers being Tom Stewart, a medical, who made the most thoughtful speech, but in the manner of discussion rather than debating, and James Weatherhead (law) who was humorous, but immature. Toronto led in the negative – the speakers being Elmer Sopha (law) and Dwight Fulford (history), both of whom spoke fluently and secured the ear of the house. We marked the Edinburgh speeches α and ß; and the Canadian α- and ß++: Toronto thus winning. There was a delightful student dinner beforehand. The President of the S.R.C., a Cambridge boy studying sociology here, impressed me most. But all made me feel young again. Selby Wright came home with me afterwards, and we talked our heads off till after midnight. He is a most unusual personality, with a knack of knowing, or acquiring conversation about, everyone. But there is a real gay originality about him which is refreshing in a world where few people risk being individualists.

The latest quip – Winston Churchill, according to Attlee, is a prima donna who occasionally comes down to the House of Commons to receive bouquets; Attlee, according to Churchill, is a sheep in sheep's clothing!

22nd February 1953 (Sunday)

It is ten years today since Gordon died. Two boys called to see us, and the house, and his little room, is full of flowers. Rosemary lends his little book to her school friends to read. Ella is full of gentle 'soft invincibility'.

This week I spent two days in Greenock hearing appeals. I stayed the night at Gourock, and motored round to Inverkip Bay, where on a clear day, such as you only get in February, I could see Holy Isle and the southern end of Arran. In the evening Mr. Peter Scott entertained Peter Thomson, interim Sheriff-substitute, and myself to stories of his experiences as Sheriff Officer in arresting ships – especially a Spanish ship with a French captain and mate put in custody by their communist crews.

I stayed at Paisley, the Brabloch Hotel, after my second day at Greenock, and proposed the toast of 'Soroptimism' at the Paisley Soroptimist Club. I took as my subject first the debt to the women of my own family (1) the generation before (mother); (2) my own generation (Ella); and (3) the next generation (Alison and Rosemary); and then discussed the opportunities for women of each of these generations in the professions. Equal rights have been secured in my own lifetime; but not equal opportunities.

The news of Normand's impending retirement from the House of Lords, known in Parliament House since the autumn, is published now. The *Scotsman* tips either Tommy Cooper or Hamish Clyde as his successor. James Walker recently delighted the Round Table by referring to the bench as including too many 'slickit politicians'. Certainly all the bad appointments of my generation have been political ones. Tommy Cooper, on merit, is the obvious choice, but, as he once said to me, he could not stand the atmosphere of 'Winchester and All Souls'. On merit, but for his health, Patrick should be next; after him, I would myself choose Keith.

9th March 1953 (Tuesday)

Last Sunday, I had the interesting experience of giving the address at the forenoon service in Greyfriars on Covenant Sunday. I spoke on 'The Renewal of the Covenant' (Heb. 8:8). The Church was full, and we sang the old Psalm Tunes, to Psalms which I was allowed to choose: Ps. 43 to Martyrs; Ps. 126 to Abbey; Ps. 46 to Stroudwater; Ps. 36 to London New (this chosen by Louden); and Ps. 103 to Coleshill. I described the first signing of the Covenant in Greyfriars on 28th February 1638, read by Johnston of Warriston from about the spot where the pulpit again stands: my two points were that, however we regarded the Covenanters, they were men who were prepared to die for their faith. I ended by asking the Congregation to stand, while I repeated the new Covenant which we took at the closing service of the World Faith and Order Conference in Lund Cathedral last August. No member of the congregation in Greyfriars would forget this part of the address. Louden, who is a modest, thoughtful and attractive personality, conducted the service most beautifully. It was a lovely warm sunny spring day and I met many friends after, including J.M. Ross, who was at Lund.

22nd March 1953 (Saturday)

The announcement was made on 17th March that the Moderator was to take part in the Coronation Service, in the Presenting of the Bible. The Archbishop gave it out at a Press Conference at 11.30 a.m., and, as his promised press 'hand-out' had not reached me by that hour, I prepared a simple statement which was issued by the Church of Scotland press bureau at noon. The announcement has been very well received in Scotland, and, so far as I can see, pretty well in England.

Last night, we had a dinner of the Round Table. The ostensible object was to welcome back Jock Cameron from his visit to Singapore as arbiter in the dock arbitration there, but the real purpose was just for us all to have a social evening. George Morton was in the chair. The Vice-Dean (Blades) proposed the toast of the Dean, who replied with a very full, hour long, account of his flight to and stay in Singapore. The description of his journey out by Constellation plane, and back by Comet, was fascinating; and also his account of post-war conditions in Singapore, of which he took a pessimistic view. He also described the arbitration itself, going into the details of the wage-structure, which was extraordinarily lucidly told, but not appropriate for after dinner. Harry Guthrie proposed the 'Round Table' to which

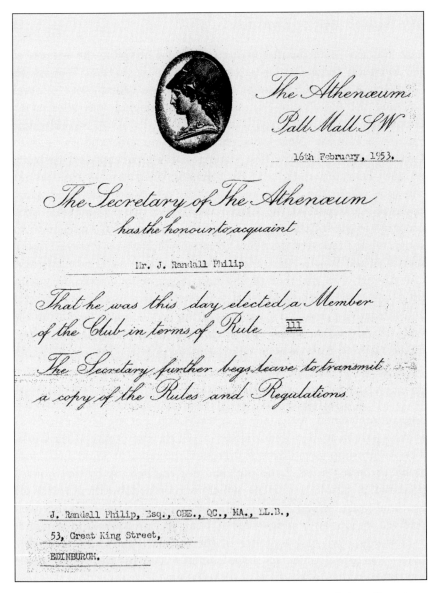

The Athenaeum
Pall Mall S.W.

16th February, 1953.

The Secretary of The Athenaeum
has the honour to acquaint

Mr. J. Randall Philip

That he was this day elected a Member
of the Club in terms of Rule III

The Secretary further begs leave to transmit
a copy of the Rules and Regulations.

J. Randall Philip, Esq., OBE., QC., MA., LL.B.,

53, Great King Street,

EDINBURGH.

I replied. John Wheatley proposed George Morton, rightly calling him 'something of a saint', and George (now eighty-three) replied. Then all the others spoke:- Bertie MacInnes (Sheriff-sub. at Glasgow) on his return to the Round Table and T.P. McDonald proposed Frank Duffy's health for having made the arrangements and the latter replied. Clifford Watt proposed John Wilson's health for his skill in choosing quotations for each guest, and John replied. His quotation for me was:

He came to ask what he had found
That was so large and smooth and round'

Southey: The Battle of Blenheim

The joviality of the dinner, while perhaps not so uproarious as Pleydell's High Jinks, had something of that quality.

On Tuesday, we are putting the allocation of seats for St. Giles' into practically final form. On Wednesday, I meet Dr. Warr and Commander Colville, Buckingham Palace Press Secretary at St. Giles'. I have heard that the two Sheriff-substitutes and I are to be presented to the Queen on June 25th at Paisley: the ceremony to be at Gilmour Street Station! I go to the Conference of the Lighthouse Authorities and the Ministry of Transport in London this week, and also to Greenock to address a municipal function on their 'Code for the Citizen', an interesting call to all citizens to remember that their citizenship is founded on Christian civilisation.

I have just been admitted a member of The Athenæum. A fortnight ago, when in London, I took Sir Basil Gibson there for lunch. Afterwards, the Secretary, Mr. Parry showed me round from the top to the bottom. It was interesting to be in this historic spot, and see the steps of the staircase, where Dickens and Thackeray became reconciled a fortnight before the latter's death, and the rooms where Thomas Carlyle and Matthew Arnold did much of their work. I met S.C. Roberts and had a chat with him. The Royal Clyde Yacht Club has also made me, as Sheriff of Argyll, an honorary member. The Epworth Press have asked permission to publish in a series of B.B.C. addresses, my 'Why I believe' address.

3rd May 1953 (Sunday)

April was a very full month. I heard two cases in Dunoon and three in Greenock at the beginning of the month, and also attended the ceremony when the Freedom of Dunoon was conferred on the Argylls (the 1st battalion is just back from Korea and the 8th is the Argyll county regiment). This led me to stay three nights in the Royal Marine Hotel which I greatly enjoyed, though apart from a walk to Sandbank, I worked solidly all the time, except when on duty elsewhere. The casket at the Freedom ceremony was received by General Scott-Eliot as deputy for General Sir Gordon Macmillan of Macmillan who is at present Governor of Gibraltar. General Scott-Eliot's way was a pleasing contrast to the Provost's bombast. There was a dinner in the evening at the Marine Hotel, where I sat between a charming Brigadier Clarke (retired) of Doune, and an equally charming Colonel Neilson, from Fort George. I had tea and a very pleasant talk with the Bruce Campbells, and the Duke of Argyll introduced me to the Duchess No. 3, and they invited me to the opening of the state rooms at Inverary. I said I was sorry I would be away on holiday at the time.

From the 18th Monday to the 25th Saturday we were on holiday. Our ostensible object was to return Alison to Oxford on the 20th and to allow myself to attend the British Council of Churches in Birmingham on the 21st and 22nd.

Perhaps the high-light of the whole holiday was our visit to Wilton House, outside Salisbury – the great house, part Holbein, mainly Inigo Jones; the Palladian Bridge over the Nadder, the trees cut away to open up a vista of Salisbury Cathedral; the stately spacious park of grass and 400 year old trees surrounding the house like a green belt; the magnificent interior, yet a place to be lived in; the Van Dycks in the large drawing-room, especially the silvery dresses in them; the exquisite proportions and surprising acoustics of that 60' × 60' room; the lovely china – I can think of no house other than Compton Winyates that I have seen to equal it. In contrast, the cafeteria in the stables for hoi polloi with radio beating out the Light Programme and 'Listen with Mother'!

I prefer Winchester to Salisbury, but this time the preference was not so marked. If only Salisbury had the red and blue stained glass of Chartres; how its cold Purbeck pilasters and white arches would warm up. All the clergy we saw in the Cathedral and its Close seemed like the aged Warden of Hiram's Hospital; but every one gave our little family a kindly smile. This was not so at Winchester, but we heard an excellent sermon from Canon Cowley, to a small congregation at Matins in the Quire. It is interesting to read the records of weekly givings in this great Cathedral – less than one-third of the Sunday offerings in St. George's West.

At the British Council of Churches in Birmingham, the Archbishop came up specially to me at lunch and gave me the warmest of welcomes. He agreed to let me photograph him still and moving. One dreadful report on the law of divorce in 'this country' (which everyone agreed, when I asked the question, referred to the United Kingdom) stated innocently that divorce was first introduced in 'this country' in 1857. How can such a document be circulated north of the Border! I pointed out that, there, it would be regarded as perpetrating a schoolboy's howler, and, I am glad to say, the Report was taken back to be reconsidered. But this kind of thing happens too often, and the trouble is that they have practically no Scotsmen on their Committees. I cannot help believing that this is due to the unfriendly attitude of that mediaeval ecclesiastic, a modern Wolsey, the Bishop of London. How different he is from the Archbishop whom I would follow through thick and thin – a great practical Christian, frank and friendly, with the gay boyish joy and humour of a first disciple.

16th May 1953

On the strength of my attendance Record at the Northern Lighthouse Board, I have just been awarded a cabin in the *Pharos* for its voyage to and from the Naval Review at Spithead. We sail down the East Coast, and return by the West, calling at the Scillies and the Isle of Man.

My seat at the Coronation will be in the South Aisle of the Abbey nave, near the West Door. Ella will be in the Royal Household Stand just almost in front of Clarence House – on the north side of the Mall.

Rosemary, nine on the 14th, had a birthday party today, with about sixteen little girl-friends; there was a conjurer, who also did a Punch-and-Judy act, and I showed my Easter and some other films. Rosemary particularly likes the film of mine which shows her doing her very first act of walking – in the garden of the 'Duke of Gordon' at Kingussie. To keep her balance she had to hold her nose! Age: 15 months; year 1945 (August).

The President asked me whether I was receiving a knighthood; I said: 'Not that I know.' He said: 'Oh then, it can't be, since it would have been intimated to you by now.' He said that the Scottish Office were working on the principle that it was not awarded to a Procurator until he had been in the office ten years. That, he said, was why Fred Strachan never got it. Campbell Black got it in his first year, and then resigned. Tommy Cooper said: 'I was responsible, and was afterwards "hauled over the coals"!' The practical effect, if this be true, is that the Procurator is almost certain not to get it; for few survive ten years of office. But then, as Jock Cameron says: 'In Scotland you are not near enough to the Fountain of Honour to be splashed by it.' I must say, I have not thought about it, remembering Fred Strachan's case. But I have been reminded of it, by so many people hinting at it – Jock Cameron, Chalmers at Oban and others. I am not going to be hypo-critical, and say I don't care. I do care, if only (a) that I would like it as a gift to Ella for all her love; and (b) that the Church in Scotland is quite inadequately recognised.

24th May 1953 (Sunday)

I am writing this in the midst of the General Assembly. The first feature of this Assembly was its opening day. The Queen's letter had a real feminine touch about it, and the references to the Church's place at the Coronation and to the National Service to be held on June 24th in St. Giles' were most tenderly expressed. The Duke of Hamilton made the best Commissioner's speech I have heard. The Moderator, Pitt Watson, is quite excellent in every department of his work, easily the best since I became Procurator. The Lord Chancellor came and made a most excellent and moving speech on the difficulties of the manse, using the material I had provided for him with great effect. By way of acknowledgment, that same afternoon, Ella and I were invited down to Holyrood to meet him and Lady Simonds, which was a kind thing to do. Last night we had our Uist Presbytery dinner at the University Club, (I acting as host). From Uist we had the Rev. Angus Morrison, Kilmull and Paible; and Mr. Donald Laing, also from South Uist. To meet them, I invited also, T.P. McDonald, John Hay Smith (both formerly Commissioners for Uist), Tommy Millar, Dr. White Anderson, Willie Tindal and Lord Stevenson, a varied company who got on well together.

27th May 1953 (Wednesday)

The General Assembly is all but completed. The closing meeting takes place this evening. It was a very busy session. We passed, I think, thirty Acts. The legal work steadily increases, and there is need of a special Law Committee. Yesterday, I presented my report on arrangements connected with the Coronation and the National Service in St. Giles'. It was very well received and there were no awkward questions asked. Sir James Fergusson seconded. In the evening Ella and I dined at Holyrood House.

4th June 1953

Ella and I have just returned from the Coronation. We travelled south on Sunday night, the 31st May, accompanied by Pitt Watson, his wife, and White Anderson. Tommy Cooper was also on the train; the last named made one of his characteristic remarks by way of disapproval of the elaborate arrangements that 'the Queen was being butchered to make a Roman holiday'. I had a talk with Pitt Watson before going off to bed. He told me one extraordinary thing: he said: 'I don't know whether to regard this as tragic or comic.' At the final Coronation rehearsal on the 29th just before the great Procession began to progress up the Abbey, the Archbishop came to him in a slightly shame-faced manner and said: 'Will you do me a favour?' Pitt Watson replied: 'Most certainly, if it is in my power.' The Archbishop explained that it was the custom after he had dispensed Communion to the Queen and the Duke of Edinburgh to give Communion also to the Arch-bishop of York and the three serving bishops (London, Norwich, and Winchester). Pitt Watson was to be sitting between York and the other three. The Archbishop: 'My difficulty, as you can well understand, is, that I do not feel enabled to give Communion to you and yet I do not like to pass along the row without doing something. Would you be willing to hold out your hands crossed and facing downwards and I shall lay my hands upon yours. This would at least be a gesture of Christian brotherhood.' Pitt Watson: 'While I understand your diffi-culty, naturally I regret it very much indeed, but will do as you ask.' At the rehearsal the actual motions were not carried through because, when the Archbishop reached the Communion service, he simply said the opening words and passed over the Communion to the closing words.

Our hotel was in Queen's Gate S.W.7, near the Albert Hall – Ashley Court Hotel – a good long way out. As Ella was to be in her stand in the Mall by 6 a.m. we thought it would be wise to test how long it took to go to it, and so after breakfast we set out to walk. We went by Kensington and down Grosvenor Place and Buckingham Palace Road to the Mall and found the Stand, viz. Stand 39, just in front of the entrance to St. James's Palace. It took 55 minutes to walk and the stand proved to be excellent when we got to it. We then crossed through St. James's Park and viewed the Stands and Decorations round Westminster Abbey and the Queen's Annexe. From there I took Ella to see the Central Land Board Board Room at Carlton House Terrace and then we went for lunch to the Athenæum Annexe where we had arranged to meet the Pitt Watsons and White Anderson. We had a very delightful lunch party and fell in with Admiral Cunningham and his wife, who were extraordinarily nice to us. Admiral Cunning-ham said that one of the amusing features of the Coronation would be that the Lord High Steward of England (himself) would carry St.

Edward's Crown wearing Thistle Robes. After lunch we returned to the hotel and were immediately joined by Alison. She had come to stay with Isobel Graham and Elspeth Milligan who now have a flat in Kensington, which for the Coronation was to be occupied not by two, but by fourteen. Our Church of Scotland party at the hotel shortly afterwards assembled. It consisted of the Pitt Watsons, White Anderson, the McKenzies, Dr. Alexander Macdonald, Principal Duncan, Dr. Johnstone Jeffrey, Dr. Caldwell, Mr. MacNicol and David Bogle.

On Coronation day, the 2nd, we rose at 4.15 a.m. and Ella left in company with Alison, who came to accompany her, at 5.15 a.m. The Church of Scotland representatives left at 6.15 a.m. We had the very greatest ease in reaching our destination at the Abbey, the entrance from the Dean's House. Our position in the Abbey was in the 3rd Bay eastwards from the West Door at the south side. The seats were well banked and we could see everything which went on in the Nave. I sat beside David Bogle with the two Clerks of Assembly in front and Dr. White Anderson and Dr. Johnstone Jeffrey behind. In front of us were the Aldermen of London and opposite the Mayors of the English Burghs. We had four hours to wait before the service began but they were anything but dull. In front and slightly to the left was the grave of the Unknown Warrior. It was uncovered, but the remainder of the floor was covered with a magnificent blue carpet and the galleries were also upholstered in blue with a crown design along the front. The general effect was rich blue coupled with the uniforms which were mostly scarlet. For the first two hours we had the entertainment of seeing the Peers and Peeresses arrive. Most of them were in their full robes but some of the newer creations wore a kind of utility robe [I learned afterwards that this was their Parliamentary robe], though oddly enough it was only the Peers and not the Peeresses, who all seemed to have the correct crimson and ermine. Someone remarked rather humorously that all the Peeresses seemed half the age of the Peers. I didn't think so, I saw quite a number of elderly Peeresses. The Peers came up on the one side of the Unknown Warrior's grave and the Peeresses up the other side. It was quite amusing because the Peers all had to wait when they passed it for the Peeresses, who were terribly afraid of tripping over each other's robes. Someone remarked that it was rather like looking into a paddock and that the horses should have been numbered. However, even so, many of them were identifiable. Amongst them came Monty in his robe of a Knight of the Garter, but in his case it was simply to hang about and talk to people. We had a very good opportunity of seeing him when he retired once more into the annexe. We saw quite a number of the Lords of Appeal, Reid and Morton of Henryton, and numerous others, amongst them the Scots peers.

While I was sitting there a very pleasant companion on my right told me that he knew Col. Hunt of the Everest Expedition, and that the Union Jack had just been planted on the top of Everest.

Then the various processions began. First there were some foreign representatives and David remarked to me that it was just as well that they were under guard, being preceded by an Officer of the Household and followed by another. They looked as though they might have been dangerous if they had been let loose. Then came some foreign rulers amongst them some colourful representatives like the Sheik of Bahrein and the Queen of Tonga, who had a most pleasant and natural way and towered above the rest of her procession like the Sanctissima Trinidad at the Battle of Trafalgar. Not merely was she 6 ft. 7 ins. but she had a most incredible head-dress consisting of two things like sticks sticking out of her hair and on the top a thing like a pink flower on which a bird might have liked to alight. Then came the Prime Ministers with Winston Churchill at the rear wearing the Garter Robes with the uniform of the Warden of the Cinque Ports. He looked exactly as if he had been blown up by a bicycle pump. Mr. Attlee and his wife slipped up the side of the nave. Then came the foreign royalties and I noticed in particular the mother of the Duke of Edinburgh, Princess Andrew of Greece, who has entered a nunnery and was dressed in a grey veil and habit. The more interesting processions began with the British royalties, the Princess Royal looking like Queen Mary and I could not help thinking it is strange to see her so elderly when my own parents had attended her marriage in this same church. She was followed by the Duchess of Kent with Princess Alexandra and the Duke of Kent, certainly amongst the most handsome of all the Royalties. Then the Duchess of Gloucester accompanied by her two boys, one of whom was gently reproved by her for staring all round the galleries. About this time the Regalia were brought from the altar right down the nave and carried into the Annexe. This was one of the most impressive scenes. The choir sang the Litany as they proceeded down the Church. They consisted of boys from the Chapel Royal, choristers from the Abbey and St. George's Chapel, Windsor, and they were followed by a group of Scholars from Westminster School, dressed in their gowns and mortar-boards. I learned later that Janet Adam Smith's boy, who is a scholar, was amongst them.

Opposite us the choir halted and then turned towards us and continued singing, and the effect was quite wonderful. One could hear every note of every part with the utmost clarity. The Dean and the Prebendaries took the Regalia into the Annexe and then, after the Litany was concluded, the remainder of the procession once more returned to the Choir. Amongst the music at this stage was Holst's 'I Vow to Thee my Country'; 'Greensleeves'; Elgar's 'Nimrod'; and the Cologne Chorale, so familiar to us in Scotland. Then came the Procession of the Queen Mother and for the first time the congregation began to bow and curtsey. Her hair is pure black, without a streak of grey in it and she behaved with all her accustomed grace. After she passed, the most surprising thing happened; a team of white-coated attendants came out with old-fashioned carpet-sweepers and swept the carpet right up and down the nave, the foreman watching his stop-watch all the time. They disappeared very quickly and then the great Procession began to form up. *[Note (25.11.53) Within the last week, strangely enough, I have been asked twice – by Dr. Johnstone Jeffrey last week, and by Dr. Warr tonight – whether there is any record made of this incredible incident. I said that I had recorded it at once – and here it is!]* It was led by an admiral, followed by the Abbey Beadle and then the Royal Chaplains with Nevile Davidson and John Baillie at their head. They had to stand for quite a time while the remainder of the Procession was forming in the Annexe. Nevile Davidson's behaviour was in marked contrast to some of the others. He stood looking to the front, while some of the others fidgeted and looked behind and whispered. Then the Procession began to move forwards very slowly – the Chaplains, the representatives of the various Orders of Knighthood – amongst them Wimberley in a cloak of what I afterwards learned was white samite (I had always wondered what white samite was) representing the Order of the Bath – the Order of St. Michael and St. George, the Victorian Order, Bath, Thistle and Garter. Then some Heralds and so on. The other Church representatives, the two ex-Moderators, Dr. McKenzie and Dr. Macdonald, the Moderator, the Archbishop of York and chaplain, the Lord Chancellor and his purse-bearer, the Archbishop of Canterbury and his chaplains, the Duke of Edinburgh, who had a midshipman to carry his coronet, then the three serving bishops carrying the Patten, Bible and Chalice, and then the Procession of the Queen. I thought, of the great Officers of State, one of the most impressive was Lord Crawford as deputy for the Steward of Scotland. I have also omitted to mention Princess Margaret who accompanied the Queen Mother, and whose train bearer was perhaps the most attractive of all the train-bearers. The Queen looked very small, wore a tiara and was very simply dressed with six train-bearers, followed by the Mistress of the Robes, the Dowager Duchess of Devonshire. The whole Procession moved very slowly and eventually passed beyond the Screen.

The words of the Service were relayed, and we heard every word including the Queen's replies, with the utmost clarity. I was surprised at how long the recognition took. The Queen and the Archbishop must have moved very slowly to the four corners of the theatre. Indeed, the actual words of the Service took relatively little time. What seemed to take time was the movement to the various stations where each ceremony took place. I was, in common with others, somewhat disappointed with the new music. I liked best Herbert Howells' 'O Taste and See'; the Gloria and Te Deum seemed to me to be a little disappointing and there was nothing which could compare with William Walton's 'Crown Imperial' for last Coronation. We of course could not see but there were some amusing incidents. During the Homage, Lord Moubray, as he was retiring down the steps, stumbled and his coronet fell and had to be picked up. At one point he was down on all fours. Evidently a little Westminster scholar was deputed to hold the coronets while each peer paid his Homage. Then at the end of the Service the various processions of the Royalties returned to the Annexe, the Queen on this occasion wearing the Imperial Crown and carrying the Orb and Sceptre. After the Service we were very quickly released from our positions and David and I went over to Church House where we found the Gold Coach and had an excellent view of it and of the coachman and postillions; the coachman looked a complete tough. I am told that not all the Commonwealth representatives were equally well received. The greatest cheers were for Canada and New Zealand. At some places, it is said, Dr. Malan was booed. Inside Church House we were supposed to have a buffet lunch on the ground floor but Dr. White Anderson and Dr. Johnstone Jeffrey were ushered to the left up a side passage and we followed them and we were taken up in a lift to where we found ourselves in the Bishops' Buffet where the food seemed to be very much better than downstairs. On the way down I ran into the Archbishop himself and he said how well the Moderator had done his part but I tried to thank him for his own part which was executed with such dignity and simplicity. We had three cars and to ensure that we did not go off and leave some of our party behind we had someone in charge of each car. I took charge of Dr. Johnstone Jeffrey, and our car was called up in ten minutes and we were back at the hotel by 4 p.m. After that we watched the Procession by TV and Ella and Alison did not arrive home till about 6.30 p.m. They had had an equally wonderful time, in quite a different way however, watching the Procession both going and coming, and were full of the thrill of it. Evidently the crowd had been very funny. A policeman on a bicycle had been cheered the whole way down the Mall and so had a cart which was picking up litter. A large number of people had fainted, but, as so often happens, no one fainted when the Procession passed.

After dinner we had a very interesting conversation in the Church of Scotland deputation about a matter which the Moderator had mentioned to me before. I refer to the point which he had previously discussed with me as we were travelling to London. 'The favour' which the Archbishop had asked of him took a rather different form at the ceremony. During the Communion Service the Archbishop administered the bread and the Dean of Westminster the wine. When the Archbishop came to the Moderator, the Moderator, as he had been asked to do, held his hands crossed, the Archbishop laid his left hand on the Moderator's crossed hands and then held the bread in front of him and uttered the words of administration 'Take, eat' etc. The Moderator felt terribly embarrassed at the action taking this form as he had already reached the understanding with the Archbishop that the Communion was not to be administered to him. It was still worse when the Dean came up to him with the wine. He held out his hands in the same way and it was to his surprise that the Dean held the Chalice right to his lips and uttered the words of administering the wine. We all agreed it could not have been subterfuge and yet it would appear to all who saw what happened as if the Moderator were offered both bread and wine, when in fact he was not being offered it. What troubled the Moderator was that it appeared that the bread and wine had been offered to him and he refused it. We all discussed what was the best course for him to take. I suggested that the Moderator should make a contemporary record of what had happened so that it could always be referred to if the question arose. I also suggested that the Moderator should, in conversation with the Archbishop, mention the embarrassment it had caused. The others were in favour of the Moderator writing to the Archbishop which I thought was a much more difficult thing to do. But it was decided that this course should be taken.

Later in the evening the Moderator told me a delightful joke about the National Service in St. Giles' on June 24th which no one seems to have noticed. He is very much hoping that no one will notice it until the day of the service. It is that the Scottish Office or the powers that be have, by accident or chance, chosen the anniversary of Bannockburn! The people in the hotel were greatly interested that one of the guests was the man who presented the Bible to the Queen and there were numerous requests for autographs not merely from himself but from the rest of the party.

Next morning Ella and I took our luggage to the Caledonian Club and then went to King's Cross to confirm our sleeper arrangements.

After lunch at King's Cross we went to the Newsreel in Piccadilly in the hopes of seeing something of the Coronation, but there was very little available yet. After some shopping we went to the Caledonian Club for dinner and fell in with dozens of friends. Alick Buchanan Smith and his sister were there, and we were afterwards joined by Wimberley and had a most lively dinner party and compared notes on what had happened. Janet Adam Smith told me that her boy, a Westminster Scholar, had worn the court dress of the Chief Justice of Hong Kong and it had to be taken in 6 ins. all round, and I told her that I was wearing my own and it had to be let out 6 ins. and Forsyths had said, when I asked would a gusset show, 'No, it will be between you and its maker.'

Immediately at the close of dinner we had to leave to catch our train.

7th June 1953

The chief news in Parliament House this week has been the information that the President, on his way to the Coronation, was stopped at the Barrier somewhere near Northumberland Avenue (where he was staying) and never reached the Abbey. He told me about it himself. He said that the crowd were fifty deep at the Barrier, and that the police in charge, not Metropolitan police but men drawn in for the occasion, would not let him through. We all felt that, with a determined effort, he could have got through somehow. He said that, though he left without breakfast at 5 a.m. he did not get his first meal until he reached the House of Commons about 12.30 p.m.!

Lord Mackay reached his 25th year on the Bench (25 years too long!) and was congratulated by the Justice-Clerk. The President told me that he (the President) said to the Justice-Clerk: 'Whatever you do, don't refer to it as his *semi*-jubilee!'

The President told me that, last autumn, he had dinner with 'Monty', and said: 'Why do you allow a general like Eisenhower to give up his vocation and become a politician?' Monty replied: 'Well, I said to him – Now you will have to learn to be dishonest!'

Though the President never reached the Abbey, he watched the Procession and was greatly entertained by Pompey, the veteran grey horse, which led one of the mounted bands. He kept pace with the drums, and when he reached Trafalgar Square, he took a knowing look down Whitehall, and then pounded down Northumberland Avenue, looking round to see that the other horses were following him. I told this story to Ella afterwards, and she said: 'Oh, I noticed one grey, almost like a circus horse, which kept in perfect time with the drums.'

The President again asked me whether I had received notice of a knighthood – a somewhat embarrassing question!

11th June 1953 (Thursday)

We left Granton Harbour this morning at 9 a.m., the *Pharos* lying in Granton Pond awaiting us. The party is:- George Morton, Robbie Maconochie, Charles Milne, Tom Simpson, myself, James Gilchrist, the new senior Bailie of Edinburgh (Bailie Mackenzie), Glen Wakelin, Mr. Campbell (the Northern Lighthouse Board accountant) and the Superintendent (Cadger).

The Forth was like a mill-pond when we went aboard, but the weather steadily worsened after Dunbar, and we had two heavy swells to land in – at Dunbar for Barns Ness; and at St. Abb's Head. Conditions may be judged by the facts that Tom Simpson in the first, and Campbell in the second landing both damaged fingers, while James Gilchrist, who has to meet the Queen the week after next, lost his lower dentures! We also started in sunshine, and now there is a haar and a north-easter. We are off the Longstone now (7.30 p.m.). Tomorrow morning, we may land at Scarborough or Bridlington.

12th June 1953 (Friday)

(11.15 a.m.) Since leaving St. Abb's yesterday at 5 p.m., we have been out of sight of land, except that some (though not I) saw Flamborough Head. We have passed Scarborough, and the idea of landing there has been abandoned. Now we are crossing the banks, and about an hour ago passed the Dowsing Light Ship, close on our port side. We have seen several cargo vessels. Last night, I did not sleep well, and then from about 3 a.m. to 5 a.m. we went through fog with our horn going every minute. The weather is cold today, though rather quieter than yesterday evening. I read Tom Johnston's *Reminiscences* during the night, a flimsy work, and G.M. Young's *Baldwin* this morning. We may call in at Yarmouth. But at present we must be level with Boston or The Wash. One cannot help noticing the complete absence of bird life here – so different from our Scottish voyages. Last night, owing to the weather, more of the party were *hors de combat* than I have seen on the *Pharos* before. In the later evening, only Maconochie, Bailie Mackenzie and myself, with Mr. Cadger and Mr. Campbell were left. I am in my usual cabin for the fifth time – a home from home now. George Morton is to be Commodore for the whole of the voyage, because of its special nature.

(Later) We passed Dowsing and Cromer and Haisboro' Lightvessels and the Caister Buoy and came into Yarmouth Roads, lying about two miles out. Beyond us was a sandbank, and, one after another running north to south they stretch out eastwards to Smith's Knolls. What a difficult stretch of water to navigate. At Yarmouth, we went ashore for a short time and did not get beyond Gorleston. In the evening, Gorleston and Yarmouth revealed their separate positions, by their brilliant Coronation lighting. But the weather was grey and disappointing.

13th June 1953 (Saturday)

We left Yarmouth about 4 a.m. The morning promised well, and the sea was calm. We felt the first real warmth. Off Harwich we began to see the north-bound traffic from the Thames. Then followed a quiet stretch; then we passed by Kentish Knock lightship and knew we were approaching the south-bound traffic stream. We kept too far east to see any land. We first knew we were level with the North Foreland, by the three two-second hoots every minute of the North Goodwin Lightship. We did not see it, but passed some distance to the east. At this point there converged on our course and crossed it a very modern trawler, which we identified as the Boston Deep Sea Fishing Company's trawler, *Princess Royal*, which was bound like ourselves for the Review at Spithead. Today's papers say that it is to represent the near and middle-water trawler fleets there. Shortly afterwards, we came right up past the East Goodwins lightship, a large vessel with a diaphone fog-signal, which gave out a tenor note sounding far away. At lunch, half-an-hour later, we passed the small South

Goodwins lightvessel. Just as we came on deck after lunch, we approached Dover Harbour. The cliffs were all but lost in the mist. Last night the 24,000 ton P.&O. liner *Chusan* collided off the Goodwins with a Harrison line freighter *Prospector*. We passed near the scene of the collision. But by then the *Chusan* had returned to London with her 1,000 Mediterranean cruise passengers. In Dover Harbour, however, we saw the *Prospector*, with her nose down in the water, and what looked like a rent in her starboard side. At Folkestone, we anchored, and went ashore for half-an-hour, when I sent telegrams to the family, as at Gorleston yesterday. But Lower Folkestone is a very ordinary place, though the harbour itself is interesting, and the *Maid of Orleans* and the *Côte d'Azur* – the cross-Channel boats – were lying at the Quay. Now we are sailing westwards along the south coast, but the land is almost blotted out by fog. No land, few birds, how ordinary it looks after magnificent days in the Orkneys, Shetlands, and West Coast of Scotland. We hope that the weather will improve for the Review itself.

(Later) We have passed Dungeness, a low wide promontory with a high but not very graceful lighthouse – it was about 2–3 miles off, as we ran a straight course for Dover to south of Beachy Head. We expect to pass the Royal Sovereign lightship and Beachy Head about 9 p.m. tonight. It is not yet determined where we will anchor for the night. The foggy weather is becoming less dense, possibly because rain has begun to fall. But the weather would require to show considerable improvement if the Review is not to be somewhat disappointing. We are now in a traffic lane, and ships proceeding up Channel have been passing us from time to time. During dinner, we had an unforgettable view of Beachy Head and its red lighthouse, cloud-capped cliffs, pink in the evening light, stretching westwards into the grey.

If I were asked what were my prevailing impressions of our journey so far, I would name first the strange knolls on sandbanks lying off the Norfolk Coast, which to the mariner are much more real than the land itself, and the areas of the lightships round Cromer (Dowsing, Cromer, Haisboro'), but even more on the Kentish Coast area (Kentish Knock, and the North, East and South Goodwins, made all the more vivid to us by last night's collision, the headlines in all today's news).

14th June 1953 (Sunday)

We lay in the Channel last night, anchored ten miles off Brighton, a novel anchorage. The fog had largely cleared, and we could see the lights of Brighton, Hove and Worthing, and, to the east, Peacehaven and still further east Newhaven. Earlier I saw Beachy Head Light switch on. We were so far out that the lights of Hove were almost over the horizon, but the promenades of Brighton, and also Worthing, showed up well.

In the morning, we proceeded westwards to Spithead. We were now accompanied by other ships converging on the Review, especially the Canadian *D'Iverville*, which let us pass her. She had two helicopters on board and afterwards, we saw one flying about in the Review area. The first sign of the Review was the faint outline of the Isle of Wight; then we passed the Nab Tower on our left, a great sea tower built of steel with all the equipment of a modern lighthouse. Then, as the channel narrowed, we could see the two old forts which guard the entrance, and, just beyond, the leading ships, at the right of each line, the *Baltimore* (U.S.A.), the *Vanguard* (Britain), and light cruisers near Portsmouth. Our station was just south of the foreign men-of-war, near the right end. But, before taking up our position there, we sailed right along the lines, westwards (on the Portsmouth-Southampton side), and then eastwards (on the Cowes-Ryde side). First, we passed *Vanguard* (on our port side), followed by four or five aircraft carriers, and then an endless line of light cruisers or frigates, almost eight miles of them. The crews were all lined up for divine service on each ship as we passed. On our starboard, we saw the *Brenda* and later a long line of submarines. Then, the Trinity House Yacht *Patricia* steamed east, passing us, and we exchanged courtesies, dipping our flags. Then three new lifeboats crossed our track, one of them the new Campbeltown lifeboat. At Cowes we turned, and came back by the south side. Here was a more entertaining variety of craft. A large Dutch liner passed us. We saw the *British Sailor*, at the moment the world's largest tanker, which quite recently I saw also in the Clyde. Well known names met us: *Scotsman*, *Largo Bay*, and *Clova*. Further on, we came to the quite fascinating foreign ships. The *pièce de résistance* was the *Amerigo Vespucci*, an Italian training ship (three master sailing), with a magnificent billowing Italian flag, which looked as if it had just returned from the Spanish main, full of treasure. Beyond it were Brazilian, Danish, Spanish, Swedish, Russian, French and American warships, the Russian especially exciting everyone's interest. Endless yachts sailed this way and that, and a helicopter went this way and that, sometimes hovering to secure a better view, but usually less than mast high. How strange to see it pass the towering masts of the Italian.

We took up our position, which is just to the south of the Russian and Swede. We can see all the big ships; out beyond us towards the sea lies the *Norge*, the Norwegian Royal Yacht. We saw all in superb sunshine, such a change after our foggy journey south, but how good that the best weather was reserved till now.

In the afternoon we went ashore to Ryde just to our south-west. But the crowds on the pier were so great that we could do little more than walk to the shore and back along the pier. Each nick of sand was occupied, and the crowds disported themselves there in little 'paddle-boats' built for two, which were propelled by the occupants after the manner of bicycles. On our return to the ship, we received a call from the Secretary of the Irish Lights Commissioners (Mr. Rowlands), inviting us to the *Grannaile*, which had just reached her station next to ours. We went over and, after refreshments, were taken round the ship. It was built in 1947, and is a little larger than the *Pharos*. But the equipment will not even bear comparison, and I have never seen the *Pharos* in such an untidy state; after our ship, always so spick and span, this was a 'come-down'. In the evening, we had Captain MacLachlan, Mr. Vass (engineer), Mr. Hunter (1st Officer) and Mr. Campbell (new 2nd Officer) at dinner, and later we saw all the lights of the fleet, and especially a nearby cable ship which was a string of lights from stern to stern, and a similarly dressed aircraft carrier over in the distance. This was for most of the time a lovely brilliantly sunny day, with freshening breeze which sent the yachts, large and small, scudding across the water.

15th June 1953 (Monday)

The Coronation Review – Lovely weather favoured us, with sunshine all day and a freshening breeze which sent all our bunting streaming in the wind.

We were up on deck at 8 o'clock, and saw every ship in the lines set free its bunting. The wind kept shifting from point to point, and, instead of the ships lying end-on in line after line, in the course of the day, they kept altering position, so that there was a constantly changing scene. One launch with Robbie Maconochie and Bailie Mackenzie left early for Portsmouth – to bring out two friends of the former, Brig. and Mrs. Philps (the first a director of Chance Brothers) and Bailie Finlay, Glasgow's senior Bailie. While they were away, the Captain put the other launch at my disposal, and we had a most wonderful sail along the lines, first to the perfectly magnificent Italian

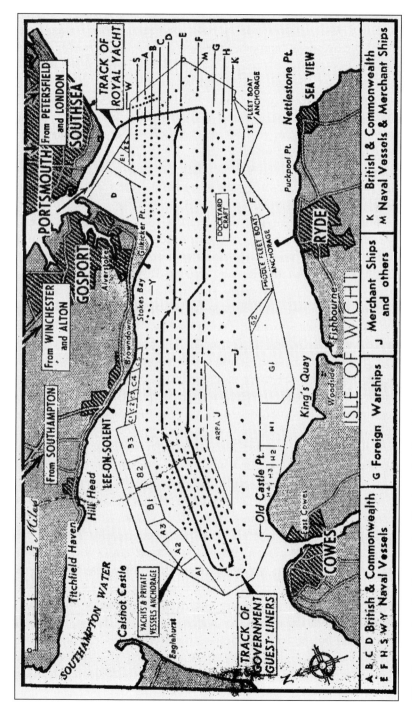

The line-up for the Coronation Review, Spithead. June 1953.

Amerigo Vespucci, a three-masted ship of pre-*Victory* type, bedecked with bunting, and a glorious large red, white and green Italian flag. We passed the Swedish, Spanish, Brazilian and Dutch (*Tromp*) on the way. Then we crossed over to a second line – of British aircraft carriers – some six to eight gigantic hulks, and so, right down to the right of the line where lay the only battleship *Vanguard*, towering above us, with its graceful bow and 15″ guns. Then across to the U.S. *Baltimore*, the Norwegian yacht *Norge*, the French cruiser *Montcalm* and the Russian cruiser *Smeddov*.

Shortly after lunch, we saw three magnificent liners coming down the lines to take up position for the inspection – the towering orange *Orcadia*, the scarlet-funnelled pink-hulled *Pretoria Castle*, and the yellow-funnelled white-hulled *Strathnaver*, all 24,000–28,000 tons. They steamed their stately way out eastwards into the open sea, and then returned to take up their position in a great sweeping curve. At 3 p.m. all the ships in the Review fired a Royal salute, and for a moment I felt, as the blue puffs appeared, as if this was another Trafalgar or Copenhagen. Then passing behind other ships, but seen between the gaps, we spied the Trinity House Yacht *Patricia* leading the frigate *Surprise* (acting as Royal Yacht) and other vessels up to the right of the line. In a few minutes they turned, and came along the lines followed by the three great liners. In *Surprise* we could see the temporary enclosed bridge erected before the mast, with the Queen standing in it. The Royal Standard flew at the foremast. An admiralty ship followed flying the Admiralty Flag. They passed westwards along the lines and while they sailed along the eight miles of the Review, we watched all the small crafts round us. On the aircraft carriers we could see thousands of men – sailors and marines – drawn up on the decks. Just to the west of us lay our Irish friends in *Grannaile*. Then back came the Royal Procession. On the way out, we could see the Queen standing in the special enclosed bridge erected for her, but she had disappeared by her return. *Surprise* anchored some way ahead of us, partly concealed by an aircraft carrier, about three lines over from us, near Lord Mountbatten's flag-ship, the *Glasgow*. Then came the fly-past, first squadrons of ordinary aircraft and then overtaking them, at incredible speed, the jets. Our guests stayed for sherry, at which we were joined by the Irish Commissioners (who all seem anxious to get a new chairman and they are more at sixes and sevens than we are). One of them whom I met for the first time was Wilson, a leading Dublin ear-throat-and-nose surgeon. They are an incredible lot, unbelievably Irish and highly amusing.

In the evening, after dinner, we had a grandstand view first of the fireworks and then of the fleet lit up. The Russian tableau with an illuminated red star was the most colourful, but for miles to the west and some distance to the east, the warships shone in outline with masses of electric bulbs. They were still lit up when I went to bed.

16th June 1953 (Tuesday)

At present we are on passage to Land's End, and just passing Portland Bill. We had a good view of Swanage, and even Bournemouth. The coast now is comparatively deserted, and almost like Shetland, though without its fine cliffs.

Epitaph for James Gilchrist:–

> When Sheriff Gilchrist died aboard
> We buried him off Portland Bill
> But fortune did one boon afford
> His teeth remain in Scotland still!

This effort of Tom Simpson's was produced at lunch today, after James Gilchrist had an attack of cramp (or so he says) this morning and was heard yelling out in his cabin.

A story of George Thomson, also from Tom Simpson. Tom was examinator for the Faculty when George Thomson came up for examination. He gave his address as The Manse, Bellshill; and his particulars disclosed that he was a Rhodes Scholar. J.A. Inglis (Jingles) remarked: 'I never knew that they gave Rhodes Scholarships to the aborigines of Bellshill!'

(Later) In the late afternoon we came to the entrance to Dartmouth and Start Point. To the north-east the coast faded away north of Torquay. A destroyer, running a measured course at top speed, overtook us and, when it was miles ahead, we saw it alter its course as if to make for Plymouth. We kept about 15 miles from Plymouth, but saw the main shipping lane away to the south with westbound ships setting their course for the Lizard. The Captain however, for my special benefit, took the other course to let me see the Eddystone. We came on it in the late afternoon, after watching it from ten miles off. There is a reef, and alongside the present red-and-white lighthouse stands the black stump of the last lighthouse. Behind – 15 miles off – lay Plymouth.

After dinner we came abreast of the Lizard Light and the coastguard signalled to enquire who we were. Night was falling as we rounded the Lizard and saw the lights of Marazion and, especially, Penzance. About midnight we reached Land's End, and, before going to bed, I went up on deck to catch a glimpse of the Wolf Rock, and also of the Land's End Light shining as yet over the cliffs.

17th June 1953 (Wednesday)

At breakfast we found ourselves more than half-way across the Bristol Channel. It was rough as we rounded Land's End, but today the weather moderated, and we had lovely conditions all day. A group of four destroyers followed by a submarine overtook us, crossing our bows, on their way northwards. We saw an American freighter going southwards, a cross-Channel Irish ship, a large tanker, and other small craft.

Before lunch, we altered course to the north-east, and went in to the Pembrokeshire coast between Milford Haven and St. Davids, to visit Skokholm Island bird sanctuary. We spent the afternoon on the island. There was fine cliff scenery, with rocks of differing colours, but relatively few birds. We met a large company of bird-watchers on the island, a Mr. Laing from Edinburgh, a Dr. Matthew from Christ's College, Cambridge, and about a dozen others, including a baby in perambulator. We inspected puffins and shearwater. One of the latter flew back to the island from America in thirteen days; another returned from Cambridge in about six hours; they have an uncanny faculty for finding their way home, not merely to their island, but to their own home on the island.

Now we have left Skokholm and passed the very distinctive South Bishop Rock, and, in brilliant sunshine, are about to cross Cardigan Bay. George and Robbie asked, was I receiving a knighthood?

(Later) A big tanker travelled alongside us to the west, and then crossed our track, making as if for Holyhead. The Snowdon group rose out of the sea to the east and the Wicklow mountains to the west. I had a long sleep on deck in the evening before dinner, and after dinner the Sheriffs of Edinburgh and Renfrew played Bailie Mackenzie and Mr. Campbell at deck-billiards. We were almost abreast of Holyhead when we went to bed.

18th June 1953 (Thursday)

Before breakfast, we were lying off the Chickens. Immediately after, all of us (except George and Robbie) set off for the rock. It was a much easier landing at the rock than last time, but somehow the lighthouse itself was no easier. The rungs of the outside ladder were damp and one had to watch. The keepers tie a rope round you, but, beyond giving you a sense of security, it would do little, unless it is passed round a bar, which it certainly was not. I watched two of my companions being let down before me, and the keeper simply held the rope as a mother might hold a baby's horse's reins. Inside there are about five or six ladder staircases to climb. Gilchrist (aged sixty-nine) stuck after reaching the top of the outside ladder, and I think it was very plucky of him to come so far, for, like myself, he is no lightweight, as well as being considerably older. Robbie, on the other hand, said: 'The Chickens is the only one I do not do.' But in making that statement he was somewhat forgetful. Glen admitted to me that the Chickens shook him a little, in spite of all his experience; and for myself, I am quite frank, it gets no easier with practice; and I find it depends rather on your mood, whether you are in a mild funk or not. So far, at least, I have not drawn back from one lighthouse and I hope to continue on that footing, until, like George, I am told that it is better for me not to go.

Later, we visited the shore-station at Port St. Mary, an attractive not over popularised holiday place, and after lunch we landed at Langness. This, normally easy, was today more difficult because the wind had freshened, but as usual Mr. Hunter (the First Officer) piloted our launch in and out with complete mastery. There was a most attractive baby boy at Port St. Mary and a most attractive baby girl at Langness. Langness is one of the few lighthouses with reflector mirrors. The station was very clean; not quite so the Chickens. We sailed on later to Douglas where we lay outside the Harbour and visited the lighthouse. For the first time on this voyage we picked up letters. Oddly enough, apart from family letters, my post included an invitation to become Hon. President of the Old Boys' Club of Dundee High School; and an invitation to present the prizes at Paisley Grammar School. I was quite moved by the first, as it is always a unique honour to be brought back to one's own school, and one where I spent the whole ten years of my school life. I read and re-read the letter as we sailed on past Laxey and Maughold Head to anchor at Ramsey.

19th June 1953 (Friday)

Yesterday was brilliantly sunny, but today began with mist on the hills which cleared later in the morning when the sun broke through. We went ashore in the morning, and visited the lighthouses, first, at Point of Ayre and, then, at Maughold. We were told that the shore north-east of the main Point of Ayre lighthouse has extended about 100 yards since we were last there three years ago. There is much shifting of gravel. I noticed that the fast Ardrossan steamer which passed us while we were there today reduced speed greatly till past the shoal. One lighthouse keeper said that sometimes its bottom just touched the bank, and great care was needed. We learned, too, that some bodies from the recent *Princess Victoria* disaster had been washed up near Castletown, on the Isle of Man. Maughold is a grandly situated light, both from the land and from the sea: this visit was the first time when I had seen it from the sea. There was a party of happy children in the keepers' houses.

In the afternoon, we returned to Douglas, where we tied up in harbour. It is curious how memory can play tricks. My recollection was that all the Isle of Man steamers had yellow funnels, but they turned out to be red. In the evening, we had a large dinner party: the new Governor (Sir Ambrose Dundas Flux Dundas), an Indian Civil Servant formerly in the North-Western Province, whose daughter turned out to be with Alison at Lady Margaret Hall (he is an Irish Dundas, but apparently related to the Scottish Dundases – of Dundas of Arniston); his aide-de-camp, a Manx man named Cain; the Chairman (Kelly) and Manager (Matthews) of the Douglas Harbour Board. Sir George and the Governor, after dinner, played Glen and myself at deck-billiards; the game was shamelessly manoeuvred to ensure that the Governor's side would win. As soon as our guests had returned to shore, we cast off from the pier and set out on our journey to Ardrossan.

Before going to bed, I had an interesting talk with Bailie Mackenzie about the ship's company. He showed me a table he had made up in which he had tried to assess the merits of his legal colleagues. It was, at all events as regards my colleagues, pretty accurate. George Morton, he gave 100 per cent for 'heart' and myself 90 per cent. Tom Simpson, he placed first in head and expression. The others had lower percentages; he was inclined to place Charles Milne level with Maconochie, then Gilchrist, and finally Wakelin. My net average on all his classifications was 82 per cent; Tom Simpson was lower in character (70 per cent), but 100 per cent in the others, and so, I think, given first place. I said I had no doubt that, in heart, old George was *facile principus*; while Tom Simpson was, indisputably, the first in intellect, though the use he had made of his might be somewhat disappointing. It was good to try to see ourselves as an outside observer had tried to assess us. Bailie Mackenzie said that he thought I was the only Commissioner to whom he would have dared to show his evaluation: I took that as a compliment.

20th June 1953 (Saturday)

In the morning, I wakened to find ourselves level with Galloway. After breakfast, we drew in to the coast at Turnberry, and visited its lighthouse, the first Commissioners' visit there since 1937. The keepers were not expecting us, and one of them was not in his uniform, but they both proved fine types of men, and the lighthouse was in excellent condition. Like Nosshead (Wick), and Langness, Turnberry had a mirror reflector.

From there it was a short run to Ardrossan, where we disembarked about 1.45 p.m. We caught a Glasgow train at 2.17 p.m. and the Edinburgh train at 4 p.m. from Glasgow (Queen Street); and were home by 5.30 p.m. So ended the Coronation Review voyage.

When I reached home I found a table covered with letters awaiting attention. Under others, I found a letter from 10 Downing Street, offering me a knighthood, in commemoration of the Queen's forthcoming visit to Scotland. I immediately took it up to show Ella. It was characteristic that she was engaged on service for another, putting her little child to bed. We read the letter over together, and then each tried to say how much we valued the honour for the other's sake. We thought, too, of the joy it would have given our parents, and Gordon, and how pleased Alison will be, and Rosemary, when she is old enough to understand.

23rd June 1953

Events move fast. W.G. Pottinger rang me up this morning to tell me that I would probably be expected to go to Holyrood tomorrow afternoon before the Garden Party to be presented to the Queen. A few minutes later I received a second letter from the Prime Minister's Secretary stating that the Queen had now approved that a knighthood be conferred.

(7.15 p.m.) A Major Ford from Holyroodhouse has just rung up and asked me to attend at Holyrood tomorrow afternoon at 3.45 p.m. when I am to be presented to the Queen to receive my knighthood.

I asked if Ella should accompany me, but apparently that is not permitted.

24th June 1953 (Wednesday)

Today the great national service took place in St. Giles'. We motored a great detour by Lothian Road, Lauriston and South Bridge to the High Street and then up to the Castle Esplanade, where we parked the car. On the way we dropped Rosemary, with our maid Muriel Mackie, who were to go to watch the procession from a window of the Destitute Sick Society at the corner of Bank Street near the Bank of Scotland. Afterwards, we heard that they saw very well, and Rosemary was delighted because the Queen looked up in her direction.

I went into the Parliament House with Ella, via the George IV Bridge Entrance, and donned my full-bottomed wig and gown. The Dean, Chris Guest, and Douglas Campbell were robing, to represent the Faculty. Then Ella and I crossed to the North Door of St. Giles', from which we obtained access to our seats. It was rather a thrill to look for them, as I had left the precise seating arrangements to the Scottish Office and the Secretary of St. Giles', and had deliberately refrained from any suggestion as to where we ourselves should have seats. Accordingly, except that I knew we were to enter by the North Door, I had no prior knowledge where our seats were to be. They turned out to be in a splendid position, facing the steps of the Communion Table, to the south thereof, and in the second row from the front. Dr. and Mrs. Caldwell were to our left. The Church of Scotland representatives were mainly in the corner of this corner of the Cathedral. Opposite us, in the corresponding north-east corner, were the representatives from St. Andrews House. The new reredos was in use for the first time, scarlet paint on a background of cloth-of-gold, the gift of the Merchant Company; it added colour to the scene. Opposite us were a newsreel and television camera. Behind us, Rogan of Paisley Abbey was placed in a corner, apparently to broadcast a commentary. One of the most interesting sights – between us and the Communion Table, a foot or two away – was Stanley Cursiter, as Queen's Limner, making sketches for a picture of the scene. The processions entered in less time than we expected, the peers and the provosts being the most impressive before the great procession. This was quite superb, the three bearers of the honours being excellent, especially Lord Crawford. The singing of the psalms and 'O Worship the King' (a favourite of the Queen's chosen by her) was full-voiced in comparison with the merely choral singing at Westminster. Pitt Watson's sermon was heard well in every corner of the building. The unusually deliberate utterance he used in order to avoid the echo was most effective, but perhaps reduced the tempo of his speaking. At the end of the service, the Queen moved from the Royal Pew to the central passage just short of the steps leading up to the Communion Table. There she stood, an almost girl-like figure, absolutely still, while Dr. Warr blessed her, and handed the Honours from off the Communion Table to her, while she in turn handed them to the three bearers, first Lord Home (the sword), then Lord Crawford (the sceptre), then the Duke of Hamilton (the Crown). The Crown rested on a small stand or tray, and the Queen obviously felt its weight. The Duke of Hamilton came quickly forward and relieved her of the weight of it. Lord Home's page made a small slip, seeking to pass in front of Lord Home when the latter was struggling with the sword, his back to the altar. But Lord Home put out his hand and stopped him, a rather amusing personal touch. After the Bearers had received the Honours, the procession filed out with the Queen and Duke of Edinburgh following them, and being in turn followed by the Countess of Erroll, as Lord High Constable. The Duke was a magnificent figure in the uniform of a Field Marshall. The Queen was in a simple blue coat; I was sorry that she did not wear formal dress; this was I think one defect in the ceremonial arrangements.

After the service, I saw hosts of friends, and Bill Milligan inveigled me up to the Crown Office for a glass of sherry with Hamish Clyde. Their respective wives and the Elphinstones were there. I did not wait long because meantime Ella was with the Pitt Watsons waiting for the latter's car. But Bill Milligan furnished me with a special police pass for the afternoon.

After a hurried lunch, we set off with the Hector McKechnies down to the Palace. I deposited Ella and the McKechnies at the North Garden Gate, and then went on to the forecourt, where I was allowed to park in the garage. I then entered the Palace and was asked up to the throne room. Shortly afterwards, I was joined by James Gilchrist, then Tom Johnston, then Lady Victoria Wemyss, then Calver, and finally Alastair Blair. After a wait for some time, the door opened at the far – south-east – corner of the room, and the Queen and the Duke crossed the floor, and went out at the other, by the door where we had entered. They had gone to the west drawing-room, and very soon we were ushered in one by one, first Tom Johnston (who was being made a Companion of Honour), then Gilchrist, then myself. When I entered the Queen and the Duke were in the centre of the room. I bowed at the door; then walked up to them; and knelt with the right knee on a little stand with rail placed in front of the Queen. Someone passed her a sword, which she rested first on my right and then on my left shoulder, and then she told me to rise up. I had previously indicated that I would be 'Sir Randall', to Major Ford. After the ceremony, the Queen and the Duke spoke to me for a little. Their opening subject was the weather, which had been so foggy yesterday when they arrived, but which was brilliantly sunny and hot today. Then they referred to the service, and the Duke was much interested when I mentioned that a boy from Gordonstoun had been invited. Then the Queen said that Gilchrist had referred to our both being at the Review. I asked their permission to tell about Tom Simpson's rhyme relating to Gilchrist, and, after explaining the circumstances, recited it to them. Both the Queen and the Duke then had a quite spontaneous laugh: they obviously enjoyed the tale. I then retired, and passed downstairs and out into the garden in face of the immense gathering awaiting the Queen. I found Ella; and Mrs. (now Lady) Gilchrist and Jock Cameron were the first to congratulate. We met so many friends whose welcome was amazing; it was good fun, too, to talk with people who had no inkling of what had happened and who learned of it from others later. After tea and much conversation, we drove the McKechnies home, and Sir James Fergusson to the New Club (he knew nothing about it). The McKechnies insisted on our joining them in a bottle of champagne. Then, after answering numerous newspaper queries, I left by car for Paisley in order to be in good time for the Queen's visit there tomorrow. I am writing this in my bedroom in the Paisley Club. No one knows anything of my news here as yet. It is nice to have been knighted at Holyrood; to see Ella's modesty and simple joy; and to realise the kindness of friends and the way they share our joy as before they shared our sorrow. One impression I retain of my visit to Holyrood – the extraordinarily attractive way in which the Queen and the Duke behaved towards each other: it left no doubt in my mind that theirs was a happy home.

25th June 1953 (Thursday)

I went to the Sheriff Court about ten o'clock and found 'Buggins' Young and Hunter, with respectively sister and wife. The good Mr. Barr gave us all a cup of tea. Then a car came to take us to Gilmour Street Station, and we smuggled Mr. Barr in with us, outwardly to lead us as bar officer, really to let him see the Queen. Sir Guy Shaw-Stewart (Lord Lieutenant) met us on the platform, and I was introduced to the ladies of his party, his wife and the wives of the two Deputy-Lieutenants. We waited about for a little, as two trains for the coast passed through (we were on the southmost platform). Then we lined up on the carpet and in came the Royal Train, a crimson affair, drawn by two large engines. Before the train had stopped, attendants jumped and began converging on the exit from the Queen's carriage, which, miraculously, stopped in the centre of the red carpet on the platform. A special set of steps was lowered from the side of the train. When all was ready, out came the Queen, followed by the Duke. She looked tired, but would scarcely be otherwise after (1) the national service (2) the investiture (3) the garden party (4) a dinner and (5) attendance at a Ball in the Music Hall, the previous day. She came quietly along the lines and shook hands with each of us. When she came to me, I stepped out and presented Buggins and Kenneth Hunter to her, and, in a flash, she was gone. The Duke followed in a more leisurely way, and in the same way I presented my two colleagues to him. He gave me a smile of recognition, and said, 'That wig must be very hot.' (It was my full-bottomed wig, and the temperature was reputed to be 80°.) He was followed by Sir Alan Lascelles, Pottinger and others who all gave me a kindly recognition; then they disappeared, and that ceremony was over. The platform was hotching with detectives.

We returned to the Sheriff Court, and after another cup of tea, and an interview with a Sheriff Officer, I set off with Kenneth Hunter, and Mr. Thomas Hunter (the doyen of the profession in Paisley) to the Brabloch Hotel, where the Honoraries, as it happened were entertaining me to lunch. It was quite a touching little function, such a welcome and kindness I received. I told them the story about reciting the verse about Gilchrist to the Queen, and I also recited to them the verse about Sir John Cheyne, my predecessor some way back as Procurator, who was the last Sheriff of Renfrew to be knighted. He was a very tall man, and was knighted by Queen Victoria on Midsummer's Day. I congratulated Mr. Hill, our respected Procurator-Fiscal, on his O.B.E. and drew attention to the fine spirit of co-operation, for Mr. Thomas Hunter had given up the chance of seeing the Queen to take the Small Debt Court and thereby release the Sheriffs to attend the presentation.

Afterwards, Mr. Walker, the Dean of Faculty, took me to see some records of Paisley Grammar School, whose prize-giving I am attending the week after next. Thereafter, I returned to the Sheriff Court to meet there Mr. Clarke, the Headmaster of the School, who was to brief me about his prize-giving. I then set out for home, calling in Glasgow for Harold on the way.

The hall-table at home was littered with greetings telegrams and Ella had answered incessant telephone rings all day.

28th June 1953 (Sunday)

On Friday, the 26th, I returned to Court, and got a great welcome. It took me an hour-and-a-half to cross the floor of Parliament House. At lunch, there was a special welcome from the Round Table, and the Dean, having already, years ago, invented the nicknames 'Puffin' and 'Sir Roundel', now suggested a new name for me 'Sir Cumference'. For the day, I found it hard to do any serious work. Ella is to be 'Lady Shrimp' (her nickname at school).

John Baillie sent me a delightful verse remembered from his schooldays, which he quoted to me at the Holyrood Garden Party. Queen Elizabeth summoned Drake to her presence and began by upbraiding him for the trouble his piracy on the high seas had caused. The poem ends:–

> He bowed his head. She rose a Queen
> A Queen to mar or make.
> 'My little pirate, rise,' said she,
> 'And be Sir Francis Drake.'

I remember my grandfather's indignation if anyone even uttered a whisper against Queen Victoria. That would be about 1911, when he was ninety, and I was eleven. I am beginning to understand the feeling. I learn now that the Queen was sick coming north in the train on Monday night. Yet she carried through her full programme.

On Friday evening, we were at the Reception at Holyroodhouse. It began at 10 p.m., and I was not in bed till 2 a.m. The Queen wore her Coronation dress, with the order and ribbon of the Thistle. We stood in the long dinner-room as she passed through her guests. The Duke of Edinburgh detached himself more informally from the procession, and lingered behind talking to friends. We stood beside the Drummond-Hays, father, son and daughter – they are an example of united friendliness. Miss Jane is a most charming frank little girl (she is taller than I am). We also met the Fergussons. Sir James's daughter is spoken of as a beauty, and she undoubtedly has a languid charm, but, for me, vivacity matters more. Her mother hung about in the background, I should judge, a bit of a tartar. Sir James could not be more friendly. W.G. Pottinger came up to me and said: 'I hear you were reciting verse to the Queen. She enjoyed it greatly, and you are going to be asked for a copy!'

When I went home, I wrote a letter to Sir Alan Lascelles sending the verse (about Gilchrist), and also the verse about Sir John Cheyne, and I also enclosed a copy of my little Gordon book, asking permission to offer it to the Queen. He was a year younger than she, just as Alison is a year younger than Princess Margaret. The more I recall it, the more pleasure I get from the investiture having taken place in Holyroodhouse, and in its loveliest room. It was a kind thought, and I shrewdly suspect that either David Milne (who once thanked me warmly for what I had done) or Sir Charles Cunningham had suggested that the ceremony should take place there and on that memorable day.

All the newspapers are enthusiastic about the National Service. But in conversation, two criticisms are made, with both of which I agree. The first is that the Queen came in informal dress. I am glad, at least, that I advised against this course, when asked by the Scottish Office. Both their view (the officials at least) and mine was that the Queen should wear a tiara, formal dress, and (I thought) some kind of mantle or train (I would have liked the Coronation robe had that been possible, and said so, but probably its train was too long). She looked a little insignificant alongside even her robed High Constable, the Countess of Erroll. Everything seems to point to Winston having wished to play down her part, but there was no constitutional issue involved in this. For some reason or other, possibly because he was thrown out at Dundee, he does not like the Scots. His public references to them recently over the Coronation question have been unkind, and in marked contrast with his studied anxiety to overcome the scruples of Malta. Undoubtedly, there has been restiveness in Scotland, particularly over the numeral in the Queen's title, but Scottish opinion was never properly consulted, and even so it is not for him to be petty. He must have known, or should have, that there were big hearts in Scotland. Many loyal Conservatives here have been much distressed by his deliberate lack of understanding. How different was the Archbishop. The second criticism of the service relates to the choice of some of the music. The preliminary music could not have been bettered. But 'Caithness', though a period piece, is not much of a tune, and was, because of its unfamiliarity, quite unsuitable for congregational singing for the 60th Paraphrase. The prose Psalm which followed was quite lovely; but it meant that two items of praise were supported only by the choir, and the real tradition of Scottish congregational singing was not disclosed until we reached 'O Worship the King'. How many people know that the hymn was written by a Scotsman, the ancestor of a recent Scottish G.O.C. 'This Sanctuary of my Soul' should have been sung to Charles Wood's setting, and not Herrick Bunney's. I have heard, I am glad to say, no serious criticism of the seating arrangements and representation at the service, for which (as I had much to do with it) I am truly thankful. The newspapers recognise that a real effort was made to make the congregation truly representative. Many of the papers have made reference to my part in this.

2nd July 1953

It was a curious accident at the National Service last week that the Primus of the Episcopal Church, Bishop Hannay, who read the second lesson, was a relative of Dean Hannay, at whom Jenny Geddes threw her historic stool in 1638, and on this occasion had with the rest of the Congregation to share in the vow extracted from the National Covenant and made part of the service!

I made my first appearance in Court today as a knight, and was congratulated by the Justice-Clerk. The cases were two big estate duty cases affecting life-policies of all the Life Assurance Companies. The Dean and M.G. Gillies were for one party; Ronald Morison, myself, and Gillies for the other; and Bill Milligan (as Sol.-Gen.) and Grieve for the Revenue. There was much chaffing, and it was strange hearing my new name being mentioned in the arguments.

18th July 1953

The Round Table are giving me a dinner in honour of my knighthood and my devils are entertaining Ella, Alison and myself to another dinner. Yesterday George Morton died of heart failure after an operation. Calver, his brother-in-law, appealed to me to arrange for a minister to take the funeral. He had been a member of the Church of Scotland, but latterly had lapsed. 'T.P.' not inaccurately described George as the finest 'non-church-going Christian' he knew. It is sad that a man so wonderfully demonstrating practical Christianity should have lost his contact with the Church and be left without friend to bury him. I asked James Stewart to stand in. Calver and the *Scotsman* both asked me to write an appreciation of George, and this I gladly did. He was a great soul. This evening I have been at the dinner of the Grotius Society, which is meeting in Edinburgh. I sat between Walter Raeburn Q.C., and Tom Smith, who was my host. Afterwards, Tom, Harald Leslie, Ian Robertson, and Archie Campbell (Professor) adjourned to my house. The chairman at the dinner was Sir Patrick Spens, a nephew of John A. Spens of Glasgow, and Sir Arnold McNair (who welcomed me) also spoke. The other week, the Central Land Board met in Edinburgh, and I received their congratulations. I took Dame Myra Curtis, Sir Basil Gibson and Mr. MacDonald to lunch, and as Dame Myra and Mr. MacDonald were at a loose end in the afternoon, I motored them to Peebles. In the evening the Board gave a sherry party to Scottish representative men connected with its work. Sir David Milne and Sir Charles Cunningham were most kind to me, and I shrewdly suspect that they were responsible for my receiving my knighthood at Holyrood on the afternoon of the National Service.

This week I attended an inspection of various sites in Edinburgh likely to prove suitable for the proposed new National Museum of Antiquities. Previously, we had considered a site to the west of Hunter Square, and two other sites further down the High Street, none of them very suitable. This time we inspected a site at the Lawnmarket, between the High Street and Victoria Terrace, which though attractive in situation proved too small. Then, in drenching rain, we inspected the corner site at the west end of the south side of Chambers Street, west of the Royal Scottish Museum. This is sufficiently large, and had much to recommend it. Provisionally, we agreed that this seemed the best available site. It has a superficial area of about 38,000 feet, with some additional space to the south for further extension.

22nd July 1953

Some time ago, the Scottish Office asked me whether, as Sheriff, I had any objection to the final closing of Inverary Court. I replied that, while the Court there could no longer be used for Sheriff Court purposes, I strongly urged that the Circuit Court should not be abolished, but transferred to Oban, which was a much better centre for road, rail, and steamer, had an adequate court with police premises adjoined, and the accommodation for judges, counsel, jurors, officials, and witnesses, which Inverary now lacked. I also spoke to the Jus-tice-General, who was enthusiastic, promised to take up the proposal at once, and said that he would preside at the first Circuit. Tonight

Miss Connor of Scottish Home Department told me that the Treasury, for its interest, had approved. It will please Argyll to retain a circuit town.

Last night my three 'devils' gave me, Ella and Alison dinner at the Albyn Rooms in honour of my knighthood. John Wilson took one end of the table with Ella, then Ronald Kydd, then Alison on his right. Arthur Matheson took the other end with Nan Wilson, then myself, then Mavis Kydd on his right. Our healths were proposed by John Wilson. I replied and later proposed our hosts. Arthur Matheson read this piece of verse, which he had composed that afternoon in half-an-hour. He has a great gift of expression:–

> Fates are unequal; life is fraught
> With varying lots and levels;
> Shepherds and sheep; teachers and taught;
> The masters and the devils.
>
> Who trains a devil must display
> Vast skill, forbearance vaster –
> And with vast gratitude today
> Three devils hail their master.
>
> A sword, on shrieval scapulae
> Descending, gives a handle;
> He knelt as Sheriff J.R.P.
> And then arose Sir Randall.
>
> Yet now we see him as before
> With his old friends consorting
> Amongst the devilish crew once more
> Convivially cavorting.
>
> Such kindly grace, human and bright,
> How can one laud it rightly?
> It makes the nobleman – or knight –
> Thrice noble – or twice knightly.
>
> And so, Sir Randall, knight indeed
> Grant our united motion;
> Accept your magisterial meed
> Of devilish devotion.

It was a most enjoyable evening, and their kindness to each of us was touching. Today I was telling Tommy Cooper about it, whereupon he said: 'My devils never gave me a dinner!' To which I replied: 'Ha! ha! The elder brother.' He smilingly admitted the impeachment. He also said that the number of those who had been invited, and had declined, the Principalship of St. Andrews University would, laid head to toes, stretch from St. Andrews to Dundee!

25th July 1953 (Saturday)

Last night there happened what I rather feared. Hamish Clyde offered me the vacant Sheriffdom of Aberdeen, Kincardine and Banff. I asked for a night to think over it, and this evening went round to see Hamish Clyde. The salary is £100 more, and the records show that there are only half the number of appeals, compared with Renfrew and Argyll. But I felt it wrong to accept. There have been too many quick changes recently in Argyll, five Sheriffs before me in about fifteen years. Renfrew has been starved of a Sheriff who took an active interest in the county, and I know that I am really beginning to reap the fruit of work done in the past five years to bring the Sheriff more into the life of the counties as he should be. To leave now, for another Sheriff, would set back all the good of the work done. So, for the second time, I asked leave to decline, though I made it plain to Hamish that, if he still considered I should go, I would. But, after hearing what I had to say, he fully understood my decision. I was greatly helped in a difficult decision by Ella, who (I know rightly) came down definitely in favour of Renfrew and Argyll. I wonder if anyone yet has, in the space of five years, had or had the chance of Renfrew, Argyll, the Lothians and Peebles, Aberdeen, Kincardine and Banff!

29th July 1953 (Wednesday)

Alison returned home today, having been in Oxford last week – the 24th – for her 'viva'. She stayed with Mary and Jim Galbraith in London, and spent the weekend with them and their parents at Aldeburgh. Today a wire came from Oxford for Alison with the short but encouraging message 'Class Two'. We all had a coffee in Browns on the strength of it – then met Douglas Duncan, also awaiting his results, with an American friend Peter, from Philadelphia. Tomorrow, we leave for our summer holiday. Rosemary is again top of her class at S. Monica's, with a perfectly lovely school report.

21st September 1953 (Monday)

Our summer holiday led us to sleep in at least fifteen different beds. We set off on 30th July for a tour round the North of Scotland, staying a night at each of Dalwhinnie, Bonar Bridge, John O'Groats, Melvich, Scourie, Lochinver, Ullapool, and Inverness (Inshes). Then we spent a fortnight at the Grey House, Nethybridge, a week at the Dell, Rothiemurchus, and a long weekend at The Lodge Hotel, Newton-more. After a night in Glasgow to let me broadcast in 'My faith and my work: By Queen's Counsel', Ella, Rosemary and I went on, first, to Dunoon for an appeal, and then to Oban for Sheriff's business there and an appeal at Campbeltown to which I motored for the day.

It was fascinating to return to the North of Scotland, where I had not been by road since 1913. Then we motored over dreadful roads in an old Darracq, which boiled over on every hill; we had sometimes to back about a mile so that another vehicle could pass; at other times, we chased sheep for miles along the road before they had cause to turn aside; then the Kylesku ferry was pulled across the narrows by a chain, hand-wound and ran only at the ferryman's pleasure at the cost of a pound. Now, the roads are, except in three places, excellent, and though narrow have ample passing places; the sheep have learned road sense; and, a month before we were there, a new £5,000 ferry had been put on the Kylesku passage, and takes cars over regularly at a cost of nil. We were blessed with almost continuous superb clear weather, saw the Dornoch peninsula laid out in sunshine before us and the Pentland Firth as blue as the Mediterranean and crystal clear. The views of Hoy from Melvich, too, were lovely; and, from Scourie, we could see, forty miles off, the whole of Lewis. Gruinard Bay, in sunshine, and Little Loch Broom, with its plentiful rowans, were also memorable. At the Portland Arms, Lybster, we fell in, at lunchtime, with the Justice-Clerk and Gracie Thomson who were staying there for fishing. I visited Morison of Canisbay's memorial at Canisbay, and we saw the Queen Mother's Castle of Mey. We had coffee with the Quarry Woods at Dunnet. Melvich was our favourite hotel, with the rather ambitious Culag at Lochinver second. We found a lovely little modernised croft – sea view – to stay in at Scourie. We called on, but missed, the Birnams at Kinlochbervie. At Ullapool, we fell in with the James Stewarts, and then with the Dean, who presented me with a walking-stick and entertained us to sherry. The Grey House at Nethybridge was a great success; as also was the Lodge at New-tonmore. We had a violent gale for our journey to Dunoon, but thereafter the most superb weather at Oban. Amongst new (or old) friends we met at the Grey House were a Mr. and Mrs. Martin from Kilmacolm, and their son Graham who had just got a First in English at Oxford; Mr. and Mrs. Andrew Young (he is Glasgow manager of the Royal Bank); the Rev. David and Mrs. Souter from Tayport (he was at the University with me); and Mr. W.R. Herdman, and their two children, from Murrayfield; and, above all, the Nevile Davidsons – all delightful companions. Mrs. Young and Mrs. Souter, sisters, were daughters of the late Mr. Murray Little, solicitor, of Annan, who used to employ me as a junior. At the Dell, we met the D.C. Munros; and at the Lodge Dr. John Sturrock and family. At Oban we met Judge Batt, formerly Professor of Commercial Law at Liverpool, and now a County Court Judge near Manchester, who knew the Thankertons; Mr. Figgures, a Treasury official, who was touring the Highlands with John Anderson of Scottish Home Department; Lady Starmer, from Darlington, a friend of many of my Durham friends, especially Mrs. Rawlinson; and Mr. J.B. Adshead (in his ninetieth year) formerly Secretary of the Royal Bank, a close neighbour of Tommy Cooper in Hermitage Drive.

On my journey from Oban to Campbeltown – I started at 7.30 a.m. – I saw no fewer than three buzzards close to the road, usually on telegraph poles. Also herons were plentiful that day, and another afternoon, when we motored to Crinan Ferry. The Trinity House *Patricia* was lying in Oban Bay when we arrived. One day we met Lord and Lady Stevenson in Oban, and they came and had lunch with us. Another day, I presided at a little ceremony at the Oban Sheriff Court when Mr. J.J. Bonar, W.S. of Edinburgh, presented a miniature bust of his grand-uncle, Sheriff Cleghorn of Argyll (son-in-law of Lord Cockburn) to Mr. Milne, as Dean for the Oban Faculty of Procurators. This gift was arranged at my suggestion.

Since then, I have paid two visits to London. The first was for the Central Land Board and War Damage Commission. But, in the afternoon, I went to the College of Arms in Queen Victoria Street, and signed the Roll of Knights Bachelor in Garter King's office. My name appears on the same page as Colonel Sir John Hunt's, of Everest fame. The College of Arms is the last building standing to the south of St. Paul's before the great 'blitzed' area begins. I had an interesting talk with Mr. Verco, Garter's secretary, as to the meaning of 'accolade'. In the end, he looked up the word in the Oxford Dictionary, and found that it means (1) a kiss, (2) an embrace, or (3) a slap on the shoulder. I decided that it was the third which the Queen gave me, in the form of a gentle tap on each shoulder!

Ballachulish Ferry

The second visit, less than a week later, was to Trinity House for a Conference of the three Lighthouse Authorities on wages. Captain Hubbard (T.H.) presided, and, afterwards, we were lunched by the Brethren, Captain Chaplin in the chair. I sat on his left, and, on my left, was a Captain from the Orient Line. The Deputy Master welcomed us on arrival, and we were shown over the magnificent premises which are to be opened by the Queen next month. The portraits were of special interest to me, especially one of the Prince Consort, which really showed what he was like. Captain Chaplin had been preparing material for a history of Trinity House, but it was all destroyed in the blitz. Maconochie was my fellow-Commissioner, and Glen Walcelin and Simpson, the Deputy Secretary, were also there.

When we were at Nethybridge, we met Tom Simpson and his

Loch Faskally, Pitlochry

brother, Robin. Ella asked, 'Was his sister not with them?' Quick as lightning, Tom Simpson made a characteristic reply: 'No – we're having a holiday!' He also told me that Tommy Cooper had again declined the Lordship of Appeal, and that he had seen the letter.

Today's *Scotsman*, however, reported that it was expected that Lord Cooper would be appointed as a Lord of Appeal, while the present Lord Advocate, Clyde, would be the new Lord President. The newspaper expressed the belief that Lord Cooper had hesitated for some time about whether or not to accept the post of Lord of Appeal. It was thought that he had perhaps been influenced by the thought that, if he declined, Scotland might lose the opportunity of having two representatives among the Lords of Appeal. I believe that Tommy Cooper is very annoyed about it!

I had the following characteristic note today from Tommy Cooper:–

Parliament House,
Edinburgh, 1.
19th Sept. 1953

My dear Philip,

Following correspondence with the the Scottish Office and the Town
Council of Inverary and Oban I am proposing an Act of Adjournal when
the Court meets transferring the Circuit Centre from Inverary to Oban.
Inverary were querulous, but after soothing treatment they have acquiesced, realising that there will never be another Circuit at Inverary
whatever happens.

Yours
T.M.C.

This last week, I have been working at perhaps the highlight of all
my practice, a Memorial regarding questions affecting the Balmoral
Estates, on behalf of the Trustees for Her Majesty the Queen.

James Walker has been made Sheriff of Aberdeen; and Hector
McKechnie Sheriff of Inverness. The latter is well due a Sheriffship,
for he is a fine lawyer in the best tradition of scholarship, as well as
a forthright counsel.

Tomorrow, I go to Inverness to address the Inverness Officebearers'
Association, and show my film, on 'Lund'. I am staying with Mr. J.D.
Michael, O.B.E., at Achtemarack, Drumnadrochit.

29th September 1953 (Tuesday)

I had a lovely visit to the North. Mr. Michael turned out to have been
an exact contemporary, and I must have played golf with him forty
years ago at Kingussie. He took a B.Sc. (Engineering) at Edinburgh,
and went into civil engineering in India, ultimately becoming manager
of an Indian Railway. About 1946, the railway wanted to have an
Indian in the senior position, and he willingly resigned, as he wanted
to return home. On his return to Scotland, he studied farming in
Kintyre for almost a year, and then bought Achtemarack – 'The place
of the Shamrock' (or wood-sorrel). He invited me out for a meal
before my Inverness meeting. Achtemarack was an amazing surprise.
You branch up Glenurquhart, and after two miles, beyond the Kiltarlity road, turn right up a steep track, like an Italian mule track.
Three miles up, 750 feet high, on a ledge of grassy bank, almost an
Alp, stands the place of the wood-sorrel, two cottages on a croft of

300 acres (40 arable). Stretched beneath is the Glen, sometimes, as I saw it next morning, with a wisp of woolly mist folded in the valley; to the east Loch Ness, and the hills beyond Errogie; to the west, Glen Affric, whose hills, snow clad in winter, remind Mr. Michael of the Himalayas. The cottage, in which he and his wife (a daughter of Dr. Main, formerly of Trinity College Church, Edinburgh and Paisley Abbey) live, is being modernised. It now has water, and most modern heating and cooking arrangements; electricity, from the North of Scotland Board, is still to come. It was strange to see this comfortable Highland cottage thickly laid with Persian rugs. Mr. Michael is gradually putting this previously almost derelict holding back into full production, with cattle, sheep, hens; and yielding now sufficient food for himself and his wife – butter, milk, meat, home-made scones, oatcakes. It was an inspiration to sense the vitality and vivacity which came to them from living close to the land amongst the Highland Hills. He runs the croft himself, with a grieve and the latter's wife, and must be the most intelligent, energetic and cultivated 'crofter' in Scotland. His faith is in regaining marginal land by crofting aided by capital, not by large landholding. His interest in the Church is also inspiring. His one holiday in the year is spent at the General Assembly, and he told me, and I saw evidence of it, that the whole glen is a church-going people. Mr. Macleod, his minister (the parish minister), a native of Lewis, had the church full, and he and the Free Church minister, also a live wire, work in close cooperation. Mr. Macleod, whom I met, told me that the arrival of Mr. Michael in the parish was like a gift from God.

When, in the evening, Mr. Michael took me to my meeting, I was astounded at the gathering. He tells me it was the largest they have had, Ness Bank Hall being full – and the elders being drawn not just from Inverness, but places like Kiltarlity, Glenurquhart, Invermoriston, Glen Affric and Petty – all come to hear about the Lund Conference. I met the Rev. Mr. Macleod of Petty, whom I last saw forty years ago, when he, a postman just turned minister, and then assistant at St. John's, Dundee, came out to preach at Invergowrie, and remembered me as a 'slim handsome youth'. *Tempora mutantur, et nos in illis*! Dr. Macdonald, the Rector of Inverness Academy, took the chair. He reminded me of Principal Knox of St. Andrews, and one had only to hear him to realise his gift of judgment and expression. There were many intelligent questions, and a lucid informative speech from the Rev. Peter Fraser, who would have put many Church leaders to shame. Next morning, as we were driving in to Inverness to catch the south-going train, we stopped at the roadside and spoke to a man driving cows along the road: he, too, was at the meeting. Where would you find such people but in Scotland, and in its country districts.

The news is published today that Oban is to be a new circuit town in place of Inverary.

Last week there died a former Premier of Queensland, Mr. Forgan Smith. He was the son of a gardener at Mylnefield, Invergowrie, one of my father's elders and a 'praying elder' at that. I remember, as a boy, a visit from this old man, with his mutton-chop whiskers, and beard. The son became a painter to trade, emigrated to Australia, and ended up as Prime Minister. When he returned to Scotland, and received the Freedom of Glasgow in the City Chambers, he told the company assembled in the hall: 'The last visit I paid this hall was when I came to paint it!' He used to come and visit Dad when in the country, and I remember him several times at Greenhill Gardens, once when he met a number of friends and made a short speech. Each year, too, a Christmas card came from him to his old minister.

Last Saturday, at the wedding of Tommy Macpherson (youngest son of Sir Stewart Macpherson of Newtonmore), I met Lord Normand. He told me that there was, as far as he knew, nothing in the *Scotsman* Report of 21st September that Tommy Cooper was, after all, going to the House of Lords. He asked me: 'Who is to be my successor?' I said that frankly I did not know, and he seemed not to know either. He thought that it would not likely yet be Master of the Rolls (Evershed). I said that I had heard Devlin's name mentioned (though he is still only a puisne judge). Normand said: 'Yes, he is a good judge.' Normand is singularly undemonstrative and uneffusive. Life must have a chill atmosphere for Giant Despair. He looks old; though singularly fit.

18th October 1953 (Sunday)

On the 14th Alison left for London, Oxford, and later Paris and the Sorbonne. She took her degree at Oxford on the 15th, and this week-end is staying in London with the Willmers, while she attended yesterday Eleanor Forshaw's wedding.

I have to be in London again myself on the 20th and 21st. I am taking Alison to Lambeth for tea on the 20th, and on to the big Bible week service in St. Paul's. On the 21st I represent the Northern Lighthouse Board at the opening of the new Trinity House by the Queen.

25th October 1953 (Sunday)

After a busy afternoon last Monday at the Church's legal sub-committee, a rush through to Glasgow, and an address to Alan Robson's Kelvinside Congregational meeting, I caught the 10.30 p.m. train from Glasgow Central to Euston. Pitt Watson and his wife were on my train, and Nevile Davidson on the earlier 10.20 p.m. We also had a mild laugh over Alan Robson: he is an 'ecclesiastical Bunthorne'.

I stayed (for the first time) at the Athenæum. Amongst other British Council delegates there were Dr. Hugh Martin, the Bishop of Sheffield and Sir Andrew Clow. I met the last for the first time, and we went on to our meeting together. This time we met in the Bishop Partridge Hall, Church House, and whether the place was overheated or not, the discussion was the most tame and sleep-producing: in fact, I had a nap. In the afternoon, I met Alison at 4.00, and after a light refreshment and a visit to Westminster Hall, we set off for Lambeth. We were welcomed by Mrs. Fisher on the stair, and in the great hall by the Archbishop. He was so kind and friendly as always, twice coming up to me and having a little conversation, first about feeling in Scotland over the Coronation, and later about the wonderful restoration of Lambeth Library. What interested me most in the great hall were the portraits of the seventeenth and eighteenth century Archbishops – from Laud even down to Manners Sutton in the nineteenth. I was particularly interested in Laud, Juxon, Sancroft and Manners Sutton (who seemed unduly young). Laud is an unattractive face, I should judge, a man fond of arranging things, but not of meeting his fellows. The Archbishop made a witty speech of welcome referring to Juxon who, after attending Charles I to the scaffold, as Bishop of London, retired to Gloucestershire and became a Master of Fox Hounds, returning at the Restoration to become Archbishop of Canterbury. I was sorry not to see portraits of the recent Archbishops.

From Lambeth, we proceeded to St. Paul's by buses for the service opening the great Bible campaign. There were five lessons, the last two, the Epistle and the Gospel, being read by the Moderator (Pitt Watson) and the Archbishop respectively. We heard all the scripture readings perfectly. But I only managed to make out one sentence of the Bishop of London's sermon, and all those whom I spoke to in the Choir had the same experience.

After lunch, I set off for Trinity House, where I found that Glen Wakelin and myself had been given quite excellent seats in the Library in the third row immediately before the platform. Glen was on my left, and a Sir George Christopher on my right. Of the platform party,

Lady Churchill was the first to arrive. She smiled professionally, but has a rather hard face. Mrs. Attlee, who came later, is much more attractive and unsophisticated. Then came the general party, amongst them Winston, Attlee, Lord Alexander, Lord Templewood, Mr. Thomas (the First Lord), and then the Duke and Duchess of Gloucester, the Duke of Edinburgh and the Queen. Poor old Winston – he shuffled across the polished floor, had to be helped up the one step on to the platform, and then slumped down breathless in his chair, only showing signs of real life after about three minutes. His colour was transparent, and he left on my mind the impression that he would not survive long, certainly not another year.

The Duke of Gloucester, dressed as Master of Trinity House, invited the Queen to perform the opening ceremony. It was interesting to watch her movements. She took a little handbag off the arm of her chair, opened it, extracted her speech from within (its only content), quietly unfolded it, laid down the bag on the chair and then approached the microphone to speak. Her voice, as always, was calm and clear, a gentle soprano conversational tone, every syllable of which would reach every corner of the Hall. Finally, Captain Curtess, the Deputy-Master, thanked the Queen, and a prayer was offered by the Chaplain. The Queen wore a little emerald feather hat, a quiet grey-blue coat, and black gloves. She looked charming.

While the Royalties were being shown around Trinity House, we remained in the Hall, and I was introduced to practically all the ordinary elder brethren. Then we went to the Court-room for refreshments, where the Queen and all the principal guests were also being entertained. There I met a number of interesting people. Sir Roderick McGregor and with him I think the Second Sea Lord, the head of the Ministry of Transport, Mr. Burleigh (the Secretary [a brother of Prof. J.H.S. Burleigh]), and many others. The refreshments took the form of afternoon tea, until her Majesty entered at one end of the room, whereupon bottles of champagne were seen to be arriving at the other end, and we soon reached a second and slightly more convivial stage in the festivities.

In the evening, Alison came to dinner to the Caledonian Club, and with her Mr. Justice Willmer and Lady Willmer, with whom she is staying. We had a happy evening, and then they drove me to King's Cross, where I said good-bye to Alison before she leaves for the Sorbonne.

Although I have scarcely mentioned the Bar, I have been in Court almost every day that I have not been away from Edinburgh, and only today I have finished an opinion dating from July. I have still two other July opinions to do, so I am heavily in arrears. This does not mean that I have not been working: on the contrary, I have been working continuously since my return from holiday, and certain work has to receive priority. But it gives some idea of the present pressures of work.

The latest rumour, which I think must now have substance to it, is that Keith is to go to the House of Lords, Bill Milligan to go on the bench in his place, and Gordon Thomson to replace Bill as Solicitor-General.

30th October 1953

Lord Keith's appointment as Lord of Appeal was announced on the 27th. I understand that Bill Milligan's elevation to the Bench was expected to be announced today. They should both be popular. James Keith, at sixty-seven, is extraordinarily youthful in appearance and spirit, able and independent, the product of a purely Scottish education, Hamilton Academy and a First in History at Glasgow University. He has a fine legal imagination, and, throughout, his promotion owed nothing to politics and everything to his own merit. Bill Milligan is a hard worker, a plodder in the best sense, and a gay and loveable personality – essentially a low-brow, almost aggressively so, but with more substance than he would ever claim. Even if politics have promoted him rather before his merits as a lawyer would have done, that does not mean that his appointment will not be universally popular.

Last Sunday, 1,400 took Communion at St. George's West, the largest number in my twenty-seven years of membership.

After two days hearing appeals in Greenock, on Wednesday I went with Beattie, to represent the National Library at the funeral of W.R. Cunningham, former Librarian of Glasgow University. It was my first visit to the University Chapel in Glasgow, which has been completed since I was a student. It is impressive, though the Gothic of Gilbert Scott does not altogether appeal to me. Cunningham was a remarkable man – he was an animated 'Who's Who'; a great enthusiast, devoted to every University activity. He had been a Trustee since the foundation of the National Library and Convener of the Books and MSS Committee, and took a great load of work. My relations with him were always happy: just last week when dying, he wrote a most kind little letter:– 'Many thanks indeed for your unfailing support. I much admired your tact and understanding on many occasions.' I shall miss his strong vital personality greatly.

Hamish Clyde told me today that the conferment of my knighthood at Holyrood was by the special arrangement of the Queen; he instanced it as an example of Her Majesty's instinct for the right occasion. Another instance he gave was that, after the parade of the 1st Argylls at Holyrood in June, the Queen deliberately congratulated the two senior Argylls officers in front of a Colonel of the Scots Guards!

22nd November 1953

To everyone's astonishment, Gordon Thomson, and not Bill Milligan, was elevated to the Bench. He told me beforehand that he was taking a territorial title. There was a Thomson already on the Bench. Skibo he could not take because that would have been discourteous to his mother-in-law. He has chosen 'Migdale' a small hamlet and fishing loch on the estate. To me it calls up midges and cleggs. The wits of the Bar have already converted it into Pigtail, and say that Chinese cases (!) are to be assigned to him. The President told me that he had suggested Embo, which would have been a known name, with character in it. But, undoubtedly, Tom Simpson's suggestion was the most ingenious – Lord Clashmore! Gordon Thomson is a decent soul, but without much of the finer sensibility. He may make a good working Clydesdale, but will never be an Arab stud. When at the age of forty, he married Louise Carnegie (granddaughter of Andrew Carnegie) it was described in Parliament House as 'the union of the sweet seventeen to the roaring Forties' (he has a loud voice). His appointment is, I think it fair to say, partly political; but he should make a solid judge, though he has not the finer points of the law. I was his fellow apprentice, thirty years ago, in Maclay, Murray and Spens, and we have always been on good, though not exactly intimate, terms, for his slightly Napoleonic manner is not exactly to my taste. He suffered a devastating loss when his wife died in two days of poliomyelitis, leaving five little children all eight or under. Four of them were at the installation, all dressed alike in kilts of Macdonald tartan, three little girls and one, the youngest, a little boy. There was an air of poignancy which we all felt. The eldest, who is now at Sherborne, could not be there. I made my first appearance before him two days later.

Incidentally, during this week, I heard the latest nickname for the President – 'Plumber's mate!' This is because of his extraordinary propensity for attending to all repairs, electrical and otherwise, required in Parliament House. It is strange that the most distinguished and scholarly judge we have had for many a day should have so undistinguished an appearance. Yet his well formed head marks him out, and the moment he speaks, one realises his true stature.

This week has been a busy one for me. On Friday a week ago I was in London at the Central Land Board and War Damage Commission. On last Sunday, I motored to Oban, with Mr. W.R. Milne, W.S., Chairman of the Church of Scotland General Trustees, Mr. Hay Downie, General Treasurer of the Church, and Mr. Mercer Robertson, Solicitor of the Church, to examine, and hold discussions over, the proposal to erect a church at Corrievore with the funds of Miss Ann McCaig's Trust, the last of the famous McCaig Trusts. They are a very competent team – the Church is well-served by them; it would be difficult to find better men for their job. We stayed till Tuesday, and that evening I returned home in superb moonlight with Mr. Milne.

On Wednesday, I was at the Commission of Assembly. On Thursday I was invited to the Installation of the new Principal (T.M. Knox) at St. Andrews University. I travelled with the President and the Editor of the *Scotsman*, with whom I had good fun, since I had launched a Sherlock Holmes correspondence in the *Scotsman* to commemorate the centenary of Holmes' birth, which 'took place' in 1854! As we passed Kinghorn, the President became quite lyrical, recalling holidays spent there as a child of five or six, and the fun he got from running up to the railway station to fetch daily the *Scotsman* for the house. He has, in the best sense, the mind of a child, and that is what makes him, though a bachelor, so understanding to children. He discussed 'Dalginch' mentioned in *Regiam Majestatem*, but untraceable now on the map, and said that he had found old lands of that name near Markinch. We were joined at Thornton by Professor J.D. Mackie of Glasgow and Sir Ernest Wedderburn. At St. Andrews, the former Rector, Sir George Cunningham, took away Cooper, and the rest of us went by a University car to United College, where I robed, and then proceeded to the Chapel. The Chapel service was most impressive. I was just sorry that, in a new era for the University which is to include both St. Andrews and Dundee, the prayer referred only to St. Andrews. It was a small error, but showed that the old spirit has still to die. The unforgettable features of the service were the Anthem 'O where shall Wisdom be found?' (Dr. William Boyce) sung by the students' choir, with a superb soprano and equally superb tenor (you could see the two throwing their whole souls into their singing); the reading of the Gospel (Matt. 25:14–30) by Lord Crawford (the Rector);

and the exquisite fourfold Amen at the conclusion of the Benediction. We were transported to the Scores Hotel for lunch, where my table-companions were Dr. Rankin (of Holy Trinity), Mr. C.D. Carlow (of the Fife Coal Co.), and a Mr. G.M. Thomson, whom I afterwards discovered to be Labour M.P. for Dundee West. Tom Johnston, in a romantic speech, proposed 'The University' to which the new Principal replied in a serious vein. In the absence of the Press, he discussed the two great difficulties facing the University: (1) the ending of the St. Andrews-Dundee dispute (which he described as a short-term problem [I hope it may be]) and (2) the difficulty of keeping the numbers of students sufficiently large. It was a true and realistic speech.

We then proceeded to the Younger Hall, on the journey to which Tom Taylor was my companion. There, amid the usual rowdy scenes, the Induction of the Principal took place. The singing of 'Gaudeamus Igitur' was impressive, but otherwise the students sang everything to hymn-tunes for some unaccountable reason, instead of using the Students' Song Book, which was born in St. Andrews. Professor Rose's promotion of the LL.D.s. – Lord Cooper and Tom Johnston – was as bad as Professor Baxter's presentation of the D.D.s – Bishop Burrowes and the Rev. J.F. Marshall of Aberdalgie – was good. The Marshall promotion could not have been better; but Professor Rose showed inexcusable ignorance of his subject, especially in relation to the President. The Principal's induction address was admirably statesmanlike, and promises well for the future of both St. Andrews and Dundee.

We returned home by the 5.05 p.m. train – Sir Ernest Wedderburn, the Editor of the *Scotsman*, Professor Mackie, Dr. J.R. Peddie and I. I had a long talk with Dr. Peddie on the way home. He asked me about a new Chairman for the Carnegie Trust, to succeed Sir John Falconer, and mentioned the President and the Dean (the latter of whom is already a Trustee). I strongly supported the latter, thinking he would make the more dependable chairman. The President would want to run the whole show, and take over Peddie's own work!

The National Museum of Antiquities Bill carrying into effect the recommendations of my Committee is published this week.

6th December 1953 (Sunday)

The last two evenings I have been twice toasted. On Friday evening I was in Dundee at the High School Old Boys' Club dinner for the first time as Hon. President of the Club. It was good to meet so many school-friends. Hugh Carlton proposed my health. I stayed with Leslie Weatherhead, and travelled to Dundee with his eldest son, James, Senior President of Edinburgh University Students' Representative Council.

Then last night the Round Table dined me at the Scotia Hotel. The Dean took the chair, and the party consisted of Blades, Boyd Berry, James Walker, T.P. McDonald, John Wheatley, George Reid, John Wilson, Frank Duffy, and our new (and excellent) member, Irvine Smith. The Dean proposed my health in a delightfully kind speech, comparing me with Henry Cockburn! and with Falstaff! (last time it was Mr. Pickwick!). John Wilson had set at my place this quotation: 'I have more flesh than another man, and therefore more faculty' [*Henry IV, Part I*]; and the Dean read *Henry IV, Part I*, Act 2, Scene 4, 438–50 (Dover Wilson's edition). Everyone spoke, and, in addition to my reply to the toast, I showed them my colour cinematograph films of the Spithead Review. They also want to see my Journal. So, at a preliminary sherry party in my house, I showed them the two folios which I so far have written. Then they believed me that the Journal did, in fact, exist. It was a jolly evening, filled with the most intimate friendship.

Today I have unveiled a plaque to the memory of Dr. John White at St. John's Extension Charge, Whitecraig, in the parish of Inveresk. David Stiven conducted the service, as parish minister. The young assistant also took part, a Rev. Mr. Ogilvie, from North Carolina, U.S.A. By strange chance, my address concluded with the account of the Gettysburg Oration – only 263 words long – as told by Truslow Adams. Mr. Ogilvie was delighted, and said any Southerner would approve of what I said about President Abe.

13th December 1953 (Sunday)

We had dinner on Friday evening at the University Club with the Birnams and the Garretts. Lord Birnam told me that he remembered Charles Warr, as a boy, playing the organ in his father's church. Later, Charles Warr came to see King Murray (as he then was) to ask his advice on whether he should go to the Bar or into the Church.

Charles Warr recently consulted me about applying for a colleague and successor. The application has now been announced. He wants as on the last occasion to have three outside consultants to aid St. Giles' in the selection of the new minister. He would like me as one, Pitt Watson as another, and the third he has not yet decided on. We discussed various names as possible choices. It was of course not a considered list, but ones that I mentioned were A.M. Hunter of Aberdeen (who would be ideal if he would let his name go forward), David Read, and John R. Gray of St. Stephen's-Buccleuch, whom John White described to me as 'the ablest young minister in Glasgow'. He asked me what I thought of Stewart McWilliam, Beechgrove, Aberdeen, but I said that I did not think this was quite the work for him. I mentioned also John Lusk of Uphall. I think Tom Taylor had desired him as Chaplain to Aberdeen University. He was a scholar of Winchester, and in many ways suitable, but I know nothing of his preaching. I have, however, a great regard for his father, and there is much ability in the family, though, I think, the father's manner suffered somewhat from a slight formality and tendency to lisp. Dr. Warr unburdened himself to me about the confidential side of his work. He keeps the Queen informed of Scottish affairs, and told her of the unfortunate incident at the Coronation [in relation to the taking of communion].

It seems now certain that Lord Mackay is about to retire. Jeffrey Cunningham told me of a delightful remark Lord Mackay made the other day. He said: 'I'm getting a little deaf, but my real difficulty is to hear the argument when there is so much cross-conversation amongst my brethren.' What seems to have brought the matter to a head is that, within the last term, he gave judgment in one undefended divorce upon the evidence in another case! The latest saying about Lord Migdale is: 'Mony a muddle makes a Migdale!'

Wimberley has been consulting me about the latest moves in the reorganisation of St. Andrews University. They propose to appoint a part-time Head of the New College in Dundee. This is contrary to Para. 85 of the Report of the Royal Commission, and half-a-man is inadequate for the immediate work to be done. It is a most unwise decision, and, if carried into effect, will undo the good impression made by Knox's installation speech. The news is not yet public, and will raise a storm in Dundee. The Lord Provost has made a wise and guarded speech of warning, and it is to be hoped that it will yet be listened to. Wimberley is not likely to be appointed. I admire his straightness and disinterestedness in the whole matter. By securing the Royal Commission, however, he has unavoidably made enemies in St. Andrews. The University Court will, however, find it difficult to secure any of his Dundee professors to supplant him, for they are loyal to him, and acknowledge how he has furthered the interests of Dundee. He has become a dear friend, and we decided to call each other by our Christian names.

CHAPTER VIII

1954

15th January 1954 (Friday)

Last Sunday evening I broadcast on the national wavelength a 52 minute radio biography of Dr. John White.

I had three days in a curious case relating to sanction of a proposed compromise by a Judicial Factor. It was attacked by one beneficiary, who had reclaimed to the First Division. Lords Cooper, Carmont and Russell heard the case. The beneficiary's argument was the exact opposite on many points of what he argued in the Outer House, and we found ourselves combating some of the contentions which we had previously made! The case was rendered still more confusing by the fact that the Division themselves, especially the President, kept altering their view from day to day! There was a great deal of shadow-boxing. But it all ended to our satisfaction. For the Division, who have taken the case to avizandum, seem now disposed to give us more than we dared to ask. So all's well that ends well. Certainly the Court realise that the Judicial Factor had acted with great skill and also forbearance.

Last night I was unanimously elected President of the Edinburgh University Graduates' Association, which I can only regard as a great and quite unexpected honour. Tonight I am going as the Dean's guest to a dinner at the Scottish Arts Club where various literary people are to be present. I gather that it will be a hilarious function.

Robbie Maconochie, Chris Guest and myself met the Lord Advocate today on the subject of the remuneration and travelling expenses of the Sheriff. I submitted a memorandum on the latter point which showed how many visits I had paid to my Sheriffdom in 1952 – 35 days and 16 nights spent there purely on judicial business, not counting visits for other purposes. It was also pointed out that, in 1952, the Sheriff disposed of 257 appeals, as against 224 cases disposed of by the Court of Session either on appeal or by reclaiming motion or remit. The Court of Session disposed of only 33 appeals from the Sheriff Court (in the total of 224). Of the 107 appeals disposed of by the part-time Sheriffs, no fewer than 92 were disposed of in the five

Central Sheriffdoms – Ayr and Bute, Renfrew and Argyll, Fife and Kinross, Perth and Angus, and Stirling, Dumbarton and Clackmannan, and certainly my portion was above the average of 18. Only 15 came from the remaining part-time Sheriffdoms together. The work done by these central Sheriffs is greatly underestimated.

Dover and Mrs. Dover entertained Ella and myself to lunch today at the George Hotel – for my birthday – but only learned after the arrangement was made that it was a month early. However, that did not affect the fun of the occasion. He talked of young 'Archie John' Wavell, who has just been killed in Kenya. Archie John went to a Shakespeare Quiz where Dover was one of those who answered questions. One question was: 'If you had to marry one of Shakespeare's heroines, which would you choose?' Archie John was greatly delighted with Dover's answer: 'Portia – because she would keep me well in order!' Anyone who knows Mrs. Dover could not but enjoy this answer, given, as Dover would always do, entirely without malice.

17th January 1954 (Sunday)

It turned out that Friday's dinner was given by Jock in honour of Compton Mackenzie who is about to be seventy. He put me at the other end of a long table. He had Compton Mackenzie on his right, and Sir Robert Bruce Lockhart on his left. I had R.J.B. Sellar on my right and Moray Maclaren on my left. Others present were Sir Frank Newsam, Permanent Secretary, Home Office, Sir David Milne, Scottish Office; from the Bar, the Vice-Dean (James Walker); T.P. McDonald; and George Walker (Treasurer of Faculty); and amongst others Wilfred Taylor (of the *Scotsman's* Log) and George Scott Moncrieff. It was my first personal encounter with Compton Mackenzie, though fifteen years ago, I was his counsel in the 'Barra motorists' case. He described himself as a 'swashbuckler', and so he is. His chief subject of conversation is himself. I liked Bruce Lockhart, and spoke to him about Cromdale and Normand: the latter was about his time at Fettes, and then enjoyed the nickname of 'Cuddy'. I took a great liking to R.J.B. Sellar. He comes from Carnoustie, and is at present producing *The Bride of Lammermuir* at the B.B.C. His theory is that Lucy Ashton is Scott's portrait of Lady Jane Stuart. I like Moray Maclaren; he has the outward resemblance of the aesthete; but, at heart, he is, I think, sincere and just, a quality shown in his estimate of the churches in Scotland in his book on *The Scots*. Wilfred Taylor has a slow rather stiff way of speaking, with a kindly smile at the corner of his lips all the time: I likened him to Professor R.W. Johnstone, and at least one other thought the same. George Scott Moncrieff suffers from a cleft palate, and I think this may account for his sometimes rather jaundiced outlook on those with whom he does not agree. The Dean proposed Compton Mackenzie's health, who then replied. As there had been much talk of the Dundonians (Sellar, Taylor and myself) Bruce Lockhart called on me to speak, whereupon Jock: 'Yes, we must have a speech from the other end of the table. The Archdeacon of Dundee.' I said: 'It should not be less than Cardinal!' So I got up and made a short *ex tempore* speech, which was well-received – as most things were by that stage in the dinner. We went home in a 90-mile-an hour gale, with the ash-buckets clattering about the streets.

24th January 1954 (Sunday)

The retirement of Lord Mackay was announced this week. He was a very friendly soul, but, as a judge, latterly a source of disorganisation to the Court. He ripened too early, and has for many years been going to seed. A scholar of King's College, Cambridge, with a First at Aberdeen University, and a First in the Moral Science Tripos at Cambridge, a mountaineer of repute (witness 'Mackay's Buttress' in Glen Einich), tennis champion of Scotland, good at all games, an amateur artist, he had got to the stage where he could not distinguish between big points and little, and therefore mentioned all as of equal importance, omitting nothing. Matters came to a head this autumn, when he decided one undefended divorce on the facts of another case. On personal grounds, I am sorry to see him go – not a day has passed without a new story about him. But his going will greatly increase the efficiency and expedition of business in the Second Division. The *Glasgow Herald* tips James Walker, Chris Guest, and myself for the vacancy. But I think that it will be filled already. I was also tipped by the *Scotsman* when Hill Watson was appointed. I don't see the Conservatives appointing anyone else, if there is even a mediocre Conservative available.

I had a wonderful visit this week to Sheffield, where Jim Anderson, my old class mate, and now a distinguished Sheffield surgeon, asked me to perform 'The Immortal Memory' at the Burns Dinner of The Caledonian Society of Sheffield. There were 350 at dinner – nearly all Scots, and most of them doctors – it is quite incredible what a strong and cohesive colony they form. I shared with Jim and his wife in receiving the guests, and was placed at dinner between the Lady Mayoress and the Mistress Cutler, the former a Yorkshire woman, the latter a very charming Glaswegian, who shares my enthusiasm for Angela Thirkell. She came from Partickhill Road, Glasgow, many years ago, and when I referred to Dr. John White having lived there a Mrs. Wallace (wife of the Society's chaplain) said: 'Oh, I heard a delightful broadcast a week ago about him, but I cannot remember the name of the broadcaster,' – so I was able to enlighten her. It was a wonderful experience to be pitchforked right into the heart of Sheffield municipal life, and everyone was most friendly, and my speech was well-received – I could tell because the laughter almost preceded the jokes, and you could have heard a pin drop. It was worth the journey to receive so much kind encouragement. The Sheffield people are not unlike Dundonians, essentially modest and friendly, and the whole left a very pleasant atmosphere. The dinner was followed by a dance, and we eventually went to bed at 4 a.m. I greatly enjoyed the journey, as I hadn't travelled by the old Midland Route between Carlisle and Sheffield for twenty years. I took my guide book with me, and looked out the various dales, Kirkstall Abbey, and the start for the Brontë Country. I also had good fun tracing the speed of the train on the return journey, by reference to the mile posts. There were messages from all sorts of Caledonian Societies from places as far apart as Retford and Penang. What a hold Scotsmen have in Yorkshire. There are no fewer than three associations of Edinburgh graduates in this county alone. The Andersons have bought a farm near Gainsborough to which they eventually mean to retire when Jim relinquishes the hospital appointment at sixty. They have five children – two boys and three girls (two of whom were with Alison at St. Leonard's). Jim was one of the first doctors to reach Belsen Camp at the end of the War. When he arrived there were 30,000 prisoners still living and 10,000 already dead. Another 10,000 died in a few days; another 10,000 were, he reckoned, permanently unfit; 10,000 would recover full health. He was given by some Germans a quite remarkable portrait of Frederick the Great, which now hangs in his dining-room. I recognised Frederick at once – vital, hard, cruel, with a strange spark of genius illuming his face. Oddly enough, the day before, in a letter to the *Scotsman*, I had been recalling the lecturing of Sir Richard Lodge on Frederick, the finest University teaching I ever encountered.

29th January 1954 (Friday)

This week there has been an interesting example of the uncertainties of judicial promotion. On Wednesday, as I returned from motoring Rosemary to school, I saw Chris Guest taking his children to school. He was wearing a brown lounge suit, and soft collar, and I immediately jumped to the conclusion that, as he was obviously not going up to Court, he must have heard that he was the new judge. I innocently spread this delightful gossip among willing ears in Parliament House. I drove Jim Shaw down from Court in the afternoon, and told him of my surmise. He told me, however, that he had just learned that there was to be a surprise appointment – John Wheatley! Today, the news is out, and the *Scotsman* adds that another appointment may be made shortly, and mentions as the likely candidates, James Walker and myself! Yesterday, I told James Walker about John Wheatley, and he said: 'I thought it was to be you.' I replied: 'Originally, I thought it was to be you.'

John Wheatley is popular and will make an excellent common law judge – rather in the style of Blades. He has great ability and vitality, and is supremely fair, honest, frank and unprejudiced. He is not a lawyer in the first rank, but well deserves his elevation. At the same time, I cannot help feeling that he could have waited, and James Walker cannot. James is sixty-three to John Wheatley's forty-six, and is, in the substance of his pleading, though not in form or manner, about our best pleader. The House of Lords hold him in very high regard. The tide has, however, never run his way, though my opinion would be the view of his brethren in Parliament House.

For a Conservative Lord Advocate to recommend a Socialist ex-Lord Advocate is unprecedented. It certainly is something of a political manoeuvre – in obverse. It removes from the Scottish opposition M.P.s their chief legal exponent, and it enables Hamish Clyde to say that the Conservatives do not always appoint Conservatives (though I do not recall any other exception to their practice). John Wheatley consistently made his appointments on merits, without regard to party, and, I see, the *Scotsman* recommends the Conservatives to do the same. John Wheatley took a share in J.S.C. Reid's (a former Conservative Lord Advocate) appointment as Lord of Appeal, and his appointments have generally been excellent, and without regard to party affiliations. He deserves his reward. Oddly enough, I am at present appearing in a case in the Second Division which he must have returned because of his impending promotion. It is an unusual habit and repute marriage case, in which the opening speech has already lasted for four days and is not yet finished.

I was told today that Lord Migdale had now no fewer than 39 cases at avizandum. He can scarcely have decided any contested case since he went on the bench. Certainly a simple case which I argued before him in his first week is still at avizandum. How different from Hill Watson, who has everything decided almost at once. The President, too, told me recently that, almost invariably, he drafts his judgment in each case on the night on which the hearing is concluded.

The National Library Trustees had their Annual Meeting this week. The only two speakers were Lord Crawford and myself. I had a very nice lunch beforehand in the University Club – Dover, Peter Alexander from Glasgow, Croft Dickinson and the President. The two first are excellent representatives of English literature – humane and generous-hearted. Their subject seems to enrich their personality in a way that, say, the classics do not; at all events, the results on classical scholars are less obvious. I congratulated Croft Dickinson on his quite charming collection of ghost stories or 'remarkable occurrents' – *The Sweet Sayers*.

13th February 1954 (Saturday)

Last Saturday, along with most of the Edinburgh members of the Inter-Church Relations Committee, I was invited by the Tindals to their house for coffee to meet Principal John Mackay, of Princeton Theological Seminary, and at present Moderator of the Presbyterian Church of the U.S.A. He was returning from a conference at Frankfurt to the U.S.A., and stopped off to spend four days in his native Scotland. He is an interesting case. A native of Inverness, and brother of the present Free Church minister of Kingussie, he still carries with him a faint impression of a Free Church minister of the old school. Yet, on the other hand, he is quite incredibly up to date, with the widest and surest knowledge of all ecumenical movements. He sat in one armchair in the Tindals' drawing room, with the rest of us grouped round him, and discoursed for I suppose about an hour quite spontaneously on the more recent developments in ecumenical growth. The ecumenical movement had two objects:- to carry the spirit of Christ more fully into the existing Churches – 'the ones occupying part of the field' – and to carry the Christian gospel to 'the fields not yet occupied'. He emphasised the distinction between those Churches which officially conducted their own missions, and those other Churches which allowed their missions to remain privately sponsored. He declared that the great contribution of the Reformed Churches to the Ecumenical Movement was their attitude to open Communion. His conversation made John Baillie sound almost commonplace – an indication of John Mackay's unquestionable stature.

On Wednesday 10th I went up to lunch at the Round Table from an interesting case in the Second Division, to learn the unexpected unofficial news that James Walker had been appointed to the fifteenth place on the Bench. Thus, for the first time in over a century, we return to the 'Auld Fifteen'.

James Walker is sixty-three, and so, I suppose, the oldest appointment since Pitman, though one does not think of him as old. He has a not very prepossessing presence, and when he pleads has a slight stammer. Yet it is no exaggeration to say that the matter of his pleading is probably the best in Parliament House, and no Scots Counsel in recent days has been more acceptable in the House of Lords. He is exceedingly subtle, with a fine mind; and, almost curiously unprejudiced about anything. He is prepared to discuss anything on its merits, and in some ways is like a stranger to this planet who has arrived without any preconceived ideas. He is also well-informed; and I have always enjoyed discussions with him. I just wonder, however, sometimes if he would not be more reliable in his opinions, if he had built for himself some marital home and some beliefs. But his point of view might well serve as a counter to those who insist on excessive dogma. Intellectually, he is in quite a different class from his two predecessors. His promotion depends on sheer merit, for he started with no personal advantages, and has won his present position simply by the respect which has grown for his intellectual qualities. If he should have a fault as a judge, it may be too great subtlety. But he is head and shoulders above some of the political appointments of the last twenty years. The wonder is that promotion has reached him so late.

Last night, as President of the Graduates' Association, I replied for the first time in my life to the toast of 'Alma Mater', at the Commerce Graduates' Association Dinner. The toast was proposed by Mr. Dan Drysdale, the famous Scots Rugby internationalist of the twenties, and was to have been replied to by the Rector, Sir Alexander Fleming, the discoverer of penicillin, who at the last moment could not come. Dan Drysdale mentioned an interesting fact about Sir Alexander – that he had served for fourteen years as a Private in the London Scottish – the kind of distinction which is seldom recorded in *Who's*

Who; yet, in Sir Alexander's case, is given a notable place. The Chairman, in introducing me, commented on the fact that I had been responsible for a lighthouse-keeper and a shepherd being amongst those invited to last year's National Service in St. Giles – a reference which I deeply appreciated.

28th February 1954 (Sunday)

I have been in one of the longest debates in which I have ever taken part. An action of declarator of marriage constituted by habit and repute is before the Second Division. The debate has already lasted seven days, and I make the fourth speech on the eighth and presumably final day, Tuesday. Since Lord Mackay demitted office, I have been in two interesting cases before the Second Division, the first a case under the Public Authorities Protection Act, in which the Court consisted of the Justice-Clerk, Mackintosh and Birnam, and now this case, in which the Court consists of the Justice-Clerk, Patrick and Mackintosh. Composed in either way, the Second Division is quite first class: and the First Division, even with the President, will have to play second fiddle. This is the second time since I came to the Bar, when the Second Division was manifestly better than the First. The other time was when the Second Division under Alness, Ormidale, Hunter and Anderson was preferred to the First Division under Clyde, Sands, Blackburn and Ashmore (or later Morison). Then, you could choose your Division, and the Second Division received all the work. Clyde, who had been humiliated by this experience, took away the right of choice in the Administration of Justice (Scotland) Act, 1933. But the right of choice served as a useful barometer; and he would have been better advised to learn a lesson from the barometer than to remove the tell-tale indicator.

I recently attended the Scott Club dinner where Principal J.J. Christie, formerly head of Repton and then Westminster, and now principal of Jesus College, Oxford, proposed the Immortal Memory, and spoke of Scott's Kings and Queens in the best address the Club has heard in my time. All the other speaking, too, was uniformly good.

Our Round Table at Court has been so reduced by the promotions of John Wheatley and James Walker, and the deaths of James Crawford and George Morton, that we decided to invite another table of four to join us. Thus our new lunch companions are Stanley Gimson, R.A. Reid, Carmichael, and Donald Macleod (the last one a Lewisman, from the manse of Uig). They are, all of them, excellent accessions to our sodality.

3rd March 1954 (Tuesday)

I finished the eighth day of the habit and repute case with my (fourth) speech. The Division were keen on the scent the whole time, and it was a pleasure to address them, even after they had had their fill, with seven previous days of the case. They were extraordinarily courteous in the way they thanked me at the end, and Patrick, whom I saw in the evening at the University Club, was most appreciative. I had dinner with Mr. Leonard Cutts of Hodder and Stoughton. I had much interesting talk with him about coming theological writers. He places James Stewart first in Scotland. He spoke highly about the young vicar of All Souls, Langham Place, as a coming writer in the Church of England, but the best seller in the C. of E. is J.B. Phillips. He says that the Archbishop of York, though almost eighty, spends most of his time from 10 a.m. till midnight at his desk. He gets a better press than Cantuar, but does not claim to be an original writer. It is rather that he thinks one step ahead of the ordinary man.

I was telling Ian Fraser about Christie's Scott address, knowing him to have been an old Repton boy. But he said that Fisher was his headmaster; he himself was headboy. Oddly enough, while paying high tribute to Fisher's efficiency and general vivacity, he regards him as, below this exterior, rather cold and unapproachable. 'He would make a splendid chairman of I.C.I.' (Imperial Chemicals). I said that his estimate scarcely agreed with mine, and that no one could have been kinder or more friendly to me than Fisher. I think that the difference may be due to the fact that Ian Fraser is possibly a little reserved himself, and that he saw Fisher as a boy sees his headmaster. He regarded Temple, however, as the more friendly and approachable; he must have had him as head in his younger days.

The Committee of Assembly took place today, and ended at 12.30 p.m., the earliest finish since I became Procurator. At lunch, Pitt Watson told a very interesting tale. When the Duke of Edinburgh was being installed as Chancellor of Edinburgh University, one day there was a civic lunch, when Pitt Watson, as Moderator, sat between the Duke of Edinburgh and the Duchess of Buccleuch. The Duchess, at one point, turned to Pitt and said: 'Who is to be the next Lord High Commissioner?' Pitt replied: 'Well, that is scarcely for me to say, but we would be very happy with a re-appointment.' (In fact the Duke of Hamilton has, since, been re-appointed.) The Duke of Edinburgh, overhearing this remark, turned to Pitt and said: 'I would rather like to be Lord High Commissioner.' Pitt, slightly taken aback, could only say how welcome that would be, but would it be possible? What about Her Majesty? Then, the Duchess chimed in, and she and the Duke thought the problem of hostess could be overcome. What about the Queen Mother, or Princess Margaret? The conversation ended with the Duke saying to Pitt: 'Remember, Moderator, it's up to you.' Pitt thinks very rightly that the possibility should be explored, and, with his approval, I am to mention the matter informally to Sir Charles Cunningham! (I have just done so this evening!)

19th March 1954 (Friday)

Skerryvore has been gutted by fire. On Wednesday morning, the three lightkeepers were found on the rocks, driven there by the flames of a fire which seems to have started on Tuesday evening. It is the worst lighthouse catastrophe since the Flannan Isles 'mystery of the Seven Hunters'. I am glad to have had the privilege of seeing Skerryvore before the catastrophe, during the lighthouse cruise of July 1950.

This week – yesterday – the Second Division decided the 'habit and repute' case, Nicol v. Bell in our favour, unanimously, with such strong judgments that the defenders will think twice before appealing to the House of Lords. [1954 SLT 314] The pursuer's Glasgow solicitor has sent me 'heartiest congratulations on the outstanding victory', with his client's thanks. This is one of the cases where, without legal aid, the pursuer would not have had a proper chance. Oddly enough, it is the only case which has ever come to me under the legal aid scheme, but that is partly because of seniority.

20th March 1954 (Saturday)

We have reached a very interesting stage in the work of constructing the new National Library, and recently the Buildings Committee has devoted much time to planning the critical arrangements. The Committee consists of Lord Crawford, the Lord President, Professor Dover Wilson, J.R. Peddie and myself. We have had one curious handicap. The original architect, Dr. Fairlie, planned the building in the conditions and taste of the Trustees, and even then he was conservative in outlook. Many of his arrangements – e.g. air-conditioning – were out of date; and Lord Crawford, who is no mean judge, described the plans for the Entrance Hall as 'Moscow underground'. The President and Crawford both considered the facade as an unhappy mixture of decoration. I must say – while no judge myself – I was very surprised at some of the schemes, the more so as he apparently never laid them fully before the Trustees of that period, and certainly did not do so fully to us now. Indeed, it was most difficult latterly to get any information out of him, though fortunately we discovered in time that he had not even provided a lift from the entrance level to the main floor above, and at once we put that right. Conlon, his partner, and successor, has been most frank and helpful, and much has been done, by the inspiration particularly of Lord Crawford, to improve the internal schemes in so far as practicable. To show the difficulty, Dr. Fairlie had, after planning three separate exhibition rooms in separate styles, agreed to throw them into one for the purposes of better supervision without even showing that they were in separate styles and with windows at entirely different levels. This difficulty will probably be overcome – without interfering with supervision – by separating the three rooms by glass partitions.

For myself, I claim to have originated one improvement. The staircase is to be illuminated by three huge windows. There were, in Dr. Fairlie's scheme, to be varied by what all of us, Conlon included, regarded as a somewhat grotesque and fussy pattern of lights. Having seen the use of armorial bearings in the New Trinity House, I suggested that the windows should be simplified, and colour obtained by the use of appropriate armorial bearings. This has been agreed to, and probably the Royal Arms will appear in the centre window, and Sir George Mackenzie's and Sir Alexander Grant's in the two side windows. The Dean has suggested the use also of the Faculty arms in the windows. Whether this is advisable remains to be seen, but I agree that it would be desirable to introduce them in some appropriate place in the building, and I should like to see them accompanied by an inscription recording that the Advocates' Library was founded in 1680 and handed over to the nation in 1925. It would be appropriate both as a historical record and also as a bibliographical record; and I think that the idea is sufficiently important to make it desirable that it should be the subject of separate treatment.

We have discussed all the woodwork, floorwork, and furniture, and have pressed hard for specially designed furniture of the highest class and taste. It looks now as if the Ministry of Works are going to meet the demand; though at first we were anxious lest we would be fobbed off with 'civil service furniture'. The prospects of a satisfactory solution have increased greatly in the last six months, and an unusual amount of work has been put into every detail, about which the public know as yet nothing. But how much more we should have liked to start from the beginning instead of having to adjust our ideas to a building already substantially erected.

26th March 1954 (Friday)

The First Division were in a puckish end-of-term mood yesterday when I went in in support of a petition for approval of a scheme relating to the Dr. Robertson Memorial Mission Chapel, Grassmarket. In addition to being senior counsel for the petitioners, as Procurator I was *ex officio* the first petitioning Trustee. Lord Carmont: 'I'm just wondering how you can appear as counsel for yourself as client, Sir Randall?' J.R.P.: 'I appear in two different legal capacities, my lord.' The President: 'Yes, I see that, but should you not appear undressed?' Lord Russell: 'I hope not!' The President: 'Well, I mean, without wig and gown.' Lord Carmont: 'I don't think that matters much. But what about this point? We may want to pass strictures on the Trustees, and how can we do so about you, in your own presence?!' J.R.P.: 'The Reporter has reported favourably, and, I think, any strictures are unlikely! But, if your Lordships should want to pass them, my back is broad enough to bear them!' Then we settled down to the case.

An unmanned light-ship has been placed off the Skerryvore rocks: but they are anxious if, in a high sea, its anchor will hold.

9th April 1954 (Friday)

Today and yesterday have brought back links with two friends whom I shall always number among the salt of the earth, each of whom triumphed over a great sorrow, the sudden loss of his wife, by tragic illness.

Yesterday, Sir John Falconer, Edinburgh's greatest Lord Provost for a generation, was laid to rest in Colinton Churchyard. He will above all be remembered for his work as inspirer of the Edinburgh Festival of Drama and Music. The project probably originated with Rudolph Bing, but it was Sir John Falconer who inspired its execution and who gave it its idealism.

It was my good fortune to know him intimately before he entered the Town Council. He probably did more than any other solicitor to give me a real start and continued support as a young advocate. Much more precious even than his support to me professionally, were his wise and disinterested advice and friendship. I still remember him saying: 'Whatever you do, keep your freedom – freedom to do what interests you. Don't be attracted by better material advantages into work you wouldn't like.' His wife died of cancer: when Mother was dying also of cancer, he said to me: 'See that she gets plenty of dope. A doctor sometimes doesn't remember. But it's the kindest thing you can do to help, when it reaches that stage.' Another time he told me that some wanted to nominate him for the Lord Provostship (this was before his nomination took place); but he considered that he was doing more useful work as Convener of the Housing Committee, and had decided not to let his name go forward.

He was a son of the Free Church Manse of Fortrose, and the best stamp of the manse was written over his character. He was not intellectually brilliant; but there was an idealism, a width of sympathy, and a charity of judgment which was infinitely dearer. His wife was an Episcopalian; and one son, Leslie, went to Marlborough; and the other, Dale, to Fettes. The first became an Anglican; and the second followed the religion of his father. But the father was entirely happy that they had each made their personal decision. Knowing that I also was a son of the manse, he even went the length of telling me some of his financial affairs, not (as some people) in self-display, but simply to give me friendly advice.

After the funeral service, George Greene (the former minister at Juniper Green) drove into town with me, and revealed more attractive traits. He would call on him after the death of his wife, and find him reading Kant's *Critique of Pure Reason*, with a note-book by his side. Five times in George Greene's Juniper Green ministry, this delightful incident took place. Mr. Falconer (as he then was) would ring up his minister on Sunday at lunch-time. J.F.: 'May I come and have tea with you this afternoon, or are you too busy with the work of your evening sermon?' G.G.: 'No – it would be a pleasure to see you. Won't you bring Mrs. Falconer with you?' J.F.: 'No – not this time; we'll just have a talk together by ourselves.' Mr. Falconer arrived, talked to his minister about his work, and then, as he slipped out through the hall, laid a sealed envelope on the table. Each time it contained £100 to send George Greene off on a special holiday.

It is good to have known such a man: even to know that such men exist.

But another of pure gold is T.McW. Millar. Margaret, his daughter, who is Alison's exact contemporary, and went right through S. Monica's and St. Leonard's with her, was married today to Muir Russell. A month ago, this young couple came and asked me to propose the health of 'the Bride and Bridegroom'. This is the second time I have had this chance in the last four months. It is a great privilege. There was a peculiar poignancy about today's marriage. Tommy's wife, Mollie, died just over a year ago – of a suddenly developed liver complaint, for which all the medical skill in Edinburgh could do nothing. For seventeen years, they have been amongst our closest friends. Mollie had a gentle, sympathetic, quiet charm; and Tommy's heart is of pure gold. My debt to them is deep: they took Alison on the day of Gordon's funeral, and there are other debts even more intimate. The whole wedding and the reception afterwards was touched with mingled joy and sorrow. My toast could not be just the ordinary toast, for I understood something of Tommy's emotions. I believe I managed to take account of the joy of the young couple, and the emotions of the bereaved father – probably because, having known them in every vicissitude of fortune for the last seventeen years, I could understand something of what was passing through all of their minds.

Tomorrow, we leave for Crinan for the weekend, and on Monday we go to the Warren, Machrihanish, for a week. I am hearing an appeal in Campbeltown next Wednesday. This will be a special holiday on the sands for Rosemary, who has still to make her acquaintance with Kintyre. I am taking a portable wireless to see whether Orpheus-like we can attract the seals inshore.

25th April 1954 (Sunday)

For the first few days of our holiday, especially at Machrihanish, the wind blew so strong, and the temperature was so low, that we could scarcely keep warm. Then, suddenly, for the Easter weekend, we had four days of the most exquisite cloudless weather. Ireland, Rathlin, Islay, Jura, Gigha and Cura all appeared clearly, and latterly we could pick out with the field glasses the monument on the Mull of Oa, 30 miles off in Islay, and a monument or lighthouse in Rathlin. Our visits included one to Southend where the footmarks at old Keil Churchyard are surely of the same character as the footmark at Dunadd, and have nothing to do with St. Columba; to Saddell and Carradale – the sculptured stones in Saddell would grace a mediaeval Cathedral, but the Abbey of Saddell is a very big ruin, though pleasantly placed (we met, incidentally, two charming old men in Saddell village with faces which would have graced any portrait gallery, who told us all we ever knew about Saddell); and to the Cauldrons (or Gauldrons as some call them) beyond Lossit, where the Atlantic breaks on the rocks in all its grandeur.

On our first Sunday we attended, at the unusual hour of 2 p.m., the tiny Church of Ballanoch, which has however recently been refitted with a beautiful little pulpit and communion table. There was a well-attended Palm Sunday service. On Easter Sunday, we went to Longrow Church, Campbeltown. Mr. Campbell Maclean, the young minister, ordained only in 1949, is unquestionably a man who will go far. He is tall, good-looking, with a beautiful voice with a lovely Highland lilt in it. But what is more important by far is that he is a born preacher with a fire and zest which is quite infectious, and the whole service, including the singing, was most inspiring. A large choir used the faux-bourdon for the 100th Psalm with wonderful effect, and the singing of the Easter hymn was unforgettable. I met Mr. Mackelvie after the service who introduced me to Mr. Maclean. I discovered that the latter came from Scourie, and was a nephew of the Mrs. Mackenzie at whose croft we stayed last summer. So much was I struck with him that, when I met Professor Riddell I asked about him (as he was a Glasgow student). Professor Riddell confirmed my impression that he will go far. Another thing – he is an old Glasgow University football blue, and a man's man.

Last night we were at the Royal Scottish Academy Reception, and saw Stanley Cursiter's picture of last summer's National Service in St. Giles' – 'The Honours of Scotland'. The Pitt Watsons were there, and we studied it together. The individual likenesses are not all good, the best being the Duke of Edinburgh, Dr. Warr, the Lyon King, the Countess of Erroll, the Earl of Home and the Heralds. Pitt Watson looks twenty years older than he is, the Earl of Crawford is not a good likeness, and the Queen's face is not the Queen. But to leave the matter there would leave a wrong impression. The composition, colouring and general lighting are magnificent. Dr. T.J. Honeyman said that he had not seen a better ceremonial picture of its kind. If some of the faces are dimmer than one would expect, one must allow for the general composition, which more than compensates. The posture of the various figures is absolutely right, not least the Queen, though her coat is made blue instead of bottle green. Dr. White Anderson was positive that he was the Royal Chaplain who appears to the left, but the figure is unquestionably that of Dr. Hutchison

Cockburn. George Maitland introduced us to the Dutch, French, Danish and Spanish consuls. But I needed no introduction to the first – Christian Van der Rijdt – for he was my class-mate at school, though we had not seen each other for 42 years – since 1912! He wore the collar of the order of Orange-Nassau.

19th May 1954 (Wednesday)

Since I wrote the last entry, a sudden overwhelming change has come in my fortunes. I had been suffering from recurring breathlessness, what I thought was indigestion; what I thought were relics of bronchitis, a cough deep down that had a strange way of recurring when I got overheated or excited. I had a bad spell at Machrihanish: one night, scarcely slept because of the breathlessness which had a most paralysing effect while it lasted; yet in the morning, I felt tolerably well. On Saturday 8th May, Dr. Brewster came and sent me to bed. Next day, he brought Dr. Cameron, general consultant, who gave me an examination for over an hour. He has sent me to bed for over a month; has directed me to stop work this term; and, beyond that, refuses to say when I will be about. He told me that first day: 'You are on the edge of a cardiac failure,' but he also indicated that, after rest, and treatment, I should be fitter than before. The chief trouble is high blood pressure; and reduction of weight will help that. I have got a little weighing machine. Last week I was just over 15½ stone; now I am definitely under that, and may shortly be under 15 (these weights are in pyjamas; but even so, they compare well with my weights on the various voyages of the *Pharos*).

To be transferred from boundless activity to complete quiet in a single day is a startling experience. It involved me dropping all legal work; the General Assembly (which began its sittings yesterday); and our American visit (to Princeton and Evanston, including Post Evanston meetings). Personally, I have almost no regrets, as I had got into a state of exhaustion from overwork, though I realised it only when I went to bed. But I am sorry to spoil Ella's hopes. But, as usual, she has taken it without thought of herself. And the last ten days, we have seen more of each other than we have seen since I don't know when, except for holidays, and it has been just like a honeymoon. Her kindness and love, as always, surround me like sunshine.

So far, time has not hung on my hands. I was so completely tired that it was enough to sleep and doze, but already I have re-read *Redgauntlet* and am now at Nevin's and Commager's short American

242

COURT OF SESSION,
SCOTLAND.
TEL. 30847.

PARLIAMENT HOUSE,

EDINBURGH, 1.

13·5·54

My dear Philip,

Very sorry to hear
that you are being decarbonised.
I shall not call on you as I
understand that the excitement
inseparable from an official
visit would be detrimental!
By the way, when exploring
old Churchyards in Devonshire
last month, I found a stone
with the name of James
Randall Philip, obiit 1875.
Are you a reincarnation?

Yours,

J.M.C.

history *The Story of a Free People*. I begin to understand some of the feelings of someone who is bedridden – wondering what the doctor is saying about you downstairs, cocking one's head like a faithful dog to try to catch any sound from next door.

By chance, I received two letters this last week which serve as contrasts. Each is from a Lord President. The first, Normand's – grave and serious – discusses comments of mine on his Notes on Legal Allusions in *Guy Mannering*. He had submitted these (and his Notes on *Waverley* earlier) to me for my views. In one note, he came down heavily for the view that Bell, as an institutional writer, came before Erskine: I suggested 'possibly'; and this letter is his rejoinder:–

> 18 May 1954
> 6 Succoth Place

My dear Philip,

Very many thanks for your comments on my Guy Mannering notes. I agree with all you say except that I think Bell a much greater writer than Erskine. We are so accustomed nowadays to thinking of Bell in terms of his Principles only that we forget what an original and great a work his 'Commentaries' was. Erskine did nothing *new* for the Scots Law: his Institute was a restatement and I think it is in some respects rather worthy. On the other hand Stair practically made the laws in many ways and Bell incorporated scientifically the Mercantile Law as it had developed. Dunedin used to say that Bell was by far the greatest Institutional writer that either Scotland or England had produced. Clyde spoke of the looseness and uncertainty which sometimes marked Erskine's writing.

I am very sorry to learn from your Clerk that you are not well and have to rest. I do hope that you will observe medical orders and that you will soon recover.

Yours aye

Wilfrid Normand

The other – Cooper's – is a characteristic gay effusion, illustrating his powers of observation, and interest in everything. He called down this week to see me, and told me that the churchyard referred to is Torre, near Torquay. He went away with a slab of Rosemary's birthday cake (she was ten on the 14th) in his pocket: what other Lord President of the Court of Session could you imagine doing that?

20th May 1954 (Thursday)

This would be Gordon's twenty-seventh birthday; it is the same day of the week again; the same sun is shining – and the same events are happening at the Assembly as happened on that day twenty-seven years ago. How well I remember every detail.

On Tuesday, Dr. White Anderson and Dr. MacNicol both made kind references to me in the Assembly.

The sub-committee of the Representation of the Church on National Occasions, set up towards the end of 1951, had completed its task. It was indeed remarkable that that committee had no sooner been established than great national occasions, entirely unforeseen at the time, brought its work into the highest prominence.

For the first time a Moderator was present in the sanctuary of St. George's Windsor, at the funeral of a British monarch; for the first time a Moderator took part, and his voice was heard in the Abbey of Westminster in the Coronation of a British monarch.

After more than 100 years, the Honours of Scotland had been again carried through their streets to Old St. Giles'; the people had seen them gleaming proudly in the sun. No one living could recall such another scene enacted in Scotland like that of June 24 last.

The conception of the service and the suggestion that the Honours of Scotland should be carried owed their origin to this committee. It was a subject of the utmost pleasure when Her Majesy expressed the wish to attend such a national service and asked that the necessary arrangements be made by the committee in association with the minister of St. Giles', under the authority of the General Assembly.

The greater burden of all these achievements fell upon the Procurator (Sir Randall Philip, Q.C.), who acted as convener of the sub-committee. The Church – and indeed the whole nation – must extend to him their deepest gratitude. It was a matter for sincere regret that, because he had been given orders to rest for a month, the Procurator was prevented from attending this Assembly.

But opportunity must be taken to congratulate Sir Randall on the knighthood which Her Majesty bestowed upon him in the Palace of Holyroodhouse. That was an honour to the Church and a fine gesture by the Queen to the Scottish nation.

(Dr. White Anderson's speech)

11th June 1954 (Friday)

It is strange, after working non-stop for twenty years, suddenly to shut off the engines for a month. I have found how easy it becomes to do nothing for a prescribed time. But this time will be remembered by me chiefly for the kindness surrounding me. No one in this house has ever entered my room without the intention to be kind and bright: Jessie, our little Highland maid from Aviemore; Mr. and Mrs. Osborne (from Kent) who occupy our basement; and Miss Johnston, my secretary, who has relieved me of every unnecessary business care. So many friends have asked for me; so many have sent flowers; so many have called. But, above all, I can never express my thanks for all Ella's wonderful love and devotion – was there ever marriage that was happier than ours!

Now that I cannot go this summer to Princeton and Evanston, the Inter-Church Relations Committee (Professor Donald Baillie) have by a master stroke secured that the Lord High Commissioner (the Duke of Hamilton) and the Duchess should, engagements permitting, take our place.

Over a fortnight ago, the Secretary of State announced that the Oath of Allegiance could be taken with the sovereign described in accordance with the judgment of the person administering the oath. Hitherto, the designation 'Elizabeth *the Second*' has been used, causing quite needless feeling in Scotland, where the Queen is, of course, not the second Elizabeth. A great deal of unnecessary harm has been done, and the Government's decision is wise. The result of the Government announcement was that, when an advocate was called to the Bar, last week, the new form of oath was used. The decision was taken in the nick of time, for Ian Hamilton, who removed the Stone of Scone from Westminster, is being called quite soon, and had presented a petition craving leave to be relieved from taking the oath in its obnoxious form. To have had such a question remitted to judicial determination would have been the height of folly, when the oath could be phrased in a harmless and correctly historical form. Happily the Government, on this occasion, saw the real light. But would that, with all their preoccupations about Malta, Cyprus, Egypt, the Sudan, Kenya and Central Africa, they could turn their eyes a little closer to home, and prevent the growth of another 'Irish' question, such as has been the fatal defect of English policy towards other people in the Commonwealth from the Stamp Act till today. How I would like Winston Churchill to get a full blast of what the Lord President thinks about it. He told the Lord Chancellor recently what he thought, and it was a bit of an eye-opener.

The Birthday Honours List yesterday brought a remarkable series of honours to the Bar: a Barony to the President; knighthoods to the Dean and Tom Taylor; a K.B.E. to Lockhart Innes; and a C.B.E. to Matthew Fisher. Now, of those called in my year – 1924 – no fewer than five have received knighthoods (out of fifteen all told) – Jock Cameron, Tom Taylor, Innes, Calver and myself, and that takes no account of Hamish Clyde, who is Lord Advocate.

17th June 1954 (Thursday)

I succeeded in getting down to 15 stone about 6th June, and the doctor began allowing me up on the 10th. Yesterday I put on my clothes for the first time for six weeks. I am glad to find that my third last suit fits me not!

21st June 1954

Dr. Cameron (with Dr. Brewster) came back today and gave a very encouraging assessment of my position. But he ordered me to give up the Life of John White. How well in my innermost heart, I knew he was right. And yet, the emotion of having to give up this work would have upset me completely but for Ella's always present sympathy. Dr. Cameron insisted on me sending off a letter to Professor Riddell this very day.

David Maxwell called immediately afterwards before I was my normal self again, and cheered me up with this ridiculous tale of a recent charge by Lord Blades to a jury:–

'The question of damages is for you, ladies and gentlemen. Just put your heads together – and apply a broad axe!'

28th June 1954 (Monday)

Last week, in spite of the very encouraging reports from the doctors, turned out to be, strangely, the most depressing of my convalescence. I am normally of cheery spirits (I think all my friends at the Round Table would say that at once). But, being up, wandering around my study, with nothing to do, made me realise the effect of prison! Yet, everyone was the soul of kindness, and I wondered – was it the drug I get as a sedative during the day and the sleeping draught? Or was it the effect of the diet (which in all conscience is strict enough over a protracted period and to which I have adhered faithfully)? Or was it the evental vacuum of doing nothing? On top of all this, came a series of about five 'nasty blows' of the kind one gets in life, but which normally one can take in one's stride. The worst was when I read in the Scottish Law Review Notes from Edinburgh from June the interesting news that as a 'notable invalid' I had at the beginning of May 'developed a coronary thrombosis' and 'accordingly' was 'not likely to be seen in harness again before October'. Incidentally the same 'news' stated that Lord Sorn was 'reported unfit' with a 'displaced disc' (which Fred Strachan today assured me is not correct) and that David Watson was 'on the sick list for a few weeks', but would be back shortly (although on the date of publication David was actually pacing the floor of Parliament House). The statement about me was flatly untrue, and Dr. Brewster gave me at once a certificate stating that he had read it and that it was 'entirely without foundation'. I rang up the publishers, to let themselves hear the voice of the person they alleged to have a coronary thrombosis. I also wrote them; reported the matter to the Dean; and let my two Sheriff Clerks have accurate particulars, so that they could authoritatively contradict idle rumours. But I mention all this not to pour out woes which are already past, but to show the damage which may be done by irresponsible statements, and, more especially, to record the amazing kindness of friends. The Dean evidently quickly took action; and, last night, J.G. Leechman, Q.C., the Clerk of Justiciary, rang up to say he was the offending author and would like to call tonight to apologise. I await him at the moment. Poor soul, he is obviously shivering in his shoes, for he has plainly made an unfounded damaging allegation against a brother advocate through mere irresponsibility, and may well be carpeted by the Dean or the President, and even lose his job if he does not take care. The publishers are to make an apology and correction; and the *Scots Law Times*, separately controlled, which comes out sooner, is likely to publish, of its good will, a correcting statement.

But the really wonderful thing was that, not merely had I a very kind visit from the Justice-Clerk, but, on Saturday 26th, the President came down out of friendship because he realised how impossible the statements were in the letter, and he wanted to assure me that they would do no harm, as they were palpably unfounded, and that he himself was going to speak to Hodge, the publisher, and see that a proper correction and apology was made. He could not have been more thoughtful and kind. He talked about all sorts of things. I told him that Selby Wright had named (1) Stuart Louden (2) Hugh Douglas (3) W. Rogan and (4) Harry Whitley as the names at present under discussion for colleague to Dr. Warr in St. Giles, and that no one could explain very adequately why the congregation by-passed David Read as a more suitable choice. Of the other four, I indicated that on the whole, I thought Stuart Louden would probably be most suitable. Then the President made one of his characteristic observations: 'The man who is fit to be colleague to Dr. Warr is not fit to be minister of St. Giles'. (I remember him saying the same of Dr. James Black and St. George's, when a colleagueship was mooted there some years before Dr. Black resigned.) The President told me that Garter King had indicated that his title should contain some reference to his father's and his mother's origins. It is to be Lord Cooper of Culross, of Dunnet in the County of Caithness – Culross for his father, Dunnet for his mother – a graceful tribute and if ambitious, nevertheless with a real Scots tang about it, appropriate for such a real Scot. Talking about a certain minister who was accused of having a 'mother-complex', I said that the truth was, the man had never married because he had to maintain his widowed mother and two sisters. 'Yes,' said the President, 'it's very unfair; my own father died when I was quite young, and I grew up as head of the house, and so never married.' His visit came at the psychological moment – cheering me beyond measure in a week of despondency. I could only write, after he left, to thank him and sign myself for this one occasion, with all due respect as 'Your appreciative friend'. I shall not forget the kindness of this visit. He is always so simple and disarmingly modest, that when he walks out of the house – with all his supreme gifts – it is as if a beloved child had left one's presence.

Today I have been out motoring around Edinburgh coming back into the world. Miss Johnston kindly drove us, to save extra strain. It dispelled my despondency, as also did some work which I surreptitiously did at my desk yesterday.

3rd July 1954

The flow of visitors has been amazing. Such kind things have happened to me. On Tuesday 29th, Miss Johnston drove the two of us in wonderful sunshine down to East Lothian. To see the hills and the blue sea and the islands of the Forth, with the *Pharos* its very self passing Fidra, was an unforgettable experience. We lunched at the Open Arms, Dirleton, my first experiment at trying to carry out a strict diet in a restaurant. On the way home, I called at the Northern Lighthouse Board to see Glen Wakelin, and he gave me the wonderful invitation to occupy a berth on the *Pharos*, even though I would not climb lighthouse stairs this year. I found I could make all arrangements without cutting into Ella's holiday. But though the plan seemed perfect, the doctor's first reaction was against it, though later he decided to take the matter to avizandum. Since then, however, Mr. Millar, Sheriff Clerk at Paisley, offered me dates for appeals at Paisley which would clash with the voyage, and it would not be fair to wait till the doctor makes up his mind. So I have fixed the appeals instead.

Then another day Riddell called in and had a long talk about John White. He fully understood my having to give it up, and was most sympathetic, even saying that he had thought of raising the matter with me himself. Another thing which touched me more than I can say was that I had had to explain to the Inspector of Taxes that certain expenses which I had been noting up as incurred over the 'Life' would not now arise. The following morning, he telephoned me to say that he himself had been Treasurer for John White's Church Extension Fund at North Morningside Church, and wished to offer me his personal sympathy, knowing what a disappointment it would be. The kind things he said about the care I took with my return, it may seem strange to say, brought tears to my eyes. I told him I had never had anything but kindness and courtesy from the Inland Revenue. I only mention these things to show what kindness seemed to spring unexpectedly from different quarters, when, because of diet or drug or nothing to do, I was in a very distressed state of mind.

I must mention also the two young advocates who came down to tea specially another day, Miss McCall Smith, and J. Irvine Smith who sent me a book on a former occasion, and now brought three others which he wanted also to give me, though I shall treat them as a loan. How kind! How amazingly kind!

Harry Whitley, it was announced yesterday, is the unanimous nominee of the congregation of St. Giles. I do not know him sufficiently to express a judgment about him. I have only sat once or twice on Committees with him. He is married to Muriel Thoms, whom Ella knew years ago in Glasgow. He is also Murdo Macdonald's successor in Old Partick, Glasgow; he came there from Newark, Port Glasgow. He has been an Iona Community man and has recently attracted newspaper attention in connection with practical work done by his congregation towards clearing up housing closes in his parish. Dr. Caldwell spoke well of him; and he is said to be a good preacher. I hope his judgment is adequate for the many difficult situations in which he will be placed as junior colleague in St. Giles'.

14th July 1954 (Wednesday)

Last week, Alison had a French friend, Agnes Blanchon, staying with her, and Miss Johnston drove us down to Manor and Peebles. In the Black Dwarf's Cottage, in the visitors' book, for August 1942, I came on the signatures of Ella, Gordon and myself. It was almost like a message from him. Another day, we drove out to Avontown and the Maconochies showed us over the house, and then Alison took Agnes to see Linlithgow Palace, the birthplace of Mary Queen of Scots. I asked Robbie Maconochie which of his ancestors he most resembled, and he said the second Lord Meadowbank but, in reality, he is the split image of the first – on his own account a much less reputable character! Alison's return from the Sorbonne has given me back a big daughter, to add to the little one. Their bright carefree vitality is in itself fresh life. Miss Johnston has been so kind, too, doing my odd jobs if I could not provide proper secretarial work all the time, and always bright and considerate. But, throughout everything, is the gentle devotion, love and encouragement of Ella, which has done so much more than anything else.

Today, the doctor has allowed me, in addition to hearing appeals at Paisley in a fortnight and going to Newtonmore for August, to take an appeal at the beginning of September in Campbeltown, to attend the Argyll Probation Committee then in Oban and best of all to pay my monthly visit to London for the Central Land Board and War Damage Commission, and to resume Church. I have been passing the time by writing letters under pseudonyms to the papers; and the Editor of the *Scotsman* wrote me a kind personal letter. The *University Journal* is to reprint my Article on Lord Cockburn.

Though I am not going on the *Pharos*, I have sent a kind message to Captain MacLachlan and also asked him to see that the Secretary finds a certain letter in his cabin after the voyage begins. Here is a copy of the letter:–

14th July 1954.

To the Honourable the Matchless
Secretary of the Aurora Borealis, C.B.E.,

Honoured Sir,
Knowing that, on your perilous voyage to faery lands forlorn, you are

likely to have taken every precaution to provide bully beef and every other requirement which your shipmates (if not yourself) may need – with the possible exception of matches,[1] I have thought it right to send you a spare box for use in the last extremity.

Since this is no longer Coronation year (at least I think not, though I have never been quite sure since Spithead), I considered that I should no longer supply the ship with Coronation matches.

With great difficulty, and after and extensive search around Houndsditch (your shopping centre) and Pidakilly (mine),[2] I have at last found one plain box, which I enclose herewith, with my most cordial good wishes, for the use of the ship's company. I hope that you will see that a fair division is made and that each Commissioner gets his share.

> Yours, for the sake of auld lang syne,
> WINSTON, K.G.
> *Frère ainé de la Trinité.*
> (His Mark)

P. S. Keep a weather eye on the Sheriff of Fife and Kinross at Tarbatness.[3]

'Winnie'

1. *I once asked for some matches on the Pharos, and since then usually get an apple-pie tin filled with empty match-boxes!*

2. *Houndsditch and Piccadilly refer to places where Glen and I were, or were near, after the re-opening of Trinity House by the Queen. Glen always swears that I had so much champagne at Trinity House, that I gave the taxi-driver the direction 'Pidakilly'!*

3. *Lillie (Sheriff of Fife) came back two years ago from Hoy High with the legend that the lightkeeper there had described his own daughter as a 'perfect smasher'. The keeper is now at Tarbatness. Lillie is a confirmed, not to say, fossilized bachelor; though one of the soundest and kindest of friends, he has never been allowed to forget his remark . . .*

The envelope also contains a Swan Vesta match-box – empty – with inside a note that the writer is sorry to find there are no matches, but perhaps the Secretary may like to keep the box as a memento of a great man!

On board the Pharos

26th July 1954 (Monday)

This morning I received a very correctly addressed envelope bearing the postmark of 'Stornoway, Isle of Lewis'. Enclosed was the Commissioners' rejoinder to my letter to the Secretary. The 'poem' is signed by all those afloat this year on the *Pharos*, including to my great delight the Provost of Greenock. Their reply was so good that I could only write and thank them for their kind remembrance of me. Aberdeen is T.P. McDonald; Roxburgh, Ross McLean; Lothians, James Gilchrist; Fife and Kinross, Jack Lillie; and Stirling, Robbie Maconochie. The 'poem' sounds like Robbie's work, with the rest helping.

THE LAMENT OF RANDALL

'Hoy High! Hoy Low! I'm no permitted,
This time to go. I'm fair upsetted.
(But I'll while tak' a trip to the Tarbatness,*
Tae keep me mem'ries green and fresh.)'

Ye'll dae nae such thing, ye idle loon,
Ye're a mairrit man an' should bide at hame.
Tae Bide at hame's what ye should dae,
And Nae gang sailin' an' on the spree.

'Hoot! Man!', says Randall, 'an' phat's a' this?
Can a no gie a lassie a wee bit kiss?'
Na, na! ye muckle doited bairn,
Ye're far ower auld for her to be carin'.

'But man, I'm twenty year nigher a bairn,
An' she's twa year aulder and mair like carin',
An' for me she wears a blodd red heart
An' a bonnie wee dice will mak' it a cert!'

Fie! Randall, man, come awa tae the ship
And gie the lassies a whilom slip,
And gar the buckies slide and slither
And slide yersel' just like anither.
An' fa' doon ladders and under the table
An' tak' yer photies as weel's ye're able.

There's an unco gap aboard the launch,
She's sair pit doon tae haud her course
For want o' a canty bit o' ballast.
Mr. Secretary's sair embarrassed,
And, man, the Captain's anxious lookin'
For frear we a' wad hae a dookin'.

Man, man, cheer up! Ye're nae forgotten!
Sae here's guid health frae a' that's floatin'
On this auld *Pharos* last Commission.
(She treats her age wi' fine derision.)

But waes us a' for Auld Lang Syne,

And one Philipian we ken fine!
And, man, we'd gie an unco hantle
To hae ye wi' us, man, Guid auld Randall!

*In case, dear man, ye canna guess,
The 'Smasher's' noo at Tarbatness.

(Sgd.)Aberdeen, Kincardine & Banff
Roxburgh, Berwick and Selkirk
Lothians and Peebles
Robert Boyd, Provost of Greenock
J. Glencorse Wakelin
Fife and Kinross
Stirling, Dumbarton and Clackmannan

12th September 1954

A wonderful holiday has ended. We four spent four weeks at Newtonmore except that Alison returned to Edinburgh to act as hostess-interpreter in the Green Room (artistes' room) of the Festival Club. She finished last night after a delightful but hectic time, and is now trying to make up time for lost sleep, as her hours of duty were 4 p.m. – 1 a.m. Ella, Rosemary and I went on for six days to the Creagdhu Hotel, Onich, where we had a mixture of bad weather, and some of the most perfect days I have ever seen in the West Highlands. One we spent in Glencoe, Rannoch Moor and by Ben Doran, on a journey to Crianlarich, where I had arranged to meet a *Glasgow Herald* staff man who was planning a religious book on church life and its place in Scotland, and asked me for my views. Another day, we motored to Fort William and Corpach to visit friends, and have lunch with the Bobby Kerrs (now Sheriff-substitute there) who have just obtained occupation of a lovely little house on the hillside at Corpach, with an unrivalled view of Ben Nevis. Incidentally, it was on journeying this time from Newtonmore to Onich that I first saw the new Commando Memorial near Spean Bridge, a most conspicuous and also satisfying monument. Another day – almost the loveliest I have seen in the West – we crossed Corran Ferry to the Lighthouse there in the morning, and, in the afternoon, visited haunts of James of the Glens, the Wood at Lettermore (where we re-enacted the Appin Murder – Rosemary being the man with the gun in the heather, and

I the 'Red Fox' – all before my ciné-camera), Acharn Farm, and his Memorial in Keil Churchyard.

On the day we went to Crianlarich, I learned of the death of Sir Bruce Campbell, and next day, in drenching rain, Sergeant Gillies of the Argyll Police motored me to Arduaine for the funeral. At Loch Creran, he said it was the wettest day he had seen there; it was as if we were not in a car, but in a motor-boat. The funeral service was held in pouring rain before the front-door of Arduaine, and the interment in the family burial ground, three-quarters of a mile up the hill overlooking the Bay. The company were swathed with Campbell tartan, and it must have been such a Highland funeral as, by its size, is rare in Argyll. Both Sir Bruce and Lady Campbell were unstinted in their service to the county. She died at Easter; he never recovered from the blow, and, after a heart-attack, was taken to the West Highland Hospital in Oban, to be brought home only to die at Arduaine. During the early summer up till July, he wrote me from time to time, and I kept in correspondence with him till the end; indeed, expressing the hope of seeing him at the beginning of September in Oban. He opened his heart to me, and he was a quietly brave and unselfish man, a member of 'the county' who could also mix with high and low. He is a great loss to Argyll. Since his death, I have been consulted as to the next Lord-Lieutenant. I went over at least eleven names in my letter to the Scottish Office and suggested either Sir Charles Maclean 11th Bart. of Duart and 27th Chief of the Clan (if a county representative was to be chosen) or Sir Gordon Macmillan of Macmillan, the present Governor of Gibraltar and Colonel of the Argylls (if a man with wide public service was to be chosen), in the latter case, if he took up residence in Argyll – with, as possible third, Colonel Campbell Preston of Ardchattan. It will be interesting to see who is chosen.

But an even greater sorrow came to my knowledge, when, as we motored home from Onich to Edinburgh, at Lochearnhead I bought a *Scotsman*, and learned that Tommy Cooper had collapsed the previous evening at a B.B.C. function in Edinburgh, and was lying gravely ill in an Edinburgh nursing home. One paper, in its first edition, even reported him 'dead'. How strange that he should so soon have become the victim of journalistic exaggeration, after consoling me about my own, minor, ill treatment. I called at the nursing home that evening and saw his brother James. He had been up all night, and I could see how anxious he was; but, because I did not want to spread any false rumour, I did not press enquiries about his precise condition. I have since learned that it is a cerebral haemorrhage, and that he is unlikely to be back at Court. If this should be correct, it is the greatest loss our law has sustained since the death of Lord President Inglis. He is not merely our first lawyer, but easily the most versatile legal scholar I have met in my career. At the same time, he is charming in his complete simplicity and modesty, without a trace of intellectual superiority, but rather a lonely little bachelor with a gift for getting along with children – yet a great counsel, great judge, perhaps our best legal scholar for two centuries, a master of thirteenth century Scottish legal history, a keen astronomer, the pioneer in Scottish hydro-electric development, and a man of untiring mental energy. I have inserted his last letter to me: it shows almost a premonition of his illness. He was so kind to me this summer, and has showed great kindness to Ella, Alison and Rosemary as well as to myself. His illness strikes me as a family calamity.

Carlton Hotel,
East Cliff,
Bournemouth.

7th Aug. 1954

My dear Philip,

It was most kind of you to write. The choice of the title was the joint effort of my brother and myself, who are the sole survivors of two large families – and both bachelors at that! It cannot be very long before both the Coopers and the Mackays are extinct! The title will at least keep the memory alive in the records of Garter and Lyon.

    I have been in this part of the world for a couple of weeks but have not enjoyed the holiday much (a) because of the wintry weather, and (b) because for some reason I too have been a little under the weather.   I am looking forward to returning home next week.

With best wishes to you all
Yours,
T. M. Cooper
(or rather Cooper of Culross)

At the nursing home, I called too on Tom Simpson. With great gifts, he also showed unique intellectual distinction with a quite unusual sense of tart humour, but ill-health dogged him, and this and a perhaps rather sharp tongue prevented him from ever acquiring a big practice. He has had a stroke, and is but a shadow of his former self. He told me that he had resigned the Sheriffdom of Perth and Angus.

I motored Ella and Rosemary home on a Friday, and the following day took a train to Oban, from there going to Campbeltown for an appeal and attending also the Probation Committee at Oban. After patient persistence, I have at last persuaded the latter to have a whole-time probation officer for Argyll. They were not unfavourable, but financial considerations had hitherto deterred them. In the Great Western Hotel, Oban, I met a very friendly Mr. and Mrs. Jeeves (London architect), who live at Lingfield, Sussex. We spent several evenings chatting together, and made a lasting friendship. From Oban I travelled to London for the Central Land Board, and returned home for the winter yesterday. I am now (by careful dieting all summer) down to 13 stone 8 lbs. and feel ever so much better.

22nd September 1954 (Wednesday)

Alison's birthday, and a very happy day for all of us, as was Ella's, on the 13th (my lucky number).

I am arranging for the appointment of five new Honorary Sheriff-substitutes at Oban. Two (one of them Sir Bruce Campbell) have died within the last few months. The five are to be the Convener of the County, Mr. J.G. Mathieson, formerly factor on the Poltalloch estate; Mr. P.A.C. Milne, Dean of the Oban Faculty of Procurators; two respected landowners, who have given much public service, Mr. T.E. Nelson of Achnacloich, and Major Struthers of Ardmaddy Castle (the latter is an intimate friend of Sheriff Chalmers); and a new precedent (for I think it is the first time in Scotland) a lady, Mrs. M.A. Campbell-Preston of Connel, the widow of the last proprietor of Ardchattan Priory, who does much County Council work and who is an active member of the Argyll Probation Committee. When Archie Chalmers, at my request, sounded her informally, her first reaction, he writes me, was conveyed in one sentence: 'My God! What have I done to deserve this!' But she is delighted to act, and I think it is just and right at this time of day to make the precedent.

Last week I had lunch one day with Dover, and his daughter, Carol, just home from her first term as a missionary-teacher on the Gold Coast. Curiously, as Dover likes to remind me, although he came of a High Anglican family and schooling (at Lancing), both his daughters have served as Church of Scotland missionaries, Audrey at Blantyre, and now Carol on the Gold Coast. In conversation, it transpired that Carol had been in touch with Rob Sutherland, now headmaster of Loanhead Public School, a friend of mine for years and an avowed admirer of Dover, whom he has never met. I told Dover of Rob's history, a typical Scots 'lad o'pairts': the son of a Caithness blacksmith; the one of a large family to be sent to the University; a bright, vivacious, warm-hearted nature, with keen intelligence and strong literary interests; his degree upset by illness as a student; then successive trials, the death of a young brother in Edinburgh Infirmary, the death of another brother in the Normandy Invasion; dogged by operations himself, over which his bright spirit has always triumphed; his wife, Constance, as much a personality as himself, with a gift of command which led her being O.C. Wrens in the large establishment during the War at Crail; he himself a born dominie, following his pupils individually through life; a devoted Church worker and office-bearer. When Dover heard all this, he said that he would like to go and address the pupils at Loanhead on Shakespeare; and this is being arranged; it is characteristic of Dover that he did not suggest waiting for an invitation, but is himself to make the offer. I said: 'This will mean far more to Loanhead than to Glenalmond, and Rob will be thrilled.'

The same afternoon, I had a visit from Dr. Lionel Smith and his brother-in-law, Sir Reader Bullard. The former came to offer a letter by R.L.S., and I suggested that he discuss with Beattie of the National Library whether it go to the National Library or to the Stevenson Museum. I was greatly interested to meet Sir Reader. He has spent most of his life in the Middle East, stationed in various consular positions any place between Leningrad and Teheran (where he ended up as Ambassador). He is short of stature, and quiet and modest in disposition. When they arrived, I was studying a question under the Foreign Marriage Act, and Sir Reader told me that, as consul, he had regularly acted as a 'marriage officer' under the Act, a term which I had only learned for the first time that evening.

Jock Cameron, whom I met the other day, told me that Tom Johnston had informed him that the President had had a cerebral haemorrhage. I have deliberately refrained from spreading any rumours, because the real hope is that no decision will be taken by, or forced on, the President until he is sufficiently well again to reach a fair view of his own condition. It will be disastrous if he is unable to resume duties. But I have also heard that the Lord Advocate is waiting for the vacant chair: I only hope that this is not as blatant a desire as it was reported to me from an authoritative quarter.

My practice is, so far, flowing back quicker than I can overtake the work. It is very cheering, as I have seen more than one forensic career ended by prolonged illness. Already, I have revised a House of Lords Case, and written several opinions, one very interesting one about St. George's Hospital, Dunkeld, for the National Trust. I have also, already, disposed of at least half a dozen opinions as Procurator.

24th September 1954 (Friday)

Members of the Faculty of Advocates learned yesterday of a quite incredible and inexplicable loss to the Bar. Ronald Morison, unquestionably the best pleader at the Scots Bar, who, ever since he was called, has stood right at the head of practice, has accepted, as from 1st October, the post to be vacated by Arthur Duffes of Deputy-Commissioner for Scotland under the National Insurances Acts. Certainly no counsel known to me has had a more complete equipment in all the art of advocacy – a mind for the essential point in his own case, and the essential weakness in his opponent's, a good adviser, a graceful presence, a full-toned voice, plausible speech which always sounded, and was, reasonable, industry, eloquence when eloquence was needed. He is exactly my own age (fifty-four). He was Dean of Faculty for a short period almost ten years ago, and has been a silk for almost twenty years. He began with the ball at his feet, the son of a judge, married to the daughter of another judge, with a family law-office behind him, mature in his forensic skill from his first year at the Bar. Why should this strange withdrawal have occurred? Undoubtedly he queered his own pitch for a time through an unfortunate domestic tragedy; he is now married to another woman whose association was the cause of his divorce. But, though this may necessarily have stayed his promotion (it certainly led to his resignation from the Deanship), may this mistake not have been kept up against him too long? Was the door finally barred to elevation to the Bench? Or has he given up practice in irritation and disappointment; or, after the stress of so many years of heavy practice, have medical reasons led him to seek a quieter life? Or is Hamish Clyde, as Lord Advocate, who is out to be Lord President, getting rid of a strong non-political rival? This seems certainly not the explanation, since, if it were offered to Ronald for that reason, he need not have accepted the post. Or does the old Clyde v. Morison and Salvesen feeling, which existed between the fathers, and is sometimes only too obvious between the sons, have a bearing? Hamish may have indicated to Ronald that the door to judicial promotion was closed, or Ronald may have inferred that so long as Hamish remained Lord Advocate? This again seems unlikely, since everything suggests that Hamish will go up 'on the dickie' himself soon and another will be Lord Advocate. These are only some of the theories suggested as lying behind this inexplicable offer to the foremost Scots pleader of a second-rate job, and his equally inexplicable acceptance of it. For my own part, I think that Ronald had been debarred from promotion for his mistake far too long. People can't throw stones indefinitely. A year ago, I went to see the President on my own initiative because I felt so strongly about it, and urged that the time had come for his elevation to the Bench. It is all the more unfortunate that he should have been passed over when some thoroughly poor political appointments have been made. My own guess is that Ronald realised that he would not get promotion at all events meantime and also felt the long stresses of a gigantic practice; and that medical advice may have led him to choose this easier life. But how the offer came to be made to a counsel of his pre-eminent standing, I do not understand. Nor does any fellow-advocate whom I have met since the appointment was announced. James Keith made the suggestion that, perhaps, this might be a stepping stone to subsequent higher promotion. But a man who has, from now onwards, to spend his whole professional time in dealing with National Insurance problems, will certainly be less fitted for higher office in a few years than he is now. I hope James Keith's surmise may prove true, but it is a hope rather than an expectation. The danger also is that Jock Cameron, who will now have more to do than ever, may also think of quitting practice because of the extra strain. It is a most deplorable anti-climax to a great career, whoever is to blame.

3rd October 1954 (Sunday)

I wrote Ronald, and have received a very friendly and kind reply.

This last week I took part in the opening meetings of the new series of Inter-Church Conversations, this time embracing four churches as equal participants:- the Church of England, the Presbyterian Church of England, the Episcopal Church in Scotland, and ourselves. Professor Donald Baillie, who should have led our representatives, is in hospital for a period; Professor Manson took his place as leader.

I found the Thursday and Friday sessions absorbingly interesting and valuable. We really did get down to brass tacks, and though the discussion ranged widely, it was of immense value, and I have not seen a better example of frank and fair cooperation in discussing differences. I did not attempt this time to take a note of the trend of discussion, but generally it led to the practical arrangement that a small committee – Ramsey, Torrance, Greenslade and Burleigh – should prepare a programme of subject-matter for the next meetings (at Durham in January) on lines suggested at the Conference. The chair was taken by Manson and Derby in turn. I was left with the impression that, if Torrance and Ramsey (the two ablest of the more theologically minded protagonists) could reach a measure of agreement, this would greatly help the Conference. Tom Torrance thinks this possible, and it would be quite an achievement were as learned a Calvinist and as learned a High Churchman to get this length. I just wonder whether Tom may not be a little over-optimistic. His general line was that the only system which would ultimately satisfy was one which gave recognition to both the individual and corporate episcopate of both Anglican and Presbyterian respectively. I think he attributes more conclusions to the theology of Presbytery, as does Ramsey to the theology of Episcopacy, than are justified. For my own part, along with others like Derby, Manson and Greenslade, I considered that historical and non-theological considerations affected our differences to a greater extent than might be realised. Ronald Williams, than whom none could be more friendly (he asked me to use his Christian name), and Manson both stressed rightly the need for keeping a practical outlook towards the sheer weight of historical atmosphere and tradition which each church had inherited, and which could not be overcome by mere theological agreement even were that possible. The man in the pew has to become gradually more and more ecumenically-minded and theologians who are continually attending ecumenical conferences are apt to assume that churches have grown together further than is the case. A sudden effort at rapprochement might produce not a loosening, but a hardening, of prejudices.

11th October 1954 (Monday)

On the 6th and 7th I was in Dublin for a conference of the three Lighthouse Authorities. The Northern Lighthouse Commissioners were represented by Robbie Maconochie, Glen Wakelin, Simpson (the deputy secretary) and myself. Going and coming we followed the Glasgow-Belfast route, taking the *Enterprise* train between Belfast and Dublin.

We indulged in the usual practical jokes and by arrangement with Glen beforehand, when Robbie entered our compartment I took out my passport (brought for the purpose) and remarked on how fortunate I was to have had it renewed for America since it would cover our entry into Eire. Glen immediately replied that his passport was in order and he was sure that Robbie's also would be. Robbie, completely taken in, said, 'Goodness, I am just back from Switzerland yesterday and here I have left my passport behind.' We assured him that even though he might be in difficulties by himself we would vouch for his credentials. After about ten minutes he discovered that no passport was necessary for entry into Eire; he took it most good- humouredly.

We crossed in the *Royal Ulsterman*, returning in the *Royal Scotsman*. The outward journey down the Clyde was most lovely as the night was clear and calm and all the lights twinkling. The ship seemed to have been refitted and looked very modern, though we all found that the diesel engines created more vibration than we were used to, and kept us for a time awake in our cabins.

The *Enterprise* train completes the journey between the two capitals in just a little over two hours for over 100 miles non-stop, and its high speed contrasted very markedly with the rather leisurely progress of so many British expresses. The blue engine and also the carriages reminded me in their outward appearance of the old Caledonian Railway. The Customs control on the southward journey was perfunctory, but on the return journey there was a careful check at Belfast, the object apparently being to prevent people buying non-dutiable articles like cigarettes etc., in large quantities in Dublin and re-selling them in Northern Ireland. Our journey south was made on a superb day. From Belfast to the frontier the country was a vivid green, which contrasted with the rather duller greens of Scotland. But south of the border the landscape was even more beautiful. The sea along which we travelled was a deep blue, the small white cabins proclaimed the lower housing standard of Eire, but also gave a picturesque character to the scene. Drogheda is exquisitely situated on rising banks on both sides of the Boyne and Louth and Meath are full of names familiar in history and legend – Tara, Cormac, Slane, the Battle of the Boyne, and Malahide, where the present heiress of James Boswell, Lady Talbot, still lives.

At Dublin we were met with a characteristic Irish welcome by the Commissionaire of the Irish Lights office. He immediately took two of our suitcases and led us down onto the street where we expected to find a car, but to our surprise he said it was only five minutes walk to the Office; we, however, realised that it was fifteen minutes walk and in any event were going first to our hotel, so instead of trundling along with suitcases we persuaded him to find a taxi, an idea which did not seem to have occurred to him.

At the Shelburne Hotel we were given most luxurious rooms; I doubt whether I have ever occupied a finer one; yet the hotel is somewhat old-fashioned. Then quickly we went to the office of the Irish Commissioners at the bridge over the Liffey which leads to O'Connell Street. There we were welcomed by Mr. Guinness, the Chairman; Mr. Rowlands, the Secretary; Col. Holloway; Mr. Benson; and Captain Colvill. From Trinity House came Commodores Hubbard and Owen. After lunch our conference began, with Captain Colvill in the Chair. The business lasted, with a break for tea, till 6.30 p.m., but we finished it and so did not require to sit the next day. It began as a conference but descended agreeably into cross-chat and characteristic of the Agenda was an Irish proposal for the appointing of light-keepers at unmanned stations! Even the Irishmen recognised the Irish bull.

We were driven at high speed (for there is no speed limit) to the Royal Irish Yacht Club at Dun Laoghaire, six miles out. Again, characteristically, by the time I had reached there all the Irish Commissioners had already left by launch for their new ship the *Isolde*, leaving the two Trinity House Commissioners and myself to come as best we might. However, the launch returned and took us out across the waters, brilliantly illuminated by moonlight. The *Isolde* has comfortable quarters for officers, commissioners and crew, but the dining room and smoke room were, we thought, in modern but very unattractive taste: it is an Irish-built ship.

Returning to the Yacht Club we all sat down together in the Club dining room at a long table for dinner; and, at the end, Dr. Poole, who was in the chair, said that he thought he would propose the toast of 'The Queen'. Robbie asked, would none of the Irishmen object to this? Poole: 'I don't mind if they do. I'm going to propose it.' So we drank the Queen's health in the heart of this Republic. On the way back it was interesting to learn that amongst other things that had happened in Dublin were the facts that a statue of George II in St. Stephen's Green had been blown up and that a statue of William of Orange had had to be removed because it was sniped at with rifle bullets. But there is a curious mixture of Irish Republicanism and also the loyalty of the old English Pale. At dinner I sat between a Professor Purser, Professor of Engineering at Trinity College, who came from Rathlin, and who strongly recommended me to spend a holiday at Ballynahinch Castle, Connemara, now a hotel, but formerly the Irish home of Ranjitsinjhi, the famous cricketer. On my other side was Col. Hollwey, a lively soldier who seems only to have to do with the sea. He invited me to come for a voyage in the Irish lighthouse-tender down the west coast of Ireland. I got all the Commissioners of the three Authorities to sign a letter to be sent to Tom Simpson, who is at present lying in an Edinburgh nursing home. Professor Purser drove me back to our hotel, again at a very high speed. He says that it is often possible to maintain 70 m.p.h. over lengthy distances on the Irish country roads as they are straight and have little traffic.

Next day, our conference having ended, we were able to do some shopping and sight-seeing, returning to the Irish Commissioners for lunch. Much to Robbie Maconochie's amusement he discovered in the Irish *Times* a 'Social' note recording that 'Sir Randall Philip had arrived at the Shelburne Hotel from Edinburgh.' Evidently this is a curious custom of the hotel, because I remember Arthur Matheson saying that the same happened when David Watson went to stay there. After lunch when Robbie and Simpson went back to their hotel, Glen and I went for a walk to Dublin Castle and St. Patrick's Cathedral, in the latter of which we found the banners of the Old Knights of St. Patrick, including a Royal Standard and the banner of the last Prince of Wales, and also a memorial to Jonathan Swift, who was a Dean of St. Patrick's. But the Cathedral is now a depressing place, little more than a mausoleum full of memorials to various benefactors of the Guinness family. We left Dublin at 5.30 p.m. and retraced our journey by the *Enterprise* to Belfast and by steamer from there to Glasgow.

12th October 1954 (Tuesday)

Last night I was present at a University dinner to the Duke of Edinburgh, as Chancellor of the University. We assembled in the Secretary's room and the dinner was held in the Senate Room. It was quite small: the Duke took the chair and there were forty others present. I was a little surprised at the composition of the party. From the Professoriate there were the Deans of the six Faculties, and only six other Professors. On the other hand, the benefactors of the University, real or prospective, were well represented as also the University Court and other University organisations. I was glad to see three students present: the Presidents of the S.R.C., University Union, and Athletic Club. We were all introduced to the Duke when we assembled. At dinner I sat between A.F. Giles on my right and Squadron

Leader Horsley, the Duke's equerry, on my left, with James Stewart opposite. There were only two Toasts: 'The Queen' which was proposed by the Duke himself (I thought a rather touching scene); and 'The Chancellor', which was proposed by Sir Edward Appleton. There were no speeches.

The Senate Room makes an ideal dining room. The five Raeburns round the walls may not individually be the very best of Raeburns, though they are not far short of that. But as a group they seemed to me to be quite unique, especially the Robison, the Robertson and Adam Fergusson.

The 'Old Quad' is now lit with beautiful lamps in keeping with the Adam building. The Dome was also illuminated and I thought the place never looked better. I said to Matthew Fisher whom I drove up that I thought some colour was needed, which could be provided either by grass or by trees. He said that the Court were advised that grass would not grow well in such an enclosed space. But there seems no reason why there should not be some trees to relieve the rather sombre grey.

13th October 1954 (Wednesday)

Last night the Duke of Edinburgh was admitted to honorary membership of the Speculative Society. He was dined by the present Ordinary Members of the Society and then the Ordinary and Extraordinary Members assembled in the Society's hall just before 9.15 p.m., when the Duke arrived, accompanied by Lord Rosebery, Sir Edward Appleton, Lt. Cdr. Michael Parker, his secretary, and Squadron Leader Horsley, his equerry. The Speculative Society premises had been redecorated for the occasion and there was a most wonderful transformation. The portrait of Lord Brougham which used to hang over the fireplace has been removed to the hall and replaced in the place of honour by a Raeburn of William Creech, first member. The scheme of decoration in the hall is now a pale green, with the wood-work of the door painted in white and this transformed the room, though there are still the old red benches and red Turkey carpet. The Society was constituted by the Senior President, J.R. Johnstone, and there must have been about sixty or so members present. Just as we were about to begin the secretary inadvertently knocked the candelabra with his head and it went spinning round. All the members except the President noticed this, and when his attention was called to it the cord holding the candelabra had twisted itself round many times. The Secretary was asked to readjust the candelabra and then turned it too far in the opposite direction. All this was received with roars from sixty throats while the Duke was standing outside. He must have wondered what was happening. Then he was admitted by two sponsors, R.D. Ireland and P.W.S. Simpson. A long Latin certificate of admission was read out recording his achievements and read by the President so clearly that it was understood. The Duke then signed the Roll and was welcomed as a member and sat down amongst us all. There followed an essay really written by Tom Simpson two years ago for the occasion when the Duke should have been admitted but was unable to be present at the last minute on account of jaundice. However, the essay could have been read 200 years before or 200 years after without its very much mattering. In Tom Simpson's absence it was delivered by Ivor Guild, who added some touches of his own. It was a very good production, the subject being the Speculative Society itself. Amongst other things it referred to the three freedoms enjoyed by the Society. Everyone expected them to be freedom of thought, discourse and the like, but they turned out to be (1) freedom from the University, (2) freedom from women, and (3) freedom from change! It was pointed out that a legal opinion had been given last century to the effect that the University held the rooms of the Society on trust for the Society (no doubt the opinion was given by a former member of the Society himself). Explicit instructions were given to the Duke as Chancellor and Sir Edward Appleton as Vice-Chancellor not to depart from this trust and a veiled threat that, if the trust were ever departed from, a judicial decision could be obtained in the Society's favour, more than half the bench being former members of the Society! The essay was then 'criticised' by R.L. Lorimer, and then the Duke was invited to speak. He spoke from notes which he prepared two years ago but added many deft touches which were obviously impromptu. He said that we must note that, though during the last two years he had been unable to take up his membership, he had not looked on the Society with a jaundiced eye! He caught the Spec atmosphere quite perfectly and his extraordinary modesty was quite admirable. Some of us thought he was looking rather tired and we also noticed that his fair hair is becoming rather sparse on the top. The Society then adjourned to the University Staff Common Room adjoining for refreshments, and a number of us were presented to the Duke. In the Staff Common Room I saw for the first time the Epstein 'the Young Communist' which David Playfair Heatley left to the University. It caused much amusement when he left it because, the most conservative of men, this turned out to be his one asset of any value. It struck me as a most impressive work of art, much more interesting than Epstein's later work.

We resumed for the Debate, at which the subject was 'Are We Further to the Fore than our Forefathers?' Douglas Foulis, Junior, opened for the affirmative and made a very good, humorous speech. P.L. Heath opened for the negative with a perfect *tour de force* in which he made great fun of modern science and psychology. He said that it was unfair to describe 'civilisation' as going to the dogs; it was an insult to a noble animal. He defined the difference between neurotics and psychotics in this way, that neurotics went to a psychoanalyst of their own free will, and psychotics had to be taken! After the two speeches the Society adjourned and the Duke left.

One other delightful episode was when the Duke referred to his two great-great-grandfathers, the Duke of Edinburgh and Prince William of Hesse having been ordinary members of the Society, and he said he was probably the only person who had two great-great-grandfathers who had been admitted on the same day, first as ordinary members and then as honorary members. Following on these remarks the secretary read out some items about the two great-great-grandfathers which he thought the Society might like to know. Not merely were they admitted on the same day but they never spoke at any time during their membership. A year after their admission it was brought to the Society's notice that they had paid no dues and the Society then decided that rather than enforce the dues it would write them off. They afterwards received honorary privileges!

The oldest member present was a Mr. Neilson, who had been a member between 1902 and 1906, but after him there were not many senior members present until my own time, except for Matthew Fisher.

19th October 1954 (Tuesday)

Yesterday I had a meeting at St. Andrew's House with Sir David Milne and Sir Charles Cunningham. The question discussed was the choice of Lord High Commissioner for next General Assembly. Several points were raised. If a member of the Royal Family were to be invited should it be the Duke of Edinburgh or should an approach be made first to the Queen Mother? My view was that it would give the Church the utmost pleasure should either be willing to accept but as the idea was known to be welcome to the Duke from his conversation with Pitt Watson, it would seem appropriate to ascertain his views first. I also thought that each might be willing to act with an interval of a few years between their holding office. Next, if the Duke were to accept office, what would be the appropriate solution of the position of hostess in the inevitable absence of the Queen? I queried whether the hostess might not be either the Queen Mother or the Duchess of Kent. It was considered that such a solution was unlikely. Probably if the Duke were to come, the hostess at Holyrood could be the wife of the senior member of his Household. This would still leave the women's meetings of the Church without the usual visit from the Lord High Commissioner's Lady. But it was felt that the Duke could himself carry out these additional functions. The views of the Queen are to be ascertained by the Prime Minister. If neither the Duke nor the Queen Mother accepts then I was asked for another suggestion. I said that, although the Duke of Hamilton had already carried out the normal two years of office, I was sure that a third term of office by him would be most acceptable, the more so that he and the Duchess had thrown themselves with great enthusiasm into all their work as delegates at the World Conference at Evanston. Failing him I mentioned as other possibilities the Earl of Selkirk or the Earl of Crawford (the latter is a member of the Episcopal Church in Scotland, but there is precedent for such an appointment). If the Duke of Edinburgh or the Queen Mother were to accept there was the additional problem that the normal allowance of £4,000 would require to be increased, but that was a financial matter which did not concern the Church, but only the Government. I was also asked whether it would be generally acceptable that the Duke should discharge his functions without the normal hostess. I replied that the Church would be most gratified to have the Duke with or without a hostess. I was also asked whether there would be any objection from the Church to a lady being the Lord High Commissioner if the Queen Mother were invited. I replied that I was quite sure there would be no such objection but on the contrary the utmost satisfaction should the Queen Mother be willing to accept, since she is immensely popular.

Amongst the Ministerial changes announced yesterday is that of the promotion of Sir David Maxwell Fyfe from Home Secretary to be Lord Chancellor. This means that a pupil of George Watson's becomes Lord Chancellor, while the speakership of the House of Commons is already held by another pupil of George Watson's, and Edinburgh University graduate, 'Shakespeare' Morrison. The elevation of Maxwell Fyfe is of personal interest to me in another direction. Though he did not attend Edinburgh University but went to Balliol, he sat the same Edinburgh University Bursary Competition in June 1917 as I did. I did notice that 'David P.M. Fyfe' beat me in the General Bursary list and in the John Welsh Classical Bursary, but that I beat him in the John Welsh Mathematical Bursary. In the General Bursary Competition and in the John Welsh Classical Competition he was beaten by Jock Cameron.

At the meeting of the Graduates' Association Executive in the same evening I suggested that consideration might be given to holding a Graduates' Dinner at which both the Lord Chancellor and the Speaker of the House of Commons should be invited as guests. The matter is to be considered by a special sub-Committee with Archie Macpherson as Convener.

Tom Simpson, unconscious since Friday, died last night. The brightest wit in Parliament House, he might have won a practice had he enjoyed good health, and avoided turning his clever tongue upon the solicitors themselves. His essays and speeches on Boswell or Pickwick, or in the Spec were the best that ever came out of Parliament House; but, there again, ill health prevented him from leaving more than fugitive precis. He was a delightful companion at meals on the *Pharos*. The order of seniority placed me at the table next to him, and no one could provide better conversation. Many of his *bons-mots* linger in one's memory. Of Lord Salvesen – 'He was always ready to strike a blow in a good cause, and, when the cause was not so good, he was still ready to strike the blow!' Or his remark last year at Nethybridge *[see entry for 21st September 1953]*. His ordinary conversation scintillated with them; they came out without effort and no one need attempt to imitate them. He was dogged by ill-health, but, unlike some, seldom mentioned it.

Tonight, Professor G.D. Henderson, Master of Christ's College, Aberdeen was nominated Moderator-Designate by the nomination Committee. Senior Professor at Aberdeen University, he is Convener of the Colonial and Continental Committee and author of numerous books on the history of the Church of Scotland and its characteristics; he is both a scholar of international reputation (the Sorbonne is conferring its doctorate of Theology upon him), and imaginative administrator; he will make a first class Moderator and representative of the Church.

The Round Table is to hold a further dinner next month – to celebrate John Wheatley's and James Walker's elevations to the Bench, and Jock Cameron's knighthood; also Tom Taylor's knighthood if he can attend.

I have now reduced my weight to 12 stone 10 lbs, more than half a hundredweight less than in January of this year. The doctors are delighted, and the tailor stupefied. It is something to reduce one's waist measurement by 10 inches in six months!

The news of the President is good. He is said to have been back at his desk already.

Last night, I had a call from Augustus Muir, the author of that delightful book *John Baxter, bookseller*. To my surprise, it appears he has been asked now to undertake the 'Life of John White'. Riddell told me that Charles Warr felt unable to tackle it; the last I had heard was that G.D. Henderson was to be asked next; but, no doubt with the Moderatorship in view, that project was, for him, out of the question. I had a long talk with Mr. Muir; if he undertakes the 'Life' and produces as attractive a result as the one short book of his that I have read, it should be good; but, of course, he did not know the Man, and that must be a handicap.

31st October 1954 (Sunday)

This weekend I appeared in a conveyancing case in Glasgow Sheriff Court. Five of us from the Bar travelled together. The Dean and Douglas Reith were appearing before Calver in a hearing on a new Glasgow Corporation bye-law allowing Sunday bowling in the parks. He was full of wrath at Calver's constant interruptions. I was appearing with Bennett before Dobie. What a contrast! Dobie seldom spoke, but, when he did, always to the point. Why is it that, almost invariably, the amount of judicial interruption is in inverse ratio to the amount of judicial brains!

On Friday evening, I went to Dundee to propose the toast of the Faculty of Procurators and Solicitors in Dundee at their Annual Dinner. I took the place of Blades, on 48 hours' notice, he having been sent to bed because of some circulation trouble. Without much time to prepare, I indulged in the same reminiscences as at the Round Table Dinner on 5th December last year, varying them slightly to suit the occasion. I recalled, as a small boy, at Dundee High School, watching from the playground a be-wigged and robed old gentleman drive past: the circuit judge (Lord Guthrie) going to the High Court. After I had spoken, Lord Provost Hughes, who was sitting on the other side of the Dean of Faculty (Pat Duncan) produced a newspaper cutting from the *Dundee Advertiser* of March 1908 with a report and photograph of the very scene I had recalled! It must have taken place in my first year at school!

On the journey to Dundee, I had as companions Principal and Mrs. Duncan, now retired from St. Mary's College, St. Andrews, and settled at Fettercairn; Principal Knox of St. Andrews; and Professor Lockhart of the Chair of Anatomy at Aberdeen. I told them an amusing story which Robbie Maconochie had given me for the Faculty Dinner. He himself had been at a Stirling Faculty Dinner. He referred to the firm of Welsh and Robb, and pointed out that they had just assumed a new partner called Cheetham! He suggested that they should also assume the former Town Clerk of Stirling, Mr. Clink. The firm could then be called Welsh and Robb, Cheetham and Clink! Principal Knox capped this tale by mentioning that there use to be an annual professorial golf match at St. Andrews – Playfair v. Cheetham! Before the journey, I had been with Principal Duncan and Professor Lockhart at my first meeting of the Trustees of the National Museum of Antiquities. The Board decided almost unanimously in favour of the new building being placed on the site at the south-east corner of the junction of Chambers' Street and George IV Bridge. It will provide 150,000 sq. feet of area, more than twice the accommodation which has so far been estimated as the requirements of the Museum. Normand, in the Chair, carried the decision through most skilfully. Thereafter, Stuart Piggott (as convener), Richardson and myself were appointed a sub-committee to recommend data of the new Museum's requirements upon which the Ministry of Works could base plans for the Museum building.

In Dundee on Saturday morning, I sent flowers with a message of kindest thoughts to Donald Baillie lying ill in Maryfield Hospital. Little did I dream that he was dying: his death occurred on Sunday. He was our foremost theologian of this generation, and a real saint. I came to know him well these last few years, and he won my heart.

On my journey back from Dundee, I fell in with Tom Taylor with whom I lunched. He was on his way to preside at the Post-Evanston Conference which took place on the afternoons and evenings of Saturday and Sunday. It was the most successful conference that I have seen there – full of life and useful discussion. The Ecumenical Movement is really beginning to catch the man in the pew.

On Sunday, there were 1,454 communicants at St. George's West, a record in my period of membership there. What other single congregation in Great Britain has had so many this century!

2nd November 1954 (Tuesday)

I have just returned from Oban, where I stayed last night with Archie
Chalmers at Kilbowie. It may be my last visit there, as he means to
retire from the office of Sheriff at Oban at the end of this Session and
move, possibly, to Dunblane. The countryside was golden with
autumn tints, especially the sunlit birches on the braes of Strathyre.
The views of Morvern and Dunollie from my bedroom window at
Kilbowie were unspeakably lovely. I received the usual kindly welcome – though I could not help feeling Archie's loneliness, now bereft
of his wife, and befriended by his little dachshund puppy which
invited us all evening to play ball with him in his master's study. The
occasion of my visit was the installation of the five new honorary
Sheriffs-substitute.

Both in Oban and Dundee, I was asked whether I was to be the

Blaven from Ord Beach, Sleat, Skye

new Sheriff of Perth and Angus. But I have certainly not been invited to be so; and it would give me a pang, if I were asked to leave my present Sheriffdom where I am so happy. There is no lovelier county in all Scotland than Argyll and its isles.

3rd November 1954 (Wednesday)

Today I had a letter from Sir Charles Cunningham, to advise me that the Prime Minister had discussed with the Queen the possibility of asking the Duke of Edinburgh to be Lord High Commissioner to the General Assembly of the Church of Scotland next year. unfortunately, Her Majesty and His Royal Highness have decided that this would not be practicable.

7th November 1954 (Sunday)

The Lord Lyon urged me to get a coat-of-arms, and recently I have been in correspondence with him about it. He now writes me that 'the Philip arms seem in general to consist of a blue shield with silver hounds' heads and a chevron, and I feel the simplest thing is to combine this motif with something relevant to books' (this because of my ancestor John Philip, my great grandfather, having been *librorum glutinator* – the creator of the Aberdeen Corner-Square binding).

26th November 1954 (Friday)

Chris Guest has been appointed to succeed Tom Simpson as Sheriff of Perth and Angus. He is a first-class counsel and has a good business-head. I have never known him intimately, though we have always been on good terms. He is quiet and unassertive, and, possibly, as a personality a little uninteresting; but has a good head, and thoroughly deserves the appointment.

Yesterday I went with Ella, on an invitation from the Sir Walter Scott Club, to see the unveiling of a plaque to John Gibson Lockhart at 25 Northumberland Street, Matthew Fisher's house. Lockhart lived there for four years from 1821 to 1825, having previously lived for the first year of his marriage at 49 Great King Street. Yesterday was the centenary of his death. The plaque was unveiled by Mrs. Maxwell-Scott, who came with her sister, Miss Jean Maxwell-Scott, and a cousin of an older generation, Father Lockhart. The Maxwell-Scotts are the great-great-great-granddaughters of Scott and great-great-granddaughters of Lockhart. Their father was Sir Walter Maxwell-Scott of Abbotsford, and their mother a MacDougall of Lunga. They are tall, handsome and vivacious, especially Miss Jean, who was most friendly and quite charming. One liked to think that perhaps her charm came from 'The Great Unknown'. Certainly, they both had heads which reminded me of that high dome and forehead. The Maxwell-Scotts live down in Abbotsford, where they have still only gas. The shoals of tourists keep them busy in the summer time, but in winter they do much reading. Miss Jean was going to reply to the toast of the 'Lassies' at the coming Edinburgh Burns Club dinner, and was full of fun about it, having never attended a Burns dinner before. Sir Walter himself would have been delighted in her unassuming vivacity and laughter.

Jim Shaw, himself an Ayr man, is the new Sheriff of Ayr and Bute. He is unquestionably one of the very ablest members of the Bar, with considerable musical talent as well, and as nice as he is able. I should have expected him to take Ronald Morison's place as leader of the Bar. But, for some reason, he has not had quite as large a senior practice as I should have expected. It may be partly his own choice, for he likes to retreat to a cottage he has acquired – a former manse – in Seil Island. Also, as Liberal, he has never been in the political tide which swept much less competent people into positions of influence which they would never reach by other means. Many of the political appointments to the Bench have made first-class judges; but nearly all the bad judges have been political appointments. The best judges just now would certainly include Patrick and Fred Strachan, neither of whom has allowed himself ever to be deflected from the law.

28th November 1954 (Sunday)

Last night, we had our Round Table dinner at the Scotia Hotel to celebrate the knighthoods to Jock and Tom Taylor; and James Walker's and John Wheatley's elevations to the Bench – not a bad record for our lunch-table in one year. We began with sherry at my house. After three-quarters of an hour, we adjourned to the dinner. Blades, as our senior member, occupied the chair. We all found our places at the table by quotations selected for us and put at the respective place by Robert Reid. This indicated my place:–

My lord, I was born about three of the clock in the afternoon with a white head and something of a round belly. For my voice I have lost it with hollaing and singing of anthems.

King Henry IV Part 2.

On Blades' right, were Jock, Robert Reid, T.P. McDonald, John Wilson, F.C. Watt, and John Wheatley, in that order. On his left, Tom Taylor, Frank Duffy, Carmichael, myself, Stanley Gimson and James Walker. Blades made a quite excellent chairman, and his speech proposing our four guests could not have been improved. Each of the guests made a first-class speech, though the high-lights of the evening were verses read (and composed) by John Wilson; and Tom Taylor's reading of 'The Charter Party' a legal skit written about twenty years ago by Tom Simpson. Frank Duffy was asked to narrate his most uncomfortable moment in Court, and selected the occasion when he found himself in London for his first appearance in the House of Lords, having with him a black jacket and waistcoat, but finding himself without the usual striped trousers, and nothing to wear around his lower limbs but the trousers of a flashy lounge-suit. He tried to borrow suitable garments from Moss Bros. but, at the last moment, found that they were closed. Robert Reid, as one of our 'new boys', proposed 'The Chairman'.

Jock mentioned two interesting points about John Wheatley, who had been his 'devil'. The 'devil', as Lord Advocate, had occupied the Chair at the Faculty meeting, where his own 'master' was elected and welcomed as Dean. The 'devil' had offered his 'master' a seat on the Bench (which Jock had declined). Blades also mentioned one interesting practice which few at the Bar know – that the judges raise their hats to the Dean of Faculty as head of the Bar.

I have, at the Editor's request, written a 'University Memory' of W.M. Gloag for the Glasgow University Courant. He was a great law lecturer, but not the equal of 'Dickie' Lodge (Sir Richard Lodge) who was definitely the first of University lecturers in my experience.

17th December 1954 (Friday)

A story of the Crown Office, when King Murray was Solicitor-General and George Thomson one of the deputes. They both had a singular faculty (quite a genuine gift) for not overworking themselves. George, about to go on holiday, and faced with the papers in a voluminous case, sent the bundle to the Solicitor-General docquetted: 'This case requires consideration', and left with an easy mind. On his return from holiday, he found the bundle back on his desk unopened, with the laconic reply: 'I agree. (Sgd) T.D.K.M.'!

The President has been seen at Church, in his car, and in Princes Street, with (unusual for him) a walking stick. I sincerely hope that he may be able to return to work. Everyone who was critical of his inexhaustible energy is now remarking on the serious gap left by his absence. Roderick Bethune, who was preaching in St. George's West last Sunday evening, told Ella, when she went to welcome him in the vestry, that he had seen him several times in North Morningside Church, first accompanied by his brother, but on the last occasion alone. This was good news; but he added that the President was still slow in his speech and seemed to have a difficulty there. To anyone who thinks of this most gifted of forensic speakers handicapped in this way the hope must be that, before he comes back, this will right itself. His loss would be the greatest we could sustain, but it would be still worse to see him other than his brilliant self. Jock and I, and not a few others, dread to think of his being replaced by Hamish Clyde. Hamish is a delightfully boyish, vivacious temperament, but, from my experience of him as an adviser at the Bar, would make a deplorably poor President. His father, the foremost pleader of his time, and a consummate intellect, was gravely deficient in the elements of judicial conduct. At that time, one could choose one's Division, and practically all the work went to the Second Division under Alness, a very much less able man, but a much better Division chairman. Father Clyde, with all his great gifts, made no impact in personal relations, and passed out without leaving friends who mourned him. How different was Craigie Aitchison, who with all his faults was both a great judge and beloved. From the first, Hamish has shown the marks of his father's dominating personality. It is as if, overshadowed by this powerful personality, he thought that the one virtue was to be quick. The result is that he is shallow and unsound. But, on the personal side, he is much more attractive than his father, who left me, as a young counsel, cold: I still remember the shock I felt that so able a man could be so unjudicial in his conduct. Intellectually, he was one of the first brains in the country; judicially, he was still in the nursery. Lord Haldane, in his autobiography, tells how Clyde's father, at the Academy, shook even the faith of boys at school. The same superficiality of conviction marked Father Clyde and also marks Hamish. I remember Craigie Aitchison once observing to me: 'The trouble with the President [Clyde] is that he has no grasp of principle'; and this remark was penetrating and true.

24th December 1954 (Friday: Christmas Eve)

The Festival of Nine Lessons and Carols is being broadcast just now from King's College, Cambridge – throughout a generation, the loveliest broadcast of each year. Today has been for me a moving day. Last evening, Ella and I went to the King's Theatre to fetch Rosemary home from the Pantomime. Whom should Ella meet coming out of the Theatre but the President and his brother James. According to her, the President looked very much himself, and full of spirit. He told her that we would hear some news of him today. I expected that it would be of his return after Christmas, and wrote him a letter expressing my delight that he was so much better.

Today, he is President no more. The *Scotsman* reports his resignation and the appointment of Hamish Clyde as his successor. I feel it as a family loss – the greatest loss to Parliament House since I came to the Bar. I wrote him again, today, trying as best I could to express my sympathy, friendship and hope that new opportunity still lay before him. He is only sixty-one, and, but for this evil fate, in the midst of his years. Yet, already, he has done so much – the best President since Inglis. What can one say to him, in face of such a blow. I wrote, too, to Hamish, my own contemporary. I remember playing in the last cricket-match between the Bar and Cargilfield, in 1924, and hearing Lord Constable say: 'The President's son [Hamish] appeared before me for the first time today.' Actually, he is two years older than myself, but was called to the Bar two months after me. In one quality, he resembles Tommy Cooper: both have always been essentially free from all intellectual pride and of youthful boyish spirits. But it is the end of a chapter, and the Courts will not be the same until another Cooper rises, perhaps not for a century.

Christmas Day 1954 (Saturday)

Last night, Cecil and Jean Mitcheson, and their son, George, now at Clare College, spent the evening with us, and saw some of my ciné films. They have had an unusual experience. Jean Macpherson, daughter of a Greenock Chartered Accountant, became Ella's friend at Grenoble University in 1923, and was one of her bridesmaids. Then Jean married Cecil, who operated one of the small Staffordshire collieries with his father – an old family business. For over twenty years their home was in a quiet corner of Warwickshire at Freasley. Then came nationalisation of the coal mines. Cecil, in middle life, seemed to have been thrown adrift, and became a mining consultant. But he

was held in such high esteem that, last year, he was appointed Professor of Mining at London University. Now they live near Walton
Heath. Cecil is a very perfect gentle knight. Of old Methodist stock,
he was educated at Bootham. He and Jean did wonderful work in the
Methodist Sunday School. They were beloved by all classes in the
community – not least by the children.

After an exciting Christmas morning – opening presents – we
attended our Christmas service, and then drove out to Melville Castle
for lunch. On the way home, Ella and I decided to call on the President
(no longer the President) to offer him our Christmas thoughts. We
were ushered in, and saw both him and his brother. We stayed only
a moment or two. He was the same kindly little man, but what a
change – no longer the clearest brain I have known, but sadly confused, with difficulty in finding the words and recollections. Yet,
through it all, shone the friendly shy spirit I have known so well. He
was cheered to see us. But he certainly is no longer fit for his work.
A sad change.

The Dean has been appointed Chairman of the Independent Court
of Inquiry into the national wages dispute in British Railways. He is
the right man for the job, but, if he goes on overworking, he risks
Tommy Cooper's fate. He should, on merit, have been the President.

28th December 1954 (Tuesday)

On reading Miss Marion Lochhead's new *Life of John Gibson Lockhart*, I was greatly delighted to read that Johnnie Hugh Lockhart, for
whom *Tales of a Grandfather* was written, was born only two doors
away, in 49 Great King Street. I wrote Miss Lochhead saying how
much I had enjoyed the book, and how, it seemed to me, Miss Jean
Maxwell-Scott has inherited both the looks and the unaffected happiness of her great-great-great-grandfather, as well as his daughter
Sophia, and Sophia's daughter, Charlotte. Miss Lochhead writes to
confirm that this is so, and that the resemblance comes out in many
ways. At Abbotsford there are still the friendly dogs – and one even
rejoices in the name of 'Apple Charlotte!'

My portrait of Lord Cockburn appears in the *University of Edinburgh Journal* today.

The likelihood is that Bill Grant, at present Senior Depute, will be
Solicitor-General to Bill Milligan, who will certainly be Lord Advocate. Bill Milligan's appointment will be most popular, and deservedly
so. He is not in the first flight intellectually, rather priding himself on

being a low-brow; but he is a hard worker, and a thorough good sort. Bill Grant is able, though with a monotonous voice. He was my junior in my last House of Lords Appeal.

CHAPTER IX

1955

New Year's Day 1955 (Saturday)

Bill Milligan's appointment as Lord Advocate was announced yesterday. What a pleasure it is to see the appointment of such a wholly loveable character as he is. I should think that he has none but friends. We certainly have been friends since our earliest days at the Bar, and our children have grown up together in like friendship.

4th January 1955 (Tuesday)

Last night I had a visit from Arthur H.C. Hope, W.S. (Hope, Todd and Kirk) who is Session Clerk of St. George's Parish Church. He came like Nicodemus in the dark to tell me that his minister the Rev. J.R. Thomson (who has only been there for about four years) is on the point of accepting an appointment as Head of a young people's Home – a sort of Quarrier's Homes – in Massachusetts, and that they are about to be faced with a vacancy. Would St. George's West consider a union with St. George's? The idea, for old association's sake, is attractive, and indeed feelers were twice put out before during our vacancy five years ago, though then they came to nothing. I could only say that, in present circumstances, the proposal, however attractive, was impracticable for two reasons. We already have a congregation of 2,000 with a church which seats only 1,300, and the congregation is growing by leaps and bounds. St. George's, with a reducing congregation, has only seats for 900, and it could not be closed and would not serve for both. Further, we have almost completed a £12,000 reconstruction scheme, and the position is radically different from five years ago. I suggested, as a possibility, that Lothian Road Church, which has a much less valuable fabric, a minister nearing the age of retirement, and a site valuable communally but rapidly deteriorating for a church, might well consider a union. But the difficulty is that St. George's rejected the much more appropriate union with St. Andrew's, Drumsheugh, only about three years ago;

and its overtures in other directions will not, at this stage, be regarded too favourably. At the same time, it would be a calamity if its building, magnificent externally, though disappointing internally (someone said that it had the second ugliest pulpit in Europe), were unable to continue in strength. My suggestion appealed to A.H.C.H. who is not blest with an inventive mind, but more often repeats, at three times the length, the views of other people. How well I remember the occasions, but not the content, of his long-winded utterances in the Spec. Yet he is amiable and industrious. Arthur 'High Class' Hope was Calver's name for him – so T.P. McDonald tells me.

The Graduates' Association Executive met this evening. We are trying to embark on a more active programme – a concert in the Music Class-room; a visit from our Glasgow branch; entertain St. Andrews and Glasgow Graduates to the University in June – with inspections of the Gymnasium, Department of Applied Mathematics, and McEwan Hall (with gymnastic display and organ recital!); a marquee and tea at the University Athletic Club meeting in May; and a big dinner at the end of June for which we might secure as guests the Duke of Edinburgh, as Chancellor, and 'Shakespeare' Morrison, the Speaker – however, the details have still to be worked out. We also hope to get a grant from the University Court in aid of *Journal*; and would like club premises and one office within the University. I put forward these proposals, and got a small executive sub-committee appointed, with powers. David Band, as Hon. Secretary, thanked me for these ideas, and the meeting was quite enthusiastic.

In the morning, we had a preliminary discussion among the Church of Scotland delegates who are to attend the resumed inter-church discussions at Durham. We are still rather at sixes and sevens, but, undoubtedly, there are signs of progress on both C. of S. and C. of E. sides.

5th January 1955 (Wednesday)

J.R. Peddie rang me up today with an invitation to become Chairman of the Carnegie Trust for the Universities of Scotland. Ella encouraged me to accept, and I think I will.

9th January 1955 (Sunday)

I did accept it.

I have just returned from spending two days at Durham. We stayed in St. John's College, not St. Chad's as on former occasions, and the weather being less icy and the college centrally-heated, did not freeze as on the two previous occasions – somehow it has, till now, always been ice-cold on my visits to Durham.

The delegates this time were:– C. of E.: Derby, Durham, Greenslade, Turner, and Hickenbotham (Secretary); C. of S.: Manson, Burleigh, Tindal, Torrance, Whitley and myself, with Stuart Louden (Secretary); Episcopal Church in Scotland: Bishop Graham and Mr. Howe; Presbyterian Church of England: Dr. Whitehorn and Mr. Connell (Welwyn Garden City).

We have really begun an adventure of faith, and have set out to try to discover practical ways and means of meeting our traditions sufficiently to enable full communion. We are really on the move, and, in no sentimental way, I can say that I really felt the Spirit working.

14th January 1955 (Friday)

I had everything arranged to go to London on the 12th – sleeper, bedroom etc. But the House of Lords cases are running slow, and now Hynd v. Hynd will not be taken before the morning of the 18th. Though bookings have to be made so long before, one is kept in a state of complete uncertainty at the end of a telephone even until the last moment. Little wonder that the matter was raised by the Faculty of Advocates before the Royal Commission on Scottish Affairs. We were talking about it at the Round Table the other day. The Dean was pulled up to London recently, kept there for four days, and then told that his case was postponed. I spent the best part of a fortnight kicking my heels in London in the thirties, just because there was a long case in front which might be disposed of on the first speech. I remember Graham Robertson setting out at short notice for the House of Lords, and then having to be pulled out of the train at Carlisle because the case was postponed. I think Ian Fraser had a similar experience at Newcastle. It is a very different matter calling up counsel from the Strand, and calling them up from 400 miles away. However – to strike a really pessimistic note – things will have to be much worse before they become better.

It is some compensation to know that, in the appeals heard this week, the House of Lords consisted of four Scotsmen and one Englishman – Lords Kilmuir, Morton, Reid and Keith; and the solitary Englishman, Lord Jowitt. I hear that there is to be one change for the hearing of my case. T.P. McDonald told me of an amusing observation made by Lord Kilmuir yesterday at the end of the day's hearing. 'You tell me that that is the law! What I want to put to you is a question Lord Macmillan once put to me: "Why is that the law? You will give me your answer on Monday!"' Incidentally, why, during a Parliamentary recess, should the House not sit on Friday in a Scots appeal, instead of putting parties to the expense of travelling a second time from Scotland?

Another point. I see that, in the North Edinburgh bye-election, in which Bill Milligan is standing in place of Hamish Clyde, he was asked the question: 'Do you believe in political appointment to judicial office?' Today's *Scotsman* quotes his answer: 'I do not know whether this question refers to the person who is recommending the appointment or the person who is being appointed. If it refers to the person who is making the recommendation, I would point out that someone has to make the recommendation, and the Prime Minister or the Secretary of State is, in my opinion, the most appropriate person to do it. If the question refers to the person being appointed, I can see no reason why a politician should not receive a judicial appointment, provided of course that the "politician" is professionally qualified. If this were not the case, either it would not be possible to have the law officers in Parliament, where it has always been acknowledged that it is most desirable to have them, or no law officer could be appointed to the Bench. Both of these propositions have only to be stated to be rejected.' That may do for the hustings, but the supposed dilemma contains a fallacy. Surely, the point is that the best equipped, in law, in judgment, in common sense and human understanding, should be appointed. But it is certainly not necessarily under existing practice. Probably, the Faculty is as well able to judge of the suitability of its professional brethren for the judicial office, and how seldom it would have chosen the politician chosen by politicians. I could give chapter and verse. One of the worst examples of political jobbery was when Pitman, whom people in Parliament House scarcely knew, and who had been out of practice for years, was appointed to the Bench, when Graham Robertson, then leader of the Bar, and Wark, most level headed of advisers, were both available. And, why is it that almost every Lord Advocate is promoted to the first convenient vacancy, although he may have cut little ice at the Bar? One can say this now, especially when I should be very glad, on personal grounds, to see Bill himself appointed. But, even there, neither he nor Bill Grant are in the same class nor having anything like the same experience of seniority as Jock Cameron, and Jock has seen one of his own devils reach the bench before him. I believe that promotions to the English bench are now much freer from political jobbery, but, here, in Scotland, one must still bow the knee to Baal! Not all political appointments have been bad – far from it – many of the best judges have been political appointments, but it is certain that all the worst ones have been so also.

This week has been a week of installations. Hamish Clyde and Bill Milligan as President and Advocate on the 11th, Bill Grant as Solicitor today. When Hamish was installed, it was the first time for over a hundred years that fifteen Scottish judges had sat together in the same Court. There was a general regret that he made no reference to Tommy Cooper's tragic breakdown in health which caused his resignation, though he had devilled for Tommy Cooper. That day the First Division finished their work before lunch, and went down to the Club for lunch. There, they met the former President – it must have been an encounter full of pathos for the former President. Hamish rightly referred to his own father, but suggested that the family succession had rather defeated the intentions of the Heritable Jurisdiction Act – whereas the fact was that each happened to be Conservative Lord Advocate when the office happened to fall vacant, and so each 'was appointed'.

I should have mentioned that the Duke of Edinburgh is, after all, not to be High Commissioner, at all events this year. The Duke of Hamilton has been appointed for a third time. His appointment will be very popular: both he and the Duchess have thrown themselves heart and soul into the work of the Church, and it is a fitting choice after their visit to Evanston.

In reading the judgment of the Lord Ordinary (Lord Mackay) in Hynd v. Hynd, in preparation for the House of Lords, I have just come on one of his priceless jewels – about the last of which he delivered himself:– 'I add that equally with Mr. Morison, Sir Randall refused to ask for any proof at all, and that both counsel were continually refusing to ask for proof of anything. They nevertheless would not renounce probation. Indeed, I have never seen a case in which so determined an attitude was taken by all Counsel, to refuse to be either encouraged or jockeyed into a proof before answer. They each persistently wished to win . . .!' In the same case, in referring to the two cases of Finlay 1948 S.C. 16 and Gorrie 1952 S.C. 1 (which decided substantially the same point in different Divisions), he observes: 'I venture to cite my own Opinions as the most crisp!'

15th January 1955 (Saturday)

Deep snow. Orkney cut off from the mainland, and Kirkwall from Stromness. Isolated villagers in Sutherland receiving emergency rations dropped by helicopters.

This last fortnight, Alison has been helping temporarily as a heraldry artist to the Lord Lyon. She has prepared the arms of Sir George Mackenzie of Rosehaugh, simply from their description, to serve as a model for the new window in the National Library; which is odd, since the inscriptions to be placed in the three staircase windows, and the two inscriptions for the entrance hall plaques, have been prepared by me. She has also painted arms for Lord Strathspey, and a Mackintosh of Daviot-Kinrara. Yesterday an amusing incident occurred in the Lyon Court. Lord Haig rang up and said that he had received a certain letter from the Lord Lyon, but his puppy, in the room at the time, had eaten it! Could he have another copy?

The University Appointments Bureau sent Alison's name to the National Library, unbeknown to herself or me, and Beattie asked her to come for an interview. He is appointing some temporary Research Assistants. He has now chosen her and several others. This does not, however, necessarily lead to an established appointment, as the latter is only made by a selection board.

21st January 1955 (Friday)

This morning, on arriving home from London, I found a 'private and confidential' letter from J.R. Peddie – writing 'more embarrassed than I can well say'. Evidently, the Executive Committee were on the point of confirming my choice as Chairman, when one member suggested that, as Jock Cameron was already a Trustee, it might seem strange if he were not approached in the first instance. After considerable discussion, they decided that Peddie must first write him giving him a formal invitation, and telling him that, failing himself, they proposed to nominate me. Peddie wrote, and Jock accepted! Why on earth they existed for a year without a chairman, when the solution was all along available to them, goodness only knows. I was very sorry for Peddie, and at once wrote to reassure him that he must not feel embarrassed. I am glad I did so at once. Quite frankly, after being invited, I felt the knock, but, from past experience, I know the wisdom of taking a disappointment, if one possibly can, without showing it, and it certainly will not be allowed to make any difference to me. It is nice to think that, although I was not even a Trustee, they went the length they did. Last night I had my old sleeper attendant friend, Mr. Duke, welcome me on the train. His son went through many air raids as a bomber pilot, and then was put to training others. One day the starboard engine failed, and he crashed from only 500 feet. I am sending him a copy of Gordon's book. He said to me: 'You never know what may happen any day: and you just have to be prepared to take it.' At Waverley, my porter turned out to be a Yorkshireman. He was pleased when I guessed his accent. He said: 'You know: my speech isn't always appreciated here. I had two elderly spinsters the other day, and, as I was directing them to the train, I said: "Come on, me luv" – which is my natural way of speaking – and they gave me a quarter-of-an-hour's lecture for being too familiar!'

I spent four days in London this week; two of them were occupied with the hearing of Hynd v. Hynd in the House of Lords. My junior was Ronald Kydd; and, against me, were Jim Shaw and Alastair Johnston. One could not have wished for a more happy combination and the whole hearing went through with honours even. It left a very pleasant taste. My own speech lasted from about 3 p.m. the first day till about 3 p.m. the second day. We were discussing the law relating to notarial execution, and it was quite fascinating to range over more than four centuries of Scots law before such a tribunal. The only previous comparable experience I have had was in the Aberdeen Ship Constructors case which also related to abstruse conveyancing – the mysteries of the *ex facie* absolute disposition. This time, the judges were the Lord Chancellor (Kilmuir), Lords Morton, Reid, Cohen and Keith. Lord Cohen retired after the first day with a cold, and the House carried on without him. It was a pity, as his comments were very much in our favour. But it was rather odd to be left with a House consisting of nothing but Scotsmen. For the first time since the War, we sat in the Chamber itself. Recently, all the Appeals in which I have been counsel have been in the Royal Robing Room or, latterly, in a Committee Room. The Chamber is infinitely more impressive. The bar consists of a low desk, inconvenient for reading from. The Lord Chancellor sits opposite at no great distance, with two of the Law Lords, nearer, on either side. The acoustics are much better than in the Committee Room, which is important because the full-bottomed wig always interferes somewhat with hearing (it is not always its warmth, but its blanketing of sound that inconveniences): but this difficulty I did not meet in the Chamber. What a magnificent place in which to appear! Opposite me, as I sat in the Respondents' place, I saw the Campbell arms – the yellow and black dice and galley of

Lorne – adorning one of the richly coloured stained glass windows. The magnificence of the surroundings contrasts with the simplicity of the Court. Only the Lord Chancellor wears wig and plain black gown. The others were dressed in lounge suits. And yet, as always, they are much more impressive than any other court. The reason is the superb judicial conduct of the judges, so extremely able, so consistently exact in their apprehension of the facts, so discriminating in their formulations of legal principle, so silent in comparison with other judges and yet always trying to help, not to obstruct, the argument, so supremely courteous and reasonable. It is an education in how to behave, and, when one has something worth saying, a thrilling experience to address them in argument. I must confess that, after being somewhat on the stocks, I found it wonderful to be back in such an atmosphere, and to know that I was holding their attention on a matter on which I could really speak with knowledge. I had the easier side of the argument, and I admired greatly the way in which Jim Shaw parodied my contentions. He is streets ahead of most counsel at the Scots Bar, and, on pure merit, should occupy an even higher position than he does. I was filled with admiration at his whole conduct, quite unaffected by those meretricious devices in which less skilful counsel sometimes indulge. The Lord Chancellor is slow and stolid, but reliable, a very different personality from the steely bloodless intellect of Simon. He has a heavy visage, slightly marked from a serious motor accident he met with some years ago. Morton is perhaps the best of all the judges, very exact and yet anything but narrow, always open to conviction, and most judicial. Reid is good too, though he did not disclose much of what he was thinking, but I know that, for old acquaintance sake, I always had his ear. Cohen is obviously a first class Chancery judge. Keith was, as usual, the independent, amiable, slightly thrawn rebel. He apologised to me afterwards for calling me 'Mr.' several times, as this was my first appearance before him in my new title: but, frankly, I was too intent on the argument ever to notice. It was a special pleasure to have Ronald Kydd as my junior, the first time I have been in the House of Lords with one of my own old 'devils', and our solicitor, Mr. Ferguson, was most appreciative of my efforts. The argument certainly went down satisfactorily – whatever may be the result of the case. After the hearing, the Lord Chancellor invited Jim Shaw and myself to have tea with him. Before the Chancellor turned up, we had a long wait while the judges were discussing the case. During this time, we sat in the room of the Chancellor's legal secretary. We also inspected all the portraits of the Chancellors from the fourteenth century onwards, and examined the boxes which carry the Chancellor's cabinet papers. It is interesting to see how many of the great families originate in a mediæval Chancellor; and also how many Colleges were founded by them. For example, there was a portrait of William of Wykeham (spelt here 'Wickham') and of Wayneflete, who, between them accounted for Eton and Winchester, Magdalen and New Colleges. In the legal secretary's room, two telephones went continuously, but not about anything but trivialities. Eventually, the Chancellor arrived (we knew this by the arrival of the mace) and then we were ushered into his room, and had a very simple tea with him. He discussed the Edinburgh University Bursary competition, when he, Jock Cameron, and myself were all competitors. Jock was ahead of us both; and he beat me, in the Open Competition and in the John Welsh Classical Competition; but I beat him in the John Welsh Mathematical Competition. I told him that I had been reading Ribbentrop's Memoirs, and he pointed to a great bundle of volumes in the corner of the room – the papers relating to the Nuremberg Trials in which he was the leading British Counsel. He is a few months younger than myself. He has a rather unhealthy pallid countenance, and Lord Keith told me of a rhyme about him which began like this:–

David Patrick Maxwell Fyfe
Looks like death though still in life.

T.P. McDonald has given me the more authentic version:–

The nearest thing to death in life
Is David Patrick Maxwell Fyfe
But 'neath the grim exterior shell
He does himself extremely well!

There is also the Watsonian rhyme about him and about 'Shakespeare' Morrison:–

For David's on the Woolsack
And 'Shakes' is in the Chair;
Most schools would covet either,
But Watson's has the pair!

(both Chancellor and Speaker)

I have been staying in the Athenæum and met various interesting people. When I arrived, the place was hotching with Bishops, attending one of their Lambeth meetings. I never realised how much time they wasted, reading the newspapers. They were forever occupying armchairs, reading newspapers and never seemed to speak, or even to notice, each other. Could one imagine three church leaders do that in a Scottish Club? No. They would be colloguing thick as thieves. On my first afternoon, I arranged to meet Janet Adam Smith for tea in the Annexe. Having just read Sir Philip Magnus's new biography of Gladstone, I was much interested when she reminded me that the Annexe, in which we were sitting, was Gladstone's old house. What a different world, when his father would give such a house to Gladstone on his marriage. Little wonder that Gladstone thought the world might come to an end if income tax rose above 6d. in the £1. On my first evening, I had Ronald Kydd for dinner, and whom should I fall in with but the Bishop of Derby and his son Anthony Rawlinson, now in the Treasury, formerly head boy at Eton, and so good a mountaineer as almost to be included in the Everest expedition. We spent, the four of us, a very pleasant evening together. Then, next evening, Lord Reid invited Lord Keith, Jim Shaw and myself to dinner, also here. Here we talked about recent changes in the Court of Session, and the coming opening of the new National Library Building. They were much interested in an idea I want to see carried out – of the National Library Trustees getting statutory powers to enter into arrangements to help in the maintenance, and possibly control, of the Abbotsford Library, Hornel Library at Kirkcudbright, Leighton Library at Dunblane, and Innerpeffray Library near Crieff. I also explained how anxious we were to find someone who could acquire for the Library the wonderful Shakespeare and eighteenth century drama collections of Major Crichton Stuart at Falkland Palace. The Shakespeare collection is at present on loan to the National Library, but it is shortly to be sold, and we are trying to find a purchaser who will buy it for the nation. It contains four early Shakespeare quartos. Lord Keith said that he had been kept so constantly on his judicial work that he had not been in Edinburgh the whole of last term. The Reids are living at Danefold, but Lord Reid spends the week in town. Lord Keith says that the Privy Council work is more varied, and on that account perhaps more interesting, than the House of Lords work, but also not so difficult. The Privy Council always issue just one judgment. 'The way never to have to write that judgment,' he added laughingly, 'is always to disagree with the majority' – a faculty which is natural to him, for he is essentially a lone and independent wolf. Another evening, at tea time, I fell in with Philip Eastman, one of the staff of the British Council of Churches, and he introduced me to Bishop Stephen

Neill, formerly Assistant-Bishop in the Diocese of Canterbury, but now associate General Secretary of the World Council of Churches, in Geneva. A Northern Irishman, he has links with Edinburgh, and was going this week to preach at St. Andrews University. I certainly did not lack friends to talk to, though the Athenæum is not exactly a clubbable place. The story is told of one member who spoke to another, whom he did not know, on the famous stair. The second (it is said) burst into tears and said: 'I have been a member here for thirty years, and you are the first person who has spoken to me!' This is an exaggeration, but I am struck by how, at breakfast, people who know each other perfectly well often sit separately, preferring to read the morning's paper to talking to each other! On my third evening, I had Ronald Kydd and Mr. Ferguson at dinner. The latter's wife is lying ill in Edinburgh, and, till that morning, he had been rather anxious, but that day received better news. At my suggestion, we joined in sending her flowers from 'the counsel and solicitors in Hynd'. We all admired the wonderful Wilton carpets in the Club, especially the one in the drawing-room, which matches the Signet Library in proportions, though it is not so beautiful a room. A replica of the Chantrey bust of Sir Walter Scott reposes on the top of a bookcase to the left of the great fire-place. From my bedroom, at the south-east corner of the top floor, I look across to Nelson on his column, and can almost see the drip on his nose.

On my last day in London, I met by chance Mr. Hugh Somerville, of Reeves Gibson & Co., the Leith Shipowners. He is Chairman of the Committee of Scottish Shipowners, with whom we of the Northern Lighthouse Board confer each year. I invited him to lunch. He is a very fine Scot of the old school, strict in his habits, with strong principles, but with, also, the most kindly and tolerant sense of humour. After lunch, I fell in with Sir Frederick Whyte, now become in appearance very like his father, the great Alexander Whyte. He was much interested that I had been Session Clerk of his father's old church, and asked for the few, the very few, members still left of his father's congregation. When he comes to Edinburgh in March, he wants me to introduce him to Murdo Macdonald, who, I told him, was maintaining the great Whyte preaching tradition.

25th January 1955 (Tuesday)

Most people in Scotland think of this as Burns' Night; but, as Murdo Macdonald said on Sunday, it is more significant as the festival of the

Conversion of St. Paul. Yesterday evening, I persuaded our Kirk Session unanimously to approve certain changes when we resume services in the reconstructed St. George's West at the end of March; it was significant in a Session numbering over ninety, and what we departed from will soon be an interesting relic of the past. Our choir are now to wear gowns; they are to enter the Church and proceed down the aisles to the new choir stalls, followed by the ministers; the congregation is to stand when they enter, and to remain standing till the ministers are seated. At the end of the service, the elders are to go to the Communion table for the salvers containing the offering; the choir will then rise, and proceed out of the Church as they came in, followed by the elders carrying the offering; followed by the ministers; the congregation will again stand. In another generation, our members will wonder how we ever did as we do now. Also, Mr. Findlay, our church-officer, is now to wear a black gown, and no longer wear evening-dress with black waistcoat and tails – a strange relic of Victorian flunkeydom! Yet Dr. Thalben-Ball, organist of the Temple, told me that, when he began as an organist in London, he too had to wear evening dress, in a Methodist chapel. Murdo Macdonald and Mr. Irvine, who is our present assistant (former minister of Dunkeld Cathedral) warmly supported me. My only object was to add reverence to the service. The Bible will still be carried in to the pulpit in the old, and it seems to me, sound Reformed tradition. That will be the signal for the choir and minister to enter, and for the congregation to stand.

This was only one event in a full day. I had lunch with Dover, Peter Alexander and Janet Adam Smith. I put my final form of the inscriptions for the windows and plaques in the new National Library to them, and got their expert literary criticisms. Then we met for the Annual Meeting of the Library Trustees at 2.30 p.m. and for the Buildings Committee at 4 p.m. The latter finally approved my inscriptions. In the evening, Ella, Alison and I attended a Municipal Reception for the Burns Federation, which is holding a special week of meetings in Scotland. The feature of the evening was the visit of Russian representatives who included a translator of Burns, whose poems are having a large circulation in Russia just now. One Russian spoke: but all that one could make out was the name Robert Burnski (it sounded like that) and another sound which was like 'Rule Britannia!' but was certainly not that. The speeches were followed by quite lovely exhibitions of Scots country dancing which must have delighted the Russians as they did everyone else

Alison started her work the same day at the National Library, and is finding it quite strenuous. It is interesting that, while the inscriptions in the windows and on the plaques are my drafting, the arms of Sir George Mackenzie in the left staircase window will be cut from a drawing prepared by Alison when at the Lyon Court.

I have had a most charming letter from Peddie. He writes 'My dear Randall, I am profoundly touched by the terms of your letter of yesterday (the 21st) . . . The matter is one which has deeply embarrassed several of my members as well as myself, and I shall let them know, privately, by word of mouth, the kind and understanding nature of your reply . . .'

26th January 1955 (Wednesday)

I made my first appearance today before the second Lord President Clyde. It was a very pleasant atmosphere, and the case went through most satisfactorily. It looks as if he will be a much better team-member than his father. After the case ended, Hamish and I had a long saunter up and down Parliament Hall. At lunch I compared notes with Jock about the 'European Masters of the 18th Century' Exhibition in Burlington House, which we both had visited last week. I was interested to find that, separately, we had arrived at the same conclusions. Sir Henry Raeburn (especially his *Sir John Sinclair*) and Allan Ramsay (*The Hon. Rachel Hamilton and her brother Charles*) stood out magnificently; Gainsborough, with his pale ladies all with the same hair, was curiously disappointing; Reynolds was only moderately impressive; Romney (especially his *Charles Grey, later 2nd Earl Grey*), was quite superb. The portraits dominated, but the landscapes and Canaletto's pictures of *Whitehall* and *The City of London from Richmond House* were historically fascinating. The buildings selected for art were all classical, and Gothic, so predominant in the nineteenth Century, was absent. The Hogarths were always interesting: *Captain Coram* especially took my fancy.

Bertie Martin told me tonight that Murdo Macdonald intends to lay the Session's recent decisions before a Congregational meeting on 13th February for its approval.

30th January 1955 (Sunday)

We had our last Communion today in St. George's West before the proposed internal rearrangement. There were 936 communicants at the morning service. I served the bread along with Mr. Barrett for the area. Our last (October) Communion was the largest in the history of the Church; and today's figure, adding to it the afternoon Communion, will not be far short of the October total.

Three interesting occurrences this week illustrate administrative duties of a Sheriff. First, although a General Election may not take place for nine months or a year yet, we are preparing the Poll Cards for the next election. Secondly, the Dean of the Faculty of Procurators at Greenock, Mr. R.M. Watson, and the Clerk of the Faculty, are coming to see me this week about 'the administration of justice in Greenock Sheriff Court'. I rather expect that they have some criticisms to state with regard to Bonnar. He is very slow in getting out his judgments, and seems unable to record arguments submitted to him. It may be rather embarrassing to deal with, as I am well aware of his inadequacies, which date from the time of Tom Taylor; yet he is, at heart, a very decent fellow, and has his own troubles to contend with. Thirdly, Mr. Stewart of Campbeltown has written the Sheriff Clerk of Argyll, asking that all the small debt cases at Lochgilphead should be taken at Dunoon. Mr. Wallace, the Sheriff Clerk, very properly replied that Lochgilphead was the proper forum. I have written to Mr. Wallace agreeing with this view, and adding that it would not be proper to depart from the usual forum merely on an *ex parte* request made extrajudicially, still less, at the request of a particular firm, to transfer all the cases in which they happen to be solicitors to a different forum. Mr. Stewart does not enter into detail as to the reasons for his request. So I have added that, if it were desired to make specific representations on any matter designed to increase efficiency in administration, I should always be most ready to consider them. But it would be better that such representations, if made, should come from the general body of solicitors in Campbeltown in order that I may know that they command general assent. I also say that, where for both parties in a particular Small Debt case, the balance of convenience would be that the case should be taken at Dunoon instead of Lochgilphead, this circumstance will always receive consideration.

3rd February 1955 (Thursday)

I was before my brother Sheriff Principal (Calver) in Glasgow on Monday with Chris Guest (Perth) against me – exactly one-quarter of the Sheriffs Principal in one Court. On Tuesday, and Wednesday,

I heard appeals in Paisley, staying on Monday night at Greenbank, Clarkston, with Buggins, and on Tuesday night (along with Ella) with the Kenneth Weatherheads. I replied to the toast of 'The University of Edinburgh' on Tuesday night at the dinner of the Glasgow branch of our Graduates' Association.

This evening, I heard a good story of Johnnie Jameson. He was asked to give Greyfriars Literary Society some years ago his often-repeated lecture on 'A member's day in the House of Commons'. He told Lord Wark, who had invited him, that he would prefer to speak on his new book *The Kingdom of Heaven*. Lord Wark went back to his Committee and reported this, but the Committee expressed their preference for the older and popular hardy-annual. So Wark returned to Johnnie and told him this, whereupon Johnnie exclaimed: 'Well, if they won't have "The Kingdom of Heaven", tell them that they can go to hell!'

7th February 1955 (Monday)

Murdo Macdonald called last Friday. It has now been arranged to have a Session Meeting tonight to give further consideration to the proposed new arrangements decided on by the Session. He finds some who were not present dislike the proposals – T.P. McDonald was the only name mentioned, who, according to Murdo, objected because they were too like St. Giles' and St. Cuthbert's!

I was just discussing last night with Professor Roy various ecclesiastical changes which had come in my own lifetime or within the memories of that period, each of which aroused different degrees of entirely trivial objections. I set them down here as recording a historical phase. (1) There was the objection to 'instrumental music' and 'human hymns', which was one of the reasons for the Free Presbyterian Church hiving off from the the Free Church in the '90s. It is only between ninety and a hundred years since organs first appeared in the Church of Scotland. (2) I remember the day myself when a morning service was not considered right unless the five items of praise included two metrical psalms and a paraphrase. (3) I remember at Newtonmore, in my boyhood, one regular church-member, who when a hymn was given out and during its singing turned in reverse, and put one foot up on the seat of the pew! (4) The use of University hoods by ministers began roughly about 1909. My own father first used one in Church, when he was presented with his D.D. hood for the graduation of 1921. (5) The use of full cassocks came in, I should say, roughly about the

'20s, though even Murdo Macdonald on his arrival in St. George's West used only a short cassock, until he was presented with a full. (6) The 'dog-collar' was never used by the older ministers of my youth. Alexander Whyte, George Adam Smith and my own father always wore a turn-over collar and white tie. The last man to maintain this dress was Dr. R.J. Drummond who died only about four years ago, but he was then over ninety years of age. (7) The freewill offering system was rejected by St. George's West twenty years ago, although congregations like my father's had adopted it with great success fifteen years earlier. Two years ago, St. George's West at length overcame its objections. The results since show that the objections earlier taken must have cost the Church over £20,000 from this one congregation alone. (8) The Christian year is only gradually being recognised. In my boyhood, we always had a service on New Year's Day, a good tradition to combat Hogmanay, but never a service on Christmas Day. In St. George's West we have only had a Christmas Day service in the last few years. Sir Frederick Ogilvie twenty years ago persuaded the Session to have, for the first time, an Easter communion. Yet, in the last year or two, it has been dropped; though this year, I have persuaded them again to hold one. To anyone who believes, as I must do, in the Resurrection, Easter without a Communion is like trying to take Gordon from me, which, however, cannot be. How can the Ecumenical movement make headway in face of such senseless adherence merely to tradition? But I know only too well that what I say about the Church I love the best is as true, if not even truer, about other churches, particularly those bound hand and foot by strangling dogma or non-theological tradition.

In the afternoon, I called on, and had tea with, Lord Cooper, and had an hour and a half with him. He is no longer allowed to drive his car; he tires after walking a quarter of a mile; and the saliva runs from the right side of his mouth. Yet, beneath the shadow of a great tragedy, and difficult as it is for him to collect his thoughts, something of his old spirit breaks through. He says that I should be on the bench. Who, a year ago, could have conceived of him a year from this talking (as he now does) of having to sell his Law Library, as he can no longer use it.

In the evening, our Kirk Session by 20 to 19(!), some abstaining, accepted the robing of the choir, but, because of the narrowness of the vote, it was decided not to proceed with this or any of the proposals unanimously agreed to at last meeting!

In spite of everything, it was for me a most encouraging day, I received a quite excellent report from Dr. Brewster on his monthly check of my condition – and this in spite of a very busy month.

10th February 1955 (Thursday)

At the Round Table yesterday, Frank Duffy mentioned an amusing incident about counsel's fees. An agent employed him regularly over a period and his fees were never forthcoming. Then recently, the practice changed; all the old fees were paid up; and in new work the fee accompanied (correctly) the instructions. Frank could not at once find the reason for this change of heart. Then one day he learned it. The solicitor in question had just been appointed to a Committee, whose remit was to consider ways and means of securing the prompt payment of counsel's fees. I was reminded of the story this morning when I received a letter from a well-known firm of solicitors in Edinburgh paying me for work done in 1948–49. It would be interesting to know when the money was received by them, and what interest had accrued on it. No explanation or apology for the delay; however, better late than never.

25th February 1955 (Friday)

I have spent one day hearing cases in Paisley, and three days hearing appeals in Greenock. Today at Greenock, I found a letter from Tom Smith informing me that the Senatus of Aberdeen University were to offer me the Honorary Degree of Doctor of Divinity. Had I not shed five stone last year, I would have fallen through the floor! But what could be more delightful than to receive this from a University which is my Alma great-grand Mater. The official letter from the Secretary of the University awaited me on my return home from Greenock this evening. Tom Smith also sent me a copy of the recommendation laid before the Senatus.

This has offset a rather worrying problem I have had this last fortnight in my Sheriffdom. On 30th January, I recorded that the Dean of the Greenock Faculty of Procurators and the Clerk of the Faculty wanted to see me about 'the administration of justice in Greenock Sheriff Court'. We had our meeting in Edinburgh on Thursday 10th February, and, as I suspected, it was about J.C. Bonnar (Sheriff-substitute). They brought unanimous representations from the Faculty that he should cease to be Sheriff-substitute at Greenock. The grounds of complaint, which I took down at the meeting, covered a wide range, which I won't record – but they showed that he was unsatisfactory on a number of grounds, of some of which I had personal confirmation. The complaints were made temperately, and they asked me to transmit them to the Lord Advocate as indeed I had no alternative but to do. I am personally very sorry for Bonnar, as our personal relations have been friendly – though I have known only too well that he was not giving satisfaction. I met the Lord Advocate (Milligan) on Saturday 12th, and discussed the position with him; he himself summoned Bonnar for a meeting with him on Saturday 19th, at which I was not present. He wrote me afterwards confirming that the views of the Faculty and of myself were well-founded. As Bonnar does not complete ten years' service until November, no immediate action is to be taken; but he has made it plain to Bonnar that he will expect his resignation in or about November. When I was in Greenock these last three days, each day Bonnar had a 'chill', and was unable to attend Court: frankly, the meeting at this point would have been embarrassing.

5th March 1955 (Saturday)

A propos the recent departures from the Bar of Ronald Morison, Harry Shewan and Norman Sloan, all to outside jobs, in the New Club this week, a certain W.S. asked me 'if there was any truth in the rumour that I was holding myself available to be the next Archbishop of Canterbury'. I replied that I had been in a state of some uncertainty as it looked as if the Papacy might fall vacant first, but that he could now give it out as official that I would prefer to remain in Great Britain! I had my own secret laugh, for I thought that, at all events, I would not require to cloak my inadequacy with a Lambeth D.D.!

On Wednesday, the House of Lords decided Hynd v. Hynd in our favour. I received a delightful letter of thanks from my solicitors.

Johnnie Jameson died this week; he went downhill in little more than a week or two with arterio-sclerosis. This district has lost its greatest character – with his snow white hair, the ruddy cheeks that always made you think of his native Galloway, the piercing blue eyes, the head reminding you of Sir Walter Scott, the deep mellow voice like a great bell, which in the old days would resound the length of the street, the sincere completely unselfconscious simplicity, the absence of any inhibitions, the rich vein of stories, the strong evangelical spirit that made him open his door to every down-and-out, sometimes to the dismay of his wife Margaret, in herself a remarkable personality, like a girl of twenty now in her seventies or late sixties, the most beautiful of the seven daughters of A.L. Smith, Master of Balliol, full of quiet shy charm as he was full of robust forthright frankness. The stories of him, and his father Lord Ardwall before him, were legion: a curious blend of port and the old Free Church tradition, Lord Ardwall was once seen dropping a number of letters into a pillar-box. A friend came up and asked him what he was doing: 'Oh, I'm delivering my Communion cards just now; but I post the cards to the teetotallers.' Once I came up from Gullane to state a plea in Edinburgh Sheriff Court before Johnnie Jameson on behalf of an accused. The Court was full of the unwashed. I was taken first. As I was leaving the Court, suddenly I heard the great bell-like voice: 'I say –' I turned round, and Johnnie, from the bench, called out: 'You're down at Gullane just now.' I replied: 'Yes, my Lord.' 'Well,' came the reply, 'give my love to your wife.' He was a keen fencer in his day, had fought in the Boer War, and was a friend of John Buchan. Till fifteen years ago, one used to see him (about sixty years of age then) sprinting short sprints, for practice, along Great King Street. When Margaret Jameson was away visiting her relatives in Oxford, Johnnie would do his own washing, and drape the three drawing-room windows with his vests and pants, hung out to dry. He kept a soap-box in the New Club, and took it over each Sunday evening to the Mound, where he gathered a crowd and spoke on religion to them. Only a fortnight ago, he struggled up to our morning service in the Usher Hall, but could scarcely move along the passage to his seat. He lost Andy, his only boy, by a streptococcal infection, when he was near the top of the Academy, just as we did Gordon eight years later. The morning after Gordon's death, the Jamesons were the first to cross the street and shake our hands. It was perhaps this link, and the friendship between Margaret and Ella in particular which has grown out of it, that led Margaret Jameson to invite us across to the little family service on Wednesday before they left for the burial at Anwoth, where Andy lies. She asked me, too, to play Crimond for them so that they might join in 'The Lord's my Shepherd' before they left, and Murdo Macdonald, who conducted the service, appropriately read Matthew 25: 31–40.

From there, I went straight on to the Commission of Assembly, and then that night to London for the conference of the three Lighthouse Authorities with the Ministry of Transport, with Robbie Maconochie and Glen Wakelin. Glen and I had breakfast at the Athenæum, and in the evening he took me to dinner at the 'In-and-Out', the Naval and Military Club, in Piccadilly, near Hyde Park Corner – my first visit there. The club has an informal charming portrait of the Queen (who was born nearby) and a lovely display of regimental emblems. It was bombed in the last War. I paid a visit to the Law Courts in the morning, and heard a delightful and rather amusing discussion before five judges in the Court of Appeal, with Evershed M.R. in the Chair. I like him much better than the Chief Justice (Goddard), who never impresses me as very judicial. I also looked in to see Pearson, J. and Willmer, J., the latter sitting in an Admiralty case with two Trinity House assessors, one of them Captain Owens whom I have met several times, and recently at Dublin.

Then we had lunch at Trinity House, the most exquisitely tasteful of modern restorations that I know. The afternoon conference at the Ministry of Transport was a solemn farce, lasting two and a half hours. As the Shipowners pay, the Ministry have little locus to interfere, and every decision taken could have been disposed of by correspondence instead of being so solemnly discussed at a conference table surrounded by about fifty persons. As usual the Irishmen, this time Dr. Poole and Colonel Holloway, came out with flying colours. They got an increase of £50,000 in an estimate for a lighthouse tender, as if they were giving something away, and persuasively obtained preliminary sanction for another tender which was not even in the estimate. We were questioned about Skerryvore, and Robbie Maconochie characteristically thrice referred to a question of future policy which had not yet arisen, and which Glen had specially asked him not to raise!

8th March 1955 (Tuesday)

The Aberdeen Honorary Degrees were announced in last night's six o'clock news and in the morning papers. I thought that, when I went up to Court today, I would be badly 'ragged'. But, on the contrary, nothing could have been kinder. Not a few referred to Lord Sands, and some to Tom Taylor, as the only two previous Scots lay D.D.s. But I think that there was genuine pleasure that I seem to be the first D.D. in practice, and walking the floor of the Parliament Hall.

Last Sunday, at lunch we had David Say and Murdo Macdonald (Betty, at the last moment, had to call off because her smaller boy, Alan, was unwell). We spent the whole afternoon in a lively talk about religious life in the United Kingdom. David Say used a good expression about Canon Wickham of Sheffield: 'Like John Collins' (of St. Paul's) 'he is an essential ingredient in the Church of England!' The same would be true of the Red Dean, and would have been true of Bishop Barnes. David Say has, for eight years, acted as General Secretary of the British Council of Churches. He is very fair, and, while not an inspired speaker, always talks with sanity and humour. This summer he becomes Rector of Bishop's Hatfield, the old parish church of Hatfield House, but now, also, the parish church of a coming 22,000 inhabitants satellite town.

(8.30 p.m.) Murdo Macdonald, kind soul, amid all his duties, has just called to give me his good wishes.

Last night, I heard one of the most pathetic tales I have heard for some time. Lord Cooper went in to a post office recently to buy stamps. He stumbled over his words, and the person behind the counter, who did not recognise him, thought he was drunk, and told him to get out of the post office. The story was confirmed today by T.P. McDonald at the Round Table. What pathos lies behind that incident.

9th March 1955 (Wednesday)

Today Ella and I travelled with most of the other Sheriffs and their wives to the launch of the sixth *Pharos* at the Caledon Yard, Dundee. It was a lovely day, and the ship went down the slip-way as smoothly as could possibly be. I thought that the first time I saw the Tay from the water was almost fifty years ago, when, at the age of about five, I sailed on the old whaling ship *Diana* from Dundee to Broughty Ferry as she left for the Antarctic. Her master, Captain Mackay, was the father of my governess. We ate oranges, solidly, the whole way! Today, we had lunch in the Royal Hotel, Dundee; the launch was at 3 p.m., just before high tide, and then we adjourned to the Shipyard dining room for tea, champagne, and speeches. I proposed the chairman. At the lunch, I sat between Gilchrist and Mrs. Bill Grant. Charles Milne, who happened, by virtue of the rota, to be our Chairman, replied to the principal toast, but neither he nor Robbie Maconochie showed any tact, though in their own way, they were amusing in spite of themselves. But it was a delightful day, my first experience of a launch, and I saw, at the Yard, many Dundee friends. The most interesting remark made was that the third *Pharos* happened to be lying in Dundee Harbour, on a rare visit there, at the time of the Tay Bridge Disaster, and her master – father of J.M. Graham, the surgeon 'goitre-king' – actually saw the Bridge collapse, and the train fall into the river.

Ella Philip

Before the ceremonies began, I had time to call on Hugh Carlton, who congratulated me on my D.D. I said that it was the least a Doctor of Divinity could do to call on the new Dean (of the Dundee Faculty of Procurators). I also called on Leslie Weatherhead, and then paid my first visit, for many a long day, to the High School, where I had a short talk with Ian Bain, the Rector, who retires this year.

I have appended the copy of a telegram sent by the old *Pharos* from Granton Harbour, wishing good fortune to her new sister!

EH 0 A92 GTG 12.15 Granton Harbour Edinburgh 54

GREETINGS

MRS. WAKELIN C/O CALEDON SHIPBUILDING COY DUNDEE

GREETINGS TO MY NEW SISTER THANK YOU FOR DELIVERING AND CHRISTENING HER STOP MAY HER GROWING UP BE FITTING OF HER STAYS GENERAL MAKE UP AND THE PUTTING ON OF PAINT RUN SMOOTHLY SO THAT SHE SHALL SOON RELIEVE ME OF KEEP-ING THE BUOYS WINKING

PHAROS

16th March 1955 (Wednesday)

Geoffrey Shaw was here on Sunday, and, in youthful exuberance, Rosemary pulled out his tie. He promptly wrote in her autograph book:–

> 'A D.D.'s daughter
> Didn't ought-ter
> Pull out the tie
> of a minister guy!'

Last night I had dinner at the New Club with Dover, Sir Alexander Gray, Professor Calder, and D.G.M. Stalker (lecturer in Biblical Studies, who is a friend of Dover's). The talk went fast and furious with a distinct theological slant. Alongside us was a dinner party of many leading Edinburgh doctors or surgeons:– Sir Sydney Smith, Sir James Learmonth, Sir Andrew Davidson, Mr. J.M. Graham, Professor Montgomery, Dr. Sinclair – to name only a few – and Carlyle Gifford, W.S., Sidney Smith, Andrew Davidson and Carlyle Gifford came over and joined us when their own party broke up.

25th March 1955 (Friday)

Today our dear spaniel Gleam died. A year younger than Rosemary, he had grown up with her, and was a faithful, loyal, patient friend to all of us. I shall miss him lying at my study fire each evening: he had the gentlest, most affectionate of 'doggy' natures. It brought back to me the loss of 'Jarpie' (J.R.P.) the little fox-terrier puppy which I had at the age of nine: his short life was only three months. Ella will miss Gleam most, for she did so much for him, the more so as he grew old.

Ronald McLarty told me an extraordinary piece of information this afternoon – that Edinburgh University were planning to offer me their D.D. and that this had only not been done, because Aberdeen's honorary degrees came out before the Edinburgh recommendations were finally issued! As he says, it seems the first time when a layman had been on the point of being offered a D.D. from two Universities. In a way, I am mildly sorry that my own Alma Mater, if it intended this, did not get in first. But it is, I feel, the greater honour to be selected by a University not one's own.

25th April 1955 (Monday)

We have just returned, Ella, Rosemary and I, from an Easter holiday in Cheltenham and London. We had almost continuous sunshine. At Cheltenham we discovered a delightful hotel – the Ellenborough – in a quiet street, Oriel Road, yet close to the Promenade. Though I have passed through Cheltenham, it exceeded my expectations as a place to stay in. The Regency architecture reminds one in some ways of Edinburgh. The buildings are less substantial; but freshly painted in cream they give an atmosphere of brightness and I know no town where there is so much lovely wrought-iron work. You get the same curved buildings as in Edinburgh. The parks were at their freshest green with the almond blossom just out and the chestnuts came out during the time we were there. The Promenade faintly reminded me of Regency Brighton though Cheltenham would not be complimented by that. It is curious to see Caryatids interspersed between the shops. The Rotunda has a squat dome of oxidised bronze recalling St. George's in Charlotte Square. The police station is the old residence of George III. There is a ridiculous statue of Edward VII in knickerbockers looking down at a small child and a much more interesting statue of Captain Wilson of the Antarctic, which recalls the statue of Captain Scott in London near the Athenæum. The Wilson statue was executed by Lady Scott. Many of the streets are named from the Peninsular and Napoleonic Wars – Vittoria, Douro, Trafalgar and Wellington. One of the most peculiar architectural features is in St. George's Road where a classical block of houses has been left, I understand deliberately, uncompleted. The excellence of the Promenade shops was only matched by the attractiveness of the second-hand bookshops in side streets. Cheltenham Ladies' College seemed to me much less attractive than St. Leonard's, overbuilt in Victorian gothic on a too-constricted site. Cheltenham (Boys') College is one of the earliest of the Victorian Public Schools with wide playing fields and a plaque recording the date when rugby football was first played there. I noted the number of legal associations. The very name of our hotel must have come from Lord Ellenborough and it bore an old coat of arms (earlier than the peerage) with the motto 'Humana vana'. In Cheltenham College Chapel there was a memorial to Lord James of Hereford, and Lord Hatherley must have taken his title from the village outside Cheltenham. One curious feature of the Promenade at Cheltenham was a record of road casualties giving the score of deaths and injuries to the various categories of road users; a rather macabre feature.

The hotel was full. I never saw so many single old ladies sitting at separate tables or for that matter so many elderly bachelors. They spent most of the time in the lounge and disappeared to bed not later than 9 p.m. They were more than usually reticent with each other and scarcely batted an eyelid at each other when they came into the dining room.

We, however, fell in with a couple, Leonard and Jane Clark, with whom we spent every evening and who got the same entertainment out of gauging our fellow-guests as we did. Leonard Clark is an Inspector of Schools but his chief interest is in poetry. He is an authority on Walter de la Mare and also knows Edith Sitwell and Edmund Blunden. He gave me two volumes of his poems and they were certainly delightful. He belonged to the Forest of Dean and his wife had spent much of her life in Worcester and also had lived for a time in St. Andrews. They now live in London. He was a most entertaining talker and liked to get quiet before he began. He had a curious theory that the first Pope of Rome after Peter – Linus – was descended from the Forest of Dean. His theory was that Caractacus (Caradoc) settled in Rome, had a daughter Caractaca, whose son was Pudens (mentioned in the New Testament) whose son was Linus, also mentioned in the New Testament. When I first met him I asked him what he took me for and he said the Professor of International Law at Bristol University. I suspected that he was either academic or a poet because he wore a crimson shirt with a brown tie! He was very clever at discovering particulars about our fellow-guests. There was, for example, Lord Parmoor, the brother of Sir Stafford Cripps; and eighty-five year old Canon Garnett late of Stow-on-the-Wold who had a German wife who had spent the war in a German concentration camp and her niece the Countess of Thuringia, a god-daughter of the Kaiserin, who also had been in a concentration camp and whose two daughters had been taken to Russia; a ninety year old Canon Raby of London, Ipswich and Leicester, who never heard a word anyone said but who liked to recount his past life *ad longum* to anyone who would listen. There was an elderly lady at the next table to us who always read a newspaper, though owing to the newspaper strike, no national papers were being published: she turned out to be a retired civil servant.

Good Friday, 8th April, in the afternoon we took a bus to Painswick, by the road which gradually mounts southwards into the Cotswolds. There is a lovely view of Gloucester tower five miles off and Prinknash Abbey, which was formerly the house of the Earl of Rothes, and is now occupied by the Benedictines from Caldey, Pluscarden being their daughter house. On the way there are two delightful inns, The Royal William and The Adam and Eve, the latter at Paradise! It was eighteen years or thereby since we had been in Painswick with its yews. It has many attractive houses but is not quite so picturesque as the best Cotswold villages. Two charming features however, are the lychgate in Tudor architecture with inscribed on one side the opening words of the Magnificat, and on the other side 'Rejoice in the Lord alway and again I say unto you rejoice'; and a little fountain in the churchyard with animals carved in the stone the whole way round, representing 'all creatures great and small'. It was obvious that Painswick had celebrated the Coronation after the fashion of Angela Thirkell for there was a plaque commemorating a celebration presided over by one of the Weld-Foresters with very little about the Coronation. After tea in an old house beside the churchyard where a little hunch-back, harassed by the Good Friday crowds, dispensed the food supplies, we walked down a lovely Cotswold lane to the west.

On 9th April we visited Bishop's Cleeve, the church of which is an amalgam of different styles and has an unusual Norman west door with a buttress on the west wall.

On Easter day, the 10th, we attended Cheltenham Parish

Church which was packed to the door. The vicar gave a quite excellent sermon.

On Monday, the 11th April, we went to Gloucester and had more time to browse round the cathedral than on previous occasions, spending a considerable time in the sunlit cloister. The most interesting new feature which I noticed was the little cross which was made and used by Lieut. Col. Carne, V.C., in Korea. After tea in the New Inn which resembles the Golden Cross in Oxford, being one of the oldest in England, we went down the Southgate to the site of the old Crypt School where there is the church of St. Mary de Crypt and St. Owen, with associations with both George Whitfield and Robert Raikes. I asked Leonard Clark afterwards if there was any connection between this St. Owen and the St. Ouen in Rouen. He said, 'Yes', and that there was a parish in Brittany called St. Ouen. It is a curious fact that two Celtic names like Owen and McLeod should both be found in Rouen. Between Gloucester and Cheltenham there is a large area of hutments containing a big section of the Foreign Office.

On Tuesday 12th April we took a bus to Tewkesbury. The interior is to me more impressive than Gloucester. On Wednesday 13th April we drove ten miles to the west of Gloucester to a wood near Four Oaks, not far from Dymock, known in the district as Newent 'Daffodil Woods'. Here wild daffodils grow in profusion amongst the trees and the public are allowed to gather as many of them as they like. There were almost a dozen motor buses there that afternoon but the people were so distributed amongst the woods that there was no sensation of being over-crowded.

On Saturday 16th April we hired a car and took the Clarks with us for a visit to many of the Cotswold villages which we love best. Our route was by Andoversford, Naunton, the Slaughters, Bourton-on-the-Water, Lower Slaughter, the Swells, Stow-on-the-Wold, Bourton-on-the-Hill, Chipping Campden, Broadway, Stanton, Stanway, Winchcombe and Cleevehill. We stopped at Upper and Lower Slaughter and renewed our acquaintance with them and at Bourton-on-the-Water Rosemary was greatly delighted with a second visit to its model village. We had tea at Chipping Campden, and spent some time there and then on the way home we looked in at Stanton Church and found our names in the visitors' book from our 1951 visit. Leonard Clark pointed out to me the site of Hayles Abbey. I was interested to find that our driver was an Ayrshire man. 'As sure as God's in Gloucestershire' is a still current Gloucestershire expression and seems to come from the days of the Holy Blood of Hayles, which made the Abbey so famous before the Dissolution of the Monasteries.

On Monday 18th, after a most wonderful holiday at Cheltenham, we left for London. On reaching London we had tea at our hotel, the Rubens, and then the three of us set out by taxi for a preliminary tour of inspection. It was the second time I had brought children for their first visit to London and it brought back the same thrill that I had on my own first visit. We went back along the Strand as far east as Bow Bells and then came back by the Embankment and then up to Piccadilly Circus and then along the Mall. The little lift-boy who took us up to our room told me that every day he cycles to the hotel and back again from his home in Walthamstow, fifteen miles away.

Tuesday, 19th April. While Ella and Rosemary spent the day shopping with Nan Currie, I went to the British Council of Churches, which, this time, met at the Y.W.C.A. at 108 Baker Street. Incidentally, Nan Currie, who is an old friend of Ella's, is an interesting example of personal enterprise. Before the war, she became head of a Department in Lewis's in London. Then she entered the Wrens during the war as a rating, and happened to be at Dover at the time of the evacuation of Dunkirk. With a good record there, she rose to be ultimately a Superintendent in the Wrens, and Wren C.O. for the Western Approaches, on the Staff of Admiral Sir Percy Noble. This position entitled her to slap Admirals on the back, act as hostess to the Duchess of Kent, and even launch a cruiser. Now, she runs a post office and general merchant's business in Chiddingstone, Kent, the whole village, on account of its interest, being a National Trust property.

Thursday 21st April. This morning I took Rosemary to the Tower, while Ella shopped. The Tower was Rosemary's first choice. She was thrilled when a Beefeater introduced her to one of the Guard, a Scots Guard from Morningside. I was much interested in a plaque commemorating the Rev. Alexander Forsyth, LL.D., Minister of Belhelvie, Aberdeenshire, who, in 1807, invented the percussion system which was adopted by the British Army in 1839. Part of Chanonry Lodge, Aberdeen, occupies the site of the former residence of the Canon of Belhelvie. It is also curious that the first notable execution at the Tower was Sir William Wallace, and the last Simon Fraser, Lord Lovat. We watched the ravens beside the place where three English Queens – Anne Boleyn, Catherine Howard, and Lady Jane Grey – met their end. Among the grim exhibits in the Tower are an iron frame used for the system of hanging in chains (so vividly described in H.M. Prescott's *Man on the Donkey*), and the room where the two little Princes were murdered. In the place where Henry VI died, representatives of King's College, Cambridge, and Eton, his foundations, each year place, respectively, red roses and white lilies, on the anniversary of his death. There is also the room occupied by Latimer, Ridley and Laud, as well as Bishop Leslie of Ross (who wrote the *History of Scotland*), and the gallery where Sir Walter Raleigh walked in his confinement. Of the Crown Jewels, I noticed particularly the ruby presented by the King of Castille to the Black Prince, the Armils first used at last Coronation, and the incomprehensible supply of salt-cellars.

In the afternoon, before meeting Ella for tea, I took Rosemary to Madame Tussaud's. The modern likenesses are not really good – many British politicians, especially Churchill and Eden, are just recognisable, and no more. The American Presidents are better. But, most interesting were the tableaux, especially 'When did you last see your Father?' with most realistic Roundheads; the capture of Guy Fawkes; the execution of Mary, Queen of Scots; and the death of Nelson. Of the other figures, I particularly noted Sir Walter Scott with Maida, and Cardinal Newman. The children's tableaux, too, were captivating, especially Robin Hood in Sherwood Forest; Long John Silver at the stockade; Snow White and the Seven Dwarfs; and Alice with the Queen of Hearts (the Cheshire cat duly smiling from an adjoining tree).

After tea, we walked back to the Hotel through St. James's Park, and watched the Scots Guards at Wellington Barracks.

Friday 22nd April. We three spent the morning watching the complete ceremony of the changing of the Guard at Buckingham Palace. Then, while Ella sat down in Westminster Abbey, I took Rosemary round the sights – not least, to the Battle of Britain window. In the afternoon, I took Rosemary to St. Paul's. We were able to go behind the temporary screen, and see the reconstructed east end. Before we left, Rosemary could recite Blake's lines on his monument in the crypt:–

> To see a world in a grain of sand
> And a Heaven in a wild flower
> Hold infinity in the palm of your hand
> And eternity in an hour.

For variation, we went by bus, and returned by three tubes, to give Rosemary a round of the escalators. We met Ella at Sloane Square for tea. Next morning, after a fortnight of sunshine, we returned home by the Flying Scotsman being pulled to Grantham by 'Scottish Union'. I noticed also 'Mons Meg' at King's Cross. But I wish British Transport would resume the use, once made by the North British Railway, of Sir Walter Scott characters for their engines – 'Redgauntlet' for example.

9th May 1955 (Thursday)

A General Election is upon us. It was suddenly announced when we were at Cheltenham, and is to take place on Thursday 26th May, right in the middle of the General Assembly – very awkward for a Procurator who is also a Returning Officer. On Saturday 7th May, I travelled to Paisley, Greenock, and Dunoon to receive the Parliamentary Writs. The Sheriff Clerk at Dunoon was distracted by a last minute suggestion from the Scottish Home Department to accelerate the Argyll declaration by bringing in the ballot boxes by air or if necessary fishery cruiser. Air was previously refused; I asked for a promise of a fishery cruiser immediately after the last General Election. But my suggestion has been 'under consideration' for four years. However, none of these worries could darken the loveliness of a spring day on the Clyde, with the trees in their freshest green, and even the rhododendrons in bloom.

The Billy Graham 'All-Scotland Crusade' has ended its six weeks in the Kelvin Hall, Glasgow, a week ago. About 14,000–18,000 attended each night; 50,000 at Ibrox Park on the second last night; and over 100,000 at Hampden Park on the final night – the largest religious meeting ever held in Scotland. One striking fact is that, successful as was Billy Graham at Harringay Stadium a year ago, the success of the All-Scotland Crusade has been still greater. Why should Scotland have thus responded, when it was almost impervious to John Wesley in the eighteenth century? It is an interesting question. But, in my view, it can only be explained by a readiness for some revival before Billy Graham ever appeared. I have never noted anything about him before in this Journal. I heard him at the beginning of May a year ago in Harringay but took ill the same week. I heard three relays broadcast from Glasgow, one in the Usher Hall, another the Hampden Park relay, and a final relay the Sunday following, gathering up the high lights of the campaign. I think that Cliff Barrows with his choir of over 1,000 was almost the most moving part – 'Just as I am' sung when the converts made their 'decisions'; 'Ye gates, lift up your heads' sung by 18,000 voices; 'The Lord's my Shepherd' sung to 'Crimond' with Dr. Baird Ross's descant. Cliff Barrows, himself, is a deservedly attractive personality. Beverly Shay, with his 'spirituals' has a magnificent 'Paul Robeson' voice, but his solos left me unaffected. The secret of Billy Graham's power is difficult to guess. He is tall, fair, and good-looking, with a strong well-modulated voice, but his characteristic is not so much charm, as immense latent energy. Despite technique which was novel to me, I could not but be impressed at my first hearing of him at Harringay with the fact that his was genuine evangelism, of a kind quite different from that of the traditional evangelist. My first impression has only been strengthened by hearing him on later occasions, and by a series of morning broadcasts which he gave on the Beatitudes – the 'Beautiful Attitudes' as he called them. He speaks as one having authority – 'The Bible says' is repeatedly on his lips. Yet, whatever his private beliefs, fundamentalism is not obtruded. Two remarkable characteristics of his preaching are that he always seeks to strengthen the Churches, by urging the converts to join them and that his gospel seems equally appealing to the Roman Catholic at one extreme and the most ardent evangelist at the other. I was asked by Nevile Davidson to meet him at a private lunch, but, unfortunately, was in London, and could not go. James Stewart says that he is a completely humble sincere Christian. Certainly, he has disarmed his critics, and brought religion right into the forefront, and, behind it all, an Unseen Power was working.

I am starting on the third week of one of the heaviest cases I have been in. Two German refugees, Meyer and Lucas, became associated with the Scottish Cooperative Wholesale Society in the production of rayon material. A company was set up, with Meyer and Lucas as minority shareholders but managing directors. Now they sue the Society, because they alleged that the latter oppressed the minority shareholders within the meaning of sec. 210 of the Companies Act, 1948. I am for the Society, and the Dean for Meyer and Lucas. I had to cross-examine Meyer for a day, and Lucas for a day and a half. My instructing solicitor, Thomas Young, gave me great encouragement today by telling me that the Society was greatly pleased with my efforts for them. The issue, however, hangs in the balance.

19th May 1955 (Thursday)

Within the last ten days, I have been at the opening, or reopening, of two distinctive Edinburgh buildings. To celebrate its internal reconstruction and the union of the New and University Clubs, the united club – the New Club – held a 'house-warming' party, which must have been attended by about 250 persons. It was certainly one of the most colourful scenes for many a day, rivalling Holyroodhouse itself – with tiaras (by special request), a great variety of military uniforms, Archers in their evening dress, and some members of the Hon. Company of Edinburgh Golfers (Robbie Maconochie) included in their scarlet tail-coats. The redecoration of the Club is on the whole very good, very much a 'period' redecoration, and, possibly, as Angela Thirkell would have said, 'too too too New Club'. Everything is almost, if not quite, right. Then, yesterday, we were at the opening of the new University 'Adam House', on the site of the old Operetta House. Here, the redecoration, notwithstanding the Adam building, is very modern, a complete contrast to the New Club, full of pastel shades in many gentle colours, and also of many modern designs. On the whole, I preferred the enterprise shown in Adam House, to the restored convention of the New Club, though they differ so much as scarcely to be comparable. They are, I understand, the work of the same architect, Mr. Kinninmonth.

After lunch today at the Round Table, I thought I would try to record what I recollected of the drift of conversation, just as an impression of an average day's table-talk, not in any way one of our best days. As usual, the talk was interspersed with fines, both Jock and I being fined for referring to work of our own. I cannot hope, or try, to reproduce the continual banter. But here was the general drift. The Lord Chancellor (Kilmuir) addressed a political meeting in Edinburgh yesterday. Was this right? The general view was that the anomaly of a judge who was also in the government had certain advantages. It saved having that anomalous creature, a Minister of Justice. On the other hand, if the political side of the Lord Chancellor's work was pressed too far, the anomaly would break down. It was one thing to handle government business in the rarefied atmosphere of the House of Lords: quite another to appear at the hustings. What about a Lord Chancellor being heckled! What impression would he create of judicial impartiality at a time when, of all times, political feeling runs high? How could a Lord Chancellor who took much part in politics ever be regarded as impartial if he had to decide a Liversidge v. Anderson, I asked? Yes, said the Dean, 'that old scoundrel Simon' decided Liversidge [1942] A.C. 206, Crofter Hand Woven Harris Tweed Co. [1942] A.C. 435, and Duncan v. Cammell, Laird & Co. [1942] A.C. 624, all in one year, 'a monstrous series of injustices!'

Stanley Gimson then referred to electioneering in Shettleston. Jack Hunter, the Conservative candidate, addresses heated meetings every night. At the end, up come some of his audience. 'That was a great speech, Mr. Hunter. Pity we can't vote for you!' Mr. McGovern, the Labour candidate, only addresses one meeting – 'comes out on the balcony once' (here with a leer at Frank Duffy, our one Roman Catholic) 'and gives his blessing *urbi et orbi*' – yet is returned easy victor. Then I introduced an incident of my own as Returning Officer at Paisley, and was promptly fined for shop. After various other subjects, we turned to the question whether law was an exact science. I argued that a case could be made for the view that it was, and therefore that a judge who followed out the law could do so equally well whether he was personally a good or bad character. This was to trail my coat, whereupon Robert Reid weighed in on the negative. This developed into a discussion on the basis that law could never be an exact science, however much that might be the ideal. Expression of thought could never quite exactly express the thought. Our words are like shoes, and our ideas often go ill-shod. Robert Reid maintained the opposite. Had we ever any ideas except those we expressed? We then discussed the difference between a good judge (say Patrick) and a bad one (say Stevenson). A good judge came nearest to expressing his ideas in accurate language. Had James Stevenson any ideas? Or if he had, was it just incapacity to express them? Did medical considerations enter into the problem? One form of aphorism was that a man thought one thing, but called it another, as for example when James Stevenson, in the Boswell MSS case, habitually called James Boswell James Ramsay. Having recently met Mr. G.A. Pollock, Consultant Orthopaedic Surgeon at Westerlea, I said that he had told me that something like this happened with spastic children. They reached out their hand for a tumbler but their hand might go a foot to the right of the object they intended to touch. Spastics also achieve greater normality sometimes under the influence of alcohol or an anaesthetic. Parents sometimes saw their spastic child coming out of an anaesthetic. At the first recovery of consciousness, he would seem relatively normal, and their hopes would rise. But, with the recovery of full consciousness, he would slip back to the usual spastic state.

It may be of interest to record the rise of counsel's fees as indicating the change in the value of money after the last war. As a junior, for a straightforward opinion, one might in 1945 receive three guineas. When I took silk the corresponding senior's fee would be five guineas. By last year, my minimum had risen to fifteen, and recently I have made it at Mr. McWhannell's suggestion twenty-one. My highest opinion fee in 1955 so far has been fifty. It is impossible to suggest the rise in tariff for appearances in Court, as these fees vary much more according to the character of the work, and the counsel engaged. But I think these minima for opinion-work are probably about as high as any, unless the Dean's. Of course, this takes no account of work which one may always do for nothing. I give opinions each week to ministers, outside my Procurator's work, for nothing, though I do like a letter of thanks, which, alas, too seldom comes. I always remember, however, that, on the minimum stipend, even a letter of thanks costs something. And, often, long afterwards, one finds the gratitude was there. I certainly receive it in personal friendship.

22nd May 1955 (Sunday)

When Gordon's class mate, Harold Nicolson (just assumed a partner in Morton, Smart, Macdonald and Prosser W.S.) was at tea this afternoon with some American friends of Alison's, we were recalling some changes in the convention of law-practice during my period at the Bar. I instanced the practice of Morton, Smart, and other leading firms, until fairly recently, still to be paying counsel's fees in cash, the shillings being carefully wrapped up in the pound notes, the latter being folded into triangular shapes to form a pocket for the shillings. Harold pointed out that, now, the firm always paid counsel's fees by cheque, but that it was still considered bad form by them, vis-à-vis counsel, to cross the cheques! I pointed out that, when I was an apprentice with Maclay, Murray & Spens in Glasgow in 1921–3 they had given up the practice of writing deeds and all their deeds were typewritten, but that, when I came to Morton, Smart in 1923–4, they were still writing deeds. 'Yes,' said Harold, 'they only gave up writing deeds when the old conveyancing clerk died recently.' I recalled receiving instructions from one firm, Henry & Scott W.S., in a still older form. The letter of instruction was simply folded round the fee, both ends and both sides, and then sealed at the join. Henry & Scott were the last firm to maintain this practice of earlier centuries. (Mr. Matthew Henry, W.S., a courteous and urbane and humorous Writer to the Signet of the old school, died the other day at the age of ninety-five!)

The General Assembly begins this week on Tuesday 24th. On Wednesday 25th I go, in the evening, for the Renfrewshire counts at Paisley next day, Polling Day, and return on Friday morning in time for the Assembly. We have a late evening sitting in the Assembly on Friday to hear the first Appeal which has come before the Assembly on the 'Act anent Congregations in an Unsatisfactory State'. On Saturday morning, I leave early for Dunoon, where the Argyll count takes place at 4 p.m. that afternoon. I am staying at the Marine Hotel, Hunter's Quay, on Saturday, and am being driven back on Sunday morning by the Argyll Police – fortunately, for a rail strike is timed to start that day.

23rd May 1955 (Monday)

This morning, Ella and I received tickets from Sir James Fergusson to attend the first election of Scottish Representative Peers to have been held in the Parliament Hall since 1707. Holyroodhouse could not be used on this occasion, since the Lord High Commissioner (the Duke of Hamilton) was taking up residence there today. The peers sat on both sides of a long table, and at a cross table at one end sat Lord Elphinstone, Lord Clerk Register, as Returning Officer, with Sir James at his side. They processed in from the W.S. Library. We sat with our backs to the door leading to the Advocates' Corridor. In front of us with their backs to us were the Dukes of Atholl and Argyll, the Earls of Elgin and Stair and Caithness and Breadalbane, Viscount Arbuthnott, the Earl of Glasgow, Lord Forbes, Marquises of Huntly and Lothian and others. Opposite were Lord Polwarth, Lord Fairfax of Cameron, Lord Gray (a callow nervous youth overdressed in a stock), the Earls of Haddington, Crawford, Home and Dundee, Lord Balfour of Burleigh, Lord Reay, the Earls of Wemyss, Strathmore and Selkirk. There were some fifty peers present; the Duke of Montrose voted for Lord Polwarth as his proxy; and several voted as absent voters. Most of the peers received between 51 and 54 votes, but there were some stragglers who received much fewer. I have never seen so many people congregated in Parliament Hall. It was a gay and colourful scene. Only Lord Elphinstone, a bent stooping figure, wore his robes. Atholl, Argyll, Breadalbane, Caithness wore their kilts. The most interesting personalities were Crawford, Home, Polwarth and Selkirk. The Lord Provost and magistrates, with city halberdiers, were opposite us at the east wall. Alison managed to find a place opposite us – to survey this museum of antiquities. It was all very picturesque, and one would be sorry to see the ceremony disappear. It must be the only election of its kind to which the Ballot Act does not apply. As usual, many peers voted for themselves. A guffaw went round the hall at the first vote so cast – by the Earl of Caithness. Amongst the peeresses, the Duchess of Argyll, (the former Mrs. Sweeney and celebrated debutante), and the Countess of Wemyss (in bright cerise) were conspicuous. Both Lord and Lady Wemyss, however, looked pale and older than a year ago – they lost their little heir Lord Elcho in the same motor accident as Sir James Fergusson lost a daughter.

In the voting each peer present, according to seniority of rank, read out his list of those for whom he votes. Then the Principal Clerk of Session (George Watson) read out the list again; after these votes, the one proxy voted; thereafter, the lists of the absent voters were read out. The peers seemed to sit in no particular order. At the head of the long table on either side, were the Duke of Atholl and Lord Polwarth. Yet the Duke of Argyll, next to Atholl, voted first, and Lord Polwarth last. The first name to be called out on his list of peers was the Duke of Rothesay, Prince and Steward of Scotland. I wonder if Prince Charles has heard anything about it!

Dr. Warr conducted prayers. At Holyroodhouse, he is referred to as 'Dean of the Thistle and of the Chapel Royal'. Here, on the advice of myself and the Clerk of Assembly, he was referred to as 'Minister of the High Kirk of Edinburgh'.

25th May 1955 (Wednesday)

The Assembly began yesterday. A curious embarrassment arose. The Duke of Hamilton, some time ago, informed Dr. White Anderson, as Convener of the General Administration Committee, that the Marquis of Salisbury was to be his guest at Holyroodhouse and would be in the Assembly yesterday. Could he speak? Dr. White Anderson agreed. Then the matter came before the General Administration Committee on Monday and they felt, not unnaturally, that it was highly embarrassing to have speaking in the Assembly, two days before the General Election, the House of Lords leader of one of the political parties, especially as the Marquis proposed to speak on the Hydrogen Bomb. This view was communicated to the Duke, who, as host, not unnaturally also, felt highly embarrassed, having invited the Marquis, especially when the American Ambassador was also to be there. We held an emergency meeting of the General Administration Committee after the forenoon session to consider further what could be done. I must say that I was most surprised that the Marquis should not have seen the unsuitability of his using such a platform for such a purpose at such a time. In the end, I proposed a solution which the Committee received with positive acclamation as a happy way out. It was that the American Ambassador, the Bishop of Durham, as a leading ecclesiastic of the Church of England, and the Marquis, as a leading layman, should *all* be invited to the floor of the Assembly. In the end the first did not come, but the other two did. The Bishop spoke first, and made a masterly and humorous short speech, which entirely caught the ear of the Assembly. Then the Marquis followed, with a long and, I regret to say, very commonplace utterance on the Hydrogen Bomb. The Assembly, which is no respecter of persons, listened courteously, but took the speech on its limited merits, and not because the speaker was the Marquis! It fell like a damp squib, and no harm was done.

In the evening, I was at Holyroodhouse with Ella for dinner. I sat between Lady Hutchison, wife of the President of the R.S.A., and Miss Hamilton, daughter of the late Rev. J.E. Hamilton and a granddaughter of the first Lord Mackay, who was one of the maids-of-honour. I found both very pleasant to talk to; Miss Hamilton was quite charming, and had been at Somerville about the same time as Alison was at L.M.H. She is an apprentice at Dundas & Wilson! I met Mrs. Billy Graham, who was amused when I was able to tell her that I had heard her on the one occasion when she herself spoke at Harringay. I asked her how her husband stood up to all the physical strain of these gigantic meetings. She said that he was not physically very strong, and could only explain by the way he was supported by people's prayers. She said this quite simply and sincerely. Ella sat with her and Dr. Billy Graham at the opening Session of the Assembly. Ella and I were both presented to the Duchess, and I thanked her for all that she and the Duke did at Evanston. The Duke made a most remarkable speech as Commissioner, saying that the last time a Hamilton Commissioner had met a Henderson Moderator was at the Great Glasgow Assembly of 1638. But the really remarkable part of the speech was on Evanston, and the need for sacrifice for greater Church unity.

29th May 1955 (Sunday)

Billy Graham, who was in the Assembly on Wednesday, came to the platform and made a speech of exactly one minute. It was so wholly admirable that it is worth quoting:–

> I have been listening to your debates this morning and yesterday with great interest, and I want to take this opportunity to thank you with all

the conviction of my heart for the encouragement you have given to the 'Tell Scotland' movement in the part that it played in the All-Scotland Crusade. We give the glory and the praise to God. The secret of any evangelism is prayer, unity, and the preaching of the Gospel of the Lord Jesus Christ. We give thanks to God and to you for your tolerance, your sympathetic understanding, your co-operation, and your prayers. God bless you, and thank you very much.

He stood at the desk immediately beside my chair as Procurator. I had the chance of judging him at a distance of three feet away. There is a fairness, modesty and sincerity about him that made his simple words memorable. Would that others, in that place, speak so little, and say so much.

I am back from the General Election. On Wednesday evening I travelled to Paisley. Next day, I attended to postal votes all morning, and squabbles between Paisley election agents. In the afternoon, I visited, with the Chief Constable (Allan) of Renfrewshire, polling stations at Bishopston, Port Glasgow, Greenock, Gourock, Inverkip and Kilmacolm. In the early evening, the Chief Constable of Paisley (Goudie) took me round Paisley polling stations, and after the close of the Polls, I superintended the West Renfrewshire count, getting to bed at 3 a.m. I was up at 7 a.m., left Paisley at 7.50 a.m., and spent all day in the General Assembly. In the evening, we heard, within closed doors the case of Arthur Memorial, New Cumnock, where, in what I should have regarded as a clear case under the Act anent Congregations in an unsatisfactory state, the General Assembly, by a narrow majority of about 104 to 94, overturned decisions of the Synod and Presbytery of Ayr. We finished at midnight, and then a cluster of newspaper reporters tried to get Longmuir and myself to tell what had happened within closed doors! We gave absolutely nothing away, and parted from them in good humour. I heard, earlier in the day, a most interesting talk on Church law and registration of votes with Mr. Fuller, Q.C., Procurator, and Mr. Hunt, law agent, of the Australian, and also the New South Wales General Assemblies.

On Saturday morning, I left at crack of dawn, and was in Dunoon by 11.30 a.m. for the Argyll count, which began at 4 p.m. and finished shortly after 7 p.m. – the smoothest and most expeditious count in which I have yet taken part. I was horribly embarrassed by Douglas Douglas, Sheriff-substitute who (1) came into the count (without any leave to do so); (2) went out to Dunoon and came in again, contrary to the regulations; and (3) went down in amongst the party agents and talked persistently to one side – a thing I studiously avoid. In the end, after trying to be patient, when he did the third thing, I asked the Sheriff Clerk to call him away, and I tried, as tactfully as I could, to remind him that the action was inadvisable. He was not even a Deputy-Returning Officer for Argyll, though, as a D.R.O. for Bute, he should have known better.

I stayed at the Royal Marine Hotel, Hunter's Quay, and in the evening was invited by Mr. Herbert Thom, the famous Clyde yachtsman, to a most fascinating lantern talk on yachting which he was giving in the Royal Clyde Yacht Club rooms (of which, as Sheriff, I am an honorary member) to yachting enthusiasts being trained by the School of Physical Recreation. I met Mr. Kerr Hunter, who runs the school, and seemed an excellent man for the job. This morning, the Argyll Police drove me back to Edinburgh, the railway strike having started at midnight last night.

We had difficulty in persuading the Post Office to get the Argyll count away quickly. They were inclined to take the view that, if it was not ready by a certain hour, they would not fly it to London till Monday. In the end, I pointed out to the Postmaster, an Englishman, that it would easily be transported to Renfrew aerodrome, if necessary by a later ferry (of which he did not seem to know) or even by car via Erskine Ferry. I asked him, if these possibilities were rejected to give me this as an official decision from Postal Headquarters in Edinburgh, as then I could report accordingly to the Scottish Office. Needless to say, this led Postal Headquarters to provide the necessary facilities. But the most astounding fact of all was that the English postmaster did not know where Renfrew lay in relation to Glasgow, and I had to explain to him, in words of one syllable, the geographical situation of Renfrew. It would be unbelievable were it not true.

The whole period of the election was one of brilliant sunshine and both shores of the Clyde were quite exquisite in the fresh green of the foliage, the rhododendrons, and the soft blues of the hills and water.

2nd June 1955 (Thursday)

The Assembly ended yesterday. G.D. Henderson's address as Moderator was the best for many a year. He stuck to his task, and examined the religious situation of 1855 as contrasted with 1955, with a wealth of entirely fresh minute historical detail, and calm detached humour. To some it might appear too much like a University lecture, but it was wise for him to take that line. It reminded me of my father's own address in 1921, when he contrasted the outlook with 1821. The difference was that Henderson remained almost entirely historical, whereas Dad used the historical contrast to look forward rather than backward. The Commissioner's closing speech was not equal to the remarkable one with which he opened the Assembly. For the first time, the Hall was only moderately full, thanks to the railway strike.

The usual Holyrood Garden Party was held in brilliant sunshine, the first time I have ever gone with tile hat without an umbrella for emergencies. For me, the most interesting day was Tuesday. In the discussion on the Anglo-Scottish Church conversations, I felt, as seldom, compelled to intervene, and appealed to brother laymen to support the conversations. I realised that I was speaking from the heart, and some incipient opposition died down, and, to my delight, two laymen came forward with supporting speeches – Sir James Fergusson and J.D. Michael. The deliverance was, in the end, carried unanimously. Alick Buchanan Smith telephoned me the same evening with his good wishes, and said that his father – George Adam Smith – had always held the view that episcopacy and Presbyterianism could be reconciled.

I was back in Court today before Lord Walker, after my fortnight of Assembly and General Election.

Two other incidents of the Assembly:– This year a letter was received from the Original Secession Church in response to overtures from our Inter-Church Relations Committee. They wish to accede to the Church of Scotland, a very timely healing of an old division. I was appointed a member of the Special Committee to confer on the arrangements for effecting the union. The other incident was the visit of Lord Lawson, whom I met at Holyrood at the garden party, and who spoke in the Assembly next day. A modest little man, he left school at the age of twelve to enter the Durham coal-mines. He has been a Methodist lay reader for fifty years, and after serving in the pits, entered Parliament, became Labour Secretary of State for War, received a barony, and was appointed Lord Lieutenant of Durham. He made a quiet kindly little speech, concluding with a quotation from Thomas a Kempis.

The *College Courant* – the Journal of the Glasgow University Graduates' Association – publishes in its Whitsun 1955 number an appreciation of W.M. Gloag which I was asked to write.

J.M. Peterson, a young advocate, who appeared with Harald Leslie and Gordon Stott in this year's Assembly, came up to me, and I asked him how he had enjoyed his first appearance in the Assembly. He made the very significant reply: 'What astonished me was the way in which some ministers, without any hesitation, impugned each other's veracity.' A just comment: happily, this characteristic is confined to a few, but they can do infinite harm. So far as my experience goes, it is not confined to the General Assembly, but there it is done so openly that it shocks those unfamiliar with it. How much the Scottish temperament requires an infusion of moderation, and, sometimes also, magnanimity. Still, I would rather have that, bad as it is, than the veiled shafts of a certain episcopal representative in the British Council of Churches, happily just retired from office. How much more attractive is the intellectual honesty and cleaner fighting of the Bar. Such behaviour would create a permanent black mark against anyone who adopted it in Parliament House.

6th June 1955 (Monday)

The death of Lord Birnam is announced today. Oddly, I dreamt last night of a vacancy on the Bench. Lord Birnam was a shrewd, hard-headed, calm, level-headed, wholly un-fussy lawyer, and a friendly quite unassuming character who was universally popular. At the end of last Session, at our Bench and Bar Party, I shook hands with him, wondering if I would see him again. He said nothing, but I knew he was entering a nursing home almost next day. He married less than ten years ago, and he and Lady Birnam were a veritable Darby and Joan, equally beloved by all the friends of either. He hid his gifts under a dormouse-like exterior: but he was much sounder in judgment than most, and his promotion owed nothing to anything except his own merit.

I called on Lord Cooper this evening. He and James Cooper were sunning themselves in their garden. Tommy Cooper seemed to me to have failed still further: I noticed a change in resonance in his voice. They twitted me about the vacant judgeship. Mr. McWhannell told me the guess of the Bar was 1. the Dean; 2. myself; 3. Chris Guest; 4. Harald Leslie. My own view is that the Dean will receive the appointment if he wants it; and that, if he does not want it, it will go to Chris Guest, if only for political reasons: he would make an excellent judge, in any event.

13th June 1955 (Monday)

Willie Tindal and I set out on a two-day journey to Portmadoc to attend the General Assembly of the Presbyterian Church of Wales as representatives of the Church of Scotland.

We travelled in a day of soft sunshine via Biggar, Carlisle, Warrington, Chester, Mold to Ruthin, where we spent the night. I have never motored south at this time of year. The country, especially Tweedsmuir, the road over Shap to Kendal, and our journey through North Wales, was quite lovely. We discoursed all the way with an unending flow of congenial talk, about everything under the sun – the Bar, the Anglo-Scottish Conversations, personalities, place-names, Wales and the Welsh.

14th June 1955 (Tuesday)

Today the weather changed for the worse, and, at the place where the mountains should have been grandest, a Scotch mist withheld their tops from view. We had some sunshine, however, in Ruthin, where we spent an hour before leaving, and later again, after lunch in Caernarvon.

In Ruthin, the most interesting building is an old Courthouse of the early fifteenth century, now used as a bank. I was struck by the scanty stock carried by most of the shops, except those selling cheap bric-a-brac. In Ruthin, they refer to Liverpool as the capital of Wales. The Liverpool *Daily Post* is the chief newspaper. I was intrigued to see a notice-board at one chapel announcing a visit (which had taken place on 12th June) of Dr. Martin Niemöller. I expected, as a result, that we should meet him at the Assembly. But, on reaching Portmadoc, we learned that he, and Frau Niemöller, had been here at the end of last week. It was strange that the meeting at which this U-boat commander of the First World War should have spoken was presided over by Mr. William George, the surviving ninety-one year old younger brother of Lloyd George, the organiser of German defeat. He still practises as a solicitor in Portmadoc, and it was in Portmadoc that Lloyd George was himself articled and practised. The name is still to be seen on the office window in Portmadoc High Street.

We left Ruthin about 11 a.m. meaning to have lunch at Bettys-y-Coed. As I left, I offered the man who had garaged our car a tip, but he would not take it: this impressed us both. On the way to Bettys, we passed a large flock of sheep and lambs. I have never seen lambs jump with such agility. They had no difficulty in clearing the wing of a car or the backs of other sheep. They were built more lightly, and had lighter coats and were relatively small. I asked the shepherd the breed, and he replied: 'Welsh'. At Cerrig-y-Druidon, an intriguing but unpronounceable name, though very beautiful when one hears it properly said, we joined the main Holyhead Road (A5). On the way we had guesses about our Portmadoc hosts. Captain Williams – Army, Navy, Air Force, Mercantile Marine? We voted Army. Ages of himself and his wife – forties, fifties, sixties? We voted for fifties.

We ran on to Portmadoc, and at a chemist's shop were directed to Aelygarth, the Williams being obviously well known. When we entered, an old gentleman greeted us – he looked like seventy, but turned out to be eighty-eight. I took him to be Captain Williams, and said I had brought some Edinburgh shortbread for his wife. He said: 'My wife is dead. Mrs. Williams is my daughter, and her husband is Captain of a big British India liner – the *Dilwara* (14,000 tons) – at present engaged as a troopship.' The old gentleman's name was also Mr. Williams. We were then met by his daughter, and given most comfortable rooms looking across to Snowdon, hidden in the mist. The Williams could not have been kinder. After a meal, in Mr. Williams' company – even at eighty-eight he was indefatigable – we set off to the Capel Saesneg for the one English service of the Assembly. The chapel was a bare building – their chapels shake our taste, as our churches must sometimes shake the taste of Anglicans. The singing was terrific. I was almost blown off my feet, and half of the last verse of every hymn was repeated as if they could not bear to leave it.

15th June 1955 (Wednesday)

The proceedings at the Assembly were nearly all in Welsh, though here and there an odd English speech was made. The Welsh Presbyterian Church has some 150,000 members. It is really, so far as its Welsh side is concerned, derived from the Calvinistic Methodists, and thus derives not from the Reformation so much as from the great Wesleyan revival of the eighteenth century, though it has had two revivals since, once in 1859, the other in 1904.

16th June 1955 (Thursday)

We left our kind hosts after breakfast, and set off by Beddgelert and the Pass of Aberglaslyn to Capel Curig. Beddgelert is to Bettys-y-coed what Kincraig is to Braemar. The Pass of Aberglaslyn was the loveliest thing we have seen in Wales, a glen in which you ascend between steep hills from one floor-bed to another higher one, each with a lake, and each lake with perfect reflections of the hills around. Except at the top, the Pass was more wooded than most Highland glens. From Capel Curig, we ran down the A5 by Bettys-y-coed and Corwen to Llangollen, and then northwards, by Ruabon and Wrexham, to the Trevor Arms, just north of Wrexham, where we stopped for lunch – a delightful wayside inn, full of interesting objects, with regard to each of which we got a full account from mine host. Then on through Chester, Wigan and Warrington till north of Preston we found a quiet wayside country-house hotel, Barton Grange, for tea, from which we telephoned for accommodation at Moss Grove, Grasmere. The Lakes were new to Willie, and he was charmed, as I was again, with Moss Grove. We came over the hill from Rydal by Dove Cottage.

The hotel was full of friendly people, particularly an Englishman who was just back after thirty years in South Africa, who asked me the best route from Grasmere to Aberfoyle, his next halt. He told us about the apartheid policy. His account, whether correct or not, was interesting. He considered that Smuts had spent too much time abroad, and while the stable door had been left open, the horse had bolted. The Nationalists had consolidated their position in his absence, and, on coming to power, had re-distributed the constituencies so as to ensure their continuance in power. A Republic of South Africa was only a matter of time. Apartheid was being pursued simply for political reasons, to secure the votes of the 'poor whites'. But the 'poor whites' were not as good workers as the natives, and, in the last resort, complete racial segregation would never be carried out, as the Afrikaners required native labour. He had great belief in Father Trevor Huddleston, who had stuck at his work among the natives, and whose views were personally disinterested. He considered the Rev. Michael Scott quite different – too much of an agitator. The Bishop of Johannesburg he regarded as not entirely disinterested, but as grinding his own axe. (Willie Tindal knew the last quite well, and said that, though an able man, he was rather apt to get a hold of particular grievances.) The Dutch Reformed Church was the only church which counted politically. Our English friend did not consider that, if South Africa became a republic, it would affect trade with Great Britain. In defence, South Africa could not allow herself to become isolated. He had walked all over the Lake District in his younger days with C.E.M. Joad.

17th June 1955 (Friday)

We visited Grasmere Church and bought some of the famous Nelson's
gingerbread and rum-butter. Then we set off to the head of Red Bank
for the view. I had never seen Grasmere in June before. The foliage
was much more profuse and the gardens were vivid with rhododendra,
azalea, laburnum and lilac. Then we set off home, by Thirlmere,
Keswick, the east side of Bassenthwaite, Carlisle, Canonbie (where
we lunched at the Cross Keys), Selkirk, Yair, Clovenfords and Stow.
We stopped for quite a time at Yair, bathed in the sunshine, with the
Tweed running softly by quite still and reflecting every tree. At Great
King Street, Ella and Elfrida were both waiting for us, at the end of
our journey of about 660 miles.

25th June 1955 (Saturday)

On Tuesday this week, the Duke of Edinburgh attended a sherry party
at the New Club. We were grouped in different rooms, and he passed
through each room, spending about quarter-of-an-hour in each. The
arrangements were quite informal. When he entered the room, we all
stood up, but, immediately thereafter, we all just proceeded with
conversation, as if he were not present. I had two interesting conversations, the one with one of the Abel-Smiths, who now lives at
Ashiestiel, and invited me to Sir Walter Scott's old home, and the
other with Squadron-Leader Horsley, the Duke's Equerry, whom I sat
next at the University Dinner to the Duke on 11th October 1954. He
is a friendly soul, discreet yet without any formality.

There is surprisingly little talk in Parliament House about the
vacancy created by Lord Birnam's death. I had a letter from Campbell
this week in which he said: 'I gather that a new judge may result in
a new Dean.' That is my own guess.

A curious instance occurred this week of the way in which ignorance
of Scotland south of the Border creates difficulties in inter-Church
relations. The Duchess of Kent is going to Stornoway on 5th July to
name a new life-boat. The parish minister of St. Columba's, Stornoway, received a letter from the assistant-secretary of the Royal
National Lifeboat Institution in London inviting him 'to assist' in the
service of dedication, and explaining that the Rev. H. Downie 'has
very kindly consented to dedicate the lifeboat'. Mr. H. Downie, it
appears, is an Episcopal clergyman. The Moderator, by chance, happened to be in Stornoway at the time, and asked the parish minister
to send on the letter of invitation to me. I immediately wrote the

Secretary of the R.N.L.I. respectfully protesting, and pointing out that, at such a public service when a member of the Royal Family was to be present, it was only right that the service should be entrusted to the parish minister. I also mentioned that the parish minister was very friendly with Mr. Downie, and would, no doubt, be very willing to have Mr. Downie associated with him. But I also pointed out that there were very few members of the Episcopal Church in the Isle of Lewis, and that, if the minister of another denomination were to be associated in the service, it would have been appropriate to invite a minister of the Free Church, which has a large membership in the Outer Hebrides. I received a telephone message from London admitting that a bad mistake had been made, and saying that Lord Saltoun, on behalf of the R.N.L.I., was sending a personal apology to the Moderator. Later, I received a letter from the Secretary of the R.N.L.I. stating that immediate steps had been taken to set the matter right. He added this extraordinary piece of information that 'the invitation to Mr. Downie was issued from this office on the recommendation of our Stornoway Branch'! It would be interesting to know who comprise the Stornoway Branch of the R.N.L.I. They must be extraordinarily ignorant of Stornoway. I have asked the parish minister to let me know. But it is very difficult to carry out inter-church conversations when things like this can happen. One well-known elder at once said to me: 'How can we make progress when this kind of thing takes place?' And that is the reaction of the man-in-the-pew. A similar incident happened when the monument to the Commandos was dedicated at Spean Bridge in presence of the Queen Mother. Then the dedication was by an Episcopal clergyman, and the parish minister was not even invited. Imagine the situation reversed on the other side of the Border. What makes it all the sadder is that, habitually, Episcopalian clergyman are invited to take part in public and national services in Scotland, for example, the National Service in St. Giles', and the Earl of Dalkeith was married in St. Giles' according to the Episcopal service, Bishop Warner conducting the service, and Dr. Warr (who had given the invitation) assisting. At the New Club this week I had an informal chat with Bishop Warner on the inter-church relations conversations. I said, quite frankly, that for me bishops, that is bishops, not prelates, constituted no great difficulty; but what I found much harder to understand was the Anglican position on intercommunion. In our preparatory talks for the next Anglo-Scottish conversations in September, Tom Torrance has prepared a paper on the mutual assimilation of the historic episcopate with Presbytery. But

I should want to see also Communion on the Anglican side a sacrament for all members of the Christian Church, and not simply for those confirmed (episcopally) or desirous of being confirmed. Surely the Lord's Supper is above the regulations of a particular denomination. On our journey to Wales, Willie Tindal used an expression which describes a certain unChristian attitude – 'Anglican thrust'. The goal must always be full unity of the Church, not mere rapprochement to a particular denomination. As Dr. Warr says in today's *Spectator*: 'Inter-communion presents no difficulties to the Church of Scotland. Accepted communicants of all branches of the Universal Church are welcomed to her Communion Tables, as are the clerics of other denominations, Anglican and non-Anglican, to her pulpits. She has never believed that this neighbourly hospitality could weaken her loyalty to her own high doctrines of the Church, its ministry, and sacraments.'

26th June 1955 (Sunday)

Over 1,000 took Communion in St. George's West at the morning Communion alone. It was my first experience of it since the reconstruction of the interior; actually the first Communion after the reconstruction was on Easter Sunday. Murdo preached a great, an unusual, sermon on 2 Cor. 13:5. 'Examine yourselves, whether ye be in the faith.' This needed (1) willingness for the costly sacrifice of a Cross; (2) a spirit of unconditional forgiveness; (3) a great assurance of faith. I looked up at the gallery where Gordon, as a boy, sat during Communion, and thought how wonderfully Ella fulfilled Murdo's words. Gentle, tender, forgiving, with her clear-shining nature and her ever-smiling courage. Was ever any man blessed as I have been?

And, then, in the afternoon, I had, as it were, communion with my own little family. At Alison's insistence, we drove down to Mellerstain, where we visited the house and had tea, returning by Kelso and St. Boswells. I have seen no lovelier taste in Scotland than the Adam rooms in Mellerstain. You cease to criticise, and can only stand in wonder. I have seen nothing like it since Wilton two years ago.

Last Friday, I went to Paisley for ceremonies connected with the retiral of John Hill, Procurator-Fiscal there for twenty-five years. We of the Sheriff Court held a little private function where we gave him the *Oxford Dictionary of Quotations* (by his own desire) and Partridge's *Dictionary of Slang* (for the lighter moments). Then the Faculty of Procurators gave him a sherry party and presented him with a box of pipes. I was asked to speak as Sheriff Principal. He is a sterling character, genial, frank, and friendly, just the kind of man for the office – and also a keen church man and Session Clerk of Sherwood Church, Paisley, to boot. Old 'Hammy' (Sheriff Hamilton) came back for the ceremony – the most Pickwickian figure Parliament House ever produced. It was like Mr. Chips revisiting his old school. We travelled home to Edinburgh together afterwards. He has an obvious bias against judges who are not Conservatives! I tried to convince him that both Harry Guthrie and John Wheatley were excellent.

2nd July 1955 (Saturday)

Today, Jock Cameron's elevation to the Bench is announced. He was more than the obvious choice. On merit, he would unquestionably be in the House of Lords, or in the Chair of one of the Divisions. For distinction in practice, as well as in wide service to the community, he is head and shoulders above his colleagues. I think that, of my own contemporaries, Ronald Morison has been the greatest counsel, but Jock was close on his heels, and, in other respects, a man of infinitely greater width of interest and versatility, besides giving endless public service, which Ronald did not do at all. Jock has also been probably the best Dean of Faculty of my time, full of vital, almost aggressive, personality, never letting the grass grow under his feet, but always devising fresh projects, for the greater benefit of the Faculty. His last act was to introduce the Duke of Edinburgh as an honorary member. Amid so many great qualities, one's only criticism might be that he is sometimes unnecessarily combative and impetuous, but with greater responsibility he has to a large extent overcome them, and grown in stature with the years. His salty, nautical language and vivid person-ality will be sadly missed at our Round Table. He is easily the most colourful personality in Parliament House. It is rather absurd that his own 'devil', John Wheatley, good though he is, should be senior on the Bench to Jock. But Jock is a big enough personality to make his presence abundantly felt wherever he is.

There is already talk about the vacant deanship. It is always difficult to judge when one is near the office. My own present impression is that Chris Guest and myself are the two names which will be most discussed. On the whole, I think that the new Dean will be Chris. I am neither going to push myself forward nor hold myself back. It is a matter for the Faculty not any individual. He has been latterly rather more in Court, and some people may feel that the Procuratorship absorbs too much of my time. I can only say that, if he is chosen, I shall be entirely satisfied.

Yesterday, we had Tom Taylor staying with us for the Holyrood Garden Party; Nellie Taylor arrived from Aberdeen, too, at 1.35 p.m. But rain involved the cancellation of the Garden Party, to everyone's chagrin. As a result, we had eleven visitors who came here instead, when the Garden Party went off – the Taylors, Rosemary Boyd (with whom Alison holidays in Norway in a fortnight), her mother, and two American friends, a Mrs. Allan and a Mrs. Granley, Archie Chalmers, from Oban, Nevile and Peggy Davidson, and Jim and Ann Aikman Smith. We were entertaining friends continuously from 2 to 7 p.m.

7th July 1955 (Thursday)

On the 5th I went to Oban and stayed the night with Archie Chalmers, going on to Lochgilphead for the Probation Committee on the 6th. The train journey to Oban was superb. I doubt if I have ever seen the country more lovely. I amused myself by taking photographs on the journey with my ciné-camera and had quite a chat with the engine driver at Balquhidder where we had to wait for the south-going train.

This was perhaps the last visit I shall pay to Kilbowie. Archie told me that the Finance Committee of the County Council were likely to resolve on the 6th to buy it as a hostel for boys from the Hebrides attending Oban High School. What a perfect situation for them with lovely grounds and a bathing slip close by. Archie himself had a bathe in the evening. This time he took me over the whole house above the fourth storey, where the view of Benderloch, Morven and Mull, with Kerrera in the foreground and fishing smacks passing up and down Oban Bay was quite superb. We also went over the whole policies. The house was built about 1884 under very different conditions from what obtain now. As we were walking past a disused tennis court I noticed a passage leading from a gate in the wall alongside the road down towards the house; it proceeded underground below the drive. I asked Archie what this was and he said: 'The entry for tradesmen and domestics. The passage-way comes out on the other side of the drive to a door in the basement.' I could not think, neither could he, of another house which had this feature. We both remarked how strange it was in these modern days of the Welfare State. But the arrangement was designed to hide from the house anyone like domestics and tradesmen who should not be seen except in their proper place. We both had a good laugh about it. He remarked to me that the Inspector of Taxes had said to him that one person in Argyll had an income of £21,000 a year, but owing to taxation received only £3,000. At the Oban end of the policies there is a little secluded corner with a garden seat where you can watch all that goes on in Oban but yet not be seen either from the garden or from the road. There, just ten feet off the rocks, we saw saithe jumping at least eighteen inches out of the calm water. The *King George V* passed up Kerrera Sound from Iona in the evening, and passed down the Sound next morning. It was a very happy visit yet tinged with the thought that very soon Archie would be leaving this lovely spot.

Archie told me an interesting fact about Craigie Aitchison and his family. Craigie used to love simply to sit indefinitely watching pictures. He never painted himself, but seemed to find an unusual fascination in art. The trait has come out in his son Ronald. Ronald decided to go to the English Bar, but, after eating some dinners, gave it up. It looked as if he would settle down to nothing. Then he tried painting, though he had no training. One day Lady Aitchison showed Sir William Hutchison some of his work. 'That boy has genius, though he can't draw,' said Sir William, 'but he should be encouraged to develop along his own line!' Ronald tried for a Slade School Scholarship. To his mother's surprise he won it. Then two of his pictures were singled out in an exhibition by an art critic. He then competed for a Rome Scholarship, and again he won it. Now he has embarked on art as a career, and it looks as if this was unquestionably his metier.

On the 6th I had a meeting with Mr. Neil MacKinnon at the Sheriff Court and provisionally planned a ceremony for Archie's retiral. It is likely to take place at the beginning of October and also a Dinner for the Faculty at which I want to be the host. Then at 11.30 a.m. a police car took me to Ardrishaig where I had lunch with Chief Constable and Mrs. Ross and then went to the Probation Committee at Lochgilphead. The police driver who took me to Ardrishaig was a new man, P.C. Carmichael, from Ballachulish. He was obviously shy and I mentioned this to the Chief Constable. He said that a police driver was very nervous the first time when he drove the Sheriff Principal! I said that I had always found the police most friendly and looked forward again to being driven by Sergeant Gillies. The Probation Committee met in Lochgilphead Courthouse, which was my first visit there. We had a short but very pleasant and useful meeting. Then at 3.30 Sergeant Gillies drove me right home to Edinburgh. We had quite a wait at Loch Lomondside where a bus was unable to pass a heavy articulated vehicle, but eventually by coaxing and some scarring of its sides the bus succeeded in getting past on the narrow road. We arrived home at 6.40 p.m. I had arranged for Sergeant Gillies to have dinner with us but he had 140 miles in front of him and decided to start on the return journey at once. He is an old friend and as he went said how much he looked forward to our drives together.

10th July 1955 (Sunday)

We returned yesterday after two days in Aberdeen for the Graduation. Ella and I motored there and back; Alison came later by train, and Harold, Kathleen and Robin motored up on Friday for the graduation itself, leaving Glasgow at 6 a.m. We were blessed with the most glorious weather. On the outward journey, we intended to cross by the Queensferry passage. But we found about sixty cars queued up for the three ferry-boats. It was useless to wait, and so we went round by Kincardine Bridge. On days like these, it would be almost better not to have the ferry, for it simply wastes time to go and see whether you can cross, and then find you can't. The Forth road bridge is long overdue. After Perth, we traversed the Carse of Gowrie to pass my old home. Then after lunch in Dundee, we proceeded by Arbroath and Montrose to Fettercairn, and then over the Cairn o'Mount. Fettercairn must have more associations with famous men than any other village in Scotland – Sir Walter Scott and Williamina Belsches, James Boswell and Samuel Johnson, the Boswell MSS found at Fettercairn House, Gladstone's old home at Fasque, and Lord Monboddo. From the Cairn o' Mount we could see the coast of Fife at St. Andrews – the most open view from any hill in Scotland, unless the road from Kildary to Ardgay. Deeside was bathed in sunshine – almost too hot. At Chanonry Lodge, our fellow guests were Admiral of the Fleet Sir Roderick MacGregor and Lady MacGregor. Sir Roderick is the new Rector of the University. He led the naval assault on Italy, and captured the first island in the northward assault – Pantilleria, which, as I read this week in Sir Walter Scott's Journal, was one of the last sights recorded by Scott. He also commanded the Russian convoys, about which his wife wants him to write a book. He was the last First Sea Lord. I had previously exchanged a few words with him at the opening of Trinity House by the Queen. It was delightful to meet a man so completely modest and unassuming, who never once talked about himself. He was exceedingly kind to me, driving me to the various ceremonies in his car. He was entertained when I described

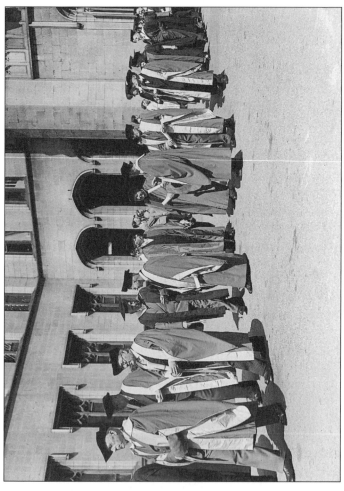

Honorary degrees, Aberdeen: leaving Mitchell Hall. Photo includes eight of those honoured: J.R. Philip (D.D.); Rev. Alexander Morrison (D.D.); Mr James J. Cargill (LL.D.); Emeritus Prof. John Cruickshank (LL.D.); Sir Thomas Ralph Merton (LL.D.); Principal Peter S. Noble (LL.D.); Prof. James R. Sutherland (LL.D.); Mr G. Fiddes Watt (LL.D.) (Courtesy of the Press and Journal, Aberdeen)

the pair of us as a sea-lawyer and a barrack-room theologian. We all had tea in the garden. Then, in the evening, there was a dinner-party in Chanonry Lodge to the honorary graduands where we regaled ourselves on a salmon caught by Tom Taylor. Dr. Morrison, my fellow D.D. (Dr. Courvoisier from Geneva was unable to be there), turned out to have many links with me. Dad had preached for him in Thurso, and he still recalled his sermon on Christ within us, 'Professor with', and all he has to teach us. We had many common friends – James Wright of Boat of Garten, R.J. Mackay of Greenock, James Cook of Dundee, R.T. Cameron, late of West St. Andrew's, Aberdeen. His brother was minister at Kincraig, and was killed in the first World War: Ella remembered him. Fiddes Watt, the artist, looked like an elderly Spanish hidalgo and smoked a cigarette from a home-made holder, made from the hind leg of a hare. He was full of stories about painting Asquith's portrait in 1912 – how Mrs. Asquith revealed all sorts of state secrets to him, while Asquith himself remained reticent and imperturbable. I had an interesting talk with Principal Noble of King's College, London. He was formerly Professor of Humanity at Aberdeen, a double first in Classics and in Oriental Languages at Cambridge, and Tom Taylor's fellow competitor when the Principalship of Aberdeen University was vacant. He was one of Tommy Cooper's assessors at the St. Andrews University Inquiry. He had unbounded admiration for Wimberley's conduct, and a very poor opinion of the St. Andrews' leaders – indeed, he thought that they had learned little since the reorganisation, and considered that the one real hope was a real change of heart towards Dundee. I sat between Lady MacGregor and Mrs. Bickersteth. She is a daughter of W.R. Sorley and of George Adam Smith's sister. She was interested when I told her that my father was a fellow student of Sorley, and that his contemporaries also included J.W. Macphail, R.B. Haldane, George Adam Smith, Andrew Pringle-Pattison and James Seth – a very remarkable group of intellectuals, especially strong in philosophy. Alison, who was staying with the Smiths at the Greek Manse, came over for the dinner, and was the only young person present; I am very proud of the charming way in which she acquitted herself.

On Friday, the day of graduation, we of Chanonry Lodge all went down to start the day with the Chapel Service. There, I met Donald Mackinnon, and introduced him to the Rector. I was glad to learn that he had been one of the D.D. Committee which had recommended my name. Then on we went to the Graduation ceremony in the Mitchell Hall, Marischal College. Tom Taylor conducted the ceremony with great dignity, giving an excellent address and conducting the remaining proceedings in clear intelligible faultless Latin. I was the second to be 'capped' after Dr. Morrison. The Rev. Professor J.M. Graham (recently Lord Provost of Aberdeen) presented me. I was delighted at the murmur of applause when he said: 'His ancestry belongs "where Gadie runs, at the back of Benachie."' Professor Cruickshanks, for thirty-five years Professor of Bacteriology, received the biggest ovation from his old students: he has reared more Professors of Bacteriology than any other Professor in Great Britain. Graham's promotion was not very happy in relation to Dr. Morrison – 'a plain parish minister, with no academic pretensions' – it could have been expressed more aptly. Farquhar MacRitchie, who promoted the LL.D.s, revealed a vein of humour comparable only to T.B. Simpson's. The proceedings as a whole were very quiet, so different from the rowdiness of other graduations I have attended. I noticed that almost all the young graduates came from Aberdeen or the North, except in Forestry, where there are only four schools in the United Kingdom, and the graduates were drawn from every corner of Great Britain. Amongst the Aberdeen Professors, I noticed particularly the blind professor of Bio-Chemistry, Kermack, who was guided to and from his place by Tom Smith, and Professor Jones, famed for having 'bent the beam' used by German night-raiders on Britain, so that, instead of unloading their bombs on crowded cities, they often dropped them on open waste-land to which their guiding radar-beam had been re-directed.

At the lunch which followed, I was placed between Lady MacGregor and Mrs. Sutherland, wife of the Lord Northcliffe Professor of English Literature at London University. Professor Bickersteth, who has retired to Chichester, was placed just beyond Mrs. Sutherland. In toasting the honorary Graduands, Tom Taylor mentioned that he and I had been called to the Bar on the same day, and had successively held the Sheriffdom of Renfrew and Argyll. Dr. Morrison replied for the D.D.s, and Sir Thomas Merton and Professor Sutherland for the LL.D.s. When we came out after lunch, we found the Rector's car imprisoned between two locked cars, fore and aft. We suggested that a depth charge would have been useful to an Admiral of the Fleet in such a situation. The lunch did not end till 3.45 p.m. We were pretty exhausted by then, and, after tea, Ella and I both had an hour's sleep.

Then we went to the Tom Smith's for dinner, where we met the Daubes. David Daube has just been appointed to the All Souls Chair of Civil Law at Oxford. He is the most learned and powerful intelligence in Aberdeen. He embarked, first of all, on a fascinating discussion on the historical background of nursery-rhymes, which he has made a special study, and then on a wonderful explanation of the Jewish Passover in its relation to New Testament teaching. We could scarcely bear to leave for the University Reception. At dinner, as a new D.D., I was asked to say grace – a difficult duty where a devout Jew was present. I chose the French grace from the 103rd Psalm: '*Mon âme, béni l'Eternel, et n'oublie aucun de ses bienfaits!*' Daube asked me to repeat it, so that he could memorise it. He promised to introduce me to C.H. Dodd, and invited me to All Souls. He showed me great friendship, and said how much his old master, Professor Kunkel of Heidelberg, had enjoyed staying with us. Daube is one of the most striking of personalities – a heavy shock of black hair, a countenance full of deep thought, dark penetrating eyes, a piercing mind, philosophical like Donald Mackinnon, yet, unlike Donald, always on the point, and a vivid intensity of conversation which compels attention – the most interesting face in the Aberdeen senatus; next to him, I place the luminous eyes and changing expression of Jones and the penetrating gaze and air of command of Tom Taylor himself.

From the Smiths we went on to the University Reception in the Mitchell Hall, a delightful function because it included not merely staff and honorary graduands, but also all the young graduates and I think some of their families. One part of the Hall was devoted to dancing, and in the other part, nearer the entrance, guests were received by Tom and Nellie Taylor and by the Rector and Lady MacGregor. We said our goodbyes to the MacGregors, as they were going straight from the Reception to their new home at Tarland. Of all the Senior Admirals, he is the only one, I believe, who has not chosen to settle, in his leisure, near Portsmouth or Southampton. For me, the Reception was one long series of meeting new friends, and old, and of conversations always being interrupted by the next. Among the Professors, I met Roe (French); Wittle (German); Graham (Systematic Theology); Duthie (English Literature: student of Dover Wilson); Farquhar MacRitchie and his wife. Earlier in the day, at the lunch I met again Donald and Lois Mackinnon, and my old University fellow student J.M. Henderson (British History) and his wife. I found many Durham common links with Angus, the University Secretary; and I met a young philosophy lecturer, Stein, from Caius College, Cambridge, a grandson of Mr. William Walker who formerly lived in Greenhill Gardens, Edinburgh; I was able to tell him that I met his mother in Genoa in 1923. (I did not add that I had been her counsel in a litigation with his father more recently!) He seemed a bright, vivacious, young don, and I liked his easy frank manner. I had a talk, too, with the Moderator (G.D. Henderson) and with Sheriffs Laing and Hamilton, the latter of whom instructed me in the first steps of Sheriff Court Practice in Maclay, Murray and Spens in 1921–3. Tom Taylor told me afterwards that he was a dull speaker, impervious to atmosphere. But, in defence, I pointed out that Hamilton had not had the ordinary advantages open to most lawyers, begun as a dogsbody of a process clerk running around in circles at the behest of a big Glasgow firm of solicitors, and had gradually risen, by his own un-aided efforts, first to partnership in the foremost Glasgow firm, and then to be Sheriff-substitute first at Dunfermline and now in Aberdeen.

On the following (Saturday) morning, we left our kind hosts shortly after breakfast and came, once again, over Cairn o' Mount, in broiling sunshine, to Fettercairn, where Mrs. Duncan gave us lunch at Inch-dowrie. Principal Duncan was away on one of his visits to Cambridge as one of the general committee concerned in the new translation of the New Testament. Through Strathmore, we ran at high speed, and reached home in time to go on to a sherry party being given by my old class-mate, Christian Van der Rijdt, Dutch Consul-General, for the officers of the Dutch cruiser *De Riyter*, now stationed in the Forth. On our arrival home, we found Douglas Duncan with Alison and Rosemary to greet us on the doorstep. Douglas is with the Aircraft Carrier *Theseus* in the Forth. Some of the senior Officers, and also some American officers were also at the Van de Rijdts. I found the Dutchmen and Americans more naturally friendly than our own naval men. Magnus Magnusson, one of Gordon's old schoolmates, was there as a *Daily Express* journalist. He took a photograph of Christian and myself, and took particulars about our being fellow-Dundonians and classmates from 1907 to 1912 for a feature article in his paper.

This afternoon we have been to a garden party for a Summer School for foreign students. It was held at Carlyle Hostel, and we met shoals of Americans, and also a Swede, some Norwegians, a German, a Jap and a student from Iraq. The hostels at Craigmillar are the most splendidly planned of Edinburgh University's buildings; yet few Edin-burgh people know much about them or have even seen their beautiful campus.

13th July 1955 (Wednesday)

While I was away from Parliament House last week, I decided to let the question of the Deanship simmer. I was very glad to be out of all the discussion. The last two days I have been in an extraordinary legitimacy case, where a man had thirteen children in two families. There was no marriage registered in the case of the first family; in the case of the second, a marriage by declaration was registered after there were three children. One of these three children has no birth certificate. All this happened in the seventies and eighties of last century, and there was, apart from documents, no direct evidence. The author of all this was himself born in Tasmania about 1842. The fact that his father had gone there from Scotland so early suggests that there was a strange background to the family history and the details of the various birth-certificates were themselves very illuminating. This has kept me out of the talk of Parliament House. But, after discussing the position with T.P. McDonald, Harald Leslie, Hector McKechnie, Douglas Johnston and John Wilson, and after considering my various commitments (Sheriffdom, Procuratorship, Convener of the Standing Committee of the National Library at a critical stage just before the opening of the new building) I have decided not to stand. It is difficult to judge accurately. No one would vote against either Chris Guest or myself. But on the whole, I think he would be likely to receive rather more votes. So last night, I rang him up and told him that I had decided not to go forward, and that I thought, with his calm, clear, judicial outlook, he would make a first-class Dean, and I warmly supported him. I am sure that this was the right course, though it is always difficult to be near such an office, and decide not to stand. Hector McKechnie urged me to let my name go forward; and T.P. McDonald, though wisely taking no active part as Faculty Librarian, would also have liked me to stand. But I think my conclusion is in accordance with the general feeling, and I cannot say that I have any serious regrets. What delighted me greatly was that, today, the Round Table made me Chairman, in succession to Jock – a personal honour which I value perhaps much more than they know. Gilchrist told me this evening that he would have voted for me, and I would see that Jeffrey Cunningham was very friendly towards me. I met them both at a Reception in the National Gallery (the first of its kind to be held there) given by the Government to the Commonwealth and Empire Law Conference. I met Professor Goodhart, Master of University College, Oxford, and various representatives from Canada, South Africa, Australia and New Zealand. Bill and Muriel Milligan received the guests. It was lovely to see Constable's 'Dedham Vale' and the Raeburns and Gainsboroughs looking down on us.

Dr. Kenneth MacLeod, author of 'The Road to the Isles', has died. Probably, there is no song of this century, whose words are more often on the lips of young people. It was composed not on the road to the Isles, of which the song tells, but at Crianlarich. I only met Kenneth MacLeod once, at Iona; but the fey charm of his island personality one could never forget. I have a photograph taken of him holding Rosemary by her arm on Iona jetty. He had a beautiful spirit, which charmed everyone, not least children, for he had the simplicity of a child, and yet, at the same time, shrewd humorous insight into human nature. When an old lady complained to him of young people whistling secular songs on their way to Iona Cathedral on Sunday, he replied: 'Why object? They are whistling their way into the Kingdom of Heaven.' He was like Conan Doyle with Sherlock Holmes – the work he created lived in the minds of everyone, so that people to whom 'The Road to the Isles' was the most familiar song scarce knew the name of its creator. He never sought royalties on its use; the royalties to him were the warmth it kindled in the hearts of the young. His name will always be linked with Gigha, his last parish. At one time he was at Straloch near Pitlochry, and I used to hear of him there, many years ago, from my uncle Donald Stewart-Fergusson of Dunfallandy. The most unassuming of the Church's sons, he has perhaps left, in this generation, the loveliest legacy to the youth of Scotland.

15th July 1955 (Friday)

Alison flew to Norway yesterday for her summer holiday.

I had scarcely reached Court this morning before Mr. McWhannell, my clerk, whispered to me: 'There's a rumour, not yet confirmed, that Lord Cooper has just died.' In half-an-hour he passed in a note to me, working in the law room, that Lord Cooper's death was confirmed. The news cast a hush over Parliament House. Later, Lillie told me that Tommy Cooper had had a second stroke at Kinloch Rannoch last Friday, and had been brought back to the Strathearn Nursing Home (where he was last autumn) by ambulance. His loss is the biggest loss to Scots law this century. In the late afternoon, the *Glasgow Herald* telephoned asking me to write an appreciation. I wrote it at once, and then went out to a Bar and Law Society Reception to the Commonwealth Law Conference in Parliament House. Since returning home, I have just, while writing this, received another telephone message from the *Herald*, when they read over my appreciation as recorded for teleprinter. At the Reception, I met Judge Batt of one of the County Courts near Manchester – centred on Stockport: I met him some years ago at Oban. He is a Commercial specialist; and has invited me to stay with him when I go to Manchester in October.

Mr. William Scoon, who takes my brief-bag up to and down from Court each day, still remembers the little red-faced apprentice of Macpherson and Mackay, W.S. rushing about on the affairs of their very large Court practice forty years ago – the future Lord President Cooper. My first sight of him was one day in 1923 when I was walking through the courtyard of the Royal Bank with Sir John Prosser, in whose office I then was. A figure dashed past, and Sir John said: 'That's the coming Lord President.' Cooper was then still only a junior. Cooper and I were ordained elders of St. George's West, side by side, next to each other in 1931. Scoon, or 'Scoonie', as he is usually called, is one of the well-known figures in Parliament House. He has a pale worn face, so that you might almost take him for a Continental refugee or displaced person. He has taken the brief-bags up and down each day as long as I can remember. He used to carry them by horse cab; but now an old-fashioned taxi-cab is used – which reminds me – I well remember the last hansom-cab in Edinburgh: it used to ply for hire from a stance at the foot of the Mound.

17th July 1955 (Sunday)

Mention of Mr. Scoon reminds me of another equally well-known Parliament House character, Mr. William Robertson, bookbinder, 369 High Street (just beside the West door of St. Giles'). He is one of the real old craftsmen. All his binding is still hand-worked. He binds my law-reports. Yesterday, he came down for the usual batch, and I also gave him various private papers to bind, and certain old volumes of reports – a number of them need periodic re-binding, and I like to keep my library in good repair. He also periodically varnishes the backs of the 'law calf'. The great feature of Mr. Robertson is both his beautiful workmanship, and his old-world courtesy. He is one of nature's gentlemen, and is as interested in my family as in my books. He had a heavy load of books to take yesterday, so I motored him back with the books to his shop. He asked me why I did not go in for active politics: it was the avenue to the Bench. I said quite frankly that I was very happy as I am, which is true; and that, if I reached the Bench, I would rather reach it on merit, without political aid. Many good judges have been politicians; but politicians have provided all the bad ones! Mr. Robertson is often seen crossing the Parliament Hall, with a load of books on his shoulder. He always wears an apron, the sign of his trade – like a bishop.

A third character, unconnected with the law but interested in it and in literature, is Mr. Martin, the little greengrocer in Dundas Street. He is another nature's gentleman. His shop has the grubby look of a little French market booth, and I am afraid trade does not come easily his way. But he is always ready to talk about Sir Walter Scott, and his one hobby is taking day motor-excursions to different parts of Scotland, in the lore of which he is unusually well-versed.

Yesterday, after discussing the matter with Beattie, I approached Miss Mena Whigham (niece of Sir John Lorne MacLeod, once Lord Provost, and one of Edinburgh's leading solicitors), who is acting for the executors of Kenneth MacLeod to see whether the National Library could acquire some of his MSS, and in particular the MS of 'The Road to the Isles'. She told me, what my Uncle Donald told me thirty years ago, that Kenneth MacLeod had been sorely treated by the Kennedy-Frasers. His method was to whistle or hum to them the airs he knew in the Isles, and to provide the words. They obtained the copyright. More recently, he has provided similar airs for Mrs. Mackintosh (wife of the Rev. Dr. Robert Mackintosh) to take down. Apparently, a copy of these is among his papers; and she also has a copy. But these latter have never been published. I said that I thought the National Library Trustees might be able to help in finding suitable means of publication through Dr. Peddie, Secretary of the Carnegie Universities Trust.

Ella and I went out to see the Binns yesterday afternoon. It is the home of General 'Tam' Dalzell and has some magnificent Italian ceilings of the seventeenth century. The custodian was at pains to whitewash General Dalzell, emphasising his clemency to the prisoners after Rullion Green. I thought I would see what W.L. Mathieson said about him, since Mathieson was certainly not pro-Covenanter. 'General Dalzell, astonished that men of loyal professions should be "so mercifully inclined to that damned crew", expressed his conviction that the west would never be settled "without the inhabitants be removed or destroyed"' (*Politics and Religion in Scotland*, vol. ii pp. 214, 215); and he goes on to refer to Dalzell as 'this ruffian'. However, the dark reputation of Dalzell has perhaps rendered his home all the more interesting, since it probably isolated it from the general flow of Scottish life, so that it retained its own character; and is, to this day, still full of legends about Dalzell's meetings with the devil. In one of the ceilings, of the King's room, David and Alexander are specially singled out as famous kings, but, for some reason, while 'Alexander' is correctly spelt in the ceiling work, 'David' is spelt with the two 'Ds' being turned the wrong way!

James Cooper last night invited me to the house for his brother's funeral.

Beattie tells me that the Appointments Committee of the National Library have recommended Alison for one of the vacant Research Assistant-ships in the Printed Books side.

18th July 1955 (Monday)

I went out with Hector McKechnie to 16 Hermitage Drive for the house service at Tommy Cooper's funeral. There was only one close relative left, his brother James. Gracie Thomson, who is some kind of cousin, was there. The others, apart from his staff, were Normand, Hamish Clyde, George Thomson, Lawrence Hill Watson, Albert Russell, John Wheatley, Bill Milligan, Sir David Milne, Dr. Meikle, Prof. A.H. Campbell, Mr. Watson (James Cooper's former partner), Hector and myself. Dr. Warr conducted the service in the house, and Roderick Bethune the service at the graveside in the Grange, where a very large crowd was assembled. He was buried in the grave of his mother and her relatives, like a boy who had never grown up. Douglas Wimberley was there – Tommy Cooper had a great respect of his disinterested attitude over the Reorganisation of St. Andrews University, and the respect was mutual. From there, I drove Hector, Dover, and Beattie to a meeting of the Books and MSS Committee of the National Library.

Then, in the evening, we went down to a sherry-party on the new *Pharos*, lying at Granton West Pier, and saw over our new ship. She is much broader in the beam than the old *Pharos*, and has an extra deck, and more deck-space for the Commissioners. The new cabins are even more sumptuous than the old. The new dining-room, in reddish-veneer, has not the distinction of the old; the smoke-room is larger and more comfortable. But the real difference is in the quite wonderful accommodation for the crew, which is vastly superior to that on the old ship, and illustrates the progress in employees' welfare since the last *Pharos* was built in 1909. We met Mr. and Mrs. Anderson (the former is the head of Canadian lighthouses).

19th July 1955 (Tuesday)

Today I attended a Conference of the three Lighthouse authorities on board the *Pharos*:– Robbie Maconochie ('Skinflats' is his new nick-name: he received his knighthood last week, so must have a territorial designation); Lillie; Glen Wakelin; and Simpson (Assistant-Secretary) representing the Northern Lights; Captains Hubbard and Drake (two fine types) and McLennan (Assistant-Secretary) representing Trinity House; and Captain Colville and Mr. England (Secretary) representing the Irish Lights. We conferred all morning about lighthouse keepers' wages, while the new *Pharos* cruised out to the Isle of May. We circled it, then made a wide sweep southwards, and came in to the south of the Bass, blowing our horn to startle the solan geese in their myriads. The new *Pharos* does 16 knots an hour to the old *Pharos*' 9. She is diesel-engined, but vibrates very little. It was a calm sunny day. A slight breeze descended in the afternoon to about a hundred feet above the water. Near Inchkeith we looked back, and saw something I have never seen before – a mirage. The haze cut off the top of Fidra making it look like Fingal's Cave from the distance. Between Fidra and the Lothian shore, a line ran across from the upper end of Fidra to the shore, exactly like the Tay Bridge, if it had no supporting piers. Unkind people might suggest that we had had too good a lunch! But there was no mistaking the sight. But for its being so far off, it could have been photographed.

20th July 1955 (Wednesday)

Today Chris Guest became Dean of Faculty.

I went to lunch with the Copyright Librarians in the Laigh Parliament Hall – the first function of its kind there. I was in the Chair, and had Creswick of Cambridge University Library (an inveterate visitor to Inchnadamph) on my right, and John Sparrow, Warden of All Souls, whom I met before at Dobie's and also in the Garrick Club, on my left. Myres of the Bodleian, and also Park, the Vice-Provost and Librarian of Trinity College, Dublin, were there too, and Hamish Clyde, as President, and Jock Cameron, as (at the time of the invitation) Dean of Faculty, were also at my end of the table. Afterwards, we inspected the new Library building, now nearing completion. The advocates' reading-room – woodwork and ceiling – is most tasteful. I like, too, the large reading-room. On the whole, the building is beginning to look more like what it should. It should be completed by October. Then the books and furniture will be moved in, and, in the early summer of 1956, the Queen is expected to open the New Library.

3rd August 1955

At the end of my last *Pharos* cruise, I came home to find the office of knighthood waiting. This time, it was the offer of the Sheriffdom of Perth and Angus, vacant through Chris Guest's election as Dean. The offer came by telephone from Bill Milligan at Heriot. '*Scotia me genuit: Anglia me docuit*' is written on Duns Scotus' tomb in Cologne. Perth gave me birth and nurtured me: Angus was my teacher. I immediately decided that I could do no other than accept, though it will tear both our hearts to leave the Sheriffdom where we have been so amazingly happy. It will, at least, remain a second home; for Oban is where I should like to retire. I have to tell Bill Milligan my decision tomorrow. But my mind was made up at once: quite different from the previous offers of Edinburgh and Aberdeen.

4th August 1955 (Thursday)

Bill Milligan's observation when I accepted the counties of my birth and upbringing was: 'Local lad makes good!'

J. Harold Macdonald C.V.O., W.S. died today, the senior partner of Morton, Smart, Macdonald and Prosser, W.S., in whose office I received training in Parliament House Practice. Each of the firms in which I was trained was headed by a remarkable triumvirate – Maclay, Murray and Spens in Glasgow by David Murray, John A. Spens ('Ailsa Craig'), and James Maclay – 'Delay, Worry and Expense' or 'the Baboon, the Ape and the Missing Link'; Morton, Smart, Macdonald and Prosser by Sir John Prosser, a great conveyancer, with one of the finest heads which never found a portrait-painter, Andrew Gray Muir, and Harold Macdonald. But the really wonderful thing about Harold Macdonald was his courage; in the space of the first three months of the Second War, he lost both his sons in the Battle of Britain, and also his wife; yet he kept his faith, and never lost his wonderful smile and kindliness of heart. When I lost Gordon, a great bond was forged between us. On Sir John Prosser's death, he became the Sovereign's Scottish solicitor, and this led to the Memorial for my Opinion, of which I am most proud, one for Her Majesty in relation to the Balmoral Estates. When in London last April, I showed Rosemary the Battle of Britain window and his sons' names in the Book of

Remembrance in Westminster Abbey. He was deeply touched when I told him, and wrote: 'I thank you for remembering them, and my wife and me, in that sacred shrine. How kind of you to tell me, and I appreciate more than I can tell you what your letter means to me. This is the fifteenth year since I lost my boys and my wife. It is almost unbelievable that all this happened so long ago; or that Rosemary is now ten years old . . . With kindest remembrances. Yours affectionately (Sgd) J. Harold Macdonald.' Now, after years of struggle with heart and asthma, he is reunited with them.

16th September 1955 (Friday)

I returned from holiday on 12th September. This has been the *annus mirabilis* for summer sunshine. Since 1st July, when rain involved the cancellation of the Queen's Holyrood Garden Party, there was scarcely a drop of rain till the end of August; the ground in Inverness-shire was parched as I have never before seen it; there were wide rural areas short of water and children rejoiced in its becoming a duty to do without the usual bath; temperatures at Newtonmore soared to 85° for several days and were even higher in the immediate vicinity of Inverness. Argyll, though dry, still retained its lovely green.

We moved in an anti-clockwise direction round Scotland staying at Edzell (three nights), Huntly (two nights), Newtonmore (two and a half weeks), Isle of Eriska, Benderloch (five nights), and Gartnagrenach, near Whitehouse, West Loch Tarbert (a week).

On the way to Edzell, we crossed the two ferries, and lunched at St. Andrews, a veritable Deauville, with summer dresses and bathing costumes, in the midst of its incredible Lammas Fair; with a merry-go-round just outside St. Mary's College. Reaching Dundee, we motored out by Invergowrie, and Muirhead of Liff, to let Rosemary see my old home; then on to Tullybaccart Hill for the panorama of Strathmore, and so along 'Cloud Howe' to Edzell.

From Edzell, we crossed the Cairn o' Mount (the third time this year), to Aboyne and then missing Tarland, by Craigievar, to the Howe of Alford, where we crossed the Don and Bridge of Alford, and made for Keig. We had a picnic lunch on the roadside running up past Keig Church, with a lovely view over the Howe, bathed in soft sunshine, and to the east Castle Forbes broiling in the sun, and behind the slopes of Bennachie. My object in going to Keig was to visit the church, and to see whether I could find any stories relating to relatives far back. My great-grandfather in his Memorandum Book

for the year 1805 (which also bears the date August 3rd 1806) refers
to his grandmother at Keig (February 1805) and records her death
there on 6th March 1806. I could find no stone with the name of
'Philip' so early (if she was his paternal grandmother). I did, however,
find a Philip stone, on the south side of the church yard, recording
the death of a George Philip, Gateside, Harthill, Keig on 29th December 1845 (age fifty-eight), apparently a farmer; the other deaths
recorded on the stone, all later, included a Robert Philip, and it was
at least interesting to find on the stone two common family Christian
names. But – much more interesting – near it, I found a stone with
the simple inscription – 'In memory of/ William Robertson Smith/
Professor of Arabic/ in the/ University of Cambridge/ Born 8th Nov.
1846/ Died 31st March 1894'. That, alone, made the visit to Keig
worthwhile. From Keig we drove northwards to Auchleven, and then
up the little Strath of the Gadie to Kirkton of Clatt, and beyond it
south-westwards up a narrow farm-road to Tillyangus Farm. The
farmer's wife with some children came, inquisitively, to the door, and
I explained that my great-great-grandfather, John Philip, had lived at
Tillyangus, and his son also John Philip (the Aberdeen bookbinder)
had been born there. The present house looks to me more recent than
the eighteenth century. It is a small upland farmhouse, on the Knockespock Estate, the proprietor of which is Commander
Fellowes-Gordon. It lies 'at the back of Bennachie', but, actually, a
much more prominent landmark is the Tap o' Noth, lying to the
North-West. We then called at Clatt manse, so that I might thank the
Rev. James Mann, who had furnished me with the birth entry of my
great-grandfather from his Kirk Session Records. The entry, dated
January 25th, 1785, runs:

> John lawful son of John Philip and Elizabeth Barbray Tailor in Tilly-
> angus was baptised before witnesses James Gordon and Andrew Murray
> both in Kirkton of Clatt.

Next morning, we visited Huntly Castle and the town. Huntly Castle
is quite the finest ruined castle in the north. It has fine stone-carved
coats-of-arms – a royal coat-of-arms of James VI after he succeeded
to the English Crown, the coat-of-arms of his queen, Anne of Denmark, and the coats-of-arms of the Gordons and Lennoxes. There is
a bottle-dungeon matching that in St. Andrew's Castle. The guide
who took us round gave an excellent account, and was not put out,
as most guides are, when we asked questions. In the avenue we met
an English visitor, whose hobby is visiting every castle in the country.

Huntly does not seem to attract visitors. Indeed, in the whole of Aberdeenshire, we were impressed by the almost complete absence of the ordinary tourist motor-traffic so plentiful in August in other parts of Scotland. Why? I do not know, when there is not merely beautiful scenery and good roads, but also National Trust properties like Crathes, Craigievar, and Leith Hall.

In the afternoon, we visited Leith Hall and its gardens, seven miles south of Huntly. It has one of the loveliest rock-gardens with little paths each bearing the name of a saint (e.g. St. Patrick's Pathway, St. Januarius' Junction, and so on) and exquisite herbaceous borders. We talked to an old gardener, a veritable Aberdeenshire Andrew Fairservice, though much more genial, who not merely showed us the gardens, but secured our entry to the house. The house itself is a lovely little mansion with corner-cone-shaped turrets. Two rooms contain interesting remains of the family, including a royal pardon of a Jacobite member of the family, apparently the only example of such a pardon now extant. From there, we motored to the crest of Suie Hill, south of Clatt, where we picnicked, and had a magnificent view of the whole strath of the Gadie, Knockespock House, Tillyangus, and Tap o' Noth. Like the previous day, it was again a broiling sunny day. From there we ran down the Gadie and in to Insch, and then back to Huntly. Next morning, we motored by Dufftown and Craigellachie to Newtonmore.

A country at peace has no history, and there is little to record of Newtonmore. To me this holiday stood for family picnics, in Glenfeshie, at Loch Alvie, Loch Laggan, Boat of Garten; resumed golf – I played more golf than since before the War, thanks to renewed health; reading; friendships; and a fresh start at pen-and-ink sketching. One day, we climbed the hill behind Ralia, and Ella, Alison (who was with us for the weekend) and Rosemary went on to the old Wade Bridge a mile beyond.

After two and a half weeks in Speyside, where everything was burned brown, and where, each day, heather moors, dried up by continuous sunshine, were set on fire by passing railway trains, it was a pleasant change to move on to Argyll, where all was soft greens and blues. At Eriska, we found ourselves in a company of English people. In Speyside, all the resident visitors are Scots; for some reason, the English always choose the West. There we found the mother and small boy of my fellow-advocate C.E. Jauncey, and had tea with them at the Airds Hotel one day, when we motored round Loch Creran to Port Appin. We made a close friendship with Mr. and Mrs. C.L.

Stocks, from Betteshanger, Deal. Mr. Stocks has had an unusual career. At Oxford he was a friend of Lionel Smith, and took 'Greats'. He then entered the Treasury, and had, under him, (the now Sir) Robert Fraser, to one of whose children he was god-father. He has a strong affection for Scotland, and had met Sir John Lorne MacLeod, my old Edinburgh neighbour (ex-Lord Provost), in Mull. The Stocks had one boy, born in the same year as Gordon. At the age of eleven, he died suddenly at his school, Betteshanger, Deal; the parents could not reach him in time. Shortly afterwards, Mr. Stocks was invited to become a Director of the School. In a few months, the then headmaster died, and, *mirabile dictu*, Mr. Stocks was invited to take his place – so the Treasury official became a headmaster. He is now a man of about seventy, one of the most humane, tolerant, and friendly of beings. He seemed to be able to 'get alongside' all the children in the hotel, including Rosemary: 'If you have a ball, you can never go far wrong with a child'; and so he played 'catches' with Rosemary. In the evening, we discussed everything under the sun, especially books; we were both reading, as it happened, Clarendon's *History*, in the extracts published in the World's Classics (Oxford University Press); and he was also reading Miss Butler's *Rilke*.

One curious incident showed how the girls from the Outer Hebrides flock across to hotel work on the mainland in Summer. I asked our Eriska waitress if she came from the Outer Isles. She replied: 'Yes, from Stornoway.' I said: 'That's odd. Our waitress at Newtonmore also came from Stornoway.' 'Was that the Lodge Hotel at Newtonmore?' she asked. 'Yes,' I replied, and added that the Newtonmore waitress's name was Ann. 'Oh, she said, 'she's my sister!'

It was while I was at Eriska that, on 11th September 1955, my appointment as Sheriff of Perth and Angus was announced. I had been awaiting the announcement for a week. I felt keenly the separation from the lovely land of Argyll, all the more coming, as it did, when I was gazing out on the Lynn of Lorne, to the mountains of Mull.

19th September 1955 (Monday)

Today, the Edinburgh holiday, Ella, Rosemary and I motored out to our old haunt, Black Barony, for lunch, and walked up the hill behind. It was a place full of lovely memories, for there we had our last two holidays with Gordon, and every corner recalled something about him. There was a tiny fawn at the house, which had been made a domestic pet. It walked into the dining-room while we were at lunch, and later it came outside and ate dandelion heads and grass from Rosemary's hand. It was quite intrigued, too, by my camera. It seemed quite tame, except it would, every now and then, start away or jump nervously into the air.

Among letters of goodwishes on my appointment to Perth and Angus, the most interesting one was from Arthur Matheson, my old 'devil', now Professor of Law at (the newly named) Queen's College, Dundee. On 12th October, certain honorary graduands are to receive LL.D.s on the establishment of the new extended law-school in Dundee, and Arthur was writing to tell me that, although I was to be invited in any event as Procurator, now, better still, I would be invited as Sheriff. He went on:–

> The only galling thing is that, if we could have had our way, you would have been present in yet another capacity. With Knox's cordial approval, I had put you up to receive Hon. LL.D. at the July Graduation, and I think that at that stage we should have got in before Aberdeen! But I was asked to defer your nomination until the October Graduation as it was to have a special emphasis on Law in recognition of the new Faculty. I gladly agreed to this, thinking that you might even prefer to receive your Degree in Dundee rather than in St. Andrews. But in the meantime these (doubtless well-meaning) blighters in Aberdeen had been getting busy, and my plan aborted; because apparently there is an agreement amongst the Scottish Universities that the same person is not honoured twice within so short a space of time. Indeed, there is a rumour that another University (I don't know which) was similarly thwarted this year in its attempt to make you an LL.D! However, the D.D. was even better, and a greater honour, being as it were *ultra crepidam*; and you must have had great pleasure in joining the select company of secular divines!

Two other letters which I value, came from Mr. Stirling, Sheriff Clerk at Paisley, and Mr. Fletcher, Sheriff Clerk Depute at Greenock. Mr. Stirling wrote: 'To all of us at Paisley you have all the attributes which go to make the perfect Sheriff.' Mr. Fletcher wrote: 'Your kindness and consideration shown to me and staff will never be forgotten. It was really a sheer joy to have known you so well.'

I have been very busy with arrangements for my new work in Perth and Angus. I have to be installed in Perth (29th September); Dundee (5th October); Forfar (6th); Arbroath (7th); and Dunblane (19th October). My first work will be an Inquiry at Perth into traffic bye-laws. I have also been asked to take the Cumbernauld (New Town) Inquiry

on 10th and 11th October, and, on 12th October, there is the Graduation Ceremony in Dundee to celebrate the inauguration of the new
Law Faculty. I have invited Principal Knox to my inauguration in
Dundee. But for a previous unavoidable engagement, he would have
come; indeed, he offered to attend one of the other installations. But,
instead, it has been arranged that St. Andrews University will be
represented at my Dundee installation by the Masters of the new
Queen's College, Dundee, and St. Salvator's, St. Andrews, and by the
Principal of St. Mary's. The Rector of the High School, and the
prefects, are also coming at my suggestion. The greetings of the
Dundee Procurators will be voiced by their Dean, my old class-mate,
Hugh Carlton.

26th September 1955 (Monday)

This afternoon, I attended a Joint-Conference between our Church
and the representatives of the Original Secession Church, who now
want to accede to the Church of Scotland. It was a friendly meeting;
but Principal Watt, our convener, is not a good chairman; we did
little more than depute various aspects to sub-committees.

This evening, I participate in the resumed Conversations between
the Church of Scotland, the Church of England, the Episcopal Church
in Scotland, and the Presbyterian Church of England. Each has submitted a memorandum; those of the two large churches are much the
best, though our own is too 'Torrancial'. I managed to offer, and
secure, five pages of alterations to Tom Torrance's original draft. He
is unnecessarily provocative and lacking in tact in the expressions he
uses; sometimes he is quite unintelligible in his abstractions; but nonetheless, he is both able and, for his age, unusually learned. The
memoranda of the two smaller churches are somewhat defensive; and
that of the Episcopal Church offers little hope for discussion.

3rd October 1955 (Monday)

Last week was one of varied non-stop activity. From the evening of
the 26th until the afternoon of the 28th I took part in the Inter-Church
Conversations. The Church of Scotland memorandum, suggesting a
way of reconciling episcopacy and presbytery, was recognised as a
great act of faith. On the whole, the other three memoranda did not
go very far in proposing concrete adaptations. We came very much
to grips with the central problems. The Anglicans find an indefinable

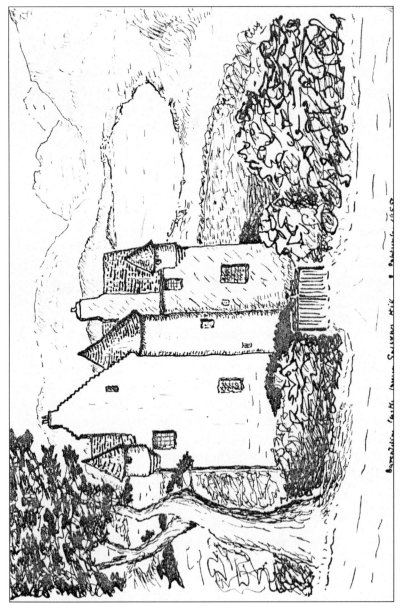

Barcaldine Castle, drawn by Randall Philip.

overtone in the bishop which is incapable of definition; we find it difficult to see in turn a 'superior person' endowed by convocation with necessarily greater wisdom than other mortals. We find an overtone in our lay office-bearers also perhaps incapable of definition; they see him as a 'near-cleric' a little detached from the general laity. We both felt that we had much to learn from the other, and their misunderstanding of the place of the lay-member in the government of the Church only suggests our misunderstanding of the place of the bishop. The C. of E. representatives, after being, at earlier conferences, dissatisfied with efforts merely for intercommunion, seemed now to be swinging back to the lesser objective, the one we have always from the start desired as a beginning. But it is too early yet to speak.

On the afternoon of the 28th, Ella and I motored to Bridge of Earn, where we stayed at the Moncrieffe Arms. Next morning, I was installed as Sheriff at Perth. Alastair Prain sat with me, and I was able to point out that Perth was the very first Court in which I had ever appeared as a young advocate and that the present occasion was unique in that both Sheriffs were not merely Perthshire men, but both born in the same parish. The ceremony was well done. Alastair and I took the Bench together. After constituting the Court, we both rose and bowed to each other, and I handed him my Commission. He announced the Commission and then handed it to Mr. Penny, the Sheriff Clerk. We also stood in loyalty and respect while it was read. Then Alastair, the Lord Provost (Smart), the Convener of the County (Sir George McGlashan), the Dean of the Faculty (Stewart), and the Sheriff Clerk made speeches of welcome, and I responded. Thereafter, I settled down to hear a local inquiry into whether High Street, Perth, should be made a one-way street. It is a difficult question, on which there has been a sharp division of opinion. At the end of two days, the inquiry had to be continued as the Town's opening case was not itself completed. During the hearing, too, I fined a hydro-electrical labourer who, when drunk, had maliciously broken a railway carriage window and an electric light on a journey across the Moor of Rannoch! He got £3! The damage came to £3 odds!

9th October 1955 (Sunday)

This week has again been a busy one. Last Monday, the Standing Committee of the National Library, and lunch with Dover Wilson at the New Club beforehand. I heard two good stories; the first from Dover. Field Marshal Smuts was staying, as Chancellor of Cambridge

University, at Christ's, of which Canon Raven, the then Vice-Chancellor, was Master. One morning, Canon Raven opened his bedroom door, and was surprised to hear childish shrieks and laughter from Marshal Smuts' bedroom. He soon detected the voice in the room of his small grandson. So he went over to Smuts' door, and pushing it open gently, found his grandson bouncing on the top of the Field Marshal, as the latter lay in bed. He was about to reprove his small grandson and call him to come away, when Smuts exclaimed: 'What's this, Vice-Chancellor? Why this interruption? "Except ye . . . become as little children, ye shall not enter into the kingdom of heaven." Now leave me to my devotions!' And so the Vice-Chancellor slunk away, leaving his small grandson playing with the Chancellor. The other story came from (Professor) Archie Campbell. He had been sitting with the Duke of Atholl at lunch, and then came over to our table. He said he had been discussing Atholl in the old days. The inns round about were usually known as 'The Duke's Arms'. The coach which plied between them was the 'Duchess of Atholl', and each inn would contain a notice stating that the 'Duchess of Atholl' left 'The Duke's Arms' at such and such an hour in the morning! Croft Dickinson, coming up at that moment and overhearing Campbell, added: 'Do you know this fact about that story? It was when Queen Victoria heard that story that she observed: "We are not amused"!'

At the Library Standing Committee, we planned to approach the Treasury, the Pilgrim Trust, and the Friends of the National Libraries, to see whether we could raise the sum – £41,000 odds – necessary to acquire the unique Falkland Palace collection of Shakespeare and seventeenth and eighteenth century dramatists. The Shakespeare portion of the collection, alone, was valued at £23,000.

On Tuesday (4th October) the Courts resumed. We had our usual service in St. Giles'; and this time it was followed by the opening of our new reading-room in the new National Library by Normand, Chris Guest occupying the chair as our new Dean. The new room is larger than the old; the yellow walls, and the inadequacy of the old carpet to cover the floor gave it at first sight a slightly bare and cold appearance. Normand paid a high tribute to the work of James Avon Clyde. The new Dean spoke and behaved with dignity.

The same afternoon, Ella and I set out by car for Dundee, for my various installations as Sheriff of Angus. The congestion at Queensferry was not quite so bad as it has been in the Summer; but the delays involved, usually from one hour to two hours especially at the north side, are little short of a public scandal. We stayed over night with the Leslie Weatherheads at 6 Adelaide Terrace, Dundee. On the way down the Carse of Gowrie, we diverted to go by the low road from Inchture to Invergowrie. What a transformation. Kingoodie, where my father conducted an afternoon service each Sunday, now almost derelict and in ruins; Invergowrie, twice its former size, and practically a suburb of Dundee. At the farm at the east side of the village, I saw my father's old member, Ben Young, now ageing, leaning against the gate as he has done for the last forty years. We stopped, and had a friendly reunion. The Weatherheads invited to meet us at dinner Mr. D.W. Erskine, the new Rector who has just taken up his duties at the High School, and his wife, and Professor and Mrs. Lendrum (pathology in Queen's College, Dundee). The new Rector is a friendly, vivacious, lively personality. He is a son of the manse at Tranent, was educated at the Royal High School, Edinburgh University (where he was second bursar and John Welsh Classical Scholar) and Oxford; and has been, for twenty-five years, a master (and latterly a house-master) at Malvern. His wife is a Forfar lady. He surprised me by saying that he found the classical tradition of the High School much stronger than Malvern. He finds the cultural side much weaker; and I am not surprised. He had entered into the spirit of my installation, and next day came to it with his wife and the five school prefects. At my installation in Dundee, there were other interesting features. The Lord Provost and Magistrates attended in their robes. Amongst other friends from my childhood were Mrs. W.L. Thoms of Benvie, Isa Cooper and her sister Annie.

Leslie Weatherhead entertained us to lunch at the Royal Hotel, to which he and Janet had invited Kenneth Cullen (Sheriff-substitute) and his wife, and Mr. McIntosh Patrick A.R.S.A. and his wife. Leslie arranged for me to meet McIntosh Patrick, whose work I particularly admire; he is swimming against the tide of modern impressionists; I had an interesting talk with him about drawing; he has a theory that the natural way to make a picture is at arm's length; that, he says, is how you see it, and the subject you are drawing, and somehow, if you imagine your subject in that way, perspective enters the picture of itself. I discussed, too, the need in landscape to exaggerate vertical measurements; otherwise you get, say, the low hills of a photograph, which is how I, personally, see them. He agreed that, in landscape, vertical measurements had often to be increased in relation to horizontal, but stressed that this must not be overdone; otherwise it distorted especially rectangular objects.

We then drove out, by Tullybaccart Hill, to Coupar Angus calling

on the Rev. J.B. Logan of Coupar Angus on the way. We stayed that
night at Foxhall, with the Wimberleys. It is a lovely rambling house,
full of interesting objects, and a military atmosphere. This was accentuated, when other guests arrived for the night, Col. Peter Hunt
(depot-commander at Fort George) and his wife, who were proceeding
south to take up a new War Office job, and transporting two ponies
with them. The whole conversation had a strong military flavour,
which I, as a lawyer, greatly enjoyed. I felt as Sir Walter Scott must
have felt when he met the Duke of Wellington. Names of well-known
generals were bandied about as I would bandy about the legal hier-
archy: but here it was in telegraphic exclamations. 'Straffer Gort – he
would never have been a Monty – a good Divisional Commander –
perhaps an Army Corp – but Monty would have come out at the top
in any event!' (Douglas is a great believer in Monty.) At dinner,
Douglas suddenly got up and, going over to the side-board, returned
with a lovely antique sugar-sifter. He then called for our healths which
were drunk by the assembled company, and then presented the sugar-
sifter to us. It dates from 1754, and was made by Dugald Ged of
Edinburgh. It bears a Hamilton crest – William Hamilton, 4th of
Wishaw (1690–1756). On the other side it now has inscribed:–

From
Douglas Wimberley
to his good friend
Randall Philip
in gratitude.
1955.

Next day, Thursday (6th October), the Wimberleys came on to my
installation at Forfar Sheriff Court, which was followed by a Recep-
tion by the County Council, and a lunch afterwards, to both of which
Douglas was invited. At Forfar, I was welcomed by Harold Ford
(Sheriff-substitute); Mr. Fred A. Ferguson, Dean of the Forfar Faculty;
Mr. James Petrie, Procurator-Fiscal Depute; the Vice- Lieutenant of
the County, Colonel Ivan D. Guthrie of Guthrie; and the Provost of
Forfar, A.C. Smith – commonly known as 'Andra' (grandson of the
station master at Glamis and himself in the railway service). Mr.
Ferguson referred to my cousin, Alex. Philip, of Will and Philip,
Brechin, as a well-known writer of the last generation. I was able to
mention in Court that I had known well Lord Trayner, who had been
Sheriff of Forfarshire from 1881 to 1885, and who was for many years
an intimate friend of my father's, visiting us frequently at the manse

at Invergowrie and on Speyside holidays, and whose portrait hangs in my study. I was able to say that I knew Angus from the Carse of Gowrie to Montrose, and from the top of Glenesk to the Bell Rock.

We spent Thursday night with the Fords at Murlingden near Brechin, a house built in 1820, with late Regency features not unlike those in the new town of Edinburgh, and full of interesting pictures including a Lavery of Lady Ford. Lucy, I knew as a little girl, the daughter of Wardlaw Burnet, Sheriff of Fife and Kinross and much-loved Vice-Dean of Faculty, who was very kind to us in our earlier days at the Bar.

From Murlingden, on Friday morning, we motored on to Arbroath, where again I was installed.

We then drove back to Edinburgh by Queensferry. I called, at Monifieth, on my old schoolmaster, Mr. James S. Stalker, now over eighty years of age, and frail and white after two shocks. But he was delighted to see me, and told me that he had been with Candlish Henderson at Morrison's Academy, Crieff, and had taught Dr. White Anderson (then still Andersen – his father was a Swede) at Bo'ness. I had not seen him for thirty years, and scarcely could recognise the old master I knew. He comes from near Keiss in Caithness. We also called on the Torrances at Invergowrie Manse, and on the MacNicols at Longforgan manse; but the latter were out.

The same evening, Eric Smith telephoned me. He has composed fresh harmonisations of 'St. George's, Edinburgh' and 'Stracathro' and asked my consent to dedicate them to me. I said that, as Ella and I share everything, I should be very grateful if he would include her also. So he agreed to dedicate 'St. George's' to me, and 'Stracathro' to Ella.

15th October 1955 (Saturday)

Last Monday, I conducted, at the Masonic Hall, Cumbernauld, the Cumbernauld New Town Inquiry. Everything went smoothly. There was a large number of objectors, and I had the feeling that they considered I had done my best to give them a full and fair hearing. I could not help being particularly sorry for those whose livelihood might be affected by the proposed new town – businesses and farms in the area. I was much interested in new governmental methods of handling such an inquiry which obviously stem from the Treasury; they are so extraordinary as to be worth recording. Two short-hand writers were sent from the Treasury Pool in London, as if no stenographers existed in Scotland! I asked them how their shorthand notes were extended. They do not extend themselves, but read their note into a dictaphone; and then another typist extends it. Here, by consent of the objectors, the witnesses were not put on oath; and so neither were the shorthand writers. But, if the second-hand method of extending the notes of Court proceedings were adopted, not merely the shorthand writers, but also the wretched typists who make the note of the proceedings should logically be put on oath. I was driven to and from Cumbernauld by a Government Pool chauffeuse. On the way home, I asked her about her work, thinking it consisted mainly of driving people in or about Edinburgh. She told me that, the previous week, she had driven the Land Court to Strontian. When I observed that such a journey must be unusual, she said: 'Oh no, I have quite often driven to and from Geneva!' It would be interesting to know what government officials require private motor transport to take them to and from Geneva. I dictated the whole of my report next day. It requires to be submitted before Parliament reassembles on the 25th.

On Wednesday, Ella and I went to the Graduation Ceremony in Dundee at which the Dundee Faculty of Law was inaugurated. There was originally a Professorship of Canon Law (and there is still a Canon Law mace); but the Professor was suppressed in 1594. A Professorship of Law was created a few years ago; Arthur Matheson, my former 'devil', is the first holder.

Yesterday, the Central Land Board and War Damage Commission held their Scottish meeting – there are normally two per year. Dame Myra Curtis always grumbles in a good-humoured way about having to come to Scotland at all. I took Sir Thomas Phillips, Sir Robert Fraser, Sir Basil Gibson and Mr. MacDonald to lunch. Mr. Mac-Donald, who is quiet at Board meetings, is in many ways the most responsive talker at such an occasion. Sir Thomas, who puts though business deftly and briefly, with the minimum of personal exertion, lapses into comparative silence in a social circle. He asked me about the religious denominations in Scotland – the strength of the Church of Scotland, the Episcopal Church, the Roman Catholic, and the Free Church. He enquired, was the Church of Scotland episcopal?! and displayed a certain ignorance in this field more characteristic of a Londoner than a Welshman – I scarcely expected it of a very distin-guished Oxford scholar and civil servant. Next week, as members of the War Damage Commission, we attend a service on the re-dedication of the restored Lambeth Palace Chapel. The invitation describes the service 'as an act of thanksgiving to Almighty God for the great assistance received by the Church of England and other Churches under the War Damage Act in the replacement and restoration of their churches destroyed or damaged during the war.' The Scottish Office brought to my notice that the Moderator of the General Assembly had not been invited. The Secretary of State for Scotland has, in view of the absence of a representative of the Church of Scotland, decided to decline the invitation sent to him. The invitation certainly did not disclose that it was a little 'domestic service'. Had I known this, as distinct from what was stated in the invitation, I would not have undertaken to travel 800 miles to attend it. Ambiguities like this harm the practical friendship which is needed to support the conversations between the Churches.

17th October 1955 (Monday)

I finished my revisal of my final draft of the Cumbernauld Report yesterday, and it has been despatched today. This has been quick work.

The Lord Lyon telephoned me on Saturday night. He has granted me my coat-of-arms, but there has been delay in issuing the parchment, partly because, in July, I received the D.D., and, on 1st September, I changed my Sheriffdom. He went on, in his intimate high-pitched squeaky humorous voice to tell me of his troubles with Garter King. A conflict first arose, before he was in office, through Garter granting arms to Lord Leverhulme 'of the Western Isles'. Recently, Sir Arnold Macnair wanted to take his title from Gleniffer in Renfrewshire. The Lyon insists, and rightly, that such a title is Scottish, and the grant of arms is for him. Garter tried to rejoin that, by some manner of means, the Act of Union in 1801 with Ireland superseded the Act of Union with Scotland, and, by some manner of means, Garter is now an arms authority for Scotland as well as England. Lyon's rejoinder rightly was: 'Come and say that publicly to an audience in Scotland!' Garter seems to have departed from this ridiculous contention. But, now, he wants that, in a grant of arms by Lyon to a peer taking a Scottish title, only Garter or his heralds should appear in the Lyon Court. Lyon, again, is making it clear that this would infringe the rights of Scottish advocates and solicitors to appear in the Court. Lyon is bringing the matter to the notice of the Dean of Faculty. I told him of my own experience during the War, when, although I was Standing Junior for the Air Ministry in Scotland, the Treasury Solicitor sought to appear through H.L. Parker (now Parker L.J.) on behalf of the Air Ministry in the Compensation Defence Tribunal in a claim against the Ministry relating to the requisition of Ayr Race Course as an aerodrome. The then Dean (McIntyre) intervened, and it was pointed out to the Treasury Solicitor that the Air Ministry had its own Standing Junior in Scotland. I was then, in a chilly way, instructed to appear with H.L. Parker and to attend a consultation with him in Edinburgh. I happened, however, to be a month or so senior to H.L. Parker – so again the Dean intervened to point out that Parker would attend a consultation with me, and that I would lead. Not content with this, the Treasury Solicitor fixed the consultation for the night before the hearing, and, whether by accident or design, sent me the wrong brief, relating to Sandown Park, not Ayr Racecourse. I was also provided with only one witness, an English valuer, admittedly a distinguished one, but he spoke only in the language of the different English valuation practice. Later, the Lord Advocate was asked questions in Parliament on behalf of the Scottish solicitors as to why the government had not been represented by a Scottish solicitor – although the Ministry had a standing Scottish solicitor, Sir Norman Macpherson. Reid came to me, and I told him the facts. Later, in his Parliamentary answer, he gave an undertaking (1) that, even if an English counsel should be instructed in a Scottish case in such a Court, he would always be led by Scottish counsel, and (2) that instructions would in future be given by a Scottish solicitor. The Lyon was much obliged for this precedent, and thought that the risk of raising questions in Parliament would be a useful deterrent to Garter's unwarranted claim. Imagine the position in reverse. Yet, I suppose, Garter will call Lyon a Scottish nationalist – whereas all he is doing is maintaining the rights of a Scottish Court and its practitioners against one form of English nationalism. How insensitive the English mind can be to smaller peoples – Buganda, Kenya, the Sudan, Egypt, and now Cyprus; yet how easy it would be to respect their closest neighbour and partner.

19th October 1955 (Wednesday)

Last night Robin Scott was nominated next year's Moderator. He received his support because of his great, almost unique, gifts as pastor, a great preacher with a gift of real eloquence, as a warm-hearted human personality and because of the wonderful work he has done in holding together and extending the loyal congregation of St.

Columba's, Pont Street, during the years from 1941 when it was blitzed till now, when the new church is about to be opened. I voted for him. He will be a splendid representative.

In the evening last night I went to Christian Van der Rijdt's, where there was a reception for the Dutch Ambassador and his wife, a most charming couple. I met Dr. J.D.S. Cameron, who attended me a year ago. He was very pleased with the results of his treatment, and when he heard I had brought my weight down to 13 stones, he said: 'I never thought you would have succeeded.' I said that it was all thanks to Ella's help, and thanked him, too, warmly for what he had done for me. He asked me what people thought when they saw me this reduced. I said: 'ninety per cent of my friends say I'm looking ten years younger: the remaining ten per cent say: "Don't overdo the slimming!"' He said, 'Very well, let me tell you this. One man said to me: "It's a pity to see Philip getting so thin – I suppose it's cancer!"'

Today, I was installed at Dunblane Sheriff Court, and also heard two appeals. Now, I am Sheriff of Perth and Angus indeed – installed five times! The Provost of Dunblane turned out in his robes, and badge of office containing emblems of St. Lawrence and St. Blane. Alastair Prain again spoke most kindly, though he laughingly said, before we entered the Court: 'I'm afraid that it will simply be "cauld kail het again"!'

20th October 1955 (Thursday)

I travelled to London last night, and this afternoon attended the War Damage Thanksgiving Service in the restored Lambeth Chapel. We first went up the main staircase of the Palace and were received there by the Archbishop and Mrs. Fisher. To be beside him always warms my heart to him. He is so frank, gay and unaffected. He stood talking to us for a while and held on to my arm like a friend; it was, to me, so attractive: he is the very antithesis of 'standoffish'. Mrs. Fisher always reminds me of the Mona Lisa: she has the same inscrutable silent smile. We then proceeded to the Chapel. Afterwards, I walked with Mr. MacDonald to Waterloo, where I caught a taxi, and was no sooner in it than, at a Belisha crossing, another taxi collided with its rear, and they became interlocked. It took four men to lift the front of the other taxi off our rear bumper. Then we proceeded on our way. Outside Clarence House, a crowd was waiting for a glimpse of either Princess Margaret or Group-Captain Peter Townsend. I spent the morning at the Athenæum and the evening at the Caledonian Club.

At the former I met Normand who has been sitting in the House of Lords. Talking about Lambeth, to my surprise he said: 'Fisher is better than Temple. Temple was such a materialist!' He praised Fisher as a Chairman: he presides at the meetings of the British Museum Trustees. He was amused when I told him of the remark of Ian Fraser (formerly head boy of Repton) who said Fisher would have made an excellent Chairman of Imperial Chemicals. But to me, he is a good example of practical Christianity.

22nd October 1955 (Saturday)

Last night, we held our big Official Dinner of the University Graduates' Association in the Upper Library Hall, Old College. Ella and I received the guests, of whom there were over two hundred. We had more applications for tickets than we could accommodate. The Taylors stayed with us for the night. I had on either side of me in the Chair, Lady Appleton and Sir Hector Hetherington. He proposed 'The University of Edinburgh'. Sir Edward Appleton replied, and in turn proposed 'The Sister Universities of St. Andrews, Glasgow and Aberdeen' to which toast, Principal Knox replied. Tom Taylor proposed our Graduates' Association, to which I replied; and then David Band informally proposed my health. All the arrangements went like clockwork: without a hitch. All the four Principals spoke equally well. I likened myself to Swithin Forsyte – 'Four-in-hand Forsyte' – cracking my whip, as ringmaster, round the heads of the four Principals! Everyone was enthusiastic; and the act of faith, on which we had embarked with trepidation, succeeded beyond our expectations. One delightful incident was when Sir Edward read a message from Edinburgh's oldest graduate, Dr. R. Cathcart Bruce, Colnside, Bibury, Glos., a man of ninety-six, who had studied at the University between 1876 and 1880. In response, I pointed out that, at the dinner, we had a recent graduate, Lady Macpherson, who had taken her Arts degree as recently as fifty-nine years ago!

30th October 1955 (Sunday)

The event of this week is best recorded in its proper sequence. Monday was devoted to a Northern Lights Conference with the Scottish Shipowners, followed by lunch on the *Pharos*. I was in the chair at both as this half-year's Chairman of the Board. The same evening, I went to Perth, and on Tuesday and Wednesday heard the remainder of the

Perth High Street Traffic Inquiry. On Thursday I travelled to Oban, where I held my dinner for Archie Chalmers in the Columba Hotel. It turned out a great success. There were twenty present. All but one, Mr. Main, denied ability to sing. But, before the evening was out half the company sang, from music tucked away in their hip-pockets. 'The Spanish Guitar', 'Riding Down to Bangor', 'Clementine', a Pibroch song, 'Polly Wolly Doodle', and a host of others – which I accompanied. Half the company made informal speeches, after I, followed by Mr. Peter A.C. Milne, Dean of the Oban Faculty, had proposed Archie's health, and he had replied. Next morning, I sat on the Bench beside him, and joined in the tribute to him on his retirement. The journey to and from Oban was in autumn sunshine: the mountains, especially Ben Lawers, had their first snow-cap of the winter, and the birches were pure gold, and the hills a warm brown, with the first frost.

In the evening, Alison, who had been out at the ballet with Ian Craddock, came in with him, and I told them about the dinner. Suddenly, there was a silence, and then Ian said: 'Alison and I would like to be married!' I could only turn to Alison and ask what she thought. She said, shyly: 'I feel that way too.' This had all developed recently. I saw faint traces of it beginning last weekend, and, since then, Ian has been at the house several times. Rosemary thinks that he comes to play with her! His father is a doctor in Holsworthy, Devon, and his mother, Mrs. Heath, wife of Gordon's master. Such a strange turn of the wheel. I do not know him well yet, but I could only say what was true: 'I like your face.' He is frank, and friendly, and straight.

10th November 1955 (Thursday)

This morning Sir Charles Cunningham rang me up with regard to next year's Lord High Commissioner – to ask my views. Names discussed were the Duke of Edinburgh, the Queen Mother, the Earl of Crawford, the Duke of Buccleuch, the Earl of Airlie, Walter Elliot, Lord Bilsland. I said my first preference would, of course be the Duke of Edinburgh or the Queen Mother, if either would consent to act. Failing either, I preferred Lord Crawford or Lord Bilsland, then the Duke of Buccleuch or the Earl of Airlie. Walter Elliot's name was suggested as a Commoner; but I was not in favour of him. He has spoken ineffectively twice within recent years in the Assembly. I said that I thought Lord Bilsland would be peculiarly fitting, as really a representative of commoners, and particularly of the best of Scotland, and mentioned his work at Alvie Church. Later, I telephoned to suggest also the name of the Admiral of the Fleet, Sir Roderick McGregor.

It looks as if the National Library Trustees may now succeed in making one of the most wonderful acquisitions in the whole history of the Library. The Crichton-Stuart Collection of Shakespeare, and of other seventeenth and eighteenth century dramatists has been valued at just over £41,000 – the Shakespeares themselves being worth £23,000. The Friends of the National Libraries have promised a grant of £500, which represents £1 per member, the equivalent of their whole year's income. The Pilgrim Trust have promised £20,000, twice what they contributed to the purchase of the Earl of Leicester's Collection at Holkham for the British Museum. We are hoping that the Treasury will provide the remaining £21,000: they gave £74,000 towards the Holkham Collection. The Falkland Shakespeares would, with the Shakespeares in Edinburgh University Library, give Edinburgh the third finest Shakespeare collection in the United Kingdom – only the British Museum and the Bodleian being better. It is hoped to achieve this in time for the opening of the Library which the Queen is expected to perform in the Summer of 1956. We held our first Committee meeting last Thursday in the New Library – an Appointments Committee, followed by the Books and MSS Committee. Today, the Standing Committee held its first meeting in the New Library. The building is almost completed. The staff and full equipment will move in in the New Year. Beattie already has his Librarian's Room in use.

9th December 1955 (Friday)

(At the Athenæum) I travelled here last night for the monthly meeting of the War Damage Commission and Central Land Board. On Waverley platform, I was hailed like an old friend by my sleeper attendant. Two of them give me always a special welcome. This one read in some London paper in 1953 the report of a speech I had made in the General Assembly about the Church of Scotland and the Coronation. He evidently thought (which was true) that I was trying to promote friendship between the Churches across the Border, and ever since he has treated me like a long lost friend! Last night, he had my hot-water bottle filled before the train had started, and loaded me with sugar lumps for my morning tea – though, for slimming reasons, I am taking saccharine! But his unaffected friendship touched me. My other sleeper attendant friend is Mr. Duke, an older man, and I learn much of Geoffrey Duke, the racing motorist. He has been a long time in the service, and, but for his peaked hat, might be a douce bank-agent or family solicitor. He has often attended the Royal family, and used to travel on the train which took Prince Philip, as he then was, to school at Gordonstoun. Our friendship began when I discovered that his boy had been killed in an air force exercise. I gave him a copy of Gordon's book for his wife, whose health is not good; he is anxious, having to be so much away from home. Both these attendants live in London, though Mr. Duke is a Newcastle man. They remind me of Dickens' characters. Incidentally, my bedside book for the journey was *In the steps of Charles Dickens* which gave many delightful pictures of London, and also of Kent and East Anglia. Dickens' London practically stopped with the Strand, just as Galsworthy's London is the West End.

At breakfast in the Athenæum, instead of the usual bevy of bishops tucked each behind his own newspaper, I was interested to see 'Monty' having coffee and a roll. I was much impressed by his trim vigorous alertness – the picture of health, with not an ounce of superfluous flesh, very smartly turned out in Field-Marshal's uniform, endless ribbons, and slacks. He drove off, before many of the late-risers had come down to breakfast.

I had lunch at the Reform Club with Mr. MacDonald, Basil Gibson, and Sir Robert Fraser, and got all the talk of the town – an undercurrent of dissatisfaction over Sir Anthony Eden's indecision, criticism of the retiring Bishop of London (Wand) accepting a Canonry at St. Paul's which would seem to embarrass his successor, and so on.

In the afternoon, I paid a visit to see the new St. Columba's, just dedicated last Sunday. It is one of the monuments of new London – most impressive, with white Portland stone, and blue decoration, shields with the coats-of-arms of every Scottish county in heraldic colours, and which is said to be the greatest vault yet built of reinforced concrete. The tower is, I think, a little dumpy; but, in every other respect, the building is a tribute to the architect, Sir Edward Maufe. The new organ (to cost £15,000) has not yet been installed; they are waiting till the building dries out. In ten years, they have raised £200,000 for the building, not counting the £80,000 received from the War Damage Commission. They have only another £8,000 to raise. I met Robin Scott just as I was leaving. He scarcely recognised me in my slimmed condition; and remarked: 'You are getting very like your

Father.' I noticed that his deafness is increasing. In the evening I had dinner at the Caledonian Club with Sheldrake, who happened to be in London on other business, and Richardson, his successor at the Central Land Board in Edinburgh.

10th December 1955 (Sunday)

Last night, we had a Round Table Dinner in the Scotia Hotel in honour of Jock on his promotion to the Bench.

Those present were:- Jock, Daniel Blades, F.C. Watt, George Carmichael, John Wilson, Stanley Gimson, James Walker, T.P. McDonald, Robert Reid, Irvine Smith, John Wheatley, Donald Macleod, Frank Duffy and myself. For the first time, I was in the Chair, as the new Chairman of the Round Table and T.P. acted as croupier. Everyone spoke, and we finished at 12.40 a.m.! I proposed Jock's health. He replied. John Wheatley proposed the 'Round Table'. George Carmichael replied for those under the Table, and T.P. for those above. John Wilson then read some verses in the style of John Dryden. James Walker proposed 'Indecent practices in the Court of Session' which gave ample scope for the Round Table's love of murmuring the judges. Harry Guthrie was to have replied, but telephoned at the last minute that the road along the Pentlands from West Linton was getting icy, and he thought it might be difficult to get home again; he may have felt that the proposer of the toast was going to indulge in a good deal of twitting at his expense. In his absence, I invited Jock to nominate a respondent to the toast, and he called on Frank Duffy who made an excellent impromptu reply, which had, as it was intended to have, nothing to do with the toast. He read a correspondence which appeared in the *Glasgow Herald* in 1937, and was a gigantic leg-pull. It was begun by one writer asking whether any of the *Herald*'s readers could give him information about the old game of 'Doogan-Rolling' on a common in Galloway. Other correspondents rushed in, and described a game something like bowls or skittles. Then one correspondent described the game as it was differently played in Ireland, with a good deal of colourful digression on folk-customs. There is, of course, no such game. Stanley Gimson proposed the toast 'Why I admire Robert Reid'; and Robert Reid, who lives in the same flat with him, replied – a well- matched exchange of deft abuse and vituperation. Then Daniel Blades, F.C. Watt, and Donald Macleod each spoke about nothing in particular, and Irvine Smith wound up, as the 'boots', by proposing my health as Chairman. John Wheatley pointed out the remarkable record of the Round Table in the last three years – Five Senators of the College of Justice, one Privy Councillor, one Lord Advocate, two Solicitor-Generals, nine Sheriffs, two Sheriff-substitutes, four knights, two LL.D.s and two D.D.s, with a part not merely in the law, but in politics, academic life, the Church and the Arts. He rightly described the Round Table as becoming in Parliament House something of a legend. Daniel Blades has not recovered from his recent illness – we all felt that the old fire had gone, and that a slight shadow hung over him. It looks as if he had suffered a mortal blow, even if he is able to carry on for a time; he was subdued, and not the old robust boisterous Daniel.

16th December 1955 (Friday)

The Court rose for the Christmas Recess on Wednesday; for our closing day, the Round Table consumed a bottle of sloe-gin furnished from fines during the term imposed on the members for talking shop. But the real news of the day came when T.P. McDonald, who had been at the Land Court that morning, brought back the news of an incredible scene there – the strangest of many in which that strange creature Robert Gibson has made himself the central figure. A stated case had gone up from the Land Court to the First Division, and the First Division decided the question of law in the landlord's favour. The case then returned to the Land Court, whereupon Lord Gibson delivered himself of an astonishing exordium, carefully prepared, in which he invoked the name of Normand, strange bed-fellow, described the decision of the superior Court as 'ultra vires, contrary to law, and of no legal effect', added that three of the First Division judges had acted as his junior when at the bar, gave judgment for the tenant, and concluded, scripturally, by asking 'the agricultural community of Scotland at the festive season to be of good cheer'. One has heard before of judicial homicide, but never yet of judicial felo da se. The Scotsman reported this extraordinary outburst on its centre page on Thursday. The same evening the Glasgow Herald telephoned me for confidential advice on the line to take. I advised 'no comment'. In Parliament House, it is generally assumed that Gibson will have to resign or be removed.

I have now, on Wednesday, received my grant of Arms, a lovely piece of heraldic art. The description runs:–

> Azure, a chevron per pale Argent and Or, between two talbots' heads
> erased of the Second, langued Gules, in chief, and an open book of the

Second, bound of the Fourth, in base, all within a bordure parted per pale, dexter invected Argent, sinister Or; Above the shield is placed an helmet befitting his degree, with a Mantling Azure doubled Argent, and on a wreath of the Liveries is set for Crest an arm, attired in a manche Sable, the hand naked grasping a burning bush eradicated and enflamed, all proper, and in an Eserd over the same the Motto 'Fide et Amore'.

The talbots are the Philip emblem, and, instead of the third talbot, there is the book, signifying that my great-grandfather was the craftsman of Aberdeen 'Corner-square' book-bindings. The arm, in legal gown, indicates my profession; and the burning-bush, my office in the Church of Scotland. I chose the motto to record the two poles in my life. I am glad to see that all those nearest and dearest to me, including Gordon, are named in the Letters Patent.

Last night, we gave a sherry party for Alison and Ian. The President, the Advocate and Dean were there, and my old classmate Christian Van der Rijdt. But three-quarters of our guests were young – which made it very vivacious. Our old Edinburgh house regained its pristine glory with over eighty guests: ninety-three accepted: it shows what a big drawing-room can contain; and there was 'a sound of revelry by night'.

CHAPTER X

1956

1st January 1956 (Sunday)

This Christmas was memorable because of the addition to our family-circle – Alison's Ian. We had an old-time Christmas Dinner on Christmas Eve, to let the staff off on Christmas: twelve sat down to turkey. On the evening of Christmas Day, the Heaths invited us all to their Christmas Dinner at Jeffrey House.

This last week, I had set apart, at Dr. Brewster's suggestion, to try ten strong new pills to reduce blood-pressure. They are liable to make one dizzy, so I understand, and therefore I have kept to the house; though the only effect they have had on me is to make me slow-witted and liable to miss out words in writing, unless I take special care. What really matters, however, was that, on Tuesday night, I was suddenly afflicted with most violent pain and sickness – which the doctor called Virus C, or possibly gastric influenza. For the next three days, I stayed in bed and ate nothing; but now it is passing. Also, the pills are doing the trick. The last pressure reading showed a marked decline. I can only say that, this upset apart, I feel extremely well, and can't help wondering if, in another hundred years, the present treatment will seem as absurd as the kind of treatment Sir Walter Scott received a century ago.

Yesterday, the death was announced of the Archbishop of York (Garbett). This makes my visit to Lambeth this week more than usually interesting. Will the new Archbishop and the new Bishop of London be among our Anglican conferrers at Lambeth? One is almost sure to be; and I would hope that one is. I should like to see William Manchester chosen as Archbishop. He is distinctly able, without perhaps having the ability to speak of Durham; what is far more important is, however, that he is a great Christian, and the soul of understanding. Durham seems to be the name most frequently mentioned; he is extraordinarily able, but, like others who have come back into the Church of England from a non-Conformist background, he has gone to the right, and is, I suppose, the one most acceptable to the

Anglo-Catholic; for all his dialectual skill, I cannot help feeling that
there is a measure of humbug about his somewhat sententious pon-
tifical manner; he conveys the impression of a man of sixty-five to
seventy, although he is only about fifty. He is also difficult to get to
know; I think, if I could have one long talk alone with him, I would
understand him better. I am not the only one who finds him inscrutable; all the others do, except possibly Torrance. He has a curious
habit of muttering approval or disapproval while others are operating,
rather after the manner of an old-fashioned Methodist with his 'Hal-
leluyahs' and 'Amens'. He does not see eye to eye with Derby, whom,
I suspect, he slightly despises; and Derby's manner vaguely suggests
fear of him. I doubt if Durham, with all his ability, would be a
sufficiently central figure. On the other hand, two things I would say:
none can put a point more exactly than he, even to the extent of
making plausible what seems somewhat pointless; and, if he wants to
state, not just his own view, but a really representative view, none
can do it better; it is this last quality which impressed me specially at
Lund, and which will have much to do with determining his future.
But how much more attractive and straightforward is the charming
frankness of Cantuar. It is probably too late now for Chichester to
be appointed Archbishop; but for this, he would seem the ideal choice.
The coming conference will study a final draft of the Conference's
Report prepared by Durham. Dr. Lionel Smith, who called this evening, backs up an earlier rumour that the new Bishop of London will
be Peterborough (Spencer Leeson).

This week I have been re-reading *The Fair Maid of Perth* – with
such a Titian background I wonder if Sir Walter Scott may not shortly
be rediscovered; the modern wordsmiths pale before his majestic
canvas. I have also been reading Winifred Peck's *Home for the Holidays*, a delightful sequel to *A Victorian Childhood*. It discusses a social
revolution in family holidays, much of which reminded me of my
mother's childhood stories. In Scotland, I have seen a somewhat similar
revolution in holidays. Before the '70s, were there family holidays at
all? A family in good middle-class circumstances might take a house
in the country; but most holidays would seem to have consisted of
(1) towns for the better-to-do; (2) holi 'days'; and (3) visits to relatives.
In the '70s, my father used to go to stay with his uncle, I think it was,
who took a house at Mains of Carr, Broomhill. It was just after then,
that the villages in Speyside began slowly to develop as holiday-centres.
Practically all the present bridges on the Spey in lower Badenoch were
built about the '90s, evidence of the growing traffic. In those days,

holidays were spent in houses let furnished for the month, or in rooms. Till the Second World War, all my summer holidays, with a few exceptions, were spent in furnished houses. Boxes of provisions were ordered in advance; and staff presented no great problem. With the Second World War, the impossibility of obtaining staff practically ended this kind of holiday. Now the same people tend to go to hotels; and this form of holiday being more expensive, holidays are shorter. In the '80s and '90s, too, continental holidays became occasional with some families. My mother visited America; my father, and later my father with my mother, made numerous continental visits – to Norway, Switzerland, Italy, and even Palestine – taking us boys, when I was 10–11, for a winter to Italy, an unforgettable experience, and all the more so at that age. This kind of family excursion has again changed. Though we have taken Alison to France, and Alison and Rosemary to Denmark and Sweden, it is now the younger generation who go off to the Continent on their own – a great advance, and one of the real benefits which derive from the Second World War, when so many people perforce saw so much of the world and caught the infection of the desire to travel. And I admire their extraordinary resource in doing all this so cheaply. They certainly know how to make the money go far, by living with foreign friends, and seeing foreign countries through their eyes, instead of as members of a Cook's conducted tour. They also take to air travel; which, to me, is strange, remembering, as I do, seeing as a child in Florence in 1911, an early air display, where it was only with the greatest difficulty that any plane succeeded in getting off the ground. I still remember, after the display was over, watching from our hotel window, with eyes agape, an aeroplane flying off over the city, the first one I ever saw able to remain airborne for any appreciable time. Another social revolution in holidays has come from the gradual supersession of the railways by the motor car. It is no longer necessary to holiday within reach of a railway station, and the transition from home to holiday and back has become simple; no longer is there the elaborate packing of luggage, the transport of it to and from the station, the crowded trains without restaurants, the long delays – for a train to be four hours late at the beginning of August on the Highland Line was nothing unusual. Also, much more of the country can now be seen from any one centre. In my early holidays at Newtonmore, a waggonette drive from Ralia, by Drumguish, to Glenfeshie in 1912, when we saw hundreds of deer at the Feshie, was the highlight. Then, just before the First Great War, in 1913, we motored round the North of Scotland in an old Darracq which boiled over on every hill. Then, between the Wars, the opportunity of our car enabled us, with Gordon and Alison, to scour every corner of England, for a fortnight, staying in nice guest-houses, at a total cost of less than £40. The same kind of holiday now costs three times that amount, and, again, another form of family-holiday is passing. It seems to me that two broad changes are taking place – the one, good; the other, bad. Far more people are now getting adequate holidays; on the other hand, those whose work requires periods of mental rest especially are economically less able to take the adequate holidays they need. And it is surprising that the fashionable disease has changed. In the twenties, everyone had apoplexy or appendicitis; now a large proportion develop coronary thrombosis!

A broadcast this evening by Gilbert Murray, on the eve of his ninetieth birthday, on 'Unfinished Battle' – the two objectives of his life, the study of Hellenism and the securing of international peace, reminds me of a remark once made to me by a cousin of the older generation – that it would be interesting for any ordinary man to collect his fragmentary meetings with the great. As an instance, he told how one day, as a young man in a hotel in Kirkwall, he was asked by a rather older, but also still young, man at the other side of the lunch-table to 'Please pass the salt.' The stranger was Robert Louis Stevenson. In the same way, my only encounter with Gilbert Murray was when, as a young advocate and honorary secretary of the then League of Nations Union, I piloted him in a taxi from Waverley Station to Sir Alfred Ewing's house in Moray Place. He had all the simplicity of real greatness. In the same way I recall three interesting occasions in my father's life:- (1) as a young post-graduate student at Leipzig, he with his School and University class-mate, George Adam Smith, attended the Congress of Berlin in 1878, and saw Bismarck and Disraeli, the latter returning with the first 'Peace with Honour'; (2) in Rome in 1923, he was the only Scottish Moderator in his official dress ever to be received by Mussolini! (3) at the University service in St. Giles' after the graduation at which Winston Churchill received Edinburgh's LL.D., he preached the sermon, and, later in the day, when he met Winston at Sir Alfred Ewing's house, Winston said: 'If I heard more sermons like that, I would be oftener in Church.' I also append a postcard to him from William Ewart Gladstone written from Crewe Station in 1895, which is of constitutional interest as showing that the Grand Old Man had still time to conduct in his own handwriting not very important correspondence.

Rev. Adam Philip
Free church
Longforgan
Perthshire
NB.

Dear Sir I thank you for the works you have kindly sent me. The production of local histories is a [one] [case] which I regard with interest, & I rejoice to see any work of this kind I think done [known to] the authors and to [both] [cards]

I remain dear Sir your very faithfully

W E Gladstone

N. 4. 95

Letter from Gladstone to Adam Philip

5th January 1956 (Thursday)

I am writing this in Bedroom No. 11 at Lambeth Palace. I travelled south by day yesterday with John Baillie, Archie Craig, Burleigh and Stuart Louden. George Gunn and Tom Torrance joined us here. It was a lovely winter's day as we crossed the Border, but, by Durham, fog was gathering, and, here, this morning, I could not even see the trees outside. On the train, there turned out to be, in the next compartment, Mrs. Gecaga, the wife of the Kikuyu friend, B.M. Gecaga, who was introduced to me two years ago by my friend, W.H. Kirkcaldy-Willis. The Gecagas had been spending the week in Edinburgh, and all the family took them to church on Sunday, except myself (as I was not out). Mrs. Gecaga recognised Rosemary on the platform and so I was introduced. I felt the least I could do to a stranger within the gates was to offer her lunch on the train. So I found myself in the unusual position of trying to act as host to a coloured lady. At King's Cross, I met her husband also, who was waiting to receive her.

This is a great gaunt building with long corridors all running at right angles to each other, decorated in quiet yellows and browns, the passages lined with portraits of archbishops. My room is a quiet austere bedroom, overlooking the archiepiscopal hen-run. A lady housekeeper, a most charming person, who might have walked out of Angela Thirkell's novels, welcomed us at the great staircase, and showed us to our rooms. From here, every ten seconds or so, I hear the dull rumbling of the trains passing in and out of Waterloo, mingled with the clucking of Archiepiscopal Rhode-Island Reds. Before me is a notice informing me that Chapel is at 8.00 a.m., Holy Communion 8.30 a.m. on Saints Days, 9.15 a.m. Matins, 7.15 p.m. Evensong; and the regrettable announcement that guests will be called at 7.15 a.m.

We sat at dinner in a large dining-room with three tables, and, at one end, a portrait of the Archbishop at the time of the Coronation: I saw it a year ago at Burlington House. Derby fell on my neck with an affectionate greeting, and I sat with him and Leicester at dinner. During dinner, in came the Archbishop, and in his friendly way, laid his hand on each of our shoulders with a word for each. He had been that day to York attending the funeral of his fellow Archbishop, and was just going out to broadcast a tribute to him. Yet amid all his preoccupations, he had time for a word for each. We began our Conference in the evening.

This morning, the Archbishop himself celebrated Communion in the chapel and invited us all to Communion. It was the first time I had ever received this invitation; that it came from him meant all the more.

On resuming our Conference, Derby announced that Durham had just been appointed Archbishop of York, and he and John Baillie gave him our good wishes. Afterwards, at morning coffee, I had the chance of offering my own good wishes, and said – what was true: 'I have always been rather afraid of you; and only hope I won't be more afraid of you now!' He was all the nicer to me for saying it; he is in some ways shy, and not easy in intercourse.

There was one new representative at the Conference – the Bishop of Exeter (Mortimer). I told him that his Dean, A.R. Wallace, the former headmaster of Cargilfield, was the only man who had ever gone off with my hat: we both take the unusual size of 7¾. John Baillie told a quip which pleased everyone. 'A bishop can never tell a lie, because a curate becomes a-c-curate if you give him a See!'

At lunch-time, I asked Derby about the new Bishop of London, Montgomery Campbell, who is somewhat disrespectfully referred to by the *Manchester Guardian* as a 'caretaker' appointment. He is sixty-eight, but had a mordant wit. Canon Prestige, having resigned the editorship of the *Church Times*, approached Montgomery Campbell to see whether he could find him a new job. 'My dear man,' said M-C., 'after you have vituperated the episcopate for so many years, you can scarcely expect them to leap at you with open arms!'

In the later discussion, Leicester, by a slip of the tongue, at one point referred to a bishop-coadjutor as a 'bishop-coagitator'! Whereupon, John Baillie recalled the foreign journalist at Lund who wrote what had impressed him so much about the Lund Conference was the 'unanimosity' of the delegates.

Actually, however, the day was devoted to most serious and fruitful discussion. We have now completed the discussion of the first draft of our report – in which the suggestions are being made that the Presbyterian churches might consider adopting a system of a bishop *in presbyterio* and the Episcopal Churches a system of synodical government in which laity as well as clergy and bishops took a full part, and also greater use of laity after the Presbyterian model. The suggestion is being examined whether the Anglican deacon – at present a rather useless office – could be assimilated in some degree to the Presbyterian elder. I miss William Manchester, but Leicester is another great soul, with whom I feel complete friendship, so that we can discuss anything, each with the desire to help the other. I took quite a fair share in the discussion, and he helped me to make more effective some points I desired to make. But the feature of the Conference was the share taken by everyone, and the quite extraordinary frankness and friendliness of it all. How I wish that the same spirit could animate each of the members of all four Churches.

6th January 1956 (Friday)

This afternoon, I went with Burleigh to see Carlyle's House in Cheyne Row. I thought our taxi driver would know of it. But he could not find it, and we wandered up and down asking passers-by and policemen. Finally, I suggested going on a little further and we might find 'some intelligent person' – not meaning to be sarcastic. To which, our driver responded with true Cockney wit: 'That's more than you can expect in this town!' The house itself was not as interesting as I had hoped, or, say, as interesting as Dickens' or Johnston's houses. The main room had no lighting, and it was a dark January afternoon. The exhibits were very numerous, but the subjects not indicated. However, with difficulty, we found a fragment of the MS of *The French Revolution* and some pages of the MS of *Frederick the Great*. It surprised me to discover that so great a work was composed in the dull top room of this ancient house, part of which I understand goes back for centuries. I then took Burleigh for tea at The Athenæum. We resumed our Conference at 5 p.m. and, with a break for dinner, have just completed our present work, with the usual uncommunicative press communiqué.

19th January 1956 (Thursday)

It has been announced today what I learned some days ago – confidentially – that the Queen is to open the National Library building on 4th July, and to dine with the Faculty of Advocates in the Parliament Hall in the evening of 6th July. In anticipation of these two events, Lord Crawford has been elected, yesterday, an honorary member of the Faculty.

At yesterday's meeting of the Northern Lighthouse Board, when I was in the Chair, we received a full report of the recent accident in which a helicopter hit the top of a lighthouse, and the pilot and his companion were both lost. The light was put out, and the seas were so high that days passed before a landing could be effected, two ships standing by all the time to make the landing as soon as it became possible. One of the assistant-lightkeepers behaved very heroically.

He was let down by rope from the top of the lighthouse to try to save the pilot. A great wave flung the helicopter, however, out into deep water, and the lightkeeper was only saved by the rope holding. The Superintendent, Mr. Cadger, also did magnificent work, carrying out repairs on the roof of the lighthouse in a howling gale. Both are being recommended for suitable recognition.

24th January 1956 (Tuesday)

On 16th December I mentioned the extraordinary scene which had taken place in the Land Court. The final upshot was reached last Friday. It appears that Lord Gibson, although he made his astonishing pronouncement, pronounced no order in the case. Indeed, his lay colleagues would not come into Court to be present at his pronouncement and had tried to dissuade him from making it. The sequel was that the landlord petitioned the Court of Session that the case should be remitted to the Land Court so that they could bring their decision into conformity with that of the First Division. The petition was served on the Land Court which is, as well as being a Court, a statutory incorporation. Apparently on service of this petition, Lord Gibson immediately retained the Dean of Faculty and Duffes – the Dean presumably to plead his case if anything could be said for it and Duffes to plead his case if nothing could be said for it. However, no sooner had the petition been served than the lay majority of the Land Court, showing courage and independence, signed an order giving effect to the judgment of the First Division. To this order Gibson added a dissent and then, realising that his position was hopeless, withdrew his retainer to counsel. No answers were given to the petition and because of the order pronounced by the lay members of the Land Court no further procedure was necessary in the petition. But when the case next came up before the First Division to enable counsel to explain that an order by the First Division was now no longer necessary, the First Division gave their comments on the position. The Lord President referred to the 'extravagant and unjudicial language in which the pronouncement was couched'; and commented that persistence by Gibson in his attitude would only damage the credit and respect that the Land Court must retain if it was to perform its important role. It is generally agreed in the legal profession that Gibson's behaviour is the most unjudicial which has occurred for a very long time. At the Annual Dinner of the Perth Society of Solicitors which I attended last Friday, I was told that two of the lay members of the Land Court had decided to resign. But there is no public confirmation of this and nothing otherwise to indicate that this rumour is confirmed.

3rd February 1956 (Friday)

On 24th January, I presided at an interesting students' meeting in the Common Room, Old College. About four hundred students were present; the subject was 'Our Church'; the standpoint of (1) the Roman Catholic Church; (2) the Anglican Communion and (3) the Reformed Churches were put in three speeches – by Father Ginns, a Dominican; Bishop Warner; and Principal Baillie; the first occasion, I believe, when the three churches had been represented thus together on the same platform. There was an hour of animated questioning afterwards. All the speakers were good. In some ways, the least defensible position, logically, the Anglican, was put the best – by Bishop Warner. Principal Baillie tended to speak from an individual standpoint; the Dominican, whom I liked much, tended, almost too much, not unnaturally, in the other direction. But they were well-balanced. And the questions put were serious – it shows how the present generation of students is keenly interested in Church Unity. I had a similar experience of this at Oxford in 1952, when I spoke to the Iona Society there, and was bombarded with questions for an hour and a half.

7th February 1956 (Tuesday)

In a letter from Principal John A. Allan of Dunedin, N.Z., congratulating me on becoming Sheriff of Perth and Angus and a D.D., he writes: 'I am reading just now J.F. Mozley's *William Tyndale*, and the night after I got your letter learned that, in 1 Kings 20:17, Tyndale has 'the sheriffs of the shires', where the Authorised Version has 'the princes of the provinces'!, so I presume that scripturally a sheriff is equivalent to a prince! At any rate, you will agree with me that a D.D. is the Presbyterian equivalent of a prince of the Church!'

Last Friday, before lunch, the Bishop of Derby came up to me in the Athenæum. I had seen in the papers that day that he was to reach the 20th anniversary of his consecration as a bishop on St. Matthias' Day. When I congratulated him, he said: 'Yes, my predecessor did not like my choice of St. Matthias' Day for my consecration, for the collect for that day runs: "O Almighty God, who into the place of the traitor Judas didst choose thy faithful servant Matthias!"'

17th February 1956 (Friday)

Last night the House of Commons decided to end capital punishment for murder. The Government motion, to retain the death penalty, with a promise of amending legislation, was defeated by 293 to 262. The amendment in favour of abolition was carried by 292 to 246. It is interesting to see how people react to a question like this. The division was roughly all Labour, all Liberal, a few Conservatives on one side: practically all Conservative on the other. Those who support abolition are, to some extent, embarrassed by cranks and sentimentalists – those who oppose abolition are equally embarrassed by some 'die-hards'. Personally I have come to be in favour of abolition with the last few years. We are one of the last civilised countries to retain the death penalty, although the United States also retain it. I can't find any reliable evidence to show that murder increases when there is no death penalty; also I do think that those who oppose abolition of the death penalty sometimes defend it on grounds not very different from those on which it was defended a century ago for lesser crimes, even in relation to the hanging of children of nine. It is, I think, regrettable too, that the present Lord Chief Justice (Goddard) expresses himself on matters affecting the judicial office in a way which is sometimes unjudicial and certainly injudicious. I imagine that Lord Chief Justices have usually thrown in their weight, all the time, against reforms which are now accepted as right and proper. 'The establishment' – to use a phrase current at the present time – have nearly always been against Social reform. My forecast is that shortly we shall all be wondering why we retained this form of penalty as long as we did, and the people who opposed its abolition will simply not be understood by future generations. This makes it all the more regrettable that its abolition should have been opposed by some responsible people, and that the government itself should have so mis-gauged public opinion.

The Government propose to take powers to appoint additional High Court judges, and one additional Court of Session judge, in connection with a Bill to create tribunals to deal with restrictive practices in trade. If appointments are made, it is to be hoped that the new judges will hold office on the same footing as the existing judges, and not be merely judges of the new tribunal.

18th February 1956 (Saturday)

I had a call this morning from John Anderson, the Deputy-Secretary of Scottish Home Department, about various matters. One was to let me know that the possibility had arisen of the Queen attending service in Iona Cathedral on 12th August, and what would be the best approach to the matter. Evidently, the Lord Lieutenant of Argyll and others had raised the point of the tension in Iona between the residents and the Iona Community. No difficulty would have arisen had the parish not at present been vacant, as the parish minister, if there had been one, would have been approached. But at least two parish ministers have found it difficult to work with George MacLeod, and have left, and no one now seems to relish stepping into a difficult situation; the Community themselves, with more understanding, could end the tension by helping the parish minister instead of holding competing services. I suggested as the best course, that an approach should be made from the Palace to Dr. Warr. He is both the senior royal chaplain and also the Chairman of the Iona Cathedral Trustees. I suggested also that he or Nevile Davidson, also a Trustee, might be invited to preach; that George MacLeod should be invited to take part; and that the Moderator of the Presbytery, or another neighbouring minister as representing the Presbytery (for example, the Interim-Moderator), might be asked to pronounce the Benediction. I think that this course may well be followed.

26th February 1956 (Sunday)

A Spoonerism from Cambridge. Cambridge divine, not too sure about the woman undergraduate, misreads Abishag the Shunamite (1 Kings 1,2): 'Shabby hag the Newnhamite!'

3rd March 1956 (Saturday)

Last night C. S. Lewis proposed 'The Immortal Memory' at the Sir Walter Scott Dinner. The most memorable passage in his oration was where he argued that Scott had *created* something which had not existed in historical literature to the same extent before – the 'sense of period'. He recalled a conversation which he had had with G.M. Trevelyan in which the latter contrasted the historical writing of Gibbon and Macaulay. Gibbon, with all his range and mastery had tended to cloak his historical personages with the modes of thought of his own, the Augustan, age. Macaulay, with all his Whig leanings, had nevertheless penetrated more deeply into the thoughts and idioms of his chosen period. Why this difference? 'Because,' said Trevelyan, 'between Gibbon and Macaulay, the Waverley Novels had appeared, and, with them, historians had discovered a new sense of period.' The whole oration was a remarkable instance of sustained and concentrated argument, freshly expressed, and if obviously 'donnish' in technique, none the less natural for that. He is, I believe, at his best in literary criticism; I consider this address and his 'Preface to Paradise Lost' better than his religious books, certainly much better than his spiritual apologia *Surprised by Joy*, which both Ella and I had just finished reading. In the latter works, his acute dialectic gets the better of him, and I have always the feeling that, like Dr. Johnston, he could, if so minded, present an equally convincing argument for the opposite view. He is a most genial personality, a chain smoker, and obviously fond of creature comforts, anything but a desiccated don. One might forget his face after an interval, as, while a strong personality, he is not so obviously distinguished in appearance. But one would never forget his intellectual make-up, and unusual combination of power of mind and power of expression. I proposed the 'City of Edinburgh' and took as my theme Scott's view of the magistracy. I knew it went down, for repeatedly I had to allow pauses until the laughter had subsided.

Allan Fraser, the Secretary of the Club, told me that the number present at the Dinner was 235, apparently the largest attendance since the War. It would be fair to say that the Scott Dinner is, at present, the first of Edinburgh's dinners: certainly, at no other dinner in Scotland, does one see anything like so many of her representative citizens. This is, I think, an interesting demonstration of the hold Scott has at the citadel of his affections. But, I think partly because of the debunking school of modern criticism, of which Lytton Strachey was an early monument, and because the modern critic thinks nothing serious unless the writer reveals the morbidity of his own soul, Scott is in partial eclipse. Yet, to me, his greatest Scottish characters and their conversations have a Shakespearean or Chaucerian quality, and the greatest of his historical descriptions have all the quality of Titian. But, the best of his novels should more often be read aloud. When I was a child, my mother read aloud to us, lying on the fireside rug, *Ivanhoe*, *The Talisman*, *Rob Roy*, *Old Mortality* and *Redgauntlet*. Lord Rosebery told me that his father, the Prime Minister, did the same with his family. I read practically all the others myself while still at school – even *Anne of Geierstein*, which introduced me to mediaeval Europe east of France. The Lord Provost, in an unaffected speech, said that he had done the same, and he read the moving description of Edinburgh given in *The Abbot*, the public reading of which was deeply impressive. Scott's *Journal* has still to be published in a cheap edition which will make it available for wider consumption.

5th March 1956 (Monday)

This evening, after a day at Perth Sheriff Court, I met little Mr. Martin, our charming little greengrocer who, with never failing spirits, carries on a decaying little business at the corner of Dundas Street. He is full of literary knowledge and reminiscences. Tonight he said: 'I see you were speaking at the Scott Dinner. I would like fine to have heard you. You know I knew a man who had known Sir Walter Scott. He was Jimmie Bell of Galashiels. He died at the age of ninety-five, when I was ten. He lived through the last ten years of Scott's life, and attended his funeral at Dryburgh. I though nothing of this then, as I was a mere laddie. But I wish now I had asked him what he thought of Scott himself.'

11th March 1956 (Sunday)

Yesterday was memorable for the astounding news that the British Government have deported Archbishop Makarios from Cyprus to the Seychelles, surely one of the biggest blunders ever made by a British Government.

17th March 1956 (Saturday)

Last night, the first dinner of the Stair Society was held (timed nicely to fit in with the Calcutta Cup match today at Murrayfield), to mark its 21st birthday. Normand occupied the chair, and Lord Evershed, Master of the Rolls, was the principal speaker, proposing the toast of the Society, to which Normand replied. I have always admired particularly Evershed's work in Court, and there is no judge I enjoy more hearing in action. My impression from a distance was confirmed on meeting him. It gives you new faith in human nature to find one whose distinction is matched by his naturalness and modesty. His speech, too, was the best of the evening. He has an unusually soft mellow voice, which reminds me in a way of the bell-tones of Cosmo Gordon Lang. Not a word is wasted, and each sentence is deftly constructed, and there is always a humorous flavour which kindles rather than sparkles. Normand, too, was good; he looked old and rugged, but to use a word which he himself used, he was, at times, 'facetious', a delightful variation from 'Giant Despair'; he has mellowed with age. Hector McKechnie made a clever speech full of puns, though perhaps too consciously smelling of midnight oil. He referred to an imaginary tramway accident in which an old lady descending the Stair had Bankton the conductor sounding the Bell, and had fallen, just saving 'Er-skine': the tramway manager was Dalrymple (there was, I think, a Glasgow tramway manager who had that name). He proposed the 'Imperial Form' to which Bernard Fergusson replied in an amusing speech. Sir Leslie Farrer, the Queen's solicitor in London and President of the Selden Society, proposed 'The Legal Profession in Scotland' – his matter was excellent, but he has a most embarrassing and disabling stutter. Bill Milligan, proposing the Chairman, was, as always, entertainingly low-brow. Hamish Clyde, who proposed the guests, and Harry Whitley, who replied, were depressingly common-place. Hamish, in spite of his incisive mind, is just not an after-dinner speaker, and repeats himself, and has no artistry in words, at all events for that kind of speech. Harry Whitley, though exuberant and genial, was scarcely what one would expect of such an occasion. He pointed out, however, that the great Lord Stair was buried, none knew where, in St. Giles', and John Knox in Parliament Square, and suggested that Scotland did less than justice to its great men. Everyone agreed that Evershed was pre-eminent, with Normand a good second. The rest of the speaking was not what one might expect from a legal dinner. I was rather surprised at the small representation of the bar; though most of the Bench were there.

18th March 1956 (Sunday)

One strangely moving incident (for those who knew what lay behind it) occurred in church this morning. In a prayer of intercession, Murdo Macdonald prayed for those who, having fought the good fight, and with their work done, stood on the brink of eternity, that they might remember that they were surrounded by a cloud of witnesses and encompassed by the love of God. His old mother, aged eighty-three, is dying of cancer, and is being flown from the croft in Harris to Renfrew, to be brought to his house in Succoth Place, where she may receive the necessary attention at the close of her life. The old father is meantime remaining in Harris, so that the mother will only think that she is being brought here for necessary treatment. He will follow later. The decision was only taken a day or two ago, and I do not imagine that half-a-dozen people in the congregation knew what lay behind the prayer.

25th March 1956 (Sunday)

On Friday, Lord Crawford was introduced as an honorary member of the Faculty; the first honorary member (omitting Royalty) was Lord Morton of Henryton, but Lord Crawford is the first layman to receive the honour. He will be present at the dinner of the Faculty to be attended by the Queen on July 6th. I went up to give him my good wishes after the meeting, as few of the Faculty know him. He fainted in his London club the other day, and told me that he has not been up to scratch, having felt rather 'light-headed' recently. I said: 'You and I are the same age. You should have your blood pressure taken.' It seemed not to have occurred to him. I think he was grateful for the suggestion. He really does give himself to public service.

The same evening, I was elected President of the Edinburgh Angus Club. There I met Mr. Scott, a member of the English Bar, a native of Arbroath, and a brother of an old schoolmate of mine. He told me that Sir William Hutchison had been completing a portrait of Tommy Cooper, and that for the final sittings, his brother James had sat in his judicial robes. It was announced at the Faculty meeting on Friday that James Cooper was presenting the portrait to the Faculty. This will be a great occasion. From the reproduction in yesterday's Scotsman, I judge the portrait to be a better likeness than that by Stanley Cursiter of Craigie Aitchison.

I have finished another week of the proof in Meyer v. Scottish Cooperative Wholesale Society. [1957 SLT 250; 1958 SLT 241] It began in March 1955, and this is now the fourth week of the proof. Another week in May has been set apart for it. It will be my longest Court of Session proof ever. On the whole, this week's evidence went well for us. Friday's evidence was devoted to accounting witnesses, and we had a day of surprises.

Knowing that this case would keep me late on Wednesday, I asked Miss Johnston my secretary to telephone the Northern Lighthouse Board to say that I would not be in time for the start of the Board Meeting, and would they proceed without me (as I should have been there to take the Chair). When I did arrive at the meeting, I was greeted with consternation, and Gilchrist, who had taken the Chair in my place, said that they all wanted to know how I was feeling! I asked the cause of their concern, and it then transpired that the

Northern Board clerkess who had received the message had recorded it as follows:–

21st March 1956 at 11.25 a.m.
Received telephone message from Sir Randall Philip.

Sir Randall is in an iron case and corset and it might prevent him from getting to the meeting on time. You have just to start the meeting without him and he will come as soon as he can.

D.I.B.

We have taken rooms at Iona from 9th to 13th August, in the hope of seeing the Queen on her visit there, which is expected to be on the 12th. Now, I hear that, on the 13th, she is to visit Oban, and then probably visit Lismore Lighthouse on her way to lunch at Duart Castle. The Commissioner of Northern Lights may have the *Pharos* in attendance, and I just wonder whether I can cross to Mull that morning, in the hope of seeing her at Lismore Light. Their arrangements are not yet published.

28th March 1956 (Wednesday)

Still another royal occasion pending. I learned yesterday that there is a possibility that the foundation stone of Strathy Point Lighthouse (for which the Northern Lighthouse Board agitated for fifty years) may be laid this summer by the Queen Mother, when she is staying at the Castle of Mey.

I had an interesting letter from James Cooper about the circumstances in which his brother's portrait was painted. 'Lord Crawford (whom I approached),' he writes, 'persuaded Sir William [Hutchison] to risk his reputation on a posthumous portrait. I am so glad that all the experts who have seen the painting consider it one of Sir William's best works. I gave him two very big enlarged photographs from Elliot and Fry of London, and I myself sat for Sir William in the Justice-General's robes. At my request, Sir William went to London and purchased a very old and very rare carved wood frame and the final product is more pleasing. After hanging in the Academy, the site for the painting in P.H. falls to be determined, and my one hope all along has been that it would hang in the Hall. I thought that the Dean would decide, but apparently the L.P. has the final word and he will not finally commit himself. Certainly there are far worse portraits of much less famous men hanging in the Hall already. The volume of

Tom's "Selected Papers" which I have been working on with assistance should shortly be ready for the printers.'

11th April 1956 (Wednesday)

We have just returned from a ten days' Easter holiday spent at the Green Park Hotel, Pitlochry, surely the hotel with the loveliest situation in Scotland. We had a broiling Easter weekend, when Alison and Ian joined Ella, Rosemary and myself. On Easter Sunday, it happened to be April Fool's Day. We had afternoon tea outside overlooking Faskally Loch.

Certainly Pitlochry is one place which has gained in amenity from the Hydro-Electric Schemes. But I note two points:– The amenities have been much better preserved under the Hydro-Electric Board, than under the pre-Board Schemes. No doubt, this is because of the strenuous amenity objectives stated at the Tummel Garry and Loch Sloy Inquiries, and the formation of the Amenity Committee under the North of Scotland Board Act. The Board stations blend much better with the countryside. The pre-Board stations are a blot on the landscape. Tummel Bridge was finally ruined by the works carried out there. It does, however, appear that the Board itself can be ruthless, in Schemes where there is no powerful opposition. I was horrified at the new unsightly mess made for two miles on the Lochside at St. Fillans, and also at the piles of rubbish near the Errochty Power Station. It will take years for these areas to recover, if they ever do. But certainly the east end of Loch Tummel is not spoiled, but rather improved by the dam there, and Loch Faskally has given Pitlochry a 'new look'.

We made many memorable excursions – to Straloch and Kirkmichael; to the Queen's View; to Crieff (to see the Prains), visiting Glenalmond, Fowlis Wester, and myself (with Alastair Prain and his boy Kenneth) Innerpeffray Library and the Drummond Chapel; to Dunfallandy to see the Celtic stone, and the burial place of my Stewart-Fergusson relatives; to Strathtay, and Aberfeldy; to Dunkeld Cathedral, Tenandry Church, and Shierglas; to Coillebhrochan; to Kinloch Rannoch; and to the Braes of Foss. We returned home by Strathbraan, Crieff, Comrie, St. Fillans and Lochearnhead.

We saw, particularly on the moor above Moulin, many birch in their spring plumage, a grouse cock (with red crop) and hen, a pair of peewits, with soft green feathers, white fronts, and caps, for all the world like school masters with mortar-boards, a solitary curlew with long beak and grey feathers making flights from point to point in the heather, and lower down a very tame cock and peahen pheasant. In the hotel grounds there was a peacock and pea hen the former of which delighted Rosemary by opening his fan tail on numerous occasions. But most interesting of all was the Prains' golden Labrador 'Saunders' which performed astonishing feats of intelligence and telepathy. If you spelt any of the numbers from O-N-E to F-I-V-E, he would bark the correct number of times. If you mentioned one of these numbers to Margaret Prain, and she then looked at Saunders without saying anything, he would again bark the correct number of times.

Some of our discoveries, too, were quite unusually interesting. Rosemary and I searched out 'Coillebhrochan' near Bonskeid – the 'wood of the brose' – though, alas, the wood is now simply stumps of trees cut down apparently by the Hydro- Electric Board. Here stands the gate of an old cottage with an inscription stating:–

COILLEBRUCHAIN
ROBERT THE BRUCE
RESTED HERE AFTER
THE BATTLE OF METHVEN
MCCCVI

The story is a lovely one. On his flight northwards, he stumbled wearily out of the forest into an open glade, where stood a cottage. The housewife, seeing the fugitive, gave him a bowl of brose, to restore his weary spirit; and he went out encouraged to ultimate victory. I have heard this beautiful story used to illustrate Ps. 23:5:–

> Thou preparest a table before me in the presence of mine enemies; thou anointest my head with oil; my cup runneth over.

Not far off, near Fincastle, is a wayside well, with the inscription:–

> Whosoever drinketh of this water shall thirst again. But whosoever drinketh of the water that I shall give him shall never thirst; but the water that I shall give him shall be in him a well of water springing up into everlasting life.
>
> St. John c. IV. vv. 13,14.

It is in memory of R.W. Barbour of Bonskeid, a fellow student of my own father.

One of our unexpected discoveries was Fowlis Wester, with its pre-Reformation Church, and two Celtic stones – one on the village green, the other inside the Church. The latter stone depicts two figures seated facing each other in a similar manner to the figures on the Dunfallandy stone. I believe that the Dunfallandy stone is supposed to represent the inauguration of a Chief and tanist; it would be interesting if the stone at Fowlis Wester depicts a similar subject.

Innerpeffray Library, which I saw for the first time, is in good order; the building has been restored with the aid of a grant from the Pilgrim Trust and our Edinburgh Perthshire Association has given, in all so far, about £400 to balance the Library accounts. But I was sorry to see the principal treasures lying in a glass case on which the sun was beating; and the custodian is much too free in his methods of handling them. He turned over the pages of the unique Clement Marot for our supposed benefit, and also the 'Treacle Bible' [so called as 'Balm from Gilead' appears translated as 'Treacle from Gilead' – Ed.]; and I noticed that the pages of both, where he had been handling them, were unnecessarily crumpled. It is sad to see this. I have already been in touch with the Scottish Home Department to see whether the National Library might not get additional powers to take over, by agreement, or at least to share in the management of the four special Libraries which exist in Scotland – Innerpeffray; the Leighton Library at Dunblane; the Hornel Library at Kirkcudbright; and the Abbotsford Library. We opened overtures about a year ago; but, with the additional work entailed in the forthcoming opening of the National Library, Beattie has asked that this other proposal should be deferred meantime. I hope something can be done before Innerpeffray's finest treasures have decayed through mis-handling. The Drummond Chapel is now in a state of almost complete decay. But recently some first aid repairs have been done, and the Earl of Perth is anxious to see it restored. One of the curious relics in Innerpeffray was a note to intending emigrants (dating from the early days of Queen Victoria) offering passages to Canada for 9 guineas, and to Queensland for 13.

On our first Sunday – Easter – we attended Dunkeld Cathedral; on our second, the little parish church of Tenandry. We returned another day to see the Cathedral itself. The two most interesting remains in it are the tomb of the Wolf of Badenoch, with its gigantic recumbent figure, and an early stone carving representing Christ feeding the five thousand. Though it was partly erected at the time of the Reformation, the fishes, the loaf, the disciples, and the serried ranks of the crowd can still be made out clearly. I was interested, too, to see, for the first time, the eighteenth century houses being restored by the National Trust; I am personally concerned in it as Sheriff, for in that capacity

I am patron of St. George's Hospital, a pre-Reformation mortification which holds certain of the houses. These the National Trust want to acquire; and the problem is, how to give them a title, as I have not a feudal title, and the intervention of the Court is needed; but, so far, the Treasury refuses to finance the application to the Court. I am just negotiating about the matter this very month. The odd thing is that over a year ago, the National Trust instructed me as their counsel; and I advised such procedure; now, as Sheriff, I have become the patron, and can no longer act for them!

Tenandry Church is a squat little not unattractive building in a lovely site on the incredibly steep twisting narrow road between Bonskeid and Killiecrankie. The singing there would have done credit to any great congregation.

In the hotel, one of the guests was Arthur Howard, brother of the late Leslie Howard, a charming young actor who is taking the leading part in the five plays being produced at this year's Festival at the Pitlochry Theatre. He was getting-up his five parts for the plays which begin at the end of the month.

22nd April 1956 (Sunday)

Our thirtieth wedding anniversary. One of the loveliest days in our home. Yesterday, I gave Ella narcissus and irises; and a posy from each of her children, Gordon, Alison-and-Ian, and Rosemary. In the afternoon, yesterday, we two with Rosemary and her little friend Jenny McIlwaine gathered spring buds near Gifford. On my pillow in the evening was a book with a message from Ella. Today, at our Sunday-morning prayers, I thought I must read something special, and chose the 13th chapter of First Corinthians, saying to the children that this described their Mother. We said our thanks for these wonderful thirty years of love, and for the little ones who had come into our home, at Church, I could not help telling our pew-neighbours of a generation, the Bunces, of this memorable day for us. Ian joined us at dinner, and we interchanged healths in a special bottle of hock. In the afternoon Ella and I went to tea at the John Baillies – on the way slipping in to the Grange to stand for a moment beside Gordon's grave. The kindly attendant came up, as always with a friendly word. At the Baillies our fellow guests were Sir John Maud, Permanent Secretary of the Ministry of Fuel and Power, and Professor John Macmurray. The former was preaching at the evening University Service in St. Giles'. We had not intended to go, but we were so captivated by his personality that we changed our minds. I had a long intimate talk with him, and found him one of the most unassuming and modest of Civil Servant heads. He is the son of a former Bishop of Kensington, and has had an unusual career:- King's Scholar at Eton; Scholar of New College (like Ian); a Scholar at Harvard; Fellow and Dean of Univ; Master of Birkbeck College, London. Then he switched over, at the beginning of the last War, to the Civil Service. He prefers it to the life of a don. He told me that all his life he had spoken at Christian conferences and services. His very expression marked the man. At St. Giles', he preached on God reconciling the World to Himself, and how that reconciliation was wrought through men. He drew his illustration from life in the modern state – an unusual and original theme, which the students would not forget.

1st May 1956 (Tuesday)

My father, who died in 1945, was born a hundred years ago today. His recollections carried me back to the early days of the Disruption. He remembered, for example, Dr. Candlish, of Free St. George's, and once when Dr. Candlish came to visit my grandfather in the early '60s at 52 Blacket Place, my father, then a very small boy, looked out from an upstairs window and shouted down at him 'Jehovah' – he was so small, then, that he hadn't the faintest idea what the words meant. But, in those days, with family prayers morning and evening, Old Testament names were household words to children. Throughout my own childhood, and in my one family home, the Bible continued to be read morning and evening. Times have changed. In our home, I have always tried to hold family prayers on Sunday morning. With the more strenuous conditions of modern life, it would be difficult to maintain the old practice; it might only produce in the present day child an adverse reaction to religion. One of the greatest problems of life is the wisest way to help children to come to know the Bible. I have never yet had any difficulty in maintaining with absolute regularity family attendance at the Sunday morning service, and, I think, the family accept the practice, and would not break from it, though, again, attendance at evening service is not, except in the case of Ella, a regular practice. I certainly maintained it till two years ago when I was ill. But, again, I think, to ask it of children might, under present conditions, produce the wrong reactions. What I do try to practise is to keep Sunday different from other days. How much, however, the atmosphere of our home here depends on Ella. Every night, through each child's childhood, she has read the Bible to them at bedtime and trained them to say a prayer. Oddly enough, Rosemary has quite enjoyed reading for herself J.B. Phillips' version of the New Testament in modern English, just as, earlier, Gordon set himself with youthful zeal, to read Moffatt from cover to cover, though the Pentateuch was all that he could take, at that stage. Recently, I have greatly enjoyed reading the flow of modern historical studies on evidence relating to the New Testament and the early church.

I have just returned from Perth and Dundee Sheriff Courts, the third visit to my Sheriffdom in the last three weeks. One of these visits was to see the Queen Mother receive the Freedom of Forfar. She has a quite natural simple spontaneous charm. The Provost of Forfar, a booking clerk at Forfar Railway Station, and son of a former station master at Glamis, excelled himself. I met a number of interesting people, especially Brigadier Bernard Fergusson (of Kilkerran). At the Freedom Ceremony and at lunch I sat next the young Earl of Strath-more – a rather pathetic figure, with almost nothing to say, but well-intentioned.

Another interesting recent ceremony at which I was present was the bestowal of the Order of Orange-Nassau to the Rev. R.P.R. Anderson, who has just retired from the Scots Church at Rome, where he ministered to many Dutch people. Christian Van de Rijdt, my old classmate, and Dutch Consul-General, made the presentation. His speech, and Mr. Anderson's reply, could not have been bettered. Mrs. Anderson was the daughter of my father's old School and University classmate, George Henderson, minister at Monzie. She belonged to two well-known families: her mother was an Ormond, and her an-cestors included Trails from Orkney, one of whom, the Rev. Robert Trail, was minister of the Scots Church at Rotterdam in, I think, the seventeenth century. It is interesting how many country ministers of the last generations came to be known by their charges as almost household names – Henderson of Crieff, Henderson of Monzie, and (my own father) Philip of Longforgan. One letter from England was once addressed to him as 'the Rev. A.P. Longforgan'. The prestige of the country parish has tended to decline: I can recall no minister of the present generation who is thus popularly linked with his parish, though, in towns, the connection is still maintained, as 'White of the Barony', or 'MacGregor of St. Cuthbert's', or 'Whyte of Free St. George's' (though the last two are scarcely recent either). The practice may still remain in some country parishes in the Highlands. In another direction, I have often noted that streets are no longer named after

City and Royal Burgh of Perth

Clarissa Eden

Anthony Eden

Presentation

of the

Freedom of the City

to

The Rt. Hon. Sir Anthony Eden
K.G., M.C., M.P.

Luncheon

in

STATION HOTEL
SATURDAY, 12th MAY, 1956

✿

Chairman:
LORD PROVOST JAMES A. SMART, D.L., J.P.

statesmen. In Edinburgh, we have Gladstone Terrace and Palmerston Place, but no twentieth century statesman has given his name to a street. The stock of politicians has gone down in public estimation; and it is perhaps not surprising, for, in a generation where long training is now the avenue to any profession, the one occupation for which no qualification seems necessary is that of Member of Parliament.

12th May 1956 (Saturday)

After a day in London at the Central Land Board and War Damage Commission, I returned early this morning, and then set out with Ella by car for Perth to see the Prime Minister receive the Freedom of the City. We met him beforehand with the immediate platform party, consisting of Lady Eden, the Lord and Lady Provost, Lord Kinnaird (the Lord-Lieutenant) and Lady Kinnaird, the Secretary of State (James Stuart), and the Rev. W.A. Smellie of St. John's Church. Anthony Eden has a curiously nervous restless, almost fidgety manner, like a man highly strung – his movements reminded me of George MacLeod, though more agitated. Lady Eden, on the other hand, is placid. The Freedom Ceremony was more humdrum than the one a fortnight ago at Forfar. The Lord Provost referred to the previous statesmen who had received the burgess ticket. The last was Winston Churchill. Before that, they were all Gladstonic or Gladstonian Liberals – Palmerston, Cobden, Gladstone himself and the like. At lunch, afterwards, I was seated between Lady Eden on my right, and Lady Kinnaird on my left. Lady Eden was delightful. We discussed the Royal Academy. I said, I thought Pietro Annigoni was the best portrait painter. She said that Christ Church, Oxford, was having the Prime Minister's portrait painted, but that, while she agreed with me about Annigoni, it was thought that the portrait should be by a British artist. She said that her husband was a greater reader than she was; that she preferred when he was still at the Foreign Office, and that the Prime Ministership was one problem after another. The Russians her husband found easier to meet than the Germans. They had a greater sense of humour, though with a cynical turn too. She thought political life was becoming more difficult because political leaders had not the same common will now as those who had served together in the First World War. She autographed my menu, and, without my asking for it, very kindly asked Sir Anthony to give me his autograph as well. I was, quite frankly, a little disappointed with him. His language is rather commonplace, and I missed the great gifts which I have seen

in many other men. He is, however, at his best when informal. Lady
Eden spoke a few words. Sir Anthony said: 'This is the first time I
have heard my wife make a speech, and, if she does it oftener, I will
not require to speak as much.' They were going on to stay the night
at Balcarres, for he and Lord Crawford were at 'The House' together.
Lady Kinnaird said that now at Rossie Priory there were only two
maids, whereas, when she first knew it, there were twenty-eight. Ella
sat between Lord Lansdowne and Lord Kinnaird, and found the
former a charming table companion. I was much attracted by both
Lansdownes, and also by Lady Mansfield. Lord Mansfield told me
that he had seen the fee-books of his famous ancestor, and that he
made 40,000 guineas a year – a remarkable figure for the eighteenth
century. I said, I doubted if, even now, any Scottish counsel exceeded
6,000 guineas. Looking back on the whole ceremony, the two thoughts
which specially impressed me in the Prime Minister's words were:–
1. 'Foreign policy is not a case of doing what you want, but doing
what you can.' 2. 'A Prime Minister moves from one problem to
another. What always reassures me and all my anxieties is to come
to a meeting like this and know that, behind me, is the loyalty and
support of the ordinary British citizen.' These are not his exact words,
but they convey the thought.

14th May 1956 (Monday)

We had our last Annual meeting of the National Library Trustees
before the official opening of the new Library building. Actually, it
was our first Trustees' meeting in the new building – it was held in
the Board Room; and the expectation for the future created a fresh
optimism. I took as my theme, in presenting the Annual Report, the
contrast between 1955 and 1925, when the National Library Trustees
took over. Whereas 'Joshua the son of Nun and Caleb the son of
Jephunneh were the only two to enter in to the land of milk and
honey' – five of those who were Trustees in 1925 still survived. Of
the five, only one was a Trustee now, Lord Normand, and even he
had been absent for a time while holding high office elsewhere. The
staff, seven in 1925, was, at the end of 1955, sixty-three. Accessions
had risen by almost 50 per cent since the beginning of the Second
World War – the figure now being 74,000 a year. Lord Crawford told
me of the Edens' visit to Balcarres, and that they had mentioned
meeting us at Perth. Over the weekend, the Prime Minister had before
him the anxieties of meeting the opposition in debate today about the

mysterious disappearance of the 'frogman' Lieut-Commander Crabb while engaged in unauthorised secret service work round the Russian battleship at Portsmouth, and about the situation in Cyprus. How trying for him, with these anxieties facing him, to have to go through the ceremonial of a presentation of a city's freedom. Lord Crawford said, when I remarked on how fit the P.M. looked: 'Yes, but he is a very tired man. He hopes for some respite at the Whitsun Recess. He hoped to have a Mediterranean holiday, but, at the present time, he could not think of going near Greece.' I suggested that, instead, in Summer, he should cruise up the West Coast of Scotland to Orkney and Shetland: he would find peace there. Lord Crawford was so taken with the idea that he said he would pass on the suggestion.

18th May 1956 (Friday)

On Wednesday, Kathleen rang up before breakfast to speak to me. She told me that Harold had had a heart attack and was seriously ill. She suggested that, if I came to Glasgow to see him at once, it might only alarm him. She promised to telephone me in the evening. Before I reached home after our Lighthouse Board meeting, another telephone message came that he had died (at 4.50 p.m. on 16th). I set off at once by car for Glasgow, and spent that evening and most of yesterday helping with the arrangements. Ella joined me in the afternoon there, and we came home together last night.

Last Saturday, he had played two rounds of golf at Gleneagles. Then on Tuesday, after a day in the office, he went out for another round. Early in the game, he felt a pain across his chest. He played round to the 17th hole, and then he and his friend stopped. He came home, pottered about the house, ate an apple (and complained of indigestion), then, after going to bed, wakened in pain. The doctor was called. He advised Kathleen: 'I think your son should come.' Robin and Rosemary arrived. Harold was given morphine. He was able to talk then. His colour became bad, and he almost looked even then as if he were dying. Later he said in extremity: 'I'm frightened – I'm frightened.' Then he rallied, and told the others: 'I looked a good way into the dark valley – and it's not so terrible after all.' He talked about golfing competitions with Robin. 'I'm afraid we won't meet again in mortal combat,' (meaning golf struggles between father and son). He even began talking about Rome, to which he and Kathleen were to set out in ten days. Dr. Olav Kerr, his friend and heart specialist, came in the morning. He received more morphine, and there was just a chance for him if he could survive for anything from one to five days. He asked what was the matter, and was told direct: 'A coronary thrombosis.' He talked on at length till noon, and was quite prepared and calm. After noon, Dr. Kerr returned. The cardiograph then showed the position to be hopeless. He received another injection, and though sometimes opening his eyes and looking at his loved ones, was unable to speak more and gradually slipped into final unconsciousness. K is very brave, as I knew she would be, and Robin, though he had never seen serious illness or death before, behaved quite wonderfully, cheering up his father in the darkening hours.

I am only beginning to realise the loss: he was the last member of my family home. The relation of big and little brother remained throughout life. Only three weeks ago, we had a lovely meeting together in Glasgow – so lovely that we each wrote a letter of thanks to the other afterwards. He was so generous-hearted to me, never envying my outward success. I wrote to him saying how, after years of swimming against the current, in his business he had come finally into his own kingdom. Strangely enough, I said: 'Very likely you will survive, and I know Ella will turn to you.' Now, he has gone, but the memory of such a lovely parting will always remain. I have tried to help K in the part I thought he would have to take with Ella. Many friends from all kinds of walks of life have said how much he inspired love and how generous-hearted he was. All the younger generation thought of him as their nicest uncle. I can only limp behind him. I telephoned the *Glasgow Herald*, and they kindly took a short tribute from me to him for tomorrow's paper.

19th May 1956 (Saturday)

A strange day. Ella, Alison, Ian and I travelled to Glasgow by the 7.30 a.m. train, and we paid our last duty to Harold at 10.30 at the Glasgow Crematorium. The large chapel was crammed to overflowing with his friends – some of whom I had scarcely seen since childhood. Driving back to the house, we chanced to discuss strikes, and Ian remarked that only large categories could strike. I said, Yes, but there were some groups of which it was unthinkable that they should strike: I instanced doctors, crematorium attendants, and mothers! – the last presumably a larger category than the whole T.U.C.!

We returned to Edinburgh by the 1 p.m. train, and at 3.30 p.m. began Rosemary's belated birthday party. Harold would certainly have wished it so. After the sadness of the morning, it was good to see a dozen little bright girls full of unfeigned joy.

Tomorrow, brings another emotion: it would have been Gordon's 29th birthday.

23rd May 1956 (Wednesday)

The General Assembly began yesterday. So far as its business is concerned, there have been as yet no highlights. At the opening, the singing of 'Ye gates, lift up your heads' to 'St. George's, Edinburgh' was one of the most wonderful acts of praise I have ever heard. I was glad that the Archbishop of Canterbury was there amongst others to hear such praise. The Commissioner (Walter Elliot) was dressed as a Privy Councillor; but the voice was the voice of a politician; and the curious smile which he puts on at the end of a well-turned sentence is the smile on the face of a tiger. The ring of sincerity in the Moderator (Robin Scott) was much more telling. The Commissioner spoke of the work of the Church in Africa, a most apt subject. He is, I feel, an abler man than Anthony Eden; yet I could understand why he fell out of the running for the Premiership, for which he used to be 'tipped' before the start of the last War. His most telling sentence was: 'Arrogance is the besetting sin of the politician.'

At dinner at Holyroodhouse on Tuesday evening, I again had as my partner Lady Hutchison, wife of the P.R.S.A. He has just completed his portrait of the Queen in the robes of the Thistle. To do it, he spent a week at Windsor, and some further days at Buckingham Palace. The children running in and out to see their mother helped him greatly in his task. I am told that the picture is a considerable success, though of course it has not yet been exhibited. I had a long talk with Sir John Colquhoun, after the ladies withdrew from the dinner-table. His wife made a most graceful lady in waiting. Afterwards, I talked to both the Archbishop and Mrs. Fisher. He was at his best at Holyrood, vivacious like a schoolboy, friendly and full of fun. Mrs. Fisher, too, was most friendly to Ella and myself.

This morning the Archbishop spoke in the Assembly. His opening remarks, full of fun and point, won him completely the ear of the Assembly. Then, for a few moments, he spoke on Inter-Church relations, his speech obviously hinging on the Lambeth Quadrilateral (to anyone who was familiar with this). Here, I felt that he just missed creating the impression which I should like him to have created. The Assembly was ready for something just a little more solid from him, and I sensed the feeling that it missed that. However, he was in a very delicate position. His best thought was that the real hope of growing unity was that both Churches were 'on the move' – from that he derived real optimism. But he scarcely measured up, in this speech, to a great Church statesman; and yet I feel that he has done more, in sheer practical Christianity, to further good relations than any other recent Church of England leader.

27th May 1956 (Sunday)

The High Commissioner of the Gold Coast, a magnificent figure, in pale pink satin robe, covered by a gorgeous yellow, blue and scarlet sari, addressed the Assembly yesterday.

31st May 1956 (Thursday)

The General Assembly ended last night. In the second week, the thing that stands out in my memory was the Inter-Church Relations Report in relation to the Anglo-Scottish Church Conversations. It could scarcely have been better introduced than it was – by Archie Craig, undoubtedly one of the most gifted of Assembly speakers. Stuart Louden seconded well, though a little long, and, for some tastes, too theological – though I did not feel this myself – for he always brings a real sense of the spiritual to what he says. But what followed was quite deplorable. After one or two of the extreme left had spoken, introducing matters supposed to be in our Conversations report (not to be presented till next year), the Moderator gave various assurances about the contents of the Report, of which he knew nothing, and of which the delegates have only considered one draft as yet. Then, worse still, Tom Torrance rose and described the Church of Scotland as 'a belligerent Church' (approving of this), said that he thought the delegates should be 'aggressive' and added that he hoped 'they would do all they could to reform the Church of England and bring it into line with Presbytery'. It was a most truculent speech; had one of the Anglicans used corresponding words of us, I should have mistrusted them thereafter. His outburst shook myself and his other fellow delegates to the core. Personally I am not concerned with either Presbyterianism or Episcopacy, except insofar as they are truly Christian, and his speech was certainly not. He apologised next day to the Assembly, but the harm has been done. Tonight, Professor Manson tells me that Tom Torrance is sending an apologetic letter to the

Scotsman. Having made a mistake, he would be better to say nothing more, least of all to say it in print. He will just put his feet further into the mire. He is as injudicious as he is able. Someone remarked to me afterwards: 'Torrance would like to impose the Solemn League and Covenant all over again.' He will only begin a violent series of newspaper counterblasts, and I could almost guarantee that the correspondence will end with mutual recriminations between T.M. Dunn (for the Presbyterians) and Miss M.E.M. Donaldson (for the Episcopalians), two of the most ardent counter-agitators of denominational rivalries.

1st June 1956 (Friday)

Today, Tom Torrance has a letter in the *Scotsman* 'offering an interpretation' which, he 'feels sure', is 'genuinely in accordance with the facts' of 'the confused debate in the General Assembly on Inter-Church relations and the difficulty of reporting it accurately in the Press'. Unfortunately, the debate was only too clear, and the Press reports quite accurate. Having himself made a first-class blunder, he would be well to observe a discreet silence, instead of trying to gloss over his own too unfortunate intervention. 'Facts are chiels that winna ding.'

To turn to a pleasanter subject, here is one episode which I found delightful. On the opening day of the Assembly, the Assembly Precentor (Philip Malcolm) came up to me and said: 'I see we are to sing "Wetherby" on the last day of the Assembly. Will the Assembly be familiar with it? I do not know it myself. How does it go?' I assured him that the Assembly would be familiar with it. We then entered to the inner passage between the Assembly Hall and the Outer Vestibule, and the Procurator proceeded to sing 'Wetherby' for the benefit of the Precentor! Needless to say, when the closing day came, the tune was sung by the Assembly quite magnificently. I told the Moderator and his daughter Nancy Scott (who sang for the Glyndebourne Opera Company) about the incident, and they were greatly entertained.

The Moderator was quite excellent (except for his one gaffe in the Inter-Church debate). The Lord High Commissioner was fair, never quite shaking off the atmosphere of the House of Commons for that of Royal Representative. In his closing speech, he made the incredible mistake of referring to the present Speaker, W.S. Morrison, as a 'son of the manse'. Mrs. Speaker is, however, a daughter of the manse, and this may account for his mistake, but it showed up his superficiality.

Yesterday and today, I have been in an extraordinarily interesting case before Harry Guthrie. Yesterday, he was against us, and I went up to make the fourth speech today, saying to another advocate in the Robing Room that, at least, I had something to say, and intended to go down with all guns firing. Very shortly after I began, Harry Guthrie said: 'This is one of the most interesting and difficult cases on the law of damages which has been in the Courts for a very long time. Don't hesitate to address me as fully as you can upon it.' I agreed that it was difficult, but I should ask him to consider in detail the true application of the second rule in Hadley v. Baxendale. With the aid of three unfamiliar English decisions, I eventually persuaded him round to our point of view, and he decided in our favour this afternoon. It was a real win, and shows that it never does to lose heart, when you have something really worth saying.

19th June 1956 (Tuesday)

I have seen two private tragedies at the Bar this term. One of the best loved members of the Bar, Vice-Dean of Faculty and Sheriff-substitute, suddenly resigned both offices. Vague rumours started to spread, which personally I at once denied. Now, it seems they hold some truth. He has done a courageous piece of work for which we all admire him. He has devoted himself to supporting his old mother for years, and remained single on her account. His health became none too good. But at least he received a Sheriffdom and we felt, at last, he had come into his own. Only three months later, he had to give it up, not for any evil-doing, but simply for an aberration in conduct which a doctor understands. I am deeply sorry for the personal suffering he must have gone through, and retain my friendship and respect for him.

A fortnight ago, a young advocate called here late in the evening and asked for an immediate loan of £200. Only a month ago, he used my name for a bank reference without asking me beforehand. At the time, I had no reason to believe him other than comfortably off. He told me then that he wanted an introduction to another bank in the country, where he has rented a country cottage. I now fear this explanation was untrue. I felt it my duty to withdraw my certificate to the bank. He seems to have pledged every asset he has: yet he still runs a motor car, and two of his children are at boarding-school. He said that the Revenue were pressing him. I doubt this explanation. In the end, I lent him £50 on an I.O.U. knowing that I would be unlikely ever to see it again. What is at the root of it I don't know. But rumour is associating his wife's name with that of another advocate, also married. If this is true, he may be more sinned against than sinning. But it is sad, as I know both the couples well.

A week ago, I went to Longforgan to read the lessons at a service where the Moderator (R.V.F. Scott) preached, and a new window was dedicated. It was my first experience of reading lessons in church, and I found no better way of myself coming to understand the passages:– the latter portion of Isaiah 40; and the wonderful picture of the new Jerusalem in the second last chapter of Revelations. I read, and re-read, and re-read, these beforehand, and was enthralled by the sublime language and imagery of both. Afterwards, the Kirk Session of Longforgan gave us lunch at Inchture Hotel, a very happy and somewhat unusual occasion. Next day, I installed three new Sheriffs-substitute in Dundee, and gave them a little lunch. Hugh Carlton was one of them. He introduced me to his father, now aged ninety, whose legal memories went back well into last century. He recited a delightful rhyme composed at a legal dinner, by Colin Mackenzie of Portmore, about the firm of John C. Brodie:

> Gibson Craig can take his glass
> And James Dalziel his toddy
> But George Dalziel can go to hell
> And so can John Clerk Brodie!

Margaret Kidd, who is one of a small committee making personal arrangements for the Queen at the coming Faculty dinner, has rung me up to say that I shall be one of the members of Faculty to be presented by the Dean to Her Majesty. She was preparing a little note about each member who is to be presented.

Today, we lunched on the *Pharos* and held one of our periodic conferences with Trinity House and the Commissioners of Irish Lights. It was the last visit of Commodore Hubbard of Trinity House, who has led their delegation each year. May we find another like him: he will not be easy to replace.

Sunday 1st July 1956

In connection with the opening of the National Library by the Queen on Wednesday, Lord Crawford is giving a private exhibition of the Library treasures at Balcarres. Today, he gave a special preview for the National Library staff, and Ella and I also went, taking with us W. Park, Keeper of MSS, and his wife. Alison was also there with the staff; she finished her duties as Research Assistant yesterday in view of her coming marriage. We and the Parks motored to Elie for lunch, stopping at the Alexander III monument at Kinghorn on the way. After lunch, we went on to Balcarres where the staff, travelling by bus, had already arrived.

Balcarres stands on rising ground, looking southwards over the Forth, a pleasant mansion, built at different periods, the oldest part being the most attractive – of yellowish sandstone – the new parts of grey rather jarring with the warm yellow. Lady Crawford came out to meet us in the friendliest way. When one passed into the interior, one entered one of the most amazing exhibitions one could possibly see in private hands – room after room, beautiful in themselves, filled with the most unique and varied library treasures – early Chinese works of the Jesuit missionaries, Boswelliana and Johnsoniana, incunabula by the score, a special table of early works relating to Russia, another of pre-Reformation and Reformation papal-bulls, indulgences, and Roman and Lutheran missals, Shakepeariana, bloodstained pages from Marat's bathroom after his assassination, a tiny Pittenweem newspaper published a century ago for ½d., the smallest newspaper ever, early works on language and dictionaries, a unique pictorial work of the fifteenth century depicting chapters of the Bible (open at the Book of Exodus – with the plagues, the Red Sea, and the Burning Bush), early astronomical works – above records of the Lyndsey family, one book dating from 1322, a lovely picture of the Hon. William Pitt (as a boy) by Romney, wonderful Florentine art. I asked Lord Crawford what were the earliest incunabula. He showed me pages from the Gutenburg Bible, the Gutenburg Psalms, and the earliest Italian book, Lactantius. The family came from Normandy: there were De Colleys from near Windermere, and their papers; they took the Crawford from Lanarkshire; the next Lindsays occupied Edzell and Invermarck; then the Crawfords and Balcarres Lindsays united. The exhibition was the most amazing private collection I have seen – gathered by centuries of devotion to culture by one family. Yet, with it all, nothing could have been more beautiful than the quite unaffected simplicity of Lord and Lady Crawford. They entertained thirty of us without any household help whatsoever, treating us to strawberries and cream, cherries, cake, sherry and lemon drinks, all by their own hand. At the end, I thanked them for us all. It was an unforgettable afternoon spent amid amazing treasures and the kindest of hosts and hostesses.

4th July 1956 (Wednesday)

Today the National Library Building was opened by the Queen. The day opened with threatening rain, but the sun came out in the afternoon, and, inside the building, it was exceedingly hot. In the morning, I went up with Ella to Court, and took her and the Dean to go over the part each of us had to take in the afternoon.

Then Ella, Alison and I went up again to the Library after lunch. The crowds of guests poured in before 2.30, when they had to be seated in the Library Reading Room, which looked bright and gay, with a string quartet performing Mozart. After helping many friends to find their seats, I gathered the group (including Ella and myself) who were to be presented to the Queen before she entered the Hall – Dover and Mrs. Wilson; the Moderator and Mrs. R.F.V. Scott; Hamish and Margaret Clyde; the Dean and Mrs. Guest; myself and Ella, in that order. We rehearsed our positions and then retired for half-an-hour to the room of Mr. Lloyd, Keeper of Printed Books. Just before 3 p.m., we returned and took our places. One amusing incident was that the Secretary of State (James Stuart) and his wife, who were to drive from the Signet Library to the main entrance, were mistakenly shepherded along the corridor of the Advocates' Library, and I found them standing at the head of the great staircase wondering where to go. I quickly had them conducted back to their proper starting point.

At 3 p.m. we heard the cheering from the entrance as the Queen opened the door. In a few moments, she had ascended the staircase, and the presentations of our group began. When the Queen reached us, Lord Crawford very kindly gave a special word about me, saying that I was Convener of the Committee which did the real work; and the Queen gave me a most charming smile which was a complete reward for the years' work. The Duke, too, gave us such a warm handshake. Then a fanfare heralded the Queen's entry to the Hall, and we proceeded to the platform. I was sitting on the left of the platform, with the Duke just in front of me to the right, and the Queen just beyond. The Queen wore a lovely brocade summer dress, with turquoise hat to match – a quite charming young figure, with fresh complexion, a beautiful string of pearls, and immaculate white gloves and white bag. The Moderator dedicated the building and gave an opening prayer. Lord Crawford, with his characteristic charm and dignity addressed her, announcing the marvellous acquisition of the Bute Collection – of Shakespeare, and a whole range of English drama of the seventeenth and eighteenth centuries – and invited the Queen to declare the Library open. The Queen then made a short simple speech, in her usual quiet clear voice, a tone lower than formerly, declaring the Library open. Then she led the platform party down the Hall. She proceeded to visit the Hopkinson Berlioz Collection, the Handel Collection, and the Mozart bi-centenary exhibition. Meantime, I marshalled those whom I was to present to her in the Catalogue Hall – Professor Alexander (Convener of the Books and MSS Committee) and Mrs. Alexander, Hector McKechnie (Convener of the Finance Committee) and Dorothy McKechnie, Mrs. Beattie (who could not at first be found), Mr. A.R. Conlon (the Trustees' architect), Mr. Hew Lorimer A.R.S.A. (the sculptor), Park (Keeper of MSS), and Loudon (Assistant-Keeper in charge of Buildings). The Queen had quite a talk with the last five. She was much interested when I told her that Hew Lorimer had carved the figures on the facade *in situ*, working like Michelangelo on a scaffolding for eighteen months. 'How do you like working at a height?' she asked. She also asked Loudon, who is our Spanish expert, about the Astorga Collection, and I told her how it had come to us through John Gibson Lockhart. Then she went on to see the MSS Collections, especially the Bute Collection, where Dover was to explain the Shakespeare acquisitions.

When she left, I was then free to return to the Hall, where I announced to the audience that tea for the majority was to be served in the Parliament Hall. Those who were to wait for the Queen's unveiling of the commemorative inscription in the entrance hall, had tea in the Board Room and the microfilm room. The Queen's visit to the Special Collections and to the General Exhibitions took twenty minutes longer than was expected. We were also in the entrance hall when she emerged from the exhibition room, and unveiled the inscription drafted by myself.

At six o'clock, we went, with the McKechnies, to the Secretary of State's Reception in the Banqueting Hall, Edinburgh Castle. There we met another host of new friends. I had long talks with Sir Edward Bridges, and was photographed with him. He was much interested when I said I thought the Scottish organisation in the War Damage Commission and Central Land Board was a useful model of administrative devolution and probed me with questions about it. Sir Charles Cunningham also told me that the Scottish Office would be raising with me a possible representation of the Church of Scotland in the House of Lords.

1956

7th July 1956 (Saturday)

Yesterday was another day full of interest, and certainly a red letter day in the history of the Faculty, for the Sovereign, as sovereign member of Faculty, dined with the Faculty for the first time; and certainly in my time there has been no such social occasion, the nearest to it having been the Scott Centenary Dinner in Parliament Hall in 1932.

The day began with the University Graduations, conducted by the Duke as Chancellor of the University. Ella and I had seats near the centre in the second row, and saw everything well. Two personalities dominated the whole proceedings – not one in the McEwan Hall would disagree with that. The one was the Duke himself; and the other Karl Barth, who received an LL.D. The Duke starts with Lord Crawford's advantage of being so handsome as to put every other man into the shade. But, like Lord Crawford, it is much more than being supremely good-looking. This time I particularly remarked the lively warm-hearted expression on his face full of vivacity and expression, and his courtesy to each graduand. He is quite unselfconscious and unaffected. He never has to call up a smile; it is rather that he is always at the point of a smile; an immutably happy nature. His spontaneous friendliness must be a great help to the Queen, who is so much shyer than he is, but who always does everything so beautifully and quietly, and, like her father, symbolises the spirit of service. She often looks rather serious, but has a lovely smile when it comes; the difference between the two is the difference between the charm of shyness and the charm of spontaneity. Karl Barth is a vivid powerful personality. One look at him was sufficient to realise his strength. Intelligence and vivacious changes of mood flit across his countenance; among theologians, I have only seen one who had the same natural genius – W.P. Paterson. He has, too, the same wayward shock of hair, though still brown, not white like W.P.'s.

From the graduation, I went to a lunch at New College to the new D.D.s – William Barclay, Principal H. Cunliffe-John (Bradford Independent College), David Read, and Selby Wright – and to Karl Barth. Again, Karl Barth was the dominant personality. He referred to himself as a Doctor of Laws and made a witty speech from that standpoint. He said that he had learned English through his fondness of 'police' (detective) stories. He also referred to the Garden of Eden and the 'snake' (correcting himself to 'serpent' amid much laughter) and to the offer of the power to choose between good and evil. He added: 'That was good law – but bad theology! The lawyer must accept the

Fall of Man, and devise laws accordingly. The theologian does not need to accept the Fall of Man. He knows that God is supreme, and that He, who alone is Judge, is wholly good.' A dramatic moment came when Sir Thomas Clark, who is publishing Karl Barth's classics, rose and presented him with his latest published translation – just out at this very time. I was interested to hear Barth placed alongside Aquinas and Luther. John Baillie introduced me to Karl Barth after lunch. He said: 'I want to introduce you to a fellow lawyer!' I said laughingly: 'Oh no – a Doctor of Divinity!'

From there, I fetched Ella, Alison, and Dorothy McKechnie and took them to the Holyrood Garden Party – the largest I have seen, held in brilliant sunshine, with a lovely fresh breeze, showing up the Gardens and Arthur's Seat at their very best. We saw endless friends, but there is always to me a sense of exasperation on these occasions at the number of friends one sees, while engaged in conversation with someone else, and is unable to talk to also.

At 7.30 I went up to Parliament House. The robing room was packed with advocates, old and young, and all the judges. I was surprised to see some old advocates whose faces even I did not know, John Peter Grant for example. The two veterans were A.J. Louttit

Faculty Dinner 6th July 1956 (Courtesy of the Scotsman Publications).

Laing (about eighty-five), and 'Hammy' (A.M. Hamilton). The fathers of the Bar, G.W. Wilton Q.C. and Lord Hunter – both over ninety – were absent. We then trooped in to the Parliament Hall about 8 o'clock, and drank sherry at our seats for almost half-an-hour. The royal party were to sit on a dais on the east side of the Hall. There ran eleven cross tables – A to L. Tables E, F, and G ran across from the dais towards the main fire-place, F (in the centre) containing the old members of Faculty, E the next, and G (where I sat) the next after that. From my seat I had a good and uninterrupted view of the Queen. The great south window was flood-lit from behind. My own immediate neighbours, on either side, were George Montgomery and Lockhart Innes (now Sir Andrew Innes), and, opposite, Ronald Morison, Gordon McIntyre, and Calver. They also signed my menu, Ronald and Gordon, jokingly, 'without prejudice'. A notable absentee was Tom Taylor: my immediate junior in call: we were the only two called to the Bar on 14th March 1924.

At 8.25, we all stood, and the royal entourage entered. A few minutes later, we stood again, and, led by Mr. Brown, the Faculty Officer, entered the Queen, the Dean and the Duke. From north to south, at the High Table, there sat the Earl of Scarborough (Lord Chamberlain); the Justice-Clerk; Mary, Duchess of Devonshire (Mistress of the Robes); Lord Crawford; the Queen; the Dean; the Duke; the President; the Secretary of State (James Stuart); Lady Alice Egerton (Lady in waiting); the Advocate. The Dean said grace: *Benedictus benedicat*. The dinner then proceeded with lashings of champagne. The toast of 'The Queen' was proposed, formally, by the Dean. He then intimated that Her Majesty gave permission to smoke (which, by prior notice, was to be cigarettes only), and the dinner ended. The Royal party then retired, Margaret Kidd acting as hostess to the Queen. We then all lined the Corridor and new Reading Room, half the Company being allocated to each. I was in the Corridor. Then, very efficiently, a committee of young advocates marshalled those who were to be presented. Kermack, Alex Thomson, myself, Robbie Maconochie, and Douglas Johnston were placed on the southside of the Corridor to be presented to the Duke (my stance was near the Dean's Room). Then, in came the Queen accompanied by the Dean, and the Duke by Hamish. Hamish presented me as Procurator of the Church of Scotland. The Duke asked exactly what that involved, and I replied that, according to the Archbishop of Canterbury, it was roughly the Scottish Dean of the Arches. He then referred to Mr. Willinck, who one moment seemed to be Vice-Chancellor of Cambridge University, and, the next, Dean of the Arches. I said: 'Yes, but he remained throughout Master of Magdalene College.' He was full of light, friendly banter, and I enjoyed it greatly. I saw many Faculty friends whom I had not seen for years.

When the presentations were over, the Royal party retired to the Judges' Retiring Room, from which they ultimately left, by the main door. Meantime, some of us went out to the square, and Douglas Johnston and I and some others found ourselves just beneath the statue of Charles II as the Queen and the Duke, seen off by the Dean, entered their car. I raised 'Three Cheers' and we gave them a 'hearty farewell'. After they had gone, I went out and congratulated the Dean. He said: 'You will be interested to know that the Queen wanted to see a full-bottomed wig, and yours was picked from the Robing Room.' I believe the Duke tried it on. I got the same story from my old friend, the Robing Room attendant, when I returned there. He had sent mine in, because it was in nice condition! Then Douglas Johnston drove me home.

14th July 1956 (Saturday)

I heard more about the 'wig' episode at the Faculty Dinner a week ago. Apparently the Queen met all the lady members of the Faculty, and conversation was not flowing very easily, as none of them thought fit to speak until Her Majesty had first done so. The Queen apparently did not find an easy topic for conversation. At length one of the lady advocates said: 'We are just sorry, ma'am, that your Majesty could not have seen us wearing our wigs, and Miss Kidd her full-bottomed wig.' The Queen immediately expressed a desire to see both types of wig, and an ordinary wig and my full-bottomed wig were obtained by Lord Walker from the Robing-Room. Characteristically, the ice for feminine discussion was broken by the introduction of the reference to apparel.

This week I learned that Belgium had issued a series of anti-tuberculosis stamps, one of which contains a portrait of my Uncle Robert, as a tuberculosis pioneer. It is apparently the first time that a British physician's head has been the subject of a postage stamp. The June 1956 Bulletin of the National Association for the Prevention of Tuberculosis has drawn attention to this. I have today received a letter about the matter from J.H. Harley Williams the Secretary of the National Association telling me that the Association has, in prospect, a commemorative volume of essays and impressions to mark the centenary

of Uncle Robert's birth, on 29th December 1857. He sends me a list
of the projected chapters, and asks my suggestions:–

SIR ROBERT PHILIP

SOME MEMORIES BY HIS FRIENDS AND PUPILS

1. Fergus Hewat: Philip and the Edinburgh School of Medicine.
2. Halliday Sutherland: Philip, creator of the modern anti-tuberculosis movement.
3. D.P. Marais: Philip's ideas overseas.
4. Charles Cameron: My predecessor in the first Chair of Tuberculosis.
5. G. Lissant Cox: The Edinburgh Dispensary and those which followed.
6. Derek Dunlop: Philip as teacher of Preventive Medicine.
7. J.B. Simpson: Philip's interest in Bovine Tuberculosis.
8. Christopher Clayson: Philip as clinician.
9. Bruce Dick: Philip as an inspirer of men.
10. Donald Stewart: Philip and modern Social Medicine.
11. John Crofton: Philip's tradition in Edinburgh.
12. Harley Williams: A Visit to Forty-five, Charlotte Square.

I wonder how much these men, most of them more than a generation
younger, will reveal the man himself. Dr. Fergus Hewat is the one
who would have the best claim to know him well. As the one younger
member of the family connection who had reasonable contact with
him, it may be worth while for me to set down my impressions. There
is no question that he was a man of great ability in many directions –
in diagnosis, in personality, in literature, in public spirit, in the art of
cultivated conversation, as a connoisseur of art and wine, in administration, above all in directing all his gifts to one central objective. I
first came to know him well when, in 1917, I came up to Edinburgh
as a student. He wanted me to follow him in medicine, and, indeed,
said that he had collected certain material which he thought would
be useful for me. But my mind was already set on the law, and he
recognised this at once. In those days, he rather liked to browbeat
me; I think that he imagined that this was the way to impress any
raw new student. He rather tended to browbeat everyone, though his
bark was worse than his bite. But even in those days, I felt slightly
sorry for his (first) wife, my Aunt Bessie, a warm-hearted Irishwoman,
infinitely kind to me, who always spoke with such admiration of his
infinite capacity and industry, and yet who, I always felt, was left a

lonely soul, her husband absorbed in his profession with little home life. I often lunched with her, and much oftener dined alone with him: I think I remember only once dining with him when she was also there. When I did dine with him, it was always, I felt, arranged almost as a part of my education. He was a first-class conversationalist, and believed that the art of conversation consisted in a series of rallies. You should never argue with the last remark, but rather disagree, qualify, or try to enlarge upon it. A conflict of view was, he considered, the spice of conversation, and certainly he cultivated it to a fine art. He was well-versed in many fields outside his own profession. For example, in his view, to be a good public speaker, to be a good conversationalist, was almost as important to higher medical practice as to be experienced in medicine itself. In his sixties, he kept up weekly French conversation to improve his French. He had, like my father, taken the medal in David Masson's English Literature Class, and had in his bookshelves Masson's *Life of Milton* as a University Prize. He would use every gift, and sacrifice every irrelevant interest, in the pursuit of his profession. He was, in my view, a lonely figure. His wife held him in awe; I never met a friend in his house; but he was surrounded by a wide circle of acquaintances; and there were always younger doctors prowling about, I sometimes thought, anxious to bathe in reflected glory. I could not possibly describe him as a loveable man. I remember him saying: 'If you make a mistake, forget it.' Also, 'Don't always be saying Thank you: it's a sign of weakness.' Frankly, I thought this a very extraordinary point of view, and I reacted strongly against it, comparing the generous humility, simplicity and disinterested forgetfulness of self of my father (his immediately elder brother) with his devotion to his one central objective, a great but also rather self-centred worldly objective. The two brothers had much in common, but, in the adventures of life, they had followed different objectives. One good side was, however, his inflexible determination to succeed in anything he did. He imparted some of this quality to me in my student days. For example, he knew that I was doing well in Sir Richard Lodge's History class in my first year. He said: 'Make up your mind to be first, and let nothing interfere with that objective.' And, partly thanks to this advice, I did secure first place, and, more important, a love of history which has affected my whole outlook ever since. His one acute disappointment in life was when the Victoria Hospital which was his own child was taken over by the city. He then formed the Victoria Hospital Tuberculosis Trust, and started Southfield Sanatorium. He invited me to the Royal College of Physicians

Einar Holbøll (1865–1927), a postal clerk on the outskirts of Copenhagen, is remembered in the history of tuberculosis as the originator of the Christmas Seal Sale. Under the patronage of King Christian, the first 'Christmas Stamp' in the world was sold in Denmark at Christmas 1904 to raise money for a children's sanitorium. More than four million seals were sold.

John D. Rockefeller, Senior (1839–1937), at one time the world's richest man, made an immense fortune out of oil refining. In 1890 he began to organise a system of philanthropy, now carried on by the Rockefeller Foundation, and in his lifetime he gave more than five hundred million dollars to charities and to education. After reading Osler's Principles and Practice of Medicine, the Rev. F.T. Gates, a member of his philanthropic staff, suggested to Rockefeller the idea of the Rockefeller Institute of Medical Research.

Sir Robert W. Philip (1857–1939) opened the first tuberculosis dispensary in the world in Edinburgh in 1887. He was first to develop a system of open-air treatment of tuberculosis in a city, from the teaching of the pioneers Bodington and Brehmer, and the first to start a farm colony. Knighted in 1913, he received the Trudeau Medal of the National Tuberculosis Association of America in 1928 and held the chair of tuberculosis at the University of Edinburgh from 1917 until his death. He was an original Member of the Council of the NAPT, and held office as Vice-Chairman and Chairman. It is believed that this is the first time a British physician has ever been depicted on a postage stamp.

Dinner when he was President, and put me beside Dr. Fergus Hewat, his assistant, at the dinner. It was obvious to me that he was the best after-dinner speaker amongst the Edinburgh doctors of his day. He also invited me to the meetings of the British Medical Association in Edinburgh, when he was President. Many is the acquaintance who has come up to me in, for example, my own profession of the law, and said how much some member of the family owed to Uncle Robert's treatment. This curious circumstance shows his meticulous attention to detail. When he made his rounds in his Infirmary Ward, he used to carry tied round his neck a tiny hot-water bottle, to which he applied his fingers before touching a patient, so that the patient should not be pained by the contact of cold hands of the doctor. He was full of the grand professorial manner, and never appeared until the caller had been waiting for quarter of an hour at least. He had admirers and detractors, and the latter would have called him a faddist and sometimes a humbug – he was not loved by any of his nephews or nieces, though they admired his services and gifts. On the whole, I tended to be repelled by him as a man, while yet admiring his talents and his judgment, in matters of the mind rather than the heart. When he married a second time at the age of eighty, I saw little of him, and he died a year later. One curious circumstance showing lack of fore-sight occurred at the end of his life. He left everything to his second wife, and she left everything to him. He died one month, and she a month later; with the result that everything belonging to both became intestate estate in her succession. All his possessions, and even his pictures were interesting, were disposed of by his second wife's Aus-tralian relatives, and apart from a card-case and some of his medals, nothing remains of him in his family's heirlooms. He passed from this life, a man who never had any real home life, a lonely figure like Cosmo Gordon Lang, and who never won the affection of the younger generation; but one whose achievement was his career, as a pioneer in prevention of tuberculosis. With all his achievement, I feel that he had missed the loveliest things in life – a real home, the love of children and younger friends, those personal affections and loyalties which mean so much in later life; but, in the balance, he had gained a name which is destined to be remembered, a hollow shell when all is dust.

22nd July 1956 (Sunday)

Yesterday, Alison was married in St. George's West to Ian Craddock, by Murdo Macdonald, assisted by Donald Beattie. The best man was

Stewart Fowlie. The bridesmaids were Rosemary (aged twelve), 'D' (Dorothy) Craddock (aged ten), and Judy Heath (aged fourteen). Rosemary acted as principal bridesmaid. The Reception was in the Freemasons' Hall, where we had some 330 guests. Four made a special journey of 500 miles from Holsworthy by road to be there, and Alison's friend, Jeanne Quénu, came all the way from Paris. What kindness we received on all hands – from Eric Smith, who threw his whole heart into the music, playing Handel's 'Water Music' and 'Holsworthy Bells' by S.S. Wesley beforehand and the Trumpet Voluntary for the entry of the Bride; his own anthem 'O Thou who gavest power to love' (words by Mandell Creighton), of which he gave the score to Alison and Ian, and Walton's 'Crown Imperial' as the wedding march, a novelty in place of Mendelssohn's Wedding March (the hymns 'Come down, O love divine' and 'Now thank we all our God' were the choice of Ian and Alison respectively); from Murdo, who came back all the way from holiday in Skye; from the choir, who furnished a quartet for the anthem; from Mr. Findlay (church officer) who behaved like a guide, philosopher, and friend; from all our friends who filled the area of the church, and part of the galleries. In the evening, the best man, ushers, and young people dined at the Golf Tavern and went on to the theatre; the 'old folks' and the very young had a family dinner at the Roxburghe Hotel. Alison and Ian flew to London; from there they go to North Devon for their honeymoon, and Alison is to meet all her new Holsworthy friends when she presents the prizes at this summer's Holsworthy Flower Show. We were charmed with our new connections, 'Giles' and Ursula Craddock, and with Ian's little sister D. Ursula and D came this morning to church with us, and, during the day, we entertained Jeanne Quénu, and an Oxford friend of Ian's, John Gundry (they were Mathematical Scholars of New College, in successive years). The sun came out on the wedding in all its brilliance as the young couple left the church.

A wedding such as this is a period piece, and it is worth recording the changes which have come about in the last generation. On the one hand, weddings seem now much more completely organised than before, and larger. We invited some 600 friends, and I could have invited another 600. Then the character of wedding presents has changed. There is less silver than formerly, but, on the other hand, presents are now far more useful, and, I think, tasteful. Certainly, Alison and Ian lack nothing. The Reception involved a contract for the hall, a contract with MacVities for the refreshments, a contract with wine-merchants for nine cases of champagne, and also for soft drinks. The decoration of hall and church are now done by a lady, Mrs. Oliver, who acts in a professional capacity, sharing this work for large weddings in Edinburgh with Lady Macmillan, wife of Sir Gordon Macmillan till recently Governor at Gibraltar. Commercial photographers, of their own volition, haunted our house before the wedding, the entrance of the Church before and after the wedding, even the Freemasons' Hall. A fleet of cars was necessary; I very nearly could not procure them, and had to try four firms before I could obtain the cars; American tourists took up most of the cars on a summer's Saturday afternoon. There were the dresses all made by a Mrs. Craig, who is again a specialist. Alison wore a lovely simple cream white dress, with Mechlin veil lent by Mrs. John Baillie. The three little bridesmaids wore white dresses flecked with delicate colours and bows with long ribbons down their backs: Rosemary's yellow, D's blue, and Judy's pink. Alison and Ian asked that they repeat in full the vows. Never have I seen to many of my personal friends present at one time. Dover proposed 'the Bride and Bridegroom' – referring to how the link of friendship with us and adoption as an 'uncle' of the family was sealed by the loss of his son and my Gordon in successive years. Dover quoted the saying: 'The quarrels of lovers are the renewals of love' and later reminded me that it came from Terence, *Andria*, 555: '*Amantium irae amoris integratio est.*' It was a day of unalloyed happiness for us all.

30th August 1956 (Thursday)

We returned two days ago from holiday. The week following the wedding, when Rosemary's school term ended, we set out for the Grey House, Nethybridge, where we stayed ten days. As the weather was exceptionally bad at the beginning, we slept and read and were thrown much in the company of our fellow-guests, who included two 'originals' – a man we called 'the Mayor' who had the voice and manner of a 'Pukka Sahib' from 'Poona' and engaged everyone in conversation, cross-examining the ladies in the most direct manner, sometimes to their confusion, and a youngish blue-stocking who was always drawling out for all to hear in a calm elocution that she was climbing 'Cairngorm and Macdui' or 'going through the Lairig' next day, but whose peregrinations never in fact reached beyond the Green Loch. Much more enterprising were a modest young couple up for a week's holiday, who, never daunted by the weather, set off each day by motor cycle and pillion. We ourselves had two delightful excursions – the first, over the Lecht to Gairnshot Lodge, Gairnside to visit Dr. A.K. Walton of St. Andrews (Drumsheugh), a church now defunct, but for a generation the pulpit of the preacher's preacher – W.M. Macgregor – and latterly known, because of its ageing congregation, as the 'Ancient Society of Retired Christians!' Dr. Walton himself is one of the best examples of the scholarly type of preacher, who made the ministry of the United Free Church between 1900 and 1929 so remarkable. Another day, a young student friend, Colin Bell, who has given up business to enter the ministry, and was taking the summer services at Glenlivet, came down to see us, and then we motored him back to Glenlivet manse, where he showed us Glenlivet Church. He is one of the best types at present preparing for the ministry. Glenlivet is a curious district – half Roman Catholic, half Protestant – with the most famous distillery in Scotland, where, at the moment, there is said to be a stock of 1½ million gallons of proof whisky. Mrs. Smith Grant of Glenlivet is keen Church of Scotland, and her husband keen Roman Catholic. She has set about restoring the whole interior of Glenlivet Church (most acceptably to the congregation) but has insisted in placing therein a Smith Grant pew with her coat-of-arms (most unacceptably). We were for the first time in Abernethy Church, a plain building with the pulpit in the old central position. Its chief feature is an absurdly laudatory memorial to a certain Captain Grant, who, according to the inscription, seems to have possessed every virtue, but who, one suspects, was the landlord of more humble and insecure tacksmen, who could do no other than plaster him with admiration. We met old friends, notably Donnie Mackenzie, the charming and friendly owner of 'the' shop at Nethybridge. The first weekend, the Nethy rose almost to the arches of the Bridge, and the Spey flooded the low ground between Nethybridge and Broomhill. The main railway near Inverness was undermined by flooding, and the line at first closed, and then limited to single-line traffic for a short period. We also met Mr. W.H.L. Paterson, a former president of the S.S.C. Society, and a first-class example of the older school of Edinburgh Chamber lawyers. He spent his evenings in crocheting fireplace rugs.

From Nethybridge, we motored to Oban for two nights at the Great Western Hotel, where we received a warm welcome from Miss MacPhee, the manageress, and Alex, the friendly and competent head porter. There we made a delightful friendship with Mr. Campbell, the Dundee surgeon, and his wife and family. His daughter, Mary, starts at St. Leonard's at the same time as Rosemary. They took Rosemary away for a wonderful day's run to Appin and Glencoe.

Oban was gay with bunting in preparation for the Queen's visit on 13th August, and I have never seen more yachts in the Bay. We met various friends, Mrs. M.A. Campbell-Preston, Canon Mackenzie (commodore of the Royal Highland Yacht Club), and Mr. Cameron of the *Oban Times*. Also, in the hotel, Major Ian Campbell, elder son of the late Sir Bruce Campbell, came up in a most friendly way, and greeted us as his parents' friends, giving us a standing invitation to Arduaine. One evening, Mr. Cameron took me with the Dundee Campbells to see the *Oban Times* being printed by its new printing-machine. For a provincial paper, it has an extraordinary circulation – 22,000 – as against the *Scotsman*'s 56,000, and the *Glasgow Herald*'s 63,000.

On 10th August, we sailed on a lovely sunny day to Iona. At Rosemary's request, I took her and Ella ashore at Fingal's Cave, our first landing there. Iona, where we stayed at the Columba Hotel, was crowded with visitors and campers for the Queen's Visit on the 12th. I had seats for the three of us at the Cathedral service, and on the 11th a meeting of the Trustees was held on the island, attended by Dr. Warr, Mr. Longmuir (Principal Clerk of Assembly) and myself. Afterwards, at tea in the Refectory, I found myself sitting beside Ronnie Falconer, Religious Director (Scotland) of the B.B.C. He told me that, next day, Ella and I were to be presented to the Queen, and that I was to join with Dr. Warr and Mr. Longmuir in receiving the Queen at the gate of the Cathedral precincts and to escort the Duke of Edinburgh round the various sites. This was the first intimation I had of this, but, immediately after, Dr. Warr confirmed the information. I rushed back to the Hotel, and 'mugged up' the Blue Guide, while Mrs. Tindal of the Columba Hotel kindly pressed my ancient holiday suit!

Sunday morning turned out fine, though the previous evening the rain had come down in buckets. I repaired to the jetty and saw *Britannia*, followed by the frigate *Orwell* and the minelayer *Clyde* anchor in the sound a good way southwards of the jetty. Ella and Rosemary went up to the Cathedral at 10.30, to the seats provided for them on the southside of the chancel, close to the Communion Table. From the jetty, I went to the main gate and was soon joined by Dr. Warr and Mr. Longmuir. Very few people were there – some grown-ups and some children mostly in perambulators. The main assemblage of people was at the jetty, where Ross MacLean's yacht was lying, and where he, with Sir Charles MacLean, received the Queen. Just as the Queen landed at the jetty, miraculously the sun came out in all his brilliance, and favoured us with his presence through the Royal visit.

By and by, a quiet little procession came up the Pilgrim's Way past the Reilig Oran to the gate of the Cathedral. Here, Dr. Warr welcomed her, as Chairman of the Cathedral Trustees, and then presented myself and Mr. Longmuir. The Duke then darted round the Queen's right, and Princess Margaret darted round her left, and each shook hands with us in turn. I remember being momentarily sorry that I had given the Queen too strong a handshake – the intention was good, but I think it unkind to one who has to face so many handshakes. The Duke and Princess Margaret then walked abreast behind the Queen, and the disposition of the Royal Party placed me, by chance, on Princess Margaret's left, so I escorted her instead of the Duke. She began to talk in a lovely manner, and my first intelligent remark was to point out the St. Martin's Cross, and tell her (from the guide book) that it was ninth-tenth century. 'Is that a fact I ought to know?' she asked. I felt inclined to say: 'No – I only "mugged it up" myself last night.' Out of respect for Royalty, I did not say so, but I wish I had, as I think she would have appreciated that more than some of my more painstaking observations. At the West Door of the Cathedral, George MacLeod (who was to preach), Mr. Macdonald (of Ardna-murchan: Moderator of the Mull Presbytery) and Mr. Macleod (of Tobermory: interim-moderator in the vacancy in the Parish of Iona and Ross of Mull) were presented to the Queen. Then we all proceeded in order down the nave, the Queen and the Duke taking their seats at the front of the nave, on the right, and the Princess and the Countess of Leicester (lady-in-waiting) on the left. Mr. Longmuir and I followed to seats in the South Chancel stalls.

The service was chiefly memorable for the wonderful singing of the Gaelic hymn 'Child in the Manger' to the Gaelic melody 'Bunessan', and of 'St. Patrick's Breastplate' and of the 'Gloria in Excelsis' all led by a choir of young people; the moving prayers of Mr. Macleod; the reading of one lesson by the Duke; and the Gaelic benediction given by Mr. Macdonald. George MacLeod's sermon was vigorous and dynamic, but too full of clichés and somewhat political.

The service ended, Mr. Longmuir and I followed the Royal Party out of the Cathedral to the monastic buildings, the Library, the Re-fectory (where members of the Iona Community and Associates were drawn up, and representatives of the Community were presented), the cloister, and the Chapter-House (where Ella and others were presented); and back into the now empty Cathedral. At the Library,

Randall Philip accompanying Princess Margaret during Queen's visit to Iona, 12th August 1956 (Courtesy of The Herald and Evening Times, Glasgow).

I fell into the company of Lady Leicester, whom both Ella and I found quite delightful and both intelligent and full of fun. It was interesting for me to watch Ella being presented. The Queen talked with her about the recent opening of the National Library. To Princess Margaret, Ella expressed the hope that she had not had too rough a voyage,

The Princess replied that she had never noticed anything, as she had slept all night.

We came out into the sunshine, and proceeded through the assembled people to the Reilig Oran, I again escorting the Princess. On the way, Dr. Warr whispered to me jokingly: 'What are we to tell them about the Reilig Oran?' 'Tell them,' I suggested, 'that, according to legend, the murdered Duncan and Macbeth himself are buried here.' Primed by Rosemary, I was also reminded that 48 Scottish, 4 Irish, 8 Norse, and 2 French kings are said to have been buried there. Whatever the truth of that be, it was at least memorable to accompany a Queen round the most ancient and hallowed burial place of Kings, the first sovereign to visit Iona for 900 years, the last having been Malcolm Canmore. The Queen and Dr. Warr stood leaning over the railing on one side, the Princess and I leaning over the railing at the other (which almost gave way under our, or rather, my weight) gazing down on the resting place of ancient kings. The Queen then entered St. Oran's Chapel which has just been reroofed with funds gifted by the late Sir David Russell; his son David and the latter's wife were here presented. At this point, inside the Chapel, I had an opportunity to take in her dress. She was wearing a pale turquoise-blue fitted coat, a coral straw-hat with dainty pink and blue flowers, pearls and diamond brooch, and quiet black low-heeled shoes, with broad laces. Princess Margaret wore a navy-blue fitted coat, tightly drawn round a diminutive waist and then opening out in a very full skirt, a diamond lapel brooch, a navy-blue and white 'pudding-basin' hat, and shoes to match. Both looked rather white, and, I could not help thinking, needed some fresh sea-breezes; but both were quite charming and unaffected.

From the Reilig Oran, we all walked down to the Nunnery, where Ian Lindsay, our architect, showed the Royal party round the ruins. We all went into St. Ronan's Chapel, now covered in with a glass-roof, and spent some time examining the Celtic stones. At the entrance, Dr. Warr asked the Queen's leave to present Mr. Rodger, the Episcopal clergyman, and an Anglican nun, who were standing by. He said to me afterwards: 'You know how, in a land where one is in a minority church, the largest church is apt to overlook its smaller sisters. I asked the Queen's special leave to present Mr. Rodger to show our desire to bring in our episcopal friends.' At the exit from the Nunnery, the Queen came up to us and shook hands with Dr. Warr, myself, and Mr. Longmuir, and our duties ended as she left the Nunnery, and walked to the jetty to return to *Britannia*. Admiral Abel-Smith told me that the Royal Yacht would not attempt to sail through the Sound of Iona. Instead, it disappeared by the way it came, sailed round the west of Iona, and on by Fingal's Cave to Loch-na-Keal.

In our hotel were a Major and Mrs. Wilson and their sons Robin and James. Mrs. Wilson, and her sister Mrs. Lingard Guthrie of Torosay, whom we also met, are cousins of Lady Maclean, and the Wilsons were to go to lunch next day at Duart Castle with the Queen. In the middle of the Sunday night, however, a gale (force 7) and torrential rain developed. All the campers on the island had their tents blown down and streamed into the hotels and houses, like refugees, for shelter. All Monday, the gale blew, and all communications by steamer and ferry with Iona were cut, and we could not leave that day, as we had planned.

There were two other memorable facts about the Queen's visit. Last February, she laid a wreath, in Nigeria, at the memorial to Mary Slessor, the Dundee factory-girl who became a missionary to Calabar and 'the uncrowned Queen of Okoyong'. Two Nigerian girls who saw that ceremony were also at the service in Iona Cathedral. The little Prince and Princess did not come ashore, but were attending the ship's service on *Britannia*. How much rather would the Queen have remained with her own little children!

It was only by 'bush-telegraph' that, on the Monday, we were able to learn of the Queen's adventures on her visit to Oban. The rain came down in buckets and she was soaked; the *Britannia* dragged her anchor in Oban Bay while the Queen was ashore, and had to make for the open Firth of Lorne beyond Kerrera; the Queen could not re-embark on the Royal Barge at Oban, and had to re-embark at the Kerrera ferry near Gallanach over an improvised gangway of fish-boxes; the *Britannia* was, in consequence, unable to fulfil the lunch engagement at Duart Castle; but the Queen managed to get ashore in the late afternoon at Craignure (it is said she was slung ashore), and spent forty minutes at tea at Duart, ending up her adventures by motoring to Tobermory and rejoining the Royal Yacht there. Yet the following day, we sailed into Oban in brilliant unclouded sunshine, the place looking like a sunny Riviera resort. We had delightful companions in Dr. Warr, Professor Garth Macgregor, and the Rev. Peter Fraser of Glenmoriston. On our arrival at 6 p.m., I retrieved my car at the Great Western Hotel, where Alex, the porter, had everything ready for me, and we drove on in a wonderful evening of lengthening shadows through Appin, and on, by moonlight, past Laggan to Newtonmore, which we reached at 10.30 p.m.

Rosemary had a lovely time on Iona with a pet-lamb – Balloch – which she fed by milk-bottle, a baby calf – Gracie – which would put its hoof on her arm, two six-weeks old collie puppies, and a tiny kitten – Mulloch (inhabitant of Mull) – which was the delight of the hotel. She also had two little Stevenson girls (also going to St. Leonard's) to play with. These matched her experience at Nethybridge, where two tame squirrels – Johnnie and Jimmy – came out of the woods each day to have protracted meals on a bird-house just situated outside the dining-room window where we had our meals.

Our final fortnight, at the Lodge Hotel, Newtonmore, was cold and wet, one of the worst summers ever. But this did not damp our spirits. One day, we were visited by Mr. and Mrs. Lake, our friends from Jamaica, whom we met in 1949 at the Loch Awe Hotel. Another day, with Kathleen, Mary, Donald, Jean and Catherine, we laid Harold's ashes in the little churchyard of St. Bride, Glen Banchor, within sound of the Calder, where forty years before, we two brothers had so often bathed together as boys. Another day, we took Kathleen for a lovely drive to Drumnadrochit, where we visited, first, the Rev. John Campbell formerly of Lochboisdale and Dulnain Bridge, and, then, my friends the Michaels at their beautiful upland croft of Achtemarack – 'the place of the Shamrock'. We met, there, a daughter of Canon Raven's, camping with her husband and family.

Our holiday ended with a journey home by that romantic route – Dalnacardoch, Trinafour, Fortingall, Killin and Callander. On our return, we found Alison and Ian, back from their honeymoon in North Devon, full of the joys of getting their new home into ship-shape, the pleasures of house-keeping on a small income, and all the adventures of the newly-wed.

2nd September 1956 (Sunday)

Last night, Ella, Rosemary and I were entertained to dinner by Alison and Ian in their new home, 22 India Street. It is a moving thing for a parent to be received as a guest for the first time in his own child's home. It was lovely to see their evident happiness, and to realise how much they had done in hospitality. They have decorated three parts of their flat themselves – the hall, the lounge, their bedroom; and the kitchen was decorated during their honeymoon. The lounge has a light, almost white paper, with delicate pattern, a gay blue carpet, two comfortable modern armchairs and a sofa; and is to have yellow curtains. We looked out to the sunset in the north-west through a tracery of trees. Their bedroom has three light walls, with the fourth a warm red, and red curtains and golden quilts on the two beds. The hall is in pastel shades, with two grey, two yellow, and two light blue doors, the archway crossing the hall having a strip of bright red on the underside of the arch. The kitchen is in light blue, with white cupboards, and a yellow ceiling. The dining-room is not yet ready. After sherry in the lounge, we sat down to a dinner prepared by Alison at their oak table in the kitchen, with their new silver and crystal, and seated on Ian's Chippendale chairs – soup, ragout Bolognese, and guavas, with a bottle of Beaujolais. Afterwards we had coffee in the lounge, and heard about North Devon, Parracombe, Combe Martin, Lee Abbey, the Three Maids of Lee, Lynton and Lynmouth.

I believe that, in this Journal, I may never yet have mentioned the Edinburgh Festival – now in its tenth year. This is chiefly due to our usually having been away in August and only having returned for the close of the Festival. What I remember best of past years are the 'Thrie Estates', Kathleen Ferrier singing to Bruno Walker's accompaniment, the symphony orchestra rather than Glyndebourne, and of the past three years, first Jean Louis Barrault and Madeleine Renault. This year, having been back for less than a week, I have seen little, though in new directions, the Raeburn bi-centenary exhibition, the exhibition of Braque, an international photographic exhibition, the flower-show, and an exhibition of musical boxes! – the choice partly dictated because of twelve-year-old Rosemary. In spite of some supercilious London critics (still a little jealous of the Festival's success) looking down their noses at the robust Raeburns, I found it fascinating to see grouped together so many Raeburns which I had seen before in different places, and also some I had not seen before – e.g. the Paterson of Castle Huntly children and the artist's wife. I came to the conclusion that Lord Abercromby, one of the finest Raeburns from Parliament House, and also the Braxfield are not quite equal to the best; that the portrait of Newton (perhaps because of familiarity with it) is more satisfying than the full-length Rosebery Newton, and that, if a choice had to be made, I would select Professor Robison as the finest of the characteristic Raeburns, and the group of the Clanranald children as the liveliest if not so characteristic. The Braque exhibition is difficult to understand, but perhaps its strength is best judged by a layman, when one looks from his work to the conventional R.S.A. exhibits in the adjoining rooms. The best of the musical boxes was a 200 year old German disc machine which played a selection from 'Hansel and Gretel' and the 'Old Hundred' in deep melodious tones. But this year,

I have only heard the greater concerts over the wireless, notably a Boston Symphony concert conducted by Pierre Monteux. The idealism of Sir John Falconer still inspires and lingers over the Festival, and I am glad to see that a memorial to him is to be placed at Colinton where he lived. The London critics say that the Raeburn Exhibition attracts countrified Scots who see in his portraits reflections of themselves, and that the intelligentsia go only to Braque. It was certainly not so on the day of my visit. The visitors to both exhibitions were extraordinarily like each other, with more visitors to Raeburn than to Braque.

9th September 1956 (Sunday)

After hearing appeals in Dundee Sheriff Court for two days, I went on (joined by Ella) to Aberdeen for the ceremony of opening the new Kirk House of West St. Nicholas, the mother church of Aberdeen. We had a full round of engagements:– a visit to see the new Kirk House and later coffee with the Rev. Anderson Nicol and his wife (when he showed me his boy's electric railway) – this on the Friday night; on the Saturday – in the morning, we went to Queen St. so that I might show Ella Edmond and Spark, the successors of the business founded by my great grandfather, who took Edmond into partnership with him well over a century ago: it is almost 150 years to this year, since my great grandfather, John Philip, set up his book-binding business first 'in the Lodge Walk near the New Inn' (somewhere near the present Police Station). From there, Ella took me to Provost Skene's House, restored a few years ago and now the Town Museum – the nearest approach to a Folk Museum of the first class Scandinavian order that I have seen in Scotland. The house is seventeenth century. Its finest room has a wonderful painted ceiling, finer than those at Culross. Three scenes – the Annunciation, the Crucifixion, the Burial, survive. Even more interesting are the 'Armorial Bearings of Christ' with the emblem of the Five Wounds of Christ, the pierced Hands, Feet, and Heart, an example of which I had never seen before. There are numerous examples in Germany, Holland, and the North-East of Scotland – some of the last being collected in the museum in photographs – one which particularly interested me was the Font at Meigle – in relation to which I am trying to settle a dispute between the local parish church and the Episcopal Church – the font having formerly been in the parish church, but later transferred by one of the Kinlochs to the local Episcopal Church (now closed down). The Bishop of St.

Andrews (Howe) is cooperating with me, and we were trying to work out a peaceful solution last summer. We then were entertained by the Lord Provost (Stephen) and the Lady Provost at the City Chambers, after which they lunched us with a party of friends at the Station Hotel. The Lord Provost struck me as a fine example of the best type of Aberdonian, interested, understanding, tolerant, with a depth of character, and keenly sympathetic to the Church, in which he sometimes acts as a lay preacher. After lunch, Mr. Nicol showed me over the West Church, which Dr. Francis Eccles regards as the finest ecclesiastical building planned in the old Reformed Tradition, with its central Communion Table; certainly I have seen nothing of the kind to compare with it. The present building was re-built by Gibbs in 1763, but the foundations go back to 1060, and the dedication is to St. Nicholas of Myra. The transepts, lying between the West and East Churches, contain the oldest part of the building, including some of the original Norman arches. There are also wonderful tapestries in the vestibule of the West Church, especially the Return of Jephthah. We also climbed the Tower to see and hear the carillon which was being played at the time. The carilloneur, Mr. Knox, who was trained at Malines, was finishing just as we arrived. I noticed among his music S.S. Wesley's 'Holsworthy Bells', and, at my special request, he kindly played the first movement of it as he finished. The largest bell in the Tower weighs 4 tons. We ascended to the bells, while they were sounding, but could not stay there because of the clanging din. Beneath the place where Mr. Knox plays is another chamber containing an instrument for practice. The instrument is like a pipe-organ with pedals, except that the manuals consist of lever-like keys, which can be depressed sharply or lightly, according to the degree of sound which it is desired to produce. From there we went to the Kirk House, which is the fine old granite South Church, reconstructed in the very latest manner as a magnificent suite of Church Halls, at a cost of £20,000. I have seen nothing like it, except the halls of St. Columba's, Pont Street, London. The opening ceremony went well. After an opening prayer by Dr. Wilson Baird of St. Machar's as Moderator of the Presbytery, Mr. Anderson Nicol from the Chair gave an introductory account of the work of reconstruction. Then I made my speech opening the Halls, and that was followed by a prayer of dedication by the Very Rev. Professor G.D. Henderson. Thereafter, the Lord Provost spoke, and there was a vote of thanks from Mr. Reid, whose father gave £4,000 to start the work of reconstruction. After tea, we caught the 5.17 p.m. train back to Edinburgh.

Round Table Dinner, 1956. Left to Right: Back Row: Randall Philip, Stanley Gimson, Donald Macleod, Robert Reid, John G. Wilson, Frank Duffy, T.P. McDonald. Front Row: George Carmichael, Jock Cameron, Daniel Blades, Clifford Watt, James Walker, John Wheatley, Tom Taylor.

16th September 1956 (Sunday)

It is delightful to pick up threads with an old University friend. Thirty-seven years ago I was a member, at Edinburgh University, of the Diagnostic Society, and there met R.D. Maclennan, son of the minister of Kintail. Many a time we have walked home together in the late evening across the Meadows to our 'digs', and discussed all manner of deep things. In those days, he had pain every day from a war wound in the First World War, and, even yet, I can see his face with just a suggestion in his expression of suffering, though few knew the reason. He was a quiet, thoughtful, reflective type, with a soft West Highland voice. After the University, our ways led in separate directions. He became a lecturer in Philosophy at Edinburgh, and the first Warden of Cowan House. Then he received the Professorship of Moral Philosophy at McGill University, Montreal, and I saw nothing of him for thirty years. Recently, I learned that he had retired, and returned to the old family home in Kintail, now a widower, with a small daughter. I suggested to our Graduates' Association that he would be an ideal corresponding secretary to keep liaison with the daughter societies of the Association scattered throughout the Dominions, and, when I broached this subject with him, he seemed taken with the idea. My first meeting with him after a generation was when he appeared as a Commissioner at this year's General Assembly, just the same quiet, kindly, thoughtful personality as when I first met him. Next, I learned that he had been invited to become Gifford Lecturer at Edinburgh University for the next course but one. Now this week, he has been ordained and inducted to his own father's former parish of Kintail.

22nd September 1956 (Saturday)

Alison's birthday. We went round after breakfast to wish the young couple Many Happy Returns. She was thrilled over the arrival of a University Undergraduate's 'Tuck-Box' which had just arrived from Fortnums and Mason, where I ordered it on Wednesday.

On Wednesday I was in London for a meeting of the International Department of the British Council of Churches. Except for Dame Kathleen Courtney, it was a meeting of well-intentioned but ineffective people, with an almost pathetic faith in passing and publishing resolutions. We passed five resolutions on the Suez Canal Situation. As the Suez Canal Conference (Second London Conference) was meeting that very day, I urged that the final decision to publish these should be taken only in light of the conclusions the Conference might reach. However, the others all were for immediate publication. Dame Courtney, now an old lady, had a most refreshing sense of precision in language.

In the morning, I looked in to St. Paul's to see how the repair of war damage was proceeding, but the east end and north transept are still boarded up. Afterwards, I found my way into the Old Bailey, where I heard three apparently fraud cases being tried by the Recorder (Sir Gerald Dodson); the Common Sergeant (Sir Anthony Hawke); and the Judge of the Mayor's and City of London Court (Judge Aarvold). The Recorder wears a black gown edged with red; the others two plain black gowns. Sir Gerald talked a good deal, and there was a good deal of laughter; Sir Anthony Hawke impressed me least of the three; Judge Aarvold struck me as quiet and to the point.

I discovered one new feature of Club Life on this visit to London. I came away inadvertently without my spectacles for reading. But both the Union Club, and The Athenæum, were able to offer me a selection for my use during the day. Evidently, I am not the only member who forgets his spectacles.

Two interesting developments concerning the Church occurred this week. Pitt Watson invited me to an informal conference (to which I cannot go, unfortunately) about the proposed representation of the Church in the House of Lords. Apparently, the government are shortly to introduce a Bill for Reform of the House of Lords; Sir Charles Cunningham indicated as much to me on July 4th, but now practical measures are to be taken. Problems will be: (1) the extent of Church of Scotland representation and (2) the method of appointment; it seems clear, however, that the principle of giving the Church of Scotland representation is settled; apparently, only the two established churches are to have this representation. Lord Selkirk had spoken to Pitt Watson; by chance, I saw Lord Selkirk myself the very next day in the Athenæum, but, as he was with a friend and was leaving for Japan next day (!), we had no chance to talk about the matter, though he hoped that, later that same day, he might be able to come back to the Athenæum to have a word with me about it.

The other news I can only regard as, in a human sense, slightly ominous. It relates to the Inter-Church Conversations. The Church of Scotland delegates, at last conversations, showed how they thought it might be possible to contemplate modifications in their polity with a view to fuller union. The main step was that it was thought not impossible that Presbyteries might choose permanent moderators who would be 'consecrated' in a manner which would, from the Anglican standpoint, bring them into the 'historical episcopate' – a step which the Church of England delegates described as 'generous'. Corresponding modifications were discussed in the Anglican polity, in particular (1) the introduction of lay-representation in the Conversations and also synodically, and (2) the sharing of all representatives in the full government of the Church. These suggestions were entertained sympathetically by the Church of England delegates, though the matter still remained somewhat unspecific. It being the Church of Scotland's turn to re-revise the proposed draft report, we made the proposals specific. I pressed for a fuller representation of each panel at the next two series of conversations, for the simple reason that, on our side, it is essential that our delegation should contain an adequate representation not merely of theologians, but of the parish ministry, if the report is to command attention by the Church. As a result, each of the Church of England and Church of Scotland delegations at the resumed conversations next week is to consist of nine representatives; instead of six. But, whereas hitherto the Church of England delegation has consisted of at least three bishops and three others, the number of bishops at the coming conversations will, I understand, be reduced to one – the Bishop of Derby, who must attend as Joint Chairman. It looks very much as if the more authoritative English voices were to be – diplomatically – absent at this stage – an ill omen. [24th September 1956: Since writing this, I have learned that the Bishop of Leicester is also coming; and I understand that the Archbishop of York is staying out, because he is now Archbishop. It is, however, interesting that the C. of E. delegates this time are to be predominantly Evangelical. What the significance of this is, appears doubtful.] Then, although the discussions have been expressly decided to be confidential until the report in its concluded form is issued, the Bishop of Brechin has, in a pastoral charge, discussed the Church of Scotland standpoint, and his charge has been reported in detail in the Dundee Courier and Advertiser. Naturally, this has aroused uneasiness among ministers of the Church of Scotland, whose own delegates have carefully adhered to the understanding of confidentiality (as have the Church of England delegates), sometimes to their great embarrassment.

3rd October 1956 (Wednesday)

The Inter-Church Conversations took place last week, and, on the whole, went well. It was a great help, on one side, having Pitt Watson present for the first time. Archie Craig and he made a first-class combination, full of practical sense. The Anglicans had two excellent new delegates, Archdeacon Harrison of Sheffield, forthright, honest, practical, and friendly, and Alan Richardson, now Professor at Nottingham, whom I had met when a canon at Durham, a theologian with his feet firmly on the ground, with, too, a fresh stimulating point of view. I was much touched by his manifest trust and friendliness shown towards myself. Derby, Leicester, John Taylor (present for the first time at this present series of conferences) always accepted any view I expressed in the most generous-hearted way, I think, because, through long friendship now, they trust me. Others whose friendship I felt very marked were Harrison, Richardson, Tomkins, and, on our side, I felt the special trust of Pitt Watson and Archie Craig. I gave a long statement, *ex tempore*, on the practical value of the pastoral side of the eldership, and was asked to supply a special paragraph on this for the Report, for the information of Anglicans. I also proposed a practical step of wider occasional inter-communion in the form of Presbyterians being welcomed as occasional communicants in the interim in Anglican Churches; we, of course, have no difficulty with this, but on the contrary already welcome them. Archie Craig entertained some of us and our wives at tea the first afternoon. The second afternoon, Ella and I entertained Derby, Leicester, John Taylor, Harrison, Alan Richardson, Oliver Tomkins, Pitt Watson, Principal Whitehorn, George Gunn, Donald Mackay, Willie and Elfrida Tindal, and Canon and Mrs. Greenslade, and the Bishop of St. Andrews (Howe). (The Craigs could not join us that day.) Derby and John Taylor told me of their visit to Moscow.

At the weekend, Ella and I went to my old class reunion at Dunblane Hydro, where there was a large assemblage on Saturday evening and on Sunday. We returned by the Macrae Memorial at Sheriffmuir, and the high road from there to Bridge of Allan, a magnificent prospect.

These last two days, I have spent in Angus, installing Bob Inglis as a Sheriff-substitute in Dundee, and attending a conference on Forfar Polling Places.

2nd November 1956 (Friday)

The British Council of Churches met in October at Wellington Church, Glasgow, the first time it has met in Scotland for over ten years. It will not be truly a 'British' Council, until its meetings in Scotland are in proper ration to its meetings elsewhere. I rather suspect a certain Anglican reluctance to meet in Scotland, because, here, the President is on an 'away' pitch as he is not even in Northern Ireland or Wales. Unfortunately, for the first time in my experience, the Archbishop was definitely not at his best. At the lunch in Glasgow City Chambers, the Lord Provost made one of the best municipal speeches I have ever heard – humorous, pointed, sympathetic, full of his own personality. The Archbishop, in reply, seemed very ill at ease, referred to his pleasure in being 'here in *Edinburgh*', and, then, followed that up by saying that he had noticed his train kept going slower and slower as it approached Glasgow as if it were reluctant ever to reach there. Said in one way, this might have passed off as a poor joke, but he was so ill at ease, fidgety, and even stammering that it sounded very gauche. He followed it up by 'debating' points referred to by the Lord Provost, and, after trying to stop but not finding a happy finish, ended with the remark, capable of misinterpretation, that the Kingdom of Heaven, and the Welfare State, rightly interpreted were one and the same.

The next day, Dr. Robert Nelson, Secretary of the Faith and Order Department of the World Council of Churches addressed the British Council at its forenoon session. His speech was the best contribution to the meetings. Yet, at the end of it, the Archbishop rose, and, without ever even thanking the guest speaker, spent twenty minutes in controversial comment from the Chair. He then abruptly closed the session, leaving no one, not even Dr. Nelson, a chance to say anything, and left for London. There was so much indignation that Dr. Hugh Martin, Chairman of the executive, in the afternoon made a statement to the effect that the remarks on Dr. Nelson's speech were to be taken as personal observations, and not as the expression of views on behalf of the Council.

I wrote to both Dr. Nelson and Dr. Martin next day, thanking the latter for what he had done.

In his appreciative reply, Hugh Martin said that he had felt it imperative to say something both on his own judgement and because of representations from other Council members. He expressed the wish that the Archbishop would adopt the Church of Scotland practice whereby the Moderator does not intervene controversially in a debate unless he has first left the Chair.

Pitt Watson has also written to me expressing similar views about the conduct of the Archbishop.

Nevile Davidson, always charitable in his judgments, said to me: 'Sometimes Fisher seems to appear as Archbishop of the Council, and sometimes addresses them as Headmaster of Repton addressing the School!'

Today, Ella and I were present at the opening of the new Museum Gallery in Shandwick Place, attached to the National Museum of Antiquities of Scotland. It is most attractively planned, after the fashion of the London Museum, and shows what can be produced out of a simple building. I also attended a Committee, and the Board Meeting, of the National Museum Trustees. At both I saw one of the most wonderful accessions which has just been received by the Museum, on permanent loan from the Roman Catholic Bishop of Aberdeen. It is said to be the oldest ecclesiastical banner not merely in Britain, but in Northern Europe, and, as yet, the public knows nothing of it. It was in the possession of the Leslies of Fetternear, who had it in their Chapel, and both Chapel and banner were handed over to the Roman Catholic diocese of Aberdeen. It is probably dated shortly before 1520, and is believed to have belonged to a con-fraternity of the then Collegiate Church of St. Giles. The arms of Gavin Douglas, who was Bishop of Dunkeld till 1520, appear at the top left corner. He was also Provost of St. Giles'. At the top right corner, there is a space, unworked but possibly meant to have sewn in the arms of the Archbishop of St. Andrews. At the foot are the arms of Graham of Fintry, and Graham is known to have been one of the masters of the con-fraternity. Down the centre is first, a dove, symbolising probably the Holy Spirit; then a blank space, in which perhaps the Father was to be represented. Below that there is the Cross, with the figure of Our Lord covered with marks of blood: the con-fraternity was of the Holy Blood. There is, beneath, a sepulchre; on one side, a cock in colours still wonderful; above, the instruments of the Cross, hammer etc; and two curious heads, one believed to be Judas, with a money-bag round his neck, the other the Jew who spat at Christ, with spittal on his protruding lips; there is also a ladder, a spear, and a sponge with vinegar. The colours are wonderfully preserved, especially the reds, and then the blues; some black has gone. Outside the central portion, hang portions of a rosary; and outside that, probably the emblems of the con-fraternity.

George MacLeod is to be next year's Moderator of the General Assembly. The *Manchester Guardian* had a leader congratulating the Church on its courage. George MacLeod himself wrote me that it was strange to see the 'Prophet being Praised and not Pelted.' It is certainly a venture. I hope that it will do the Church good, and also George MacLeod good. He needs both to come, and to be brought, central.

11th November 1956 (Sunday)

Last weekend I paid two flying visits to Angus. The first was on Saturday morning to take the Chair at the Edinburgh Angus Club dinner held at the Glenesk Hotel, Edzell. The Club had, apparently, not dined in the evening since 1927. I had as guest Douglas Duncan, just back from R.N.V.R. service extended by being seconded for about a year to instruct Italian naval-cadets on their wonderful sailing ship *Amerigo Vespucci*, which I saw at the Coronation Revue in 1953 – Douglas sailed on her to the Azores – now, he has just been appointed Lecturer in English at Aberdeen University. He sat on my left, and Lord Airlie, as Lord Lieutenant, on my right. Lord Airlie went out of his way to be most kind to me. Harold Duke, the Secretary of the Club, and almost my kinsman, through the Dukes of Brechin, motored me to Edzell on Saturday morning, and back on Sunday morning. There were almost no autumn tints either here or in Perthshire, but, in Angus, the browns and reds were gorgeous. The explanation of no autumn tints elsewhere seems to be the lack of sunshine this summer, with no sharp October frost to follow.

On the Monday Ella and I set off for Forfar, where that afternoon I opened the new West School, a splendid functional building. It was, in every way, a most happy and well-planned day – so different from the previous evening. The Director of Education drove us from Dundee to Forfar, and we took the high road by Kingennie, which gave us a panorama of Strathmore and the entrance to Glen Prosen and Glen Clova. (I was able to tell the Angus Dinner that, the previous day, I had seen two spear-heads of 700 BC (Bronze Age) which had been found in Glen Clova by the children of the Rev. J.M. Haddow, parish minister of Glamis; almost as old as Romulus and Remus.) At Forfar, the county council entertained us to lunch, Mr. R.W.L. McCaig, the County Convener, in the Chair, a charming diminutive bachelor, courteous and efficient. The name of 'McCaig' is held in honour in Angus, different from Argyll. At the ceremony of opening the School, I found an old school-mate, whom I had not seen since school-days, Col. Scott of Letham, in the Chair. The large school-hall was full of county councillors, teachers, pupils and the public. I felt my speech went down well, if only because the small children listened well. It is a real test to speak to children, and, in the right circumstances, I think it is something which I can do, perhaps because I have now known the child-mind for thirty years. I spoke to children, teachers, parents, and ended with the words: 'A school is like a garden. The parents are the soil. The teachers are the gardeners. The children are the flowers – and what lovely flowers they are!' Both Lord and Lady Airlie came up to me afterwards, and thanked me warmly; they have six children of their own. Lord Airlie pressed us with a standing invitation to come and stay at Cortachy.

At lunch, Mrs. Eadie, wife of the Director of Education, sitting next me, apologised that she was deaf. So I told her: 'I have been stone-deaf in my right ear' (the one next her) 'as long as I can remember. Fortunately, my left ear is so good that, so far, I have been able to 'hear round the corner!' I first learned that I was deaf in the right ear when I was about seven, and was punished by 'Big Bob', our writing master, for not hearing what he said. But, so far, I have managed to conceal the infirmity, and, I think, very few people know. The great embarrassment of deafness is that a person affected by it is often taken for stupid, when the truth is, that he has not heard. Many a time, I have answered 'Yes' or 'No' or non-committally to a lady on my right, or tried to maintain a monologue myself to avoid having to try to hear. But, latterly, with ladies at a public lunch or dinner, I have found it better to confess the fact at the beginning; men's voices are more resonant, and there is less difficulty with them. In the army, I used to have great difficulty when numbering took place, as the numbering always came from the right, my deaf side, and sometimes I was 'ticked off' for turning my head, to hear; but no one ever guessed the reason. It is strange how hearing aids are still not quite *comme il faut*; it will be a good thing when they are as readily accepted as spectacles.

Overshadowing all these trivialities of the past week has been the Suez Crisis. Israel, after years of sporadic attacks from Arab neighbours, declared war on Egypt. Then Britain and France, to protect the Suez Canal, gave a twenty-four-hour ultimatum to both, and landed at Port Said. The fighting ended in about four days, and Egypt was ignominiously put out of action. But the British-French 'police' measure has divided the nation as I have never in my lifetime seen it divided, and brought most countries in the world against us. Then in the same week, Russian forces moved into Hungary, and put down resistance there in the most harsh manner in modern times. Public opinion in the country, which tended at first to be shocked by the action of Sir Anthony Eden, has, since, been gradually swinging round to realise that he was probably right. It has certainly stimulated the United Nations to take action in Suez, whereas they have done nothing in relation to the Russian action in Hungary. The crisis is not yet over – the worst may still be to come. But Suez has absorbed every moment of conversation. The country has, I think, behaved much more calmly than the House of Commons, where there has been hysterical abuse and counter-abuse which has only lowered our representatives in the judgment of the public.

19th November 1956 (Monday)

This last week three interesting things occurred. Sir William Hutchison's portrait of Lord Cooper was hung in the Parliament Hall, just to the left of the great window and beside the passage-way which leads to the First Division. Seeing it now *in situ*, I can only regard it as a remarkable achievement for a posthumous portrait. The rich mellow colouring contrasts favourably with the more sketchy effects of the colouring in Stanley Cursiter's portrait of Craigie Aitchison. At the same time, the portrait of Lord Birnam was also placed in position, an excellent likeness, with his calm dormouse expression, almost asleep, yet full of life – yet, as portraiture, not quite in the same class of painting.

The last Edinburgh electric tramcar ran last Friday evening. A special car, decked in white, was prepared for the occasion. I saw it running down Dundas Street earlier in the week. The final run started from Morningside Station at 7.45 p.m. We expected it to follow the usual route, and Rosemary and I went out at 8 p.m. to watch for it at the corner of Great King Street and Pitt Street. But it went along Princes Street instead – where thousands watched it. The last tramcar in Dundee ran earlier this autumn.

I received a letter from 10 Downing Street stating that I had been nominated on behalf of the Scottish Institutions to serve on the Standing Commission on Museums and Galleries, in place of Normand, and that, if I was willing to act, the Prime Minister proposed to appoint me. I have accepted. The list of Institutions with which the Standing Commission is concerned is fascinating:-

The National Gallery; The Tate Gallery; The National Portrait Gallery; The British Museum (Bloomsbury and Natural History); The Wallace Collection; The London Museum; The Imperial War Museum; The Victoria and Albert Museum; The Bethnal Green Museum; The National Maritime Museum; The Science Museum; The Royal Botanic Gardens, Kew; The Geological Museum; The National Gallery, Scotland; The National Portrait Gallery, Scotland; The National Library of Scotland; The National Museum of Antiquities in Scotland;

The Royal Scottish Museum; The National Museum of Wales; and The National Library of Wales.

Almost simultaneously, came a request from the Trustees of the National Portrait Gallery in London that I should give a sitting for a portrait by Mr. Walter Stoneman, F.R.P.S., to be included in their National Record of Distinguished Persons!

25th November 1956 (Sunday)

Last night we had another Round Table Dinner – it only ended at 1.30 a.m. this morning; and I am jotting this down before breakfast, while awaiting the descent from his bedroom of Tom Taylor, who was also at the dinner. The excuse for the dinner was to celebrate T.P. McDonald's election as Vice-Dean. James Walker occupied the Chair. The company in their order round the table were:- James Walker; T.P.; George Carmichael; Jock Cameron; Donald Macleod; John Wilson; Stanley Gimson; Harry Guthrie; Tom Taylor; Robert Reid; John Wheatley; Frank Duffy; myself; Daniel Blades. John Wilson, our sennachie, read a poem about T.P. in the Hiawatha strain. Jock proposed 'East of Suez' (the Suez crisis being still in everyone's mind) – coupled with the name of the 'Abbot of Katmandu' – Stanley. Robert Reid proposed 'The Vice-Admiral of the Pentland Firth' – which was to have been replied to by F.C. Watt; but he had a chill, and so Frank Duffy was appointed at the last moment. Frank read an imaginary page from this Journal! – about which they all know, though no one has ever seen it. Every one spoke before the night was over.

30th December 1956

This must be one of the longest gaps in the Journal for some time. It is explained partly by the fact that I have been very busy, busier than usual, and partly by the fact that I was laid up for about a week, and have, since then, had to go slow – just tiredness affecting my heart, and it was wise to nip it in time. Then there have been the Christmas Festivities, with, for the first time, a child's home to celebrate in as well as in my own. I had, too, a solid week in Court, a visit to Dundee in connection with a new polling-station, and to Forfar, for a Sheriff Court Appeal; and a day in London at the Central Land Board and War Damage Commission. Mr. Stoneman, the photographer, proved to be a most delightful old man – in his eighties. He told me that he had photographed everyone, starting with Sir Hiram Maxim. Once he lectured in 'Portraiture' in the Assembly Hall, Edinburgh, with Lord Sands as chairman. He noticed Lord Sands' notes of Chairman's Remarks beforehand, and that they related to some other subject. So he tactfully mentioned to Lord Sands what his subject was to be. To his surprise, Lord Sands, in making his Chairman's remarks, just used the notes which should have been rejected. Mr. Stoneman was interested when I told him that I now held two of the offices which Lord Sands had formerly held (the Procuratorship; and the Sheriffdom of Perth).

That evening, Sir Harold Claughton called to see me at the Athenæum. He turned out to be an entertaining talker. His wife is Helen Henschel, the elder daughter of George Henschel, whose book *When Soft Voices Die* I had read some years ago. I was able to tell him that I knew Allt-na-Criche, and had, in my youthful days, transported Georgina Henschel on the pillion of my old motor-cycle; also of the link I had with the Henschels through Druimenlochan. His grandfather was first Bishop of St. Albans, and a grand-aunt, strangely enough, was a Duchess of Argyll!

Sitting alone, afterwards, at dinner, I was joined by an older man, who engaged in friendly conversation, and, after a little, observed: 'You come from north of the Border, don't you? So do I.' He turned out to be Sir Francis Richard Fraser, Professor-Emeritus of Medicine at London University, and a son of Sir Thomas Fraser who was Professor of Materia Medica at Edinburgh when I went up to the University. He knew my Uncle Robert well, and we discussed many old Edinburgh Associations.

I have been pressed to take the Public Inquiry into the proposed Nuclear Generating Station at Hunterston, West Kilbride, which, if it goes ahead, will be the largest station of its kind in the world. The request came just when I had to lie up, but I could not refuse.

6th January 1957 (Sunday)

I have just returned from three days in London. On Thursday and Friday and the corresponding nights I was at Lambeth attending the final inter-church conference of this series between the two Episcopal and two Presbyterian Churches. We succeeded in completing a unanimous report – a great achievement. At this final meeting, all attended who could, and not a mere representation of the panel.

13th January 1957 (Sunday)

I heard three Sheriff Court Appeals this week – one from Dunblane, in my house here (the first time I have done this), and two from Dundee, in Dundee. I have gone on the practice of never hearing Sheriff Court Appeals in Edinburgh, unless the parties jointly seek this. In the present instance, the request came from Dunblane. I also had an informal hearing in connection with the Hunterston Inquiry, an objector seeking advance production of certain documents from the South of Scotland Electricity Board, the promoters. It seemed doubtful whether I could competently order production in advance of the inquiry. But, in the end, counsel for the Board undertook to see that certain production was made.

Last night I was present, for the first time, at a Festival (dinner) of the Monks of St. Giles. The dinner was held in Surgeons' Hall, surely one of Edinburgh's finest interiors, though acoustically bad. I went as John Sturrock's guest. There were about twenty-five, out of the thirty, monks present, and about the same number of guests. The atmosphere was not unlike the Spec, except that it was older men, instead of young men, renewing their youth; and the membership was made up mainly of doctors and surgeons, schoolmasters, and a smattering of military men and lawyers, instead of the overwhelming legal membership of the Spec. We all took our seats at table. Then the lights were put out, and we were left with only three candles. The retiring Prior, Father Veitch (D. Crichton Miller of Fettes), opened the proceedings with a long rigmarole, just nonsense. The new Prior, Father Corrie (Dr. Douglas Allan of the Royal Scottish Museum) was then installed. Father Nestor (Dr. Eggeling), the Secretary, made various announcements, and produced two small medicine bottles, reputed to contain vodka and to have arrived from Moscow as presents to 'Wattie' Mercer and Professor John Bruce, each of whom had recently visited Russia. They were appointed to drink the 'contents'. Meantime Father Ares (Brigadier Freddie Johnston, late of the Royal Scots) and others made various boyish interruptions, which were visited by fines proposed by the 'Fiscal', Father Figaro (Pilkington-Jackson, the sculptor), the fines being collected by the 'Bursar' Father Papingo (Douglas Watson, W.S., Queen's Archer). Then followed various contributions in verse or song, accompanied by piano, banjo, etc. – for example, a song by Father Roland (J.W. Oliver, D. Litt), verse by Father Ulysses (R.C. Watt of Edinburgh Academy), an Auditor's Report on the Accounts sung by Fathers Longinus and Rhadamanthus (R.M. Carnegie and T.G. Dempster). Thereafter, some guests were invited to make a contribution – including myself, Dr. Brewster, and R.H. Law, the civil servant whom I met in connection with Hunterston. All the contributions were collected for record purposes by the Father Librarian. R.H. Law's contribution was perhaps the best. It was based on the comment in some newspaper that the present petrol shortage (owing to the Suez Crisis) might create difficulties for the Boat-Race! The theme was that Cambridge's recent successes must have been attributable to their obtaining assistance from an outboard motor (which would not be available this year!); and his verse was labelled 'Two Stroke'. In sheer desperation, I struggled to compose a Canterbury Tales Fragment.

19th January 1957 (Saturday)

I have just returned from hearing appeals in Dundee and Forfar. An interesting experience occurred. When we were boys at Invergowrie Manse some forty years ago, my Father used to take out a little volume from one of the bookcases in his study, and read us some lines to which he was much attached. I never knew whether the book was one of his own, or one from the little endowed library in the Manse. After his death, however, there was no trace of the tome amongst his own books. All I could remember of the verse was:- 'Feeding full hardy on brown bread, Yet were . . . [something] . . . But . . . [and the same kind of promise].' My own impression was that it was from a Scots version of the Psalms, but though I asked Beattie of the National Library, and other knowledgeable people, they have been unable to trace it; and the very frustration of this kept what I recalled fresh in my mind.

Two nights ago, in Dundee, James Torrance, my father's successor (with three ministers in between) called to see me at the Eastern Club, and I quoted what I remembered to him, and raised the question whether the book was not in the Manse Library. I was able to describe exactly where it used to lie forty years ago – on the top of a series of folio volumes of a Polyglot Bible; I could even give a rough description of what the little book looked like.

Next evening, when I returned from Forfar Sheriff Court to Dundee, to my great delight, what should I find awaiting me at the Club, but the volume itself. James Torrance had found the volume and the verse, and left it at the Club for me to peruse. The volume turned out to be *The Psalms of David in Meeter, with the Prose*: Printed by Andro Hart, 1611. The verse occurred in Ps. 12/. Nisl Dominus aedificamunt.

The title was followed by these initials, presumably of the author of the verse:– 'W.W.' (Whittingham, Dean of Durham? – author of the Old 124). The verse in question was No. 2, and it ran:–

Though ye rise earlie in the morne,
And so at night go late to bed,
Feeding full hardlie with browne bread
Yet were your labour lost and worne,
But they whom God doth love and keep
Receive all things with quiet sleepe.

A quaint homely rendering, it is not surprising that a fragment of it lingers in a boy's memory. (The book itself is catalogued 'Longforgan F(ree) C(hurch) Library C. II 1; and is bound in olive green leather, with gilt panels in the spine, one of the panels being red; and the title outside is 'John Knox's Prayers', for the volume contains more than just that metrical version of the Psalms).

Index of Selected Names

to be presented to the Queen to receive my knighthood. I asked if Ella should accompany me, but apparently that is not permitted.

24th June 1953
(Wednesday)

Today the great national service took place in St. Giles. We made a great detour by Holyrood Road, Lauriston, and South Bridge to the High Street and then up to the Castle Esplanade, where we parked the car. On the way we dropped Rosemay, with our maid Muriel Mackie, who were to go to watch the procession from a window of the Destitute Sick Society at the corner of Bank Street near the Bank of Scotland. Afterwards we heard that they saw very well, and Rosemay was delighted because the Queen looked up in her direction.

I went into the Parliament House with Ella, via the George IV Bridge Entrance, and donned my full-bottomed wig and gown. The Dean, Chree Guest, and Douglas Campbell were acting to represent the Faculty. Then Ella & I crossed to the North Door of St. Giles, from which we obtained access to our seats. They turned out to be a splendid position, facing the steps of the Communion Table to the south thereof, and we the second row from the front. Dr. & Mrs. Caldwell were to our left. The Church of Scotland representatives were nearing the outer corner of the Cathedral. Opposite us, in the corresponding north-east corner were the representatives from St. Andrews House. The new reredos was in use for the first time, scarlet panels on a background of clothing-gold, the gift of the Merchant Company: it added colour to the scene. Opposite us were a news reel and television cameras. Behind us, Regan of Paisley Abbey was placed in a corner, apparently to broadcast a commentary. One of the more interesting sights – between us and the Communion Table, a portion has away – was Stanley Cursiter, the Queen's Limner, making sketches for a picture of the scene. The processions entered in less time than we expected, the peers and the provosts being the most impressive before the great procession. This was quite superb, the three bearers of the honours being excellent, especially Lord Crawford. The singing of the psalms and 'O worship the King' (a favourite of the Queen, chosen by her) was full-voiced in comparison with the never ... Mr. Watson's sermon was heard well in every corner of the building. The ...

(margin) It was rather a thrill to look for them, as I had left the precise arrangements to the Scottish office and the Secretary of St. Giles, who had deliberately refrained from any suggestion as to where we ourselves should have seats. Accordingly except that I knew we were to enter by the North Door, I had no prior knowledge where our seats were to be.